A TEXTBOOK OF MATRICES

Hari Kishan

ATLANTIC

PUBLISHERS & DISTRIBUTORS (P) LTD

Published by
ATLANTIC
PUBLISHERS & DISTRIBUTORS (P) LTD
7/22, Ansari Road, Darya Ganj, New Delhi-110002
Phones : +91-11-40775252, 40775214, 23273880, 23275880
Fax: +91-11-23285873
Web: www.atlanticbooks.com
E-mail: orders@atlanticbooks.com

Printed & bound in India by Atlantic Print Services

PREFACE

Matrices were invented in the latter half of the 19th century and introduced in the study of transformation Geometry, especially in translation, rotation, reflexion, enlargement and contraction, etc. Today, the knowledge of matrices is considered necessary in various areas of Mathematics and a wide variety of other subjects, like Chemistry, Sociology, Genetics and Electrical Engineering.

Matrix Theory has a special importance in modern scientific study based on precision and pinpoint accuracy. Its importance has greatly increased with the invention of Electronic Brain—Computer. It has become a powerful tool of modern Mathematics and is now extensively used in the allied fields of Mathematics including Probability, Statistics, Quantum Mechanics, Mechanics, etc. Space scientists are using matrices in the study of perturbation of planetary motion and making new discoveries in Astronomy.

A Textbook of Matrices covers all the important topics on matrices. The subject matter has been divided into nine chapters. Chapter 1 explains multiplication and addition by scalar, commutative and associative matrices. In addition, cancellation laws, zero divisors, difference between a matrix and a determinant and various kinds of matrices and their applications have been explained. Special kinds of matrices like Symmetric, Skew-Symmetric, Hermitian, Skew-Hermitian, Involutary, Orthogonal and Unitary have been dealt with in chapter 2. Determinants of matrices have been taken up in chapter 3 which also explains various types of permutations and inversions, Sarrus's rule, cofactor of an element, properties and working rules of determinants besides complementary minor and Laplace's expansion of a determinant. Chapter 4 takes up adjoint and inverse of a matrix and explains elementary operations and symbols.

A matrix has two identical rows which are not independent of each other. The rank of a matrix is the maximum number of independent rows or columns. The rank of a matrix, invariance of rank through elementary transformations and reduction to normal form have been dealt with in chapter 5. Since matrices are widely used to understand different forms and systems of linear equations, chapter 6 has been devoted to the study of linear equations in relation to matrices. A matrix can also be understood as a set of row vectors arranged in various columns, and a set of column vectors arranged in various rows. Chapter 7 deals with linear independence and dependence of vectors and explains the difference in vectors, fundamental unit vectors, vector space over a field and basis and dimension of a vector space. Characteristic roots and vectors in Cayley-Hamilton Theorem have been analysed in chapter 8. The concept of homogeneous forms is extremely important in Mathematics. Since quadratic forms are one of the three most frequently encountered homogeneous forms, chapter 9 explains quadratic form as a matrix product, linear transformations and reduction of quadratic forms into sum of square forms.

The book is an ideal textbook on matrices. The language is simple and approach thoroughly illustrative. Several examples and theorems have been included for complete understanding of various concepts. A number of exercises have been added to provide sufficient practice to the students. It will prove immensely useful to the students and teachers of matrices.

Hari Kishan

CONTENTS

Preface .... *iii*

1. Definitions, Addition and Multiplication 1
2. Special Matrices 67
3. Determinants 135
4. Adjoint and Inverse of a Matrix 229
5. Rank 337
6. Linear Equations 390
7. Linear Independence and Dependence of Vectors 427
8. Characteristic Roots and Vectors—Cayley-Hamilton Theorem 450
9. Quadratic Forms 508

1 DEFINITIONS, ADDITION AND MULTIPLICATION

1.1. Introduction

The word matrices is plural of the word matrix. The term matrix was apparently coined by British Mathematician J.J. Sylvester in about 1850, but was first introduced by the mathematician Arther Cayley in 1860. Matrices were invented in the study of transformation Geometry, specifically in translation, rotation, reflexion, enlargement and contraction, etc. of geometrical shapes. The knowledge of matrices is necessary in various areas of Mathematics and in a wide variety of other subjects. Matrix theory has a special importance in modern scientific study. It has widely been used in Molecular Physics and Engineering. It has become a powerful tool of modern mathematics. Its importance has greatly increased by the invention of Electronic Brain Computer. In network and communication of confidential informations from one place to the other, it has established its specific place. It has been most widely used in the solution of system of linear algebraic equations, linear differential equations and non-linear differential equations. Matrices are also used in Chemistry, Sociology, Genetics, Electrical Engineering. The other areas of Mathematics where matrices occur include Probability, Statistics, Mathematical Economics, Quantum Mechanics, Electrical Networks, Curve Fitting, Transportation Problems, Frame works in Mechanics, etc. Matrices are easily amenable for computers. French Mathematician Pierre Simon Laplace (1749-1827) used this theory in the study of perturbation of planetary motion. Thus, matrix theory finds an important place in modern age and has become an integral part of mathematics. The use of matrices helps a lot in mathematical investigations.

1.2. Elementary Idea

Let Meenu, Saroj, Praveen and Apala appear in tests in the subjects of Mathematics, English and Science. Let the marks obtained by Meenu be 12, 18 and 15 in Mathematics, English and Science, respectively. Let the marks obtained in these subjects by Saroj, Praveen and Apala be 10, 19 and 11; 13, 17 and 14; 18, 16 and 20, respectively. Then, the marks obtained by Meenu, Saroj, Praveen and Apala can be represented in the tabular form as follows:

$$\begin{array}{l} \\ \text{Meenu} \\ \text{Saroj} \\ \text{Praveen} \\ \text{Apala} \end{array} \begin{array}{c} \begin{array}{ccc} \text{Mathematics} & \text{English} & \text{Science} \end{array} \\ \begin{bmatrix} 12 & 18 & 15 \\ 10 & 19 & 11 \\ 13 & 17 & 14 \\ 18 & 16 & 20 \end{bmatrix} \end{array}$$

In the above arrangement, the marks obtained by Meenu, Saroj, Praveen and Apala are arranged in the first row, second row, third row and the fourth row, respectively. The first column in the arrangement represents the marks in Mathematics. Similarly, the second and the third columns represent the marks in English and Science, respectively. From the above arrangement, the marks obtained by any of the candidates in any of the subjects can be read very easily. An arrangement of this type is called a matrix.

1.3. Rectangular Array

We know that a horizontal line is called a row and a vertical line is called a column. If we arrange some numbers in rows and columns, then this arrangement is called an array. More specifically, if the arrangement is rectangular, then it is called a rectangular array. We can visualise a rectangular array in a class, price list, coach, parade or cinema hall, etc.

1.4. Scalars

The numbers which obey the algebraic laws of addition, subtraction, multiplication and division are called scalars. These may be real or complex.

1.5. Definition of a Matrix

A matrix is a rectangular array of scalars or functions.

These scalars or functions known as elements or entries are enclosed in brackets [ ] or ( ) or || ||.

For example:

$$\begin{bmatrix} 1 & 2 & 3 \end{bmatrix}$$

$$\begin{bmatrix} 1 \\ 2 \\ 3 \end{bmatrix}$$

$$\begin{bmatrix} a & b & c \\ d & e & f \end{bmatrix}$$

$$\begin{bmatrix} 1 & 1 \\ 1 & 1 \end{bmatrix}$$

$$\begin{bmatrix} 0 & 0 & 0 \\ 0 & 0 & 0 \\ 0 & 0 & 0 \end{bmatrix}$$

$$\begin{bmatrix} \cos\theta & \sin\theta \\ -\sin\theta & \cos\theta \end{bmatrix}$$

are all matrices.

Note: *It is not necessary that the number of rows is equal to the number of columns.*

1.6. An $m \times n$ Matrix

If we arrange mn scalars in a rectangular array of m rows and n columns, then the matrix so formed is called an $m \times n$ matrix or a matrix of order $m \times n$ or a matrix of order m by n. The elements of a matrix are located by the double suffix notation ij where i denotes the row and j the column. Thus, an $m \times n$ matrix is given below:

$$\begin{bmatrix} a_{11} & a_{12}\cdots\cdots a_{1j}\cdots\cdots a_{1n} \\ a_{21} & a_{22}\cdots\cdots a_{2j}\cdots\cdots a_{2n} \\ \cdots\cdots & \cdots\cdots\cdots\cdots \\ a_{i1} & a_{i2}\cdots\cdots a_{ij}\cdots\cdots a_{in} \\ a_{m1} & a_{m2}\cdots\cdots a_{mj}\cdots\cdots a_{mn} \end{bmatrix}_{m\times n}$$

1.7. Notations

Matrices are usually denoted by capital letters of the English alphabet such as $A, B, C, \ldots\ldots, X, Y, Z, \ldots\ldots$, etc. Their elements are denoted by the small letters such as $a, b, c, \ldots\ldots, x, y, z, \ldots\ldots, a_{11}, a_{12}, a_{13}, \ldots\ldots$, etc. The general element of an $m \times n$ matrix is denoted by a_{ij} where $i = 1, 2, \ldots\ldots, m$; $j = 1, 2, \ldots\ldots, n$. It should be understood that a_{ij} is the element situated in the ith row and jth column. In other words, the element a_{ij} is situated at the intersection of ith row and jth column. In practice, we write the $m \times n$ matrix given in Section 1.6 as

$$A = [a_{ij}]_{m \times n}$$

Examples

1. $\begin{bmatrix} 2 & 1 & -1 & -2 \\ 3 & -2 & -1 & -1 \\ 2 & -5 & -1 & 0 \end{bmatrix}$ is a matrix of order 3×4 over the set I of integers. Here, $a_{23} = -1$, $a_{33} = -1$, $a_{34} = 0$

2. $\begin{bmatrix} 3 & 2-3i & 3+5i \\ 2+3i & 5 & i \\ 3-5i & -i & 7 \end{bmatrix}$ is a matrix of order 3×3 over the set C of complex numbers. Here $a_{12} = 2 - 3i$, $a_{22} = 5$, $a_{31} = 3 - 5i$

1.8. Salient Features of an *m* × *n* Matrix

(i) It has m rows.

(ii) It has n columns.

(iii) Each row has n elements.

(iv) Each column has m elements.

(v) Total number of elements is mn.

1.9. A Matrix Over a Number Field

If all the elements of a matrix belong to a field F, we say that the matrix is over the field F. In particular, if all the elements are natural numbers, then we say that the matrix is over the field of natural numbers.

1.10. Difference Between a Matrix and a Determinant

Although we find some similarity in the way of writing a matrix and a determinant, yet the two are entirely different.

(i) Whereas a determinant has a numerical value, a matrix has no numerical value. A matrix is merely a convenient and abbreviated way of storing informations.

(ii) In case of a determinant, the number of rows must be equal to the number of columns. However, in case of a matrix, it is not essential.

(iii) The values of the determinants $\begin{vmatrix} 0 & 0 & 1 \\ 2 & 2 & 3 \\ 2 & 4 & 7 \end{vmatrix}$ and $\begin{vmatrix} 0 & 0 & 2 \\ 2 & 0 & 9 \\ 3 & 1 & 11 \end{vmatrix}$ are the same, i.e. they are equal determinants but the matrices $\begin{bmatrix} 0 & 0 & 1 \\ 2 & 2 & 3 \\ 2 & 4 & 7 \end{bmatrix}$ and $\begin{bmatrix} 0 & 0 & 2 \\ 2 & 0 & 9 \\ 3 & 1 & 11 \end{bmatrix}$ are not equal.

(iv) The value of the determinant $\begin{vmatrix} 0 & 0 & 1 \\ 2 & 2 & 3 \\ 4 & 4 & 7 \end{vmatrix}$ is zero but the matrix $\begin{bmatrix} 0 & 0 & 1 \\ 2 & 2 & 3 \\ 4 & 4 & 7 \end{bmatrix}$ is not a zero matrix.

1.11. Kinds of Matrices

1. Real matrix

A matrix whose all the elements are real is called a real matrix. For example:

$$\begin{bmatrix} 0 & 1 & 2 & 3 \\ 4 & -4 & -9 & 8 \\ \frac{1}{2} & -\frac{1}{2} & \sqrt{2} & \frac{3}{4} \end{bmatrix}_{3\times 4} \quad \text{is a real matrix.}$$

2. Complex matrix

A matrix whose at least one element is complex is called a complex matrix. For example:

$$\begin{bmatrix} 1 & 1+i \\ 1-i & -1 \end{bmatrix}_{2\times 2} \quad \text{is a complex matrix.}$$

3. Rectangular matrix

Any $m \times n$ $(m \neq n)$ matrix is called a rectangular matrix. For example:

(i) $\begin{bmatrix} 2 & -3 & 1 \\ 2 & -2 & 0 \end{bmatrix}_{2\times 3}$ is a rectangular matrix.

(ii) $\begin{bmatrix} 1+i & 2-3i & 2 & -7 \\ 3-4i & 4+5i & 1 & 0 \\ 5 & 3 & 3-i & 6i \end{bmatrix}_{3\times 4}$ is a rectangular matrix.

4. Single element matrix

A matrix of order 1×1 is called a single element matrix. For example:

$[a]_{1\times 1}$ is a single element matrix.

5. Horizontal matrix

A matrix of order $m \times n$ $(m < n)$ is called a horizontal matrix. For example:

$$\begin{bmatrix} 1 & 2 & 3 & 4 \\ 7 & 9 & 14 & 13 \end{bmatrix}_{2\times 4}$$ is a horizontal matrix.

Here,

$m = 2$

$n = 4$

Clearly, $m < n$

6. Vertical matrix

A matrix of order $m \times n$ $(m > n)$ is called a vertical matrix. For example:

$$\begin{bmatrix} 3 & -2 \\ 5 & 9 \\ 7 & 11 \\ 8 & 17 \end{bmatrix}_{4\times 2}$$ is a vertical matrix.

Here,

$m = 4$

$n = 2$

Clearly, $m > n$

7. Row matrix

A matrix is said to be a row matrix or row vector if it has only one row. However, it may have any number of columns. Thus, any $1 \times n$ matrix is called a row matrix. For example:

(i) $[a_1 \quad a_2 \quad a_3.....a_n]_{1\times n}$ is a row matrix.

(ii) $[5 \quad 0 \quad 3]_{1\times 3}$ is a row matrix.

(iii) $[2]_{1\times 1}$ is a row matrix.

8. Column matrix

A matrix is said to be a column matrix or column vector if it has only one column. However, it may have any number of rows. Thus, any $m \times 1$ matrix is called a column matrix.

For example:

(i) $\begin{bmatrix} a_1 \\ a_2 \\ a_3 \\ \vdots \\ a_m \end{bmatrix}_{m\times 1}$ is a column matrix

(ii) $\begin{bmatrix} 1 \\ 2 \\ 3 \end{bmatrix}_{3\times 1}$ is a column matrix

(iii) $[2]_{1\times 1}$ is a column matrix

Note 1: *Sometimes it is convenient to write a column matrix as a row matrix and enclose the elements by curly brackets or by putting a dash (') over the right hand square bracket. Thus, we may write*

$$\begin{bmatrix} a_1 \\ a_2 \\ a_3 \\ \vdots \\ a_m \end{bmatrix} = \{a_1, a_2, a_3, ..., a_m\} \text{ or } [a_1\ a_2\ a_3\ ...\ a_m]'$$

Note 2: *A single element matrix is a row matrix as well as a column matrix.*

9. Zero matrix or Null matrix

A matrix is said to be a zero matrix or null matrix if all its elements are zero. It is denoted by $O_{m\times n}$ or O_{mn} or by O simply. For example:

$[0]_{1\times 1}$, $\begin{bmatrix} 0 & 0 \\ 0 & 0 \end{bmatrix}_{2\times 2}$, $\begin{bmatrix} 0 & 0 & 0 \\ 0 & 0 & 0 \\ 0 & 0 & 0 \end{bmatrix}_{3\times 3}$, $[0\ \ 0]_{1\times 2}$ are all zero matrices.

10. Square matrix

A matrix in which the number of rows is equal to the number of columns is called a square matrix. Thus, any $n \times n$ matrix is called a square matrix of order n or an n-square matrix. For example:

$$[5]_{1\times 1}, \begin{bmatrix} 2 & 3 \\ 5 & 0 \end{bmatrix}_{2\times 2}, \begin{bmatrix} -3 & 2 & 5 \\ 0 & 6 & -1 \\ 7 & 5 & 2 \end{bmatrix}_{3\times 3}$$ are all square matrices.

Note: *In a square matrix, the elements a_{ij} for which $i = j$, i.e. the elements $a_{11}, a_{22}, \ldots\ldots, a_{mn}$ are called diagonal elements. The line along which these elements lie is called the leading diagonal (or principal diagonal or main diagonal). Moreover, the pair of elements a_{ij} and a_{ji} are said to be conjugate elements.*

11. Diagonal matrix

If all the elements of a square matrix except the leading diagonal elements are zero, then the matrix is called a diagonal matrix. Thus, a square matrix $A = [a_{ij}]$ is said to be diagonal matrix if $a_{ij} = 0$ for $i \neq j$. For example:

$$[5]_{1\times 1}, \begin{bmatrix} 2 & 0 \\ 0 & -3 \end{bmatrix}_{2\times 2}, \begin{bmatrix} 5 & 0 & 0 \\ 0 & -1 & 0 \\ 0 & 0 & 6 \end{bmatrix}_{3\times 3}$$ are all diagonal matrices.

If $A = [a_{ij}]$ is a diagonal matrix of order n, then it must be of the following form:

$$A = \begin{bmatrix} a_{11} & 0 & 0 & \ldots\ldots & 0 \\ 0 & a_{22} & 0 & \ldots\ldots & 0 \\ \ldots\ldots & \ldots\ldots & \ldots\ldots & \ldots\ldots & \ldots\ldots \\ 0 & 0 & 0 & \ldots\ldots & a_{nn} \end{bmatrix}_{n\times n}$$

Sometimes, a diagonal matrix of order n with diagonal elements $d_1, d_2, d_3, \ldots\ldots, d_n$ is denoted by

diag $(d_1, d_2, d_3, \ldots\ldots, d_n)$

12. Scalar matrix

A diagonal matrix, whose all the diagonal elements are equal, is called a scalar matrix. Thus, if $A = [a_{ij}]_{n \times n}$ is a square matrix and

$$a_{ij} = \begin{cases} \alpha, \text{ if } i \neq j \\ 0, \text{ if } i = j \end{cases}$$

where α is some number, then A is called a scalar matrix.

For example:

$$[2]_{1\times1}, \begin{bmatrix} 1 & 0 \\ 0 & 1 \end{bmatrix}_{2\times2}, \begin{bmatrix} 5 & 0 & 0 \\ 0 & 5 & 0 \\ 0 & 0 & 5 \end{bmatrix}_{3\times3} \text{ are all scalar matrices.}$$

13. Identity matrix or Unit matrix

A scalar matrix of order n in which each diagonal element is 1 (unity) is called an identity matrix of order n. It is denoted by I_n.

Thus, if $A = [a_{ij}]_{n \times n}$ is a square matrix and

$$a_{ij} = \begin{cases} 1, \text{ if } i \neq j \\ 0, \text{ if } i = j \end{cases}, \text{ then } A \text{ is called an identity matrix. Thus,}$$

$$I_1 = [1]$$

$$I_2 = \begin{bmatrix} 1 & 0 \\ 0 & 1 \end{bmatrix}$$

$$I_3 = \begin{bmatrix} 1 & 0 & 0 \\ 0 & 1 & 0 \\ 0 & 0 & 1 \end{bmatrix}$$

Note: *Unit matrix and null matrix are scalar matrices.*

14. Triangular matrix

If every element above or below the leading diagonal of a square matrix is zero, the matrix is called a triangular matrix.

(i) Upper triangular matrix. If every element below the leading diagonal of a square matrix is zero, the square matrix is called an upper triangular matrix. Thus, if $A = [a_{ij}]_{n \times n}$ is an upper triangular matrix, then

$a_{ij} = 0$ for $i > j$

For example:

$$\begin{bmatrix} 1 & 2 & 4 & 8 \\ 0 & 3 & 7 & 9 \\ 0 & 0 & 5 & 6 \\ 0 & 0 & 0 & 8 \end{bmatrix}$$ is an upper triangular matrix.

(ii) Lower triangular matrix. If every element above the leading diagonal of a square matrix is zero, the square matrix is called a lower triangular matrix. Thus, if $A = [a_{ij}]_{n \times n}$ is a lower triangular matrix, then

$a_{ij} = 0$ for $i < j$

For example:

$$\begin{bmatrix} 3 & 0 & 0 & 0 \\ 4 & 1 & 0 & 0 \\ 0 & 2 & 6 & 0 \\ 5 & 7 & 0 & 8 \end{bmatrix}$$ is a lower triangular matrix.

Note: *A diagonal matrix is an upper triangular matrix as well as a lower triangular matrix.*

(iii) Strictly triangular matrix. If every element above or below the leading diagonal of a square matrix is zero, then the square matrix is called a strictly triangular matrix. Thus, if $A = [a_{ij}]_{n \times n}$ is a strictly triangular matrix, then

$a_{ij} = 0$ for $i < j$ or $i > j$

For example:

$$\begin{bmatrix} 1 & 0 & 0 & 0 \\ 0 & 2 & 0 & 0 \\ 0 & 0 & 3 & 0 \\ 0 & 0 & 0 & 4 \end{bmatrix}$$ is a strictly triangular matrix.

Note: *A strictly triangular matrix is essentially a diagonal matrix.*

15. Sub-matrix

A matrix which is obtained from a given matrix by deleting any number of rows or columns or both is called a sub-matrix of the given matrix. For example: $\begin{bmatrix} 1 & 2 & 3 & 1 \\ 2 & 4 & 6 & 2 \end{bmatrix}$ is a sub-matrix of $\begin{bmatrix} 1 & 2 & 3 & 1 \\ 2 & 4 & 6 & 2 \\ 1 & 2 & 3 & 2 \end{bmatrix}$

1.12. Equality of Matrices

Two matrices $A = [a_{ij}]$ and $B = [b_{ij}]$ are said to be equal if

(i) they are of the same order

(ii) their corresponding elements are equal, i.e. $a_{ij} = b_{ij}\ \forall$ i and j.

Note: *If only condition (i) is satisfied, then A and B are said to be comparable matrices. Thus, any two matrices of the same order are comparable.*

For example:

(i) The matrices $\begin{bmatrix} 1 & 2 \\ 3 & 4 \end{bmatrix}_{2\times 2}$ and $\begin{bmatrix} 1 & 2 & 3 \\ 4 & 5 & 6 \end{bmatrix}_{2\times 3}$ are not comparable.

(ii) The matrices $\begin{bmatrix} 1 & 2 & 3 \\ 4 & 5 & 6 \end{bmatrix}_{2\times 3}$ and $\begin{bmatrix} 3 & 4 & 5 \\ 6 & 7 & 8 \end{bmatrix}_{2\times 3}$ are comparable but not equal.

(iii) The matrices $\begin{bmatrix} 1 & 2 & 3 \\ 4 & 5 & 6 \end{bmatrix}_{2\times 3}$ and $\begin{bmatrix} 1 & 2 & 3 \\ 2\times 2 & 10\div 2 & 2\times 3 \end{bmatrix}_{2\times 3}$ are equal.

Note: *If A and B are any two matrices, then using the definition of equality of matrices we can verify the following easily.*

(i) if A is any matrix, then A = A (Reflexivity)

(ii) if A = B, then B = A (Symmetry)

(iii) if A = B and B = C, then A = C (Transitivity)

In view of (i), (ii) and (iii), we may conclude that the relation of equality in the set of matrices is an equivalence relation.

1.13. Multiplication of a Matrix by a Scalar

Let $A = [a_{ij}]_{m \times n}$ be an $m \times n$ matrix. Let K be a scalar quantity belonging to a field over which A is defined. Then the product of K and A is denoted by KA and is defined to be the $m \times n$ matrix whose $(i, j)^{th}$ element is $K\, a_{ij}$. Thus,

$$KA = [K\, a_{ij}]_{m \times n}$$

$$= \begin{bmatrix} K\,a_{11} & K\,a_{12} & \cdots\cdots & K\,a_{1n} \\ K\,a_{12} & K\,a_{22} & \cdots\cdots & K\,a_{2n} \\ \cdots\cdots & \cdots\cdots & \cdots\cdots & \cdots\cdots \\ K\,a_{m1} & K\,a_{m2} & \cdots\cdots & K\,a_{mn} \end{bmatrix}_{m \times n}$$

Note 1: *The commutative law holds for the product of a matrix and a scalar.*

Note 2: *If K = –1, then (–1) A = [$-a_{ij}$]. Generally, (–1)A is denoted by –A and is called the negative or additive inverse of matrix A. Thus, the negative of a matrix is obtained by changing the sign of every element of the given matrix.*

For example:

If $A = \begin{bmatrix} 1 & 2 & -3 \\ -7 & 8 & 9 \end{bmatrix}_{2 \times 3}$, then

$$-A = \begin{bmatrix} -1 & -2 & 3 \\ 7 & -8 & -9 \end{bmatrix}_{2 \times 3}$$

and $4A = \begin{bmatrix} 4 & 8 & -12 \\ -28 & 32 & 36 \end{bmatrix}_{2 \times 3}$

1.14. Addition of Matrics

Two matrices are said to be conformable for addition if they are of the same order. If A and B are two matrices of the same order then their sum denoted by $A + B$ is a matrix of the same order obtained by adding the corresponding elements of A and B. Thus, if $A = [a_{ij}]_{m \times n}$ and $B = [b_{ij}]_{m \times n}$, then

$A + B = [a_{ij} + b_{ij}]_{m \times n}$

For example:

If $A = \begin{bmatrix} 1 & 4 & -1 \\ 2 & 6 & 5 \end{bmatrix}$ and $B = \begin{bmatrix} 3 & -2 & -6 \\ 2 & 0 & -7 \end{bmatrix}$

$$\text{then } A + B = \begin{bmatrix} 1 & 4 & -1 \\ 2 & 6 & 5 \end{bmatrix} + \begin{bmatrix} 3 & -2 & -6 \\ 2 & 0 & -7 \end{bmatrix}$$

$$= \begin{bmatrix} 1+3 & 4-2 & -1-6 \\ 2+2 & 6+0 & 5-7 \end{bmatrix}$$

$$= \begin{bmatrix} 4 & 2 & -7 \\ 4 & 6 & -2 \end{bmatrix}$$

If $C = \begin{bmatrix} 1 & 2 \\ 3 & 4 \end{bmatrix}$, then neither $A + C$ nor $B + C$ is defined.

Note: *If two matrices are not of the same order, then their sum cannot be found out.*

1.15. Subtraction of Matrices

Two matrices are said to be conformable for subtraction if they are of the same order. If A and B are two matrices of the same order then their difference denoted by $A - B$ is a matrix of the same order obtained by subtraction from each element of A the corresponding element of B.

Thus, if $A = [a_{ij}]_{m \times n}$ and $B = [b_{ij}]_{m \times n}$, then

$A - B = [a_{ij} - b_{ij}]_{m \times n}$

For example:

If $A = \begin{bmatrix} 1 & 4 & -1 \\ 2 & 6 & 5 \end{bmatrix}$ and $B = \begin{bmatrix} 3 & -2 & -6 \\ 2 & 0 & -7 \end{bmatrix}$,

$$\text{then} \quad A - B = \begin{bmatrix} 1 & 4 & -1 \\ 2 & 6 & 5 \end{bmatrix} - \begin{bmatrix} 3 & -2 & -6 \\ 2 & 0 & -7 \end{bmatrix}$$

$$= \begin{bmatrix} 1-3 & 4+2 & -1+6 \\ 2-2 & 6-0 & 5+7 \end{bmatrix}$$

$$= \begin{bmatrix} -2 & 6 & 5 \\ 0 & 6 & 12 \end{bmatrix}$$

If $C = \begin{bmatrix} 1 & 2 \\ 3 & 4 \end{bmatrix}$, then neither $A - C$ nor $B - C$ is defined.

Note: *By definition, $A - B$ is the same as the matrix $A + (-B)$.*

1.16. Properties of Matrix Addition (Subtraction)

1. Matrix addition is commutative

If A and B are two matrices of the same order, then $A + B = B + A$.

Proof. Let $A = [a_{ij}]_{m \times n}$ and $B = [b_{ij}]_{m \times n}$

Then,

$$\begin{aligned} A + B &= [a_{ij}]_{m \times n} + [b_{ij}]_{m \times n} \\ &= [a_{ij} + b_{ij}]_{m \times n} \\ &= [b_{ij} + a_{ij}]_{m \times n} && \because \text{Addition of scalars} \\ &= [b_{ij}]_{m \times n} + [a_{ij}]_{m \times n} && \text{is commutative.} \\ &= B + A \end{aligned}$$

2. Matrix addition is associative

If A, B and C are three matrices of the same order, then

$$(A + B) + C = A + (B + C)$$

Proof. Let $A = [a_{ij}]_{m \times n}$, $B = [b_{ij}]_{m \times n}$ and $C = [c_{ij}]_{m \times n}$. Then,

$$\begin{aligned} (A + B) + C &= \left\{ \left[a_{ij} \right]_{m \times n} + \left[b_{ij} \right]_{m \times n} \right\} + \left[c_{ij} \right]_{m \times n} \\ &= \left[a_{ij} + b_{ij} \right]_{m \times n} + \left[c_{ij} \right]_{m \times n} \end{aligned}$$

$$= \left[\left(a_{ij} + b_{ij}\right) + c_{ij}\right]_{m \times n}$$

$$= \left[a_{ij} + \left(b_{ij} + c_{ij}\right)\right]_{m \times n} \quad \because \text{Addition of scalars is associative.}$$

$$= \left[a_{ij}\right]_{m \times n} + \left[b_{ij} + c_{ij}\right]_{m \times n}$$

$$= \left[a_{ij}\right]_{m \times n} + \left\{\left[b_{ij}\right]_{m \times n} + \left[c_{ij}\right]_{m \times n}\right\}$$

$$= A + (B + C)$$

3. Existence of additive identity

If A is a matrix of order $m \times n$ and O is a null matrix of the same order, then

$A + O = A = O + A$

Thus, the null matrix is the additive identity for the matrix addition.

Proof. Let $A = [a_{ij}]_{m \times n}$ and $O = [0]_{m \times n}$, then,

$$A + O = \left[a_{ij}\right]_{m \times n} + [0]_{m \times n}$$

$$= \left[a_{ij} + 0\right]_{m \times n}$$

$$= \left[a_{ij}\right]_{m \times n}$$

$$= A$$

$$O + A = [0]_{m \times n} + \left[a_{ij}\right]_{m \times n}$$

$$= \left[0 + a_{ij}\right]_{m \times n}$$

$$= \left[a_{ij}\right]_{m \times n}$$

$$= A$$

Thus, $A + O = A = O + A$

Note: *Additive identity is unique.*

4. Existence of additive inverse

If A is a matrix of order $m \times n$, then $-A$ is the additive inverse of A because $A + (-A) = O = (-A) + A$

Proof. Let $A = [a_{ij}]_{m \times n}$

Then, $-A = [-a_{ij}]_{m \times n}$

$$\therefore A + (-A) = \left[a_{ij}\right]_{m\times n} + \left[-a_{ij}\right]_{m\times n}$$

$$= \left[a_{ij} + \left(-a_{ij}\right)\right]_{m\times n}$$

$$= [0]_{m\times n} = O$$

$$(-A) + A = \left[-a_{ij}\right]_{m\times n} + \left[a_{ij}\right]_{m\times n}$$

$$= \left[\left(-a_{ij}\right) + a_{ij}\right]_{m\times n}$$

$$= [0]_{m\times n}$$

$$= O$$

Thus, $A + (-A) = O = (-A) + A$

Note: *Additive inverse is unique.*

5. Cancellation laws

If A, B and C are three matrices of the same order, then

$A + B = A + C \Rightarrow B = C$ [Left cancellation]

and $B + A = C + A \Rightarrow B = C$ [Right cancellation]

Proof. Let $A\ [a_{ij}]_{m \times n}$, $B = [b_{ij}]_{m \times n}$ and $C = [c_{ij}]_{m \times n}$ be three matrices of the same order. Then,

$A + B = A + C$

$\Rightarrow -A + (A + B) = -A + (A + C)$ | Adding $-A$ to both sides

$\Rightarrow (-A + A) + B = (-A + A) + C$ | Associative property

$\Rightarrow O + B = O + C$ | $\because -A + A = O$

$\Rightarrow B = C$ | $\because O + B = B$ and $O + C = C$

Similarly, we can prove that

$$B + A = C + A \Rightarrow B = C$$

6. Properties of negative of a matrix

(i) $-(-A) = A$

(ii) $-O = O$

(iii) $-(A + B) = (-A) + (-B)$

Proof.

(i) Let $A = [a_{ij}]_{m \times n}$, then,

$$\begin{aligned} -(-A) = -[-a_{ij}]_{m \times n} &= [-(-a_{ij})]_{m \times n} \\ &= [a_{ij}]_{m \times n} \\ &= A \end{aligned}$$

(ii) Let $O = [0]_{m \times n}$, then,

$$-O = -[0]_{m \times n} = [-0]_{m \times n} = [0]_{m \times n} = O$$

(iii) Let $A = [a_{ij}]_{m \times n}$ and $B = [b_{ij}]_{m \times n}$, then,

$$\begin{aligned} -(A + B) &= -[a_{ij} + b_{ij}]_{m \times n} \\ &= -\{[a_{ij}]_{m \times n} + [b_{ij}]_{m \times n}\} \\ &= -[a_{ij}]_{m \times n} - [b_{ij}]_{m \times n} \\ &= -A - B \\ &= (-A) + (-B) \end{aligned}$$

7. The equation A + X = O has a unique solution

Let $A = [a_{ij}]_{m \times n}$ and $X = [x_{ij}]_{m \times n}$

Then,

$$A + X = O$$

$$\Rightarrow [a_{ij}] + [x_{ij}]_{m \times n} = [0]_{m \times n}$$

$$\Rightarrow [a_{ij} + x_{ij}]_{m \times n} = [0]_{m \times n}$$

$$\Rightarrow a_{ij} + x_{ij} = 0$$

$$\Rightarrow x_{ij} = -a_{ij}$$

$$\Rightarrow [x_{ij}] = [-a_{ij}]$$

$$\Rightarrow [x_{ij}] = -[a_{ij}]$$

$$\Rightarrow X = -A$$

Uniqueness

Let X_1 and X_2 be two different solutions of $A + X = O$. Then,

$$A + X_1 = O$$

and $A + X_2 = O$

Therefore, $A + X_1 = A + X_2$ | Each $= O$

$\Rightarrow X_1 = X_2$ | Using left cancellation law

1.17. Properties of Scalar Multiplication of a Matrix

1. Scalar multiplication is distributive over matrix addition

If A and B are two matrices of the same order and K is any scalar, then

$$K(A + B) = KA + KB$$

Proof. Let $A = [a_{ij}]_{m \times n}$ and $B = [b_{ij}]_{m \times n}$. Then,

$$\begin{aligned} K(A + B) &= K\left\{\left[a_{ij}\right]_{m\times n} + \left[b_{ij}\right]_{m\times n}\right\} \\ &= K\left[a_{ij} + b_{ij}\right]_{m\times n} \\ &= \left[K\left(a_{ij} + b_{ij}\right)\right]_{m\times n} \\ &= \left[K\,a_{ij} + K\,b_{ij}\right]_{m\times n} \\ &= \left[K\,a_{ij}\right]_{m\times n} + \left[K\,b_{ij}\right]_{m\times n} \\ &= K\left[a_{ij}\right]_{m\times n} + K\left[b_{ij}\right]_{m\times n} \\ &= KA + KB \end{aligned}$$

2. If K_1 and K_2 are any two scalars and A is any matrix,

then, $(K_1 + K_2)A = K_1A + K_2A$

Proof. Let $A = [a_{ij}]_{m \times n}$. Then,

$$(K_1 + K_2)A = (K_1 + K_2)\left[a_{ij}\right]_{m\times n}$$

$$= \left[(K_1 + K_2)\, a_{ij}\right]_{m \times n}$$

$$= \left[K_1\, a_{ij} + K_2\, a_{ij}\right]_{m \times n}$$

$$= \left[K_1\, a_{ij}\right]_{m \times n} + \left[K_2\, a_{ij}\right]_{m \times n}$$

$$= K_1 \left[a_{ij}\right]_{m \times n} + K_2 \left[a_{ij}\right]_{m \times n}$$

$$= K_1 A + K_2 A$$

3. If K_1 and K_2 are any two scalars and A is any matrix

then, $K_1(K_2A) = (K_1K_2)A$

Proof. Let $A = [a_{ij}]_{m \times n}$. Then,

$$K_1(K_2A) = K_1 \left\{K_2 \left[a_{ij}\right]_{m \times n}\right\}$$

$$= K_1 \left[K_2\, a_{ij}\right]_{m \times n}$$

$$= \left[K_1 \left(K_2\, a_{ij}\right)\right]_{m \times n}$$

$$= \left[(K_1K_2)\, a_{ij}\right]_{m \times n}$$

$$= (K_1K_2) \left[a_{ij}\right]_{m \times n}$$

$$= (K_1K_2)A$$

4. If A is any matrix and K is any scalar

then, $(-K)A = -(KA) = K(-A)$

Proof. Let $A = [a_{ij}]_{m \times n}$

Then,

$$(-K)A = (-K) \left[a_{ij}\right]_{m \times n}$$

$$= \left[(-K)\, a_{ij}\right]_{m \times n}$$

$$= \left[-(K\, a_{ij})\right]_{m \times n}$$

$$= -\left[K\, a_{ij}\right]_{m\times n}$$

$$= -(KA) \qquad \text{... (1.1)}$$

$$K(-A) = K\left[-a_{ij}\right]_{m\times n}$$

$$= \left[-K\, a_{ij}\right]_{m\times n}$$

$$= -\left[K\, a_{ij}\right]_{m\times n}$$

$$= -(KA) \qquad \text{... (1.2)}$$

In view of Eqs. (1.1) and (1.2), we get

$$(-K)A = -(KA) = K(-A)$$

ILLUSTRATIVE EXAMPLES

Example 1. Does the sum $\begin{bmatrix} 3 & 2 & 1 \\ 1 & 3 & 2 \\ 2 & 1 & 2 \end{bmatrix} + \begin{bmatrix} 0 & 0 \\ 0 & 0 \\ 0 & 0 \end{bmatrix}$ make sense?

Solution: The order of the 1st matrix is 3 × 3, while the order of the 2nd matrix is 3 × 2. Since the orders of the two matrices are not the same, therefore, the given matrices are not conformable for addition. Hence, the given sum does not make sense.

Example 2. Express $\begin{bmatrix} 2 & 5 & -7 \\ -9 & 12 & 4 \\ 15 & -13 & 6 \end{bmatrix}$ as the sum of a lower triangular matrix and an upper triangular matrix with zero leading diagonal.

Solution: Let $L = \begin{bmatrix} a & 0 & 0 \\ b & c & 0 \\ d & e & f \end{bmatrix}$ be the lower triangular matrix and

$U = \begin{bmatrix} 0 & p & q \\ 0 & 0 & r \\ 0 & 0 & 0 \end{bmatrix}$ be the upper triangular matrix with zero leading diagonal such that

$$\begin{bmatrix} 2 & 5 & -7 \\ -9 & 12 & 4 \\ 15 & -13 & 6 \end{bmatrix} = \begin{bmatrix} a & 0 & 0 \\ b & c & 0 \\ d & e & f \end{bmatrix} + \begin{bmatrix} 0 & p & q \\ 0 & 0 & r \\ 0 & 0 & 0 \end{bmatrix}$$

$$\Rightarrow \begin{bmatrix} 2 & 5 & -7 \\ -9 & 12 & 4 \\ 15 & -13 & 6 \end{bmatrix} = \begin{bmatrix} a+0 & 0+p & 0+q \\ b+0 & c+0 & 0+r \\ d+0 & e+0 & f+0 \end{bmatrix}$$

$$\Rightarrow \begin{bmatrix} 2 & 5 & -7 \\ -9 & 12 & 4 \\ 15 & -13 & 6 \end{bmatrix} = \begin{bmatrix} a & p & q \\ b & c & r \\ d & e & f \end{bmatrix}$$

Equating the corresponding elements on both sides, we get

$a = 2,\ p = 5,\ q = -7,\ b = -9,\ c = 12,\ r = 4,\ d = 15,\ e = -13,\ f = 6$

$$\therefore \quad L = \begin{bmatrix} 2 & 0 & 0 \\ -9 & 12 & 0 \\ 15 & -13 & 6 \end{bmatrix} \text{ and } U = \begin{bmatrix} 0 & 5 & -7 \\ 0 & 0 & 4 \\ 0 & 0 & 0 \end{bmatrix}$$

Example 3. Find X and Y if $2X + Y = \begin{bmatrix} 4 & 4 & 7 \\ 7 & 3 & 4 \end{bmatrix}$ and $X - 2Y = \begin{bmatrix} -3 & 2 & 1 \\ 1 & -1 & 2 \end{bmatrix}$.

Solution: We have,

$$2X + Y = \begin{bmatrix} 4 & 4 & 7 \\ 7 & 3 & 4 \end{bmatrix} \qquad \dots (1.3)$$

$$\text{and} \quad X - 2Y = \begin{bmatrix} -3 & 2 & 1 \\ 1 & -1 & 2 \end{bmatrix} \qquad \dots (1.4)$$

Multiplying Eq. (1.3) by 2, we get

$$4X + 2Y = 2\begin{bmatrix} 4 & 4 & 7 \\ 7 & 3 & 4 \end{bmatrix}$$

$$\Rightarrow \quad 4X + 2Y = \begin{bmatrix} 8 & 8 & 14 \\ 14 & 6 & 8 \end{bmatrix} \qquad \text{... (1.5)}$$

Adding Eqs. (1.4) and (1.5), we get

$$5X = \begin{bmatrix} -3 & 2 & 1 \\ 1 & -1 & 2 \end{bmatrix} + \begin{bmatrix} 8 & 8 & 14 \\ 14 & 6 & 8 \end{bmatrix}$$

$$\Rightarrow \quad 5X = \begin{bmatrix} -3+8 & 2+8 & 1+14 \\ 1+14 & -1+6 & 2+8 \end{bmatrix}$$

$$\Rightarrow \quad 5X = \begin{bmatrix} 5 & 10 & 15 \\ 15 & 5 & 10 \end{bmatrix}$$

$$\Rightarrow \quad X = \frac{1}{5}\begin{bmatrix} 5 & 10 & 15 \\ 15 & 5 & 10 \end{bmatrix}$$

$$\Rightarrow \quad X = \begin{bmatrix} 1 & 2 & 3 \\ 3 & 1 & 2 \end{bmatrix}$$

Putting the value of X in Eq. (1.3), we get

$$2\begin{bmatrix} 1 & 2 & 3 \\ 3 & 1 & 2 \end{bmatrix} + Y = \begin{bmatrix} 4 & 4 & 7 \\ 7 & 3 & 4 \end{bmatrix}$$

$$\Rightarrow \quad \begin{bmatrix} 2 & 4 & 6 \\ 6 & 2 & 4 \end{bmatrix} + Y = \begin{bmatrix} 4 & 4 & 7 \\ 7 & 3 & 4 \end{bmatrix}$$

$$\Rightarrow \quad Y = \begin{bmatrix} 4 & 4 & 7 \\ 7 & 3 & 4 \end{bmatrix} - \begin{bmatrix} 2 & 4 & 6 \\ 6 & 2 & 4 \end{bmatrix}$$

$$\Rightarrow \quad Y = \begin{bmatrix} 4-2 & 4-4 & 7-6 \\ 7-6 & 3-2 & 4-4 \end{bmatrix}$$

$$\Rightarrow \quad Y = \begin{bmatrix} 2 & 0 & 1 \\ 1 & 1 & 0 \end{bmatrix}$$

Example 4. If $[a_1 \quad a_2 \quad a_3]\, x + [b_1 \quad b_2 \quad b_3]\, y + [c_1 \quad c_2 \quad c_3]\, z = [0 \quad 0 \quad 0]$, where x, y, z are scalars, not all zero, then prove that

$$\begin{vmatrix} a_1 & b_1 & c_1 \\ a_2 & b_2 & c_2 \\ a_3 & b_3 & c_3 \end{vmatrix} = 0$$

Solution: We have

$$[a_1 \quad a_2 \quad a_3]\, x + [b_1 \quad b_2 \quad b_3]\, y + [c_1 \quad c_2 \; c_3]\, z = [0 \quad 0 \quad 0]$$

$$\Rightarrow \quad [a_1x \quad a_2x \quad a_3x] + [b_1y \quad b_2y \quad b_3y] + [c_1z \quad c_2z \quad c_3z] = [0 \quad 0 \quad 0]$$

$$\Rightarrow \quad [a_1x + b_1y + c_1z \quad a_2x + b_2y + c_2z \quad a_3x + b_3y + c_3z] = [0 \quad 0 \quad 0]$$

This equality is equivalent to the three equations

$$a_1x + b_1y + c_1z = 0 \qquad \text{... (1.6)}$$

$$a_2x + b_2y + c_2z = 0 \qquad \text{... (1.7)}$$

$$a_3x + b_3y + c_3z = 0 \qquad \text{... (1.8)}$$

On eliminating x, y, z from Eqs. (1.6), (1.7) and (1.8) determinantically, we get

$$\begin{vmatrix} a_1 & b_1 & c_1 \\ a_2 & b_2 & c_2 \\ a_3 & b_3 & c_3 \end{vmatrix} = 0$$

Example 5. Solve the matrix equation

$$\begin{bmatrix} x^2 \\ y^2 \end{bmatrix} - 3\begin{bmatrix} x \\ 2y \end{bmatrix} = \begin{bmatrix} -2 \\ 9 \end{bmatrix}$$

Solution: We have

$$\begin{bmatrix} x^2 \\ y^2 \end{bmatrix} - 3\begin{bmatrix} x \\ 2y \end{bmatrix} = \begin{bmatrix} -2 \\ 9 \end{bmatrix}$$

$$\Rightarrow \quad \begin{bmatrix} x^2 \\ y^2 \end{bmatrix} - \begin{bmatrix} 3x \\ 6y \end{bmatrix} = \begin{bmatrix} -2 \\ 9 \end{bmatrix}$$

$$\Rightarrow \quad \begin{bmatrix} x^2 - 3x \\ y^2 - 6y \end{bmatrix} = \begin{bmatrix} -2 \\ 9 \end{bmatrix}$$

$$\Rightarrow \quad x^2 - 3x = -2;\ y^2 - 6y = 9$$

$$\Rightarrow \quad x^2 - 3x + 2 = 0;\ y^2 - 6y - 9 = 0$$

$$\Rightarrow \quad x = 1, 2;\ y = 3 \pm 3\sqrt{2}$$

EXERCISE 1.1

1. If $A = \begin{bmatrix} 2 & -5 & 1 \\ -2 & -1 & 4 \end{bmatrix}$, $B = \begin{bmatrix} 3 & 4 & 0 \\ 5 & -2 & 3 \end{bmatrix}$, $C = \begin{bmatrix} 7 & -6 & 2 \\ 1 & -4 & 11 \end{bmatrix}$,

then evaluate

(i) $A + B$

(ii) $A - B$

(iii) $2A + B - C$

2. If $A = \begin{bmatrix} 2 & 3 & 1 \\ 0 & -1 & 5 \end{bmatrix}$ and $B = \begin{bmatrix} 1 & 2 & -1 \\ 0 & -1 & 3 \end{bmatrix}$, then find $2A - 3B$.

3. Find a matrix X such that

$$4X = \begin{bmatrix} 1 & 2 & 1 \\ 4 & 2 & 3 \\ -1 & 9 & 7 \end{bmatrix}$$

4. If $A = \begin{bmatrix} 1 & 2 \\ 3 & 4 \\ 5 & 6 \end{bmatrix}$ and $B = \begin{bmatrix} -3 & -2 \\ 1 & -5 \\ 4 & 3 \end{bmatrix}$, then find $D = \begin{bmatrix} p & q \\ r & s \\ t & u \end{bmatrix}$ so that $A + B - D = O$.

5. Given $A = \begin{bmatrix} 1 & 2 & -3 \\ 5 & 0 & 2 \\ 1 & -1 & 1 \end{bmatrix}$ and $B = \begin{bmatrix} 3 & -1 & 2 \\ 4 & 2 & 5 \\ 2 & 0 & 3 \end{bmatrix}$, find the matrix C such that $A + 2C = B$.

6. If $A = \begin{bmatrix} 2 & -2 \\ 4 & 2 \\ -5 & 1 \end{bmatrix}$, $B = \begin{bmatrix} 8 & 0 \\ 4 & -2 \\ 3 & 6 \end{bmatrix}$, then find the matrix X such that $2A + 3X = 5B$.

7. Find x, y, z and w if

$$3\begin{bmatrix} x & y \\ z & w \end{bmatrix} = \begin{bmatrix} x & 6 \\ -1 & 2w \end{bmatrix} + \begin{bmatrix} 4 & x+y \\ 3+w & 3 \end{bmatrix}$$

8. Find X and Y, if $X + Y = \begin{bmatrix} 5 & 2 \\ 0 & 9 \end{bmatrix}$ and $X - Y = \begin{bmatrix} 3 & 6 \\ 0 & -1 \end{bmatrix}$

9. Solve the following equations for A and B

$$2A - B = \begin{bmatrix} 3 & -3 & 0 \\ 3 & 3 & 2 \end{bmatrix}$$

$$2B + A = \begin{bmatrix} 4 & 1 & 5 \\ -1 & 4 & -4 \end{bmatrix}$$

10. Simplify

$$\cos\theta\begin{bmatrix} \cos\theta & \sin\theta \\ -\sin\theta & \cos\theta \end{bmatrix} + \sin\theta\begin{bmatrix} \sin\theta & -\cos\theta \\ \cos\theta & \sin\theta \end{bmatrix}$$

11. If $A = \text{diag}\,[2, 9, 4]$, $B = \text{diag}\,[-3, 7, 6]$, then find $A + B$, $A - B$, $7A + 2B$ and $9A - 11B$.

12. Find the additive inverse of the matrix

$$A = \begin{bmatrix} 1 & 2 & -3 & 7 \\ 2 & -5 & 6 & -9 \\ 3 & 4 & 5 & -4 \end{bmatrix}$$

13. If w is a complex cube root of unity, show that

$$\begin{bmatrix} 1 & w & w^2 \\ w & w^2 & 1 \\ w^2 & 1 & w \end{bmatrix} + \begin{bmatrix} w & w^2 & 1 \\ w^2 & 1 & w \\ 1 & w & w^2 \end{bmatrix} + \begin{bmatrix} w^2 & 1 & w \\ 1 & w & w^2 \\ w & w^2 & 1 \end{bmatrix}$$ is a null matrix.

14. Solve the matrix equation $X + \begin{bmatrix} 0 & 1 & 5 \\ 1 & 0 & 4 \\ 2 & -6 & 8 \end{bmatrix} = \begin{bmatrix} 1 & 2 & 3 \\ 2 & 3 & 1 \\ 3 & 2 & 1 \end{bmatrix}$

15. If $[a_{ij}]$, $[b_{ij}]$, $[c_{ij}]$ be the matrices of the same order, and x be a scalar, show that

$$\left[a_{ij}\right]x^2 + \left[b_{ij}\right]x + \left[c_{ij}\right] = \left[a_{ij}x^2 + b_{ij}x + c_{ij}\right]$$

ANSWERS

1. (i) $\begin{bmatrix} 5 & -1 & 1 \\ 3 & -3 & 7 \end{bmatrix}$

(ii) $\begin{bmatrix} -1 & -9 & 1 \\ -7 & 1 & 1 \end{bmatrix}$

(iii) $\begin{bmatrix} 0 & 0 & 0 \\ 0 & 0 & 0 \end{bmatrix}$

2. $\begin{bmatrix} 1 & 0 & 5 \\ 0 & 1 & 1 \end{bmatrix}$

3. $\begin{bmatrix} \frac{1}{4} & \frac{1}{2} & \frac{1}{4} \\ 1 & \frac{1}{2} & \frac{3}{4} \\ -\frac{1}{4} & \frac{2}{4} & \frac{2}{4} \end{bmatrix}$

4. $\begin{bmatrix} -2 & 0 \\ 4 & -1 \\ 9 & 9 \end{bmatrix}$

5. $\begin{bmatrix} 1 & -\frac{3}{2} & \frac{5}{2} \\ -\frac{1}{2} & 1 & \frac{3}{2} \\ \frac{1}{2} & \frac{1}{2} & 1 \end{bmatrix}$

6. $\begin{bmatrix} 12 & \frac{4}{3} \\ 4 & -\frac{14}{3} \\ \frac{25}{3} & \frac{28}{3} \end{bmatrix}$

7. $x = 2, y = 4, z = 1, w = 3$

8. $X = \begin{bmatrix} 4 & 4 \\ 0 & 4 \end{bmatrix}, Y = \begin{bmatrix} 1 & -2 \\ 0 & 5 \end{bmatrix}$

9. $A = \begin{bmatrix} 2 & -1 & 1 \\ 1 & 2 & 0 \end{bmatrix}, B = \begin{bmatrix} 1 & 1 & 2 \\ -1 & 1 & -2 \end{bmatrix}$

10. $\begin{bmatrix} 1 & 0 \\ 0 & 1 \end{bmatrix}$

11. diag [–1, 16, 10]
diag [5, 2, –2]
diag [8, 77, 40]
diag [51, 4, –30]

12. $\begin{bmatrix} -1 & -2 & 3 & -7 \\ -2 & 5 & -6 & 9 \\ -3 & -4 & -5 & 4 \end{bmatrix}$

14. $\begin{bmatrix} 1 & 1 & -2 \\ 1 & 3 & -3 \\ 1 & 8 & -7 \end{bmatrix}$

1.18. Multiplication of Two Matrices

Two matrices A and B are said to be conformable for multiplication if the number of columns of A is equal to the number of rows of B. In the product, A is called the pre-multiplier or pre-factor of B and B is called the post-multiplier or post-factor of A.

Let $A = [a_{ij}]_{m \times n}$ and $B = [b_{jk}]_{n \times p}$. Then the product of the matrices A and B is defined as

$C = [c_{ik}]_{m \times p}$, where

$$c_{ik} = \sum_{j=1}^{n} a_{ij} b_{jk} = a_{i1} b_{ik} + a_{i2} b_{2k} + a_{i3} b_{3k} + \dots + a_{in} b_{nk}$$

Here, j is called the dummy suffix and

$$i = 1, 2, \dots, m;\ k = 1, 2, \dots, p$$

The process of multiplication can be understood by the following diagram:

$$\xrightarrow{i} \begin{bmatrix} a_{11} & a_{12} & \dots & a_{1j} & \dots & a_{1n} \\ a_{21} & a_{22} & \dots & a_{2j} & \dots & a_{2n} \\ \dots\dots & \dots\dots & \dots & \dots\dots & \dots & \dots\dots \\ a_{i1} & a_{i2} & \dots & a_{ij} & \dots & a_{in} \\ a_{m1} & a_{m2} & \dots & a_{mj} & \dots & a_{mn} \end{bmatrix}_{m \times n}$$

$$\downarrow k$$

$$\begin{bmatrix} b_{11} & b_{12} & \dots & b_{1k} & \dots & b_{1p} \\ b_{21} & b_{22} & \dots & b_{2k} & \dots & b_{2p} \\ \dots\dots & \dots\dots & \dots & \dots\dots & \dots & \dots\dots \\ b_{j1} & b_{j2} & \dots & b_{jk} & \dots & b_{jp} \\ b_{n1} & b_{n2} & \dots & b_{nk} & \dots & b_{np} \end{bmatrix}_{n \times p}$$

$$\downarrow k$$

$$= \xrightarrow{i} \begin{bmatrix} c_{11} & c_{12} & \dots & c_{1k} & \dots & c_{1p} \\ c_{21} & c_{22} & \dots & c_{2k} & \dots & c_{2p} \\ \dots\dots & \dots\dots & \dots & \dots\dots & \dots & \dots\dots \\ c_{i1} & c_{i2} & \dots & c_{ik} & \dots & c_{ip} \\ c_{m1} & c_{m2} & \dots & c_{mk} & \dots & c_{mp} \end{bmatrix}_{m \times p}$$

Note: *This method of multiplying two matrices is called row by column rule.*

1.19. Properties of Matrix Multiplication

1. Matrix multiplication is not commutative, in general

Proof.

(i) If the product AB is defined, it is not at all necessary that the product BA is defined. For example, if A is a matrix of order 4×3 and B is a matrix of order 3×2, then AB is defined but BA is not defined.

(ii) Even if AB and BA are both defined, it is not necessary that the order of AB and BA are the same. For example, if A is a matrix of order 4×3 and B is a matrix of order 3×4, then the order of AB is 4×4 whereas the order of BA is 3×3 so that $AB \neq BA$.

(iii) Even if AB and BA are both defined and also their orders are the same, it is not necessary that $AB = BA$.

For example, if $A = \begin{bmatrix} 1 & 1 \\ 0 & 0 \end{bmatrix}$ and $B = \begin{bmatrix} 0 & 1 \\ 0 & 0 \end{bmatrix}$, then

$AB = \begin{bmatrix} 0 & 1 \\ 0 & 0 \end{bmatrix}$ and $BA = \begin{bmatrix} 0 & 0 \\ 0 & 0 \end{bmatrix}$ so that $AB \neq BA$.

(iv) Matrix multiplication is not commutative does not at all mean that there exist no two matrices A and B such that $AB = BA$. It simple means that $AB = BA$ is not always true. Actually, there exist some pairs of matrices A and B for which $AB = BA$. For example, if A is a square matrix and B is an identity matrix of the same order, then

$$AB = AI = A$$

and $$BA = IA = A$$

so that $$AB = BA \ (=A)$$

As an other example, if $A = \begin{bmatrix} p & q \\ -q & p \end{bmatrix}$ and $B = \begin{bmatrix} r & s \\ -s & r \end{bmatrix}$, then $AB = BA$.

Note: *Two square matrices of the same order are said to be anti-commutative, if* $AB = -BA$.

Example

Let $A = \begin{bmatrix} 1 & 0 \\ 0 & -1 \end{bmatrix}$ and $B = \begin{bmatrix} 0 & -1 \\ 1 & 0 \end{bmatrix}$, then $AB = -BA$.

2. Matrix multiplication is associative

If A, B and C are three matrices such that the products AB and BC are defined, then

$(AB)\,C = A\,(BC)$

Proof. Let $A = [a_{ij}]_{m \times n}$, $B = [b_{jk}]_{n \times p}$ and $C = [c_{kl}]_{p \times q}$.

Then, order of AB is $m \times p$ so that the order of $(AB)\,C$ is $m \times q$. Also, order of BC is $n \times q$ so that the order of $A\,(BC)$ is $m \times q$. Thus, $(AB)\,C$ and $A\,(BC)$ have the same order.

Now, $(i, k)^{\text{th}}$ element of AB

$$= \sum_{j=1}^{n} a_{ij} b_{jk} \qquad \left| \begin{array}{l} i = 1, 2, \ldots, m; \\ k = 1, 2, \ldots, p \end{array} \right.$$

$$\therefore \quad AB = \left[\left(\sum_{j=1}^{n} a_{ij} b_{jk} \right) \right]$$

$\therefore$ $(i, l)^{\text{th}}$ element of $(AB)C$

$$= \sum_{k=1}^{p} \left(\sum_{j=1}^{n} a_{ij} b_{jk} \right) c_{kl}$$

$$\therefore \quad (AB)C = \left[\sum_{k=1}^{p} \left(\sum_{j=1}^{n} a_{ij} b_{jk} \right) c_{kl} \right] \text{ where } l = 1, 2, \ldots, q$$

$$= \left[\sum_{k=1}^{p} \left(\sum_{j=1}^{n} a_{ij} b_{jk} c_{kl} \right) \right]$$

Similarly,

$$A(BC) = \left[\sum_{k=1}^{n} \left(\sum_{j=1}^{p} a_{ij} b_{jk} c_{kl} \right) \right]$$

Since the sums are finite and involve elements, we can change the order of summation in the last expression. Hence,

$$A(BC) = \left[\sum_{k=1}^{n}\left(\sum_{j=1}^{n} a_{ij}b_{jk}c_{kl}\right)\right] = (AB)C$$

3. Distribution law

(i) $A(B + C) = AB + AC$ | Left distribution law

and

(ii) $(B + C)A = BA + CA$ | Right distribution law

where the order of A, B and C are such that they are conformable for the operations involved.

Proof.

(i) Let $A = [a_{ij}]_{m \times n}$

$B = [b_{jk}]_{m \times p}$

and $C = [c_{jk}]_{n \times p}$.

Then, the order of $B + C$ is $m \times p$ so that the order of $A(B + C)$ is $m \times p$. Also, the order of AB and AC each is $m \times p$ so that the order of $AB + AC$ is $m \times p$. Thus, $A(B + C)$ and $AB + AC$ have the same order.

Now, $(i, k)^{\text{th}}$ element of $A(B + C)$

$$= \sum_{j=1}^{n} a_{ij}\left(b_{jk} + c_{jk}\right)$$

$$= \sum_{j=1}^{n} a_{ij}b_{jk} + \sum_{j=1}^{n} a_{ij}c_{jk}$$

$$\therefore\ A(B + C) = \left[\left(\sum_{j=1}^{n} a_{ij}b_{jk} + \sum_{j=1}^{n} a_{ij}c_{jk}\right)\right]$$

$$= \left[\sum_{j=1}^{n} a_{ij}b_{jk}\right] + \left[\sum_{j=1}^{n} a_{ij}c_{jk}\right]$$

$$= AB + AC$$

(ii) Let $A = [a_{kl}]_{m \times p}$

$B = [b_{jk}]_{m \times n}$

and $C = [c_{jk}]_{m \times n}$.

Then, the order of $B + C$ is $m \times n$ so that the order of $(B + C)A$ is $m \times p$. Also, the order of BA and CA each is $m \times p$ so that the order of $BA + CA$ is $m \times p$. Thus, $(B + C)A$ and $BA + CA$ have the same order.

Now, $(j, l)^{\text{th}}$ element of $(B + C)A$

$$= \sum_{k=1}^{n} \left(b_{jk} + c_{jk}\right) a_{kl}$$

$$\therefore\ (B + C)A = \left[\sum_{k=1}^{n} \left(b_{jk} + c_{jk}\right) a_{kl}\right]$$

$$= \left[\sum_{k=1}^{n} b_{jk}a_{kl}\right] + \left[\sum_{k=1}^{n} c_{jk}a_{kl}\right]$$

$$= BA + CA$$

4. Zero divisors

If A and B are two non-null matrices such that $AB = O$ where O is a null matrix, then A and B are called the divisors of O.

Theorem 1. The product of two non-zero matrices can be a zero matrix.

Proof. We shall prove this theorem by taking an example in its support.

$$\text{Let}\quad A = \begin{bmatrix} 0 & c & -b \\ -c & 0 & a \\ b & -a & 0 \end{bmatrix} \neq O$$

$$\text{and,}\quad B = \begin{bmatrix} a^2 & ab & ac \\ ab & b^2 & bc \\ ac & bc & c^2 \end{bmatrix} \neq O$$

Then, we have

$$AB = \begin{bmatrix} 0 & c & -b \\ -c & 0 & a \\ b & -c & 0 \end{bmatrix} \begin{bmatrix} a^2 & ab & ac \\ ab & b^2 & bc \\ ac & bc & c^2 \end{bmatrix}$$

$$= \begin{bmatrix} (0)(a^2) & (0)(ab) & (0)(ac) \\ +(c)(ab) & +(c)(b^2) & +(c)(bc) \\ +(-b)(ac) & +(-b)(bc) & +(-b)(c^2) \\ (-c)(a^2) & (-c)(ab) & (-c)(ac) \\ +(0)(ab) & +(0)(b^2) & +(0)(bc) \\ +(a)(ac) & +(a)(bc) & +(a)(c^2) \\ (b)(a^2) & (b)(ab) & (b)(ac) \\ +(-a)(ab) & +(-a)(b^2) & +(-a)(bc) \\ +(0)(ac) & +(0)(bc) & -(0)(c^2) \end{bmatrix}$$

$$= \begin{bmatrix} 0 & 0 & 0 \\ 0 & 0 & 0 \\ 0 & 0 & 0 \end{bmatrix} = O$$

Theorem 2. Cancellation law does not hold for matrix multiplication, i.e. $AB = AC$ ($A \neq O$, $A \neq I$) does not imply $B = C$.

Proof. We shall prove this thorem by taking an example in its support.

Let $$A = \begin{bmatrix} 1 & 2 & 0 \\ 1 & 1 & 0 \\ -1 & 4 & 0 \end{bmatrix}$$

$$B = \begin{bmatrix} 1 & 2 & 3 \\ 1 & 1 & -1 \\ 2 & 2 & 2 \end{bmatrix}$$

and $$C = \begin{bmatrix} 1 & 2 & 3 \\ 1 & 1 & -1 \\ 1 & 1 & 1 \end{bmatrix}$$

$$\text{Then, } AB = \begin{bmatrix} 3 & 4 & 1 \\ 2 & 3 & 2 \\ 3 & 2 & -7 \end{bmatrix} = AC$$

Thus, $AB = AC$ ($A \neq O$, $A \neq I$); but $B \neq C$.

1.20. Positive Integral Powers of a Square Matrix

If A is any matrix, then the product AA is defined only when A is a square matrix. We write A^2 for AA.

Now, by associative law,

$$A^2A = (AA)A = A(AA) = AA^2$$

We write A^2A or AA^2 as A^3.

In general, if m and n are arbitrary positive integers, then

AAA ..... (m factors) is denoted by A^m.

Again,

$$\begin{aligned} A^mA^n &= \{AAA \text{ ..... } (m \text{ factors})\}\{AAA \text{ ..... } (n \text{ factors})\} \\ &= AAA \text{ ..... } \{(m+n) \text{ factors}\} \\ &= A^{m+n} \end{aligned}$$

and,

$$\begin{aligned} (A^m)^n &= A^m\, A^m\, A^m \text{ ..... } (n \text{ factors}) \\ &= \{AAA \text{ ..... } (m \text{ factors})\}\{AAA \text{ .... } (m \text{ factors})\} \\ &\qquad \{AAA \text{ ..... } (m \text{ factors})\} \text{ ..... } (n \text{ factors}) \\ &= AAA \text{ ..... } (mn \text{ factors}) \\ &= A^{mn} \end{aligned}$$

Similarly, $(A^n)^m = A^{mn}$

Therefore,

$$(A^m)^n = A^{mn} = (A^n)^m$$

Note 1: *In particular, we define $A^0 = I_n$, where $n \times n$ is the order of the square matrix A.*

Note 2: *If I is a unit matrix of any order, say n, then $I^2 = I$ and hence*

$I^3 = II^2 = II = I^2 = I$, *and so on*

Hence, $I = I^2 = I^3 = \ldots\ldots = I^m$

Note 3: *Let* A *be any matrix of order* $m \times n$. *Then,*

$$I_m A = A = AI_n$$

where suffix in I *represents the order of the identity matrix.*

Note that in case of no doubt about the order of the identity matrix, we simply use the symbol I *for the identity matrix.*

1.21. Matrix Polynomial

Let A be a square matrix of order n. An expression of the form $a_0 A^m + a_1 A^{m-1} + \ldots\ldots + a_m I_n$, where $a_0, a_1, \ldots\ldots, a_m$ are scalars, is called a matrix polynomial.

If $f(x) = a_0 x^m + a_1 x^{m-1} + \ldots\ldots + a_m$, then for a square matrix A of order n, we define

$$f(A) = a_0 A^m + a_1 A^{m-1} + \ldots\ldots + a_m I_n.$$

1.22. Mathematical Induction

Mathematical induction is a very useful device for proving results for all positive integers. If the result to be proved involves a positive integer n, then the proof by mathematical induction consists of the following two steps:

Step 1. Verify the result for $n = 1$.

Step 2. Assume the result to be true for $n = k$, where k is a positive integer and then prove that it is true for $n = k + 1$.

Now, the result is true for $n = 1$.

Using step 2,

the result is true for $n = 1 + 1 = 2$

$\Rightarrow$ the result is true for $n = 2 + 1 = 3$

$\Rightarrow$ the result is true for $n = 3 + 1 = 4$ and so on.

Hence, the result is true for all positive integral values of n.

ILLUSTRATIVE EXAMPLES

Example 1. If A, B, C are three matrices such that

$$A = [x \quad y \quad z],\ B = \begin{bmatrix} a & h & g \\ h & b & f \\ g & f & c \end{bmatrix} \text{ and } C = \begin{bmatrix} x \\ y \\ z \end{bmatrix},$$

evaluate ABC.

Solution: $AB = [x \quad y \quad z]\begin{bmatrix} a & h & g \\ h & b & f \\ g & f & c \end{bmatrix}$

$$= [ax + hy + gz \quad hx + by + fz \quad gx + fy + cz]$$

Therefore,

$$ABC = [ax + hy + gz \quad hx + by + fz \quad gx + fy + cz]\begin{bmatrix} x \\ y \\ z \end{bmatrix}$$

$$= \left[x(ax + hy + gz) + y(hx + by + fz) + z(gx + fy + cz)\right]$$

$$= \left[ax^2 + hxy + gzx + hxy + by^2 + fyz + gzx + fyz + cz^2\right]$$

$$= \left[ax^2 + by^2 + cz^2 + 2hxy + 2fyz + 2gzx\right]$$

Example 2. Prove that the product of matrices

$$A = \begin{bmatrix} \cos^2\theta & \cos\theta\sin\theta \\ \cos\theta\sin\theta & \sin^2\theta \end{bmatrix},$$

$$B = \begin{bmatrix} \cos^2\varphi & \cos\varphi\sin\varphi \\ \cos\varphi\sin\varphi & \sin^2\varphi \end{bmatrix}$$

is zero when θ and φ differ by an odd multiple of $\frac{\pi}{2}$.

Solution:

$$AB = \begin{bmatrix} \cos^2\theta & \cos\theta\sin\theta \\ \cos\theta\sin\theta & \sin^2\theta \end{bmatrix} \begin{bmatrix} \cos^2\varphi & \cos\varphi\sin\varphi \\ \cos\varphi\sin\varphi & \sin^2\varphi \end{bmatrix}$$

$$= \begin{bmatrix} \begin{matrix}\cos^2\theta\cos^2\varphi + \\ \cos\theta\sin\theta\cos\varphi\sin\varphi\end{matrix} & \begin{matrix}\cos^2\theta\cos\varphi\sin\varphi + \\ \cos\theta\sin\theta\sin^2\varphi\end{matrix} \\ \begin{matrix}\cos\theta\sin\theta\cos^2\varphi + \\ \sin^2\theta\cos\varphi\sin\varphi\end{matrix} & \begin{matrix}\cos\theta\sin\theta\cos\varphi\sin\varphi + \\ \sin^2\theta\sin^2\varphi\end{matrix} \end{bmatrix}$$

$$= \begin{bmatrix} \begin{matrix}\cos\theta\cos\varphi \\ (\cos\theta\cos\varphi + \sin\theta\sin\varphi)\end{matrix} & \begin{matrix}\cos\theta\sin\varphi \\ (\cos\theta\cos\varphi + \sin\theta\sin\varphi)\end{matrix} \\ \begin{matrix}\sin\theta\cos\varphi \\ (\cos\theta\cos\varphi + \sin\theta\sin\varphi)\end{matrix} & \begin{matrix}\sin\theta\sin\varphi \\ (\cos\theta\cos\varphi + \sin\theta\sin\varphi)\end{matrix} \end{bmatrix}$$

$$= \begin{bmatrix} \cos\theta\cos\varphi\cos(\theta \sim \varphi) & \cos\theta\sin\varphi\cos(\theta \sim \varphi) \\ \sin\theta\cos\varphi\cos(\theta \sim \varphi) & \sin\theta\sin\varphi\cos(\theta \sim \varphi) \end{bmatrix}$$

If $\theta \sim \varphi$ is an odd multiple of $\frac{\pi}{2}$, then

$$\cos(\theta \sim \varphi) = 0$$

Therefore,

$$AB = \begin{bmatrix} 0 & 0 \\ 0 & 0 \end{bmatrix} = O$$

where O is a zero matrix of order 2 × 2.

Example 3. If $A = \begin{bmatrix} 1 & 2 & 2 \\ 2 & 1 & 2 \\ 2 & 2 & 1 \end{bmatrix}$, show that $A^2 - 4A - 5I = O$

Solution:

$$A^2 = AA$$

$$= \begin{bmatrix} 1 & 2 & 2 \\ 2 & 1 & 2 \\ 2 & 2 & 1 \end{bmatrix} \begin{bmatrix} 1 & 2 & 2 \\ 2 & 1 & 2 \\ 2 & 2 & 1 \end{bmatrix}$$

$$= \begin{bmatrix} 1+4+4 & 2+2+4 & 2+4+2 \\ 2+2+4 & 4+1+4 & 4+2+4 \\ 2+4+2 & 4+2+2 & 4+4+1 \end{bmatrix}$$

$$= \begin{bmatrix} 9 & 8 & 8 \\ 8 & 9 & 8 \\ 8 & 8 & 9 \end{bmatrix}$$

$$4A = 4\begin{bmatrix} 1 & 2 & 2 \\ 2 & 1 & 2 \\ 2 & 2 & 1 \end{bmatrix} = \begin{bmatrix} 4 & 8 & 8 \\ 8 & 4 & 8 \\ 8 & 8 & 4 \end{bmatrix}$$

$$5I = 5\begin{bmatrix} 1 & 0 & 0 \\ 0 & 1 & 0 \\ 0 & 0 & 1 \end{bmatrix} = \begin{bmatrix} 5 & 0 & 0 \\ 0 & 5 & 0 \\ 0 & 0 & 5 \end{bmatrix}$$

$\therefore A^2 - 4A - 5I$

$$= \begin{bmatrix} 9 & 8 & 8 \\ 8 & 9 & 8 \\ 8 & 8 & 9 \end{bmatrix} - \begin{bmatrix} 4 & 8 & 8 \\ 8 & 4 & 8 \\ 8 & 8 & 4 \end{bmatrix} - \begin{bmatrix} 5 & 0 & 0 \\ 0 & 5 & 0 \\ 0 & 0 & 5 \end{bmatrix}$$

$$= \begin{bmatrix} 9-4-5 & 8-8-0 & 8-8-0 \\ 8-8-0 & 9-4-5 & 8-8-0 \\ 8-8-0 & 8-8-0 & 9-4-5 \end{bmatrix}$$

$$= \begin{bmatrix} 0 & 0 & 0 \\ 0 & 0 & 0 \\ 0 & 0 & 0 \end{bmatrix} = O$$ where O is a zero matrix of order 3×3

Example 4. If $A = \begin{bmatrix} 0 & 2 & 0 & 0 \\ 0 & 0 & 3 & 0 \\ -2 & 0 & 0 & -3 \\ 0 & 5 & 4 & 0 \end{bmatrix}$, $B = \begin{bmatrix} 1 & 2 & 3 \\ 3 & 4 & 5 \\ 5 & -4 & 0 \\ 0 & 7 & 8 \end{bmatrix}$, find the elements c_{23}, c_{32}, c_{42}, c_{43} in the product $C = AB$ where $C = [c_{ij}]$.

Solution: Here, the matrix A is of order 4×4 and the matrix B is of order 4×3. Therefore, the matrix $C = AB$ will be of order 4×3.

Now,

c_{23} = Element in the second row and third column of C

$$= \begin{bmatrix} 0 & 0 & 3 & 0 \end{bmatrix} \begin{bmatrix} 3 \\ 5 \\ 0 \\ 8 \end{bmatrix}$$

$$= (0)\ (3) + (0)\ (5) + (3)\ (0) + (0)\ (8)$$

$$= 0$$

c_{32} = Element in the third row and second column of C

$$= \begin{bmatrix} -2 & 0 & 0 & -3 \end{bmatrix} \begin{bmatrix} 2 \\ 4 \\ -4 \\ 7 \end{bmatrix}$$

$$= (-2)\ (2) + (0)\ (4) + (0)\ (-4) + (-3)\ (7)$$

$$= -25$$

c_{42} = Element in the fourth row and second column of C

$$= \begin{bmatrix} 0 & 5 & 4 & 0 \end{bmatrix} \begin{bmatrix} 2 \\ 4 \\ -4 \\ 7 \end{bmatrix}$$

$$= (0)\ (2) + (5)\ (4) + (4)\ (-4) + (0)\ (7)$$

$$= 4$$

c_{43} = Element in the fourth row and third column of C

$$= \begin{bmatrix} 0 & 5 & 4 & 0 \end{bmatrix} \begin{bmatrix} 3 \\ 5 \\ 0 \\ 8 \end{bmatrix}$$

$$= (0)(3) + (5)(5) + (4)(0) + (0)(8)$$
$$= 25$$

Example 5. If A is any $m \times n$ matrix such that AB and BA are both defined, show that B is a $n \times m$ matrix.

Solution: $\because$ AB is defined

$\therefore$ Number of columns of B = Number of rows of $A = m$

$\because$ BA is defined

$\therefore$ Number of rows of B = Number of columns of $A = n$

Hence, B is a $n \times m$ matrix.

Example 6. If A and B are two matrices such that AB and $A + B$ are both defined, then show that A and B are square matrices of the same order.

Solution: Let the order of matrix A be $m \times n$ and the order of the matrix B be $n \times p$ so that AB is defined.

Now, in order that $A + B$ is defined, their orders must be the same.

$\therefore$ $m = n$

and $n = p$

This shows that A and B are square matrices of the same order n each.

Example 7. Show that the only matrices commutative with a diagonal matrix with distinct diagonal elements are diagonal matrices.

Solution: Let $A = [a_{ij}]$ and $B = \text{diag}\ (d_{11}, d_{22}, \ldots, d_{nn})$ be square matrices of order $n \times n$ each.

Then,

$(i, j)^{\text{th}}$ element of $AB = a_{ij}\ d_{jj}$

and $(i, j)^{th}$ element of $BA = d_{ii}\, a_{ij}$

Since A and B commute, therefore

$$AB = BA$$

$$\Rightarrow a_{ij}\, d_{jj} = d_{ii}\, a_{ij}$$

$$\Rightarrow a_{ij}\,(d_{jj} - d_{ii}) = 0$$

Since $d_{ii} \neq d_{jj}$, except when $i = j$, therefore,

$$a_{ij} = 0 \text{ when } i \neq j$$

Hence, A is a diagonal matrix.

Example 8. Show that if a matrix is commutative with every matrix of the same order, it is necessarily a scalar matrix.

Solution: Let a matrix A be commutative with every matrix of the same order. Then, in order that AB and BA may exist, A and B, both must be square matrices here. Hence, let us suppose that

$$A = [a_{ij}]$$

and $B = [b_{ij}]$

where $i, j = 1, 2, \ldots\ldots, n$

Then,

$$(i, j)^{th} \text{ element of } AB = \sum_{k=1}^{n} a_{ik}\, b_{kj}$$

$$\text{and } (i, j)^{th} \text{ element of } BA = \sum_{k=1}^{n} b_{ik}\, a_{kj}$$

If A and B commute, then

$$AB = BA$$

and, therefore,

$$\sum_{k=1}^{n} a_{ik}\, b_{kj} = \sum_{k=1}^{n} b_{ik}\, a_{kj} \qquad \ldots (1.9)$$

for every set of values of b's.

Now b_{ij} is the only element of B which occurs in both the members of Eq. (1.9), Also, since b_{ij} is arbitrary, the coefficients of b_{ij} on the two sides must be equal and the coefficients of all other b's must be zero.

$\therefore \quad a_{ii} = a_{jj}$

and, $a_{ik} = 0$, when $i \neq k$

Finally, since i and j are arbitrary, we must have

$$a_{11} = a_{22} = a_{33} = \ldots\ldots = a_{nn}$$

and, $a_{ij} = 0$, when $i \neq j$

Hence, A is a scalar matrix.

Example 9. If $A = \begin{bmatrix} 1 & 2 & 3 \\ 3 & 2 & 5 \\ 1 & 9 & 7 \\ 4 & 5 & 1 \end{bmatrix}$, $B = \begin{bmatrix} 1 & 2 & 3 \\ 5 & 4 & 6 \\ 1 & 2 & 7 \end{bmatrix}$ and

$C = \begin{bmatrix} 1 & 2 \\ 5 & 4 \\ 3 & 0 \end{bmatrix}$, then find q_{42} where $ABC = Q = [q_{ij}]$

Solution:

$$AB = \begin{bmatrix} 1 & 2 & 3 \\ 3 & 2 & 5 \\ 1 & 9 & 7 \\ 4 & 5 & 1 \end{bmatrix}_{4\times 3} \begin{bmatrix} 1 & 2 & 3 \\ 5 & 4 & 6 \\ 1 & 2 & 7 \end{bmatrix}_{3\times 3}$$

$$= \begin{bmatrix} 14 & 16 & 36 \\ 18 & 24 & 56 \\ 53 & 52 & 106 \\ 30 & 30 & 49 \end{bmatrix}_{4\times 3}$$

$ABC = (AB)\ C$

$\therefore q_{42}$ = Element of fourth row and second column of Q

$$= \begin{bmatrix} 30 & 30 & 49 \end{bmatrix} \begin{bmatrix} 2 \\ 4 \\ 0 \end{bmatrix}$$

$$= (30)\ (2) + (30)\ (4) + (49)\ (0)$$

$= 60 + 120 + 0$
$= 180$

Example 10. Show that $(i, l)^{th}$ element of the product ABC is the (1×1) matrix $R_i\, B\, C_l$, where R_i and C_l respectively denote the matrices of the ith row and l^{th} column of the matrices A and C, respectively.

Solution: $(i, l)^{th}$ element of ABC

= Product of the matrices of ith row of (AB) and l^{th} column of C

= Product of the matrices of ith row of $(AB) \times C_l$

Hence, the matrix of ith row of AB

$$= \left[a_{i1}\, b_{1k} + a_{i2}\, b_{2k} + \ldots\ldots + a_{in}\, b_{nk}\right]$$

where $k = 1, 2, \ldots\ldots, p$, if $A = [a_{ij}]$ and $B = [b_{jk}]$ be $m \times n$ and $n \times p$ matrices, respectively.

$$= \left[a_{i1}, a_{i2}, \ldots\ldots, a_{in}\right] B$$

$$= (R_i\, B)$$

Hence, $(i, l)^{th}$ element of ABC

$$= (R_i\, B)\, C_l = R_i\, B\, C_l$$

Example 11. Show that the product of two upper (lower) triangular matrices is upper (lower) triangular.

Solution: Let $A = [a_{ij}]_{m \times n}$ and $B = [b_{jk}]_{m \times p}$ be two upper triangular matrices.

Then, by definition,

$$a_{ij} = 0 \text{ when } i > j \qquad \ldots (1.10)$$

and, $$b_{jk} = 0 \text{ when } j > k \qquad \ldots (1.11)$$

Clearly, the order of $C = AB$ is $m \times p$.

Let $C = [c_{ik}]_{m \times p}$ where

$$c_{ik} = \sum_{j=1}^{n} a_{ij}\, b_{jk}$$

Then,

$c_{ik} = 0$ when $i > j,\ j > k$ | Using Eqs. (1.10) and (1.11)

$\Rightarrow\ c_{ik} = 0$ when $i > k$

Hence, C (= AB) is an upper triangular matrix.

Similarly, we can prove for lower triangular matrices.

Example 12. If $A = \begin{bmatrix} 0 & 1 \\ -1 & 0 \end{bmatrix}$, determine α, β such that $(\alpha I + \beta A)^2 = A$.

Solution: We have,

$$A = \begin{bmatrix} 0 & 1 \\ -1 & 0 \end{bmatrix}$$

$$\therefore\ A^2 = AA$$

$$= \begin{bmatrix} 0 & 1 \\ -1 & 0 \end{bmatrix}\begin{bmatrix} 0 & 1 \\ -1 & 0 \end{bmatrix} = \begin{bmatrix} -1 & 0 \\ 0 & -1 \end{bmatrix} = -\begin{bmatrix} 1 & 0 \\ 0 & 1 \end{bmatrix} = -I$$

Now,

$$(\alpha I + \beta A)^2 = (\alpha I + \beta A)\ (\alpha I + \beta A)$$

$$= \alpha^2 I^2 + \alpha\beta IA + \beta\alpha AI + \beta^2 A^2$$

| by distributive law

$$= \alpha^2 I + \alpha\beta A + \beta\alpha A + \beta^2 (-I)$$

$\because I^2 = I,\ IA = A,\ AI = A,\ A^2 = -I$

$$= \alpha^2 I + \alpha\beta A + \alpha\beta A - \beta^2 I$$

$$= \alpha^2 I + 2\alpha\beta A - \beta^2 I$$

$$= (\alpha^2 - \beta^2)I + 2\alpha\beta A$$

$$= A \text{ iff}$$

$$\alpha^2 - \beta^2 = 0 \ \Rightarrow \alpha^2 = \beta^2$$

and $2\alpha\beta = 1$

These relations give

$$\alpha = \beta = \pm \frac{1}{\sqrt{2}} \text{ or } \alpha = -\beta = \pm \frac{i}{\sqrt{2}}$$

Example 13. Show that all possible square roots of the two rowed unit matrix I are

$$\pm I \text{ and } \begin{bmatrix} \alpha & \beta \\ \gamma & -\alpha \end{bmatrix}$$

where α, β, γ are any three numbers related by the relation $1 - \alpha^2 = \beta\gamma$.

Solution: Let $\begin{bmatrix} \alpha & \beta \\ \gamma & \delta \end{bmatrix}$ be a possible square root of the two rowed unit matrix I. Then,

$$\begin{bmatrix} \alpha & \beta \\ \gamma & \delta \end{bmatrix}\begin{bmatrix} \alpha & \beta \\ \gamma & \delta \end{bmatrix} = I = \begin{bmatrix} 1 & 0 \\ 0 & 1 \end{bmatrix}$$

$$\Rightarrow \begin{bmatrix} \alpha^2 + \beta\gamma & \alpha\beta + \beta\delta \\ \gamma\alpha + \delta\gamma & \gamma\beta + \delta^2 \end{bmatrix} = \begin{bmatrix} 1 & 0 \\ 0 & 1 \end{bmatrix}$$

$$\Rightarrow \alpha^2 + \beta\gamma = 1 \quad \text{... (1.12)}$$

$$\alpha\beta + \beta\delta = 0 \quad \text{... (1.13)}$$

$$\gamma\alpha + \delta\gamma = 0 \quad \text{... (1.14)}$$

$$\gamma\beta + \delta^2 = 1 \quad \text{... (1.15)}$$

Equations (1.12) and (1.15) give,

$$\alpha^2 + \beta\gamma = 1 = \gamma\beta + \delta^2$$

$$\Rightarrow \alpha^2 = \delta^2$$

$$\Rightarrow \alpha = \pm\delta$$

Case I: *When* $\alpha = +\delta$

Equations (1.13) and (1.14) give,

$$\delta\beta + \beta\delta = 0 \text{ and } \gamma\delta + \delta\gamma = 0$$

$$\Rightarrow \beta = 0 = \gamma$$

Also, Eq. (1.12) gives $\alpha = \pm 1$, Eq. (1.15) gives $\delta = \pm 1$. Thus, $\alpha = \delta = \pm 1$

Therefore, the square root matrix becomes $\begin{bmatrix} \pm 1 & 0 \\ 0 & \pm 1 \end{bmatrix}$,

i.e. $\pm I$.

Case II: *When* $\alpha = -\delta$

Equations (1.13) and (1.14) are automatically satisfied.

Also, Eq. (1.12) or (1.15) reduces to

$$1 - \alpha^2 = \beta\gamma$$

Therefore, the square root matrix becomes

$$\begin{bmatrix} \alpha & \beta \\ \gamma & -\alpha \end{bmatrix}, \text{ where } 1 - \alpha^2 = \beta\gamma.$$

Example 14. Show that the solution of the equation

$$\begin{bmatrix} x & y \\ z & t \end{bmatrix}^2 = \begin{bmatrix} 0 & 0 \\ 0 & 0 \end{bmatrix} \text{ is } \begin{bmatrix} x & y \\ z & t \end{bmatrix} = \begin{bmatrix} \pm\sqrt{\alpha\beta} & -\beta \\ \alpha & \mp\sqrt{\alpha\beta} \end{bmatrix}$$

where α, β are arbitrary.

Solution: The given matrix equation is

$$\begin{bmatrix} x & y \\ z & t \end{bmatrix}^2 = \begin{bmatrix} 0 & 0 \\ 0 & 0 \end{bmatrix}$$

$$\Rightarrow \begin{bmatrix} x & y \\ z & t \end{bmatrix}\begin{bmatrix} x & y \\ z & t \end{bmatrix} = \begin{bmatrix} 0 & 0 \\ 0 & 0 \end{bmatrix}$$

$$\Rightarrow \begin{bmatrix} x^2 + yz & xy + yt \\ zx + tz & zy + t^2 \end{bmatrix} = \begin{bmatrix} 0 & 0 \\ 0 & 0 \end{bmatrix}$$

$$\Rightarrow x^2 + yz = 0 \quad \text{... (1.16)}$$

$$xy + yt = 0 \quad \text{... (1.17)}$$

$$zx + tz = 0 \quad \text{... (1.18)}$$

$$zy + t^2 = 0 \quad \text{... (1.19)}$$

Equations (1.16) and (1.19) give

$$x^2 = t^2$$

$$\Rightarrow x = \pm t$$

Case I: *When* $x = +t$

Then, Eqs. (1.17) and (1.18) give

$$y = 0 = z$$

Hence, Eqs. (1.16) and (1.19) give $x = 0$, $t = 0$ respectively

Case II: *When* $x = -t$

Then Eqs. (1.17) and (1.18) are automatically satisfied for all values of y and z.

If we choose $y = -\beta$, $z = \alpha$, then Eq. (1.16) gives,

$$x = \pm\sqrt{\alpha\beta} = -t$$

Clearly, Case I is included in Case II (if we choose $\alpha = 0$, $\beta = 0$).

Therefore, the general solution of the given equation is

$$x = -t = \pm\sqrt{\alpha\beta}$$

$$y = -\beta$$

$$z = \alpha$$

i.e., $$\begin{bmatrix} x & y \\ z & t \end{bmatrix} = \begin{bmatrix} \pm\sqrt{\alpha\beta} & -\beta \\ \alpha & \pm\sqrt{\alpha\beta} \end{bmatrix}$$

where α, β are arbitrary.

Example 15. If $A = \begin{bmatrix} 3 & -4 \\ 1 & -1 \end{bmatrix}$, then prove that $A^n = \begin{bmatrix} 1+2n & -4n \\ n & 1-2n \end{bmatrix}$ where n is any positive integer.

Solution: We shall prove that result by mathematical induction.

When $n = 1$,

$$A^n = \begin{bmatrix} 1+2n & -4n \\ n & 1-2n \end{bmatrix}$$

$$\Rightarrow A^1 = \begin{bmatrix} 1+2.1 & -4.1 \\ 1 & 1-2.1 \end{bmatrix} = \begin{bmatrix} 3 & -4 \\ 1 & -1 \end{bmatrix} = A$$

$\Rightarrow$ The result is true for $n = 1$.

Let us assume that the result is true for any positive integer K. Then,

$$A^K = \begin{bmatrix} 1+2K & -4K \\ K & 1-2K \end{bmatrix}$$

Now,

$$A^{K+1} = A^K \cdot A = \begin{bmatrix} 1+2K & -4K \\ K & 1-2K \end{bmatrix}\begin{bmatrix} 3 & -4 \\ 1 & -1 \end{bmatrix}$$

$$= \begin{bmatrix} 3(1+2K)-4K & -4(1+2K)+4K \\ 3K+1-2K & -4K-1+2K \end{bmatrix}$$

$$= \begin{bmatrix} 3+2K & -4-4K \\ 1+K & -1-2K \end{bmatrix}$$

$$= \begin{bmatrix} 1+2(K+1) & -4(K+1) \\ K+1 & 1-2(K+1) \end{bmatrix}$$

$\Rightarrow$ The result is true for $n = K + 1$

Hence, by mathematical induction, the result is true for all positive integral value of n.

Example 16. Let $A = \begin{bmatrix} 0 & 1 \\ 0 & 0 \end{bmatrix}$. Show that $(aI + bA)^n = a^nI + na^{n-1}bA$, where I is the identity matrix of order 2, $n \in N$ and a, b are scalars.

Solution:

$$aI + bA = a\begin{bmatrix} 1 & 0 \\ 0 & 1 \end{bmatrix} + b\begin{bmatrix} 0 & 1 \\ 0 & 0 \end{bmatrix}$$

$$= \begin{bmatrix} a & 0 \\ 0 & a \end{bmatrix} + \begin{bmatrix} 0 & b \\ 0 & 0 \end{bmatrix}$$

$$= \begin{bmatrix} a & b \\ 0 & a \end{bmatrix}$$

$$a^nI + na^{n-1}bA = a^n\begin{bmatrix}1 & 0\\0 & 1\end{bmatrix} + na^{n-1}b\begin{bmatrix}0 & 1\\0 & 0\end{bmatrix}$$

$$= \begin{bmatrix}a^n & 0\\0 & a^n\end{bmatrix} + \begin{bmatrix}0 & na^{n-1}b\\0 & 0\end{bmatrix}$$

$$= \begin{bmatrix}a^n & na^{n-1}b\\0 & a^n\end{bmatrix}$$

So, we are to prove that

$$\begin{bmatrix}a & b\\0 & a\end{bmatrix}^n = \begin{bmatrix}a^n & na^{n-1}b\\0 & a^n\end{bmatrix} \text{ for } n \in N.$$

We shall prove the result by mathematical induction.

When $n = 1$,

$$\begin{bmatrix}a & b\\0 & a\end{bmatrix}^1 = \begin{bmatrix}a & b\\0 & a\end{bmatrix}$$

and, $$\begin{bmatrix}a^n & na^{n-1}b\\0 & a^n\end{bmatrix} = \begin{bmatrix}a^1 & 1a^{1-1}b\\0 & a^1\end{bmatrix} = \begin{bmatrix}a & b\\0 & a\end{bmatrix}$$

Hence, the result is true for $n = 1$.

Let us assume that the result is true for any positive integer K. Then,

$$\begin{bmatrix}a & b\\0 & a\end{bmatrix}^K = \begin{bmatrix}a^K & Ka^{K-1}b\\0 & a^K\end{bmatrix}$$

Now,

$$\begin{bmatrix}a & b\\0 & a\end{bmatrix}^{K+1} = \begin{bmatrix}a & b\\0 & a\end{bmatrix}^K \begin{bmatrix}a & b\\0 & a\end{bmatrix}$$

$$= \begin{bmatrix}a^K & Ka^{K-1}b\\0 & a^K\end{bmatrix}\begin{bmatrix}a & b\\0 & a\end{bmatrix}$$

$$= \begin{bmatrix} a^{K+1} & a^K b + K a^K b \\ 0 & a^{K+1} \end{bmatrix}$$

$$= \begin{bmatrix} a^{K+1} & (K+1)a^K b \\ 0 & a^{K+1} \end{bmatrix}$$

$$= \begin{bmatrix} a^{K+1} & (K+1)a^{(K+1)-1} b \\ 0 & a^{K+1} \end{bmatrix}$$

$\Rightarrow$ The result is true for $n = K + 1$.

Hence, by mathematical induction, the result is true for all positive integral values of n.

Example 17. If $I = \begin{bmatrix} 1 & 0 \\ 0 & 1 \end{bmatrix}$ and $E = \begin{bmatrix} 0 & 1 \\ 0 & 0 \end{bmatrix}$, prove that $(aI + bE)^3 = a^3 I + 3a^2 bE$, where a and b are arbitrary scalars.

Solution:

$$aI + bE = a\begin{bmatrix} 1 & 0 \\ 0 & 1 \end{bmatrix} + b\begin{bmatrix} 0 & 1 \\ 0 & 0 \end{bmatrix}$$

$$= \begin{bmatrix} a & 0 \\ 0 & a \end{bmatrix} + \begin{bmatrix} 0 & b \\ 0 & 0 \end{bmatrix}$$

$$= \begin{bmatrix} a & b \\ 0 & a \end{bmatrix}$$

$\therefore \quad (aI + bE)^2 = (aI + bE)\,(aI + bE)$

$$= \begin{bmatrix} a & b \\ 0 & a \end{bmatrix}\begin{bmatrix} a & b \\ 0 & a \end{bmatrix}$$

$$= \begin{bmatrix} a^2 & ab + ba \\ 0 & a^2 \end{bmatrix}$$

$$= \begin{bmatrix} a^2 & 2ab \\ 0 & a^2 \end{bmatrix}$$

$\therefore \quad (aI + bE)^3 = (aI + bE)^2 (aI + bE)$

$$= \begin{bmatrix} a^2 & 2ab \\ 0 & a^2 \end{bmatrix} \begin{bmatrix} a & b \\ 0 & a \end{bmatrix}$$

$$= \begin{bmatrix} a^3 & a^2b + 2a^2b \\ 0 & a^3 \end{bmatrix}$$

$$= \begin{bmatrix} a^3 & 3a^2b \\ 0 & a^3 \end{bmatrix}$$

Also,

$$a^3I + 3a^2bE = a^3 \begin{bmatrix} 1 & 0 \\ 0 & 1 \end{bmatrix} + 3a^2b \begin{bmatrix} 0 & 1 \\ 0 & 0 \end{bmatrix}$$

$$= \begin{bmatrix} a^3 & 0 \\ 0 & a^3 \end{bmatrix} + \begin{bmatrix} 0 & 3a^2b \\ 0 & 0 \end{bmatrix}$$

$$= \begin{bmatrix} a^3 & 3a^2b \\ 0 & a^3 \end{bmatrix}$$

Hence, $(aI + bE)^3 = a^3I + 3a^2bE$

Example 18. Under what conditions is the matrix equation $A^2 - B^2 = (A - B)(A + B)$ true?

Solution:

$A^2 - B^2 = (A - B)(A + B)$

$\Rightarrow A^2 - B^2 = (A - B)A + (A - B)B$ | Distributive Law

$= AA - BA + AB - BB$ | Distributive Law

$= A^2 - BA + AB - B^2$

$\Rightarrow (A^2 - A^2) + (B^2 - B^2) - AB + BA = O$

$\Rightarrow O + O - AB + BA = O$

$\Rightarrow -AB + BA = O$

$\Rightarrow AB = BA$

Example 19. If e^A is defined as $I + A + \frac{A^2}{\underline{|2}} + \frac{A^3}{\underline{|3}} + ...$, show that

$$e^A = e^x \begin{bmatrix} \cos hx & \sin hx \\ \sin hx & \cos hx \end{bmatrix}, \text{ where } A = \begin{bmatrix} x & x \\ x & x \end{bmatrix}$$

Solution:

$$A^2 = AA = \begin{bmatrix} x & x \\ x & x \end{bmatrix}\begin{bmatrix} x & x \\ x & x \end{bmatrix} = \begin{bmatrix} 2x^2 & 2x^2 \\ 2x^2 & 2x^2 \end{bmatrix} = 2\begin{bmatrix} x^2 & x^2 \\ x^2 & x^2 \end{bmatrix}$$

$$\Rightarrow \quad \frac{A^2}{\underline{|2}} = \begin{bmatrix} x^2 & x^2 \\ x^2 & x^2 \end{bmatrix}$$

$$A^3 = A^2A = 2\begin{bmatrix} x^2 & x^2 \\ x^2 & x^2 \end{bmatrix}\begin{bmatrix} x & x \\ x & x \end{bmatrix}$$

$$= 2\begin{bmatrix} 2x^3 & 2x^3 \\ 2x^3 & 2x^3 \end{bmatrix}$$

$$= 4\begin{bmatrix} x^3 & x^3 \\ x^3 & x^3 \end{bmatrix}$$

$$\therefore \quad \frac{A^3}{\underline{|3}} = \frac{A^3}{6} = \frac{2}{3}\begin{bmatrix} x^3 & x^3 \\ x^3 & x^3 \end{bmatrix}$$

$$\therefore e^A = I + A + \frac{A^2}{\underline{|2}} + \frac{A^3}{\underline{|3}} + ...$$

$$= \begin{bmatrix} 1 & 0 \\ 0 & 1 \end{bmatrix} + \begin{bmatrix} x & x \\ x & x \end{bmatrix} + \begin{bmatrix} x^2 & x^2 \\ x^2 & x^2 \end{bmatrix} + \frac{2}{3}\begin{bmatrix} x^3 & x^3 \\ x^3 & x^3 \end{bmatrix} + ...$$

$$= \begin{bmatrix} 1 + x + x^2 + \frac{2}{3}x^3 + ... & x + x^2 + \frac{2}{3}x^3 + ... \\ x + x^2 + \frac{2}{x}x^3 + ... & 1 + x + x^2 + \frac{2}{3}x^3 + ... \end{bmatrix}$$

$$= \frac{1}{2}\begin{bmatrix} 2+2x+\frac{(2x)^2}{\lfloor 2} + \frac{(2x)^3}{\lfloor 3} + \ldots & 2x+\frac{(2x)^2}{\lfloor 2} + \frac{(2x)^3}{\lfloor 3} + \ldots \\ 2x+\frac{(2x)^2}{\lfloor 2} + \frac{(2x)^3}{\lfloor 3} + \ldots & 2+2x+\frac{(2x)^2}{\lfloor 2} + \frac{(2x)^3}{\lfloor 3} + \ldots \end{bmatrix}$$

$$= \frac{1}{2}\begin{bmatrix} e^{2x}+1 & e^{2x}-1 \\ e^{2x}-1 & e^{2x}+1 \end{bmatrix}$$

$$= \frac{1}{2}\begin{bmatrix} e^{x}\left(e^{x}+e^{-x}\right) & e^{x}\left(e^{x}-e^{-x}\right) \\ e^{x}\left(e^{x}-e^{-x}\right) & e^{x}\left(e^{x}+e^{-x}\right) \end{bmatrix}$$

$$= e^{x}\begin{bmatrix} \frac{e^{x}+e^{-x}}{2} & \frac{e^{x}-e^{-x}}{2} \\ \frac{e^{x}-e^{-x}}{2} & \frac{e^{x}+e^{-x}}{2} \end{bmatrix}$$

$$= e^{x}\begin{bmatrix} \cos hx & \sin hx \\ \sin hx & \cos hx \end{bmatrix}$$

Example 20. A is the $n \times n$ matrix whose elements are all unity and B is a square matrix of order n with all diagonal elements equal to n and other elements $(n - r)$, show that A^2 is a scalar multiple of A and deduce that

$$(B - rI)\,[B - (n^2 - nr + r)\,I] = O$$

Solution: We have

$$A = \begin{bmatrix} 1 & 1 & \ldots & 1 \\ 1 & 1 & \ldots & 1 \\ \ldots & \ldots & \ldots & \ldots \\ 1 & 1 & \ldots & 1 \end{bmatrix}$$

$\therefore \quad A^2 = AA$

$$= \begin{bmatrix} 1 & 1 & ..... & 1 \\ 1 & 1 & ..... & 1 \\ ..... & ..... & ..... & ..... \\ 1 & 1 & ..... & 1 \end{bmatrix} \begin{bmatrix} 1 & 1 & ..... & 1 \\ 1 & 1 & ..... & 1 \\ ..... & ..... & ..... & ..... \\ 1 & 1 & ..... & 1 \end{bmatrix}$$

$$= \begin{bmatrix} n & n & ..... & n \\ n & n & ..... & n \\ ..... & ..... & ..... & ..... \\ n & n & ..... & n \end{bmatrix} = n \begin{bmatrix} 1 & 1 & ..... & 1 \\ 1 & 1 & ..... & 1 \\ ..... & ..... & ..... & ..... \\ 1 & 1 & ..... & 1 \end{bmatrix}$$

$$= nA \qquad \text{... (1.20)}$$

Hence, A^2 is a scalar multiple of A.

Deduction

From Eq. (1.20)

$$A^2 - nA = 0$$

$$\Rightarrow A(A - nI) = 0 \qquad \text{... (1.21)}$$

Now,

$$B = \begin{bmatrix} n & n-r & ..... & n-r \\ n-r & n & ..... & n-r \\ ..... & ..... & ..... & ..... \\ n-r & n-r & ..... & n \end{bmatrix}$$

$$= \begin{bmatrix} n-r+r & n-r+0 & ..... & n-r+0 \\ n-r+0 & n-r+r & ..... & n-r+0 \\ ..... & ..... & ..... & ..... \\ n-r+0 & n-r+0 & ..... & n-r+r \end{bmatrix}$$

$$= \begin{bmatrix} n-r & n-r & ..... & n-r \\ n-r & n-r & ..... & n-r \\ ..... & ..... & ..... & ..... \\ n-r & n-r & ..... & n-r \end{bmatrix} + \begin{bmatrix} r & 0 & ..... & 0 \\ 0 & r & .... & 0 \\ ..... & ..... & ..... & ..... \\ 0 & 0 & ..... & r \end{bmatrix}$$

$$= (n - r)\, A + rI \qquad \dots (1.22)$$

$$\therefore \quad (B - rI)\,[B - (n^2 - nr + r)\, I]$$

$$= (n-r)A\left[(n-r)A + rI - \left(n^2 - nr + r\right)I\right]$$

$$= (n-r)A\left[(n-r)A - n\,(n-r)I\right]$$

$$= (n-r)^2\, A\,(A - nI)$$

$$= (n-r)^2\, O \qquad \text{| Using Eq. (1.21)}$$

$$= O$$

EXERCISE 1.2

1. If $A = \begin{bmatrix} 1 & 2 & -3 \\ -2 & 1 & 7 \end{bmatrix}$ and $B = \begin{bmatrix} 2 & 3 & 1 \\ 5 & 4 & 2 \\ 1 & 6 & 3 \end{bmatrix}$, find AB.

2. Find the product of the matrices

$$A = \begin{bmatrix} 2 & 1 & 2 & 1 \\ 1 & 1 & 1 & 1 \end{bmatrix} \text{ and } B = \begin{bmatrix} 2 & -1 & 0 \\ 0 & 4 & 1 \\ -2 & 1 & 0 \\ 1 & -3 & 2 \end{bmatrix}$$

3. If $A = \begin{bmatrix} 2 & 3 & 4 \\ 1 & 2 & 3 \\ -1 & 1 & 2 \end{bmatrix}$ and $B = \begin{bmatrix} 1 & 3 & 0 \\ -1 & 2 & 1 \\ 0 & 0 & 2 \end{bmatrix}$, evaluate AB, BA whichever exists.

4. If $A = \begin{bmatrix} 1 & -2 & 3 \\ 2 & 3 & -1 \\ -3 & 1 & 2 \end{bmatrix}$, $B = \begin{bmatrix} 1 & 0 & 2 \\ 0 & 1 & 2 \\ 1 & 2 & 0 \end{bmatrix}$, show that $AB \neq BA$.

5. If $A = \begin{bmatrix} 1 & -2 & 3 \\ -4 & 2 & 5 \end{bmatrix}$ and $B = \begin{bmatrix} 2 & 3 \\ 4 & 5 \\ 2 & 1 \end{bmatrix}$, find AB, BA and show that $AB \neq BA$.

6. If $A = \begin{bmatrix} 1 & -3 & 2 \\ 2 & 1 & -3 \\ 4 & -3 & -1 \end{bmatrix}$, $B = \begin{bmatrix} 1 & 4 & 1 & 0 \\ 2 & 1 & 1 & 1 \\ 1 & -2 & 1 & 2 \end{bmatrix}$,

$C = \begin{bmatrix} 2 & 1 & -1 & -2 \\ 3 & -2 & -1 & -1 \\ 2 & -5 & -1 & 0 \end{bmatrix}$, show that

(i) $AB = AC$

(ii) $A(B + C) = AB + AC$

7. (a) If $A = \begin{bmatrix} 2 & 1 & -1 & 2 \\ -2 & -2 & 1 & -1 \\ -3 & 0 & 0 & 3 \\ 0 & 1 & 4 & 4 \end{bmatrix}$, $B = \begin{bmatrix} 1 & 2 & 3 & 4 \\ 2 & 3 & 4 & -1 \\ -3 & 4 & 1 & 2 \\ 4 & 1 & 2 & 3 \end{bmatrix}$,

show that $AB \neq BA$.

(b) If $A = \begin{bmatrix} 1 & 1 & -1 \\ 2 & -3 & 4 \\ 3 & -2 & 3 \end{bmatrix}$, $B = \begin{bmatrix} -1 & -2 & -1 \\ 6 & 12 & 6 \\ 5 & 10 & 5 \end{bmatrix}$,

$C = \begin{bmatrix} -1 & -1 & 1 \\ 2 & 2 & -2 \\ -3 & -3 & 3 \end{bmatrix}$, show that AB, CA are null matrices but BA, AC are not null matrices.

8. If the Pauli spin components s_x, s_y, s_z are given by

$$s_x = \begin{bmatrix} 0 & 1 \\ 1 & 0 \end{bmatrix}, s_y = \begin{bmatrix} 0 & -i \\ i & 0 \end{bmatrix}, s_z = \begin{bmatrix} 1 & 0 \\ 0 & -1 \end{bmatrix}$$

show that they anti-commute with each other and that

$$s_x^2 = s_y^2 = s_z^2 = I^2 = I, \text{ where } I = \begin{bmatrix} 1 & 0 \\ 0 & 1 \end{bmatrix}$$

9. If $I = \begin{bmatrix} 1 & 0 \\ 0 & 1 \end{bmatrix}, i = \begin{bmatrix} \sqrt{-1} & 0 \\ 0 & -\sqrt{-1} \end{bmatrix}, j = \begin{bmatrix} 0 & 1 \\ -1 & 0 \end{bmatrix},$

$k = \begin{bmatrix} 0 & \sqrt{-1} \\ \sqrt{-1} & 1 \end{bmatrix}$, show that

$ij = k,\ jk = i,\ ki = j,\ ji = -k,\ kj = -i,\ ik = -j,\ i^2 = j^2 = k^2 = -I$

10. If $A = \begin{bmatrix} i & 0 \\ 0 & -i \end{bmatrix}$, $B = \begin{bmatrix} 0 & -1 \\ 1 & 0 \end{bmatrix}$, $C = \begin{bmatrix} 0 & i \\ i & 0 \end{bmatrix}$, prove that

$A^2 = B^2 = C^2 = -I$

and $AB = -C = BA$,

where $I = \begin{bmatrix} 1 & 0 \\ 0 & 1 \end{bmatrix}$

11. If $E = \begin{bmatrix} 0 & 1 & 0 \\ 0 & 0 & 1 \\ 0 & 0 & 0 \end{bmatrix}$, $F = \begin{bmatrix} 0 & 0 & 0 \\ 1 & 0 & 0 \\ 0 & 1 & 0 \end{bmatrix}$, calculate the matrices EF and FE and show that $E^2F + FE^2 = E$. Also prove that $(E + xF)^2 = xI$; x being a scalar and I being the identity matrix.

12. If $\begin{bmatrix} 2 & -1 & 3 \\ 1 & 2 & -4 \\ -1 & 3 & -2 \end{bmatrix} \begin{bmatrix} x \\ y \\ z \end{bmatrix} = \begin{bmatrix} 1 \\ -3 \\ 0 \end{bmatrix}$, find the values of x, y and z.

13. Find x, if

$$\begin{bmatrix} x & 1 \end{bmatrix} \begin{bmatrix} 1 & 0 \\ -2 & -3 \end{bmatrix} \begin{bmatrix} x \\ 3 \end{bmatrix} = O$$

14. If A and B be n-rowed square matrices, then show that

(i) $(A + B)^2 = A^2 + AB + BA + B^2$

(ii) $(A - B)^2 = A^2 - AB - BA + B^2$

(iii) $(A + B)(A - B) = A^2 - AB + BA - B^2$

(iv) $(A - B)(A + B) = A^2 + AB - BA - B^2$

(v) $(A + B)^3 = A^3 + ABA + A^2B + AB^2 + BA^2 + B^2A + BAB + B^3$

What happens when A and B commute?

15. If A and B are square matrices of the same order, show that unless $AB = BA$, $(A - 2B)(A - 3B) \neq A^2 - 5AB + 6B^2$.

16. If $A = \begin{bmatrix} 2 & -1 \\ 0 & 1 \end{bmatrix}$, $B = \begin{bmatrix} 1 & 0 \\ -1 & -1 \end{bmatrix}$, show that

$(A + B)^2 = A^2 + AB + BA + B^2 \neq A^2 + 2AB + B^2$

17. If $A = \begin{bmatrix} -1 & 1 & -1 \\ -2 & 0 & 1 \\ 0 & -1 & 1 \end{bmatrix}$, $B = \begin{bmatrix} 1 & -1 & 1 \\ 4 & 0 & -1 \\ 4 & -2 & 1 \end{bmatrix}$, $C = \begin{bmatrix} 1 & 0 & 1 \\ 2 & 1 & 1 \\ 2 & 1 & 2 \end{bmatrix}$,

find p_{23}, p_{32}, p_{22}, where p_{ij} is the $(i, j)^{\text{th}}$ element of ABC.

18. If $A = \begin{bmatrix} 1 & -1 \\ 2 & -1 \end{bmatrix}$, $B = \begin{bmatrix} a & 1 \\ b & -1 \end{bmatrix}$ and $(A + B)^2 = A^2 + B^2$, find a and b.

19. If $A = \begin{bmatrix} 4 & 3 \\ 2 & 5 \end{bmatrix}$, find x and y such that $A^2 - xA + yI = O$.

20. If $A = \begin{bmatrix} -1 & 1 & -1 \\ 3 & -3 & 3 \\ 5 & -5 & 5 \end{bmatrix}$, $B = \begin{bmatrix} 0 & 4 & 3 \\ 1 & -3 & -3 \\ -1 & 4 & 4 \end{bmatrix}$, compute A^2B^2.

21. If $f(x) = \begin{bmatrix} \cos x & -\sin x & 0 \\ \sin x & \cos x & 0 \\ 0 & 0 & 1 \end{bmatrix}$, show that $f(\alpha)\, f(\beta) = f(\alpha + \beta)$.

22. If $A = \begin{bmatrix} 0 & -\tan\frac{\alpha}{2} \\ \tan\frac{\alpha}{2} & 0 \end{bmatrix}$ and I is a unit matrix, show that

$$I + A = (I - A)\begin{bmatrix} \cos\alpha & -\sin\alpha \\ \sin\alpha & \cos\alpha \end{bmatrix}$$

23. If $A = \begin{bmatrix} 1 & 1 & -1 \\ 2 & 0 & 3 \\ 3 & -1 & 2 \end{bmatrix}$, $B = \begin{bmatrix} 1 & 3 \\ 0 & 2 \\ -1 & 4 \end{bmatrix}$ and $C = \begin{bmatrix} 1 & 2 & 3 & -4 \\ 2 & 0 & -2 & 1 \end{bmatrix}$, show that $(AB)C = A(BC)$.

24. If $A = \begin{bmatrix} 0 & 1 & 0 \\ 0 & 0 & 1 \\ p & q & r \end{bmatrix}$ and I is the unit matrix of order 3, show that

$$A^3 = pI + qA + rA^2$$

25. If $A = \begin{bmatrix} 1 & -2 & 3 \\ 2 & 3 & -1 \\ 3 & 1 & 2 \end{bmatrix}$, show that

$$6A^2 + 25A - 42I = O$$

26. Show that if A is the matrix $\begin{bmatrix} 2 & -1 & 1 \\ -1 & 2 & -1 \\ 1 & -1 & 2 \end{bmatrix}$, then $A^3 - 6A^2 + 9A - 4I = O$, where I is the unit matrix of order 3 and O is the null matrix of order 3×3.

27. If $I = \begin{bmatrix} 1 & 0 \\ 0 & 1 \end{bmatrix}$, $i = \begin{bmatrix} 0 & 1 \\ -1 & 0 \end{bmatrix}$, $E(\theta) = \begin{bmatrix} \cos\theta & \sin\theta \\ -\sin\theta & \cos\theta \end{bmatrix}$, show that

(i) $E(\theta) = I\cos\theta + i\sin\theta$

(ii) $E(\alpha)\,E(\beta) = E(\beta)\,E(\alpha) = E(\alpha + \beta)$

(iii) $\{E(\theta)\}^n = E(n\theta)$, where n is a positive integer.

28. If $A_\alpha = \begin{bmatrix} \cos\alpha & \sin\alpha \\ -\sin\alpha & \cos\alpha \end{bmatrix}$, show that

(i) $A_\alpha A_\beta = A_\beta A_\alpha$

(ii) $A_\alpha A_\beta = A_{\alpha+\beta}$

(iii) $A_\alpha A_{-\alpha} = I$

(iv) $A_\alpha^n = A_{n\alpha}$

29. If $A = \begin{bmatrix} 1 & 1 \\ 0 & 1 \end{bmatrix}$, show that $A^n = \begin{bmatrix} 1 & n \\ 0 & 1 \end{bmatrix}$ where n is a positive integer.

30. If $A = \text{diag}\,(a, b, c)$, show that $A^n = \text{diag}\,(a^n, b^n, c^n)$

31. If $A = \begin{bmatrix} \cos\theta & \sin\theta \\ -\sin\theta & \cos\theta \end{bmatrix}$, show that $A^n = \begin{bmatrix} \cos n\theta & \sin n\theta \\ -\sin n\theta & \cos n\theta \end{bmatrix}$,

$n \in N$.

32. If $H = \begin{bmatrix} \cos hu & \sin hu \\ \sin hu & \cos hu \end{bmatrix}$, show that $H^n = \begin{bmatrix} \cos hnu & \sin hnu \\ \sin hnu & \cos hnu \end{bmatrix}$,

$n \in N$.

33. If $A = \begin{bmatrix} 1 & 1 & 1 \\ 1 & 1 & 1 \\ 1 & 1 & 1 \end{bmatrix}$, show that $A^n = \begin{bmatrix} 3^{n-1} & 3^{n-1} & 3^{n-1} \\ 3^{n-1} & 3^{n-1} & 3^{n-1} \\ 3^{n-1} & 3^{n-1} & 3^{n-1} \end{bmatrix}$,

$n \in N$.

34. If $A = \begin{bmatrix} \lambda & 1 \\ 0 & \lambda \end{bmatrix}$, show that $A^n = \begin{bmatrix} \lambda^n & n\lambda^{n-1} \\ 0 & \lambda^n \end{bmatrix}$, $n \in N$.

35. If $A = \begin{bmatrix} a & b \\ 0 & 1 \end{bmatrix}$, $a \neq 1$, show that $A^n = \begin{bmatrix} a^n & b\left(a^{n-1}\right) \\ 0 & 1 \end{bmatrix}$,

$n \in N$.

36. If A and B are square commutative matrices of the same order, prove that

(i) $AB^n = B^nA,\ n \in N$

(ii) $(AB)^n = B^nA^n,\ n \in N$

37. If $A = \begin{bmatrix} 1 & 1 & 0 \\ 0 & 1 & 1 \\ 0 & 0 & 1 \end{bmatrix}$, prove that $A^n = \begin{bmatrix} 1 & n & \frac{1}{2}n(n-1) \\ 0 & 1 & n \\ 0 & 0 & 0 \end{bmatrix}$,

$n \in N.$

38. Prove that

$$\begin{bmatrix} \cos\theta + \sin\theta & \sqrt{2}\sin\theta \\ -\sqrt{2}\sin\theta & \cos\theta - \sin\theta \end{bmatrix}^n = \begin{bmatrix} \cos n\theta + \sin n\theta & \sqrt{2}\sin n\theta \\ -\sqrt{2}\sin n\theta & \cos n\theta - \sin n\theta \end{bmatrix},$$

$n \in N.$

39. Given $A_1 = \begin{bmatrix} 0 & 0 & 0 & 1 \\ 0 & 0 & 1 & 0 \\ 0 & 1 & 0 & 0 \\ 1 & 0 & 0 & 0 \end{bmatrix}$, $A_2 = \begin{bmatrix} 0 & 0 & 0 & i \\ 0 & 0 & -i & 0 \\ 0 & i & 0 & 0 \\ -i & 0 & 0 & 0 \end{bmatrix}$,

$A_3 = \begin{bmatrix} 0 & 0 & 1 & 0 \\ 0 & 0 & 0 & -1 \\ 1 & 0 & 0 & 0 \\ 0 & -1 & 0 & 0 \end{bmatrix}$, $A_4 = \begin{bmatrix} 1 & 0 & 0 & 0 \\ 0 & 1 & 0 & 0 \\ 0 & 0 & -1 & 0 \\ 0 & 0 & 0 & -1 \end{bmatrix}$,

show that $A_i A_k + A_k A_i = 2I$ or zero according as $i = k$ or $i \neq k$ and I is the unit matrix of order 4 and i, k take the values 1, 2, 3 and 4.

40. If A, B, C are n-rowed square matrices and if $A = B + C$, $BC = CB$, $C^2 = O$, then show that for every positive integer p,

$A^{p+1} = B^p\,[B + (p + 1)\,C]$

ANSWERS

1. $\begin{bmatrix} 9 & -7 & -4 \\ 8 & 40 & 21 \end{bmatrix}$

2. $\begin{bmatrix} 1 & 1 & 3 \\ 1 & 1 & 3 \end{bmatrix}$

3. $AB = \begin{bmatrix} -1 & 12 & 11 \\ -1 & 7 & 8 \\ -2 & -1 & 5 \end{bmatrix}$

$BA = \begin{bmatrix} 5 & 9 & 13 \\ -1 & 2 & 4 \\ -2 & 2 & 4 \end{bmatrix}$

5. $AB = \begin{bmatrix} 14 & 4 \\ 4 & 14 \end{bmatrix}$

$BA = \begin{bmatrix} 9 & 6 & 3 & 0 \\ 6 & 5 & 4 & 3 \\ 3 & 4 & 5 & 6 \\ 0 & 3 & 6 & 9 \end{bmatrix}$

11. $EF = \begin{bmatrix} 0 & 0 & 0 \\ 1 & 1 & 0 \\ 0 & 0 & 0 \end{bmatrix}$

$FE = \begin{bmatrix} 0 & 0 & 0 \\ 0 & 1 & 0 \\ 0 & 0 & 1 \end{bmatrix}$

12. $x = -1$

$y = 3$

$z = 2$

13. $1 \pm \sqrt{10}$

14. (i) $(A + B)^2 = A^2 + 2AB + B^2$

(ii) $(A - B)^2 = A^2 - 2AB + B^2$

(iii) $(A + B)(A - B) = A^2 - B^2$

(iv) $(A - B)(A + B) = A^2 - B^2$

(v) $(A + B)^3 = A^3 + 3A^2B + 3AB^2 + B^3$

17. 0, 0, –1

18. $a = 1$, $b = 4$

19. $x = 9$, $y = 14$

20. $\begin{bmatrix} -1 & 1 & -1 \\ 3 & -3 & 3 \\ 5 & -5 & 5 \end{bmatrix}$

1.23. Trace of Matrix

The trace of a square matrix is defined as the sum of its principal diagonal elements. Thus, if $A = [a_{ij}]$ is a square matrix of order n, then,

$$\text{trace } A = \text{tr. } A = a_{11} + a_{22} + \ldots\ldots + a_{nn}$$

$$= \sum_{i=1}^{n} a_{ii}$$

Example

Let $A = \begin{bmatrix} -5 & -8 & 0 \\ 3 & 5 & 0 \\ 1 & 2 & -1 \end{bmatrix}$. Then, trace of $A = (-5) + (5) + (-1) = -1$.

Note 1. The German word 'spur' is also used for the trace of a matrix.

Note 2. For the identity matrix I_n, trace $I_n = n$.

ILLUSTRATIVE EXAMPLES

Example 1. Show that

(i) trace $(KA) = K$ trace A, K being a scalar.

(ii) trace $(KA + lB) = K$ (trace A) $+ l$ (trace B), K, l being scalars.

Solution:

(i) Let $A = [a_{ij}]_{n \times n}$

Then,

$$KA = K\,[a_{ij}]_{n \times n}$$
$$= [K\,a_{ij}]_{n \times n}$$
$$\therefore \text{ trace } KA = \sum_{i=1}^{n} Ka_{ii}$$
$$= K\sum_{i=1}^{n} a_{ii}$$
$$= K \text{ trace } A$$

(ii) Let $A = [a_{ij}]_{n \times n}$ and $B = [b_{ij}]_{n \times n}$

Then,

$$KA + lB = K\,[a_{ij}]_{n \times n} + l\,[b_{ij}]_{n \times n}$$
$$= [Ka_{ij}]_{n \times n} + [l\,b_{ij}]_{n \times n}$$
$$= [Ka_{ij} + l\,b_{ij}]_{n \times n}$$
$$\therefore \text{ trace } (KA + lB) = \sum_{i=1}^{n}\left(K a_{ii} + l b_{ii}\right)$$
$$= \sum_{i=1}^{n} K a_{ii} + \sum_{i=1}^{n} l b_{ii}$$
$$= K\sum_{i=1}^{n} a_{ii} + l\sum_{i=1}^{n} b_{ii}$$
$$= K \text{ (trace } A) + l \text{ (trace } B)$$

Example 2. Show that trace AB = trace BA, provided AB and BA co-exist.

Solution: Let $A = [a_{ij}]_{m \times n}$ and $B = [b_{ij}]_{m \times m}$ so that AB and BA, both, exist and their orders are $m \times m$ and $n \times n$ respectively. Now, let $AB = [c_{ij}]_{m \times n}$. Then,

$$c_{ij} = \sum_{k=1}^{n} a_{ik}\, b_{kj}$$

$$\therefore \text{ trace } AB = \sum_{i=1}^{n} c_{ii}$$

$$= \sum_{i=1}^{m} \sum_{k=1}^{n} a_{ik} b_{ki} \qquad \text{... (1.23)}$$

Again, let $BA = [d_{ij}]_{n \times n}$. Then,

$$d_{ij} = \sum_{k=1}^{m} b_{ik} a_{kj}$$

$$\therefore \text{ trace } BA = \sum_{i=1}^{n} d_{ii}$$

$$= \sum_{i=1}^{n} \sum_{k=1}^{m} b_{ik} a_{ki}$$

$$= \sum_{k=1}^{n} \sum_{i=1}^{m} b_{ki} a_{ik} \qquad | \text{ on interchanging } i \text{ and } k$$

$$= \sum_{i=1}^{m} \sum_{k=1}^{n} a_{ik} b_{ki} \qquad \text{... (1.24)}$$

In view of Eqs. (1.23) and (1.24),

trace AB = trace BA.

EXERCISE 1.3

1. Show that trace A' = trace A, where A' is the matrix obtained from A by interchanging rows and columns.
2. Show that trace $AA' \geq 0$.
3. Show that trace $A^2 = \sum_{i=1}^{n} \sum_{j=1}^{n} a_{ij}^2$, if $A' = A = [a_{ij}]_{n \times n}$.
4. Show that trace $(AX) = O$ for all X implies that $A = O$.
5. If A is nilpotent, show that trace $A = 0$.
6. If C is an orthogonal matrix, show that trace $(C'AC)$ = trace A.

2 SPECIAL MATRICES

2.1. Transpose of a Matrix

The transpose of a matrix A is defined as the matrix obtained by interchanging the rows and columns of the given matrix A and is denoted by A' or A^t (read as A transpose). For example,

$$\text{If } A = \begin{bmatrix} 2 & 3 & 4 \\ -1 & 1 & 2 \end{bmatrix}_{2 \times 3}, \text{ then } A' = \begin{bmatrix} 2 & -1 \\ 3 & 1 \\ 4 & 2 \end{bmatrix}_{3 \times 2}$$

Symbolically,

If $A = [a_{ij}]_{m \times n}$, then $A' = [a'_{ji}]_{n \times m}$, where $a'_{ji} = a_{ij}$, i.e. $(i, j)^{\text{th}}$ element of $A = (j, i)^{\text{th}}$ element of A'.

See: A dash has been employed over $(j, i)^{\text{th}}$ element of A' in order to distinguish it from $(j, i)^{\text{th}}$ element of A. Thus, a'_{ji} shows that it is the $(j, i)^{\text{th}}$ element of A' and not of A.

Notes

(1) If A is of order $m \times n$, then A' will be of order $n \times m$.

(2) $(i, j)^{\text{th}}$ element of $A = (j, i)^{\text{th}}$ element of A'.

(3) The transpose of a row matrix is a column matrix.

(4) The transpose of a column matrix is a row matrix.

(5) $A' = A$ if A is a 1×1 matrix (single element matrix).

2.2. Theorems Related to Transpose of Matrices

Theorem 1. If A is any matrix, then $(A')' = A$, i.e. the transpose of transpose of a matrix is the matrix itself.

Proof. Let $A = [a_{ij}]_{m \times n}$. Then, the order of A' is $n \times m$ so that the order of $(A')'$ is $m \times n$. Thus, the matrices A and $(A')'$ are comparable.

Now,

$$A' = [a'_{ji}]_{n \times m} \text{ where } a'_{ji} = a_{ij}$$

$$\therefore \quad (A')' = [a''_{ij}]_{m \times n} \text{ where } a''_{ij} = a'_{ji}$$

But $a'_{ji} = a_{ij}$

$$\therefore \ a''_{ij} = a'_{ji} = a_{ij}$$

$$\therefore \ (A')' = [a_{ij}]_{m \times n}$$

Hence, the two matrices $(A')'$ and A are comparable and their corresponding elements are equal each to each. Therefore, they are equal, i.e. $(A')' = A$.

Theorem 2. The transpose of the sum of two matrices is equal to the sum of their transposes, i.e. $(A + B)' = A' + B'$.

Proof. Let $A = [a_{ij}]_{m \times n}$ and $B = [b_{ij}]_{m \times n}$ so that $A + B$ exists and is of order $m \times n$. So, $(A + B)'$ will be of order $n \times m$. Now, A' will be of order $n \times m$ and B' will be of order $n \times m$ so that $A' + B'$ will also be of order $n \times m$. Thus, the orders of $(A + B)'$ and $A' + B'$ are the same. Hence, they are comparable. Now,

$$\begin{aligned} A + B &= [a_{ij}]_{m \times n} + [b_{ij}]_{m \times n} \\ &= [a_{ij} + b_{ij}]_{m \times n} \\ &= [c_{ij}]_{m \times n}, \text{ where } c_{ij} = a_{ij} + b_{ij} \end{aligned}$$

$$\therefore \ (A + B)' = [c'_{ji}]_{n \times m}, \text{ where } c'_{ji} = c_{ij} = a_{ij} + b_{ij}$$

Again,

$$A' = [a'_{ji}]_{n \times m} \text{ where } a'_{ji} = a_{ij}$$

and,

$$B' = [b'_{ji}]_{n \times m} \text{ where } b'_{ji} = b_{ij}$$

$$\begin{aligned} \therefore \quad A' + B' &= [a'_{ji}]_{n \times m} + [b'_{ji}]_{n \times m} \\ &= [a'_{ji} + b'_{ji}]_{n \times m} \end{aligned}$$

$$= [c'_{ji}]_{n \times m}, \text{ where } c'_{ji} = a'_{ji} + b'_{ji}$$
$$= a_{ij} + b_{ij}$$

Hence, the two matrices $(A + B)'$ and $A' + B'$ are comparable and their corresponding elements are equal each to each. Therefore, they are equal, i.e.,

$$(A + B)' = A' + B'$$

Theorem 3. If K is a scalar, then $(KA)' = KA'$, i.e. the transpose of a matrix multiplied by a scalar K is scalar K times the multiple of the transpose of the matrix A.

Proof. Let $A = [a_{ij}]_{m \times n}$. Let K be any scalar then, the order of KA is $m \times n$ so that the order of $(KA)'$ is $n \times m$. Again, the order of A' is $n \times m$ so that the order of KA' is $n \times m$. Thus, the orders of $(KA)'$ and KA' are the same. Hence, they are comparable.

Now,

$$KA = K\ [a_{ij}]_{m \times n}$$
$$= [Ka_{ij}]_{m \times n}$$
$$\therefore \quad (KA)' = [Ka'_{ji}]_{n \times m}, \text{ where } Ka'_{ji} = Ka_{ij}$$

Again, $A' = [a'_{ji}]_{n \times m}$, where $a'_{ji} = a_{ij}$

$$\therefore \quad KA' = K\ [a'_{ji}]_{n \times m} = [Ka'_{ji}]_{n \times m}$$

Hence, the two matrices $(KA)'$ and KA' are comparable and their corresponding elements are equal each to each. Therefore, they are equal, i.e.

$$(KA)' = KA'$$

Theorem 4. *Reversal Law of Transpose:* The transpose of the product of two matrices is the product in the reverse order of their transposes, i.e.

$$(AB)' = B'A'$$

Proof. Let $A = [a_{ij}]_{m \times n}$ and $B = [b_{jk}]_{n \times p}$ so that the product AB exists and is a matrix of order $m \times p$ so that $(AB)'$ is a matrix of order $p \times m$. Again, B' is of order $p \times m$ and A' is of order $n \times m$ so that $B'A'$ exists and is a matrix of order $p \times m$. Thus, the orders of $(AB)'$ and $B'A'$ are the same. Hence, they are comparable.

Now,

$$AB = \left[\sum_{j=1}^{n} a_{ij}\, b_{jk}\right]_{m \times p}$$

$$= [c_{ik}]_{m \times p}, \text{ where } c_{ik} = \sum_{j=1}^{n} a_{ij}\, b_{jk}$$

$$\therefore\ (AB)' = [c'_{ki}]_{p \times m}, \text{ where } c'_{ki} = c_{ik} = \sum_{j=1}^{n} a_{ij}\, b_{jk}$$

Again, $B' = [b'_{kj}]_{p \times n}$, where $b'_{kj} = b_{jk}$
and, $A' = [a'_{ji}]_{n \times m}$ where $a'_{ji} = a_{ij}$

$$\text{so that } B'A' = \left[\sum_{j=1}^{n} b'_{kj}\, a'_{ji}\right]_{p \times m}$$

$$= [c'_{ki}]_{p \times m}$$

$$\text{where, } \quad c'_{ki} = \sum_{j=1}^{n} b'_{kj}\, a'_{ji}$$

$$= \sum_{j=1}^{n} b_{jk}\, a_{ij}$$

$$= \sum_{j=1}^{n} a_{ji}\, b_{jk} \qquad \mid \because a_{ij} \text{ and } b_{jk} \text{ are scalars}$$

$$= c_{ik}$$

Hence, the two matrices $(AB)'$ and $B'A'$ are comparable and their corresponding elements are equal each to each. Therefore, they are equal, i.e. $(AB)' = B'A'$.

Generalisation. This result can be generalised to the product of any finite number of matrices with suitable orders, i.e.

$$(A_1\, A_2 \ldots\ldots A_n)' = A'_n\, A'_{n-1} \ldots\ldots A'_2\, A'_1$$

2.3. Symmetric Matrix

A square matrix A is said to be symmetric if $A' = A$, i.e. the transpose of the matrix A is the matrix A itself. Hence, the matrix $A = [a_{ij}]_{m \times n}$ is symmetric if $a_{ij} = a_{ji}\ \forall\ i, j$. For example, the matrices

$$\begin{bmatrix} 1 & 4 & 5 \\ 4 & 2 & 6 \\ 5 & 6 & 3 \end{bmatrix}_{3\times 3} \text{ and } \begin{bmatrix} a & h & g \\ h & b & f \\ g & f & c \end{bmatrix}_{3\times 3} \text{ are both symmetric.}$$

2.4. Skew-Symmetric Matrix

A square matrix A is said to be skew-symmetric if $A' = -A$, i.e. the transpose of the matrix A is scalar (–1) multiple of A. Hence, the matrix $A = [a_{ij}]_{n \times n}$ is skew-symmetric if $a_{ij} = -a_{ji}\ \forall\ i, j$.

For the diagonal elements, we have

$$i = j$$

$$\therefore\ a_{ii} = -a_{ii}$$

$$\Rightarrow\ 2a_{ii} = 0$$

$$\Rightarrow\ a_{ii} = 0$$

$\Rightarrow$ Every diagonal element of a skew-symmetric matrix is zero.

Examples of skew-symmetric matrices are $\begin{bmatrix} 0 & 1 & 2 \\ -1 & 0 & -3 \\ -2 & 3 & 0 \end{bmatrix}$, $\begin{bmatrix} 0 & h & -g \\ -h & 0 & -f \\ g & f & 0 \end{bmatrix}$, etc.

Note: If K is any scalar and A is symmetric (skew-symmetric), then KA is also symmetric (skew-symmetric).

2.5. Theorem

The necessary and sufficient condition for a matrix A to be symmetric is that $A' = A$.

Proof. *(1) The condition is necessary*

Let $A = [a_{ij}]_{n \times n}$ be a square matrix of order n.

Then, $A' = [a'_{ji}]_{n \times n}$ where $a'_{ji} = a_{ij}$

Thus, A and A' have the same order.

$\because$ A is symmetric

$\therefore$ $a_{ij} = a_{ji} \; \forall \; i, j$ ... (2.1)

Now, $(i, j)^{\text{th}}$ element of A'

$= (j, i)^{\text{th}}$ element of A

$= a_{ji}$

$= a_{ij}$ | From Eqn. (2.1)

$= (i, j)^{\text{th}}$ element of A.

Thus, the corresponding elements of A and A' are equal each to each. Hence, $A = A'$.

(2) The condition is sufficient

Here,

$A' = A$ | Given ... (2.2)

To Prove: A is symmetric.

Let the order of A be $m \times n$.

Then the order of A' is $n \times m$.

But $A' = A$ | Given

$\therefore$ Order of A' = Order of A

$\therefore$ $m = n$

$\Rightarrow$ A is a square matrix of order n.

Now,

$a_{ij} = (i, j)^{\text{th}}$ element of A

$= (i, j)^{\text{th}}$ element of A' | $\because A' = A$

$= (j, i)^{\text{th}}$ element of A | by definition of transpose

$= a_{ji}$

Thus, $a_{ij} = a_{ji} \; \forall \; i, j$

Hence, A is symmetric.

Note: Every diagonal matrix is symmetric.

2.6. Theorem

The necessary and sufficient condition for a matrix A to be skew-symmetric is that $A' = -A$.

Proof.

(1) The condition is necessary

Let $A = [a_{ij}]_{n \times n}$ be a square matrix of order n.

Then, $A' = [a'_{ji}]_{n \times n}$ where $a'_{ji} = a_{ij}$

and, $-A = [-a_{ij}]_{n \times n}$

Thus, A' and $-A$ have the same order.

$\because$ A is skew-symmetric

$\therefore$ $a_{ij} = -a_{ji} \ \forall \ i, j$ ... (2.3)

Now, $(i, j)^{th}$ element of A'

$= (j, i)^{th}$ element of A

$= a_{ji}$

$= -a_{ij}$ | From Eq. (2.3)

$= -(i, j)^{th}$ element of A

$= (i, j)^{th}$ element of $(-A)$

Thus, the corresponding elements of A' and $-A$ are equal each to each. Hence,

$A' = -A$

(2) The condition is sufficient

Here, $A' = -A$ | Given ... (2.4)

To Prove: A is skew-symmetric.

Let the order of A be $m \times n$.

Then the order of $-A$ is $m \times n$ and the order of A' is $n \times m$.

But $A' = -A$ | Given

$\therefore$ Order of A' = Order of $-A$

$\therefore$ $m = n$

$\Rightarrow$ A is a square matrix of order n.

Now,

$a_{ij} = (i, j)^{th}$ element of A

$= (i, j)^{th}$ element of $-A'$ | $\because A' = -A$

$= -\ (i, j)^{th}$ element of A'

$= -\ (j, i)^{\text{th}}$ element of A | by definition of transpose

$= -a_{ji}$

Thus, $a_{ij} = -a_{ji}\ \forall\ i, j$

Hence, A is skew-symmetric.

ILLUSTRATIVE EXAMPLES

Example 1. Prove that $I' = I$.

Solution: We know that

$$I = [a_{ij}]_{n \times n} \qquad \text{where } a_{ij} = \begin{cases} 0 \text{ when } i \neq j \\ 1 \text{ when } i = j \end{cases}$$

$$\therefore\ I' = [a'_{ji}]_{n \times n} \qquad \text{where } a'_{ji} = a_{ij} = \begin{cases} 0 \text{ when } i \neq j \\ 1 \text{ when } i = j \end{cases}$$

Hence, I and I' are identical, i.e. $I' = I$.

Example 2. If $A = \begin{bmatrix} 3 & 4 \\ 1 & 1 \\ 2 & 0 \end{bmatrix}$, $B = \begin{bmatrix} 2 & 1 & 2 \\ 1 & 2 & 4 \end{bmatrix}$, find $(AB)'$. Hence, verify that $(AB)' = B'A'$.

Solution:

$$AB = \begin{bmatrix} 3 & 4 \\ 1 & 1 \\ 2 & 0 \end{bmatrix}_{3 \times 2} \begin{bmatrix} 2 & 1 & 2 \\ 1 & 2 & 4 \end{bmatrix}_{2 \times 3}$$

$$= \begin{bmatrix} 6+4 & 3+8 & 6+16 \\ 2+1 & 1+2 & 2+4 \\ 4+0 & 2+0 & 4+0 \end{bmatrix}_{3 \times 3}$$

$$= \begin{bmatrix} 10 & 11 & 22 \\ 3 & 3 & 6 \\ 4 & 2 & 4 \end{bmatrix}_{3 \times 3}$$

$$\therefore \quad (AB)' = \begin{bmatrix} 10 & 3 & 4 \\ 11 & 3 & 2 \\ 22 & 6 & 4 \end{bmatrix}_{3\times 3} \qquad \text{... (2.5)}$$

Now,

$$B'A' = \begin{bmatrix} 2 & 1 & 2 \\ 1 & 2 & 4 \end{bmatrix}' \begin{bmatrix} 3 & 4 \\ 1 & 1 \\ 2 & 0 \end{bmatrix}'$$

$$= \begin{bmatrix} 2 & 1 \\ 1 & 2 \\ 2 & 4 \end{bmatrix}_{3\times 2} \begin{bmatrix} 3 & 1 & 2 \\ 4 & 1 & 0 \end{bmatrix}_{2\times 3}$$

$$= \begin{bmatrix} 6+4 & 2+1 & 4+0 \\ 3+8 & 1+2 & 2+0 \\ 6+16 & 2+4 & 4+0 \end{bmatrix}_{3\times 3}$$

$$= \begin{bmatrix} 10 & 3 & 4 \\ 11 & 3 & 2 \\ 22 & 6 & 4 \end{bmatrix} \qquad \text{... (2.6)}$$

In view of Eqs. (2.5) and (2.6),

$(AB)' = B'A'$

Example 3. If A be any matrix, show that AA' and $A'A$ are symmetric.

Solution: Let $A = [a_{ij}]_{m \times n}$

Then $A' = [a'_{ji}]_{n \times m}$, where $a'_{ji} = a_{ij}$

Clearly, AA' is a square matrix of order $m \times m$.

Let $AA' = [c_{ij}]_{m \times m}$. Then

$$c_{ij} = \Sigma a_{ik}\, a'_{kj}$$

$$= \Sigma a_{ik}\, a_{jk} \qquad \text{... (2.7)} \mid \because a'_{kj} = a_{jk}$$

$$\therefore \quad c_{ji} = \Sigma a_{jk}\, a_{ik} = \Sigma a_{ik}\, a_{jk} \qquad \text{... (2.8)}$$

In view of Eqs. (2.7) and (2.8),

$$c_{ij} = c_{ji}$$

This shows that AA' is symmetric.

Similarly, we can show that $A'A$ is also symmetric.

Aliter. By reversal law of transpose of matrices, we have

$$(AA')' = (A')'A' = AA'$$

and $(A'A)' = A'(A')' = A'A$

Hence, AA' and $A'A$ both are symmetric.

Note: The matrix $A'A$ (or AA') is called the Gram-matrix of A (or A').

Example 4. If A and B are both symmetric, then AB is symmetric iff A and B commute.

Solution:

$\because$ A and B are both symmetric

$\therefore$ $A' = A$ and $B' = B$ ... (2.9)

$\therefore$ $(AB)' = B'A'$ | By Reversal Law of Transposes of Matrices

$= BA$ | By Eq. (2.9)

$= AB$ | iff A and B commute

This shows that AB is symmetric iff A and B commute.

Aliter. Since A and B are both symmetric and AB exists, therefore, A and B both must be square matrices of the same order.

Let $A = [a_{ij}]_{n \times n}$ and $B = [b_{ij}]_{n \times n}$

Since A and B are both symmetric, therefore,

$$a_{ij} = a_{ji} \text{ and } b_{ij} = b_{ji} \ \forall\ i, j \qquad \text{... (2.10)}$$

Let $AB = [c_{ij}]_{n \times n}$. Then,

$$c_{ij} = \sum_{k=1}^{n} a_{ik}\, b_{kj}$$

so that $c_{ji} = \sum_{k=1}^{n} a_{jk}\, b_{ki}$ ... (2.11)

Let $BA = [d_{ij}]_{n \times n}$. Then,

$$d_{ij} = \sum_{k=1}^{n} b_{ik}\, a_{kj}$$

$$= \sum_{k=1}^{n} a_{kj}\, b_{ik}$$

$$= \sum_{k=1}^{n} a_{jk}\, b_{ki} \qquad | \text{ From Eq. (2.10)}$$

$$= c_{ji} \qquad | \text{ From Eq. (2.11)} \quad \dots (2.12)$$

If A and B commute, then $AB = BA$, so that

$c_{ij} = d_{ij}\ \forall\ i, j$

$\Rightarrow\ c_{ij} = c_{ji}\ \forall\ i, j$ | From Eq. (2.12)

$\Rightarrow\ AB = [c_{ij}]$ is symmetric, i.e. $(AB)' = B'A'$

Conversely

If $AB = [c_{ij}]_{n \times n}$ is symmetric, then

$c_{ij} = c_{ji}\ \forall\ i, j$

$\Rightarrow\ c_{ij} = d_{ij}\ \forall\ i, j$ | From Eq. (2.12)

$\Rightarrow\ [c_{ij}]_{n \times n} = [d_{ij}]_{n \times n}$

$\Rightarrow\ AB = BA$

$\Rightarrow$ A and B commute.

Example 5. If A and B are symmetric (skew-symmetric), show that $A + B$ is symmetric (skew-symmetric).

Solution:

Case I: Let A and B be symmetric. Then,

$A' = A$ and $B' = B$ ... (2.14)

$\because$ A and B are symmetric

$\therefore$ A and B are square matrices

$\because$ $A + B$ is defined

$\therefore$ Order of A = Order of B.

Now,

$$(A + B)' = A' + B'$$

$$= A + B \qquad | \text{ By Eq. (2.14)}$$

$\Rightarrow A + B$ is symmetric.

Case II: Let A and B be skew-symmetric. Then,

$$A' = -A \text{ and } B' = -B \qquad \ldots (2.15)$$

Now,

$$(A + B)' = A' + B'$$
$$= -A - B \qquad | \text{ From Eq. (2.15)}$$
$$= -(A + B)$$

$\Rightarrow A + B$ is skew-symmetric.

Example 6. Show that every square matrix can be uniquely expressed as the sum of a symmetric matrix and a skew-symmetric matrix.

Solution: Let A be any square matrix.

Now,

$$A = \frac{1}{2}A + \frac{1}{2}A$$
$$= \frac{1}{2}A + \frac{1}{2}A' + \frac{1}{2}A - \frac{1}{2}A'$$
$$= \frac{1}{2}(A + A') + \frac{1}{2}(A - A')$$
$$= P + Q \qquad \ldots (2.16)$$

where,

$$P = \frac{1}{2}(A + A')$$

and, $Q = \frac{1}{2}(A - A')$

Now,

$$P' = \left\{\frac{1}{2}(A + A')\right\}'$$
$$= \frac{1}{2}(A + A')'$$
$$= \frac{1}{2}\{A' + (A')'\}$$

$$= \frac{1}{2}(A' + A)$$

$$= \frac{1}{2}(A + A')$$

$$= P$$

$\Rightarrow$ P is symmetric.

Again,

$$Q' = \left\{\frac{1}{2}(A - A')\right\}'$$

$$= \frac{1}{2}(A - A')'$$

$$= \frac{1}{2}\left\{A' - (A')'\right\}$$

$$= \frac{1}{2}(A' - A)$$

$$= -\frac{1}{2}(A - A')$$

$$= -Q$$

$\Rightarrow$ Q is skew-symmetric.

From Eq. (2.16), we conclude that the matrix A can be expressed as the sum of a symmetric matrix and a skew-symmetric matrix.

Uniqueness

If possible, Let $A = P_1 + Q_1$ ... (2.17)

be another such representation where P_1 is symmetric and Q_1 is skew-symmetric. Then,

$$P_1' = P_1 \text{ and } Q_1' = -Q_1$$

Now,

$$A' = (P_1 + Q_1)'$$

$$= P_1' + Q_1'$$

$$= P_1 - Q_1 \qquad \text{... (2.18)}$$

From Eqs. (2.17) and (2.18),

$$A + A' = 2P_1 \Rightarrow P_1 = \frac{1}{2}(A + A')$$

and, $A - A' = 2Q_1 \Rightarrow Q_1 = \frac{1}{2}(A - A')$

Thus, $A = \frac{1}{2}(A + A') + \frac{1}{2}(A - A')$ which is the same as the earlier one.

Hence, the uniqueness is established.

Example 7. If A is a skew-symmetric matrix, then show that $AA' = A'A$ and A' is symmetric.

Solution:

$\because$ A is a skew-symmetric matrix

$\therefore$ $A' = -A$ ... (2.19)

Pre-multiplying both sides of Eq. (2.19) by A, we have

$AA' = -AA = -A^2$ ... (2.20)

Post-multiplying both sides of Eq. (2.19) by A, we have

$A'A = -AA = -A^2$ ... (2.21)

In view of Eqs. (2.20) and (2.21), we have

$AA' = A'A$

Again, from Eq. (2.20),

$A^2 = -AA'$

$\Rightarrow A^2 = (-)AA'$

But AA' is symmetric by Example 3.

Therefore, $(-)AA'$ is also symmetric.

| $\because$ A symmetric matrix remains symmetric when multiplied by any scalar quantity.

Hence, A^2 is symmetric.

Example 8. If $A_1, A_2, \ldots, A_n$ be of suitable sizes for $A_1 A_2 \ldots A_n$ to exist, prove with the help of finite induction that $(A_1 A_2 \ldots A_n)' = A_n' A_{n-1}' \ldots A_2' A_1'$.

Solution: We know that

$$(A_1\ A_2)' = A_2'\ A_1' \quad \text{... (2.22)}$$

| By Reversal Law of Transposes of Matrices

Let us assume that the result is true for $n = k$. Then,

$$(A_1 A_2 \ldots\ldots A_{k-1}\ A_k)' = A_k'\ A_{k-1}' \ldots\ldots A_2'\ A_1' \quad \text{... (2.23)}$$

Now,

$$(A_1\ A_2 \ldots\ldots A_{k-1}\,A_k\ A_{k+1})'$$

$$= \left\{(A_1 A_2 \ldots\ldots A_{k-1} A_k)\, A_{k+1}\right\}'$$

| $\because$ Products of matrices is associative

$$= A_{k+1}'\ (A_1\ A_2 \ldots\ldots A_{k-1}\ A_k)'$$

| By Reversal Law of Transposes of Matrices

$$= A_{k+1}'\ A_k'\ A_{k-1}' \ldots\ldots A_2'\ A_1'$$

| Using Eq. (2.23)

Hence, the result is true for $n = k + 1$.

Hence, by mathematical induction, the result is true for any finite number of matrices.

Example 9. If A is a skew-symmetric matrix and X is a column matrix, show that $X'AX = O$.

Solution:

$\because$ A is a skew-symmetric matrix

$\therefore$ $A' = -A$ ... (2.24)

Now,

$$(X'AX)' = X'A'(X')'$$

| By Reversal Law of Transposes of Matrices

$$= X'\ (-A)X$$

$$= -(X'AX)$$

$\Rightarrow$ $X'AX$ is a skew-symmetric matrix

$\Rightarrow$ All the diagonal elements of $X'AX$ are zero.

Let the order of X be $n \times 1$.

Then the order of X' is $1 \times n$.

$\therefore$ The order of $X'AX$ is 1×1, i.e. $X'AX$ is a single element matrix.

But since $X'AX$ is a skew-symmetric matrix, therefore, it must have that single element also as zero.

Hence, $X'AX$ is a null matrix, i.e. $X'AX = O$

EXERCISE 2.1

1. If $A = \begin{bmatrix} 2 & 4 & -1 \\ -1 & 0 & 2 \end{bmatrix}$ and $B = \begin{bmatrix} 3 & 4 & 5 \\ -1 & 2 & 7 \\ 2 & 1 & 0 \end{bmatrix}$, compute $(AB)'$ and $B'A'$. Hence, verify that $(AB)' = B'A'$.

2. If $A = \begin{bmatrix} \cos\alpha & \sin\alpha \\ -\sin\alpha & \cos\alpha \end{bmatrix}$, verify that $AA' = A'A = I_2$.

3. If $A = \begin{bmatrix} i & 0 \\ 0 & -i \end{bmatrix}$ and $B = \begin{bmatrix} 0 & i \\ -i & 0 \end{bmatrix}$, prove that $(AB)' = B'A'$.

4. If $A = \begin{bmatrix} 2 & 3 & 4 \\ 5 & 7 & 9 \\ -2 & 1 & 1 \end{bmatrix}$ and $B = \begin{bmatrix} 4 & 0 & 5 \\ 1 & 2 & 0 \\ 0 & 3 & 1 \end{bmatrix}$, verify that $(AB)' = B'A'$.

5. If $A = \begin{bmatrix} 1 & 2 & 0 \\ 3 & -1 & 4 \end{bmatrix}$, find AA' and $A'A$ and show that AA' and $A'A$ are symmetric but $AA' \neq A'A$.

6. If A is a symmetric matrix, prove that KA is also a symmetric matrix, where K is a scalar.

7. If A is a skew-symmetric matrix, prove that KA' is also skew-symmetric, where K is any scalar.
8. If A is any square matrix, show that $A + A'$ is symmetric and $A - A'$ is skew-symmetric.
9. If A and B are symmetric, show that $AB + BA$ is symmetric and $AB - BA$ is skew-symmetric.
10. If A is symmetric (skew-symmetric), show that $B'AB$ is symmetric (skew-symmetric).
11. Show that A^2 is symmetric, if either A is symmetric or A is skew-symmetric.
12. Show that all positive integral powers of a symmetric matrix are symmetric.
13. Show that all positive integral power of a skew-symmetric matrix are skew-symmetric.
14. Express $\begin{bmatrix} 4 & 3 & 7 \\ 6 & 5 & -8 \\ 1 & 2 & 6 \end{bmatrix}$ as the sum of a symmetric matrix and a skew-symmetric matrix.
15. Express the matrix $A = \begin{bmatrix} 2 & 4 & -6 \\ 7 & 3 & 5 \\ 1 & -2 & 4 \end{bmatrix}$ as the sum of a symmetric and a skew-symmetric matrix.

ANSWERS

1. $\begin{bmatrix} 0 & 1 \\ 15 & -2 \\ 38 & -5 \end{bmatrix}, \begin{bmatrix} 0 & 1 \\ 15 & -2 \\ 38 & -5 \end{bmatrix}$

5. $\begin{bmatrix} 5 & 1 \\ 1 & 26 \end{bmatrix}, \begin{bmatrix} 10 & -1 & 12 \\ -1 & 5 & -4 \\ 12 & -4 & 16 \end{bmatrix}$

14. $\begin{bmatrix} 4 & 9/2 & 4 \\ 9/2 & 5 & -3 \\ 4 & -3 & 6 \end{bmatrix} + \begin{bmatrix} 0 & -3/2 & 3 \\ 3/2 & 0 & -5 \\ -3 & 5 & 0 \end{bmatrix}$

15. $\begin{bmatrix} 2 & 11/2 & -5/2 \\ 11/2 & 3 & 3/2 \\ -5/2 & 3/2 & 4 \end{bmatrix} + \begin{bmatrix} 0 & -3/2 & -7/2 \\ 3/2 & 0 & 7/2 \\ 7/2 & -7/2 & 0 \end{bmatrix}$

2.7. Conjugate of a Matrix

Let A be any matrix. If we replace each element of A by its complex conjugate (obtained by replacing i by $-i$), then the matrix so obtained is called the conjugate matrix of A and is symbolically denoted by $\overline{A}$.

Thus, if $A = [a_{ij}]_{m \times n}$, then

$\overline{A} = \left[\overline{a_{ij}}\right]_{m\times n}$ where $\overline{a_{ij}}$ is the complex conjugate of a_{ij}.

For example,

$$\text{If } A = \begin{bmatrix} 2-3i & 4 & -5i \\ 0 & -4i & 8 \\ 4-3i & 0 & 7-3i \end{bmatrix}, \text{ then}$$

$$\overline{A} = \begin{bmatrix} 2+3i & 4 & 5i \\ 0 & 4i & 8 \\ 4+3i & 0 & 7+3i \end{bmatrix}$$

Note: A matrix A is real (i.e. all the elements of A are real) if and only if $\overline{A} = A$.

2.8. Transposed Conjugate of a Matrix or Tranjugate of a Matrix

Let A be any matrix. The transpose of the conjugate of A is called the transposed conjugate of A. This is also known as tranjugate. We denote the tranjugate of A by A^* symbolically. Thus,

$$(\overline{A})' = A^*$$

Evidently, $(\overline{A})' = \overline{(A')} = A^*$

For example,

If $A = \begin{bmatrix} 3+4i & 5-6i & 2+3i \\ 4-5i & 7 & 8i \\ 6 & 5+6i & 2-3i \end{bmatrix}$, then

$$\overline{A} = \begin{bmatrix} 3-4i & 5+6i & 2-3i \\ 4+5i & 7 & -8i \\ 6 & 5-6i & 2+3i \end{bmatrix}$$

and $A^* = (\overline{A})' = \begin{bmatrix} 3-4i & 4+5i & 6 \\ 5+6i & 7 & 5-6i \\ 2-3i & -8i & 2+3i \end{bmatrix}$

Again, $A' = \begin{bmatrix} 3+4i & 4-5i & 6 \\ 5-6i & 7 & 5+6i \\ 2+3i & 8i & 2-3i \end{bmatrix}$

and $A^* = \overline{(A')} = \begin{bmatrix} 3-4i & 4+5i & 6 \\ 5+6i & 7 & 5-6i \\ 2-3i & 8i & 2+3i \end{bmatrix}$

2.9. Hermitian Matrix

A square matrix A is said to be hermitian if its tranjugate is equal to the matrix itself, i.e. if $A^* = A$. Thus,

$A = [a_{ij}]_{n \times n}$ is hermitian if

$$a_{ij} = \overline{a_{ji}} \ \forall \ i, j$$

For example,

$$\begin{bmatrix} a & c+id \\ c-id & b \end{bmatrix} \text{ and } \begin{bmatrix} a & \alpha+i\beta & \gamma+i\delta \\ \alpha-i\beta & b & x+iy \\ \gamma-i\delta & x-iy & c \end{bmatrix}$$

are hermitian matrices.

Theorem. Every diagonal element of a hermitian matrix is real.

Proof. For diagonal elements

$i = j$

$\therefore\ a_{ii} = \overline{a_{ii}}$ | By definition

$\Rightarrow\ a_{ii}$ is real.

2.10. Skew-Hermitian Matrix

A square matrix A is said to be skew-hermitian if its tranjugate is equal to scalar (–1) multiple of the matrix itself, i.e. if $A^* = -A$. Thus, $A = [a_{ij}]_{n \times n}$ is skew-hermitian if

$a_{ij} = -\overline{a_{ji}}\ \forall\ i, j$

For example,

$$\begin{bmatrix} 0 & 1-i \\ -1-i & 5i \end{bmatrix} \text{ and } \begin{bmatrix} i & 1-i & 2 \\ -1-i & 3i & i \\ -2 & i & 0 \end{bmatrix} \text{ are}$$

skew-hermitian matrices.

Theorem. Diagonal elements of a skew-hermitian matrix are either zero or purely imaginary numbers.

Proof. For diagonal elements

$i = j$

$\therefore\ a_{ii} = -\overline{a_{ii}}$ | By definition

$\Rightarrow\ a_{ii} + \overline{a_{ii}} = 0$

$\Rightarrow\ a_{ii}$ is zero or purely imaginary number.

2.11. Some Theorems

Theorem 1. $\overline{(\overline{A})} = A$

Proof. Let $A = [a_{ij}]_{m \times n}$

Then,

$$\overline{A} = \left[\overline{a_{ij}}\right]_{m \times n}$$ where $\overline{a_{ij}}$ is the complex conjugate of a_{ij}.

Now,

$(i, j)^{\text{th}}$ element of $\overline{(\overline{A})}$

= Complex conjugate of $(i, j)^{\text{th}}$ element of $\overline{A}$

= Complex conjugate of $\overline{a_{ij}}$

$= \overline{\left(\overline{a_{ji}}\right)}$

$= a_{ij}$

$= (i, j)^{\text{th}}$ element of A.

Thus, A and $\overline{(\overline{A})}$ are comparable matrices with their corresponding elements equal each to each.

Therefore, $\overline{(\overline{A})} = A$.

Theorem 2. If A and B are two matrices such that they are conformable for addition, then

$$\left(\overline{A + B}\right) = \overline{A} + \overline{B}$$

Proof. Let $A = [a_{ij}]_{m \times n}$ and $B = [b_{ij}]_{m \times n}$

Then,

$$\overline{A} = \left[\overline{a_{ij}}\right]_{m \times n} \text{ and } \overline{B} = \left[\overline{b_{ij}}\right]_{m \times n}$$

Now,

$$A + B = [a_{ij}]_{m \times n} + [b_{ij}]_{m \times n}$$
$$= [a_{ij} + b_{ij}]_{m \times n}$$

$\therefore$ Order of $\left(\overline{A + B}\right) = m \times n$

Again,

Order of $\overline{A} = m \times n$

Order of $\overline{B} = m \times n$

$\therefore$ Order of $\overline{A} + \overline{B} = m \times n$

Thus, the matrices $(\overline{A+B})$ and $\overline{A} + \overline{B}$ are comparable. ... (2.25)

Now,

$(i, j)^{th}$ element of $(\overline{A+B})$

$=$ Complex conjugate of $(i, j)^{th}$ element of $A + B$

$=$ Complex conjugate of $(a_{ij} + b_{ij})$

$= \overline{(a_{ij} + b_{ij})}$

$= \overline{a_{ij}} + \overline{b_{ij}}$

$= (i, j)^{th}$ element of $\overline{A}$ + $(i, j)^{th}$ element of $\overline{B}$

$= (i, j)^{th}$ element of $(\overline{A} + \overline{B})$

Thus, the corresponding elements of $(\overline{A+B})$ and $\overline{A} + \overline{B}$ are equal each to each. .... (2.26)

In view of Eqs. (2.25) and (2.26),

$$(\overline{A+B}) = \overline{A} + \overline{B}$$

Theorem 3. $(\overline{KA}) = \overline{K}\,\overline{A}$ where K is a scalar.

Proof. Let $A = [a_{ij}]_{m \times n}$

Then,

$$KA = K\,[a_{ij}]_{m \times n} = [K\,a_{ij}]_{m \times n}$$

$\therefore$ Order of $(\overline{KA}) = m \times n$

Also, order of $\overline{K}\,\overline{A} = m \times n$

Thus, the matrices $(\overline{KA})$ and $\overline{K}\,\overline{A}$ are comparable. ... (2.27)

Now,

$(i, j)^{th}$ element of $(\overline{KA})$

$= \text{Complex conjugate of } (i, j)^{th} \text{ element of } KA$

$= \text{Complex conjugate of } K\, a_{ij}$

$= \left(\overline{K\, a_{ij}}\right)$

$= \overline{K}\, \overline{a_{ij}}$

$= \overline{K}\ (i, j)^{th} \text{ element of } \overline{A}$

$= (i, j)^{th} \text{ element of } \overline{K}\,\overline{A}$

Thus, the corresponding elements of $\overline{(KA)}$ and $\overline{K}\,\overline{A}$ are equal each to each. ... (2.28)

In view of Eqs. (2.27) and (2.28),

$$\overline{(KA)} = \overline{K}\,\overline{A}$$

Theorem 4. If A and B are two matrices conformable for multiplication, then

$$(\overline{AB}) = \overline{A}\,\overline{B}$$

Proof. Let $A = [a_{ij}]_{m \times n}$ and $B = [b_{jk}]_{n \times p}$

Then, $AB = [c_{ik}]_{m \times p}$ where $c_{ik} = \sum_{j=1}^{n} a_{ij}\, b_{jk}$; $\overline{A} = \left[\overline{a_{ij}}\right]_{m \times n}$ and $\overline{B} = \left[\overline{b_{jk}}\right]_{n \times p}$.

Now, order of $AB = m \times p$

$\therefore$ Order of $(\overline{AB}) = m \times p$

Also,

Order of $\overline{A} = m \times n$

Order of $\overline{B} = m \times p$

$\therefore$ Order of $\overline{A}\,\overline{B} = m \times p$

Thus, the matrices $(\overline{AB})$ and $\overline{A}\,\overline{B}$ are comparable. ... (2.29)

Now,

$(i, k)^{\text{th}}$ element of $(\overline{AB})$

$= \text{Complex conjugate of } (i, k)^{\text{th}} \text{ element of } AB$

$= \text{Complex conjugate of } \sum_{j=1}^{n} a_{ij}\, b_{jk}$

$= \overline{\left(\sum_{j=1}^{n} a_{ij}\, b_{jk}\right)}$

$= \sum_{j=1}^{n} \overline{a_{ij}\, b_{jk}}$

$= \sum_{j=1}^{n} \overline{a_{ij}}\, \overline{b_{jk}}$ $\quad\Big|\ \because\ \overline{z_1 z_2} = \overline{z_1}\,\overline{z_2};\ z_1, z_2$ being complex numbers

$= (i, k)^{\text{th}}$ element of $\overline{A}\,\overline{B}$

Thus, the corresponding element of $(\overline{AB})$ and $\overline{A}\overline{B}$ are equal each to each. ... (2.30)

In view of Eqs. (2.29) and (2.30),

$$(\overline{AB}) = \overline{A}\overline{B}$$

Theorem 5. Prove that $(A^*)^* = A$.

Proof. We know that

$$A^* = (\overline{A})'$$

$$\therefore \quad (A^*)^* = \left((\overline{A})'\right)^*$$

$$= \overline{\left((\overline{A})'\right)'} \qquad \Big|\ \because A^* = \overline{(A')}$$

$$= (\overline{\overline{A}}) \qquad \Big|\ \because (A')' = A$$

$$= A$$

Theorem 6(a). Prove that

$(KA)^* = \overline{K}A^*$ where K is a scalar.

Proof.

$$(KA)^* = \left(\overline{KA}\right)'$$

$$= \left(\overline{K}\,\overline{A}\right)'$$

$$= \overline{K}\left(\overline{A}\right)'$$

$$= \overline{K}\,A^*$$

Theorem 6(b). If A is real matrix, then

$$A^* = A'$$

Proof. $\because$ A is real matrix

$$\therefore \quad \overline{A} = A \qquad \text{| By definition} \qquad \ldots (2.31)$$

Now,

$$A^* = \left(\overline{A}\right)' \qquad \text{| By definition}$$

$$= A' \qquad \text{| Using Eq. (2.31)}$$

Theorem 7. If A and B are two matrices such that they are conformable for addition, then

$$(A + B)^* = A^* + B^*$$

Proof.

$$(A + B)^* = \left(\overline{A + B}\right)'$$

$$= \left(\overline{A} + \overline{B}\right)'$$

$$= \left(\overline{A}\right)' + \left(\overline{B}\right)'$$

$$= A^* + B^*$$

Theorem 8. If A and B are two matrices, conformable for multiplication, then

$$(AB)^* = B^*A^*$$

Proof.

$$(AB)^* = \left(\overline{AB}\right)'$$

$$= \left(\overline{A}\,\overline{B}\right)'$$

$$= (\overline{B})' (\overline{A})'$$
$$= B^* A^*$$

Generalisation. The above result can be extended to the product of any finite number of matrices with proper orders. Thus,

$(A_1 A_2 \ldots\ldots A_{n-1} A_n)^* = A_n^* A_{n-1}^* \ldots\ldots A_2^* A_1^*$

Put $A_1 = A_2 = \ldots\ldots = A_{n-1} = A_n = A_1$ we obtain

$(A^n)^* = A^* A^* \ldots\ldots n$ times

$\Rightarrow (A^n)^* = (A^*)^n$

This is known as reversal law for tranjugate.

Theorem 9. The necessary and sufficient condition for a square matrix A to be hermitian is that $A^* = A$.

Proof. ***The condition is necessary***

Let $A = [a_{ij}]_{n \times n}$ be any n-rowed square matrix.

$\because$ A is hermitian

$\therefore$ $a_{ij} = \overline{a_{ij}}$ | By definition ... (2.32)

Also, A^* is an n-rowed square matrix.

Thus, A and A^* are comparable. ... (2.33)

Now,

$(i, j)^{\text{th}}$ element of A^*

$= (i, j)^{\text{th}}$ element of $(\overline{A})'$

$= (j, i)^{\text{th}}$ element of $\overline{A}$

$= \overline{a_{ij}}$

$= a_{ij}$ | Using Eq. (2.32)

$= (i, j)^{\text{th}}$ element of A

Thus, the corresponding elements of A^* and A are equal each to each. ... (2.34)

In view of Eqs. (2.33) and (2.34),

$$A^* = A$$

The condition is sufficient

We are given that $A^* = A$

We are to prove that A is hermitian.

Let A be of order $m \times n$.

Then $\overline{A}$ is also of order $m \times n$.

$\therefore$ $(\overline{A})'$ is of order $n \times m$

$\Rightarrow$ A^* is of order $n \times m$

$\because$ $A^* = A$ | Given

$\therefore$ Order of A^* = Order of A

$\therefore$ $m = n$

$\Rightarrow$ A is a square matrix.

Again,

$\because$ $A^* = A$ | Given

$\therefore$ $(\overline{A})' = A$ | By definition

$\Rightarrow$ $\left(\overline{(\overline{A})'}\right) = \overline{A}$

$\Rightarrow$ $\left(\overline{(\overline{A})}\right)' = \overline{A}$

$\Rightarrow$ $A' = \overline{A}$

$\Rightarrow$ $(j, i)^{\text{th}}$ element of A' = $(j, i)^{\text{th}}$ element of $\overline{A}$

$\Rightarrow$ $(i, j)^{\text{th}}$ element of A = $(j, i)^{\text{th}}$ element of $\overline{A}$

$\Rightarrow$ $a_{ij} = \overline{a_{ij}} \quad \forall\, i, j$

Hence, A is hermitian.

Theorem 10. The necessary and sufficient condition for a matrix A to be skew-hermitian is that $A^* = -A$.

Proof. ***The condition is necessary***

Let $A = [a_{ij}]_{n \times n}$ be any n-rowed square matrix.

$\because$ A is skew-hermitian

$\therefore$ $a_{ij} = -\overline{a_{ji}}$ | By definition

$\Rightarrow$ $(i, j)^{\text{th}}$ element of A = $-(j, i)^{\text{th}}$ element of $\overline{A}$

$\Rightarrow$ $(j, i)^{\text{th}}$ element of A' = $(j, i)^{\text{th}}$ element of $(-\overline{A})$

$\Rightarrow$ $A' = -\overline{A}$

$\Rightarrow$ $\overline{(A')} = -(\overline{\overline{A}})$

$\Rightarrow$ $A^* = -A$

The condition is sufficient

We are given that $A^* = -A$.

We are to prove that A is skew-hermitian.

Let A be of order $m \times n$.

Then $\overline{A}$ is also of order $m \times n$.

$\therefore$ $(\overline{A})'$ is of order $n \times m$

$\Rightarrow$ A^* is of order $n \times m$

$\because$ $A^* = -A$ | Given

$\therefore$ Order of A^* = Order of $(-A)$

$\Rightarrow$ Order of A^* = Order of A

$\Rightarrow$ $m = n$

$\Rightarrow$ A is a square matrix.

Again,

$A^* = -A$ | Given

$\therefore$ $(\overline{A})' = -A$ | By defintion

$\Rightarrow$ $\overline{\left((\overline{A})'\right)} = -\overline{A}$

$\Rightarrow$ $\left(\overline{(\overline{A})}\right)' = -\overline{A}$

$\Rightarrow$ $A' = -\overline{A}$

$\Rightarrow$ $(j, i)^{th}$ element of A' = $(j, i)^{th}$ element of $\left(-\overline{A}\right)$

$\Rightarrow$ $(i, j)^{th}$ the element of A = $-$ $(j, i)^{th}$ element of $\overline{A}$

$\Rightarrow$ $a_{ij} = -\overline{a_{ji}} \quad \forall\, i, j$

Hence, A is skew-hermitian.

Theorem 11. Show that every square matrix can be uniquely expressed as the sum of a hermitian and a skew-hermitian matrix.

Proof. Let A be any square matrix.

Then,

$$A = \frac{1}{2}\left(A + A^*\right) + \frac{1}{2}\left(A - A^*\right)$$

$$= P + Q \qquad \text{... (2.35)}$$

where

$$P = \frac{1}{2}\left(A + A^*\right)$$

and $Q = \frac{1}{2}\left(A - A^*\right)$

Now,

$$P^* = \left(\frac{1}{2}\left(A + A^*\right)\right)^*$$

$$= \frac{1}{2}\left(A + A^*\right)^*$$

$$= \frac{1}{2}\left(A^* + \left(A^*\right)^*\right)$$

$$= \frac{1}{2}\left(A^* + A\right)$$

$$= \frac{1}{2}\left(A + A^*\right)$$

$$= P$$

$\Rightarrow$ P is hermitian.

and,

$$Q^* = \left(\frac{1}{2}\left(A - A^*\right)\right)^*$$

$$= \frac{1}{2}\left(A - A^*\right)^*$$

$$= \frac{1}{2}\left(A^* - \left(A^*\right)^*\right)$$

$$= \frac{1}{2}\left(A^* - A\right)$$

$$= -\frac{1}{2}\left(A - A^*\right)$$
$$= -Q$$

$\Rightarrow$ Q is skew-hermitian.

Hence, from Eq. (2.35) we conclude that the matrix A can be expressed as the sum of a hermitian and a skew-hermitian matrix.

Uniqueness

Let $A = P_1 + Q_1$ ... (2.36)

be another such representation

$\because$ P_1 is hermitian

$\therefore$ $P_1^* = P_1$ ... (2.37)

$\because$ Q_1 is skew-hermitian

$\therefore$ $Q_1^* = -Q_1$ ... (2.38)

Now,

$$A^* = (P_1 + Q_1)^*$$
$$= P_1^* + Q_1^*$$
$$= P_1 - Q_1 \quad \text{... (2.39)}$$

| Using Eqs. (2.37) and (2.38)

Adding Eqs. (2.36) and (2.39), we obtain

$$A + A^* = 2P_1$$
$$\Rightarrow P_1 = \frac{1}{2}\left(A + A^*\right) = P$$

Subtracting Eq. (2.39) from Eq. (2.36), we obtain

$$A - A^* = 2Q_1$$
$$\Rightarrow Q_1 = \frac{1}{2}\left(A - A^*\right) = Q$$

$\therefore$ From Eq. (2.36),

$$A = P_1 + Q_1 = P + Q$$

Hence, the representation is unique.

Theorem 12. Show that every square matrix can be uniquely expressed as $P + iQ$, where P and Q are hermitian.

Proof. Let A be any square matrix. Then,

$$A = \frac{1}{2}\left(A + A^*\right) + i\left(\frac{1}{2i}\left(A - A^*\right)\right)$$

$$\Rightarrow A = P + iQ \qquad \text{... (2.40)}$$

where

$$P = \frac{1}{2}\left(A + A^*\right)$$

and $Q = \dfrac{1}{2i}\left(A - A^*\right)$

Now,

$$\begin{aligned} P^* &= \left(\frac{1}{2}\left(A + A^*\right)\right)^* \\ &= \frac{1}{2}\left(A + A^*\right)^* \\ &= \frac{1}{2}\left(A^* + \left(A^*\right)^*\right) \\ &= \frac{1}{2}\left(A^* + A\right) \\ &= \frac{1}{2}\left(A + A^*\right) \\ &= P \end{aligned}$$

$\Rightarrow$ P is hermitian

and,

$$\begin{aligned} Q^* &= \left(\frac{1}{2i}\left(A - A^*\right)\right)^* \\ &= \left(\overline{\frac{1}{2i}}\right)\left(A - A^*\right)^* \\ &= -\frac{1}{2i}\left(A^* - \left(A^*\right)^*\right) \\ &= -\frac{1}{2i}\left(A^* - A\right) \end{aligned}$$

$$= \frac{1}{2i}\left(A - A^*\right)$$
$$= Q$$

$\Rightarrow$ Q is hermitian.

Hence, from Eq. (2.40) we conclude that the matrix A can be expressed as $P + iQ$ where P and Q are hermitian.

Uniqueness

Let $A = P_1 + iQ_1$ ... (2.41)

be another such representation.

$\because$ P_1 is hermitian

$\therefore$ $P_1^* = P$ ... (2.42)

$\because$ Q_1 is hermitian

$\therefore$ $Q_1^* = Q$ ... (2.43)

Now,

$$\begin{aligned} A^* &= (P_1 + iQ_1)^* \\ &= (P_1)^* + (iQ_1)^* \\ &= P_1 + \bar{i}\, Q_1^* \\ &= P_1 + (-i)\, Q_1 \\ &= P_1 - iQ_1 \end{aligned}$$

| Using Eqs. (2.42) and (2.43) ... (2.44)

Adding Eqs. (2.41) and (2.44), we obtain

$$A + A^* = 2P_1$$

$$\Rightarrow P_1 = \frac{1}{2}\left(A + A^*\right) = P$$

Subtracting Eq. (2.44) from Eq. (2.41), we obtain

$$A - A^* = 2iQ_1$$

$$\Rightarrow Q_1 = \frac{1}{2i}\left(A - A^*\right) = Q$$

$\therefore$ From Eq. (2.41)

$$A = P_1 + iQ_1 = P + iQ$$

Hence, the representation is unique.

Theorem 13. Show that every hermitian matrix H can be uniquely expressed as $P + iQ$, where P is real and symmetric and Q is real and skew-symmetric. Also, H^*H is real iff $PQ = -QP$.

Proof. Let $H = [a_{rs} + ib_{rs}]_{n \times n}$; $r, s = 1, 2, 3, ..., n$ where a_{rs}, b_{rs} are real and $i = \sqrt{-1}$.

$\because$ H is hermitian | Given

$\therefore$ $H^* = H$

$\therefore$ $a_{rs} + ib_{rs} = \overline{a_{sr} + ib_{sr}}$

$= a_{sr} - ib_{sr}$

$$\left.\begin{aligned} \Rightarrow \quad a_{rs} &= a_{sr} \\ \text{and, } b_{rs} &= -b_{sr} \end{aligned}\right\} \quad \text{... (2.45)}$$

$\therefore$ $H = [a_{rs} + i\,b_{rs}]_{n \times n}$

$= [a_{rs}]_{n \times n} + [i\,b_{rs}]_{n \times n}$

$= [a_{rs}]_{n \times n} + i\,[b_{rs}]_{n \times n}$

$= P + iQ$ ... (2.46)

where,

$P = [a_{rs}]_{n \times n}$

and, $Q = [b_{rs}]_{n \times n}$

Clearly P and Q are real matrices.

Also,

$P' = [a'_{rs}]_{n \times n}$ where

$a'_{rs} = a_{sr} = a_{rs}$ | From Eq. (2.45)

$\therefore$ $P' = [a_{rs}]_{n \times n} = P$

$\Rightarrow$ P is symmetric.

Again,

$Q' = [b'_{rs}]_{n \times n}$ where

$b'_{rs} = b_{sr} = -b_{rs}$

$\therefore$ $Q' = [-b_{rs}]_{n \times n} = -[b_{rs}]_{n \times n} = -Q$

$\Rightarrow$ Q is skew-symmetric.

Thus, Eq. (2.46) expresses H in the form of $P + iQ$ where P is real and symmetric and Q is real and skew-symmetric.

Uniqueness

Let $H = R + iS$ ... (2.46)

be another such representation where R is real and symmetric, Q is real and skew-symmetric and at least one of the inequalities $R \neq P$, $S \neq Q$ holds.

Then,

$$H = [a_{rs} + i\ b_{rs}]_{n \times n} = R + iS \quad \text{... (2.47)}$$

$$\therefore \quad \overline{H} = [a_{rs} - i\ b_{rs}]_{n \times n} = R - iS \quad \text{... (2.48)}$$

Adding Eqs. (2.47) and (2.48), we obtain

$$\begin{aligned} 2R &= [a_{rs} + i\ b_{rs}]_{n \times n} + [a_{rs} - i\ b_{rs}]_{n \times n} \\ &= [2a_{rs}]_{n \times n} \\ &= 2\ [a_{rs}]_{n \times n} \end{aligned}$$

$$\Rightarrow \quad R = [a_{rs}]_{n \times n} = P$$

Similarly on subtraction, we obtain

$$\begin{aligned} 2iS &= [a_{rs} + i\ b_{rs}]_{n \times n} - [a_{rs} - i\ b_{rs}]_{n \times n} \\ &= [2\ i\ b_{rs}]_{n \times n} \\ &= 2i\ [b_{rs}]_{n \times n} \end{aligned}$$

$$\Rightarrow \quad S = [b_{rs}]_{n \times n} = Q$$

Thus, we reach a contradiction. Hence, the representation is unique.

Lastly,

$$\begin{aligned} H^*H &= HH \qquad | \because H \text{ is hermitian} \\ &= (P + iQ)\ (P + iQ) \\ &= P^2 - Q^2 + i\ (PQ + QP) \end{aligned}$$

Hence, H^*H is real, iff

$$PQ + QP = O$$

i.e. iff $PQ = -\ QP$

ILLUSTRATIVE EXAMPLES

Example 1. Prove that the matrix $A = \begin{bmatrix} 1 & 1-i & 2 \\ 1+i & 3 & i \\ 2 & -i & 0 \end{bmatrix}$ is hermitian. If K is a complex number, examine whether KA is hermitian.

Solution: We have,

$$A = \begin{bmatrix} 1 & 1-i & 2 \\ 1+i & 3 & i \\ 2 & -i & 0 \end{bmatrix}$$

$$\therefore \quad A' = \begin{bmatrix} 1 & 1+i & 2 \\ 1-i & 3 & -i \\ 2 & i & 0 \end{bmatrix}$$

$$\therefore \quad \overline{(A')} = \begin{bmatrix} 1 & 1-i & 2 \\ 1+i & 3 & i \\ 2 & -i & 0 \end{bmatrix}$$

$$\Rightarrow \quad A^* = \begin{bmatrix} 1 & 1-i & 2 \\ 1+i & 3 & i \\ 2 & -i & 0 \end{bmatrix}$$

$\Rightarrow \quad A^* = A$

$\Rightarrow \quad A$ is hermitian.

Now,

$(KA)^* = \overline{K}A^* = \overline{K}A$ | $\because A^* = A$

$\neq KA$ | $\because \overline{K} \neq K$; K being a complex number

Hence, KA is not hermitian.

Example 2. Show that all positive integral powers of a hermitian matrix are hermitian.

Solution: It is evident that for the existence of the integral powers of a hermitian matrix, the matrix must be square. Let A be a square hermitian matrix of order $n \times n$.

Then,

$A^* = A$ ... (2.49)

Let n be a positive integer. Then,

$A^n = A\ A\ A\ .....\ n$ times

$\therefore\ (A^n)^* = (A\ A\ A\ .....\ n \text{ times})^*$

$= A^*\ A^*\ A^*\ .....\ n$ times | By reversal law of tranjugate

$= A\ A\ A\ .....\ n$ times | Using Eq. (2.49)

$= A^n$

$\Rightarrow A^n$ is hermitian.

Example 3. If A is a hermitian (skew-hermitian) matrix, show that iA is a skew-hermitian (hermitian) matrix.

Solution: Let $B = iA$

Then,

$B^* = (iA)^*$

$= \bar{i}A^*$

$= -\ iA^*$ ... (2.50)

Case I. If A is a hermitian matrix, then

$A^* = A$

Therefore,

$B^* = -\ iA$ | From Eq. (2.50)

$\Rightarrow B^* = -\ B$ | $\because B = iA$

$\Rightarrow B$ is skew-hermitian

$\Rightarrow iA$ is skew-hermitian | $\because B = iA$

Case II. If A is a skew-hermitian matrix, then

$A^* = -\ A$

Therefore,

$B^* = -i\ (-A)$ | From Eq. (2.50)

$= iA$

$= B$ | $\because B = iA$

$\Rightarrow$ B is hermitian

$\Rightarrow$ iA is hermitian | $\because B = iA$

Example 4. If A is hermitian (skew-hermitian), show that B^*AB (or $\bar{B}'AB$) is hermitian (skew-hermitian).

Solution: If A is hermitian, then

$A^* = A$

Now,

$(B^*AB)^* = B^*A^*(B^*)^*$ | By reversal law for tranjugate

$= B^* A B$ | $\because A^* = A$ and $(B^*)^* = B$

$\Rightarrow$ B^*AB is hermitian

If A is skew-hermitian, then

$A^* = -A$

Now,

$(B^*AB)^* = B^*A^*(B^*)^*$ | By reversal law for tranjugate

$= B^*(-A)B$ | $\because A^* = -A$ and $(B^*)^* = B$

$= -(B^*AB)$

$\Rightarrow$ B^*AB is skew-hermitian.

Example 5. If A is hermitian such that $A^2 = O$, show that $A = O$.

Solution: Let $A = [a_{ij}]_{n \times n}$; $i, j = 1, 2, \ldots, n$

$\because$ A is hermitian

$\therefore$ $a_{ij} = \overline{a_{ji}}\ \forall\ i, j$ ... (2.51)

Let $A^2 = C = [c_{ij}]_{n \times n}$. Then,

$$c_{ij} = \sum_{k=1}^{n} a_{ik}\, a_{kj}$$

For a diagonal element of C, $j = i$.

Therefore,

$$c_{ii} = \sum_{k=1}^{n} a_{ik}\, a_{ki}$$

$$= \sum_{k=1}^{n} a_{ik}\, \overline{a_{ik}} \qquad \text{| From Eq. (2.51)}$$

$$= \sum_{k=1}^{n} |a_{ik}|^2 \qquad \text{where } |a_{ik}| \text{ is the modulus of } a_{ik}.$$

$$= |a_{i1}|^2 + |a_{i2}|^2 + |a_{i3}|^2 + \ldots + |a_{in}|^2$$

But $A^2 = O$ | Given

$\therefore \quad c_{ii} = 0 \ \forall \ i$

$\Rightarrow \quad |a_{i1}|^2 + |a_{i2}|^2 + |a_{i3}|^2 + \ldots + |a_{in}|^2 = 0$

$\Rightarrow \quad a_{i1} = a_{i2} = a_{i3} = \ldots = a_{in} = 0$

where

$i = 1, 2, \ldots, n$

Hence, if A is hermitian and $A^2 = O$, then all the elements of A must be zero, i.e. $A = O$.

EXERCISE 2.2

1. If $A = \begin{bmatrix} 1+i & 2-3i & 2 \\ 3-4i & 4+5i & 1 \\ 5 & 3 & 3-i \end{bmatrix}$, find $\overline{A}$ and A^*.

2. Show that $\begin{bmatrix} 3 & 1+2i \\ 1-2i & 2 \end{bmatrix}$ is hermitian.

3. Show that $\begin{bmatrix} 0 & 1+i \\ -1+i & 0 \end{bmatrix}$ is skew-hermitian.

4. Show that $\begin{bmatrix} 3 & 7-4i & -2+5i \\ 7+4i & -2 & 3+i \\ -2-5i & 3-i & 4 \end{bmatrix}$ is hermitian.

5. Show that $\begin{bmatrix} i & 3+2i & -2-i \\ -3+2i & 0 & 3-4i \\ 2-i & -3-4i & -2i \end{bmatrix}$ is skew-hermitian.

6. If $A = \begin{bmatrix} 3 & 2-3i & 3+5i \\ 2+3i & 5 & i \\ 3-5i & -i & 7 \end{bmatrix}$, then prove that $\bar{A}$ is hermitian.

7. If $A = \begin{bmatrix} i & 1+i & 2-3i \\ -1+i & 2i & 1 \\ -2-3i & -1 & 0 \end{bmatrix}$, then show that $\bar{A}$ is skew-hermitian.

8. Give an example of a matrix which is
   (i) Symmetric but not hermitian.
   (ii) Skew-symmetric but not skew-hermitian.

9. Show that if A and B are hermitian (skew-hermitian), so is also $A + B$.

10. If A is any square matrix, prove that AA^* and A^*A are both hermitian.

11. Show that A is skew-hermitian if and only if $\bar{A}$ is skew-hermitian.

12. If A and B are hermitian matrices, show that $AB + BA$ is hermitian and $AB - BA$ is skew-hermitian.

13. If A is a hermitian matrix, examine whether KA and iKA are hermitian matrices, where K is a real number.

14. If A is a square matrix, show that $A + A^*$ is hermitian and $A - A^*$ is skew-hermitian.

15. If A and B are hermitian, show that AB is hermitian iff A and B commute.

16. If A and B are hermitian matrices, show that BAB is also hermitian.

17. Show that the determinant of a hermitian matrix is real.

18. If A and B are hermitian such that $A^2 + B^2 = O$, show that $A = O$ and $B = O$.

ANSWERS

1. $\bar{A} = \begin{bmatrix} 1-i & 2-3i & 2 \\ 3+4i & 4-5i & 1 \\ 5 & 3 & 3+i \end{bmatrix}$

$A^* = \begin{bmatrix} 1-i & 3+4i & 5 \\ 2-3i & 4-5i & 3 \\ 2 & 1 & 3+i \end{bmatrix}$

8. (i) $\begin{bmatrix} 1 & 2-i & 3+i \\ 2-i & 2 & 4 \\ 3+i & 4 & 3 \end{bmatrix}$

(ii) $\begin{bmatrix} 0 & 2i & 4i \\ -2i & 0 & 3 \\ -4i & -3 & 0 \end{bmatrix}$

13. KA is hermitian, iKA is skew-hermitian.

2.12. Nilpotent Matrix

A square matrix A is said to be nilpotent if $A^2 = O$. For example, $\begin{bmatrix} 0 & 0 \\ 1 & 0 \end{bmatrix}$ is a nilpotent matrix.

A square matrix A is said to be nilpotent matrix of index p if p is the least positive integer such that $A^p = O$. Thus, the matrix $\begin{bmatrix} 0 & 0 \\ 1 & 0 \end{bmatrix}$ is a nilpotent matrix of index 2.

2.13. Idempotent Matrix

A square matrix A is said to be idempotent if $A^2 = A$. For example, $\begin{bmatrix} 1 & 0 \\ 0 & 1 \end{bmatrix}$ is an idempotent matrix. Similarly, I is an idempotent matrix.

A square matrix A is said to be idempotent matrix of index p if p is the least positive integer such that $A^{p+1} = A$.

Thus, the matrix $\begin{bmatrix} 1 & 0 \\ 0 & 1 \end{bmatrix}$ is an idempotent matrix of index 1.

2.14. Involutory Matrix

A square matrix A is said to be involutory if $A^2 = I$, where I is the unit matrix. For example, $\begin{bmatrix} 1 & 0 \\ 0 & 1 \end{bmatrix}$ is an involutory matrix. Similarly, I is an involutory matrix.

2.15. Orthogonal Matrix

A square matrix A is said to be orthogonal if $AA' = A'A = I$, where I is the identity matrix. For example, $\begin{bmatrix} \cos\theta & \sin\theta \\ -\sin\theta & \cos\theta \end{bmatrix}$ is an orthogonal matrix. Similarly, I is an orthogonal matrix.

Note: If A is an orthogonal matrix, then $|A|^2 = 1$ so that $|A| = \pm 1$. If $|A| = 1$, then A is called a proper matrix.

2.16. Unitary Matrix

A square matrix A is said to be unitary of $AA^* = A^*A = I$, where I is the identity matrix. For example,

$$\begin{bmatrix} \frac{1}{2}(1+i) & -\frac{1}{2}(1-i) \\ \frac{1}{2}(1+i) & \frac{1}{2}(1-i) \end{bmatrix}$$ is a unitary matrix.

Note: If A is real, then $\bar{A} = A$ so that $A^* = A'$. In this case, A is unitary if $AA' = A'A = I$, i.e. if A is orthogonal.

2.17. Determinant of a Matrix

If $A = [a_{ij}]_{n \times n}$ is a square matrix, then the determinant of A is written as det A in brief and is denoted by $|A|$. It is defined as follows:

$|A| = |a_{ij}|$

$$= \begin{vmatrix} a_{11} & a_{12} & \dots\dots & a_{1n} \\ a_{21} & a_{22} & \dots\dots & a_{2n} \\ \dots\dots & \dots\dots & \dots\dots & \dots\dots \\ a_{n1} & a_{n2} & \dots\dots & a_{nn} \end{vmatrix}$$

The determinant of a square matrix of order $n \times n$ is called a determinant of order n.

2.18. Unimodular Matrix

A square matrix A is called unimodular if $|A| = 1$.

2.19. Singular Matrix

A square matrix A is said to be singular if $|A| = 0$.

2.20. Non-singular or Regular or Invertible Matrix

A square matrix A is said to be non-singular if $|A| \neq 0$.

2.21. Some Theorems

Theorem 1. Every non-singular idempotent matrix is an identity matrix.

Proof. Let A be a non-singular idempotent matrix. Then,

$$A^2 = A \qquad | \text{ By definition}$$

$$\Rightarrow AA = A \qquad \dots (2.52)$$

Note that a square matrix B of the same order as A such that $AB = BA = I$ is called the inverse matrix of the matrix A and is denoted by A^{-1}. Also, the inverse of a square matrix A exists if and only if A is non-singular.

Since A is non-singular, therefore, A^{-1} exists and

$$AA^{-1} = A^{-1}A = I$$

Now, pre-multiplying both sides of Eq. (2.52) by A^{-1}, we get

$$A^{-1}(AA) = A^{-1}A$$

$$\Rightarrow (A^{-1}A)A = I \qquad | \text{ By Associative Law of Multiplication}$$

$$\Rightarrow IA = I$$

$$\Rightarrow A = I$$

Theorem 2. If A and B are idempotent matrices, then AB is idempotent if and only if A and B commute.

Proof. $\because$ A and B are idempotent matrices

$\therefore$ We have,

$$A^2 = A \quad \text{and,} \quad B^2 = B \qquad \text{By definition} \qquad \ldots (2.53)$$

Now,

$$(AB)^2 = (AB)(AB)$$
$$= A(BA)B \qquad | \text{ By Associative Law of Multiplication}$$
$$= A(AB)B \qquad | \text{ if } A \text{ and } B \text{ commute}$$
$$= (AA)(BB)$$
$$= A^2 B^2$$
$$= A B \qquad | \text{ From Eq. (2.53)}$$

$\Rightarrow$ AB is idempotent if A and B commute.

Theorem 3. If A and B are idempotent matrices, then $A + B$ will be idempotent if and only if $AB = BA = O$.

Proof. $\because$ A and B are idempotent matrices

$\therefore$ We have,

$$A^2 = A \quad \text{and,} \quad B^2 = B \qquad \text{By definition} \qquad \ldots (2.54)$$

Now,

$$(A + B)^2 = (A + B)(A + B)$$
$$= (A + B)A + (A + B)B \qquad | \text{ By Distributive Law}$$
$$= A^2 + BA + AB + B^2 \qquad | \text{ By Distributive Law}$$
$$= A + BA + AB + B \qquad | \text{ From Eq. (2.54)}$$
$$= A + B \qquad | \text{ If } AB = BA = O$$

$\Rightarrow$ $(A + B)$ is idempotent if $AB = BA = O$.

Again, if $(A + B)$ is idempotent, then

$$(A + B)^2 = A + B \qquad | \text{ By definition}$$

$\Rightarrow$ $(A + B)(A + B) = A + B$

$\Rightarrow$ $(A + B)A + (A + B)B = A + B$

| By Distributive Law

$\Rightarrow$ $A^2 + BA + AB + B^2 = A + B$

$\Rightarrow$ $A + BA + AB + B = A + B$

$\Rightarrow$ $A + B + (AB + BA) = A + B$

$\Rightarrow$ $AB + BA = O$

$\Rightarrow$ $AB = -BA$ ... (2.55)

$\Rightarrow$ $A(AB) = -A(BA)$ | Pre-multiplying both sides by A

$\Rightarrow$ $(AA)B = -(AB)A$

$\Rightarrow$ $(AA)B = (BA)A$ | $\because AB = -BA$

$\Rightarrow$ $(AA)B = B(AA)$

$\Rightarrow$ $A^2B = BA^2$

$\Rightarrow$ $AB = BA$ ... (2.56) | From Eq. (2.54)

$\therefore$ $AB = BA = O$ | From Eqs. (2.55) and (2.56)

$\Rightarrow$ If $(A + B)$ is idempotent, then

$AB = BA = O$

Thus, if A and B are idempotent matrices, then $(A + B)$ will be idempotent iff $AB = BA = O$.

Theorem 4. If A is idempotent and $A + B = I$, then B is idempotent and $AB = BA = O$.

Proof. $\because$ A is idempotent

$\therefore$ We have,

$A^2 = A$ ... (2.57)

Also,

$A + B = I$

$\Rightarrow$ $B = I - A$

$\Rightarrow$ $B^2 = (I - A)^2$

$\Rightarrow$ $B^2 = (I - A)(I - A)$

$\Rightarrow$ $B^2 = (I - A)I - (I - A)A$ | By Distributive Law

$\Rightarrow$ $B^2 = II - AI - IA - AA$

$\Rightarrow \; B^2 = I^2 - A - A + A^2$

$\Rightarrow \; B^2 = I - A - A + A$ | From Eq. (2.57)

$\Rightarrow \; B^2 = I - A$

$\Rightarrow \; B^2 = B$

$\Rightarrow$ B is an idempotent matrix.

Again,

$A + B = I$

Pre-multiplying both sides by A, we get

$A\,(A + B) = AI$

$\Rightarrow \; AA + AB = A$

$\Rightarrow \; A^2 + AB = A$

$\Rightarrow \; A + AB = A$ | From Eq. (2.57)

$\Rightarrow \; A + AB = A + O$

$\Rightarrow \; AB = O$ | By Cancellation Law

Lastly,

$A + B = I$

Pre-multiplying both sides by B, we get

$B\,(A + B) = BI$

$\Rightarrow \; BA + BB = B$

$\Rightarrow \; BA + B^2 = B$

$\Rightarrow \; BA + B = B$ | $\because$ B is an idempotent matrix

$\Rightarrow \; BA + B = O + B$

$\Rightarrow \; BA = O$ | By Cancellation Law

Theorem 5. If A and B are n-square orthogonal matrices, then AB and BA are orthogonal matrices.

Proof. $\because$ A and B are n-square orthogonal matrices

$\therefore \quad AA' = A'A = I_n$

and, $BB' = B'B = I_n$ | By definition ... (2.58)

Now,

$(AB)\,(AB)' = (AB)\,(B'A')$ | By Reversal Law of Transpose

$= A(BB')A'$ | By Associative Law of Multiplication

$= A\ I_n\ A'$ | From Eq. (2.58)

$= AA'$

$= I_n$ | From Eq. (2.58)

and,

$$(AB)'\ (AB) = (B'A')\ (AB)$$
$$= B'\ (A'A)\ B$$
$$= B'\ I_n\ B$$
$$= B'\ B$$
$$= I_n$$

$\therefore\ (AB)\ (AB)' = (AB)'\ (AB) = I_n$

$\Rightarrow$ AB is an orthogonal matrix.

Similarly,

$$(BA)\ (BA)' = (BA)\ (A'B')$$
$$= B\ (AA')\ B'$$
$$= B\ I_n\ B'$$
$$= BB'$$
$$= I_n$$

and,

$$(BA)'\ (BA) = (A'B')\ (BA)$$
$$= A'\ (B'B)\ A$$
$$= A'\ I_n\ A$$
$$= A'A$$
$$= I_n$$

$\therefore\ (BA)\ (BA)' = (BA)'\ (BA) = I_n$

$\Rightarrow$ BA is an orthogonal matrix.

Theorem 6. If $AB = A$ and $BA = B$, then show that A and B are idempotent.

Proof. We have,

$$AB = A$$

$\Rightarrow\ (AB)\ A = AA$

$\Rightarrow A\,(BA) = A^2$

$\Rightarrow AB = A^2$

$\Rightarrow A = A^2$

$\Rightarrow A^2 = A$

$\Rightarrow A$ is idempotent.

Again,

$BA = B$

$\Rightarrow (BA)B = BB$

$\Rightarrow B(AB) = B^2$

$\Rightarrow BA = B^2$

$\Rightarrow B = B^2$

$\Rightarrow B^2 = B$

$\Rightarrow B$ is idempotent.

Theorem 7. Show that the matrix $B = n^{-1}A$, where A is of order $n \times n$ and has every element $a_{ij} = 1$, is idempotent.

Proof. We have

$$A = \begin{bmatrix} 1 & 1 & \ldots\ldots & 1 \\ 1 & 1 & \ldots\ldots & 1 \\ \ldots & \ldots & \ldots\ldots & \ldots \\ 1 & 1 & \ldots\ldots & 1 \end{bmatrix}_{n \times n}$$

$$\Rightarrow \quad A^2 = AA = \begin{bmatrix} 1 & 1 & \ldots\ldots & 1 \\ 1 & 1 & \ldots\ldots & 1 \\ \ldots & \ldots & \ldots\ldots & \ldots \\ 1 & 1 & \ldots\ldots & 1 \end{bmatrix}_{n \times n} \begin{bmatrix} 1 & 1 & \ldots\ldots & 1 \\ 1 & 1 & \ldots\ldots & 1 \\ \ldots & \ldots & \ldots\ldots & \ldots \\ 1 & 1 & \ldots\ldots & 1 \end{bmatrix}_{n \times n}$$

$$= \begin{bmatrix} n & n & \ldots\ldots & n \\ n & n & \ldots\ldots & n \\ \ldots & \ldots & \ldots\ldots & \ldots \\ n & n & \ldots\ldots & n \end{bmatrix}_{n \times n}$$

$$= n \begin{bmatrix} 1 & 1 & \cdots\cdots & 1 \\ 1 & 1 & \cdots\cdots & 1 \\ \cdots & \cdots & \cdots\cdots & \cdots \\ 1 & 1 & \cdots\cdots & 1 \end{bmatrix}_{n \times n}$$

$$= nA \qquad \text{... (2.59)}$$

Now,

$$B^2 = (n^{-1}A)^2 = n^{-2}\, A^2 = n^{-2}\, nA = n^{-1}A = B$$

$\Rightarrow$ B is idempotent.

Theorem 8. Show that A is involutory iff

$$(I + A)\,(I - A) = O$$

Proof. Let A be an involutory matrix of order $n \times n$.

Then,

$A^2 = I$ | By definition ... (2.60)

$\Rightarrow$ $I - A^2 = O$

$\Rightarrow$ $I^2 - A^2 = O$

$\Rightarrow$ $(I + A)\,(I - A) = O$ | $\because IA = AI = A$

Conversely,

Let $(I + A)\,(I - A) = O$

Then,

$II - IA + AI - AA = O$ | By distributive law

$\Rightarrow$ $I^2 - IA + AI - A^2 = O$

$\Rightarrow$ $I^2 - A + A - A^2 = O$ | $\because IA = AI = A$

$\Rightarrow$ $I - A^2 = O$

$\Rightarrow$ $A^2 = I$

$\Rightarrow$ A is involutory.

ILLUSTRATIVE EXAMPLES

Example 1. Prove that the matrix $A = \begin{bmatrix} 1 & 1 & 3 \\ 5 & 2 & 6 \\ -2 & -1 & -3 \end{bmatrix}$ is a nilpotent matrix of index 3.

Solution:

$$A^2 = AA$$

$$= \begin{bmatrix} 1 & 1 & 3 \\ 5 & 2 & 6 \\ -2 & -1 & -3 \end{bmatrix} \begin{bmatrix} 1 & 1 & 3 \\ 5 & 2 & 6 \\ -2 & -1 & -3 \end{bmatrix}$$

$$= \begin{bmatrix} 1+5-6 & 1+2-3 & 3+6-9 \\ 5+10-12 & 5+4-6 & 15+12-18 \\ -2-5+6 & -2-2+3 & -6-6+9 \end{bmatrix}$$

$$= \begin{bmatrix} 0 & 0 & 0 \\ 3 & 3 & 9 \\ -1 & -1 & -3 \end{bmatrix}$$

$$A^3 = A^2A$$

$$= \begin{bmatrix} 0 & 0 & 0 \\ 3 & 3 & 9 \\ -1 & -1 & -3 \end{bmatrix} \begin{bmatrix} 1 & 1 & 3 \\ 5 & 2 & 6 \\ -2 & -1 & -3 \end{bmatrix}$$

$$= \begin{bmatrix} 0 & 0 & 0 \\ 0 & 0 & 0 \\ 0 & 0 & 0 \end{bmatrix} = O$$

$\Rightarrow$ A is a nilpotent matrix of index 3.

Example 2. Show that diag (1, 1, ..., 1) is an idempotent matrix.

Solution: We know that

diag (1, 1, ..., 1) = I

and $I^2 = I$

Hence, diag (1, 1, ..., 1) is an idempotent matrix.

Example 3. Show that the matrix $A = \begin{bmatrix} 1 & -2 & -6 \\ -3 & 2 & 9 \\ 2 & 0 & -3 \end{bmatrix}$ is an idempotent (periodic) matrix of index (period) 2.

Solution:

$$A^2 = AA$$

$$= \begin{bmatrix} 1 & -2 & -6 \\ -3 & 2 & 9 \\ 2 & 0 & -3 \end{bmatrix} \begin{bmatrix} 1 & -2 & -6 \\ -3 & 2 & 9 \\ 2 & 0 & -3 \end{bmatrix}$$

$$= \begin{bmatrix} 1+6-12 & -2-4+0 & -6-18+18 \\ -3-6+18 & 6+4+0 & 18+18-27 \\ 2+0-6 & -4+0+0 & -12+0+9 \end{bmatrix}$$

$$= \begin{bmatrix} -5 & -6 & -6 \\ 9 & 10 & 9 \\ -4 & -4 & -3 \end{bmatrix}$$

$$A^3 = A^2A$$

$$= \begin{bmatrix} -5 & -6 & -6 \\ 9 & 10 & 9 \\ -4 & -4 & -3 \end{bmatrix} \begin{bmatrix} 1 & -2 & -6 \\ -3 & 2 & 9 \\ 2 & 0 & -3 \end{bmatrix}$$

$$= \begin{bmatrix} -5+18-12 & 10-12+0 & 30-54+18 \\ 9-30+18 & -18+20+0 & -54+90-27 \\ -4+12-6 & 8-8+0 & 24-36+9 \end{bmatrix}$$

$$= \begin{bmatrix} 1 & -1 & 6 \\ -3 & 2 & 9 \\ 2 & 0 & -3 \end{bmatrix}$$

$$= A$$

$\Rightarrow \; A^{2+1} = A$

$\Rightarrow$ A is an idempotent (periodic) matrix of index (period) 2.

Example 4. Show that the matrix $A = \begin{bmatrix} 0 & 1 & -1 \\ 4 & -3 & 4 \\ 3 & -3 & 4 \end{bmatrix}$ is involutory.

Solution:

$$A^2 = AA$$

$$= \begin{bmatrix} 0 & 1 & -1 \\ 4 & -3 & 4 \\ 3 & -3 & 4 \end{bmatrix}\begin{bmatrix} 0 & 1 & -1 \\ 4 & -3 & 4 \\ 3 & -3 & 4 \end{bmatrix}$$

$$= \begin{bmatrix} 0+4-3 & 0-3+3 & 0+4-4 \\ 0-12+12 & 4+9-12 & -4-12+16 \\ 0-12+12 & 3+9-12 & -3-12+16 \end{bmatrix}$$

$$= \begin{bmatrix} 1 & 0 & 0 \\ 0 & 1 & 0 \\ 0 & 0 & 1 \end{bmatrix} = I$$

$\Rightarrow$ A is involutory.

Example 5. Prove that the matrix $A = \begin{bmatrix} \cos\alpha & \sin\alpha \\ -\sin\alpha & \cos\alpha \end{bmatrix}$ is orthogonal.

Solution: We have

$$A = \begin{bmatrix} \cos\alpha & \sin\alpha \\ -\sin\alpha & \cos\alpha \end{bmatrix}$$

$$\therefore \quad A' = \begin{bmatrix} \cos\alpha & \sin\alpha \\ -\sin\alpha & \cos\alpha \end{bmatrix}' = \begin{bmatrix} \cos\alpha & -\sin\alpha \\ \sin\alpha & \cos\alpha \end{bmatrix}$$

$$\therefore \quad AA' = \begin{bmatrix} \cos\alpha & \sin\alpha \\ -\sin\alpha & \cos\alpha \end{bmatrix} \begin{bmatrix} \cos\alpha & -\sin\alpha \\ \sin\alpha & \cos\alpha \end{bmatrix}$$

$$= \begin{bmatrix} \cos^2\alpha + \sin^2\alpha & \begin{matrix} -\cos\alpha\sin\alpha + \\ \sin\alpha\cos\alpha \end{matrix} \\ \begin{matrix} -\sin\alpha\cos\alpha + \\ \cos\alpha\sin\alpha \end{matrix} & \sin^2\alpha + \cos^2\alpha \end{bmatrix}$$

$$= \begin{bmatrix} 1 & 0 \\ 0 & 1 \end{bmatrix} = I$$

Similarly,

$$A'A = I$$

Thus,

$$AA' = A'A = I$$

$\Rightarrow$ A is orthogonal.

Example 6. Prove that the matrix $A = \dfrac{1}{5}\begin{bmatrix} -1+2i & -4-2i \\ 2-4i & -2-i \end{bmatrix}$ is unitary.

Solution: We have

$$A = \frac{1}{5}\begin{bmatrix} -1+2i & -4-2i \\ 2-4i & -2-i \end{bmatrix}$$

$$\therefore \quad \bar{A} = \frac{1}{5}\begin{bmatrix} -1-2i & -4+2i \\ 2+4i & -2+i \end{bmatrix}$$

$$\therefore \quad (\bar{A})' = \frac{1}{5}\begin{bmatrix} -1-2i & 2+4i \\ -4+2i & -2+i \end{bmatrix}$$

$$\Rightarrow \quad A^* = \frac{1}{5}\begin{bmatrix} -1-2i & 2+4i \\ -4+2i & -2+i \end{bmatrix}$$

$$\therefore \quad AA^* = \frac{1}{5}\begin{bmatrix} -1+2i & -4-2i \\ 2-4i & -2-i \end{bmatrix} \times \frac{1}{5}\begin{bmatrix} -1-2i & 2+4i \\ -4+2i & -2+i \end{bmatrix}$$

$$= \frac{1}{25}\begin{bmatrix} (-1+2i)(-1-2i)+ & (-1+2i)(2+4i)+ \\ (-4-2i)(-4+2i) & (-4-2i)(-2+i) \\ (2-4i)(-1-2i)+ & (2-4i)(2+4i)+ \\ (-2-i)(-4+2i) & (-2-i)(-2+i) \end{bmatrix}$$

$$= \frac{1}{25}\begin{bmatrix} 25 & 0 \\ 0 & 25 \end{bmatrix} = \begin{bmatrix} 1 & 0 \\ 0 & 1 \end{bmatrix} = I$$

Similarly, we can show that

$$A^*A = I$$

Thus,

$$AA^* = A^*A = I$$

$\Rightarrow$ A is unitary.

Example 7. Show that the matrix A defined by

$$A = I_n - X(X'X)^{-1} X'$$

is a symmetric and idempotent matrix.

Solution:

$$A = I_n - X(X'X)^{-1} X'$$

$= I_n - X(X^{-1} (X')^{-1})X'$ | By reversal law of inverse

$= I_n - (XX^{-1}) ((X')^{-1}X')$ | By associative law

$= I_n - I_n I_n$

$= I_n - I_n$

$= O$

$\Rightarrow$ $A' = O$ and $A^2 = O$

$\therefore$ $A' = A$ and $A^2 = A$

$\Rightarrow$ A is symmetric and idempotent.

Example 8. If A is a real skew-symmetric matrix such that $A^2 + I = O$, show that A is orthogonal and is of even order.

Solution:

$\because$ A is a real skew-symmetric matrix

$\therefore$ $A' = -A$

$\Rightarrow AA' = -AA$

$\Rightarrow AA' = -A^2$

$\Rightarrow A^2 = -AA'$

$\Rightarrow O - I = -AA'$ $\quad | \because A^2 + I = O$

$\Rightarrow -I = -AA'$

$\Rightarrow I = AA'$

$\Rightarrow AA' = I$

Similarly, we can prove that $A'A = I$

Thus, $AA' = A'A = I$

$\Rightarrow A$ is orthogonal.

Again, we know that

$|A| = |A'|$

Also, $|KA| = K^n |A|$ where n is the order of A

Now,

$\Rightarrow A' = -A$

$\Rightarrow A' = (-1)A$

$\Rightarrow |A'| = |(-1)A|$

$\Rightarrow |A'| = (-1)^n |A|$

$\Rightarrow |A| = (-1)^n |A|$ $\quad | \because |A| = |A'|$

$\Rightarrow \{1 - (-1)^n\} |A| = 0$

$\Rightarrow$ Either $|A| = 0$

or $1 - (-1)^n = 0$

But $A^2 = O - I$

$\Rightarrow A^2 = -I$

$\Rightarrow |A^2| = |-I|$

$\Rightarrow |AA| = |(-1)I|$

$\Rightarrow |A||A| = (-1)^n |I|$ $\quad | \because |A||B| = |AB|$

$\Rightarrow |A|^2 = (-1)^n 1$

$\Rightarrow |A|^2 = (-1)^n \neq 0$

$\Rightarrow |A| \neq 0$

Therefore,

$1 - (-1)^n = 0$

$\Rightarrow \quad (-1)^n = 1$

$\Rightarrow \quad n$ is even

$\Rightarrow \quad A$ is of even order.

Example 9. Show that the product of two unitary matrices is a unitary matrix.

Solution: Let A and B be two unitary matrices, Then,

$$\left.\begin{aligned} AA^* &= A^*A = I \\ \text{and} \quad BB^* &= B^*B = I \end{aligned}\right| \text{ By definition} \qquad \ldots (2.61)$$

Now,

$$\begin{aligned} (AB)\,(AB)^* &= (AB)\,(B^*A^*) \\ &= A\,(BB^*)A^* \\ &= A\,I\,A^* && \mid \text{From Eq. (2.61)} \\ &= A\,A^* \\ &= I \end{aligned}$$

Similarly, we can show that

$$(AB)^*\,(AB) = I$$

Thus,

$$(AB)\,(AB)^* = (AB)^*\,(AB) = I$$

$\Rightarrow \quad AB$ is unitary.

Example 10. Show that if U is unitary, then U^* and $\bar{U}$ are also unitary.

Solution:

$\because \quad U$ is unitary | Given

$\therefore \quad UU^* = U^*U = I$ | By definition ... (2.61)

Now,

$$U^*\,(U^*)^* = U^*U = I$$

and,

$$(U^*)^*U^* = UU^* = I$$

Thus,

$$U^*(U^*)^* = (U^*)^*U^* = I$$

$\Rightarrow \quad U^*$ is unitary.

Again,

$$\bar{U}(\bar{U})^* = \bar{U}\left(\overline{(\bar{U})}\right)'$$

$$= \left(\bar{U}'\right)'\left(\overline{(\bar{U})}\right)'$$

$$= \left(\overline{(\bar{U})}\left(\bar{U}'\right)\right)' \qquad | \because (AB)' = B'A'$$

$$= (UU^*)' \qquad | \because U \text{ is unitary}$$

$$= I^1$$

$$= I$$

Similarly, we can show that

$$(\bar{U})^*\bar{U} = I$$

Thus,

$$\bar{U}(\bar{U})^* = (\bar{U})^*\bar{U} = I$$

$\Rightarrow$ $\bar{U}$ is unitary.

Example 11. If A be a unitary matrix of order 2 such that $|A| = 1$, show that it must be of the form $\begin{bmatrix} a & -b \\ \bar{b} & \bar{a} \end{bmatrix}$ where $a\bar{a} + b\bar{b} = 1$.

Solution: Let $A = \begin{bmatrix} a_{11} & a_{12} \\ a_{21} & a_{22} \end{bmatrix}$

Then,

$$\bar{A} = \begin{bmatrix} \overline{a_{11}} & \overline{a_{12}} \\ \overline{a_{21}} & \overline{a_{22}} \end{bmatrix}$$

$$\therefore \quad (\bar{A})' = \begin{bmatrix} \overline{a_{11}} & \overline{a_{12}} \\ \overline{a_{21}} & \overline{a_{22}} \end{bmatrix}' = \begin{bmatrix} \overline{a_{11}} & \overline{a_{21}} \\ \overline{a_{12}} & \overline{a_{22}} \end{bmatrix}$$

$$\Rightarrow \quad A^* = \begin{bmatrix} \overline{a_{11}} & \overline{a_{21}} \\ \overline{a_{12}} & \overline{a_{22}} \end{bmatrix}$$

$\because$ A is unitary.

$\therefore$ $AA^* = A^*A = I$

Now,

$$AA^* = I$$

$$\Rightarrow \begin{bmatrix} a_{11} & a_{12} \\ a_{21} & a_{22} \end{bmatrix} \begin{bmatrix} \overline{a_{11}} & \overline{a_{12}} \\ \overline{a_{21}} & \overline{a_{22}} \end{bmatrix} = I$$

$$\Rightarrow \begin{bmatrix} a_{11}\overline{a_{11}} + a_{12}\overline{a_{12}} & a_{11}\overline{a_{21}} + a_{12}\overline{a_{22}} \\ a_{21}\overline{a_{11}} + a_{22}\overline{a_{12}} & a_{21}\overline{a_{21}} + a_{22}\overline{a_{22}} \end{bmatrix} = \begin{bmatrix} 1 & 0 \\ 0 & 1 \end{bmatrix}$$

$$\Rightarrow a_{11}\overline{a_{11}} + a_{12}\overline{a_{12}} = 1 \qquad \text{... (2.62)}$$

$$a_{21}\overline{a_{21}} + a_{22}\overline{a_{22}} = 1 \qquad \text{... (2.63)}$$

Again,

$$A^*A = I$$

$$\Rightarrow \begin{bmatrix} \overline{a_{11}} & \overline{a_{21}} \\ \overline{a_{12}} & \overline{a_{22}} \end{bmatrix} \begin{bmatrix} a_{11} & a_{12} \\ a_{21} & a_{22} \end{bmatrix} = I$$

$$\Rightarrow \begin{bmatrix} \overline{a_{11}}\, a_{11} + \overline{a_{21}}\, a_{21} & \overline{a_{11}}\, a_{12} + \overline{a_{21}}\, a_{22} \\ \overline{a_{12}}\, a_{11} + \overline{a_{22}}\, a_{21} & \overline{a_{12}}\, a_{12} + \overline{a_{22}}\, a_{22} \end{bmatrix} = \begin{bmatrix} 1 & 0 \\ 0 & 1 \end{bmatrix}$$

$$\Rightarrow \overline{a_{11}}\, a_{11} + \overline{a_{21}}\, a_{21} = 1 \qquad \text{... (2.64)}$$

$$\overline{a_{12}}\, a_{12} + \overline{a_{22}}\, a_{22} = 1 \qquad \text{... (2.65)}$$

Eqs. (2.62) and (2.64) give,

$$a_{12}\, \overline{a_{12}} = \overline{a_{21}}\, a_{21}$$

$$\Rightarrow a_{12}\, \overline{a_{12}} = a_{21}\, \overline{a_{21}}$$

$$|a_{12}| = |a_{21}| \qquad \text{... (2.66)}$$

Eqs. (2.62) and (2.65) give,

$$a_{11}\, \overline{a_{11}} = \overline{a_{22}}\, a_{22}$$

$$a_{11}\, \overline{a_{11}} = a_{22}\, \overline{a_{22}}$$

$$|a_{11}| = |a_{22}| \qquad \text{... (2.67)}$$

In view of Eqs. (2.66) and (2.67), we may take

$$A = \begin{bmatrix} r_1\, e^{i\alpha} & -r_2\, e^{i\beta} \\ r_2\, e^{i\theta} & r_1\, e^{i\varphi} \end{bmatrix}$$

Then,

$$A^* = \begin{bmatrix} r_1\, e^{-i\alpha} & r_2\, e^{-i\theta} \\ -r_2\, e^{-i\beta} & r_1\, e^{-i\varphi} \end{bmatrix}$$

$\because$ A is unitary

$\therefore$ $AA^* = I$

$$\Rightarrow \begin{bmatrix} r_1\, e^{i\alpha} & -r_2\, e^{i\beta} \\ r_2\, e^{i\theta} & r_1\, e^{i\varphi} \end{bmatrix}\begin{bmatrix} r_1\, e^{-i\alpha} & r_2\, e^{-i\theta} \\ -r_2\, e^{-i\beta} & r_1\, e^{-i\varphi} \end{bmatrix} = I$$

$$\Rightarrow \begin{bmatrix} r_1^2 + r_2^2 & r_1 r_2 e^{i(\alpha-\theta)} - r_1 r_2 e^{i(\beta-\varphi)} \\ r_2 r_1 e^{i(\theta-\alpha)} - r_1 r_2 e^{i(\varphi-\beta)} & r_2^2 + r_1^2 \end{bmatrix} = \begin{bmatrix} 1 & 0 \\ 0 & 1 \end{bmatrix}$$

$$\Rightarrow r_1^2 + r_2^2 = 1$$

and

$$e^{i\,(\alpha - \theta)} = e^{i\,(\beta - \varphi)}$$

$$\Rightarrow \alpha - \theta = \beta - \varphi$$

$$\Rightarrow \alpha + \varphi = \beta + \theta$$

Also,

$$|A| = 1$$

$$\Rightarrow \begin{vmatrix} r_1 e^{i\alpha} & -r_2 e^{i\beta} \\ r_2 e^{i\theta} & r_1 e^{i\varphi} \end{vmatrix} = 1$$

$$\Rightarrow r_1^2\, e^{i(\alpha+\varphi)} + r_2^2 e^{i(\theta+\beta)} = 1$$

$$\Rightarrow \left(r_1^2 + r_2^2\right) e^{i(\alpha+\varphi)} = 1 \qquad | \because \alpha + \varphi = \beta + \theta$$

$$\Rightarrow e^{i(\alpha+\varphi)} = 1 \qquad | \because r_1^2 + r_2^2 = 1$$

$$\Rightarrow e^{i(\alpha+\varphi)} = e^{i0}$$

$$\Rightarrow \alpha + \varphi = 0$$
$$\varphi = -\alpha$$

Now,

$$\alpha + \varphi = \beta + \theta$$
$$0 = \beta + \theta$$
$$\theta = -\beta$$

Hence,

$$A = \begin{bmatrix} r_1 e^{i\alpha} & -r_2 e^{i\beta} \\ r_2 e^{-i\beta} & r_1 e^{-i\alpha} \end{bmatrix} \text{ which is clearly of the form } \begin{bmatrix} a & -b \\ \overline{b} & \overline{a} \end{bmatrix}$$

EXERCISE 2.3

1. Prove that the matrix $A = \begin{bmatrix} ab & b^2 \\ -a^2 & -ab \end{bmatrix}$ is nilpotent.

2. Show that the matrix $A = \begin{bmatrix} 1 & 2 & 3 \\ 1 & 2 & 3 \\ -1 & -2 & -3 \end{bmatrix}$ is a nilpotent matrix of index 2.

3. Show that the matrix $A = \begin{bmatrix} 2 & -2 & -4 \\ -1 & 3 & 4 \\ 1 & -2 & -3 \end{bmatrix}$ is idempotent.

4. Show that the matrix $A = \frac{1}{6}\begin{bmatrix} 1 & -2 & 1 \\ -2 & 4 & -2 \\ 1 & -2 & 1 \end{bmatrix}$ is symmetric and idempotent.

5. Show that the matrix $A = \frac{1}{3}\begin{bmatrix} -1 & 2 & 2 \\ 2 & -1 & 2 \\ 2 & 2 & -1 \end{bmatrix}$ is orthogonal.

6. Show that the matrix $A = \begin{bmatrix} \frac{1}{\sqrt{3}} & \frac{1}{\sqrt{6}} & -\frac{1}{\sqrt{2}} \\ \frac{1}{\sqrt{3}} & -\frac{2}{\sqrt{6}} & 0 \\ \frac{1}{\sqrt{3}} & \frac{1}{\sqrt{6}} & \frac{1}{\sqrt{2}} \end{bmatrix}$ is orthogonal.

7. Show that the matrix $A = \frac{1}{2}\begin{bmatrix} 1+i & -(1-i) \\ 1+i & 1-i \end{bmatrix}$ is unitary.

8. Show that the matrix $A = \begin{bmatrix} -5 & -8 & 0 \\ 3 & 5 & 0 \\ 1 & 2 & -1 \end{bmatrix}$ is involutory.

9. Show that the matrix $A = \begin{bmatrix} 4 & 3 & 3 \\ -1 & 0 & -1 \\ -4 & -4 & -3 \end{bmatrix}$ is involutory.

10. Prove that the matrix $A = \frac{1}{3}\begin{bmatrix} 1 & 2 & 2 \\ 2 & 1 & -2 \\ -2 & 2 & -1 \end{bmatrix}$ is unimodular.

11. Show that the matrix $A = \begin{bmatrix} 1 & 0 & 0 & 0 \\ 1 & -1 & 0 & 0 \\ 1 & -2 & 1 & 0 \\ 1 & -3 & 3 & -1 \end{bmatrix}$ is involutory.

12. Prove that the matrix $A = \frac{1}{\sqrt{2}}\begin{bmatrix} 1 & i \\ -i & -1 \end{bmatrix}$ is unitary.

13. Prove that the matrix $A = \begin{bmatrix} 2 & -3 & -5 \\ -1 & 4 & 5 \\ 1 & -3 & -4 \end{bmatrix}$ is idempotent.

14. If A and B are orthogonal matrices, prove that AB is also orthogonal.

15. Prove that the matrix $A = \begin{bmatrix} \dfrac{1+i}{2\sqrt{2}} & \dfrac{\sqrt{3}(1-i)}{2\sqrt{2}} \\ \dfrac{\sqrt{2}+i}{2} & \dfrac{i\sqrt{2}-1}{2\sqrt{3}} \end{bmatrix}$ is unitary.

16. Prove that the matrix $A = \begin{bmatrix} a & b & c \\ c & a & b \\ b & c & a \end{bmatrix}$ is orthogonal if a, b, c are the roots of an equation of the form $x^3 \pm x^2 + P = 0$.

17. If A is a square matrix and $A - \dfrac{1}{2}I$ and $A + \dfrac{1}{2}I$ are orthogonal, prove that A is skew-symmetric and $A^2 = -\dfrac{3}{4}I$. Deduce that A is of even order.

18. Show that if A is an orthogonal matrix, then A' is also orthogonal.

2.22. Polynomials in a Square Matrix with Scalar Coefficients

Let A be a square matrix of order n. Let I be the identity matrix of order n. We know that $I^p = I$ and $IA^q = A^qI$ where p and q are positive integers. Also, the distributive law holds good for matrix multiplication. It follows that any polynomial identity in a scalar x will remain an identity when x is replaced by a square matrix A and every term independent of x is multiplied by I. Consequently, the algebra of matrix polynomials in one square matrix A with scalar coefficients is the same as the algebra of ordinary polynomials.

For example, consider the ordinary polynomial identity

$$x^2 - (\alpha + \beta)\, \alpha + \alpha\beta \equiv (x - \alpha)\,(x - \beta)$$

Then, the corresponding identity for square matrix A is

$$A^2 - (\alpha + \beta)\, A + \alpha\beta I \equiv (A - \alpha I)\,(A - \beta I)$$

In general, if

$$x^n + p_1 x^{n-1} + \ldots + p_{n-1}\, x + p_n$$
$$\equiv (x - \alpha_1)\,(x - \alpha_2)\, \ldots\, (x - \alpha_n)$$

Then the parallel identity for A is given by

$$A^n + p_1\, A^{n-1} + \ldots + p_{n-1} A + p_n I$$
$$\equiv (A - \alpha_1 I)\,(A - \alpha_2 I)\, \ldots\, (A - \alpha_n I)$$

ILLUSTRATIVE EXAMPLES

Example 1. Find the scalar solution of the matrix equation $A^2 - 5A + 7I = O$ and show that $\begin{bmatrix} 3 & 1 \\ -2 & 2 \end{bmatrix}$ is a non-scalar solution.

Solution: The algebraic equation corresponding to $A^2 - 5A + 7I = O$ is

$$x^2 - 5x + 7 = 0$$

$$\Rightarrow \quad x = \frac{5 \pm i\sqrt{3}}{2}$$

Hence, the corresponding scalar solutions are

$$A = \frac{5 \pm i\sqrt{3}}{2} I \text{ where } I = \begin{bmatrix} 1 & 0 \\ 0 & 1 \end{bmatrix}$$

Thus,

$$A = \begin{bmatrix} \dfrac{5 + i\sqrt{3}}{2} & 0 \\ 0 & \dfrac{5 + i\sqrt{3}}{2} \end{bmatrix}$$

and,

$$A = \begin{bmatrix} \frac{5 - i\sqrt{3}}{2} & 0 \\ 0 & \frac{5 - i\sqrt{3}}{2} \end{bmatrix}$$

2nd Part

If $A = \begin{bmatrix} 3 & 1 \\ -2 & 2 \end{bmatrix}$, then

$$A^2 = \begin{bmatrix} 8 & 5 \\ -5 & 3 \end{bmatrix}$$

$$\therefore \quad A^2 - 5A = \begin{bmatrix} 8 & 5 \\ -5 & 3 \end{bmatrix} - 5\begin{bmatrix} 3 & 1 \\ -2 & 2 \end{bmatrix}$$

$$= \begin{bmatrix} -7 & 0 \\ 0 & -7 \end{bmatrix}$$

$$= (-7)\begin{bmatrix} 1 & 0 \\ 0 & 1 \end{bmatrix}$$

$$= -7I$$

$$\Rightarrow \quad A^2 - 5A + 7I = O$$

Hence, $\begin{bmatrix} 3 & 1 \\ -2 & 2 \end{bmatrix}$ is a non-scalar solution.

Example 2. Find all the scalar matrices which satisfy the matrix equation $A^3 - I = O$.

Solution: The algebraic equation corresponding to

$A^3 - I = O$ is

$x^3 - 1 = 0$

$\Rightarrow \quad (x - 1)\ (x^2 + x + 1) = 0$

$\Rightarrow \quad x = 1, \ \frac{-1 \pm i\sqrt{3}}{2}$

Hence, the corresponding scalar solutions are

$$A = I_3, \quad \frac{-1 \pm i\sqrt{3}}{2} I_3$$

where I_3 is a unit matrix of order 3.

Example 3. Show that $A - \lambda I$ is a factor of $f(A) - f(\lambda)I$, where A is a square matrix of order n, I a unit matrix of order n, λ a scalar and f denotes a polynomial.

Solution: The ordinary polynomial corresponding to the matrix polynomial $f(A) - f(\lambda)I$ is $f(x) - f(\lambda)$.

Let $F(x) = f(x) - f(\lambda)$

Putting $x = \lambda$, we get

$$F(\lambda) = f(\lambda) - f(\lambda) = 0$$

$\Rightarrow$ $(x - \lambda)$ is a factor of $f(x) - f(\lambda)$

$\Rightarrow$ $A - \lambda I$ is a factor of $f(A) - f(\lambda)I$.

Example 4. If A is a nilpotent matrix of index 2, show that $A\,(1 \pm A)^n = A$ where n is any positive integer.

Solution:

$\because$ A is a nilpotent matrix of index 2

$\therefore$ $A^2 = O$

$\therefore$ $A^3 = A^4 = \ldots\ldots = A^n = O$

Now,

$$A\,(1 \pm A)^n$$

$$A\left(1 \pm nA + \frac{n\,(n-1)}{\underline{|2}} A^2 + \ldots\ldots + A^n \text{or}\,(-1)^n A^n\right)$$

$$= A(1 \pm nA)$$

$$= A \pm nAA$$

$$= A \pm nA^2$$

$$= A \pm nO$$

$$= A$$

Example 5. Show that if A is idempotent, then $(I + A)^n = I + (2^n - 1)A$.

Solution:

$\because$ A and I both are idempotent

$\therefore$ $A^2 = A,\ I^2 = I$

Now,

$$A^3 = A^2A = AA = A^2 = A$$

$$A^4 = A^2A^2 = AA = A$$

Similarly,

$$A^5 = A^6 = \ldots = A^n = A$$

and,

$$I = I^2 = I^3 = \ldots = I^n = I$$

Also,

$$AI = IA = A$$

By Binomial Theorem,

$$\begin{aligned}(I + A)^n &= I^n + nC_1\, I^{n-1}A + nC_2\, I^{n-2}A^2 + \ldots + nC_nA^n \\ &= I + nC_1A + nC_2A + \ldots + nC_nA \\ &= I + (nC_1 + nC_2 + \ldots + nC_n)A \\ &= I + (2^n - 1)A\end{aligned}$$

Example 6. Show that every triangular matrix A, such that $AA' = A'A$, is diagonal.

Solution: Let $A = [a_{ij}]_{n \times n}$

Then,

$$A' = \left[a'_{ij}\right]_{n\times n} \quad \text{where } a'_{ij} = a_{ji} \qquad \ldots (2.68)$$

Now,

$$AA' = \left[\sum_{k=1}^{n} a_{ik}a'_{kj}\right]$$

$$= \left[\sum_{k=1}^{n} a_{ik}a_{jk}\right] \qquad |\ \text{Using Eq. (2.68)}$$

and,

$$A'A = \left[\sum_{k=1}^{n} a'_{ik}\, a_{kj}\right]$$

$$= \left[\sum_{k=1}^{n} a_{ki} \, a_{kj} \right] \qquad | \text{ Using Eq. (2.68)}$$

$\because \quad AA' = A'A$ | Given

$$\therefore \quad \sum_{k=1}^{n} a_{ik} \, a_{jk} = \sum_{k=1}^{n} a_{ki} \, a_{kj} \ \forall \ i, j$$

$\Rightarrow \quad a_{ik} = a_{ki}$ | $\because$ A is a triangular matrix

and $a_{jk} = a_{kj}$

$\Rightarrow$ A is symmetric.

Thus, A is symmetric as well as triangular. Consequently, A is a diagonal matrix.

Example 7. If A is a diagonal matrix with diagonal elements all different, then prove that A and B commute iff B is a diagonal matrix.

Solution: Since A is a diagonal matrix, therefore, AB and BA both will exist only where B is a square matrix of the same order as A.

Let $A = \text{diag}\,(a_{11}, a_{22}, ..., a_{nn})$ where

$$a_{ii} \neq a_{jj} \text{ if } i \neq j$$

and

$$B = [b_{ij}]_{n \times n}; \ i, j = 1, 2, ..., n$$

Then,

$$AB = [c_{ij}]_{n \times n} \text{ where } c_{ij} = a_{ii} \, b_{ij}$$

and,

$$BA = [d_{ij}]_{n \times n} \text{ where } d_{ij} = b_{ij} \, a_{jj}$$

If $AB = BA$, then

$$c_{ij} = d_{ij}$$

$$\Rightarrow a_{ii} \, b_{ij} = b_{ij} \, a_{jj}$$

$$\Rightarrow b_{ij} \, (a_{ii} - a_{jj}) = 0$$

$$\Rightarrow b_{ij} = 0, \text{ if } i \neq j \qquad | \because a_{ii} \neq a_{jj}$$

$\Rightarrow$ B is a diagonal matrix of the same order as A.

Hence, if A and B commute, then B is a diagonal matrix of the same order as A.

Conversely

If B is a diagonal matrix of the same order as A, then

$$b_{ij} = 0, \text{ if } i \neq j$$

and,

$$a_{ii} - a_{jj} = 0, \text{ if } i \neq j$$

$$\therefore \quad b_{ij}(a_{ii} - a_{jj}) = 0$$

$$\Rightarrow \quad a_{ii}\, b_{ij} = b_{ij}\, a_{jj}$$

$$\Rightarrow \quad c_{ij} = d_{ij}$$

$$\Rightarrow \quad AB = BA$$

$\Rightarrow$ A and B commute

Hence, A and B commute if B is a diagonal matrix of the same order as A.

Example 8. Show that, if an orthogonal matrix is triangular, then it is diagonal with all its diagonal elements equal to ± 1.

Solution: Let A be an orthogonal matrix. Then,

$$AA' = A'A = I \qquad \text{... (2.69)}$$

$\because$ A is triangular | Given

$\therefore$ A is a diagonal matrix | See Ex. 6, page 131

2nd Part

Let $A = \text{diag}\,(a_{11}, a_{22}, ..., a_{nn})$

Then,

$$A' = A$$

Therefore,

$$AA' = A'A = I$$

$$\Rightarrow \quad A^2 = I$$

$$\Rightarrow \quad \text{diag}\,(a_{11}^2, a_{22}^2, ..., a_{nn}^2) = I$$

$$\Rightarrow \quad a_{11}^2 = a_{22}^2 = ... = a_{nn}^2 = 1$$

$$\Rightarrow \quad a_{11} = a_{22} = ... = a_{nn} = \pm 1$$

Hence, each diagonal element of A is equal to ± 1.

EXERCISE 2.4

1. Find all the scalar matrices, which satisfy the matrix equation $A^2 + I = O$ and show that $\begin{bmatrix} 1 & 2 \\ -1 & -1 \end{bmatrix}$ is a non-scalar solution.
2. Find all the scalar matrices which satisfy the matrix equation $2A^3 + 3A^2 - 4A - 6I = O$.
3. Prove that the product of two upper (lower) triangular matrices of the same order is itself an upper (lower) triangular matrix.
4. Show that
   (a) The product of two or more diagonal matrices is diagonal.
   (b) The product of two or more lower (upper) triangular matrices is also a lower (upper) triangular matrix.

ANSWERS

1. $\begin{bmatrix} i & 0 \\ 0 & i \end{bmatrix}, \begin{bmatrix} -i & 0 \\ 0 & -i \end{bmatrix}$

2. $I_3, \frac{1}{2}(-1 \pm i\sqrt{3})I_3$, where $I_3 = \begin{bmatrix} 1 & 0 & 0 \\ 0 & 1 & 0 \\ 0 & 0 & 1 \end{bmatrix}$

3 DETERMINANTS

3.1. Permutations and Inversions

Let 1, 2, 3 be three positive integers. Then, they can be taken together in $\lfloor 3 = 3 \times 2 \times 1 = 6$ ways as follows:

1 2 3
1 3 2
2 3 1
2 1 3
3 1 2
3 2 1

These are called the permutations of three positive integers 1, 2, 3.

Similarly, let 1, 2, 3, 4 be four positive integers. Then, they can be taken together in $\lfloor 4 = 4 \times 3 \times 2 \times 1 = 24$ ways as follows:

1 2 3 4	2 1 3 4	3 1 2 4	4 1 2 3
1 2 4 3	2 1 4 3	3 1 4 2	4 1 3 2
1 3 2 4	2 3 1 4	3 2 1 4	4 2 1 3
1 3 4 2	2 3 4 1	3 2 4 1	4 2 3 1
1 4 2 3	2 4 1 3	3 4 1 2	4 3 1 2
1 4 3 2	2 4 3 1	3 4 2 1	4 3 2 1

These are the permutations of four positive integers 1, 2, 3, 4.

Rigorously,

Let X be a finite set having n distinct elements. Then, the one-one mapping of the set X onto itself is called a permutation of degree n.

Let X be a set defined by

$$X = \{a_1, a_2, a_3, ..., a_n\};\ a_m \neq a_k \text{ for } m \neq k$$

Let P be the transformation (mapping) on X such that

$$P(a_1) = b_1$$
$$P(a_2) = b_2$$
$$P(a_3) = b_3$$
$$\vdots$$
$$P(a_n) = b_n$$

where $a_1, a_2, a_3, ..., a_n$ is some arrangement of n-elements $a_1, a_2, a_3, ..., a_n$ of X. Then, a two-line notation for the permutation is

$$P = \begin{pmatrix} a_1 & a_2 & a_3 & \cdots & a_n \\ b_1 & b_2 & b_3 & \cdots & b_n \end{pmatrix}$$

Note: The order of columns in this notation is immaterial.

A set of n positive integers 1, 2, 3, ..., n is said to be in natural order if no larger integer preceds a smaller one.

If in a given permutation, a larger integer preceds a smaller one, then the permutation is said to contain an inversion. For example, in permutation 3 2 1, we see that the larger integer 2 preceds the smaller integer 1, so it is one inversion in permutation 3 2 1 and other such inversions are also possible in a permutation. If the total number of inversions in a permutation is odd (or even), the permutation is called odd (or even). If there is no inversion in a permutation, then it is called an identity permutation denoted by I. The identity permutation is regarded as an even permutation. For example, in permutation 5 3 1 2, 5 preceds 3, 5 preceds 1, 5 preceds 2, 3 preceds 1 and 3 preceds 2, i.e. there are 5(odd) inversions in the permutation 5 3 1 2. So, the permutation 5 3 1 2 is odd. Again, in permutation 6 4 3 2, 6 preceds 4, 6 preceds 3,

6 precedes 2, 4 preceds 3, 4 preceds 2 and 3 preceds 2, i.e. there are six (even) inversions in the permutation 6 4 3 2. So, the permutation 6 4 3 2 is even. Lastly, in permutation 1 2 3 4, there is no inversion. So, this permutation is an identity permutation. (It is also regarded as an even permutation.)

The interchange of any two integers of a permutation, whether adjacent or not, is called a transposition. The interchange of two adjacent integers of a permutation is called an adjacent transposition.

3.2. Determinant

The theory of determinants has originated from the study of system of linear equations. Later, it was found that it has several other applications.

First of all, consider the following system of two linear equations in two variables x and y (both not zero):

$$a_1x + b_1y = 0 \quad \text{... (3.1)}$$

$$a_2x + b_2y = 0 \quad \text{... (3.2)}$$

Equation (3.1) gives,

$$\frac{x}{y} = -\frac{b_1}{a_1} \quad \text{... (3.3)}$$

Equation (3.2) gives,

$$\frac{x}{y} = -\frac{b_2}{a_2} \quad \text{... (3.4)}$$

From Eqs. (3.3) and (3.4), we can eliminate x and y to get

$$-\frac{b_1}{a_1} = -\frac{b_2}{a_2}$$

$$\Rightarrow a_1b_2 - a_2b_1 = 0$$

The number $a_1b_2 - a_2b_1$ is represented more conveniently by the symbol

$$\begin{vmatrix} a_1 & a_2 \\ b_1 & b_2 \end{vmatrix}$$

and is called a determinant of order two. It has two rows and two columns. The scalars a_1, a_2, b_1, b_2 are called the constituents or elements of the determinant and $a_1b_2 - a_2b_1$ is called the value of the determinant. The elements a_1, b_2 constitute the principal (leading) diagonal. If the matrix of coefficients $\begin{bmatrix} a_1 & b_1 \\ a_2 & b_2 \end{bmatrix}$ is denoted by A, then we wite

$$|A| \text{ or } \det A = \begin{vmatrix} a_1 & b_1 \\ a_2 & b_2 \end{vmatrix} = a_1b_2 - a_2b_1.$$

It may be observed that the value of a determinant of order 2 is equal to the product of the elements along the principal diagonal minus the product of the off-diagonal elements.

Note: Although there is some similarity in the ways of writing a determinant and a matrix, however, the two are entirely different. Whereas a determinant has a numerical value, a matrix is merely a representation in a rectangular array.

Now, let us consider the following system of three linear equations in three variables x, y and z (not all zero):

$$a_1x + b_1y + c_1z = 0 \qquad \text{... (3.5)}$$

$$a_2x + b_2y + c_2z = 0 \qquad \text{... (3.6)}$$

$$a_3x + b_3y + c_3z = 0 \qquad \text{... (3.7)}$$

Equations (3.6) and (3.7) give,

$$(a_2b_3 - a_3b_2)x + (c_2b_3 - c_3b_2)z = 0 \qquad \text{... (3.8)}$$

$$(a_3b_2 - a_2b_3)y + (a_3c_2 - a_2c_3)z = 0 \qquad \text{... (3.9)}$$

Equation (3.5) gives,

$$a_1(a_2b_3 - a_3b_2)x + b_1(a_2b_3 - a_3b_2)y + c_1(a_2b_3 - a_3b_2)z = 0$$

$$\Rightarrow a_1(b_2c_3 - b_3c_2)z + b_1(a_3c_2 - a_2c_3)z + c_1(a_2b_3 - a_3b_2)z = 0$$

| Using Eqs. (3.8) and (3.9)

$$\Rightarrow [a_1(b_2c_3 - b_3c_2) + b_1(a_3c_2 - a_2c_3) + c_1(a_2b_3 - a_3b_2)]z = 0$$

$\Rightarrow \quad \Delta z = 0$

where

$$\Delta = a_1(b_2c_3 - b_3c_2) + b_1(a_3c_2 - a_2c_3) + c_1(a_2b_3 - a_3b_2)$$

Δ is represented more conveniently by the symbol $\begin{vmatrix} a_1 & b_1 & c_1 \\ a_2 & b_2 & c_2 \\ a_3 & b_3 & c_3 \end{vmatrix}$ and is called a determinant of order three.

Similarly, we can show that

$$\Delta x = 0$$

and $\Delta y = 0$

But x, y, z are not all zero

$\therefore \quad \Delta = 0$

$$\rightarrow \begin{vmatrix} a_1 & b_1 & c_1 \\ a_2 & b_2 & c_2 \\ a_3 & b_3 & c_3 \end{vmatrix} = 0$$

Δ is called the determinant of the matrix of coefficients of the system of Eqs. (3.5), (3.6) and (3.7).

If the matrix of coefficients is denoted by A, i.e.

$$A = \begin{bmatrix} a_1 & b_1 & c_1 \\ a_2 & b_2 & c_2 \\ a_3 & b_3 & c_3 \end{bmatrix}, \text{ then we write}$$

$$|A| \text{ or } \det A = \begin{vmatrix} a_1 & b_1 & c_1 \\ a_2 & b_2 & c_2 \\ a_3 & b_3 & c_3 \end{vmatrix} = \Delta$$

det A has three rows and three columns. Its leading diagonal is $a_1\ b_2\ c_3$.

Generalisation

If there are n linear equations in n variables (not all zero) given by

$$a_1x_1 + b_1x_2 + \dots + k_1x_n = 0$$
$$a_2x_1 + b_2x_2 + \dots + k_2x_n = 0$$
$$\dots\dots\dots\dots\dots\dots\dots\dots\dots\dots$$
$$a_nx_1 + b_nx_2 + \dots + k_nx_n = 0$$

then, we have on eliminating $x_1, x_2, \dots, x_n$, that

$$\begin{vmatrix} a_1 & b_1 & \dots & k_1 \\ a_2 & b_2 & \dots & k_2 \\ \dots & \dots & \dots & \dots \\ a_n & b_n & \dots & k_n \end{vmatrix} = 0$$

LHS is a function of $a_1, a_2, \dots, a_n; b_1, b_2, \dots, b_n; \dots, k_1, k_2, \dots, k_n$ and is called a determinant of order n denoted by Δ_n.

Characteristics of Δ_n

1. The value of Δ_n is $\Sigma \pm a_r\, b_s \,\dots\dots\, k_\theta$ where +ve or –ve sign is taken according as $r, s, \dots, \theta$ is an even or odd permutation of 1, 2, 3, ..., n, the summation being extended over all the possible $\underline{|n}$ permutations of the column subscripts 1, 2, 3, ..., n and none of the terms is repeated. This is called column-wise expansion of Δ_n.
2. The term $a_1b_2 \dots k_n$ formed by the elements situated in the leading diagonal drawn from the left-hand top corner to the right-hand bottom corner is +ve. This is called the leading term.
3. The sign of any other term is +ve if the number of inversions is even or –ve if the number of inversions is odd in the permutation $r, s, \dots, \theta$.

Determinants of a square matrix

Let $A = \begin{bmatrix} a_{11} & a_{12} & \dots\dots & a_{1n} \\ a_{21} & a_{22} & \dots\dots & a_{2n} \\ \dots\dots & \dots\dots & \dots\dots & \dots\dots \\ a_{n1} & a_{n2} & \dots\dots & a_{nn} \end{bmatrix}_{n \times n}$ be a square matrix of order $n \times n$, where n is some positive integer. Then, the determinants of A denoted by $|A|$ is defined as follows:

$$|A| = \begin{bmatrix} a_{11} & a_{12} & \cdots & a_{1n} \\ a_{21} & a_{22} & \cdots & a_{2n} \\ \cdots & \cdots & \cdots & \cdots \\ a_{n1} & a_{n2} & \cdots & a_{nn} \end{bmatrix}$$

$$= \Sigma \pm a_{1i}\, a_{2j}\, a_{3k} \,\ldots\, a_{nt} \qquad \ldots (3.10)$$

where +ve or –ve sign is taken according as the permutation $i, j, k, \ldots, t$ of positive integers 1, 2, 3, ..., n is an even or odd permutation, the summation being extended over all the possible $\lfloor n$ permutations of the row subscripts 1, 2, 3, ..., n. The order of the determinant of a square matrix is the same as that of the given matrix. Equation (3.10) is the row-wise expansion of $|A|$ since the row subscripts are kept in the natural order in the formation of each term in the sum. Another formula for $|A|$ is

$$|A| = \Sigma \pm a_{i1}\, a_{j2}\, a_{k3} \ldots a_{tn} \qquad \ldots (3.11)$$

where +ve or –ve sign is taken according as $i, j, k, \ldots, t$ is an even or an odd permutation of 1, 2, 3, ..., n, the summation being extended over all the possible $\lfloor n$ permutations of the column subscripts 1, 2, 3, ..., n. This is the column-wise expansion of $|A|$.

Thus, for a second order determinant, we have

$$\Delta = \begin{vmatrix} a_{11} & a_{12} \\ a_{21} & a_{22} \end{vmatrix} = a_{11}\, a_{22} - a_{12}\, a_{21}$$

and, for a third order determinant, we have

$$\Delta = \begin{vmatrix} a_{11} & a_{12} & a_{13} \\ a_{21} & a_{22} & a_{23} \\ a_{31} & a_{32} & a_{33} \end{vmatrix}$$

$$= a_{11}\, a_{22}\, a_{33} - a_{11}\, a_{32}\, a_{23} + a_{21}\, a_{32}\, a_{13} - a_{21}\, a_{12}\, a_{33} + a_{31}\, a_{12}\, a_{23} - a_{31}\, a_{22}\, a_{13}$$

$$= a_{11}\,(a_{22}\, a_{33} - a_{23}\, a_{32}) - a_{12}\,(a_{21}\, a_{33} - a_{23}\, a_{31}) + a_{13}\,(a_{21}\, a_{32} - a_{22}\, a_{31})$$

$$= a_{11}\begin{vmatrix} a_{22} & a_{23} \\ a_{32} & a_{33} \end{vmatrix} - a_{12}\begin{vmatrix} a_{21} & a_{23} \\ a_{31} & a_{33} \end{vmatrix} + a_{13}\begin{vmatrix} a_{21} & a_{22} \\ a_{31} & a_{32} \end{vmatrix}$$

(row-wise expansion)

3.3. Sarrus's Rule for Expanding a Determinant of Third Order

Let $|A| = \begin{vmatrix} a_{11} & a_{12} & a_{13} \\ a_{21} & a_{22} & a_{23} \\ a_{31} & a_{32} & a_{33} \end{vmatrix}$

Then, $|A| = a_{11}\, a_{22}\, a_{33} + a_{12}\, a_{23}\, a_{31} + a_{13}\, a_{21}\, a_{32}$
$- a_{31}\, a_{22}\, a_{13} - a_{32}\, a_{23}\, a_{11} - a_{33}\, a_{21}\, a_{12}$

Below we are giving a scheme which enables us to write the value of $|A|$ more conveniently.

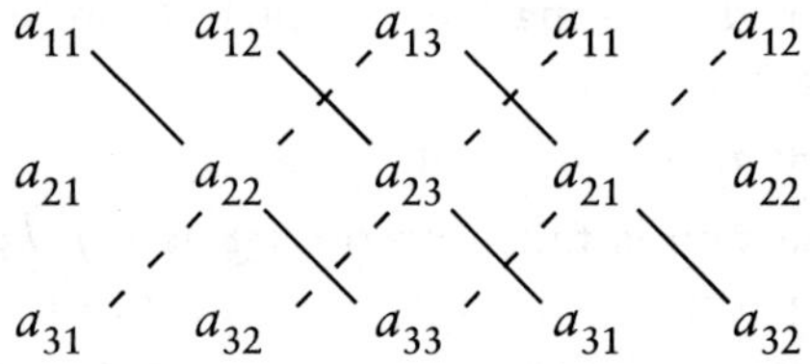

If we take the product of the terms joined by continuous lines as +ve and the product of the terms joined by broken lines as –ve, then we may very easily write the value of $|A|$. This diagram is known as Sarrus's diagram.

3.4. Minor Determinants

Let Δ be a determinant of order n. If any number of rows and the same number of columns are deleted in Δ, the determinant formed by the remaining elements with their relative positions unchanged, is called a minor determinant.

If only one row and one column are deleted in any determinant, the corresponding minor is called a first minor, its order is $(n - 1)$. If two rows and two columns are deleted, the corresponding minor is called a second minor, its order is $(n - 2)$ and so on. The deleted rows and columns have common elements forming a determinant and the minor obtained after this deletion is said to be complementary to this determinant. The minor complementary to the first leading element a_1 is called the leading first minor and its leading first minor again is the leading second minor of the original determinant. Any minor of the determinant whose leading diagonals consists of elements from leading diagonal of the determinant is called a leading minor of that determinant.

The first minor obtained by deleting, in any determinant Δ, the row and column which contain any element α is denoted by Δ_α; the second minor obtained by deleting two rows and two columns which contain α and β is denoted by $\Delta_{\alpha, \beta}$ and so on.

Thus, Δ_{a_1} is the leading first minor; Δ_{a_1, b_2} or Δ_{a_2, b_1} represents the leading second minor.

3.5. Cofactor of an Element

While expanding a determinant A, we collect all the terms containing the fixed element a_{ij} as a factor and write their sum in the factorised form as $a_{ij} A_{ij}$. A_{ij} is called the cofactor of the element a_{ij} in determinant A. The above definition suggests that if $A = [a_{ij}]$ be the $n \times n$ matrix whose determinant is $|a_{ij}|$, then if from $[a_{ij}]$, the elements of its ith row and j^{th} column are removed, the terms of A_{ij} are then composed of the elements of the remaining $(n - 1) \times (n - 1)$ sub-matrix M_{ij} of $[a_{ij}]$.

From the above definition, it is evident that exactly one element from each row and one element from each column appear in each term in the expansion of det A. Thus, A_{ij} contains no elements either from the ith row or the jth column of A. Since det A is a linear and homogeneous function of the elements of any row or any column, hence if we repeat the process described above for each element of a fixed row (column), then det A can be expressed as a function of the elements of the ith row, given by, $a_{i1}, a_{i2}, \ldots, a_{in}$ as

$$\det A = a_{i1} A_{i1} + a_{i2} A_{i2} + \ldots + a_{in} A_{in}$$

$$= \sum_{j=1}^{n} a_{ij} A_{ij}$$

Similarly, det A can be expressed as a function of the elements of jth column, namely, $a_{1j}, a_{2j}, \ldots, a_{nj}$ as

$$\det A = a_{1j} A_{1j} + a_{2j} A_{2j} + \ldots + a_{nj} A_{nj}$$

$$= \sum_{i=1}^{n} a_{ij} A_{ij}$$

Remark. If M_{ij} is the minor determinant corresponding to the element a_{ij} where $A = [a_{ij}]_{n \times n}$, then it can be shown that

$$A_{ij} = (-1)^{i+j} M_{ij}$$

where A_{ij} is the cofactor of the element a_{ij} in determinant A.

3.6. Properties of the Determinants

Property 1. If two rows or columns of a determinant are interchanged, the sign of the determinant is changed, the absolute value (numerical value) remaining unaltered.

OR

If a matrix B is obtained from a square matrix A by interchanging two rows or columns, then

$$|B| = -|A|$$

Proof.

$$\text{Let } A = \begin{bmatrix} a_{11} & a_{12} & \ldots & a_{1s} & \ldots & a_{1t} & \ldots & a_{1n} \\ a_{21} & a_{22} & \ldots & a_{2s} & \ldots & a_{2t} & \ldots & a_{2n} \\ \ldots & \ldots & \ldots & \ldots & \ldots & \ldots & \ldots & \ldots \\ a_{i1} & a_{i2} & \ldots & a_{is} & \ldots & a_{it} & \ldots & a_{in} \\ a_{n1} & a_{n2} & \ldots & a_{ns} & \ldots & a_{nt} & \ldots & a_{nn} \end{bmatrix}$$

Then, the product of the principal diagonal elements of $A = a_{11}\, a_{22} \ldots\ldots a_{ss} \ldots\ldots a_{tt} \ldots\ldots a_{nn}$.

Let s^{th} and t^{th} columns of A be interchanged $(s < t)$. Then,

$$B = \begin{bmatrix} a_{11} & a_{12} & \ldots & a_{1t} & \ldots & a_{1s} & \ldots & a_{1n} \\ a_{21} & a_{22} & \ldots & a_{2t} & \ldots & a_{2s} & \ldots & a_{2n} \\ \ldots & \ldots & \ldots & \ldots & \ldots & \ldots & \ldots & \ldots \\ a_{i1} & a_{i2} & \ldots & a_{it} & \ldots & a_{is} & \ldots & a_{in} \\ a_{n1} & a_{n2} & \ldots & a_{nt} & \ldots & a_{ns} & \ldots & a_{nn} \end{bmatrix}$$

Then, the product of the principal diagonal elements of $B = a_{11}\ a_{22}\ .....\ a_{tt}\ .....\ a_{ss}\ .....\ a_{nn}$. In order to have a term of $|A|$, let us operate on the row subscripts of the product of the principal diagonal elements of A by the permutation

$$p = \begin{pmatrix} 1 & 2 & \ldots & s & \ldots & t & \ldots & n \\ i_1 & i_2 & \ldots & i_s & \ldots & i_t & \ldots & i_n \end{pmatrix}$$

Then we get $a_{i_1} 1\, a_{i_2} 2 \ldots a_{i_s} s \ldots a_{i_t} t \ldots a_{i_n} n$ as one of the terms of $|A|$.

This term can also be obtained from the product of the principal diagonal elements of B by operating on its row subscripts by the permutation

$$p' = \begin{pmatrix} 1 & 2 & \ldots & t & \ldots & s & \ldots & n \\ i_1 & i_2 & \ldots & i_t & \ldots & i_s & \ldots & i_n \end{pmatrix}$$

Hence, we observe that $p' = p\ (i_s\ i_t)$ since $(i_s\ i_t)$ is a transposition. Therefore, p' is odd or even according as p is even or odd. Hence, the term $\pm\, a_{i_1} 1\ a_{i_2} 2\ \ldots\ a_{i_s} s\ \ldots\ a_{i_t} t\ \ldots\ a_{i_n} n$ is also a term of $|B|$ but with its sign changed. Thus, everyone of the $\lfloor n$ terms of $|A|$ is a term of $|B|$ but with sign changed.

Hence, $|B| = -|A|$

Example

$$\text{Let } |A| = \begin{vmatrix} a_1 & a_2 & a_3 \\ b_1 & b_2 & b_3 \\ c_1 & c_2 & c_3 \end{vmatrix}$$

Let the determinant B be formed by interchanging second and third columns. Then,

$$|B| = \begin{vmatrix} a_1 & a_3 & a_2 \\ b_1 & b_3 & b_2 \\ c_1 & c_3 & c_2 \end{vmatrix}$$

$$= a_1 \begin{vmatrix} b_3 & b_2 \\ c_3 & c_2 \end{vmatrix} - a_3 \begin{vmatrix} b_1 & b_2 \\ c_1 & c_2 \end{vmatrix} + a_2 \begin{vmatrix} b_1 & b_3 \\ c_1 & c_3 \end{vmatrix}$$

| Expanding $|B|$ in terms of the elements of its first row

$$= a_1 (b_3c_2 - b_2c_3) - a_3 (b_1c_2 - b_2c_1) + a_2 (b_1c_3 - b_3c_1)$$

$$= -[a_1 (b_2c_3 - b_3c_2) - a_2 (b_1c_3 - b_3c_1) + a_3 (b_1c_2 - b_2c_1)]$$

$$= -\left[a_1 \begin{vmatrix} b_2 & b_3 \\ c_2 & c_3 \end{vmatrix} - a_2 \begin{vmatrix} b_1 & b_3 \\ c_1 & c_3 \end{vmatrix} + a_3 \begin{vmatrix} b_1 & b_2 \\ c_1 & c_2 \end{vmatrix}\right]$$

$$= -\begin{vmatrix} a_1 & a_2 & a_3 \\ b_1 & b_2 & b_3 \\ c_1 & c_2 & c_3 \end{vmatrix}$$

$$= -|A|$$

Note. By repeated application of this property, it is clear that the sign of the determinant will or will not change according as there are an odd or even number of interchanges of the rows or columns.

Property 2. If every element in any row (or column) of a determinant be multiplied by the same factor, then the determinant is multiplied by that factor.

Proof.

Let $A = [a_{ij}]_{n \times n}$

Then,

$$|A| = \sum_{j=1}^{n} a_{in} A_{ij}; \ A_{ij} \text{ being the cofactor of } a_{ij}.$$

Let every element of the ith row of the determinant be multiplied by K. Then, the resulting determinant

$$\begin{vmatrix} a_{11} & a_{12} & \dots & a_{in} \\ a_{21} & a_{22} & \dots & a_{2n} \\ \dots & \dots & \dots & \dots \\ Ka_{i1} & Ka_{i2} & \dots & Ka_{in} \\ \dots & \dots & \dots & \dots. \\ a_{n1} & a_{n2} & \dots & a_{nn} \end{vmatrix} = \sum_{j=1}^{n} K \, a_{ij} \, A_{ij}$$

$$= K \sum_{j=1}^{n} a_{ij} A_{ij}$$

$$= K |A|$$

Similarly, we can prove the statement when every element of kth column is multiplied by K.

Example

$$\text{Let } |A| = \begin{vmatrix} a_1 & b_1 & c_1 \\ a_2 & b_2 & c_2 \\ a_3 & b_3 & c_3 \end{vmatrix}$$

Let every element of first column be multiplied by K. Then,

$$\begin{vmatrix} Ka_1 & b_1 & c_1 \\ Ka_2 & b_2 & c_2 \\ Ka_3 & b_3 & c_3 \end{vmatrix} = Ka_1 (b_2c_3 - b_3c_2) - Ka_2 (b_1c_3 - b_3c_1) + Ka_3 (b_1c_2 - b_2c_1)$$

$$= K [a_1(b_2c_3 - b_3c_2) - a_2 (b_1c_3 - b_3c_1) + a_3 (b_1c_2 - b_2c_1)]$$

$$= K \begin{vmatrix} a_1 & b_1 & c_1 \\ a_2 & b_2 & c_2 \\ a_3 & b_3 & c_3 \end{vmatrix}$$

Hence the proposition.

Corollary 1. If A be a n-rowed square matrix and K be any scalar, then

$$|KA| = K^n |A|$$

Note. If the matrix B is obtained from the matrix A by multiplying all the elements of one row (or one column) by the non-zero scalar K, then

$$|B| = K |A|$$

Corollary 2. If the signs of all the elements in any row (or column) in a determinant be changed, the sign of the determinant is changed, because it implies multiplying the row (or column) by a scalar (–1).

Property 3. If in a determinant rows be changed into columns and columns into rows, the value of the determinant remains unchanged.

OR

If $A = [a_{ij}]$ is a $n \times n$ matrix, then $|A'| = |A|$, where A' is the transpose of matrix A.

Proof. Let $A = [a_{ij}]$. Then,

$$A' = [a'_{ij}] \text{ where } a'_{ij} = a_{ji}$$

Now, the product of the principal diagonal elements of A'

$$= a'_{11}\, a'_{22}\, a'_{33} \ldots a'_{nn}$$

Operating on the row subscripts of the elements of this product by the permutation $p = \begin{pmatrix} 1 & 2 & 3 & \ldots & n \\ i_1 & i_2 & i_3 & \ldots & i_n \end{pmatrix}$ where $i_1, i_2, i_3, \ldots, i_n$ are in some order, we see that $\pm\, a'_{i_1} 1\, a'_{i_2} 2\, a'_{i_3} 3 \ldots a'_{i_n} n$ is a term of $|A'|$; positive or negative sign to be taken according as p is even or odd.

$\because \quad a'_{ij} = a_{ji}$

$\therefore \quad$ We have

$$a'_{i_1} 1\, a'_{i_2} 2\, a'_{i_3} 3 \ldots a'_{i_n} n$$
$$= a_{1_i} 1\, a_{2_i} 2\, a_{3_i} 3 \ldots a_{n_i} n$$

The term $a_{1_i} 1\, a_{2_i} 2\, a_{3_i} 3 \ldots a_{n_i} n$ can be obtained from the term $a_{i_1}\, a_{i_1}\, a_{i_2 i_2}\, a_{i_3 i_3} \ldots a_{i_n}\, a_{i_n}$ by operating on its row subscripts, the permutation

$$p' = \begin{pmatrix} i_1 & i_2 & i_3 & \ldots & i_n \\ 1 & 2 & 3 & \ldots & n \end{pmatrix} = p^{-1}$$

Hence, p' is even or odd according as p is even or odd. Therefore, the term $\pm\, a'_{i_1} 1\, a'_{i_2} 2\, a'_{i_3} 3 \ldots a'_{i_n} n$ of $|A'|$ is also a term of $|A|$. Thus, we can prove that each one of the $\lfloor n$ terms of $|A'|$ is a term of $|A|$ and vice-versa.

Hence, the result.

Example. Let $|A| = \begin{vmatrix} a_1 & a_2 & a_3 \\ b_1 & b_2 & b_3 \\ c_1 & c_2 & c_3 \end{vmatrix}$

Then, $|A| = a_1 \begin{vmatrix} b_2 & b_3 \\ c_2 & c_3 \end{vmatrix} - a_2 \begin{vmatrix} b_1 & b_3 \\ c_1 & c_3 \end{vmatrix} + a_3 \begin{vmatrix} b_1 & b_2 \\ c_1 & c_2 \end{vmatrix}$

$$= a_1b_2c_3 - a_3b_3c_2 - a_2b_1c_3 + a_2b_3c_1 + a_3b_1c_2 - a_3b_2c_1$$

Again,

$$|A'| = \begin{vmatrix} a_1 & b_1 & c_1 \\ a_2 & b_2 & c_2 \\ a_3 & b_3 & c_3 \end{vmatrix}$$

$$= a_1 \begin{vmatrix} b_2 & c_2 \\ b_3 & c_3 \end{vmatrix} - b_1 \begin{vmatrix} a_2 & c_2 \\ a_3 & c_3 \end{vmatrix} + c_1 \begin{vmatrix} a_2 & b_2 \\ a_3 & b_3 \end{vmatrix}$$

$$= a_1b_2c_3 - a_1b_3c_2 - b_1a_2c_3 + b_1a_3c_2 + c_1a_2b_3 - c_1a_3b_2$$

$\therefore \quad |A'| = |A|$

Property 4. If two rows or columns of a determinant are identical, the value of the determinant is zero.

Proof. Let Δ be the value of a determinant of any order. Then by interchanging two rows (two columns) which are identical, we obtain a determinant whose value is –Δ (by Property 1). But the interchanged rows (columns) of the given determinant are identical, so that the absolute value of the determinant remains unchanged. Hence,

$$\Delta = -\Delta$$

$$\Rightarrow 2\Delta = 0$$

$$\Rightarrow \Delta = 0$$

Example. Let $\Delta = \begin{vmatrix} a_1 & b_1 & c_1 \\ a_2 & b_2 & c_2 \\ a_2 & b_2 & c_2 \end{vmatrix}$

Then, $\Delta = a_1 (b_2c_2 - b_2c_2) - b_1 (a_2c_2 - a_2c_2)$
$+ c_1 (a_2b_2 - a_2b_2)$
$= 0$

Property 5. If each consituent of any row or any column be the sum (or difference) of two quantities, the determinant can be expressed as the sum (or difference) of two determinants of the same order.

Proof. To prove the property, we start with taking a determinant of order 3.

$$\text{Let } \Delta = \begin{vmatrix} a_1 + \alpha_1 & b_1 & c_1 \\ a_2 + \alpha_2 & b_2 & c_2 \\ a_3 + \alpha_3 & b_3 & c_3 \end{vmatrix}$$

Then,

$$\Delta = (a_1 + \alpha_1)\begin{vmatrix} b_2 & c_2 \\ b_3 & c_3 \end{vmatrix} - (a_2 + \alpha_2)\begin{vmatrix} b_1 & c_1 \\ b_3 & c_3 \end{vmatrix} + (a_3 + \alpha_3)\begin{vmatrix} b_1 & c_1 \\ b_2 & c_2 \end{vmatrix}$$

$$= \left\{a_1\begin{vmatrix} b_2 & c_2 \\ b_3 & c_3 \end{vmatrix} - a_2\begin{vmatrix} b_1 & c_1 \\ b_3 & c_3 \end{vmatrix} + a_3\begin{vmatrix} b_1 & c_1 \\ b_2 & c_2 \end{vmatrix}\right\} + \left\{\alpha_1\begin{vmatrix} b_2 & c_2 \\ b_3 & c_3 \end{vmatrix} - \alpha_2\begin{vmatrix} b_1 & c_1 \\ b_3 & c_3 \end{vmatrix} + \alpha_3\begin{vmatrix} b_1 & c_1 \\ b_2 & c_2 \end{vmatrix}\right\}$$

$$= \begin{vmatrix} a_1 & b_1 & c_1 \\ a_2 & b_2 & c_2 \\ a_3 & b_3 & c_3 \end{vmatrix} + \begin{vmatrix} \alpha_1 & b_1 & c_1 \\ \alpha_2 & b_2 & c_2 \\ \alpha_3 & b_3 & c_3 \end{vmatrix}$$

Hence, the result.

This property holds if each element of any row of a determinant is the sum of two quantities because $|A| = |A'|$.

Generalisation. Now, let us consider a determinant of order n.

$$\text{Let } \Delta = \begin{vmatrix} a_{11}+\alpha_{11} & a_{12}+\alpha_{12} & a_{1n}+\alpha_{1n} \\ a_{21} & a_{22} & a_{2n} \\ a_{n1} & a_{n2} & a_{nn} \end{vmatrix}$$

Then, $\Delta = \sum_{j=1}^{n} \left(a_{ij} + \alpha_{ij}\right) A_{ij}$ where A_{ij} is the cofactor of the element $(a_{ij} + \alpha_{ij})$

$$= \sum_{j=1}^{n} a_{ij}\, A_{ij} + \sum_{j=1}^{n} \alpha_{ij}\, A_{ij}$$

$$= \begin{vmatrix} a_{11} & a_{12} & \ldots & a_{in} \\ a_{21} & a_{22} & \ldots & a_{2n} \\ \ldots & \ldots & \ldots & \ldots \\ a_{n1} & a_{n2} & \ldots & a_{nn} \end{vmatrix} + \begin{vmatrix} \alpha_{11} & \alpha_{12} & \ldots & \alpha_{in} \\ a_{21} & a_{22} & \ldots & a_{2n} \\ \ldots & \ldots & \ldots & \ldots \\ a_{n1} & a_{n2} & \ldots & a_{nn} \end{vmatrix}$$

Hence, the proposition.

Note. If the consituents of three rows (or columns) consist of p, q, r terms respectively, then the determinant can be expressed as the sum of $p \times q \times r$ determinants and so on.

For Property 6 and Property 7, see Sections 3.10 and 3.11.

3.7. Theorem

The cofactor A_{ij} of the element a_{ij} in the determinant $|A| = |a_{ij}|$ is given by

$$A_{ij} = (-1)^{i+j}\, |M_{ij}|$$

where M_{ij} is the sub-matrix of the matrix $A = [a_{ij}]$ obtained by deleting the ith row and j^{th} column.

Proof. Let us first of all prove the case

$$A_{11} = (-1)^{1+1}\, |M_{11}|$$

$$\Rightarrow A_{11} = |M_{11}|$$

The terms of A_{11} are composed of the elements taken from the $(n-1) \times (n-1)$ sub-matrix M_{11} of A.

The general term of $a_{11}\, A_{11} = \pm\, a_{11}\, a_{i22}\, a_{i33} \ldots a_{inn}$ where $i_2, i_3, \ldots, i_n$ are 2, 3, ..., n in some order.

This term can also be obtained from the product of the diagonal elements of the matrix A, i.e. $a_{11}\ a_{22}\ a_{33} \dots a_{nn}$ by operating on its row subscripts by the permutation

$$p = \begin{pmatrix} 1 & 2 & 3 & \dots & n \\ 1 & i_2 & i_3 & \dots & i_n \end{pmatrix}$$

where $i_2, i_3, \dots, i_n$ are defined as above.

Hence, the permutation p may be regarded as a permutation on the symbols 2, 3, ..., n; and therefore all the terms of $a_{11}A_{11}$ can be obtained by running p through the $\lfloor n-1$ permutations of the symbols 2, 3, ..., n keeping 1 fixed.

Thus, the term of A_{11} can be obtained by operating on the row subscripts of the elements of the product $a_{22}\ a_{33} \dots a_{nn}$, which is actually the product of the elements of the diagonal of sub-matrix M_{11}.

Hence, $A_{11} = |M_{11}|$

Now, we shall proceed to prove that

$$A_{ij} = (-1)^{i+j}\ |M_{ij}|$$

Let us move the jth column of the matrix A to the first column by performing $(j - 1)$ successive interchanges of adjacent columns and also let us move the ith row of the matrix A to the first row by performing $(i - 1)$ successive interchanges of adjacent rows. Then, the element a_{ij} is in the first row and first column of the resulting matrix B (say). The sub-matrix of B obtained by removing the first row and first column is the sub-matrix M_{ij} of the matrix A. Hence, $a_{ij}\ |M_{ij}|$ is the term of $|B|$ containing a_{ij}. Also, we know that interchange of any two rows (or two columns) of a determinant changes its sign, the absolute value remaining the same. Thus, in view of the number of movements,

$$\begin{aligned} |B| &= (-1)^{i-1+j-1}\ |A| \\ &= (-1)^{i+j}\ (-1)^{-2}\ |A| \\ &= (-1)^{i+j}\ |A| \qquad \Big|\ \because (-1)^{-2} = 1 \end{aligned}$$

Equating the coefficients of a_{ij} from both sides, we get

$$A_{ij} = (-1)^{i+j}\ |M_{ij}|$$

3.8. Theorem

If A_{ij} is the cofactor of a_{ij} in the determinant $|A| = |a_{ij}|$ of order n, then

(i) The sum of the products of the elements of the ith row with the cofactors of the corresponding elements of the kth row is zero provided $i \neq k$.

(ii) Also, the sum of the products of the elements of the jth column with the cofactors of the corresponding elements of the kth column is zero provided $j \neq k$.

i.e. symbolically we have to prove that

(i) $\sum_{j=1}^{n} a_{ij} A_{kj} = 0$, if $i \neq k$

(ii) $\sum_{j=1}^{n} a_{ij} A_{ik} = 0$, if $j \neq k$

Proof.

(i) We know that,

$$|A| = \sum_{j=1}^{n} a_{kj} A_{kj}$$

If we replace k^{th} row by i^{th} row, we get a new determinant whose value is $\sum_{j=1}^{n} a_{ij} A_{kj}$.

But the kth and i^{th} $(i \neq k)$ rows of the new determinant are identical, hence its value is zero, i.e.

$$\sum_{j=1}^{n} a_{ij} A_{kj} = 0$$

(ii) The given determinant $|A| = \sum_{i=1}^{n} a_{ik} A_{ik}$. If we replace the kth column by j^{th} column, we get a new determinant whose value is $\sum_{j=1}^{n} a_{ij} A_{ik}$. But the kth and j^{th} $(j \neq k)$ columns of the new determinant and identical, hence its value is zero, i.e.

$$\sum_{j=1}^{n} a_{ij} A_{ik} = 0$$

3.9. An Important Example

In the determinant $|A| = \begin{vmatrix} a_1 & b_1 & c_1 \\ a_2 & b_2 & c_2 \\ a_3 & b_3 & c_3 \end{vmatrix}$, prove that

$$a_1A_2 + b_1B_2 + c_1C_2 = 0,$$
$$b_1C_1 + b_2C_2 + b_3C_3 = 0,$$
and $$c_1B_1 + c_2B_2 + c_3B_3 = 0,$$

where capital letters denote the cofactors of the corresponding small letters. Also, prove that

$$a_1A_1 + b_1B_1 + c_1C_1 = |A| = a_2A_2 + b_2B_2 + c_2C_2$$
$$= a_3A_3 + b_3B_3 + c_3C_3$$

Solution: We have,

$$|A| = \begin{vmatrix} a_1 & b_1 & c_1 \\ a_2 & b_2 & c_2 \\ a_3 & b_3 & c_3 \end{vmatrix}$$

$$\therefore \quad A_1 = \begin{vmatrix} b_2 & c_2 \\ b_3 & c_3 \end{vmatrix}$$

$$A_2 = -\begin{vmatrix} b_1 & c_1 \\ b_3 & c_3 \end{vmatrix}$$

$$A_3 = \begin{vmatrix} b_1 & c_1 \\ b_2 & c_2 \end{vmatrix}$$

$$B_1 = -\begin{vmatrix} a_2 & c_2 \\ a_3 & c_3 \end{vmatrix}$$

$$B_2 = \begin{vmatrix} a_1 & c_1 \\ a_3 & c_3 \end{vmatrix}$$

$$B_3 = -\begin{vmatrix} a_1 & c_1 \\ a_2 & c_2 \end{vmatrix}$$

$$C_1 = \begin{vmatrix} a_2 & b_2 \\ a_3 & b_3 \end{vmatrix}$$

$$C_2 = -\begin{vmatrix} a_1 & b_1 \\ a_3 & b_3 \end{vmatrix}$$

$$C_3 = -\begin{vmatrix} a_1 & b_1 \\ a_2 & b_2 \end{vmatrix}$$

$\therefore \quad a_1A_2 + b_1B_2 + c_1C_2$

$$= -a_1\begin{vmatrix} b_1 & c_1 \\ b_3 & c_3 \end{vmatrix} + b_1\begin{vmatrix} a_1 & c_1 \\ a_3 & c_3 \end{vmatrix} - c_1\begin{vmatrix} a_1 & b_1 \\ a_3 & b_3 \end{vmatrix}$$

$$= -a_1(b_1c_3 - b_3c_1) + b_1(a_1c_3 - a_3c_1) - c_1(a_1b_3 - a_3b_1)$$

$$= 0$$

Similarly, we can prove that

$$b_1C_1 + b_2C_2 + b_3C_3 = 0$$

and $\quad c_1B_1 + c_2B_2 + c_3B_3 = 0$

This shows that the sum of the products of elements of any row (or any column) by the cofactors of the corresponding elements of a different row (or column) is always zero.

Also,

$$|A| = \begin{vmatrix} a_1 & b_1 & c_1 \\ a_2 & b_2 & c_2 \\ a_3 & b_3 & c_3 \end{vmatrix}$$

$$= a_1\begin{vmatrix} b_2 & c_2 \\ b_3 & c_3 \end{vmatrix} - b_1\begin{vmatrix} a_2 & c_2 \\ a_3 & c_3 \end{vmatrix} + c_1\begin{vmatrix} a_2 & b_2 \\ a_3 & b_3 \end{vmatrix} \quad \text{... (3.12)}$$

| Expanding in terms of the elements of first row

and,

$$a_1A_1 + b_1B_1 + c_1C_1$$

$$= a_1 \begin{vmatrix} b_2 & c_2 \\ b_3 & c_3 \end{vmatrix} + b_1 \left\{ - \begin{vmatrix} a_2 & c_2 \\ a_3 & c_3 \end{vmatrix} \right\} + c_1 \begin{vmatrix} a_2 & b_2 \\ a_3 & b_3 \end{vmatrix}$$

$$= a_1 \begin{vmatrix} b_2 & c_2 \\ b_3 & c_3 \end{vmatrix} - b_1 \begin{vmatrix} a_2 & c_2 \\ a_3 & c_3 \end{vmatrix} + c_1 \begin{vmatrix} a_2 & b_2 \\ a_3 & b_3 \end{vmatrix} \qquad \ldots (3.13)$$

In view of Eqs. (3.12) and (3.13),

$$a_1A_1 + b_1B_1 = c_1C_1 = |A|$$

Similarly, we can show that

$$a_2A_2 + b_2B_2 + c_2C_2 = |A|$$

and, $a_3A_3 + b_3B_3 + c_3C_3 = |A|$

3.10. Property 6

(i) If A_i, the ith row of a determinant $|A| = |a_{ij}|$ of order n be replaced by $A_i + \lambda A_k$, where λ is a scalar and A_k denotes the kth row of the determinant $|A|$, then the value of the determinant is not changed.

Proof. We know that

$$|A| = \sum_{j=1}^{n} a_{ij} A_{ij}, \text{ where } A_{ij} \text{ is the cofactor of } a_{ij}.$$

If we replace A_i by $A_i + \lambda A_k$, we get the new determinant, $|B|$ say. Then,

$$|B| = \sum_{j=1}^{n} \left(a_{ij} + \lambda a_{kj}\right) A_{ij}$$

$$= \sum_{j=1}^{n} a_{ij} A_{ij} + \lambda \sum_{j=1}^{n} a_{kj} A_{ij}$$

$$= |A| + \lambda\, 0 \qquad | \text{ By Theorem 3.9}$$

$$= |A|$$

Property 6(ii) If C_i, the ith column of a determinant $|A| = |a_{ij}|$ of order n be replaced by $C_i + \mu C_k$, where μ is a scalar and C_k denotes the kth column of the determinant $|A|$, then the value of the determinant is not changed.

Proof. We know that $|A| = |A'|$ | By Property 3

Hence, the result is evident.

3.11. Property 7

If the constituents of a determinant Δ which involve x are polynomials in x and if $\Delta = 0$, when $x = a$, then $x - a$ is a factor of Δ.

Proof. Since the elements of Δ are polynomials in x, therefore, the expansion of Δ will also be a polynomial in x. Now, since Δ vanishes for $x = a$, therefore, $(x - a)$ is a factor of Δ by Factor Theorem for polynomials.

Note. In general, if in a determinant of order n, r rows (or columns) become identical by putting $x = a$, then $(x - a)^{r-1}$ is a factor of the determinant.

3.12. Working Rule

Alongwith applying the above 7 properties while evaluating a determinant, an attempt should be made

(i) to reduce the size of the elements as far as possible

(ii) to reduce at least one of the elements to unity

(iii) to bring as many zeros as possible in a certain row or column. To achieve this, an element of unit value will greatly help.

3.13. Notations

(i) $R_1, R_2, R_3, \ldots$ denote first, second, third, ... rows, respectively.

(ii) $C_1, C_2, C_3, \ldots$ denote first, second, third, ... columns respectively.

(iii) $R_1 + 3R_2 - 2R_3$ means: Add 3 times the second row to the first row and then substract from this 2 times the third row.

(iv) $C_1 + 3C_2 - 4C_3$ means: Add three times the second column to the first column and then substract from this four times the third column.

ILLUSTRATIVE EXAMPLES

Example 1. Find the value of the determinant

$$\begin{vmatrix} 265 & 240 & 219 \\ 240 & 225 & 198 \\ 219 & 198 & 181 \end{vmatrix}$$

Solution:

$$\text{Let } \Delta = \begin{vmatrix} 265 & 240 & 219 \\ 240 & 225 & 198 \\ 219 & 198 & 181 \end{vmatrix}$$

Operating $R_1 + R_3 - 2R_2$, we get

$$\Delta = \begin{vmatrix} 4 & -12 & 4 \\ 240 & 225 & 198 \\ 219 & 198 & 181 \end{vmatrix}$$

$$= 4\begin{vmatrix} 1 & -3 & 1 \\ 240 & 225 & 198 \\ 219 & 198 & 181 \end{vmatrix} \qquad | \text{ Taking 4 common from } R_1$$

$$= 4\begin{vmatrix} 1 & -3 & 1 \\ 3\times 80 & 3\times 75 & 3\times 66 \\ 219 & 198 & 181 \end{vmatrix}$$

$$= 4\times 3\begin{vmatrix} 1 & -3 & 1 \\ 80 & 75 & 66 \\ 219 & 198 & 181 \end{vmatrix} \qquad | \text{ Taking 3 common from } R_2$$

$$= 4\times 3\begin{vmatrix} 1 & -3 & 1 \\ 80 & 3\times 25 & 66 \\ 219 & 3\times 66 & 181 \end{vmatrix}$$

$$= 4 \times 3 \times 3 \begin{vmatrix} 1 & -1 & 1 \\ 80 & 25 & 66 \\ 219 & 66 & 181 \end{vmatrix}$$ | Taking 3 common from C_2

$$= 4 \times 3 \times 3 \begin{vmatrix} 1 & 0 & 0 \\ 80 & 105 & 91 \\ 219 & 285 & 247 \end{vmatrix}$$ | Operating $C_2 + C_1$, $C_3 + C_2$

$$= 4 \times 3 \times 3 \begin{vmatrix} 105 & 91 \\ 285 & 247 \end{vmatrix}$$ | Expanding in terms of elements of R_1

$$= 36 \begin{vmatrix} 105 & 91 \\ 285 & 247 \end{vmatrix}$$

$$= 36 \begin{vmatrix} 14 & 91 \\ 38 & 247 \end{vmatrix}$$ | Operating $C_1 - C_2$

$$= 36 \times 19 \begin{vmatrix} 14 & 91 \\ 2 & 13 \end{vmatrix}$$ | Taking 19 common from R_2

$$= 36 \times 19 \times 2 \times 13 \begin{vmatrix} 7 & 7 \\ 1 & 1 \end{vmatrix}$$ | Taking 2 common from C_1 and 13 from C_2

$= 0$ | $\because$ C_1 and C_2 are identical

Example 2. Find the value of

$$\begin{vmatrix} 1^2 & 2^2 & 3^2 & 4^2 \\ 2^2 & 3^2 & 4^2 & 5^2 \\ 3^2 & 4^2 & 5^2 & 6^2 \\ 4^2 & 5^2 & 6^2 & 7^2 \end{vmatrix}$$

Solution:

Let $\Delta = \begin{vmatrix} 1^2 & 2^2 & 3^2 & 4^2 \\ 2^2 & 3^2 & 4^2 & 5^2 \\ 3^2 & 4^2 & 5^2 & 6^2 \\ 4^2 & 5^2 & 6^2 & 7^2 \end{vmatrix}$

Then,

$$\Delta = \begin{vmatrix} 1 & 4 & 9 & 16 \\ 4 & 9 & 16 & 25 \\ 9 & 16 & 25 & 36 \\ 16 & 25 & 36 & 49 \end{vmatrix}$$

Operating $C_4 - C_3$, $C_3 - C_2$, $C_2 - C_1$,

$$\Delta = \begin{vmatrix} 1 & 3 & 5 & 7 \\ 4 & 5 & 7 & 9 \\ 9 & 7 & 9 & 11 \\ 16 & 9 & 11 & 13 \end{vmatrix}$$

Operating $C_4 - C_3$, $C_3 - C_2$,

$$\Delta = \begin{vmatrix} 1 & 3 & 2 & 2 \\ 4 & 5 & 2 & 2 \\ 9 & 7 & 2 & 2 \\ 16 & 9 & 2 & 2 \end{vmatrix} = 0 \quad \big| \because C_3 \text{ and } C_4 \text{ are identical}$$

Example 3. Evaluate $\begin{vmatrix} 1 & 2 & 3 & 4 \\ 2 & 3 & 4 & 1 \\ 3 & 4 & 1 & 2 \\ 4 & 1 & 2 & 3 \end{vmatrix}$

Solution:

$$\text{Let } \Delta = \begin{vmatrix} 1 & 2 & 3 & 4 \\ 2 & 3 & 4 & 1 \\ 3 & 4 & 1 & 2 \\ 4 & 1 & 2 & 3 \end{vmatrix}$$

Operating $C_1 + C_2 + C_3 + C_4$,

$$\Delta = \begin{vmatrix} 10 & 2 & 3 & 4 \\ 10 & 3 & 4 & 1 \\ 10 & 4 & 1 & 2 \\ 10 & 1 & 2 & 3 \end{vmatrix}$$

$$\Rightarrow \quad \Delta = 10 \begin{vmatrix} 1 & 2 & 3 & 4 \\ 1 & 3 & 4 & 1 \\ 1 & 4 & 1 & 2 \\ 1 & 1 & 2 & 3 \end{vmatrix}$$ | Taking 10 common from C_1

Operating $R_2 - R_1$, $R_3 - R_1$, $R_4 - R_1$,

$$\Delta = 10 \begin{vmatrix} 1 & 2 & 3 & 4 \\ 0 & 1 & 1 & -3 \\ 0 & 2 & -2 & -2 \\ 0 & -1 & -1 & -1 \end{vmatrix}$$

$$\Rightarrow \quad \Delta = 10 \begin{vmatrix} 1 & 1 & -3 \\ 2 & -2 & -2 \\ -1 & -1 & -1 \end{vmatrix}$$ | Expanding in terms of the elements of C_1

Operating $R_2 - 2R_1$, $R_3 + R_1$,

$$\Delta = 10 \begin{vmatrix} 1 & 1 & -3 \\ 0 & -4 & 4 \\ 0 & 0 & -4 \end{vmatrix}$$

$$\Rightarrow \quad \Delta = 10\begin{vmatrix} -4 & 4 \\ 0 & -4 \end{vmatrix}$$

$$\Rightarrow \quad \Delta = 10\ (16 - 0) = 160$$

Example 4. Prove that

$$\begin{vmatrix} -a^2 & ab & ac \\ ba & -b^2 & bc \\ ac & bc & -c^2 \end{vmatrix} = 4a^2b^2c^2$$

Solution:

$$\text{Let } \Delta = \begin{vmatrix} -a^2 & ab & ac \\ ba & -b^2 & bc \\ ac & bc & -c^2 \end{vmatrix}$$

Taking a, b, c common from R_1, R_2, R_3 respectively,

$$\Delta = abc\begin{vmatrix} -a & b & c \\ a & -b & c \\ a & b & -c \end{vmatrix}$$

Taking a, b, c common from C_1, C_2, C_3 respectively,

$$\Delta = (abc)\,(abc)\begin{vmatrix} -1 & 1 & 1 \\ 1 & -1 & 1 \\ 1 & 1 & -1 \end{vmatrix}$$

Operating $C_2 + C_1$, $C_3 + C_1$

$$\Delta = a^2b^2c^2\begin{vmatrix} -1 & 0 & 0 \\ 1 & 0 & 2 \\ 1 & 2 & 0 \end{vmatrix}$$

$$\Rightarrow \quad \Delta = (-1)\,a^2b^2c^2\begin{vmatrix} 0 & 2 \\ 2 & 0 \end{vmatrix}$$

$$\Rightarrow \quad \Delta = (-1)\ (a^2b^2c^2)\ (0 - 4) = 4a^2b^2c^2$$

Example 5. Prove that

$$\begin{vmatrix} 0 & c & b \\ -c & 0 & a \\ -b & -a & 0 \end{vmatrix} = 0$$

Solution:

$$\text{Let } \Delta = \begin{vmatrix} 0 & c & b \\ -c & 0 & a \\ -b & -a & 0 \end{vmatrix}$$

Then,

$$\Delta = (-1)(-1)(-1)\begin{vmatrix} 0 & -c & -b \\ c & 0 & -a \\ b & a & 0 \end{vmatrix}$$ | Taking (–1) common from each row

$$\Rightarrow \quad \Delta = (-1)^3 \begin{vmatrix} 0 & c & b \\ -c & 0 & a \\ -b & -a & 0 \end{vmatrix}$$ | Interchanging all the rows and columns

$$\Rightarrow \quad \Delta = (-1)^3 \, \Delta$$
$$\Rightarrow \quad \Delta = -\Delta$$
$$\Rightarrow \quad 2\Delta = 0$$
$$\Rightarrow \quad \Delta = 0$$

Example 6. Show that

$$\begin{vmatrix} a-b-c & 2a & 2a \\ 2b & b-c-a & 2b \\ 2c & 2c & c-a-b \end{vmatrix} = (a+b+c)^3$$

Solution:

$$\text{Let } \Delta = \begin{vmatrix} a-b-c & 2a & 2a \\ 2b & b-c-a & 2b \\ 2c & 2c & c-a-b \end{vmatrix}$$

Operating $R_1 + R_2 + R_3$,

$$\Delta = \begin{vmatrix} a+b+c & a+b+c & a+b+c \\ 2b & b-c-a & 2b \\ 2c & 2c & c-a-b \end{vmatrix}$$

$$\Rightarrow \quad \Delta = (a+b+c)\begin{vmatrix} 1 & 1 & 1 \\ 2b & b-c-a & 2b \\ 2c & 2c & c-a-b \end{vmatrix}$$ | Taking $(a + b + c)$ from R_1

Operating $C_2 - C_1$, $C_3 - C_1$,

$$\Delta = (a+b+c)\begin{vmatrix} 1 & 0 & 0 \\ 2b & -a-b-c & 0 \\ 2c & 0 & -a-b-c \end{vmatrix}$$

$$\Rightarrow \quad \Delta = (a+b+c)\begin{vmatrix} -a-b-c & 0 \\ 0 & -a-b-c \end{vmatrix}$$ | Expanding in terms of the elements of R_1

$\Rightarrow \quad \Delta = (a + b + c)\ (-a - b - c)\ (-a - b - c)$

$\Rightarrow \quad \text{D} = (a + b + c)^3$

Example 7. Show that

$$\begin{vmatrix} (b+c)^2 & a^2 & a^2 \\ b^2 & (c+a)^2 & b^2 \\ c^2 & c^2 & (a+b)^2 \end{vmatrix} = 2abc\,(a+b+c)^3$$

Solution:

$$\text{Let } \Delta = \begin{vmatrix} (b+c)^2 & a^2 & a^2 \\ b^2 & (c+a)^2 & b^2 \\ c^2 & c^2 & (a+b)^2 \end{vmatrix}$$

Operating $C_1 - C_3$, $C_2 - C_3$,

$$\Delta = \begin{vmatrix} (b+c)^2 - a^2 & 0 & a^2 \\ 0 & (c+a)^2 - b^2 & b^2 \\ c^2 - (a+b^2) & c^2 - (a+b)^2 & (a+b)^2 \end{vmatrix}$$

$$= \begin{vmatrix} \begin{matrix}(b+c-a)\\(b+c+a)\end{matrix} & 0 & a^2 \\ 0 & \begin{matrix}(c+a+b)\\(c+a-b)\end{matrix} & b^2 \\ \begin{matrix}(c-a-b)\\(c+a+b)\end{matrix} & \begin{matrix}(c+a+b)\\(c-a-b)\end{matrix} & (a+b)^2 \end{vmatrix}$$

$$= (a+b+c)(a+b+c) \begin{vmatrix} b+c-a & 0 & a^2 \\ 0 & c+a-b & b^2 \\ c-a-b & c-a-b & (a+b)^2 \end{vmatrix}$$

| Taking $(a + b + c)$ common from C_1 and C_2 each

$$= \frac{(a+b+c)^2}{ab} \begin{vmatrix} a(b+c-a) & 0 & a^2 \\ 0 & b(c+a-b) & b^2 \\ a(c-a-b) & b(c-a-b) & (a+b)^2 \end{vmatrix}$$

| Multiplying C_1, C_2 by a, b respectively and dividing the whole by ab, so that the value of the determinant is not altered

Operating $R_3 - (R_1 + R_2)$,

$$\Delta = \frac{(a+b+c)^2}{ab} \begin{vmatrix} a(b+c-a) & 0 & a^2 \\ 0 & b(c+a-b) & b^2 \\ -2ab & -2ab & 2ab \end{vmatrix}$$

Operating $C_1 + C_3$, $C_2 + C_3$,

$$\Rightarrow \Delta = \frac{(a+b+c)^2}{ab}\begin{vmatrix} a(b+c) & a^2 & a^2 \\ b^2 & b(c+a) & b^2 \\ 0 & 0 & 2ab \end{vmatrix}$$

$$= \frac{(a+b+c)^2}{ab} 2ab \begin{vmatrix} a(b+c) & a^2 \\ b^2 & b(c+a) \end{vmatrix}$$

| Expanding along R_3

$$= 2(a+b+c)^2\, ab \begin{vmatrix} b+c & a \\ b & c+a \end{vmatrix}$$

| Taking a, b common from R_1, R_2 respectively

$= 2ab\ (a + b + c)^2\ \{(b + c)\ (c + a) - ab\}$
$= 2ab\ (a + b + c)^2\ (bc + c^2 + ac)$
$= 2abc\ (a + b + c)^3$

Aliter

$$\text{Let } \Delta = \begin{vmatrix} (b+c)^2 & a^2 & a^2 \\ b^2 & (c+a)^2 & b^2 \\ c^2 & c^2 & (a+b)^2 \end{vmatrix}$$

Putting $a = 0$, we find that C_2 and C_3 become identical, so that $\Delta = 0$. Hence, a is a factor of the determinant. Similarly, b and c are also the factors of the given determinant.

Again, on putting $a + b + c = 0$, we have,

$$\Delta = \begin{vmatrix} (-a)^2 & a^2 & a^2 \\ b^2 & (-b)^2 & b^2 \\ c^2 & c^2 & (-c)^2 \end{vmatrix}$$

$$= \begin{vmatrix} a^2 & a^2 & a^2 \\ b^2 & b^2 & b^2 \\ c^2 & c^2 & c^2 \end{vmatrix}$$

$$= a^2b^2c^2 \begin{vmatrix} 1 & 1 & 1 \\ 1 & 1 & 1 \\ 1 & 1 & 1 \end{vmatrix}$$

$$= 0 \qquad | \because C_1, C_2 \text{ and } C_3 \text{ are identical}$$

Hence, $(a + b + c)^2$ is a factor of the determinant. Now, the principal diagonal terms of the determinant reveal the fact that the given determinant is of sixth degree in a, b, c. Therefore, alongwith the factors obtained above, we must have another linear factor symmetrical in a, b, c. Therefore, let

$$\begin{vmatrix} (b+c)^2 & a^2 & a^2 \\ b^2 & (c+a)^2 & b^2 \\ c^2 & c^2 & (a+b)^2 \end{vmatrix} = K\, abc\, (a+b+c)^3$$

Now, putting $a = b = c = 1$ on both sides, we get

$$\begin{vmatrix} 4 & 1 & 1 \\ 1 & 4 & 1 \\ 1 & 1 & 4 \end{vmatrix} = 27K$$

$$\Rightarrow \; 54 = 27K$$

$$\Rightarrow \; K = 2$$

Hence, $\Delta = 2abc\,(a + b + c)^3$

Example 8. Evaluate the following determinant:

$$\begin{vmatrix} 1+a_1 & 1 & 1 & 1 \\ 1 & 1+a_2 & 1 & 1 \\ 1 & 1 & 1+a_3 & 1 \\ 1 & 1 & 1 & 1+a_4 \end{vmatrix}$$

Solution:

$$\text{Let } \Delta = \begin{vmatrix} 1+a_1 & 1 & 1 & 1 \\ 1 & 1+a_2 & 1 & 1 \\ 1 & 1 & 1+a_3 & 1 \\ 1 & 1 & 1 & 1+a_4 \end{vmatrix}$$

Taking a_1, a_2, a_3, a_4 common from C_1, C_2, C_3, C_4 respectively, we get

$$\Delta = a_1a_2a_3a_4 \begin{vmatrix} \frac{1}{a_1}+1 & \frac{1}{a_2} & \frac{1}{a_3} & \frac{1}{a_4} \\ \frac{1}{a_1} & \frac{1}{a_2}+1 & \frac{1}{a_3} & \frac{1}{a_4} \\ \frac{1}{a_1} & \frac{1}{a_2} & \frac{1}{a_3}+1 & \frac{1}{a_4} \\ \frac{1}{a_1} & \frac{1}{a_2} & \frac{1}{a_3} & \frac{1}{a_4}+1 \end{vmatrix}$$

Operating $C_1 + C_2 + C_3 + C_4$,

$$\Delta = a_1a_2a_3a_4 \begin{vmatrix} 1+\frac{1}{a_1}+\frac{1}{a_2}+\frac{1}{a_3}+\frac{1}{a_4} & \frac{1}{a_2} & \frac{1}{a_3} & \frac{1}{a_4} \\ 1+\frac{1}{a_1}+\frac{1}{a_2}+\frac{1}{a_3}+\frac{1}{a_4} & \frac{1}{a_2}+1 & \frac{1}{a_3} & \frac{1}{a_4} \\ 1+\frac{1}{a_1}+\frac{1}{a_2}+\frac{1}{a_3}+\frac{1}{a_4} & \frac{1}{a_2} & \frac{1}{a_3}+1 & \frac{1}{a_4} \\ 1+\frac{1}{a_1}+\frac{1}{a_2}+\frac{1}{a_3}+\frac{1}{a_4} & \frac{1}{a_2} & \frac{1}{a_3} & \frac{1}{a_4}+1 \end{vmatrix}$$

$$= a_1a_2a_3a_4\left(1+\frac{1}{a_1}+\frac{1}{a_2}+\frac{1}{a_3}+\frac{1}{a_4}\right)\begin{vmatrix} 1 & \frac{1}{a_2} & \frac{1}{a_3} & \frac{1}{a_4} \\ 1 & \frac{1}{a_2}+1 & \frac{1}{a_3} & \frac{1}{a_4} \\ 1 & \frac{1}{a_2} & \frac{1}{a_3}+1 & \frac{1}{a_4} \\ 1 & \frac{1}{a_2} & \frac{1}{a_3} & \frac{1}{a_4}+1 \end{vmatrix}$$

| Taking $\left(1+\frac{1}{a_1}+\frac{1}{a_2}+\frac{1}{a_3}+\frac{1}{a_4}\right)$ common from C_1

Operating $R_2 - R_1$, $R_3 - R_4$, $R_4 - R_1$,

$$\Delta = a_1a_2a_3a_4\left(1+\frac{1}{a_1}+\frac{1}{a_2}+\frac{1}{a_3}+\frac{1}{a_4}\right)\begin{vmatrix} 1 & \frac{1}{a_2} & \frac{1}{a_3} & \frac{1}{a_4} \\ 0 & 1 & 0 & 0 \\ 0 & 0 & 1 & 0 \\ 0 & 0 & 0 & 1 \end{vmatrix}$$

$$= a_1a_2a_3a_4\left(1+\frac{1}{a_1}+\frac{1}{a_2}+\frac{1}{a_3}+\frac{1}{a_4}\right)\begin{vmatrix} 1 & 0 & 0 \\ 0 & 1 & 0 \\ 0 & 0 & 1 \end{vmatrix}$$

| Expanding along C_1

$$= a_1a_2a_3a_4\left(1+\frac{1}{a_1}+\frac{1}{a_2}+\frac{1}{a_3}+\frac{1}{a_4}\right)\begin{vmatrix} 1 & 0 \\ 0 & 1 \end{vmatrix}$$

| Expanding along C_1

$$= a_1a_2a_3a_4\left(1+\frac{1}{a_1}+\frac{1}{a_2}+\frac{1}{a_3}+\frac{1}{a_4}\right)(1-0)$$

| Expanding along C_1

$$= a_1a_2a_3a_4\left(1+\frac{1}{a_1}+\frac{1}{a_2}+\frac{1}{a_3}+\frac{1}{a_4}\right)$$

Example 9. If A, B, C are the angles of a triangle, show that

$$\begin{vmatrix} -1 & \cos C & \cos B \\ \cos C & -1 & \cos A \\ \cos B & \cos A & -1 \end{vmatrix} = 0$$

Deduce that $\cos^2 A + \cos^2 B + \cos^2 C + 2 \cos A \cos B \cos C = 1$

Solution:

$$\text{Let } \Delta = \begin{vmatrix} -1 & \cos C & \cos B \\ \cos C & -1 & \cos A \\ \cos B & \cos A & -1 \end{vmatrix}$$

Multiplying C_1 by a, C_2 by b, C_3 by c and dividing the whole determinant by abc, we have

$$\Delta = \frac{1}{abc}\begin{vmatrix} -a & b\cos C & c\cos B \\ a\cos C & -b & c\cos A \\ a\cos B & b\cos A & -c \end{vmatrix}$$

Operating $C_1 + C_2 + C_3$,

$$\Delta = \frac{1}{abc}\begin{vmatrix} -a + b\cos C + c\cos B & b\cos C & c\cos B \\ a\cos C - b + c\cos A & -b & c\cos A \\ a\cos B + b\cos A - c & b\cos A & -c \end{vmatrix}$$

$$= \frac{1}{abc}\begin{vmatrix} -a + a & b\cos C & c\cos B \\ -b + b & -b & c\cos A \\ -c + c & b\cos A & -c \end{vmatrix}$$

| $\because b \cos C + c \cos B = 0$, etc.

$$= \frac{1}{abc}\begin{vmatrix} 0 & b\cos C & c\cos B \\ 0 & -b & c\cos A \\ 0 & b\cos A & -c \end{vmatrix}$$

$$= 0 \qquad \text{... (3.14)}$$

Deduction

Expanding the given determinant in terms of R_1, we obtain

$$\Delta = -1\ (1 - \cos^2 A) - \cos C\ (-\cos C - \cos A \cos B) + \cos B\ (\cos C \cos A + \cos B)$$

$$= -1 + \cos^2 A + \cos^2 C + \cos A \cos B \cos C + \cos A \cos B \cos C + \cos^2 B$$

$$= -1 + \cos^2 A + \cos^2 B + \cos^2 C + 2 \cos A \cos B \cos C \quad \ldots (3.15)$$

In view of Eqs. (3.14) and (3.15),

$$-1 + \cos^2 A + \cos^2 B + \cos^2 C + 2 \cos A \cos B \cos C = 0$$

$$\Rightarrow \cos^2 A + \cos^2 B + \cos^2 C + 2 \cos A \cos B \cos C = 1$$

Example 10. If w is one of the imaginary cube roots of unity, prove that $a + bw + cw^2$ is a factor of the determinant

$$\begin{vmatrix} a & b & c \\ b & c & a \\ c & a & b \end{vmatrix}$$

Hence, evaluate the determinant.

Solution:

$$\text{Let } \Delta = \begin{vmatrix} a & b & c \\ b & c & a \\ c & a & b \end{vmatrix}$$

Operating $C_1 + wC_2 + w^2C_3$, we have

$$\Delta = \begin{vmatrix} a + bw + cw^2 & b & c \\ b + cw + aw^2 & c & a \\ c + aw + bw^2 & a & b \end{vmatrix}$$

$$= \begin{vmatrix} a + bw + cw^2 & b & c \\ w^2\left(a + bw + cw^2\right) & c & a \\ w\left(a + bw + cw^2\right) & a & b \end{vmatrix} \quad \Big|\ \because w^3 = 1$$

$$= \left(a + bw + cw^2\right)\begin{vmatrix} 1 & b & c \\ w^2 & c & a \\ w & a & b \end{vmatrix} \quad \begin{array}{|l} \text{Taking } (a + bw + cw^2) \\ \text{common from } C_1 \end{array}$$

$\Rightarrow$ $a + bw + cw^2$ is a factor of Δ.

Again, operating $C_1 + w^2C_2 + wC_3$, we have

$$\Delta = \begin{vmatrix} a + bw^2 + cw & b & c \\ w\left(a + bw^2 + cw\right) & c & a \\ w^2\left(a + bw^2 + cw\right) & a & b \end{vmatrix}$$

$$= \left(a + bw^2 + cw\right)\begin{vmatrix} 1 & b & c \\ w & c & a \\ w^2 & a & b \end{vmatrix} \quad \begin{array}{|l} \text{Taking } (a + bw^2 + cw) \\ \text{common from } C_1 \end{array}$$

$\Rightarrow$ $a + bw^2 + cw$ is a factor of Δ.

Also, operating $C_1 + C_2 + C_3$, we have

$$\Delta = \begin{vmatrix} a + b + c & b & c \\ b + c + a & c & a \\ c + a + b & a & b \end{vmatrix}$$

$$= (a + b + c)\begin{vmatrix} 1 & b & c \\ 1 & c & a \\ 1 & a & b \end{vmatrix}$$

$\Rightarrow$ $a + b + c$ is a factor of Δ.

Since Δ is of third degree in a, b, c as is revealed on looking at the principal diagonal elements, there cannot be any other factor other than a numerical constant. Therefore, let

$\Delta = K\,(a + b + c)\,(a + bw + bw^2)\,(a + bw^2 + cw)$

Now, putting $a = 1$, $b = 0$, $c = 0$ or either side, we have

$$\begin{vmatrix} 1 & 0 & 0 \\ 0 & 0 & 1 \\ 0 & 1 & 0 \end{vmatrix} = K$$

$\Rightarrow K = -1$

Hence,

$$\Delta = -(a + b + c)\ (a + bw + cw^2)\ (a + bw^2 + cw)$$
$$= -(a + b + c)\ [a^2 + b^2 + c^2 + ab\ (w + w^2) + bc\ (w + w^2) + ca\ (w + w^2)]$$
$$= -(a + b + c)\ (a^2 + b^2 + c^2 - ab - bc - ca) \quad | \because 1 + w + w^2 = 0$$
$$= -(a^3 + b^3 + c^3 - 3abc)$$

Example 11. If $a + b + c = 0$, solve the equation

$$\begin{vmatrix} a-x & c & b \\ c & b-x & a \\ b & a & c-x \end{vmatrix} = 0$$

Solution: We have,

$$\begin{vmatrix} a-x & c & b \\ c & b-x & a \\ b & a & c-x \end{vmatrix} = 0$$

Operating $C_1 + C_2 + C_3$, we get

$$\begin{vmatrix} a+b+c-x & c & b \\ a+b+c-x & b-x & a \\ a+b+c-x & a & c-x \end{vmatrix} = 0$$

$$\Rightarrow \quad (a+b+c-x)\begin{vmatrix} 1 & c & b \\ 1 & b-x & a \\ 1 & a & c-x \end{vmatrix} = 0$$

Operating $R_2 - R_1$, $R_3 - R_1$, we get

$$(a+b+c-x)\begin{vmatrix} 1 & c & b \\ 0 & b-c-x & a-b \\ 0 & a-c & c-b-x \end{vmatrix} = 0$$

$$\Rightarrow (-x)\begin{vmatrix} 1 & c & b \\ 0 & b-c-x & a-b \\ 0 & a-c & c-b-x \end{vmatrix} = 0 \quad | \because a+b+c=0$$

$$\Rightarrow x\begin{vmatrix} b-c-x & a-b \\ a-c & c-b-x \end{vmatrix} = 0 \quad | \text{ Expanding along } C_1$$

$$\Rightarrow x\left[(b-c-x)(c-b-x)-(a-b)(a-c)\right]=0$$

$$\Rightarrow x\left[-(b-c-x)(b-c+x)-(a-b)(a-c)\right]=0$$

$$\Rightarrow x\left[-(b-c)^2+x^2-(a-b)(a-c)\right]=0$$

$$\Rightarrow x\left[-b^2-c^2+2bc+x^2-a^2+ac+ab-bc\right]=0$$

$$\Rightarrow x\left[x^2-a^2-b^2-c^2+ab+bc+ca\right]=0$$

$$\Rightarrow x=0 \text{ or } x^2=a^2+b^2+c^2-ab-bc-ca$$

$$\Rightarrow x=0 \text{ or } x^2=\left(a^2+b^2+c^2\right) - \frac{1}{2}\left\{(a+b+c)^2-\left(a^2+b^2+c^2\right)\right\}$$

$$\Rightarrow x=0 \text{ or } x^2=\left(a^2+b^2+c^2\right)+\frac{1}{2}\left(a^2+b^2+c^2\right) \quad | \because a+b+c=0$$

$$\Rightarrow x=0 \text{ or } x^2=\frac{3}{2}\left(a^2+b^2+c^2\right)$$

$$\Rightarrow x=0 \text{ or } x=\pm\sqrt{\frac{3}{2}\left(a^2+b^2+c^2\right)}$$

EXERCISE 3.1

1. Show that $\begin{vmatrix} 3 & 2 & 1 \\ 4 & 2 & 2 \\ 1 & 3 & 1 \end{vmatrix} = -6$

2. Show that $\begin{vmatrix} 1^2 & 2^2 & 3^2 \\ 2^2 & 3^2 & 4^2 \\ 3^2 & 4^2 & 5^2 \end{vmatrix} = -8$

3. Show that $\begin{vmatrix} 13 & 16 & 19 \\ 14 & 17 & 20 \\ 15 & 18 & 21 \end{vmatrix} = 0$

4. Show that $\begin{vmatrix} 67 & 19 & 21 \\ 39 & 13 & 14 \\ 81 & 24 & 26 \end{vmatrix} = -43$

5. Show that $\begin{vmatrix} 29 & 26 & 22 \\ 25 & 31 & 27 \\ 63 & 54 & 46 \end{vmatrix} = 132$

6. Show that $\begin{vmatrix} 12 & 5 & -3 & 2 \\ 8 & 6 & 4 & 6 \\ 8 & 3 & -1 & -1 \\ 12 & 4 & 2 & 4 \end{vmatrix} = 616$

7. Show that $\begin{vmatrix} 1 & a & b+c \\ 1 & b & c+a \\ 1 & c & a+b \end{vmatrix} = 0$

8. Show that $\begin{vmatrix} 1 & bc & a(b+c) \\ 1 & ca & b(c+a) \\ 1 & ab & c(a+b) \end{vmatrix} = 0$

9. Show that $\begin{vmatrix} 1 & w & w^2 \\ w & w^2 & 1 \\ w^2 & w & 1 \end{vmatrix} = 0$

10. Show that $\begin{vmatrix} 1 & w^3 & w^2 \\ w^3 & 1 & w \\ w^2 & w & 1 \end{vmatrix} = 3$

11. Show that $\begin{vmatrix} a-b & b-c & c-c \\ b-c & c-a & a-b \\ c-a & a-b & b-c \end{vmatrix} = 0$

12. Show that $\begin{vmatrix} a^2 & bc & ac+c^2 \\ a^2+ab & b^2 & ca \\ ab & b^2+bc & c^2 \end{vmatrix} = 4a^2b^2c^2$

13. Show that $\begin{vmatrix} b+c & a & a \\ b & c+a & b \\ c & c & a+b \end{vmatrix} = 4abc$

14. Show that $\begin{vmatrix} y+z & x & y \\ z+x & z & x \\ x+y & y & z \end{vmatrix} = (x+y+z)(x-z)^2$

15. Show that

$$\begin{vmatrix} a+b+2c & a & b \\ c & b+c+2a & b \\ c & a & c+a+2b \end{vmatrix} = 2(a+b+c)^3$$

16. Show that $\begin{vmatrix} b+c & a-c & a-b \\ b-c & c+a & b-a \\ c-b & c-a & a+b \end{vmatrix} = 8abc$

17. Show that $\begin{vmatrix} b+c & a-b & a \\ c+a & b-c & b \\ a+b & c-a & c \end{vmatrix} = 3abc - a^3 - b^3 - c^3$

18. Show that $\begin{vmatrix} x+a & b & c \\ a & x+b & c \\ a & b & x+c \end{vmatrix} = x^2(x+a+b+c)$

19. Show that $\begin{vmatrix} b+c & a+b & a \\ c+a & b+c & b \\ a+b & c+a & c \end{vmatrix} = a^3+b^3+c^3-3abc$

20. Show that

$$\begin{vmatrix} a+b+c & -c & -b \\ -c & a+b+c & -a \\ -b & -a & a+b+c \end{vmatrix} = 2(a+b)(b+c)(c+a)$$

21. Show that

$$\begin{vmatrix} a & b+c & a^2 \\ b & c+a & b^2 \\ c & a+b & c^2 \end{vmatrix} = -(a+b+c)(a-b)(b-c)(c-a)$$

22. Show that $\begin{vmatrix} a+3b & a+5b & a+7b \\ a+4b & a+6b & a+8b \\ a+5b & a+7b & a+9b \end{vmatrix} = 0$

23. Prove that $\begin{vmatrix} b+c & c+a & a+b \\ q+r & r+p & p+q \\ y+z & z+x & x+y \end{vmatrix} = 2\begin{vmatrix} a & b & c \\ p & q & r \\ x & y & z \end{vmatrix}$

24. Show that $\begin{vmatrix} x & y & z \\ x^2 & y^2 & z^2 \\ yz & zx & xy \end{vmatrix} = \begin{vmatrix} 1 & 1 & 1 \\ x^2 & y^2 & z^2 \\ x^3 & y^3 & z^3 \end{vmatrix}$

$$= (y-z)(z-x)(x-y)(xy+yz+zx)$$

25. Show that $\begin{vmatrix} 1 & 1 & 1 \\ a & b & c \\ a^2 & b^2 & c^2 \end{vmatrix} = (a-b)(b-c)(c-a)$

26. Show that $\begin{vmatrix} 1 & 1 & 1 \\ a & b & c \\ a^3 & b^3 & c^3 \end{vmatrix} = (a-b)(b-c)(c-a)(a+b+c)$

27. Show that $\begin{vmatrix} 1 & 1 & 1 \\ 1 & 1+x & 1 \\ 1 & 1 & 1+y \end{vmatrix} = xy$

28. Show that $\begin{vmatrix} 1 & 1 & 1 & 1 \\ 1 & 1+x & 1 & 1 \\ 1 & 1 & 1+y & 1 \\ 1 & 1 & 1 & 1+z \end{vmatrix} = xyz$

29. Show that $\begin{vmatrix} 1 & a & a^2-bc \\ 1 & b & b^2-ca \\ 1 & c & c^2-ab \end{vmatrix} = 0$

30. Show that $\begin{vmatrix} -2a & a+b & a+c \\ b+c & -2b & b+c \\ c+a & c+b & -2c \end{vmatrix} = 4(a+b)(b+c)(c+a)$

31. Show that $\begin{vmatrix} (b+c)^2 & a^2 & bc \\ (c+a)^2 & b^2 & ca \\ (a+b)^2 & c^2 & ab \end{vmatrix}$

$$= (b-c)(c-a)(a-b)(a+b+c)\left(a^2+b^2+c^2\right)$$

32. Without expanding the determinant, prove that

$$\begin{vmatrix} a & b & c \\ x & y & z \\ p & q & r \end{vmatrix} = \begin{vmatrix} y & b & q \\ x & a & p \\ z & c & r \end{vmatrix} = \begin{vmatrix} x & y & z \\ p & q & r \\ a & b & c \end{vmatrix}$$

33. Prove that $\begin{vmatrix} y^2z^2 & yz & y+z \\ z^2x^2 & zx & z+x \\ x^2y^2 & xy & x+y \end{vmatrix} = 0$

34. Show that $\begin{vmatrix} a^2 & a^2-(b-c)^2 & bc \\ b^2 & b^2-(c-a)^2 & ca \\ c^2 & c^2-(a-b)^2 & ab \end{vmatrix}$

$$= (b-c)(c-a)(a-b)(a+b+c)(a^2+b^2+c^2)$$

35. Show that $\begin{vmatrix} b^2c^2+a^2 & bc+a & 1 \\ c^2a^2+b^2 & ca+b & 1 \\ a^2b^2+c^2 & ab+c & 1 \end{vmatrix}$

$$= (a-b)(b-c)(c-a)(a-1)(b-1)(c-1)$$

36. Show that $\begin{vmatrix} 1 & 1 & 1 \\ bc(b+c) & ca(c+a) & ab(a+b) \\ b^2c^2 & c^2a^2 & a^2b^2 \end{vmatrix}$

$$= abc(a-b)(b-c)(c-a)$$

37. Show that $\begin{vmatrix} 1 & bc+ad & b^2c^2+a^2d^2 \\ 1 & ca+bd & c^2a^2+b^2d^2 \\ 1 & ab+cd & a^2b^2+c^2d^2 \end{vmatrix}$

$$= (c-d)(a-b)(b-d)(a-c)(a-d)(b-c)$$

38. Show that $\begin{vmatrix} (a+b)^2 & ca & bc \\ ca & (b+c)^2 & ab \\ bc & ab & (c+a)^2 \end{vmatrix} = 2abc(a+b+c)^3$

39. Show that $\begin{vmatrix} (b+c)^2 & c^2 & b^2 \\ c^2 & (c+a)^2 & a^2 \\ b^2 & a^2 & (a+b)^2 \end{vmatrix} = 2(ab+bc+ca)^3$

40. If $2s = a + b + c$, prove that

$$\begin{vmatrix} a^2 & (s-a)^2 & (s-a)^2 \\ (s-b)^2 & b^2 & (s-b)^2 \\ (s-c)^2 & (s-c)^2 & c^2 \end{vmatrix} = 2s^3(s-a)(s-b)(s-c)$$

41. Prove that $x = -1$ is a root of the equation

$$\begin{vmatrix} 2-x & 3 & 3 \\ 3 & 4-x & 5 \\ 3 & 5 & 4-x \end{vmatrix} = 0$$

42. Prove that $x = 1$ is a root of the equation

$$\begin{vmatrix} x+1 & 3 & 5 \\ 2 & x+2 & 5 \\ 2 & 3 & x+4 \end{vmatrix} = 0$$

43. Show that

$$\begin{vmatrix} a & b & ax+by \\ b & c & bx+ay \\ ax+by & bx+cy & 0 \end{vmatrix} = (b^2-ac)(ax^2+2bxy+cy^2)^2$$

44. Show that $\begin{vmatrix} a & b & c \\ a' & b' & c' \\ a'' & b'' & c'' \end{vmatrix} = \dfrac{1}{abc}\begin{vmatrix} 1 & 1 & 1 \\ a'bc & b'ca & c'ab \\ a''bc & b''ca & c''ab \end{vmatrix}$

45. Show that

$$\begin{vmatrix} 1 & yz & y+z \\ 1 & zx & z+x \\ 1 & xy & x+y \end{vmatrix} = \begin{vmatrix} 1 & x & x^2 \\ 1 & y & y^2 \\ 1 & z & z^2 \end{vmatrix} = (x-y)(y-z)(z-x)$$

46. Solve the following equations:

(i) $\begin{vmatrix} a & a & x \\ m & m & m \\ b & x & b \end{vmatrix} = 0$

(ii) $\begin{vmatrix} x & -6 & -1 \\ 2 & -3x & x-3 \\ -3 & 2x & x+2 \end{vmatrix} = 0$

(iii) $\begin{vmatrix} x-2 & 2x-3 & 3x-4 \\ x-4 & 2x-9 & 3x-16 \\ x-8 & 2x-27 & 3x-64 \end{vmatrix} = 0$

(iv) $\begin{vmatrix} 4x & 6x+2 & 8x+1 \\ 6x+2 & 9x+2 & 12x \\ 8x+1 & 12x & 16x+2 \end{vmatrix} = 0$

(v) $\begin{vmatrix} a+x & a-x & a-x \\ a-x & a+x & a-x \\ a-x & a-x & a+x \end{vmatrix} = 0$

(vi) $\begin{vmatrix} p+x & q+r & r+x \\ q+r & r+x & p+x \\ r+x & p+x & q+x \end{vmatrix} = 0$

(vii) $\begin{vmatrix} x & c+x & b+x \\ c+x & x & a+x \\ b+x & a+x & x \end{vmatrix} = 0$

(viii) $\begin{vmatrix} x+2 & 2x+3 & 3x+4 \\ 2x+3 & 3x+4 & 4x+5 \\ 3x+5 & 5x+8 & 10x+17 \end{vmatrix} = 0$

47. Show that

(i) $\begin{vmatrix} 3 & 2 & 1 & 4 \\ 15 & 29 & 2 & 14 \\ 16 & 19 & 3 & 17 \\ 33 & 39 & 8 & 38 \end{vmatrix} = 6$

(ii) $\begin{vmatrix} 3 & 7 & 9 & 6 \\ 8 & 4 & 5 & 8 \\ 7 & 10 & 3 & 5 \\ 6 & 2 & 9 & 8 \end{vmatrix} = -500$

(iii) $\begin{vmatrix} 5 & 7 & 10 & 14 \\ 2 & 3 & 7 & 6 \\ 3 & 3 & 6 & 9 \\ 5 & 6 & 11 & 20 \end{vmatrix} = 96$

(iv) $\begin{vmatrix} 21 & 17 & 7 & 10 \\ 24 & 22 & 6 & 10 \\ 6 & 8 & 2 & 3 \\ 5 & 7 & 1 & 2 \end{vmatrix} = 0$

48. If $\begin{vmatrix} x & x^2 & 1+x^3 \\ y & y^2 & 1+y^3 \\ z & z^2 & 1+z^2 \end{vmatrix} = 0$, show that $xyz = -1$

49. Show that $\begin{vmatrix} 1+x & 2 & 3 & 4 \\ 1 & 2+x & 3 & 4 \\ 1 & 2 & 3+x & 4 \\ 1 & 2 & 3 & 4+x \end{vmatrix} = x^3(x+10)$

50. Prove that $x = 0$ or $x + a + b + c + d = 0$, if

$$\begin{vmatrix} x+a & b & c & d \\ a & x+b & c & d \\ a & b & x+c & d \\ a & b & c & x+d \end{vmatrix} = 0$$

51. Show that

$$\begin{vmatrix} 0 & -c & b & -l \\ c & 0 & -a & -m \\ -b & a & 0 & -n \\ x & y & z & 0 \end{vmatrix} = (al + bm + cn)(ax + by + cz)$$

52. Prove that $\begin{vmatrix} x^3 & 3x^2 & 3x & 1 \\ x^2 & x^2+2x & 2x+1 & 1 \\ x & 2x+1 & x+2 & 1 \\ 1 & 3 & 3 & 1 \end{vmatrix} = (x-1)^6$

53. Prove that $\begin{vmatrix} a & b & c & d \\ -b & a & -d & c \\ -c & d & a & -b \\ -d & -c & b & a \end{vmatrix} = (a^2 + b^2 + c^2 + d^2)^2$

54. Prove that $\begin{vmatrix} 1 & a & a^2 & a^3+bcd \\ 1 & b & b^2 & b^3+cda \\ 1 & c & c^2 & c^3+dab \\ 1 & d & d^2 & d^3+abc \end{vmatrix} = 0$

55. Show that

$$\begin{vmatrix} a^2+\lambda & ab & ac & ad \\ ba & b^2+\lambda & bc & bd \\ ca & cb & c^2+\lambda & cd \\ da & db & dc & d^2+\lambda \end{vmatrix}$$

$$= \lambda^3\left(a^2+b^2+c^2+d^2+\lambda\right)$$

$$= \begin{vmatrix} a^2+\lambda & a^2 & a^2 & a^2 \\ b^2 & b^2+\lambda & b^2 & b^2 \\ c^2 & c^2 & c^2+\lambda & c^2 \\ d^2 & d^2 & d^2 & d^2+\lambda \end{vmatrix}$$

ANSWERS

46. (i) a, b

(ii) $1, 2, -3$

(iii) 4

(iv) $-\dfrac{19}{89}$

(v) $0, 3a$

(vi) $-\dfrac{1}{3}(p+q+r)$

(vii) $\dfrac{2abc}{a^2+b^2+c^2-2(ab+bc+ca)}$

(viii) $-1, -1, -2$

3.14. Product of Two Determinants (Row by Row Rule)

Theorem 1. The product of two determinants, each of second order, is itself, a determinant of the second order.

Proof. Let $A = \begin{vmatrix} a_{11} & a_{12} \\ a_{21} & a_{22} \end{vmatrix}$ and $B = \begin{vmatrix} b_{11} & b_{12} \\ b_{21} & b_{22} \end{vmatrix}$

We shall prove that

$$AB = \begin{vmatrix} a_{11}b_{11}+a_{12}b_{12} & a_{11}b_{21}+a_{12}b_{22} \\ a_{21}b_{11}+a_{22}b_{12} & a_{21}b_{21}+a_{22}b_{22} \end{vmatrix}$$

The determinant on RHS can be expressed as the sum of 2 × 2, i.e. 4 determinants as

$$\begin{vmatrix} a_{11}b_{11}+a_{12}b_{12} & a_{11}b_{21}+a_{12}b_{22} \\ a_{21}b_{11}+a_{22}b_{12} & a_{21}b_{21}+a_{22}b_{22} \end{vmatrix}$$

$$= \begin{vmatrix} a_{11}b_{11} & a_{11}b_{21} \\ a_{21}b_{11} & a_{21}b_{21} \end{vmatrix} + \begin{vmatrix} a_{11}b_{11} & a_{12}b_{22} \\ a_{21}b_{11} & a_{22}b_{22} \end{vmatrix} + \begin{vmatrix} a_{12}b_{12} & a_{11}b_{21} \\ a_{22}b_{12} & a_{21}b_{21} \end{vmatrix} + \begin{vmatrix} a_{12}b_{12} & a_{12}b_{22} \\ a_{22}b_{12} & a_{22}b_{22} \end{vmatrix}$$

$$= a_{11}a_{21}\begin{vmatrix} b_{11} & b_{21} \\ b_{11} & b_{21} \end{vmatrix} + b_{11}b_{22}\begin{vmatrix} a_{11} & a_{12} \\ a_{21} & a_{22} \end{vmatrix} + b_{12}b_{21}\begin{vmatrix} a_{12} & a_{11} \\ a_{22} & a_{21} \end{vmatrix} + b_{11}b_{22}\begin{vmatrix} a_{11} & a_{12} \\ a_{21} & a_{22} \end{vmatrix}$$

$$= a_{11}a_{21}(0) + b_{11}b_{22}\begin{vmatrix} a_{11} & a_{12} \\ a_{21} & a_{22} \end{vmatrix} - b_{12}b_{21}\begin{vmatrix} a_{11} & a_{12} \\ a_{21} & a_{22} \end{vmatrix} + b_{12}b_{22}(0)$$

$$= \begin{vmatrix} a_{11} & a_{12} \\ a_{21} & a_{22} \end{vmatrix}(b_{11}\, b_{12} - b_{12}\, b_{21})$$

$$= \begin{vmatrix} a_{11} & a_{12} \\ a_{21} & a_{22} \end{vmatrix}\begin{vmatrix} b_{11} & b_{12} \\ b_{21} & b_{22} \end{vmatrix}$$

Hence, the theorem.

The rule by which the product *AB* is constructed from the elements of *A* and *B* is called row-by-row rule.

According to this rule, we multiply the elements of R_1 in *A* (first determinant) with the corresponding elements of R_1 in *B* (second determinant) and add them up. We get the first element of R_1 in *AB*. Similarly, for second element of R_1. Similarly, elements of R_2 in *AB* can be found out.

Theorem 2. The product of two determinants, each of third order, is itself a determinant of third order.

Proof. Let $\Delta_1 = \begin{vmatrix} a_1 & b_1 & c_1 \\ a_2 & b_2 & c_2 \\ a_3 & b_3 & c_3 \end{vmatrix}$ and $\Delta_2 = \begin{vmatrix} \alpha_1 & \beta_1 & \gamma_1 \\ \alpha_2 & \beta_2 & \gamma_2 \\ \alpha_3 & \beta_3 & \gamma_3 \end{vmatrix}$

We shall prove that

$$\Delta_1\Delta_2 = \begin{vmatrix} a_1\alpha_1 + b_1\beta_1 + c_1\gamma_1 & a_1\alpha_2 + b_1\beta_2 + c_1\gamma_2 & a_1\alpha_3 + b_1\beta_3 + c_1\gamma_3 \\ a_2\alpha_1 + b_2\beta_1 + c_2\gamma_1 & a_2\alpha_2 + b_2\beta_2 + c_2\gamma_2 & a_2\alpha_3 + b_2\beta_3 + c_2\gamma_3 \\ a_3\alpha_1 + b_3\beta_1 + c_3\gamma_1 & a_3\alpha_2 + b_3\beta_2 + c_3\gamma_2 & a_3\alpha_3 + b_3\beta_3 + c_3\gamma_3 \end{vmatrix}$$

The determinant on RHS can be expressed as the sum of 3 × 3 × 3, i.e. 27 determinants. These determinants can be grouped in three ways. One group having the first column as $a_1\alpha_1, a_2\alpha_1, a_3\alpha_1$ is

$$\begin{vmatrix} a_1\alpha_1 & a_1\alpha_2 & a_1\alpha_3 \\ a_2\alpha_1 & a_2\alpha_2 & a_2\alpha_3 \\ a_3\alpha_1 & a_3\alpha_2 & a_3\alpha_3 \end{vmatrix}, \begin{vmatrix} a_1\alpha_1 & a_1\alpha_2 & b_1\beta_3 \\ a_2\alpha_1 & a_2\alpha_2 & b_2\beta_3 \\ a_3\alpha_1 & a_3\alpha_2 & b_3\beta_3 \end{vmatrix},$$

$$\begin{vmatrix} a_1\alpha_1 & a_1\alpha_2 & c_1\gamma_3 \\ a_2\alpha_1 & a_2\alpha_2 & c_2\gamma_3 \\ a_3\alpha_1 & a_3\alpha_2 & c_3\gamma_3 \end{vmatrix}, \begin{vmatrix} a_1\alpha_1 & b_1\beta_2 & a_1\alpha_3 \\ a_2\alpha_1 & b_2\beta_2 & a_2\alpha_3 \\ a_3\alpha_1 & b_3\beta_2 & a_3\alpha_3 \end{vmatrix},$$

$$\begin{vmatrix} a_1\alpha_1 & b_1\beta_2 & b_1\beta_3 \\ a_2\alpha_1 & b_2\beta_2 & b_2\beta_3 \\ a_3\alpha_1 & b_3\beta_2 & b_3\beta_3 \end{vmatrix}, \begin{vmatrix} a_1\alpha_1 & b_1\beta_2 & c_1\gamma_3 \\ a_2\alpha_1 & b_2\beta_2 & c_2\gamma_3 \\ a_3\alpha_1 & b_3\beta_2 & c_3\gamma_3 \end{vmatrix},$$

$$\begin{vmatrix} a_1\alpha_1 & c_1\gamma_2 & a_1\alpha_3 \\ a_2\alpha_1 & c_2\gamma_2 & a_2\alpha_3 \\ a_3\alpha_1 & c_3\gamma_2 & a_3\alpha_3 \end{vmatrix}, \begin{vmatrix} a_1\alpha_1 & c_1\gamma_2 & b_1\beta_3 \\ a_2\alpha_1 & c_2\gamma_2 & b_2\beta_3 \\ a_3\alpha_1 & c_3\gamma_2 & b_3\beta_3 \end{vmatrix},$$

$$\begin{vmatrix} a_1\alpha_1 & c_1\gamma_2 & c_1\gamma_3 \\ a_2\alpha_1 & c_2\gamma_2 & c_2\gamma_3 \\ a_3\alpha_1 & c_3\gamma_2 & c_3\gamma_3 \end{vmatrix}$$

Out of these nine, seven vanish	Two or three lines being identical

Thus, we are left with two determinants

$$\begin{vmatrix} a_1\alpha_1 & b_1\beta_2 & c_1\gamma_3 \\ a_2\alpha_1 & b_2\beta_2 & c_2\gamma_3 \\ a_3\alpha_1 & b_3\beta_2 & c_3\gamma_3 \end{vmatrix} \text{ and } \begin{vmatrix} a_1\alpha_1 & c_1\gamma_2 & b_1\beta_3 \\ a_2\alpha_1 & c_2\gamma_2 & b_2\beta_3 \\ a_3\alpha_1 & c_3\gamma_2 & b_3\beta_3 \end{vmatrix}$$

$$\text{or, } \alpha_1\beta_2\gamma_3 \begin{vmatrix} a_1 & b_1 & c_1 \\ a_2 & b_2 & c_2 \\ a_3 & b_3 & c_3 \end{vmatrix} \text{ and } \alpha_1\beta_3\gamma_2 \begin{vmatrix} a_1 & c_1 & b_1 \\ a_2 & c_2 & b_2 \\ a_3 & c_3 & b_3 \end{vmatrix}, \text{ i.e.}$$

$$-\alpha_1\beta_3\gamma_2 \begin{vmatrix} a_1 & b_1 & c_1 \\ a_2 & b_2 & c_2 \\ a_3 & b_3 & c_3 \end{vmatrix}$$

Their sum

$$= (\alpha_1\beta_2\gamma_3 - \alpha_1\beta_3\gamma_2) \begin{vmatrix} a_1 & b_1 & c_1 \\ a_2 & b_2 & c_2 \\ a_3 & b_3 & c_3 \end{vmatrix}$$

Similarly, the sum of second group

$$= (\alpha_2\beta_3\gamma_1 - \alpha_2\beta_1\gamma_3) \begin{vmatrix} a_1 & b_1 & c_1 \\ a_2 & b_2 & c_2 \\ a_3 & b_3 & c_3 \end{vmatrix}$$

and, the sum of third group

$$= (\alpha_3\beta_1\gamma_2 - \alpha_3\beta_2\gamma_1) \begin{vmatrix} a_1 & b_1 & c_1 \\ a_2 & b_2 & c_2 \\ a_3 & b_3 & c_3 \end{vmatrix}$$

Therefore, the sum of all 27 determinants

$$= \left[\alpha_1(\beta_2\gamma_3 - \beta_3\gamma_2) + \alpha_2(\beta_3\gamma_1 - \beta_1\gamma_3) + \alpha_3(\beta_1\gamma_2 - \beta_2\gamma_1)\right] \begin{vmatrix} a_1 & b_1 & c_1 \\ a_2 & b_2 & c_2 \\ a_3 & b_3 & c_3 \end{vmatrix}$$

$$= \begin{vmatrix} \alpha_1 & \beta_1 & \gamma_1 \\ \alpha_2 & \beta_2 & \gamma_2 \\ \alpha_3 & \beta_3 & \gamma_3 \end{vmatrix} \begin{vmatrix} a_1 & b_1 & c_1 \\ a_2 & b_2 & c_2 \\ a_3 & b_3 & c_3 \end{vmatrix}$$

$$= \Delta_2\Delta_1$$

$$= \Delta_1\Delta_2$$

Hence, the theorem.

Again, we have multiplied the two determinants, each of third order by row-by-row rule. According to this rule, we multiply the elements of R_1 in Δ_1 (first determinant) with the corresponding elements of R_1 in Δ_2 (second determinant) and add them up. We get the first element of R_1 in $\Delta_1\Delta_2$. Similarly, for second element of R_1. Similarly, elements of R_2 and R_3 in $\Delta_1\Delta_2$ can be found out.

Remark 1. The product of two determinants can also be constructed by applying row-by-column rule or column-by-row rule or column-by-column rule. (A determinant retains its value as such even if rows are changed into columns and columns into rows.) In practice, we usually follow row-by-row rule. However, while multiplying two matrices, conformable for multiplication, only row-by-column rule is applied.

Theorem 3. The product of two determinants of any order is itself a determinant of the same order.

Proof. We have proved the result for two determinants of order 2 and order 3 in Theorem 1 and Theorem 2, respectively. However, the nature of the proof shows that it is equally applicable in general.

Theorem 4. The determinant of the product of two or more square matrices is equal to the product of their determinants.

Proof. Let $A = [a_{ij}]_{n \times n}$ and $B = [b_{ij}]_{n \times n}$ be two square matrices of the same order n. Then,

$$AB = \left[\sum_{k=1}^{n} a_{ik}\, b_{kj} \right]; \begin{array}{l} i = 1, 2, ..., n \\ j = 1, 2, ..., n \end{array}$$

$$\Rightarrow |AB| = \left| \sum_{k=1}^{n} a_{ik}\, b_{kj} \right|; \begin{array}{l} i = 1, 2, ..., n \\ j = 1, 2, ..., n \end{array}$$

$$\Rightarrow |AB| = |A|\,|B|$$ | By row-by-column rule for the multiplication of two determinants

Generalisation

The above theorem is true for more than two matrices, i.e. $|A\ B\ C\ .....\ K| = |A|\ |B|\ |C|\ .....\ |K|$

Note 1. $|AA| = |A|\ |A| = |A^2|$

Note 2. One may easily see that $|AB| = |BA|$ always. However, $AB \neq BA$, in general.

3.15. Product of Two Determinants of Different Orders

$$\begin{vmatrix} a_1 & b_1 & c_1 \\ a_2 & b_2 & c_2 \\ a_3 & b_3 & c_3 \end{vmatrix} \times \begin{vmatrix} \alpha_1 & \beta_1 \\ \alpha_2 & \beta_2 \end{vmatrix} = \begin{vmatrix} a_1 & b_1 & c_1 \\ a_2 & b_2 & c_2 \\ a_3 & b_3 & c_3 \end{vmatrix} \begin{vmatrix} \alpha_1 & \beta_1 & 0 \\ \alpha_2 & \beta_2 & 0 \\ 0 & 0 & 1 \end{vmatrix}$$

$$= \begin{vmatrix} a_1\alpha_1 + b_1\beta_1 & a_1\alpha_2 + b_1\beta_2 & c_1 \\ a_2\alpha_1 + b_2\beta_1 & a_2\alpha_2 + b_2\beta_2 & c_2 \\ a_3\alpha_1 + b_3\beta_1 & a_3\alpha_2 + b_3\beta_2 & c_3 \end{vmatrix}$$

3.16. Reciprocal Determinant or Adjoint Determinant

$$\text{Let } \Delta = \begin{vmatrix} a_{11} & a_{12} & ... & a_{1n} \\ a_{21} & a_{22} & ... & a_{2n} \\ ... & ... & ... & ... \\ a_{n1} & a_{n2} & ... & a_{nn} \end{vmatrix}$$

$$\text{and, } \Delta' = \begin{vmatrix} A_{11} & A_{12} & \dots & A_{1n} \\ A_{21} & A_{22} & \dots & A_{2n} \\ \dots & \dots & \dots & \dots \\ A_{n1} & A_{n2} & \dots & A_{nn} \end{vmatrix}$$

where A's are the cofactors of the corresponding a's. Then, the determinant Δ' is called the reciprocal (or adjoint) determinant of Δ. The cofactors A_{ij} $(i, j = 1, 2, \dots, n)$ are called *inverse elements*.

Note. Δ' may be written as adj Δ.

3.17. Theorem

If Δ is a determinant of order n, then $\Delta^1 = \Delta^{n-1}$

Proof. We have,

$$\Delta\Delta' = \begin{vmatrix} a_{11} & a_{12} & \dots & a_{1n} \\ a_{21} & a_{22} & \dots & a_{2n} \\ \dots & \dots & \dots & \dots \\ a_{n1} & a_{n2} & \dots & a_{nn} \end{vmatrix} \begin{vmatrix} A_{11} & A_{12} & \dots & A_{1n} \\ A_{21} & A_{22} & \dots & A_{2n} \\ \dots & \dots & \dots & \dots \\ A_{n1} & A_{n2} & \dots & A_{nn} \end{vmatrix}$$

$$= \begin{vmatrix} \Delta & 0 & \dots & 0 \\ 0 & \Delta & \dots & 0 \\ \dots & \dots & \dots & \dots \\ 0 & 0 & \dots & \Delta \end{vmatrix} \qquad \left| \begin{aligned} \because \sum_{k=1}^{n} a_{ik} A_{jk} &= \Delta_1 \text{ when } i = j \\ &= 0 \text{ when } i \neq j \end{aligned} \right.$$

$$= \Delta^n$$

$$\Rightarrow \Delta^1 = \Delta^{n-1}$$

Hence, the theorem.

Particularisation

For a determinant of order 3, we have

$n = 3$

$\therefore$ In this case,

$\Delta^1 = \Delta^{3-1}$

$\Rightarrow \Delta^1 = \Delta^2$

ILLUSTRATIVE EXAMPLES

Example 1. Show that

$$\begin{vmatrix} 0 & c & b \\ c & 0 & a \\ b & a & 0 \end{vmatrix}^2 = \begin{vmatrix} b^2+c^2 & ab & ac \\ ab & c^2+a^2 & bc \\ ac & bc & a^2+b^2 \end{vmatrix}$$

Hence or otherwise show that the value of the determinant on the right hand side is equal to $4a^2b^2c^2$.

Solution: Applying row-by-row rule for the multiplication of two determinants, we have,

$$\begin{vmatrix} 0 & c & b \\ c & 0 & a \\ b & a & 0 \end{vmatrix}^2 = \begin{vmatrix} 0 & c & b \\ c & 0 & a \\ b & a & 0 \end{vmatrix}\begin{vmatrix} 0 & c & b \\ c & 0 & a \\ b & a & 0 \end{vmatrix}$$

$$= \begin{vmatrix} 0.0+c.c+b.b & 0.c+c.0+b.a & 0.b+c.a+b.0 \\ c.0+0.c+a.b & c.c+0.0+a.a & c.b+0.a+a.0 \\ b.0+a.c+0.b & b.c+a.0+0.a & b.b+a.a+0.0 \end{vmatrix}$$

$$= \begin{vmatrix} b^2+c^2 & ab & ac \\ ab & c^2+a^2 & bc \\ ac & bc & a^2+b^2 \end{vmatrix}$$

Again,

$$\begin{vmatrix} 0 & c & b \\ c & 0 & a \\ b & a & 0 \end{vmatrix} = 0\begin{vmatrix} 0 & a \\ a & 0 \end{vmatrix} - c\begin{vmatrix} c & a \\ b & 0 \end{vmatrix} + b\begin{vmatrix} c & 0 \\ b & a \end{vmatrix}$$ | Expanding along R_1

$$= abc + abc$$
$$= 2abc$$

Hence, the value of the determinant on the right hand side = $(2abc)^2 = 4a^2b^2c^2$

Example 2. Find the value of

$$\begin{vmatrix} l_1 & m_1 & n_1 \\ l_2 & m_2 & n_2 \\ l_3 & m_3 & n_3 \end{vmatrix}$$

where,

$$l_1^2 + m_1^2 + n_1^2 = 1, \text{ etc.}$$

and

$$l_1 l_2 + m_1 m_2 + n_1 n_2 = 0, \text{ etc.}$$

Solution:

$$\text{Let } \Delta = \begin{vmatrix} l_1 & m_1 & n_1 \\ l_2 & m_2 & n_2 \\ l_3 & m_3 & n_3 \end{vmatrix}$$

Then,

$$\Delta^2 = \Delta\Delta$$

$$= \begin{vmatrix} l_1 & m_1 & n_1 \\ l_2 & m_2 & n_2 \\ l_3 & m_3 & n_3 \end{vmatrix} \begin{vmatrix} l_1 & m_1 & n_1 \\ l_2 & m_2 & n_2 \\ l_3 & m_3 & n_3 \end{vmatrix}$$

$$= \begin{vmatrix} l_1^2 + m_1^2 + n_1^2 & l_1 l_2 + m_1 m_2 + n_1 n_2 & l_1 l_3 + m_1 m_3 + n_1 n_3 \\ l_1 l_2 + m_1 m_2 + n_1 n_2 & l_2^1 + m_2^2 + n_2^2 & l_2 l_3 + m_2 m_3 + n_2 n_3 \\ l_3 l_1 + m_3 m_1 + n_3 n_1 & l_2 l_3 + m_2 m_3 + n_2 n_3 & l_3^2 + m_3^2 + n_3^2 \end{vmatrix}$$

| Applying row-by-row rule for the multiplication of two determinants

$$= \begin{vmatrix} 1 & 0 & 0 \\ 0 & 0 & 1 \\ 0 & 0 & 1 \end{vmatrix}$$

| $\because l_1^2 + m_1^2 + n_2^2 = 1$, etc
| and, $l_1 l_2 + m_1 m_2 + n_1 n_2 = 0$, etc.

$= 1$ | Expanding the determinant

$\Rightarrow \ \Delta = \pm 1$

Example 3. Prove that

$$\begin{vmatrix} a & b & c \\ b & c & a \\ c & a & b \end{vmatrix}^2 = \begin{vmatrix} 2bc - a^2 & c^2 & b^2 \\ c^2 & 2ac - b^2 & a^2 \\ b^2 & a^2 & 2ab - c^2 \end{vmatrix}$$

$$= \left(a^3 + b^3 + c^3 - 3abc\right)^2$$

Solution: We have,

$$\begin{vmatrix} a & b & c \\ b & c & a \\ c & a & b \end{vmatrix}^2 = \begin{vmatrix} a & b & c \\ b & c & a \\ c & a & b \end{vmatrix} \times \begin{vmatrix} a & b & c \\ b & c & a \\ c & a & b \end{vmatrix}$$

$$= \begin{vmatrix} a & b & c \\ b & c & a \\ c & a & b \end{vmatrix} \times (-1) \begin{vmatrix} a & c & b \\ b & a & c \\ c & b & a \end{vmatrix}$$

| Interchanging C_2 and C_3 in the second determinant

$$= \begin{vmatrix} a & b & c \\ b & c & a \\ c & a & b \end{vmatrix} \times \begin{vmatrix} -a & c & b \\ -b & a & c \\ -c & b & a \end{vmatrix}$$

| Multiplying C_1 by (–1)

$$= \begin{vmatrix} -a^2 + bc + cb & -ab + ba + c^2 & -ac + b^2 + ca \\ -ba + c^2 + cb & -b^2 + ca + ac & -bc + cb + a^2 \\ -ca + ac + b^2 & -cb + a^2 + bc & -c^2 + ab + ba \end{vmatrix}$$

$$= \begin{vmatrix} 2bc - a^2 & c^2 & b^2 \\ c^2 & 2ac - b^2 & a^2 \\ b^2 & a^2 & 2ab - c^2 \end{vmatrix}$$

Again,

$$\begin{vmatrix} a & b & c \\ b & c & a \\ c & a & b \end{vmatrix} = \begin{vmatrix} a+b+c & a+b+c & a+b+c \\ b & c & a \\ c & a & b \end{vmatrix}$$

| Operating $R_1 + R_2 + R_3$

$$= (a+b+c)\begin{vmatrix} 1 & 1 & 1 \\ b & c & a \\ c & a & b \end{vmatrix}$$

| Operating $C_2 - C_1$, $C_3 - C_1$

$$= (a+b+c)\begin{vmatrix} 1 & 0 & 0 \\ b & c-b & a-b \\ c & a-c & b-c \end{vmatrix}$$

$$= (a+b+c)\begin{vmatrix} c-b & a-b \\ a-c & b-c \end{vmatrix}$$

| Expanding along R_1

$$= (a+b+c)\,[(c-b)(b-c) - (a-c)(a-b)]$$
$$= (a+b+c)\,[cb - c^2 - b^2 + bc - a^2 + ab + ca - cb]$$
$$= -(a+b+c)(a^2 + b^2 + c^2 - ab - bc - ca)$$
$$= -(a^3 + b^3 + c^3 - 3abc)$$

$$\therefore \quad \begin{vmatrix} a & b & c \\ b & c & a \\ c & a & b \end{vmatrix}^2 = \{-(a^3 + b^3 + c^3 - 3abc)\}^2$$

$$= (a^3 + b^3 + c^3 - 3abc)^2$$

Example 4. Show that $\begin{vmatrix} a+ib & c+id \\ -c+id & a-ib \end{vmatrix} \times \begin{vmatrix} \alpha - i\beta & \gamma - i\delta \\ -\gamma - i\delta & -\alpha + \beta i \end{vmatrix}$ can be expressed as $\begin{vmatrix} A-iB & C-iD \\ -C-iD & A+iB \end{vmatrix}$, where $i = \sqrt{-1}$. Hence, prove Euler's Theorem. [The product of two sums each of four squares is itself the sum of four squares.]

Also, express $(9^2 + 2^2 + 3^2 + 4^2)(2^2 + 6^2 + 7^2 + 8^2)$ as sum of four squares.

Solution: By usual rule for multiplication of determinants, we have

$$\begin{vmatrix} a+ib & c+id \\ -c+id & a-ib \end{vmatrix} \times \begin{vmatrix} \alpha - i\beta & \gamma - i\delta \\ -\gamma - i\delta & -\alpha + \beta i \end{vmatrix}$$

$$= \begin{vmatrix} a\alpha + b\beta + c\gamma + d\delta & -a\gamma + b\delta + c\alpha - d\beta \\ -i(a\beta - b\alpha + c\delta - d\gamma) & -i(a\delta + b\gamma - c\beta - d\alpha) \\ a\gamma - b\delta - c\alpha + d\beta & a\alpha + b\beta + c\gamma + d\delta \\ -i(a\delta + b\gamma - c\beta - d\alpha) & +i(a\beta - b\alpha + c\delta - d\gamma) \end{vmatrix}$$

$$= \begin{vmatrix} A - iB & C - iD \\ -c - iD & A + iB \end{vmatrix}$$

where

$A = a\alpha + b\beta + c\gamma + d\delta$

$B = a\beta - b\alpha + c\delta - d\gamma$

$C = -a\gamma + b\delta + c\alpha - d\beta$

$D = a\delta + b\gamma - c\beta - d\alpha$

Now, expanding the determinants on both sides, we have

$$(a^2 + b^2 + c^2 + d^2)(\alpha^2 + \beta^2 + \gamma^2 + \delta^2) = A^2 + B^2 + C^2 + D^2$$

which is Euler's Theorem which asserts that the product of two sums, each of four squares is itself the sum of four squares.

Again, in the product

$(9^2 + 2^2 + 3^2 + 4^2)(5^2 + 6^2 + 7^2 + 8^2)$, we have

$a = 9$

$b = 2$

$c = 3$

$d = 4$

$\alpha = 5$
$\beta = 6$
$\gamma = 7$
$\delta = 8$

$\therefore \quad A = 110$
$B = 40$
$C = 56$
$D = 48$

Hence,

$$(9^2 + 2^2 + 3^2 + 4^2)(5^2 + 6^2 + 7^2 + 8^2)$$
$$= 110^2 + 40^2 + 56^2 + 48^2$$

Example 5. Show that

$$\begin{vmatrix} a_1 & b_1 & c_1 \\ a_2 & b_2 & c_2 \\ a_3 & b_3 & c_3 \end{vmatrix}^2 = \begin{vmatrix} A_1 & B_1 & C_1 \\ A_2 & B_2 & C_2 \\ A_3 & B_3 & C_3 \end{vmatrix} \text{ where}$$

A_1, B_1, C_1, etc. are the cofactors of a_1, b_1, c_1, etc. in the determinants on the left.

Solution: Let Δ and Δ^1 denote the determinants on the left hand and right hand sides respectively. Then,

$$\Delta\Delta' = \begin{vmatrix} a_1A_1 + b_1B_1 + c_1C_1 & a_2A_1 + b_2B_1 + c_2C_1 & a_3A_1 + b_3B_1 + c_3C_1 \\ a_1A_2 + b_1B_2 + c_1C_2 & a_2A_2 + b_2B_2 + c_2C_2 & a_3A_2 + b_3B_2 + c_3C_2 \\ a_1A_3 + b_1B_3 + c_1C_3 & a_2A_3 + b_2B_3 + c_2C_3 & a_3A_3 + b_3B_3 + c_3C_3 \end{vmatrix}$$

$$= \begin{vmatrix} \Delta & 0 & 0 \\ 0 & \Delta & 0 \\ 0 & 0 & \Delta \end{vmatrix} \qquad | \text{ By property of cofactors}$$

$$= \Delta^3$$

$\Rightarrow \Delta^1 = \Delta^2$

Hence, the result.

Example 6. Prove that

$$\begin{vmatrix} a & b & c \\ c & a & b \\ b & c & a \end{vmatrix}^2 = \begin{vmatrix} a^2 - bc & b^2 - ca & c^2 - ab \\ c^2 - ab & a^2 - bc & b^2 - ca \\ b^2 - ca & c^2 - ab & a^2 - bc \end{vmatrix}$$

Solution:

$$\text{Let } \Delta = \begin{vmatrix} a & b & c \\ c & a & b \\ b & c & a \end{vmatrix}$$

Then,

Δ' = Reciprocal determinant of Δ

= The determinant in which each element is the cofactor of the corresponding element of Δ

$$= \begin{vmatrix} (a^2 - bc) & -(ca - b^2) & (c^2 - ab) \\ -(ab - c^2) & (a^2 - bc) & -(ca - b^2) \\ (b^2 - ca) & -(ab - c^2) & (a^2 - bc) \end{vmatrix}$$

$$= \begin{vmatrix} a^2 - bc & b^2 - ca & c^2 - ab \\ c^2 - ab & a^2 - bc & b^2 - ca \\ b^2 - ca & c^2 - ab & a^2 - bc \end{vmatrix}$$

$= \Delta^2$ | By property of Δ'

Hence, the result.

Example 7. Prove that the determinant

$$\Delta = \begin{vmatrix} -a^2 & ab & ac \\ ab & -b^2 & bc \\ ac & bc & -c^2 \end{vmatrix}$$

is a perfect square and find its value.

Solution: By inspection, we find that the elements in the given determinant are the cofactors of the corresponding elements in the determinant

$$\begin{vmatrix} 0 & c & b \\ c & 0 & a \\ b & a & 0 \end{vmatrix}$$

$$\therefore \quad \Delta = \begin{vmatrix} 0 & c & b \\ c & 0 & a \\ b & a & 0 \end{vmatrix}^2$$

$$\Rightarrow \quad \Delta = 4a^2b^2c^2$$

Example 8. Express

$$\begin{vmatrix} (a-x)^2 & (b-x)^2 & (c-x)^2 \\ (a-y)^2 & (b-y)^2 & (c-y)^2 \\ (a-z)^2 & (b-z)^2 & (c-z)^2 \end{vmatrix}$$

as product of two determinants and find its value.

Solution:

$$\text{Let } \Delta = \begin{vmatrix} (a-x)^2 & (b-x)^2 & (c-x)^2 \\ (a-y)^2 & (b-y)^2 & (c-y)^2 \\ (a-z)^2 & (b-z)^2 & (c-z)^2 \end{vmatrix}$$

Then,

$$\Delta = \begin{vmatrix} a^2 - 2ax + x^2 & b^2 - 2bx + x^2 & c^2 - 2cx + x^2 \\ a^2 - 2ay + y^2 & b^2 - 2by + y^2 & c^2 - 2cy + y^2 \\ a^2 - 2az + z^2 & b^2 - 2bz + z^2 & c^2 - 2cz + z^2 \end{vmatrix}$$

First element $a^2 - 2ax + x^2 = a^2 \cdot 1 + (-2a) \cdot x + x^2 \cdot 1$ shows that first rows of the required determinants are

$a^2, -2a, 1$ and $1, x, x^2$

Hence, by inspection and trial,

$$\Delta = \begin{vmatrix} a^2 & -2a & 1 \\ b^2 & -2b & 1 \\ c^2 & -2c & 1 \end{vmatrix} \times \begin{vmatrix} 1 & x & x^2 \\ 1 & y & y^2 \\ 1 & z & z^2 \end{vmatrix}$$

$$= 2\begin{vmatrix} 1 & a & a^2 \\ 1 & b & b^2 \\ 1 & c & c^2 \end{vmatrix} \times \begin{vmatrix} 1 & x & x^2 \\ 1 & y & y^2 \\ 1 & z & z^2 \end{vmatrix}$$

$$= 2\ (a - b)\ (b - c)\ (c - a)\ (x - y)\ (y - z)\ (z - x)$$

EXERCISE 3.2

1. If $A = \begin{bmatrix} 1 & 2 & 1 \\ 2 & 4 & 6 \\ 3 & 1 & 2 \end{bmatrix}$ and $B = \begin{bmatrix} -1 & 2 & -3 \\ 2 & -1 & 4 \\ 3 & 4 & 1 \end{bmatrix}$, then prove that

$|AB| = |A|\ |B|$

2. If $A = \begin{bmatrix} 1 & 0 & 0 \\ 2 & 3 & 5 \\ 4 & 1 & 3 \end{bmatrix}$ and $B = \begin{bmatrix} 1 & 0 & 6 \\ 3 & 4 & 15 \\ 5 & 3 & 20 \end{bmatrix}$, then show that

$|AB| = |A|\ |B|$.

3. If $u = ax + by + cz$, $v = ay + bz + cx$ and $w = az + cx + by$, then prove that

$$\begin{vmatrix} a & b & c \\ b & c & a \\ c & a & b \end{vmatrix} \times \begin{vmatrix} x & y & z \\ y & z & x \\ z & x & y \end{vmatrix} = u^3 + v^3 + w^3 - 3uvw$$

4. Prove that

$$\begin{vmatrix} a & x & y \\ x & a & x \\ y & x & a \end{vmatrix}^2 = \begin{vmatrix} a^2 + x^2 + y^2 & 2ax + xy & x^2 + 2ay \\ 2ax + xy & a^2 + 2x^2 & 2ax + xy \\ 2ay + x^2 & 2ax + xy & a^2 + x^2 + y^2 \end{vmatrix}$$

5. Show that

$$\begin{vmatrix} 0 & \cos x & -\sin x \\ \sin x & 0 & \cos x \\ \cos x & \sin x & 0 \end{vmatrix}^2 = \begin{vmatrix} 1 & \lambda & -\lambda \\ \lambda & 1 & \lambda \\ -\lambda & \lambda & 1 \end{vmatrix}, \text{ where}$$

$\lambda = \sin x \cos x$

6. Show that

$$\begin{vmatrix} a & b & c \\ b & c & a \\ c & a & b \end{vmatrix}^2 = \begin{vmatrix} a^2+b^2+c^2 & bc+ca+ab & bc+ca+ab \\ bc+ca+ab & a^2+b^2+c^2 & bc+ca+ab \\ bc+ca+ab & bc+ca+ab & a^2+b^2+c^2 \end{vmatrix}$$

$$= (a^3 + b^3 + c^3 - 3abc)^2$$

7. Show that

$$\begin{vmatrix} 1 & \cos(\alpha-\beta) & \cos(\gamma-\alpha) \\ \cos(\alpha-\beta) & 1 & \cos(\beta-\gamma) \\ \cos(\gamma-\alpha) & \cos(\beta-\gamma) & 1 \end{vmatrix} = 0$$

[Hint. Given determinant

$$= \begin{vmatrix} \cos\alpha & \sin\alpha & 0 \\ \cos\beta & \sin\beta & 0 \\ \cos\gamma & \sin\gamma & 0 \end{vmatrix} \times \begin{vmatrix} \cos\alpha & \sin\alpha & 0 \\ \cos\beta & \sin\beta & 0 \\ \cos\gamma & \sin\gamma & 0 \end{vmatrix}\Bigg]$$

8. Show that

$$\begin{vmatrix} 1 & 1 & 1 \\ a & b & c \\ a^2 & b^2 & c^2 \end{vmatrix}^2 = \begin{vmatrix} 3 & a+b+c & a^2+b^2+c^2 \\ a+b+c & a^2+b^2+c^2 & a^3+b^3+c^3 \\ a^2+b^2+c^2 & a^3+b^3+c^3 & a^4+b^4+c^4 \end{vmatrix}$$

9. Show that

$$\begin{vmatrix} a_1 & b_1 & c_1 \\ a_2 & b_2 & c_2 \\ a_3 & b_3 & c_3 \end{vmatrix}^2 = \begin{vmatrix} A_1 & -B_1 & -C_1 \\ -A_2 & B_2 & -C_2 \\ A_3 & -B_3 & C_3 \end{vmatrix},$$

where the capital letters denote the minors of the corresponding small letters.

10. Show that

$$\begin{vmatrix} x & c & -b \\ -c & x & a \\ b & -a & x \end{vmatrix}^2 = \begin{vmatrix} a^2+x^2 & ab-cx & ac+bx \\ ab+cx & b^2+x^2 & bc-ax \\ ac-bx & bc+ax & c^2+x^2 \end{vmatrix}$$

11. Show that

$$\begin{vmatrix} a^2-bc & b^2-ca & c^2-ab \\ c^2-ab & a^2-bc & b^2-ca \\ b^2-ca & c^2-ab & a^2-bc \end{vmatrix} \times \begin{vmatrix} a & b & c \\ c & a & b \\ b & c & a \end{vmatrix} = \left(a^3+b^3+c^3-abc\right)^2$$

12. Show that

$$\begin{vmatrix} a^2+\lambda^2 & ab+c\lambda & ca-b\lambda \\ ab-c\lambda & b^2+\lambda^2 & bc+a\lambda \\ ca+b\lambda & bc-a\lambda & c^2+\lambda^2 \end{vmatrix} \times \begin{vmatrix} \lambda & c & -b \\ -c & \lambda & a \\ b & -a & \lambda \end{vmatrix} = \lambda^3\left(\lambda^2+a^2+b^2+c^2\right)$$

13. Show that

$$\begin{vmatrix} x^2+y^2+a^2 & 2ax+xy & 2ay+x^2 \\ 2ax+xy & a^2+2x^2 & 2ax+xy \\ 2ay+x^2 & 2ax+xy & x^2+y^2+a^2 \end{vmatrix} = \begin{vmatrix} a^2-x^2 & xy-ax & x^2-ay \\ xy-ax & a^2-y^2 & xy-ax \\ x^2-ay & xy-ax & a^2-x^2 \end{vmatrix}$$

14. If w is an imaginary cube root of unity, then show that

$$\begin{vmatrix} yz-x^2 & zx-y^2 & xy-z^2 \\ zx-y^2 & xy-z^2 & yz-x^2 \\ xy-z^2 & yz-x^2 & zx-y^2 \end{vmatrix} = \begin{vmatrix} r^2 & u^2 & u^2 \\ u^2 & r^2 & u^2 \\ u^2 & u^2 & r^2 \end{vmatrix} = (x+y+z)^2\,(x+wy+w^2z)^2\,(x+w^2y+wz)^2$$

where,

$$r^2 = x^2 + y^2 + x^2$$

and, $u^2 = yz + zx + xy$

15. Express

$$\begin{vmatrix} (1+ax)^2 & (1+ay)^2 & (1+az)^2 \\ (1+bx)^2 & (1+by)^2 & (1+bz)^2 \\ (1+cx)^2 & (1+cy)^2 & (1+cz)^2 \end{vmatrix}$$

as a product of two determinants and show that its value is

$$2\ (a-b)\ (b-c)\ (c-a)\ (x-y)\ (y-z)\ (z-x)$$

$$\left[\text{Hint. Given determinant } = \begin{vmatrix} 1 & 2a & a^2 \\ 1 & 2b & b^2 \\ 1 & 2c & c^2 \end{vmatrix} \times \begin{vmatrix} 1 & x & x^2 \\ 1 & y & y^2 \\ 1 & z & z^2 \end{vmatrix}\right]$$

16. Express

$$\begin{vmatrix} 0 & (\alpha-\beta)^2 & (\alpha-\gamma)^2 \\ (\alpha-\beta)^2 & 0 & (\beta-\gamma)^2 \\ (\alpha-\gamma)^2 & (\beta-\gamma)^2 & 0 \end{vmatrix}$$

as a product of two determinants of third order and hence show that its value is $-2\ (\alpha - \beta)^2\ (\beta - \gamma)^2\ (\gamma - \alpha)^2$

$$\left[\text{Hint. Given determinant } = \begin{vmatrix} \alpha^2 & -2\alpha & 1 \\ \beta^2 & -2\beta & 1 \\ \gamma^2 & -2\gamma & 1 \end{vmatrix} \times \begin{vmatrix} 1 & \alpha & \alpha^2 \\ 1 & \beta & \beta^2 \\ 1 & \gamma & \gamma^2 \end{vmatrix}\right]$$

17. If w is one of the imaginary cube root of unity, show that

$$\begin{vmatrix} 1 & w & w^2 & w^3 \\ w & w^2 & w^3 & 1 \\ w^2 & w^3 & 1 & w \\ w^3 & 1 & w & w^2 \end{vmatrix}^2 = \begin{vmatrix} 1 & 1 & -2 & 1 \\ 1 & 1 & 1 & -2 \\ -2 & 1 & 1 & 1 \\ 1 & 2 & 1 & 1 \end{vmatrix}$$

and hence show that the value of the determinant on the left is $3\sqrt{-3}$.

3.18. Complementary Minor of a Determinant

Let A be a square matrix of order n. Let B be a $r \times r$ submatrix of A. Then, the determinant $|B'|$ of the submatrix of A formed by deleting the rows and columns of A containing the elements of B is known as the complementary minor of B.

For example, in the matrix $\begin{vmatrix} a_1 & b_1 & c_1 & d_1 \\ a_2 & b_2 & c_2 & d_2 \\ a_3 & b_3 & c_3 & d_3 \\ a_4 & b_4 & c_4 & d_4 \end{vmatrix}$, the complementary minor of the determinant $\begin{vmatrix} a_1 & b_1 \\ a_2 & b_2 \end{vmatrix}$ is $\begin{vmatrix} c_3 & d_3 \\ c_4 & d_4 \end{vmatrix}$; the complementary minor of the determinant $\begin{vmatrix} b_1 & c_1 & d_1 \\ b_2 & c_2 & d_2 \\ b_3 & c_3 & d_3 \end{vmatrix}$ is a_4; moreover, the complementary minor of the determinant $\begin{vmatrix} b_2 & c_2 \\ b_3 & c_3 \end{vmatrix}$ is $\begin{vmatrix} a_1 & d_1 \\ a_4 & d_4 \end{vmatrix}$.

3.19. Laplace's Expansion of a Determinant by the Minors of First *r* Columns

Let A be a square matrix of order n. Let $|Bi|$ be a $r \times r$ minor of A formed by the elements of first r columns of A. Let

$|B_i'|$ be the complementary minor of $|Bi|$. Then,

$$A = \Sigma \pm |Bi|\ |B_i'|$$

where the summation is extended over all possible $r \times r$ minors of A which can be formed from the elements of the first r columns and positive or negative sign is taken according as an even or odd number of interchanges of adjacent rows of A is required to bring the submatrix Bi into the first r rows of A.

To understand the above concept in a better way, we take an example given below:

Example. Expand $\begin{vmatrix} a & -b & -a & b \\ b & a & -b & -a \\ c & -d & c & -d \\ d & c & d & c \end{vmatrix}$ by Laplace's expansion method by the minors of the first two columns. Hence, evaluate it.

Solution: All the possible minors of the first two columns and their complementary minors are given by

$$|B_1| = \begin{vmatrix} a & -b \\ b & a \end{vmatrix}$$

$$|B_1'| = \begin{vmatrix} c & -d \\ d & c \end{vmatrix}$$

$$|B_2| = \begin{vmatrix} a & -b \\ c & -d \end{vmatrix}$$

$$|B_2'| = \begin{vmatrix} -b & -a \\ d & c \end{vmatrix}$$

$$|B_3| = \begin{vmatrix} a & -b \\ d & c \end{vmatrix}$$

$$|B_3'| = \begin{vmatrix} -b & -a \\ c & -d \end{vmatrix}$$

$$|B_4| = \begin{vmatrix} b & a \\ c & -d \end{vmatrix}$$

$$|B_4'| = \begin{vmatrix} -a & b \\ d & c \end{vmatrix}$$

$$|B_5| = \begin{vmatrix} b & a \\ d & c \end{vmatrix}$$

$$|B_5'| = \begin{vmatrix} -a & b \\ c & -d \end{vmatrix}$$

$$|B_6| = \begin{vmatrix} c & -d \\ d & c \end{vmatrix}$$

$$|B_6'| = \begin{vmatrix} -a & b \\ -b & -a \end{vmatrix}$$

$\therefore$ The given determinant

$$= \begin{vmatrix} a & -b \\ b & a \end{vmatrix}\begin{vmatrix} c & -d \\ d & c \end{vmatrix} - \begin{vmatrix} a & -b \\ c & -d \end{vmatrix}\begin{vmatrix} -b & -a \\ d & c \end{vmatrix}$$

$$+ \begin{vmatrix} a & -b \\ d & c \end{vmatrix}\begin{vmatrix} -b & -a \\ c & -d \end{vmatrix} + \begin{vmatrix} b & a \\ c & -d \end{vmatrix}\begin{vmatrix} -a & b \\ d & c \end{vmatrix}$$

$$- \begin{vmatrix} b & a \\ d & c \end{vmatrix}\begin{vmatrix} -a & b \\ c & -d \end{vmatrix} + \begin{vmatrix} c & -d \\ d & c \end{vmatrix}\begin{vmatrix} -a & b \\ -b & -a \end{vmatrix}$$

$$= (a^2 + b^2)(c^2 + d^2) + (bc - ad)(bc - ad)$$

$$+ (ac + bd)(ac + bd) + (ac + bd)^2$$

$$+ (bc - ad)^2 + (c^2 + d^2)(a^2 + b^2)$$

$$= 2(a^2 + b^2)(c^2 + d^2) + 2(bc - ad)^2 + 2(ac + bd)^2$$

$$= 2(a^2 + b^2)(c^2 + d^2) + 2[b^2c^2 + a^2d^2 + a^2c^2 + b^2d^2]$$

$$= 2(a^2 + b^2)(c^2 + d^2) + 2[c^2(b^2 + a^2) + d^2(a^2 + b^2)]$$

$$= 2(a^2 + b^2)(c^2 + d^2) + 2(a^2 + b^2)(c^2 + d^2)$$

$$= 4(a^2 + b^2)(c^2 + d^2)$$

EXERCISE 3.3

1. Expand $\begin{vmatrix} 3 & 2 & 1 & 4 \\ 15 & 29 & 2 & 14 \\ 16 & 19 & 3 & 17 \\ 33 & 39 & 8 & 38 \end{vmatrix}$ by Laplace's expansion method by the minors of first two columns. Hence, evaluate it.

2. Evaluate the determinant $\begin{vmatrix} 3 & 5 & 7 & 2 \\ 2 & 4 & 1 & 1 \\ -2 & 0 & 0 & 0 \\ 1 & 1 & 3 & 4 \end{vmatrix}$ by Laplace's expansion method.

3. Evaluate the determinant $\begin{vmatrix} 3 & 4 & 1 & 5 \\ 2 & 8 & 7 & 6 \\ 1 & 0 & 5 & 4 \\ 9 & 9 & 1 & 3 \end{vmatrix}$ by Laplace's expansion method.

4. Expand $\begin{vmatrix} a & x & y & a \\ x & 0 & 0 & y \\ y & 0 & 0 & x \\ a & y & x & a \end{vmatrix}$ by Laplace's expansion by the minors of first two columns. Hence, evaluate it.

5. Expand $\begin{vmatrix} a & b & c & d \\ e & f & g & h \\ 0 & 0 & j & k \\ 0 & 0 & l & m \end{vmatrix}$ by Laplace's expansion by the minors of first two columns. Hence, evaluate it.

6. Expand $\begin{vmatrix} a & 1 & 0 & 0 & 0 \\ b & a & 1 & 0 & 0 \\ 0 & b & a & 1 & 0 \\ 0 & 0 & b & a & 1 \\ 0 & 0 & 0 & b & a \end{vmatrix}$ by Laplace's expansion by the minors of first two columns. Hence, evaluate it.

7. Expand $\begin{vmatrix} a_1 & a_2 & a_3 & a_4 \\ b_1 & b_2 & b_3 & b_4 \\ c_1 & c_2 & c_3 & c_4 \\ d_1 & d_2 & d_3 & d_4 \end{vmatrix}$ by Laplace's expansion by the minors of first two columns.

ANSWERS

1. –10754
2. 156
3. –1125
4. $(x^2 - y^2)^2$
5. $(af - be)\ (jm - lk)$
6. $a(a^2 - b)\ (a^2 - 3b)$
7. $\begin{vmatrix} a_1 & a_2 \\ b_1 & b_2 \end{vmatrix}\begin{vmatrix} c_3 & c_4 \\ d_3 & d_4 \end{vmatrix} - \begin{vmatrix} a_1 & a_2 \\ c_1 & c_2 \end{vmatrix}\begin{vmatrix} b_3 & b_4 \\ d_3 & d_4 \end{vmatrix} + \begin{vmatrix} a_1 & a_2 \\ d_1 & d_2 \end{vmatrix}\begin{vmatrix} b_3 & b_4 \\ c_3 & c_4 \end{vmatrix}$

$+ \begin{vmatrix} b_1 & b_2 \\ c_1 & c_2 \end{vmatrix}\begin{vmatrix} a_3 & a_4 \\ d_3 & d_4 \end{vmatrix} - \begin{vmatrix} b_1 & b_2 \\ d_1 & d_2 \end{vmatrix}\begin{vmatrix} a_3 & a_4 \\ c_3 & c_4 \end{vmatrix} + \begin{vmatrix} c_1 & c_2 \\ d_1 & d_2 \end{vmatrix}\begin{vmatrix} a_3 & a_4 \\ b_3 & b_4 \end{vmatrix}$

3.20. Use of Determinants in Solving a System of Non-Homogeneous Linear Eqations (Cramer's Rule)

Let the n simultaneous equations in n unknown quantities $x_1, x_2, ..., x_n$ be

$$a_{11}\, x_1 + a_{12}\, x_2 + ... + a_{1j}\, x_j + ... + a_{1n}\, x_n = b_1$$
$$a_{21}\, x_1 + a_{22}\, x_2 + ... + a_{2j}\, x_j + ... + a_{2n}\, x_n = b_2$$

$$a_{31}\, x_1 + a_{32}\, x_2 + \dots + a_{3j}\, x_j + \dots + a_{3n}\, x_n = b_3$$

....

$$a_{i1}\, x_1 + a_{i2}\, x_2 + \dots + a_{ij}\, x_j + \dots + a_{in}\, x_n = b_i$$

....

$$a_{n1}\, x_1 + a_{n2}\, x_2 + \dots + a_{nj}\, x_j + \dots + a_{nn}\, x_n = b_n$$

These equations can be written as

$$\sum_{j=1}^{n} a_{ij}\, x_j = b_i; \quad i = 1, 2, \dots, n \qquad \dots (3.15)$$

Let the determinants of the coefficients $|A| = |a_{ij}| \neq 0$.

Multiplying Eq. (3.15) by the cofactor of a_{ij} in $|a_{ij}|$, i.e. A_{ij}; $i = 1, 2, \dots, n$ and summing up with respect to i, we obtain

$$\sum_{i=1}^{n} a_{ij}\, A_{ij}\, x_j = \sum_{i=1}^{n} b_i\, A_{ij}$$

$$\Rightarrow \quad |A|\, x_j = \sum_{i=1}^{n} b_i\, A_{ij} \qquad \left|\ \because |A| = \sum_{i=1}^{n} a_{ij}\, A_{ij}\right.$$

= Determinant formed by replacing the jth column of the determinant $|A|$ by the constants $b_1, b_2, \dots, b_n$

$$= \begin{vmatrix} a_{11} & a_{12} & \dots & a_{1j-1} & b_1 & a_{1j+1} & \dots & a_{1n} \\ a_{21} & a_{22} & \dots & a_{2j-1} & b_2 & a_{2j+1} & \dots & a_{2n} \\ \dots & \dots & \dots & \dots & \dots & \dots & \dots & \dots \\ a_{i1} & a_{i2} & \dots & a_{ij-1} & b_i & a_{ij+1} & \dots & a_{in} \\ \dots & \dots & \dots & \dots & \dots & \dots & \dots & \dots \\ a_{n1} & a_{n2} & \dots & a_{nj-1} & b_n & a_{nj+1} & \dots & a_{nn} \end{vmatrix}$$

$$\Rightarrow \quad x_j = \frac{1}{|A|} \begin{vmatrix} a_{11} & a_{12} & \dots & a_{1j-1} & b_1 & a_{1j+1} & \dots & a_{1n} \\ a_{21} & a_{22} & \dots & a_{2j-1} & b_2 & a_{2j+1} & \dots & a_{2n} \\ \dots & \dots & \dots & \dots & \dots & \dots & \dots & \dots \\ a_{i1} & a_{i2} & \dots & a_{ij-1} & b_i & a_{ij+1} & \dots & a_{in} \\ \dots & \dots & \dots & \dots & \dots & \dots & \dots & \dots \\ a_{n1} & a_{n2} & \dots & a_{nj-1} & b_n & a_{nj+1} & \dots & a_{nn} \end{vmatrix}$$

Particular Case (Three simultaneous equations in three variables x, y and z)

Let a system of three simultaneous non-homogeneous linear equations in three unknown quantities x, y, z be

$$a_1x + b_1y + c_1z = d_1 \quad \text{... (3.16)}$$

$$a_2x + b_2y + c_2z = d_2 \quad \text{... (3.17)}$$

$$a_3x + b_3y + c_3z = d_3 \quad \text{... (3.18)}$$

Let A_1, A_2, A_3, etc. be the cofactors of a_1, a_2, a_3, etc. respectively in the determinant of coefficients given by

$$\Delta = \begin{vmatrix} a_1 & b_1 & c_1 \\ a_2 & b_2 & c_2 \\ a_3 & b_3 & c_3 \end{vmatrix}$$

Then, multiplying Eqs. (3.16), (3.17) and (3.18) by A_1, A_2 and A_3 respectively and adding, we obtain

$$(a_1A_1 + a_2A_2 + a_3A_3)x + (b_1A_1 + b_2A_2 + b_3A_3)y + (c_1A_1 + c_2A_2 + c_3A_3)z = d_1A_1 + d_2A_2 + d_3A_3$$

$$\Rightarrow \Delta x + 0y + 0z = \begin{vmatrix} d_1 & b_1 & c_1 \\ d_2 & b_2 & c_2 \\ d_3 & b_3 & c_3 \end{vmatrix}$$

$$\Rightarrow \Delta x = \begin{vmatrix} d_1 & b_1 & c_1 \\ d_2 & b_2 & c_2 \\ d_3 & b_3 & c_3 \end{vmatrix}$$

$$\Rightarrow x = \frac{\begin{vmatrix} d_1 & b_1 & c_1 \\ d_2 & b_2 & c_2 \\ d_3 & b_3 & c_3 \end{vmatrix}}{\begin{vmatrix} a_1 & b_1 & c_1 \\ a_2 & b_2 & c_2 \\ a_3 & b_3 & c_3 \end{vmatrix}}, \text{ provided } \Delta \neq 0 \quad \text{... (3.19)}$$

Similarly, multiplying Eqs. (3.16), (3.17) and (3.18) by B_1, B_2 and B_3 respectively and adding, we get

$$y = \frac{\begin{vmatrix} a_1 & d_1 & c_1 \\ a_2 & d_2 & c_2 \\ a_3 & d_3 & c_3 \end{vmatrix}}{\begin{vmatrix} a_1 & b_1 & c_1 \\ a_2 & b_2 & c_2 \\ a_3 & b_3 & c_3 \end{vmatrix}}, \text{ provided } \Delta \neq 0 \quad \ldots (3.20)$$

In the last, multiplying Eqs. (3.16), (3.17) and (3.18) by C_1, C_2 and C_3 respectively and adding, we get

$$z = \frac{\begin{vmatrix} a_1 & b_1 & d_1 \\ a_2 & b_2 & d_2 \\ a_3 & b_3 & d_3 \end{vmatrix}}{\begin{vmatrix} a_1 & b_1 & c_1 \\ a_2 & b_2 & c_2 \\ a_3 & b_3 & c_3 \end{vmatrix}}, \text{ provided } \Delta \neq 0 \quad \ldots (3.21)$$

Thus, to obtain the value of any unknown, the known quantities d_1, d_2, d_3 on the right-hand side of the given equations are to be substituted in Δ for the coefficients of the required unknown and the determinant so formed is divided by Δ.

In view of Eqs. (3.19), (3.20) and (3.21), we obtain

$$\frac{x}{\begin{vmatrix} d_1 & b_1 & c_1 \\ d_2 & b_2 & c_2 \\ d_3 & b_3 & c_3 \end{vmatrix}} = \frac{y}{\begin{vmatrix} a_1 & d_1 & c_1 \\ a_2 & d_2 & c_2 \\ a_3 & d_3 & c_3 \end{vmatrix}} = \frac{z}{\begin{vmatrix} a_1 & b_1 & d_1 \\ a_2 & b_2 & d_2 \\ a_3 & b_3 & d_3 \end{vmatrix}} = \frac{1}{\begin{vmatrix} a_1 & b_1 & c_1 \\ a_2 & b_2 & c_2 \\ a_3 & b_3 & c_3 \end{vmatrix}}$$

The above method of solving a system of non-homogeneous linear equations is known as Cramer's Rule.

ILLUSTRATIVE EXAMPLES

Example 1. Solve the following system of linear equations by Cramer's Rule:

$$x + y + z = 9$$
$$2x + 5y + 7z = 52$$
$$2x + y - z = 0$$

Solution: Here,

$$\Delta = \begin{vmatrix} 1 & 1 & 1 \\ 2 & 5 & 7 \\ 2 & 1 & -1 \end{vmatrix}$$

Operating $C_2 - C_1$, $C_3 - C_1$

$$\Delta = \begin{vmatrix} 1 & 0 & 0 \\ 2 & 3 & 5 \\ 2 & -1 & -3 \end{vmatrix}$$

$$= \begin{vmatrix} 3 & 5 \\ -1 & -3 \end{vmatrix} = -9 + 5 = -4 \neq 0$$

Hence, Cramer's Rule can be applied and the given system of equations possesses a unique solution given by

$$\frac{x}{\begin{vmatrix} 9 & 1 & 1 \\ 52 & 5 & 7 \\ 0 & 1 & -1 \end{vmatrix}} = \frac{y}{\begin{vmatrix} 1 & 9 & 1 \\ 2 & 52 & 7 \\ 2 & 0 & -1 \end{vmatrix}} = \frac{z}{\begin{vmatrix} 1 & 1 & 9 \\ 2 & 5 & 52 \\ 2 & 1 & 0 \end{vmatrix}} = \frac{1}{\begin{vmatrix} 1 & 1 & 1 \\ 2 & 5 & 7 \\ 2 & 1 & -1 \end{vmatrix}}$$

$$\Rightarrow \quad \frac{x}{-4} = \frac{y}{-12} = \frac{z}{-20} = \frac{1}{-4}$$

$$\Rightarrow \quad x = \frac{-4}{-4} = 1; \; y = \frac{-12}{-4} = 3 \text{ and } z = \frac{-20}{-4} = 5$$

Example 2. If a, b, c are all different, solve the following equations by the application of Cramer's Rule:

$x + y + z = 1$
$ax + by + cz = K$
$a^2x + b^2y + c^2z = K^2$

Solution: By Cramer's Rule,

$$\frac{x}{\begin{vmatrix} 1 & 1 & 1 \\ K & b & c \\ K^2 & b^2 & c^2 \end{vmatrix}} = \frac{y}{\begin{vmatrix} 1 & 1 & 1 \\ a & K & c \\ a^2 & K^2 & c^2 \end{vmatrix}} = \frac{z}{\begin{vmatrix} 1 & 1 & 1 \\ a & b & K \\ a^2 & b^2 & K^2 \end{vmatrix}} = \frac{1}{\begin{vmatrix} 1 & 1 & 1 \\ a & b & c \\ a^2 & b^2 & c^2 \end{vmatrix}}$$

$$\Rightarrow \frac{x}{(K-b)(b-c)(c-K)} = \frac{y}{(a-K)(K-c)(c-a)}$$

$$= \frac{z}{(a-b)(b-K)(K-a)}$$

$$= \frac{1}{(a-b)(b-c)(c-a)}$$

$$\Rightarrow x = \frac{(K-b)(b-c)(c-K)}{(a-b)(b-c)(c-a)} = \frac{(K-b)(c-K)}{(a-b)(c-a)}$$

Similarly, $y = \dfrac{(a-K)(K-c)}{(a-b)(b-c)}$ and $z = \dfrac{(b-K)(K-a)}{(b-c)(c-a)}$

Example 3. Find λ if the following equations are consistent:

$ax + hy + g = 0$
$hx + by + f = 0$
$gx + fy + c = \lambda$

Solution: The given equations are

$ax + hy + g = 0$ ... (3.22)
$hx + by + f = 0$ ... (3.23)
$gx + fy + (c - \lambda) = 0$ ... (3.24)

The equations are consistent if

$\Delta = 0$

$$\Rightarrow \begin{vmatrix} a & h & g \\ h & b & f \\ g & f & c-\lambda \end{vmatrix} = 0$$

$$\Rightarrow \begin{vmatrix} a & h & g \\ h & b & f \\ g & f & c \end{vmatrix} + \begin{vmatrix} a & h & 0 \\ h & b & 0 \\ g & f & -\lambda \end{vmatrix} = 0$$

$$\Rightarrow \left(abc + 2fgh - af^2 - bg^2 - ch^2\right) - \lambda\left(ab - h^2\right) = 0$$

$$\Rightarrow \lambda = \frac{abc + 2fgh - af^2 - bg^2 - ch^2}{ab - h^2},$$

provided $ab - h^2 \neq 0$

Example 4. Show that the equations

$$a_1x^2 + b_1x + c_1 = 0$$

and $a_2x^2 + b_2x + c_2 = 0$

possess a common root only if

$$\begin{vmatrix} a_1 & b_1 \\ a_2 & b_2 \end{vmatrix} \times \begin{vmatrix} b_1 & c_1 \\ b_2 & c_2 \end{vmatrix} = \begin{vmatrix} a_1 & c_1 \\ a_2 & c_2 \end{vmatrix}^2$$

Solution: Let α be a common root. Then,

$$a_1\alpha^2 + b_1\alpha = -c_1$$

$$a_2\alpha^2 + b_2\alpha = -c_2$$

Solving these simultaneous equations by Cramer's Rule, we obtain

$$\frac{\alpha^2}{\begin{vmatrix} -c_1 & b_1 \\ -c_2 & b_2 \end{vmatrix}} = \frac{\alpha}{\begin{vmatrix} a_1 & -c_1 \\ a_2 & -c_2 \end{vmatrix}} = \frac{1}{\begin{vmatrix} a_1 & b_1 \\ a_2 & b_2 \end{vmatrix}}$$

$$\Rightarrow \alpha^2 = \frac{\begin{vmatrix} b_1 & c_1 \\ b_2 & c_2 \end{vmatrix}}{\begin{vmatrix} a_1 & b_1 \\ a_2 & b_2 \end{vmatrix}} \qquad \ldots (3.25)$$

$$\text{and } \alpha = -\frac{\begin{vmatrix} a_1 & c_1 \\ a_2 & c_2 \end{vmatrix}}{\begin{vmatrix} a_1 & b_1 \\ a_2 & b_2 \end{vmatrix}} \qquad \ldots (3.26)$$

In view of Eqs. (3.25) and (3.26), we have

$$\frac{\begin{vmatrix} b_1 & c_1 \\ b_2 & c_2 \end{vmatrix}}{\begin{vmatrix} a_1 & b_1 \\ a_2 & b_2 \end{vmatrix}} = \frac{\begin{vmatrix} a_1 & c_1 \\ a_2 & c_2 \end{vmatrix}^2}{\begin{vmatrix} a_1 & b_1 \\ a_2 & b_2 \end{vmatrix}^2}$$

$$\Rightarrow \begin{vmatrix} a_1 & b_1 \\ a_2 & b_2 \end{vmatrix} \times \begin{vmatrix} b_1 & c_1 \\ b_2 & c_2 \end{vmatrix} = \begin{vmatrix} a_1 & c_1 \\ a_2 & c_2 \end{vmatrix}^2$$

EXERCISE 3.4

Solve the following systems of equation by Cramer's Rule:

1. $x + y + z = 7$
$x + 2y + 3z = 16$
$x + 3y + 4z = 22$

2. $x + y + z = 7$
$x + 2y + 3z = 16$
$x + 3y + 4z = 20$

3. $x + 2y + 3z = 6$
$2x + 4y + z = 7$
$3x + 2y + 9z = 14$

4. $x + y + z = 11$
$2x - 6y - z = 0$
$3x + 4y + 2z = 0$

5. $3x + 5y - 7z = 13$
$4x + y - 12z = 6$
$2x + 9y - 3z = 20$

6. $x + y + z = 1$
$x + 2y + 3z = 2$
$x + 4y + 9z = 4$

7. $x + y + z = 3$
$x + 2y + 3z = 4$
$x + 4y + 9z = 6$

8. $x + 3y - 5z = 0$

$2x + y + 2z = 7$

$x - y = 1$

9. $x_1 + 2x_2 + 3x_3 + 5 = 0$

$2x_1 + x_2 + x_3 + 7 = 0$

$x_1 + x_2 + x_3 = 0$

10. $2x + 3y - 4z = 2$

$3x - 2y + 5z = 5$

$x + 2y + 3z = 11$

11. $x + y + z + d = 0$

$ax + by + cz + d^2 = 0$

$a^2x + b^2y + c^2z + d^3 = 0$

12. $ax + by + cz = K$

$a^2x + b^2y + c^2z = K^2$

$a^3x + b^3y + c^3z = K^3$

13. Are the equations consistent?

$x + 6y - 5 = 0$

$2x - 3y - 1 = 0$

and $x + y - 2 = 0$

14. If $(f^2 - bc)x + (ch - fg)y + (bg - hf)z = 0$,

$(ch - fg)x + (g^2 - ca)y + (af - gh)z = 0$,

$(bg - hf)x + (af - gh)y + (h^2 - ab)z = 0$,

show that $abc + 2fgh - af^2 - bg^2 - ch^2 = 0$

15. Show that the following equations are consistent:

$(a - b)x + (b - c)y + (c - a)z = 0$

$(b - c)x + (c - a)y + (a - b)z = 0$

$(c - a)x + (a - b)y + (b - c)z = 0$

16. $x + y + z + u = 1$

$ax + by + cz + du = K$

$a^2x + b^2y + c^2z + d^2u = K^2$

$a^3x + b^3y + c^3z + d^3u = K^3$

ANSWERS

1. $x = 1, y = 3, z = 3$
2. $x = 3, y = -1, z = 5$
3. $x = 1, y = 1, z = 1$
4. $x = -8, y = -7, z = 26$
5. $x = 1, y = 2, z = 0$
6. $x = 0, y = 1, z = 0$
7. $x = 2, y = 1, z = 0$
8. $x = 2, y = 1, z = 1$
9. $x_1 = -7, x_2 = 19, x_3 = -12$
10. $x = \frac{10}{19}, y = \frac{50}{19}, z = \frac{33}{19}$
11. $x = \frac{d(c-b)(d-b)}{(a-b)(a-c)}$, etc.
12. $x = \frac{K(K-b)(K-c)}{a(a-b)(a-c)}$, etc.
13. Yes
16. $x = \frac{(K-b)(K-c)(K-d)}{(a-b)(a-c)(a-d)}$, etc.

3.21. Conjugate Elements

Any two elements of a determinant which are situated at the intersection of ith row, j^{th} column and j^{th} row, i^{th} column respectively are called conjugate elements.

In other words, two elements are said to be conjugte if they are situated in a line perpendicular to principal diagonal and equidistant from it.

Thus, in $\begin{vmatrix} a_1 & b_1 & c_1 \\ a_2 & b_2 & c_2 \\ a_3 & b_3 & c_3 \end{vmatrix}$, $a_2, b_1; a_3, c_1; b_3, c_2$ are conjugate elements.

3.22. Symmetric Determinant

A determinant in which the conjugate elements are equal is called a symmetric determinant. Thus, if $A = [a_{ij}]$ is a square matrix and $a_{ij} = a_{ji}\ \forall\ i, j$, then the determinant $|A|$ is said to be symmetric. For example,

$$\begin{vmatrix} a & h & g \\ h & b & f \\ g & f & c \end{vmatrix}$$

is a symmetric determinant.

3.23. Circulant Determinant

A determinant in which the same element occur in all the rows in circular order is called a circulant determinant. For example:

$$\begin{vmatrix} a & b & c \\ b & c & a \\ c & a & b \end{vmatrix}$$

Note: A circulant determinant is symmetric.

3.24. Alternate Determinant

A determinant in which the interchange of any two letters gives rise to a change in sign is called an alternate determinant. For example:

$$\begin{vmatrix} 1 & 1 & 1 \\ l & m & n \\ l^2 & m^2 & n^2 \end{vmatrix}$$

3.25. Theorem

Prove that the square of any determinant is a symmetric determinant.

Proof. $$\begin{vmatrix} l_1 & m_1 & n_1 \\ l_2 & m_2 & n_2 \\ l_3 & m_3 & n_3 \end{vmatrix}^2 = \begin{vmatrix} l_1 & m_1 & n_1 \\ l_2 & m_2 & n_2 \\ l_3 & m_3 & n_3 \end{vmatrix} \times \begin{vmatrix} l_1 & m_1 & n_1 \\ l_2 & m_2 & n_2 \\ l_3 & m_3 & n_3 \end{vmatrix}$$

$$= \begin{vmatrix} l_1^2 + m_1^2 + n_1^2 & l_1l_2 + m_1m_2 + n_1n_2 & l_3l_1 + m_3m_1 + n_3n_1 \\ l_1l_2 + m_1m_2 + n_1n_2 & l_2^2 + m_2^2 + n_2^2 & l_2l_3 + m_2m_3 + n_2n_3 \\ l_3l_1 + m_3m_1 + n_3n_1 & l_2l_3 + m_2m_3 + n_2n_3 & l_3^2 + m_3^2 + n_3^2 \end{vmatrix}$$

which is obviously a symmetric determinant.

3.26. Skew-Symmetric Determinant

A determinant in which the conjugate elements are equal and opposite is called a skew-symmetric determinant. Thus, if $A = [a_{ij}]$ is a square matrix and $a_{ij} = -a_{ji}\ \forall\ i, j$, then the determinant $|A|$ is said to be skew-symmetric.

For $i = j$, we have

$$a_{ii} = -a_{ii}$$

$$\Rightarrow a_{ii} = 0$$

Hence, every diagonal element in a skew-symmetric determinant is zero. For example:

$$\begin{vmatrix} 0 & h & g \\ -h & 0 & f \\ -g & -f & 0 \end{vmatrix}$$

is a skew-symmetric determinant.

3.27. Theorem

Prove that a skew-symmetric determinant of odd order vanishes.

Proof. Let $A = [a_{ij}]_{n \times n}$ be a square matrix of order $n \times n$. Let $|A|$ be a skew-symmetric determinant of order n, where n is odd. Let A' be the transpose matrix of the matrix A. Since A' is skew-symmetric, therefore

$$A' = -A$$

$$\Rightarrow A = -A'$$

$$\Rightarrow |A| = |-A'|$$

$$\Rightarrow |A| = (-1)^n\ |A'|$$

$\Rightarrow\ |A| = -|A'|$ | $\because$ n is odd

$\Rightarrow\ |A| = -|A|$ | By property of determinants

$\Rightarrow\ 2\ |A| = 0$

$\Rightarrow\ |A| = 0$

Example

$$\text{Let } A = \begin{bmatrix} 0 & h & g \\ -h & 0 & f \\ -g & -f & 0 \end{bmatrix}$$

Then,

$$|A| = \begin{bmatrix} 0 & h & g \\ -h & 0 & f \\ -g & -f & 0 \end{bmatrix}$$

$$= \begin{bmatrix} 0 & -h & -g \\ h & 0 & -f \\ g & f & 0 \end{bmatrix} \quad \text{| Interchanging rows and columns}$$

$$= (-1)^3 \begin{bmatrix} 0 & h & g \\ -h & 0 & f \\ -g & -f & 0 \end{bmatrix} \quad \text{| Taking } (-1) \text{ column from each column}$$

$= (-1)\ |A|$

$= -\ |A|$

$\Rightarrow\ 2|A| = 0$

$\Rightarrow\ |A| = 0$

3.28. Theorem

Prove that a skew-symmetric determinant of even order is a perfect square.

Proof. For the sake of definiteness, let us consider a skew-symmetric determinant of order 4 as given below:

$$\Delta = \begin{vmatrix} 0 & a_{12} & a_{13} & a_{14} \\ a_{21} & 0 & a_{23} & a_{24} \\ a_{31} & a_{32} & 0 & a_{34} \\ a_{41} & a_{42} & a_{43} & 0 \end{vmatrix}$$

where $a_{ij} = -a_{ji}$

Now, by Laplace's expansion of a determinant, we have

$$A_{11} A_{22} - A_{12} A_{21} = \begin{vmatrix} A_{11} & A_{12} & A_{13} & A_{14} \\ A_{21} & A_{22} & A_{23} & A_{24} \\ 0 & 0 & 1 & 0 \\ 0 & 0 & 0 & 1 \end{vmatrix}$$

$\therefore \quad (A_{11} A_{22} - A_{12} A_{21})\Delta$

$$= \begin{vmatrix} A_{11} & A_{12} & A_{13} & A_{14} \\ A_{21} & A_{22} & A_{23} & A_{24} \\ 0 & 0 & 1 & 0 \\ 0 & 0 & 0 & 1 \end{vmatrix} \times \begin{vmatrix} 0 & a_{12} & a_{13} & a_{14} \\ a_{21} & 0 & a_{23} & a_{24} \\ a_{31} & a_{32} & 0 & a_{34} \\ a_{41} & a_{42} & a_{43} & 0 \end{vmatrix}$$

$$= \begin{vmatrix} \Sigma a_{11}A_{11} & \Sigma a_{11}A_{21} & a_{13} & a_{14} \\ \Sigma a_{21}A_{11} & \Sigma a_{21}A_{21} & a_{23} & a_{24} \\ \Sigma a_{31}A_{11} & \Sigma a_{31}A_{21} & a_{33} & a_{34} \\ \Sigma a_{41}A_{11} & \Sigma a_{41}A_{21} & a_{43} & a_{44} \end{vmatrix}$$

$$= \begin{vmatrix} \Delta & 0 & a_{13} & a_{14} \\ 0 & \Delta & a_{23} & a_{24} \\ 0 & 0 & 0 & a_{34} \\ 0 & 0 & a_{43} & 0 \end{vmatrix} \qquad |\because a_{33} = 0 = a_{44}, \text{ etc.}$$

$$= \begin{vmatrix} \Delta & 0 \\ 0 & \Delta \end{vmatrix} \times \begin{vmatrix} 0 & a_{34} \\ a_{43} & 0 \end{vmatrix}$$

$$= -(a_{34}\,a_{43})\,\Delta^2$$

$$= (a_{34}\,\Delta)^2 \qquad \Big|\because a_{34} = -a_{43}$$

which is a perfect square.

3.29. Theorem

The reciprocal (adjugate) of a skew-symmetric determinant of the nth order is a symmetric determinant when n is odd, and, a skew-symmetric determinant when n is even.

Proof. We know that in any skew-symmetric determinant, the minors corresponding to a pair of conjugate elements differ by an interchange of rows and columns and by the signs of all elements. Therefore, the two minors are equal when their order is even, i.e. when the order of the determinant is odd. Hence, when n is odd, the reciprocal determinant is symmetric. Again, the two minors are equal with opposite signs when their order is odd, i.e. when n is even. Furthermore, in this case the minors of the leading diagonal elements are all skew-symmetric determinants of odd order and therefore vanish. Thus, when n is even, the reciprocal determinant is skew-symmetric.

ILLUSTRATIVE EXAMPLES

Example 1. Verify the following expansion for the skew-symmetric determinant of the fourth order:

$$\begin{vmatrix} 0 & x & y & z \\ -x & 0 & c & b \\ -y & -c & 0 & a \\ -z & -b & -a & 0 \end{vmatrix} = (ax - by + cz)^2$$

Solution:

$$\text{Let } \Delta = \begin{vmatrix} 0 & x & y & z \\ -x & 0 & c & b \\ -y & -c & 0 & a \\ -z & -b & -a & 0 \end{vmatrix}$$

Then,

$$\Delta = \frac{1}{a}\begin{vmatrix} 0 & ax & y & z \\ -x & 0 & c & b \\ -y & -ca & 0 & a \\ -z & -ab & -a & 0 \end{vmatrix}$$ | Multiplying C_2 by a and taking $\frac{1}{a}$ outside

Operating $C_2 - bC_3 + cC_4$

$$= \frac{1}{a}\begin{vmatrix} 0 & ax - by + cz & y & z \\ -x & 0 & c & b \\ -y & 0 & 0 & a \\ -z & 0 & -a & 0 \end{vmatrix}$$

$$= -\frac{1}{a}(ax - by + cz)\begin{vmatrix} -x & c & b \\ -y & 0 & a \\ -z & a & 0 \end{vmatrix}$$ | Expanding along C_2

$$= \frac{1}{a}(ax - by + cz)\begin{vmatrix} x & c & b \\ y & 0 & a \\ z & -a & 0 \end{vmatrix}$$

$$= \frac{1}{a^2}(ax - by + cz)\begin{vmatrix} ax & ca & ab \\ y & 0 & a \\ z & -a & 0 \end{vmatrix}$$ | Multiplying R_1 by a and taking $\frac{1}{a}$ outside

Operating $R_1 - bR_2 + cR_3$

$$= \frac{1}{a^2}(ax - by + cz)\begin{vmatrix} ax - by + cz & 0 & 0 \\ y & 0 & a \\ z & -a & 0 \end{vmatrix}$$

$$= \frac{1}{a^2}(ax - by + cz)(ax - by + cz)\left(0 + a^2\right)$$

| Expanding along R_1

$$= (ax - by + cz)^2$$

Example 2. Evaluate $\begin{vmatrix} 0 & \alpha & \beta & \gamma \\ l & 0 & c & -b \\ m & -c & 0 & a \\ n & b & -a & 0 \end{vmatrix}$

Solution:

Let $\Delta = \begin{vmatrix} 0 & \alpha & \beta & \gamma \\ l & 0 & c & -b \\ m & -c & 0 & a \\ n & b & -a & 0 \end{vmatrix}$

Then,

$$\Delta = \frac{1}{a}\begin{vmatrix} 0 & \alpha & \beta & \gamma \\ al & 0 & ca & -ab \\ m & -c & 0 & a \\ n & b & -a & 0 \end{vmatrix} \quad \left| \begin{array}{l} \text{Multiplying } R_2 \text{ by } a \text{ and} \\ \text{taking } \dfrac{1}{a} \text{ outside} \end{array} \right.$$

Operating $R_2 + bR_3 + cR_4$,

$$= \frac{1}{a}\begin{vmatrix} 0 & \alpha & \beta & \gamma \\ al + bm + cn & 0 & 0 & 0 \\ m & -c & 0 & a \\ n & b & -a & 0 \end{vmatrix}$$

$$= -\frac{1}{a}(al + bm + cn)\begin{vmatrix} \alpha & \beta & \gamma \\ -c & 0 & a \\ b & -a & 0 \end{vmatrix} \quad \Big| \text{ Expanding along } R_2$$

$$= -\frac{(al + bm + cn)}{a^2}\begin{vmatrix} a\alpha & \beta & \gamma \\ -ca & 0 & a \\ ab & -a & 0 \end{vmatrix} \quad \left| \begin{array}{l} \text{Multiplying } C_1 \text{ by } a \\ \text{and taking } \dfrac{1}{a} \text{ outside} \end{array} \right.$$

Operating $C_1 + bC_2 + cC_3$,

$$= -\frac{(al+bm+cn)}{a^2}\begin{vmatrix} a\alpha + b\beta + c\gamma & \beta & \gamma \\ 0 & 0 & a \\ 0 & -a & 0 \end{vmatrix}$$

$$= -\frac{(al+bm+cn)}{a^2}(a\alpha + b\beta + c\gamma)\begin{vmatrix} 0 & a \\ -a & 0 \end{vmatrix} \quad \text{Expanding along } C_1$$

$$= -(al+bm+cn)(a\alpha + b\beta + c\gamma)$$

Example 3. If A, B, C are the angles of a triangle, show that

$$\begin{vmatrix} -1 & \cos C & \cos B \\ \cos C & 1 & \cos A \\ \cos B & \cos A & -1 \end{vmatrix} = 0$$

Deduce that $\cos^2 A + \cos^2 B + \cos^2 C + 2 \cos A \cos B \cos C = 1$

Solution:

$$\text{Let } \Delta = \begin{vmatrix} -1 & \cos C & \cos B \\ \cos C & 1 & \cos A \\ \cos B & \cos A & -1 \end{vmatrix}$$

Then,

$$\Delta = \frac{1}{abc}\begin{vmatrix} -a & b\cos C & c\cos B \\ a\cos C & -b & c\cos A \\ a\cos B & b\cos A & -c \end{vmatrix}$$

Multiplying C_1, C_2, C_3 by a, b, c respectively and taking $\frac{1}{abc}$ outside

Operating $C_1 + C_2 + C_3$,

$$= \frac{1}{abc}\begin{vmatrix} -a + b\cos C + c\cos B & b\cos C & c\cos B \\ a\cos C - b + c\cos A & -b & c\cos A \\ a\cos B + b\cos A - c & b\cos A & -c \end{vmatrix}$$

$$= \frac{1}{abc}\begin{vmatrix} 0 & b\cos C & c\cos B \\ 0 & -b & c\cos A \\ 0 & b\cos A & -c \end{vmatrix} \quad \begin{vmatrix} \because b\cos C + c\cos B = a, \text{ etc.} \\ \text{(By Trigonometry)} \end{vmatrix}$$

$$= 0$$

Deduction. Expanding the determinant along R_1, we obtain,

$$-1\,(1 - \cos^2 A) - \cos C\,(-\cos C - \cos A \cos B) + \cos B\,(\cos A \cos C + \cos B) = 0$$

$$\Rightarrow -1 + \cos^2 A + \cos^2 C + 2\cos A \cos B \cos C + \cos^2 B = 0$$

$$\Rightarrow \cos^2 A + \cos^2 B + \cos^2 C + 2\cos A \cos B \cos C = 1$$

EXERCISE 3.5

1. Show that $\begin{vmatrix} x & a & a & a \\ a & x & a & a \\ a & a & x & a \\ a & a & a & x \end{vmatrix} = (x-a)^3(x+3a)$

2. Show that $\begin{vmatrix} a & 1 & 1 & 1 \\ 1 & a & 1 & 1 \\ 1 & 1 & a & 1 \\ 1 & 1 & 1 & a \end{vmatrix} = (a+3)(a-1)^3$

3. Show that $\begin{vmatrix} 4 & 5 & 6 & x \\ 5 & 6 & 7 & y \\ 6 & 7 & 8 & z \\ x & y & z & 0 \end{vmatrix} = (x-2y+z)^2$

4. Show that

$$\begin{vmatrix} 0 & 1 & 1 & 1 \\ 1 & b+c & a & a \\ 1 & b & c+a & b \\ 1 & c & c & a+b \end{vmatrix} = a^2 + b^2 + c^2 - 2ab - 2bc - 2ca$$

5. Show that $\begin{vmatrix} -1 & 0 & 0 & a \\ 0 & -1 & 0 & b \\ 0 & 0 & -1 & c \\ x & y & z & -1 \end{vmatrix} = 1 - ax - by - cz$

6. Show that $\begin{vmatrix} x & \beta & \gamma & 1 \\ \alpha & x & \gamma & 1 \\ \alpha & \beta & x & 1 \\ \alpha & \beta & \gamma & 1 \end{vmatrix} = (x - \alpha)(x - \beta)(x - \gamma)$

7. Show that $\begin{vmatrix} 1 & x & x^2 & x^3 \\ x^3 & 1 & x & x^2 \\ x^2 & x^3 & 1 & x \\ x & x^2 & x^3 & 1 \end{vmatrix} = (1 - x^4)^3$

8. Show that $\begin{vmatrix} a & b & b & b \\ a & b & a & a \\ a & a & b & a \\ b & b & b & a \end{vmatrix} = -(a - b)^4$

9. Show that

$$\begin{vmatrix} a^2+1 & ab & ac & ad \\ ab & b^2+1 & bc & bd \\ ac & bc & c^2+1 & cd \\ ad & bd & cd & d^2+1 \end{vmatrix} = 1 + a^2 + b^2 + c^2 + d^2$$

10. Show that

$$\begin{vmatrix} 1+x^2 & x & 0 & 0 \\ x & 1+x^2 & x & 0 \\ 0 & x & 1+x^2 & x \\ 0 & 0 & x & 1+x^2 \end{vmatrix} = 1 + x^2 + x^4 + x^6 + x^8$$

11. Show that

$$\begin{vmatrix} a & b & c & d \\ -b & a & -d & c \\ -c & d & a & -b \\ -d & -c & b & a \end{vmatrix} = \left(a^2 + b^2 + c^2 + d^2\right)^2$$

12. Show that

$$\begin{vmatrix} 0 & x & y & z \\ x & 0 & z & y \\ y & z & 0 & x \\ z & y & x & 0 \end{vmatrix} = (x + y + z)(x - y - z)(x + y - z)(x - y + z)$$

13. Show that

$$\begin{vmatrix} a^2 + \lambda & ab & ac & ad \\ ab & b^2 + \lambda & bc & bd \\ ac & bc & c^2 + \lambda & cd \\ ad & bd & cd & d^2 + \lambda \end{vmatrix} \text{ is divisible by } \lambda^3.$$

14. Show that $\begin{vmatrix} \sin^2 A & \sin A \cos A & \cos^2 A \\ \sin^2 B & \sin B \cos B & \cos^2 B \\ \sin^2 C & \sin C \cos C & \cos^2 C \end{vmatrix}$

$$= \sin(A - B)\sin(B - C)\sin(C - A)$$

15. Prove that

$$\begin{vmatrix} y^2 + z^2 + 1 & z^2 + 1 & y^2 + 1 & y + z \\ z^2 + 1 & z^2 + x^2 + 1 & x^2 + 1 & z + x \\ y^2 + 1 & x^2 + 1 & x^2 + y^2 + 1 & x + y \\ y + z & z + x & x + y & z \end{vmatrix}$$

$$= (yz + zx + xy)^2$$

and write down the determinant of which it is the square.

ANSWER

15. Given determinant $=\begin{vmatrix} y & z & 1 & 0 \\ 0 & z & 1 & x \\ y & 0 & 1 & z \\ 1 & 1 & 0 & 1 \end{vmatrix}^2$

4 ADJOINT AND INVERSE OF A MATRIX

4.1. Adjoint of a Matrix

Let $A = [a_{ij}]$ be a square matrix of order $n \times n$. Let A_{ij} denotes the cofactor of a_{ij} in the determinant $|A|$. Then, the transpose of the matrix $[A_{ij}]$ is known as the adjoint of the matrix A and is written as adj A. This is also known as adjugate of A.

$$\text{Thus, if } A = \begin{bmatrix} a_{11} & a_{12} & \ldots\ldots & a_{1n} \\ a_{21} & a_{22} & \ldots\ldots & a_{2n} \\ \ldots\ldots & \ldots\ldots & \ldots\ldots & \ldots\ldots \\ \ldots\ldots & \ldots\ldots & \ldots\ldots & \ldots\ldots \\ a_{n1} & a_{n2} & \ldots\ldots & a_{nn} \end{bmatrix}$$

$$\text{Then, } [A_{ij}] = \begin{bmatrix} A_{11} & A_{12} & \ldots\ldots & A_{1n} \\ A_{21} & A_{22} & \ldots\ldots & A_{2n} \\ \ldots\ldots & \ldots\ldots & \ldots\ldots & \ldots\ldots \\ \ldots\ldots & \ldots\ldots & \ldots\ldots & \ldots\ldots \\ A_{n1} & A_{n2} & \ldots\ldots & A_{nn} \end{bmatrix}$$

$\therefore$ Adj $A = [A_{ij}]'$

$$= \begin{bmatrix} A_{11} & A_{21} & \ldots\ldots & A_{n1} \\ A_{12} & A_{22} & \ldots\ldots & A_{n2} \\ \ldots\ldots & \ldots\ldots & \ldots\ldots & \ldots\ldots \\ \ldots\ldots & \ldots\ldots & \ldots\ldots & \ldots\ldots \\ A_{1n} & A_{2n} & \ldots\ldots & A_{nn} \end{bmatrix}$$

Working Rule

(i) Replace each element of A by its cofactor in $|A|$.

(ii) Then, take the transpose of the matrix of cofactors.

OR

(i) Take the transpose of A to obtain A'.

(ii) Then, replace each element of A' by its cofactor in $|A'|$.

Note: The cofactors of the elements of the first row of $|A|$ are the elements of the first column of adj A. Similarly, the cofactors of the elements of the first column of $|A|$ are the elements of the first row of adj A.

4.2. Some Theorems

Theorem 1. If A is a square matrix, then

A (adj A) = (adj A) A = $|A|I$

where I is the unit matrix of the same order as A.

Proof. Let $A = [a_{ij}]_{n \times n}$

Then,

adj $A = [A_{ij}]'_{n \times n} = [A'_{ji}]_{n \times n}$, where

$$A'_{ji} = A_{ij};\ i = 1, 2, \ldots\ldots, n \text{ and } j = 1, 2, \ldots\ldots, n$$

Now,

$$A\ (\text{adj } A) = \left[\sum_{j=1}^{n} a_{ij}\ A'_{jk}\right]_{n \times n}, \text{ where}$$

$$i = 1, 2, \ldots\ldots, n;\ j = 1, 2, \ldots\ldots, n \text{ and } k = 1, 2, \ldots\ldots, n$$

$$= [B_{ik}]_{n \times n}$$

where,

$B_{ik} = (i, k)^{th}$ element of the product A (adj A) = Sum of the products of ith row of A and k^{th} column of adj A

$$= \sum_{j=1}^{n} a_{ij} \cdot A'_{jk}$$

$$= a_{i1} A'_{1k} + a_{i2} A'_{2k} + \ldots + a_{in} A'_{nk}$$

$$= a_{i1} + A_{k1} + a_{i2} A_{k2} + \ldots + a_{in} A_{kn}$$

$$\Big| \because A'_{jk} = A_{kj}, \text{etc.}$$

$$= \begin{cases} |A|, \text{ if } i = k \\ 0, \text{ if } i \neq k \end{cases}$$

i.e. Each diagonal element of A (adj A) is $|A|$ while all other elements are zero, so that

$$A \cdot (\text{adj } A) = \begin{bmatrix} |A| & 0 & \ldots\ldots & 0 \\ 0 & |A| & \ldots\ldots & 0 \\ \ldots\ldots & \ldots\ldots & \ldots\ldots & \ldots\ldots \\ \ldots\ldots & \ldots\ldots & \ldots\ldots & \ldots\ldots \\ 0 & 0 & \ldots\ldots & |A| \end{bmatrix}$$

$$= |A| \, I \qquad \ldots (4.1)$$

Similarly, we can prove that

$$(\text{adj } A) \cdot A = |A| \, I \qquad \ldots (4.2)$$

In view of Eqs. (4.1) and (4.2), we obtain

$$A \cdot (\text{adj } A) = (\text{adj } A) \cdot A = |A| \, I$$

Corollary 1. If the matrix A is non-singular or regular, then $|A| \neq 0$, so that, dividing by $|A|$, we have,

$$A \cdot \left(\frac{adj\ A}{|A|} \right) = \left(\frac{adj\ A}{|A|} \right) \cdot A = I$$

Corollary 2. If $|A| \neq 0$, then

$$|\text{adj } A| = |A|^{n-1}$$

We have,

$$|A \cdot (\text{adj } A)| = |A|\ |\text{adj } A|$$

$$= \begin{vmatrix} |A| & 0 & \ldots\ldots & 0 \\ 0 & |A| & \ldots\ldots & 0 \\ \ldots\ldots & \ldots\ldots & \ldots\ldots & \ldots\ldots \\ \ldots\ldots & \ldots\ldots & \ldots\ldots & \ldots\ldots \\ 0 & 0 & \ldots\ldots & |A| \end{vmatrix}$$

$$= |A|^n$$

$$\Rightarrow \quad |\text{adj } A| = |A|^{n-1}$$

Theorem 2. If A and B are two $n \times n$ matrices, then

$$\text{adj } (AB) = (\text{adj } B) \cdot (\text{adj } A)$$

Proof. We know that

$$A \cdot (\text{adj } A) = |A|\ I$$

$$\therefore \quad (AB) \cdot (\text{adj } AB) = |AB|\ I \qquad \ldots (4.3)$$

Now,

$$(AB) \cdot (\text{adj } B) \cdot (\text{adj } A)$$

$$= A\ (B \cdot \text{adj } B) \cdot (\text{adj } A)$$

$$= A \cdot (|B|\ I|) \cdot (\text{adj } A) \qquad | \because B \cdot \text{adj } B = |B|\ I$$

$$= A \cdot |B|\ I \cdot (\text{adj } A)$$

$$= A \cdot |B|\ (\text{adj } A) \qquad | \because I \cdot (\text{adj } A) = \text{adj } A$$

$$= |B|\ A \cdot (\text{adj } A)$$

$$= |B|\ |A|\ I \qquad | \because A\ (\text{adj } A) = |A|\ I$$

$$= |A|\ |B|\ I$$

$$= |AB|\ I \qquad | \because |A|\ |B| = |AB| \qquad \ldots (4.4)$$

In view of Eqs. (4.3) and (4.4), we have

$$(AB) \cdot (\text{adj } AB) = (AB) \cdot (\text{adj } B) \cdot (\text{adj } A)$$

$$\Rightarrow \quad \text{adj } (AB) = (\text{adj } B) \cdot (\text{adj } A)$$

Generalisation. The result can be generalised for square matrices A, B, C, D,... each of order n as follows:

$$\text{adj } (ABCD\ldots) = \ldots (\text{adj } D) \cdot (\text{adj } C) \cdot (\text{adj } B) \cdot (\text{adj } A)$$

Theorem 3. Prove that adj $A' = (\text{adj } A)'$

Proof. Let A be a matrix of order $n \times n$.

Then, A' is a matrix of order $n \times n$.

Therefore, adj A' is a matrix of order $n \times n$.

Again, adj A is a matrix of order $n \times n$.

Therefore, $(\text{adj } A)'$ is a matrix of order $n \times n$.

Thus, the two matrices adj A' and $(\text{adj } A)'$ are comparable ... (4.5)

Now, $(i, j)^{\text{th}}$ element of adj A'

= The cofactor of $(j, i)^{\text{th}}$ element of A' in the determinant $|A'|$

= The cofactor of $(i, j)^{\text{th}}$ element of A in the determinant $|A|$

= $(j, i)^{\text{th}}$ element of adj A ... (4.6)

In view of Eqs. (4.5) and (4.6), we obtain

adj $A' = (\text{adj } A)'$

Theorem 4. Prove that adj $A^* = (\text{adj } A)^*$

Proof. Let $A = [a_{ij}]_{n \times n}$. Then, obviously, A^*, adj A^* and $(\text{adj } A)^*$ are all of the same order $n \times n$. Now,

$(i, j)^{\text{th}}$ element of adj A^*

$$= \text{Cofactor of } (j, i)^{\text{th}} \text{ element of } A^* \text{ in } |A^*|$$

$$= \text{Cofactor of } (i, j)^{\text{th}} \text{ element of } \bar{A} \text{ in } |\bar{A}|$$

$$= \text{Cofactor of } \overline{a_{ij}} \text{ in } |\bar{A}|$$

$$= \overline{A_{ij}}$$

$$\therefore \quad \text{adj } A^* = \left[\overline{A_{ij}}\right]$$

$$= \overline{\left[A_{ij}\right]}$$

$$= \overline{[\text{adj } A]'}$$

$$= (\text{adj } A)^*$$

Theorem 5. Show that adj $(k\,I_n) = k^{n-1}\,I_n$, where k is a scalar.

Proof. We have,

$$I_n = \begin{bmatrix} 1 & 0 & \dots & 0 \\ 0 & 1 & \dots & 0 \\ \dots & \dots & \dots & \dots \\ \dots & \dots & \dots & \dots \\ 0 & 0 & \dots & 1 \end{bmatrix}_{n \times n}$$

$$\therefore \quad kI_n = \begin{bmatrix} k & 0 & \dots & 0 \\ 0 & k & \dots & 0 \\ \dots & \dots & \dots & \dots \\ \dots & \dots & \dots & \dots \\ 0 & 0 & \dots & k \end{bmatrix}_{n \times n}$$

Matrix of cofactors of the elements of kI_n in $|kI_n|$

$$= \begin{bmatrix} k^{n-1} & 0 & \dots & 0 \\ 0 & k^{n-1} & \dots & 0 \\ \dots & \dots & \dots & \dots \\ \dots & \dots & \dots & \dots \\ 0 & 0 & \dots & k^{n-1} \end{bmatrix}_{n \times n}$$

$$= k^{n-1} \begin{bmatrix} 1 & 0 & \dots & 0 \\ 0 & 1 & \dots & 0 \\ \dots & \dots & \dots & \dots \\ \dots & \dots & \dots & \dots \\ 0 & 0 & \dots & 1 \end{bmatrix}_{n \times n}$$

$$= k^{n-1} I_n$$

Aliter

We know that

$$kI_n = \text{diag}\ (k\ a_{11},\ k\ a_{22},\ \ldots..,\ k\ a_{nn}),\ \text{where}\ a_{ii} = 1$$

Here, cofactor of the diagonal element $k\ a_{ii}$

$$= \frac{(k a_{11})(k a_{22})(k a_{33})\ldots(k a_{nn})}{k a_{ii}}$$

$$= k^{n-1} \frac{a_{11}\ a_{22}\ a_{33}\ \ldots\ a_{nn}}{a_{ii}}$$

and, cofactor of any non-diagonal element = 0

$$\therefore\ \text{adj}\ (k\ I_n) = k^n\ a_{11}\ a_{22}\ a_{33} \ldots a_{nn}\ \text{diag}\left(\frac{1}{k a_{11}}, \frac{1}{k a_{22}}, \ldots, \frac{1}{k a_{nn}}\right)$$

$$= k^{n-1}\ \text{diag}\ (1, 1, \ldots, n\ \text{times})$$

$| \because a_{ii} = 1$

$$= k^{n-1}\ I_n$$

Theorem 6. If A is any square matrix of order $n \times n$, then adj (adj A) = $|A|^{n-2}A$.

Proof. We know that

$$A \cdot (\text{adj}\ A) = |A|\ I$$

$$\therefore\ \text{adj}\ \{A \cdot (\text{adj}\ A)\} = \text{adj}\ \{|A|\ I\}$$

$$\Rightarrow \{\text{adj}\ (\text{adj}\ A)\} \cdot (\text{adj}\ A) = |A|^{n-1}$$

$| \because \text{adj}\ \{k\ I_n\} = k^{n-1}\ I_n$

$$\Rightarrow \{\text{adj}\ (\text{adj}\ A)\} \cdot (\text{adj}\ A)\ A = |A|^{n-1}\ I \cdot A$$

| Post-multiplying both sides by A

$$\Rightarrow \{\text{adj}\ (\text{adj}\ A)\} \cdot |A|\ I = |A|^{n-1}A$$

$$\Rightarrow \{\text{adj}\ (\text{adj}\ A)\}\ |A| = |A|^{n-1}A$$

$$\Rightarrow \text{adj}\ (\text{adj}\ A) = |A|^{n-2}A$$

Theorem 7. If A is a square matrix of order n and $|A| \neq 0$, then $|\text{adj}\ (\text{adj}\ A)| = |A|^{(n-1)^2}$

Proof. We know that

$$|\text{adj}\ A| = |A|^{n-1},\ \text{if}\ |A| \neq 0$$

Replacing A by adj A, we obtain

$$\begin{aligned}|\text{adj }(\text{adj } A)| &= |\text{adj } A|^{n-1} \\ &= \{|A|^{n-1}\}^{n-1} \\ &= |A|^{(n-1)^2}\end{aligned}$$

ILLUSTRATIVE EXAMPLES

Example 1. Find adj A where $A = \begin{bmatrix} 0 & 1 & 2 \\ 1 & 2 & 3 \\ 3 & 1 & 1 \end{bmatrix}$ and verify the theorem A (adj A) = (adj A) · A = $|A|$ I_3

Solution: Here,

$$A_{11} = \text{Cofactor of } a_{11} = \begin{vmatrix} 2 & 3 \\ 1 & 1 \end{vmatrix} = -1$$

$$A_{12} = \text{Cofactor of } a_{12} = -\begin{vmatrix} 1 & 3 \\ 3 & 1 \end{vmatrix} = 8$$

$$A_{13} = \text{Cofactor of } a_{13} = \begin{vmatrix} 1 & 2 \\ 3 & 1 \end{vmatrix} = -5$$

$$A_{21} = \text{Cofactor of } a_{21} = -\begin{vmatrix} 1 & 2 \\ 1 & 1 \end{vmatrix} = 1$$

$$A_{22} = \text{Cofactor of } a_{22} = \begin{vmatrix} 0 & 2 \\ 3 & 1 \end{vmatrix} = -6$$

$$A_{23} = \text{Cofactor of } a_{23} = -\begin{vmatrix} 0 & 1 \\ 3 & 1 \end{vmatrix} = 3$$

$$A_{31} = \text{Cofactor of } a_{31} = \begin{vmatrix} 1 & 2 \\ 2 & 3 \end{vmatrix} = -1$$

$$A_{32} = \text{Cofactor of } a_{32} = -\begin{vmatrix} 0 & 2 \\ 1 & 3 \end{vmatrix} = 2$$

$$A_{33} = \text{Cofactor of } a_{33} = \begin{vmatrix} 0 & 1 \\ 1 & 2 \end{vmatrix} = -1$$

$$\therefore \text{ Adj } A = \begin{bmatrix} A_{11} & A_{12} & A_{13} \\ A_{21} & A_{22} & A_{23} \\ A_{31} & A_{32} & A_{33} \end{bmatrix}'$$

$$= \begin{bmatrix} A_{11} & A_{21} & A_{31} \\ A_{12} & A_{22} & A_{32} \\ A_{13} & A_{23} & A_{33} \end{bmatrix}$$

$$= \begin{bmatrix} -1 & 1 & -1 \\ 8 & -6 & 2 \\ -5 & 3 & -1 \end{bmatrix}$$

Verification

$$|A| = \begin{vmatrix} 0 & 1 & 2 \\ 1 & 2 & 3 \\ 3 & 1 & 1 \end{vmatrix} = \begin{vmatrix} 0 & 1 & 0 \\ 1 & 2 & -1 \\ 3 & 1 & -1 \end{vmatrix} \text{ Operating } C_3 - 2C_2$$

$$= -\begin{vmatrix} 1 & -1 \\ 3 & -1 \end{vmatrix} = -(-1+3) = -2$$

$$A \cdot (\text{adj } A) = \begin{bmatrix} 0 & 1 & 2 \\ 1 & 2 & 3 \\ 3 & 1 & 1 \end{bmatrix} \cdot \begin{bmatrix} -1 & 1 & -1 \\ 8 & -6 & 2 \\ -5 & 3 & -1 \end{bmatrix}$$

$$= \begin{bmatrix} 0+8-10 & 0-6+6 & 0+2-2 \\ -1+16-15 & 1-12+9 & -1+4-3 \\ -3+8-5 & 3-6+3 & -3+2-1 \end{bmatrix}$$

$$= \begin{bmatrix} -2 & 0 & 0 \\ 0 & -2 & 0 \\ 0 & 0 & -2 \end{bmatrix} = -2\begin{bmatrix} 1 & 0 & 0 \\ 0 & 1 & 0 \\ 0 & 0 & 1 \end{bmatrix}$$

$$= |A| \; I_3$$

Similarly, we can show that

$$(\text{adj } A) \cdot A = |A| \; I_3$$

Thus,

$$A \cdot (\text{adj } A) = (\text{adj } A) \cdot A = |I| \; A_3$$

Example 2. Prove that the adjoint of a symmetric matrix is symmetric.

Solution: Let A be a symmetric matrix.

Then,

$$A' = A \qquad \text{... (4.7) | By definition}$$

Now,

$$(\text{adj } A)' = \text{adj } A' = \text{adj } A \qquad \text{| by Eq. (4.7)}$$

$\Rightarrow$ adj A is symmetric.

Example 3. Prove that the adjoint of a hermitian matrix is hermitian.

Solution: Let A be a hermitian matrix.

Then,

$$A^* = A \qquad \text{... (4.8) By definition}$$

Now,

$$(\text{adj } A)^* = \text{adj } A^*$$

$$= \text{adj } A \qquad \text{| by Eq. (4.8)}$$

$\Rightarrow$ adj A is hermitian

Example 4. Prove that the adjoint of a diagonal matrix of order 3 is a diagonal matrix.

Solution: Let A be a diagonal matrix of order 3 given by

$$A = \begin{bmatrix} a & 0 & 0 \\ 0 & b & 0 \\ 0 & 0 & c \end{bmatrix}$$

Then,

$$A_{11} = \begin{vmatrix} b & 0 \\ 0 & c \end{vmatrix} = bc$$

$$A_{12} = -\begin{vmatrix} 0 & 0 \\ 0 & c \end{vmatrix} = 0$$

$$A_{13} = \begin{vmatrix} 0 & b \\ 0 & 0 \end{vmatrix} = 0$$

$$A_{21} = -\begin{vmatrix} 0 & 0 \\ 0 & c \end{vmatrix} = 0$$

$$A_{22} = \begin{vmatrix} a & 0 \\ 0 & c \end{vmatrix} = ac$$

$$A_{23} = -\begin{vmatrix} a & 0 \\ 0 & 0 \end{vmatrix} = 0$$

$$A_{31} = \begin{vmatrix} 0 & 0 \\ b & 0 \end{vmatrix} = 0$$

$$A_{32} = -\begin{vmatrix} a & 0 \\ 0 & 0 \end{vmatrix} = 0$$

$$A_{33} = \begin{vmatrix} a & 0 \\ 0 & b \end{vmatrix} = ab$$

$$\therefore \quad \text{adj } A = \begin{bmatrix} A_{11} & A_{21} & A_{31} \\ A_{12} & A_{22} & A_{32} \\ A_{13} & A_{23} & A_{33} \end{bmatrix}$$

$$= \begin{bmatrix} bc & 0 & 0 \\ 0 & ca & 0 \\ 0 & 0 & ab \end{bmatrix}$$

which is evidently a diagonal matrix.

EXERCISE 4.1

1. If $A = \begin{bmatrix} 1 & 2 \\ 3 & -5 \end{bmatrix}$, show that adj $A = \begin{bmatrix} -5 & -2 \\ -3 & 1 \end{bmatrix}$. Verify that

$A \cdot (\text{adj } A) = (\text{adj } A) \cdot A = |A|\, I_2$

2. Find adj A, where $A = \begin{bmatrix} 1 & 0 & -1 \\ 3 & 4 & 5 \\ 0 & -6 & -7 \end{bmatrix}$. Verify that

$A \cdot (\text{adj } A) = (\text{adj } A) \cdot A = |A|\, I_3$

3. Find the adjoint of the matrix $A = \begin{bmatrix} 1 & 2 & 3 \\ 0 & 5 & 0 \\ 2 & 4 & 3 \end{bmatrix}$.

4. Find the adjoint of the matrix $A = \begin{bmatrix} -1 & -2 & 3 \\ -2 & 1 & -1 \\ 4 & -5 & 2 \end{bmatrix}$.

5. Find the adjoint of the matrix $A = \begin{bmatrix} 1 & 1 & 1 \\ 1 & 2 & -3 \\ 2 & -1 & 3 \end{bmatrix}$.

6. Find the adjoint of the matrix $A = \begin{bmatrix} 1 & 1 & 3 \\ 0 & 1 & -1 \\ 2 & 0 & 4 \end{bmatrix}$.

7. Find the adjoint of the matrix $A = \begin{bmatrix} 5 & 0 & 0 & 2 \\ 0 & 1 & 0 & 2 \\ 0 & 0 & 2 & 1 \\ 1 & 0 & 0 & 1 \end{bmatrix}$.

8. Show that
   (i) adj $O = O$
   (ii) adj $I_n = I_n$
9. Show that the adjoint of a diagonal matrix is a diagonal matrix.
10. Show that the adjoint of a triangular matrix is a triangular matrix.
11. If A is a square matrix of order n and k is a scalar, then show that
    adj $(A\ k) = (\text{Adj } A)k^{n-1}$
12. If A is a square matrix of order $n \times n$ and $B =$ adj A, then prove that
    $(AB + kI_n| = \{|A| + k\}^n$
    where k is a scalar.

ANSWERS

2. $\begin{bmatrix} 2 & 6 & 4 \\ 21 & -7 & -8 \\ -18 & 6 & 4 \end{bmatrix}$

3. $\begin{bmatrix} 15 & 6 & -15 \\ 0 & -3 & 0 \\ -10 & 0 & 5 \end{bmatrix}$

4. $\begin{bmatrix} 7 & -11 & -5 \\ 8 & -14 & -5 \\ 6 & -13 & -5 \end{bmatrix}$

5. $\begin{bmatrix} 3 & -4 & -5 \\ -9 & 1 & 4 \\ -5 & 3 & 1 \end{bmatrix}$

6. $\begin{bmatrix} 4 & -4 & -4 \\ 2 & -2 & 1 \\ -2 & 2 & 1 \end{bmatrix}$

7. $\begin{bmatrix} 2 & 0 & 0 & -4 \\ 2 & 6 & 0 & -16 \\ 1 & 0 & 3 & -5 \\ -2 & 0 & 0 & 10 \end{bmatrix}$

4.3. Inverse (or Reciprocal) of a Matrix

Let A be a square matrix of order $n \times n$. Let B be a square matrix of order $n \times n$ such that

$$AB = I_n = BA$$

where I_n is the identity matrix of order $n \times n$, then the matrix B is said to be the inverse of the matrix A and is denoted by A^{-1}.

Thus,

$$AA^{-1} = I = A^{-1}A$$

Note 1. A non-square matrix does not possess any inverse.

Note 2. If B is the inverse of A, then A is the inverse of B.

Note 3. A^{-1} is called the inverse of A because it has the property

$$AA^{-1} = I = A^{-1}A$$

Note 4. A matrix possessing an inverse is called an invertible matrix.

We have already proved that

$$A \cdot (\text{adj } A) = |A| \, I = (\text{adj } A) \cdot A$$

$$\Rightarrow \quad A \cdot \left(\frac{\text{adj } A}{|A|}\right) = I = \left(\frac{\text{adj } A}{|A|}\right) \cdot A \qquad | \text{ provided } |A| \neq 0$$

Hence, $A^{-1} = \dfrac{\text{adj } A}{|A|}$, if $|A| \neq 0$

Corollary

We have,

$$AA^{-1} = I$$

$$\Rightarrow |AA^{-1}| = |I|$$

$$\Rightarrow |A|\,|A^{-1}| = 1$$

$$\Rightarrow |A^{-1}| = |A|^{-1}$$

4.4. Some Theorems

Theorem 1. The inverse of a matrix is unique.

Proof. If possible, let there be two inverses B and C of a matrix. Then, by definition of the inverse of a matrix,

$$AB = I = BA \qquad \text{... (4.9)}$$

and, $AC = I = CA$ ... (4.10)

From Eq. (4.9),

$$C\,(AB) = CI = C$$

$$\Rightarrow (CA)\,B = C$$

$$\Rightarrow IB = C \qquad |\text{ From Eq. (4.10)}$$

$$\Rightarrow B = C$$

Hence, the inverse is unique.

Theorem 2. A square matrix A has an inverse if and only if $|A| \neq 0$, i.e. only a non-singular matrix has an inverse and every non-singular matrix has one.

Proof. *The condition is necessary*

Let B be the inverse of A.

Then,

$$AB = I$$

$$\Rightarrow |AB| = |I|$$

$$\Rightarrow |A|\,|B| = 1$$

$$\Rightarrow |A| \neq 0$$

$\Rightarrow$ A is non-singular

The condition is sufficient

Let $|A| \neq 0$, and $B = \dfrac{\text{adj } A}{|A|}$.

Then,

$$AB = A \cdot \left\{\frac{\text{adj } A}{|A|}\right\}$$

$$= \frac{A \cdot (\text{adj } A)}{|A|}$$

$$= \frac{|A| I}{|A|} = I$$

Similarly, $BA = I$

$\therefore \quad AB = I = BA$

Hence, A has in inverse.

Theorem 3. *(Reversal Law for Inverses)*: If A and B are two non-singular matrices of the same order, then their product AB is also a non-singular matrix and

$$(AB)^{-1} = B^{-1}A^{-1}$$

OR

The inverse of the product of two matrices is equal to the product of the inverse of those matrices taken in reverse order.

Proof. Let A and B be two non-singular matrices of order $n \times n$. Then, $|A| \neq 0$, $|B| \neq 0$ and A^{-1} and B^{-1} exist.

Now,

$$|AB| = |A| \; |B| \neq 0$$

$\Rightarrow$ The product matrix AB is non-singular.

Again,

Order of $AB = n \times n$

$\therefore$ Order of $(AB)^{-1} = n \times n$

Also,

Order of $B^{-1} = n \times n$

Order of $A^{-1} = n \times n$

$\therefore$ Order of $B^{-1} A^{-1} = n \times n$

Thus, matrices $(AB)^{-1}$ and $B^{-1}A^{-1}$ are comparable.

Now,

$$(AB) \; (B^{-1}A^{-1}) = A \; (BB^{-1})A^{-1} \qquad | \text{ By associative law}$$

$= A\ I\ A^{-1}$ | $\because BB^{-1} = I$

$= AA^{-1}$

$= I$ | By the definition of inverse of a matrix

and

$(B^{-1}A^{-1})\ (AB) = B^{-1}\ (A^{-1}A)B$ | By associative law

$= B^{-1}\ I\ B$ | $\because A^{-1}A = I$

$= B^{-1}\ B$

$= I$

$\therefore\ (AB)\ (B^{-1}A^{-1}) = I = (B^{-1}A^{-1})\ (AB)$

$\Rightarrow\ B^{-1}A^{-1}$ is the unique inverse of AB

i.e. $(AB)^{-1} = B^{-1}A^{-1}$

This shows that the matrix AB is non-singular.

Generalisation

Generalisation of the above result gives

$$(ABC\ ...\ LM)^{-1} = M^{-1}L^{-1}\ ...\ C^{-1}B^{-1}A^{-1}$$

Theorem 4. If A is a non-singular matrix and p is any positive integer, then

$$(A^p)^{-1} = (A^{-1})^p$$

Proof.

$\because\ A^p = A \cdot A\ ...\ p$ times

$\therefore\ (A^p)^{-1} = (A \cdot A\ ...\ A)^{-1}$

$= A^{-1} \cdot A^{-1} \cdot A^{-1}\ ...\ A^{-1}$ | By reversal law of inverses

$= (A^{-1})^p$

Theorem 5. If A is a non-singular matrix, then

$$(A^{-1})^{-1} = A$$

i.e. the inverse of the inverse of a matrix is the matrix itself.

Proof. Let A^{-1} be the inverse of the given matrix A. Then,

$AA^{-1} = I = A^{-1}A$

$\Rightarrow\ A^{-1}A = I = AA^{-1}$

$\Rightarrow$ A is the unique inverse of A^{-1}, i.e. $(A^{-1})^{-1} = A$

Theorem 6. The inverse of the transpose of a matrix is the transpose of the inverse of that matrix, i.e.

$$(A^1)^{-1} = (A^{-1})^1$$

OR

The operations of transposing and inverting are commutative.

Proof. We know that

$$AA^{-1} = I = A^{-1}A$$

$$\Rightarrow \quad (AA^{-1})' = I' = (A^{-1}A)'$$

$$\Rightarrow \quad (A^{-1})'A' = I = A'(A^{-1})' \mid \text{By reversal law of transposes}$$

$$\Rightarrow \quad A'(A^{-1})' = I = (A^{-1})'A'$$

$\Rightarrow$ $(A^{-1})'$ is the unique inverse of A'

$$\Rightarrow \quad (A^{-1})' = (A')^{-1}$$

Theorem 7. Prove that $(\text{adj } A)^{-1} = \text{adj } (A^{-1})$, where A is any $n \times n$ matrix.

Proof. By definition of the inverse of a matrix,

$$\text{LHS} = (\text{adj } A)^{-1}$$

$$= \frac{\text{adj}(\text{adj } A)}{|\text{adj } A|}$$

$$= \frac{|A|^{n-2} A}{|A|^{n-1}}$$

$$= \frac{A}{|A|} \qquad \ldots (4.11)$$

Again,

$$\text{RHS} = \text{adj } (A^{-1})$$

$$= \text{adj}\left\{\frac{\text{adj } A}{|A|}\right\}$$

$$= \text{adj}\left\{\frac{1}{|A|}\text{adj } A\right\}$$

$$= \frac{1}{|A|^{n-1}}\text{adj}(\text{adj } A)$$

$$= \frac{|A|^{n-2} A}{|A|^{n-1}}$$

$$= \frac{A}{|A|} \qquad \ldots (4.12)$$

In view of Eqs. (4.11) and (4.12), we have

$(\text{adj } A)^{-1} = \text{adj } (A^{-1})$

Theorem 8. If A is a non-singular matrix of order n such that $AX = AY$, then $X = Y$.

Proof.

$\because$ A is a non-singular matrix

$\therefore$ A^{-1} exists.

Now,

$AX = AY$	Given
$\Rightarrow A^{-1}(AX) = A^{-1}(AY)$	Pre-multiplying both sides by A^{-1}
$\Rightarrow (A^{-1}A)X = (A^{-1}A)Y$	By associative law
$\Rightarrow IX = IY$	By definition of inverse of a matrix
$\Rightarrow X = Y$	

Theorem 9. If A and B are any two $n \times n$ matrices such that $AB = O$, where O is the null matrix, then at least one of them is singular.

Solution: We have

$AB = O$ | Given

$\Rightarrow |AB| = |O|$

$\Rightarrow |A|\,|B| = 0$

$\Rightarrow |A| = 0$ or $|B| = 0$ or $|A|$ and $|B|$ both are zero.

$\Rightarrow$ A is singular

or

B is sngular

or

A and B both are singular.

$\Rightarrow$ At least one of A and B is singular.

Theorem 10. If a non-singular matrix A is symmetric, then A^{-1} is also symmetric.

Proof. If A is symmetric, then

$$A^1 = A \quad \text{... (4.13)}$$

$\because$ A is non-singular

$\therefore$ A^{-1} exists and

$$AA^{-1} = I = A^{-1}A$$

Now,

$$AA^{-1} = I$$

$\Rightarrow$ $AA^{-1} = I'$

$\Rightarrow$ $AA^{-1} = (AA^{-1})'$

$\Rightarrow$ $AA^{-1} = (A^{-1})'\,A'$

$\Rightarrow$ $AA^{-1} = (A^{-1})'A$ | Using Eq. (4.13)

$\because$ A is non-singular

$\therefore$ $A^{-1} = (A^{-1})'$ | By theorem 8

$\Rightarrow$ A^{-1} is symmetric.

Theorem 11. The universe of the tranjugate of a matrix A is the tranjugate of the inverse of the matrix A, i.e.

$$(A^*)^{-1} = (A^{-1})^*$$

Proof. We know that

$$AA^{-1} = I = A^{-1}A$$

$\Rightarrow$ $(AA^{-1})^* = I^* = (A^{-1}A)^*$

$\Rightarrow$ $(A^{-1})^*A^* = I = A^*(A^{-1})^*$

$\Rightarrow$ $A^*(A^{-1})^* = I = (A^{-1})^*A^*$

$\Rightarrow$ $(A^{-1})^*$ is the unique inverse of A^*

$\Rightarrow$ $(A^*)^{-1} = (A^{-1})^*$

ILLUSTRATIVE EXAMPLES

Example 1. Find the inverse of the matrix

$$A = \begin{bmatrix} 1 & 2 & 3 \\ 1 & 3 & 4 \\ 1 & 4 & 3 \end{bmatrix}$$

Solution: We have

$$A = \begin{bmatrix} 1 & 2 & 3 \\ 1 & 3 & 4 \\ 1 & 4 & 3 \end{bmatrix}$$

$$\therefore \quad |A| = \begin{vmatrix} 1 & 2 & 3 \\ 1 & 3 & 4 \\ 1 & 4 & 3 \end{vmatrix}$$

$$= \begin{vmatrix} 1 & 2 & 3 \\ 0 & 1 & 1 \\ 0 & 2 & 0 \end{vmatrix} \quad | \text{ Operating } R_2 - R_1 \text{ and } R_3 - R_1$$

$$= 1\begin{vmatrix} 1 & 1 \\ 2 & 0 \end{vmatrix} \quad | \text{ Expanding along } C_1$$

$$= 0 - 2$$

$$= -2 \; (\neq 0)$$

$\therefore$ The matrix A is invertible, i.e. the matrix A has an inverse.

For the matrix A, we have the cofactors of the elements of $|A|$ as follows:

$$A_{11} = \text{Cofactor of } a_{11} = (-1)^{1+1}\begin{vmatrix} 3 & 4 \\ 4 & 3 \end{vmatrix} = -7$$

$$A_{12} = \text{Cofactor of } a_{12} = (-1)^{1+2}\begin{vmatrix} 1 & 4 \\ 1 & 3 \end{vmatrix} = 1$$

$$A_{13} = \text{Cofactor of } a_{13} = (-1)^{1+3}\begin{vmatrix} 1 & 3 \\ 1 & 4 \end{vmatrix} = 1$$

$$A_{21} = \text{Cofactor of } a_{21} = (-1)^{2+1}\begin{vmatrix} 2 & 3 \\ 4 & 3 \end{vmatrix} = 6$$

$$A_{22} = \text{Cofactor of } a_{22} = (-1)^{2+2}\begin{vmatrix} 1 & 3 \\ 1 & 3 \end{vmatrix} = 0$$

$$A_{23} = \text{Cofactor of } a_{23} = (-1)^{2+3} \begin{vmatrix} 1 & 2 \\ 1 & 4 \end{vmatrix} = -2$$

$$A_{31} = \text{Cofactor of } a_{31} = (-1)^{3+1} \begin{vmatrix} 2 & 3 \\ 3 & 4 \end{vmatrix} = -1$$

$$A_{32} = \text{Cofactor of } a_{32} = (-1)^{3+2} \begin{vmatrix} 1 & 3 \\ 1 & 4 \end{vmatrix} = -1$$

$$A_{33} = \text{Cofactor of } a_{33} = (-1)^{3+3} \begin{vmatrix} 1 & 2 \\ 1 & 3 \end{vmatrix} = 1$$

$\therefore$ Matrix of cofactors

$$= \begin{bmatrix} A_{11} & A_{12} & A_{13} \\ A_{21} & A_{22} & A_{23} \\ A_{31} & A_{32} & A_{33} \end{bmatrix}$$

$$= \begin{bmatrix} -7 & 1 & 1 \\ 6 & 0 & -2 \\ -1 & -1 & 1 \end{bmatrix}$$

$$\therefore \text{Adj } A = \begin{bmatrix} -7 & 1 & 1 \\ 6 & 0 & -2 \\ -1 & -1 & 1 \end{bmatrix}'$$

$$= \begin{bmatrix} -7 & 6 & -1 \\ 1 & 0 & -1 \\ 1 & -2 & 1 \end{bmatrix}$$

$$\therefore \quad A^{-1} = \frac{\text{Adj } A}{|A|}$$

$$= -\frac{1}{2} \begin{bmatrix} -7 & 6 & -1 \\ 1 & 0 & -1 \\ 1 & -2 & 1 \end{bmatrix}$$

$$= \begin{bmatrix} \frac{7}{2} & -3 & \frac{1}{2} \\ -\frac{1}{2} & 0 & \frac{1}{2} \\ -\frac{1}{2} & 1 & -\frac{1}{2} \end{bmatrix}$$

Example 2. If $A = \begin{bmatrix} -1 & 0 & 0 & 2 \\ -9 & 1 & 0 & 1 \\ 1 & 0 & 2 & -1 \\ -4 & 1 & -3 & 1 \end{bmatrix}$, find A^{-1}.

Solution: We have

$$A = \begin{bmatrix} -1 & 0 & 0 & 2 \\ -9 & 1 & 0 & 1 \\ 1 & 0 & 2 & -1 \\ -4 & 1 & -3 & 1 \end{bmatrix}$$

$$\therefore \quad |A| = \begin{vmatrix} -1 & 0 & 0 & 2 \\ -9 & 1 & 0 & 1 \\ 1 & 0 & 2 & -1 \\ -4 & 1 & -3 & 1 \end{vmatrix}$$

$$= \begin{vmatrix} -1 & 0 & 0 & 0 \\ -9 & 1 & 0 & -17 \\ 1 & 0 & 2 & 1 \\ -4 & 1 & -3 & -7 \end{vmatrix} \qquad | \text{ Operating } C_4 + 2C_1$$

$$= -\begin{vmatrix} 1 & 0 & -17 \\ 0 & 2 & 1 \\ 1 & -3 & -7 \end{vmatrix} \qquad | \text{ Expanding along } R_1$$

$$= -\begin{vmatrix} 1 & 0 & -17 \\ 0 & 2 & 1 \\ 0 & -3 & 10 \end{vmatrix} \qquad | \text{ Operating } R_3 - R_1$$

$$= -\begin{vmatrix} 2 & 1 \\ -3 & 10 \end{vmatrix} \qquad | \text{ Expanding along } C_1$$

$$= -23 \neq 0$$

$\therefore$ The matrix A is invertible.

For the matrix A, we have the cofactors of the elements of $|A|$ as follows:

$$A_{11} = (-1)^{1+1} \begin{vmatrix} 1 & 0 & 1 \\ 0 & 2 & -1 \\ 1 & -3 & 1 \end{vmatrix}$$

$$= \begin{vmatrix} 1 & 0 & 0 \\ 0 & 2 & -1 \\ 1 & -3 & 1 \end{vmatrix} \qquad | \text{ Operating } C_3 - C_1$$

$$= \begin{vmatrix} 2 & -1 \\ -3 & 0 \end{vmatrix} = -3$$

$$A_{12} = (-1)^{1+2} \begin{vmatrix} -9 & 0 & 1 \\ 1 & 2 & -1 \\ -4 & -3 & 1 \end{vmatrix}$$

$$= -\begin{vmatrix} 0 & 0 & 1 \\ -8 & 2 & -1 \\ 5 & -3 & 1 \end{vmatrix} \qquad | \text{ Operating } C_1 + 9C_3$$

$$= -\begin{vmatrix} -8 & 2 \\ 5 & -3 \end{vmatrix} \qquad | \text{ Expanding along } R_1$$

$$= -14$$

$$A_{13} = (-1)^{1+3} \begin{vmatrix} -9 & 1 & 1 \\ 1 & 0 & -1 \\ -4 & 1 & 1 \end{vmatrix}$$

$$= \begin{vmatrix} -8 & 1 & 1 \\ 0 & 0 & -1 \\ -3 & 1 & 1 \end{vmatrix} \qquad | \text{ Operating } C_1 + C_3$$

$$= -(-1) \begin{vmatrix} -8 & 1 \\ -3 & 1 \end{vmatrix}$$

$$= -5$$

$$A_{14} = (-1)^{1+4} \begin{vmatrix} -9 & 1 & 0 \\ 1 & 0 & 2 \\ -4 & 1 & -3 \end{vmatrix}$$

$$= - \begin{vmatrix} 0 & 1 & 0 \\ 1 & 0 & 2 \\ 5 & 1 & -3 \end{vmatrix} \qquad | \text{ Operating } C_1 + 9C_2$$

$$= \begin{vmatrix} 1 & 2 \\ 5 & -3 \end{vmatrix} \qquad | \text{ Expanding along } R_1$$

$$= -13$$

$$A_{21} = (-1)^{2+1} \begin{vmatrix} 0 & 0 & 2 \\ 0 & 2 & -1 \\ 1 & -3 & 1 \end{vmatrix}$$

$$= - \begin{vmatrix} 0 & 2 \\ 2 & -1 \end{vmatrix} = 4 \qquad | \text{ Expanding along } R_1$$

$$A_{22} = (-1)^{2+2} \begin{vmatrix} -1 & 0 & 2 \\ 1 & 2 & -1 \\ -4 & -3 & 1 \end{vmatrix}$$

$$= \begin{vmatrix} -1 & 0 & 0 \\ 1 & 2 & -1 \\ -4 & -3 & -7 \end{vmatrix} \qquad | \text{ Operating } C_3 + 2C_1$$

$$= (-1)\begin{vmatrix} 2 & 1 \\ -3 & -7 \end{vmatrix} \qquad | \text{ Expanding along } R_1$$

$$= 11$$

$$A_{23} = (-1)^{2+3}\begin{vmatrix} -1 & 0 & 2 \\ 1 & 0 & -1 \\ -4 & 1 & 1 \end{vmatrix}$$

$$= -\begin{vmatrix} -1 & 0 & 0 \\ 1 & 0 & 1 \\ -4 & 1 & -7 \end{vmatrix} \qquad | \text{ Operating } C_3 + 2C_1$$

$$= -(-1)\begin{vmatrix} 0 & 1 \\ 1 & -7 \end{vmatrix} \qquad | \text{ Expanding along } R_1$$

$$= -1$$

$$A_{24} = (-1)^{2+4}\begin{vmatrix} -1 & 0 & 0 \\ 1 & 0 & 2 \\ -4 & 1 & -3 \end{vmatrix}$$

$$= (-1)\begin{vmatrix} 0 & 2 \\ 1 & -3 \end{vmatrix} \qquad | \text{ Expanding along } R_1$$

$$= 2$$

$$A_{31} = (-1)^{3+1}\begin{vmatrix} 0 & 0 & 2 \\ 1 & 0 & 1 \\ 1 & -3 & 1 \end{vmatrix}$$

$$= 2\begin{vmatrix} 1 & 0 \\ 1 & -3 \end{vmatrix} \qquad | \text{ Expanding along } R_1$$

$$= -6$$

$$A_{32} = (-1)^{3+2}\begin{vmatrix} -1 & 0 & 2 \\ -9 & 0 & 1 \\ -4 & -3 & 1 \end{vmatrix}$$

$$= -\left\{-(-3)\begin{vmatrix} -1 & 2 \\ -9 & 1 \end{vmatrix}\right\} \qquad \text{| Expanding along } C_2$$

$$= -51$$

$$A_{33} = (-1)^{3+3}\begin{vmatrix} -1 & 0 & 2 \\ -9 & 1 & 1 \\ -4 & 1 & 1 \end{vmatrix}$$

$$= \begin{vmatrix} -1 & 0 & 0 \\ -9 & 1 & -17 \\ -4 & 1 & -7 \end{vmatrix} \qquad \text{| Operating } C_3 + 2C_1$$

$$= (-1)\begin{vmatrix} 1 & -17 \\ 1 & -7 \end{vmatrix} \qquad \text{| Expanding along } R_1$$

$$= -10$$

$$A_{34} = (-1)^{3+4}\begin{vmatrix} -1 & 0 & 0 \\ -9 & 1 & 0 \\ -4 & 1 & -3 \end{vmatrix}$$

$$= -(-1)\begin{vmatrix} 1 & 0 \\ 1 & -3 \end{vmatrix} \qquad \text{| Expanding along } R_1$$

$$= -3$$

$$A_{41} = (-1)^{4+1}\begin{vmatrix} 0 & 0 & 2 \\ 1 & 0 & 1 \\ 0 & 2 & -1 \end{vmatrix}$$

$$= -2\begin{vmatrix} 1 & 0 \\ 0 & 2 \end{vmatrix} \qquad \text{| Expanding along } R_1$$

$$= -4$$

$$A_{42} = (-1)^{4+2}\begin{vmatrix} -1 & 0 & 2 \\ -9 & 0 & 1 \\ 1 & 2 & -1 \end{vmatrix}$$

$$= -2\begin{vmatrix} -1 & 2 \\ -9 & 1 \end{vmatrix} \qquad \text{| Expanding along } C_2$$

$$= -34$$

$$A_{43} = (-1)^{4+3}\begin{vmatrix} -1 & 0 & 2 \\ -9 & 1 & 1 \\ 1 & 0 & -1 \end{vmatrix}$$

$$= -\begin{vmatrix} -1 & 2 \\ 1 & -1 \end{vmatrix} \qquad \text{| Expanding along } C_2$$

$$= 1$$

$$A_{44} = (-1)^{4+4}\begin{vmatrix} -1 & 0 & 0 \\ -9 & 1 & 0 \\ 1 & 0 & 2 \end{vmatrix}$$

$$= 2\begin{vmatrix} -1 & 0 \\ -9 & 1 \end{vmatrix} \qquad \text{| Expanding along } C_3$$

$$= -2$$

$\therefore$ Matrix of cofactors

$$= \begin{bmatrix} A_{11} & A_{12} & A_{13} & A_{14} \\ A_{21} & A_{22} & A_{23} & A_{24} \\ A_{31} & A_{32} & A_{33} & A_{34} \\ A_{41} & A_{42} & A_{43} & A_{44} \end{bmatrix}$$

$$= \begin{bmatrix} -3 & -14 & -5 & -13 \\ 4 & 11 & -1 & 2 \\ -6 & -51 & -10 & -3 \\ -4 & -34 & 1 & -2 \end{bmatrix}$$

$$\therefore \quad \text{Adj } A = \begin{bmatrix} -3 & -14 & -5 & -13 \\ 4 & 11 & -1 & 2 \\ -6 & -51 & -10 & -3 \\ -4 & -34 & 1 & -2 \end{bmatrix}'$$

$$= \begin{bmatrix} -3 & 4 & -6 & -4 \\ -14 & 11 & -51 & -34 \\ -5 & -1 & -10 & 1 \\ -13 & 2 & -3 & -2 \end{bmatrix}$$

$$\therefore \quad A^{-1} = \frac{\text{Adj } A}{|A|}$$

$$= -\frac{1}{23}\begin{bmatrix} -3 & 4 & -6 & -4 \\ -14 & 11 & -51 & -34 \\ -5 & -1 & -10 & 1 \\ -13 & 2 & -3 & -2 \end{bmatrix}$$

$$= \begin{bmatrix} \frac{3}{23} & -\frac{4}{23} & \frac{6}{23} & \frac{4}{23} \\ \frac{14}{23} & -\frac{11}{23} & \frac{51}{23} & \frac{34}{23} \\ \frac{5}{23} & \frac{1}{23} & \frac{10}{23} & -\frac{1}{23} \\ \frac{13}{23} & -\frac{2}{23} & \frac{3}{23} & \frac{2}{23} \end{bmatrix}$$

Example 3. What is the reciprocal of the matrix?

$$A = \begin{bmatrix} \cos\alpha & -\sin\alpha & 0 \\ \sin\alpha & \cos\alpha & 0 \\ 0 & 0 & 1 \end{bmatrix}$$

Solution: We have

$$A = \begin{bmatrix} \cos\alpha & -\sin\alpha & 0 \\ \sin\alpha & \cos\alpha & 0 \\ 0 & 0 & 1 \end{bmatrix}$$

$$\therefore \quad |A| = \begin{vmatrix} \cos\alpha & -\sin\alpha & 0 \\ \sin\alpha & \cos\alpha & 0 \\ 0 & 0 & 1 \end{vmatrix}$$

$$= \begin{vmatrix} \cos\alpha & -\sin\alpha \\ \sin\alpha & \cos\alpha \end{vmatrix} \qquad \text{| Expanding along } C_3$$

$$= \cos^2\alpha + \sin^2\alpha = 1 \neq 0$$

$\therefore \quad A^{-1}$ exists.

Now,

$$\text{Adj } A = \begin{bmatrix} \cos\alpha & -\sin\alpha & 0 \\ \sin\alpha & \cos\alpha & 0 \\ 0 & 0 & 1 \end{bmatrix}' \qquad \text{| Replacing each element by its cofactor}$$

$$= \begin{bmatrix} \cos\alpha & \sin\alpha & 0 \\ -\sin\alpha & \cos\alpha & 0 \\ 0 & 0 & 1 \end{bmatrix}$$

$$\therefore \quad A^{-1} = \frac{\text{Adj } A}{|A|} = \begin{bmatrix} \cos\alpha & \sin\alpha & 0 \\ -\sin\alpha & \cos\alpha & 0 \\ 0 & 0 & 1 \end{bmatrix}$$

Example 4. Show that if w is one of the imaginary cube roots of unity and if

$$A = \begin{bmatrix} 1 & 1 & 1 \\ 1 & w & w^2 \\ 1 & w^2 & w \end{bmatrix}, \text{ then } A^{-1} = \frac{1}{3}\begin{bmatrix} 1 & 1 & 1 \\ 1 & w^2 & w \\ 1 & w & w^2 \end{bmatrix}$$

Solution:

$$|A| = \begin{vmatrix} 1 & 1 & 1 \\ 1 & w & w^2 \\ 1 & w^2 & w \end{vmatrix}$$

$$= \begin{vmatrix} 1 & 1 & 1 \\ 0 & w-1 & w^2-1 \\ 0 & w^2-1 & w-1 \end{vmatrix} \quad \Bigg| \text{ Operating } R_2 - R_1 \text{ and } R_3 - R_1$$

$= (w - 1)(w - 1) - (w^2 - 1)^2$ | Expanding along C_1

$= (w - 1)^2 - (w - 1)^2 (w + 1)^2$

$= (w - 1)^2 \{1 - (w + 1)^2\}$

$= (w - 1)^2 (1 - w^2 - 1 - 2w)$

$= -(w - 1)^2 (w^2 + 2w)$

$= -(w - 1)^2 (-1 - w + 2w)$ | $\because 1 + w + w^2 = 0$

$= -(w - 1)^2 (w - 1)$

$= -(w - 1)^3 \neq 0$

$\therefore$ A^{-1} exists.

Now,

$$A_{11} = \begin{vmatrix} w & w^2 \\ w^2 & w \end{vmatrix}$$

$= w^2 - w^4$

$= w^2 - w^3 w$

$= w^2 - 1 w$ | $\because w^3 = 1$

$= w^2 - w$

$$A_{12} = -\begin{vmatrix} 1 & w^2 \\ 1 & w \end{vmatrix}$$

$= w^2 - w$

$$A_{13} = \begin{vmatrix} 1 & w \\ 1 & w^2 \end{vmatrix} = w^2 - w$$

$$A_{21} = -\begin{vmatrix} 1 & 1 \\ w^2 & w \end{vmatrix} = w^2 - w$$

$$A_{22} = \begin{vmatrix} 1 & 1 \\ 1 & w \end{vmatrix} = w - 1$$

$$A_{23} = -\begin{vmatrix} 1 & 1 \\ 1 & w^2 \end{vmatrix} = -\left(w^2 - 1\right)$$

$$A_{31} = \begin{vmatrix} 1 & 1 \\ w & w^2 \end{vmatrix} = w^2 - w$$

$$A_{32} = -\begin{vmatrix} 1 & 1 \\ 1 & w^2 \end{vmatrix} = -\left(w^2 - 1\right)$$

$$A_{33} = \begin{vmatrix} 1 & 1 \\ 1 & w \end{vmatrix} = w - 1$$

$$\therefore \quad \text{Adj } A = \begin{bmatrix} A_{11} & A_{12} & A_{13} \\ A_{21} & A_{22} & A_{23} \\ A_{31} & A_{32} & A_{33} \end{bmatrix}'$$

$$= \begin{bmatrix} A_{11} & A_{21} & A_{31} \\ A_{12} & A_{22} & A_{32} \\ A_{13} & A_{23} & A_{33} \end{bmatrix}$$

$$= \begin{bmatrix} w^2 - w & w^2 - w & w^2 - w \\ w^2 - w & w - 1 & -\left(w^2 - 1\right) \\ w^2 - w & -\left(w^2 - 1\right) & w - 1 \end{bmatrix}$$

$$\therefore \quad A^{-1} = \frac{\text{Adj } A}{|A|}$$

$$= \frac{1}{-(w-1)^3} \begin{bmatrix} w^2 - w & w^2 - w & w^2 - w \\ w^2 - w & w - 1 & -\left(w^2 - 1\right) \\ w^2 - w & -\left(w^2 - 1\right) & w - 1 \end{bmatrix}$$

$$= -\frac{1}{(w-1)^3}\begin{bmatrix} w(w-1) & w(w-1) & w(w-1) \\ w(w-1) & w-1 & -(w-1)(w+1) \\ w(w-1) & -(w-1)(w+1) & (w-1) \end{bmatrix}$$

$$= -\frac{1}{(w-1)^2}\begin{bmatrix} w & w & w \\ w & 1 & -(w+1) \\ w & -(w+1) & 1 \end{bmatrix}$$

$$= \frac{1}{3w}\begin{bmatrix} w & w & w \\ w & 1 & -(w+1) \\ w & -(w+1) & 1 \end{bmatrix}$$

$\because (w-1)^2 = w^2 + 1 - 2w$
$= -w - 2w$
$= -3w$
$(\because 1 + w + w^2 = 0)$

$$= \frac{1}{3w}\begin{bmatrix} w & w & w \\ w & w^3 & w^2 \\ w & w^2 & w^3 \end{bmatrix}$$

$\because w^3 = 1$ and $1 + w + w^2 = 0$

$$= \frac{1}{3}\begin{bmatrix} 1 & 1 & 1 \\ 1 & w^2 & w \\ 1 & w & w^2 \end{bmatrix}$$

Example 5. If $A = \begin{bmatrix} 0 & 0 & 1 \\ 0 & 1 & 0 \\ 1 & 0 & 0 \end{bmatrix}$, show that $A^{-1} = A$.

Solution:

$$|A| = \begin{bmatrix} 0 & 0 & 1 \\ 0 & 1 & 0 \\ 1 & 0 & 0 \end{bmatrix} = -1 \neq 0$$

$\therefore$ A^{-1} exists.

Now,

$$A_{11} = \begin{vmatrix} 1 & 0 \\ 0 & 0 \end{vmatrix} = 0$$

$$A_{12} = -\begin{vmatrix} 0 & 0 \\ 1 & 0 \end{vmatrix} = 0$$

$$A_{13} = \begin{vmatrix} 0 & 1 \\ 1 & 0 \end{vmatrix} = -1$$

$$A_{21} = -\begin{vmatrix} 0 & 1 \\ 0 & 0 \end{vmatrix} = 0$$

$$A_{22} = \begin{vmatrix} 0 & 1 \\ 1 & 0 \end{vmatrix} = -1$$

$$A_{23} = -\begin{vmatrix} 0 & 0 \\ 1 & 0 \end{vmatrix} = 0$$

$$A_{31} = \begin{vmatrix} 0 & 1 \\ 1 & 0 \end{vmatrix} = -1$$

$$A_{32} = -\begin{vmatrix} 0 & 1 \\ 0 & 0 \end{vmatrix} = 0$$

$$A_{33} = \begin{vmatrix} 0 & 0 \\ 0 & 1 \end{vmatrix} = 0$$

$\therefore$ Matrix of cofactors

$$= \begin{bmatrix} A_{11} & A_{12} & A_{13} \\ A_{21} & A_{22} & A_{23} \\ A_{31} & A_{32} & A_{33} \end{bmatrix}$$

$$= \begin{bmatrix} 0 & 0 & -1 \\ 0 & -1 & 0 \\ -1 & 0 & 0 \end{bmatrix}$$

$$\therefore \quad \text{Adj } A = \begin{bmatrix} 0 & 0 & -1 \\ 0 & -1 & 0 \\ -1 & 0 & 0 \end{bmatrix}'$$

$$= \begin{bmatrix} 0 & 0 & -1 \\ 0 & -1 & 0 \\ -1 & 0 & 0 \end{bmatrix}$$

$$\therefore \quad A^{-1} = \frac{\text{Adj } A}{|A|} = \begin{bmatrix} 0 & 0 & -1 \\ 0 & -1 & 0 \\ -1 & 0 & 0 \end{bmatrix} = \begin{bmatrix} 0 & 0 & 1 \\ 0 & 1 & 0 \\ 1 & 0 & 0 \end{bmatrix} = A$$

Example 6. If $A = \begin{bmatrix} 3 & -3 & 4 \\ 2 & -3 & 4 \\ 0 & -1 & 1 \end{bmatrix}$, show that $A^3 = A^{-1}$.

Solution:

$$|A| = \begin{vmatrix} 3 & -3 & 4 \\ 2 & -3 & 4 \\ 0 & -1 & 1 \end{vmatrix}$$

$$= \begin{vmatrix} 1 & 0 & 0 \\ 2 & -3 & 4 \\ 0 & -1 & 1 \end{vmatrix} \qquad | \text{ Operating } R_1 - R_2$$

$$= \begin{vmatrix} -3 & 4 \\ -1 & 1 \end{vmatrix} \qquad | \text{ Expanding along } R_1$$

$$= -3 + 4$$

$$= 1 \neq 0$$

$\therefore$ A^{-1} exists.

Now,

$$A_{11} = +\begin{vmatrix} -3 & 4 \\ -1 & 1 \end{vmatrix} = 1$$

$$A_{12} = -\begin{vmatrix} 2 & 4 \\ 0 & 1 \end{vmatrix} = -2$$

$$A_{13} = +\begin{vmatrix} 2 & -3 \\ 0 & -1 \end{vmatrix} = -2$$

$$A_{21} = -\begin{vmatrix} -3 & 4 \\ -1 & 1 \end{vmatrix} = -1$$

$$A_{22} = +\begin{vmatrix} 3 & 4 \\ 0 & 1 \end{vmatrix} = 3$$

$$A_{23} = -\begin{vmatrix} 3 & -3 \\ 0 & -1 \end{vmatrix} = 3$$

$$A_{31} = +\begin{vmatrix} -3 & 4 \\ -3 & 4 \end{vmatrix} = 0$$

$$A_{32} = -\begin{vmatrix} 3 & 4 \\ 2 & 4 \end{vmatrix} = -4$$

$$A_{33} = +\begin{vmatrix} 3 & -3 \\ 2 & -3 \end{vmatrix} = -3$$

$\therefore$ Matrix of cofactors

$$= \begin{bmatrix} A_{11} & A_{12} & A_{13} \\ A_{21} & A_{22} & A_{23} \\ A_{31} & A_{32} & A_{33} \end{bmatrix}$$

$$= \begin{bmatrix} 1 & -2 & -2 \\ -1 & 3 & 3 \\ 0 & -4 & -3 \end{bmatrix}$$

$$\therefore \quad \text{Adj } A = \begin{bmatrix} 1 & -2 & -2 \\ -1 & 3 & 3 \\ 0 & -4 & -3 \end{bmatrix}'$$

$$= \begin{bmatrix} 1 & -1 & 0 \\ -2 & 3 & -4 \\ -2 & 3 & -3 \end{bmatrix}$$

$$\therefore \quad A^{-1} = \frac{\text{Adj } A}{|A|} = \begin{bmatrix} 1 & -1 & 0 \\ -2 & 3 & -4 \\ -2 & 3 & -3 \end{bmatrix} \qquad \text{... (4.14)}$$

Again,

$$A^2 = A\ A$$

$$= \begin{bmatrix} 3 & -3 & 4 \\ 2 & -3 & 4 \\ 0 & -1 & 1 \end{bmatrix} \begin{bmatrix} 3 & -3 & 4 \\ 2 & -3 & 4 \\ 0 & -1 & 1 \end{bmatrix}$$

$$= \begin{bmatrix} 9-6+0 & -9+9-4 & 12-12+4 \\ 6-6+0 & -6+9-4 & 8-12+4 \\ 0-2+0 & 0+3-1 & 0-4+1 \end{bmatrix}$$

$$= \begin{bmatrix} 3 & -4 & 4 \\ 0 & -1 & 0 \\ -2 & 2 & -3 \end{bmatrix}$$

$$\therefore A^3 = A^2 A$$

$$= \begin{bmatrix} 3 & -4 & 4 \\ 0 & -1 & 0 \\ -2 & 2 & -3 \end{bmatrix} \begin{bmatrix} 3 & -3 & 4 \\ 2 & -3 & 4 \\ 0 & -1 & 1 \end{bmatrix}$$

$$= \begin{bmatrix} 9-8+0 & -9+12-4 & 12-16+4 \\ 0-2+0 & 0+3+0 & 0-4+0 \\ -6+4+0 & 6-6+3 & -8+8-3 \end{bmatrix}$$

$$= \begin{bmatrix} 1 & -1 & 0 \\ -2 & 3 & -4 \\ -2 & 3 & -3 \end{bmatrix} \quad \text{... (4.15)}$$

From Eqs. (4.14) and (4.15), we have

$$A^3 = A^{-1}$$

Example 7. Show that if the matrix product AB of two square matrices is zero, then either $A = O$ or $B = O$ both A and B are singular matrices.

Solution: We have,

$$AB = O \qquad \text{| Given ... (4.16)}$$

$$\Rightarrow |AB| = |O| \qquad \text{| } \because A \text{ and } B \text{ are square matrices}$$

$$\Rightarrow |A|\ |B| = 0$$

$$\Rightarrow |A| = 0 \text{ or } |B| = 0$$

$$\Rightarrow A \text{ is singular or } B \text{ is singular.}$$

If A is non-singular, then A^{-1} exists.

Therefore, pre-multiplying both sides of Eq. (4.16) by A^{-1}, we have,

$$A^{-1}(AB) = A^{-1}O$$

$$\Rightarrow (A^{-1}A)B = O \qquad \text{| By associative law of multiplication}$$

$$\Rightarrow IB = O \qquad \text{| By definition of inverse of a matrix}$$

$$\Rightarrow B = O \qquad \text{| } \because IB = B$$

Similarly, if B is non-singular, then post-multiplying both sides of Eq. (4.16) by B^{-1}, we can show that $A = O$

Hence, when A is non-singular, then B is a null matrix and when B is non-singular, then A is a null matrix. Furthermore, if A is singular and non-zero, then B is also singular for otherwise $A = O$.

Thus, $AB = O$ implies that either $A = O$ or $B = O$ or both A and B must be singular matrices.

Note. If $AB = O$ and $B \neq O$, then A is known as a left zero divisor and if $AB = O$ and $A \neq O$, then B is known as a right zero divisor.

Example 8. If $A = \text{diag}\ (a_{11}, a_{22}, ..., a_{nn})$, then show that $A^{-1} = \text{diag}\ (a_{11}^{-1}, a_{22}^{-1}, ..., a_{nn}^{-1})$, provided $a_{11}, a_{22}, ... a_{nn} \neq 0$.

Solution: We have

$$A = \text{diag}\ (a_{11}, a_{22}, ..., a_{nn})$$

$$\therefore |A| = a_{11}\ a_{22} \ ...\ a_{nn} \neq 0$$

$\therefore A^{-1}$ exists.

Now,

$$A = \begin{bmatrix} a_{11} & 0 & ... & 0 \\ 0 & a_{22} & ... & 0 \\ ... & ... & ... & ... \\ 0 & 0 & ... & a_{nn} \end{bmatrix}$$

Therefore,

$$A_{ii} = a_{11}\ a_{22}\ .....\ a_{i-1,\, i-1}\ a_{i+1,\, i+1}\ .....\ a_{nn}$$

$$= \frac{a_{11}\ a_{22}\ .....\ a_{nn}}{a_{ii}}$$

$$= \frac{|A|}{a_{ii}}$$

Also, $A_{ij} = 0$, when $i \neq j$ because the elements of jth row and i^{th} column of the corresponding determinant will be all zero.

$$\therefore \quad A^{-1} = \frac{1}{|A|} \text{Adj}\ A$$

$$= \frac{1}{|A|} \begin{bmatrix} \frac{|A|}{a_{11}} & 0 & ..... & 0 \\ 0 & \frac{|A|}{a_{22}} & ..... & 0 \\ ..... & ..... & ..... & ..... \\ 0 & 0 & ..... & \frac{|A|}{a_{nn}} \end{bmatrix}$$

$$= \begin{bmatrix} \frac{1}{a_{11}} & 0 & \ldots\ldots & 0 \\ 0 & \frac{1}{a_{22}} & \ldots\ldots & 0 \\ \ldots\ldots & \ldots\ldots & \ldots\ldots & \ldots\ldots \\ 0 & 0 & \ldots\ldots & \frac{1}{a_{nn}} \end{bmatrix}$$

$$= \begin{bmatrix} a_{11}^{-1} & 0 & \ldots\ldots & 0 \\ 0 & a_{22}^{-1} & \ldots\ldots & 0 \\ \ldots\ldots & \ldots\ldots & \ldots\ldots & \ldots\ldots \\ 0 & 0 & \ldots\ldots & a_{nn}^{-1} \end{bmatrix}$$

$$= \text{diag}\left(a_{11}^{-1}, a_{22}^{-1}, \ldots\ldots, a_{nn}^{-1}\right)$$

Example 9. Show that if A and B are two non-singular symmetric matrices and commute uner multiplication, then (i) $A^{-1}B$, (ii) AB^{-1} and, (iii) $A^{-1}B^{-1}$ are symmetric.

Solution:

(i) $\because$ A and B commute under multiplication

$\therefore$ $AB = BA$ ... (4.17)

$\because$ A and B are non-singular $\therefore$ A^{-1} and B^{-1} both exist.

$\because$ A and B are symmetric $\therefore$ $A' = A$ and $B' = B$.

Pre-multiplying both sides of Eq. (4.17) by A^{-1}, we get,

$A^{-1}(AB) = A^{-1}(BA)$

$\Rightarrow$ $(A^{-1}A)B = (A^{-1}B)A$ | By associative law of multiplication

$\Rightarrow$ $IB = (A^{-1}B)A$ | $\because$ $A^{-1}A = I$

$\Rightarrow$ $B = (A^{-1}B)A$ | $\because$ $IB = B$

$\Rightarrow$ $BA^{-1} = (A^{-1}B)\ AA^{-1}$ | Post-multiplying both sides by A^{-1}

$\Rightarrow$ $BA^{-1} = (A^{-1}B)\ I$ | $\because$ $AA^{-1} = I$

$\Rightarrow$ $BA^{-1} = A^{-1}B$ ... (4.18)

Now,

$(A^{-1}B)' = B'(A^{-1})'$ | $\because (AB)' = B'A'$

$= B'(A')^{-1}$ | $\because (A^{-1})' = (A')^{-1}$

$= B'A^{-1}$ | $\because A' = A$

$= BA^{-1}$ | $\because B' = B$

$= A^{-1}B$ | Using Eq. (4.18)

Hence, $A^{-1}B$ is symmetric.

(ii) Similarly, we can show that AB^{-1} is symmetric.

(iii) Again,

$(A^{-1}B^{-1})' = (B^{-1})' (A^{-1})'$

$= (B')^{-1} (A)^{-1}$

$= B^{-1} A^{-1}$ | $\because B' = B,\ A' = A$

$= (AB)^{-1}$ | $\because (AB)^{-1} = B^{-1}A^{-1}$

$= (BA)^{-1}$ | Using Eq. (4.17)

$= A^{-1}B^{-1}$ | By reversal law of inverses

Hence, $A^{-1}B^{-1}$ is symmetric.

Example 10. If adj $B = A$ and P, Q are two unimodular matrices, i.e. $|P| = 1$, $|Q| = 1$, then show that

adj $(Q^{-1}BP^{-1}) = PAQ$

Solution:

$\because\ |P| = 1 \neq 0$

$\therefore\ P$ is non-singular

$\because\ |Q| = 1 \neq 0$

$\therefore\ Q$ is non-singular

We know that

$PP^{-1} = P^{-1}P = I$

$\therefore$ Adj (PP^{-1}) = Adj $(P^{-1}P)$ = Adj $(I) = I$

$\Rightarrow$ Adj $P^{-1} \cdot$ Adj P = Adj $P \cdot$ Adj $P^{-1} = I$

$\Rightarrow$ Adj P^{-1} = (Adj $P)^{-1}$ ... (4.19)

Also,

$(P^{-1})^{-1} \dfrac{\text{Adj } P^{-1}}{|P^{-1}|}$ ... (4.20) | By definition of inverse

Therefore,

$$\begin{aligned}
\text{Adj } (Q^{-1}BP^{-1}) &= \text{Adj } P^{-1} \cdot \text{Adj } B \cdot \text{Adj } Q^{-1} \\
&= (P^{-1})^{-1}\, |P^{-1}| \cdot A \cdot (Q^{-1})^{-1}\, |Q^{-1}| && \mid \text{Using Eq. (4.20) and adj } B = A \\
&= |P^{-1}|\, |Q^{-1}|\, (PAQ) && \mid \because (P^{-1})^{-1} = P;\ (Q^{-1})^{-1} = Q \\
&= \frac{1}{|P|} \cdot \frac{1}{|Q|} (PAQ) && \left| \begin{array}{l} \because |PP^{-1}| = |I| = 1 \\ \Rightarrow |P|\,|P^{-1}| = 1 \end{array} \right. \\
&= PAQ && \mid \because |P| = 1, |Q| = 1
\end{aligned}$$

Example 11. Find the reciprocal of the matrix

$$S = \begin{bmatrix} 0 & 1 & 1 \\ 1 & 0 & 1 \\ 1 & 1 & 0 \end{bmatrix}$$

and show that the transform of the matrix

$$A = \begin{bmatrix} b+c & c-a & b-a \\ c-b & c+a & a-b \\ b-c & a-c & a+b \end{bmatrix}$$

by S, i.e. SAS^{-1} is a diagonal matrix.

Solution:

$$|S| = \begin{vmatrix} 0 & 1 & 1 \\ 1 & 0 & 1 \\ 1 & 1 & 0 \end{vmatrix}$$

$$= \begin{vmatrix} 0 & 0 & 1 \\ 1 & -1 & 1 \\ 1 & 1 & 0 \end{vmatrix} \qquad \mid \text{Operating } C_2 - C_3$$

$$= \begin{vmatrix} 1 & -1 \\ 1 & 1 \end{vmatrix} \qquad \mid \text{Expanding along } R_1$$

$$= 2 \neq 0$$

$\therefore\ S^{-1}$ exists.

$$\text{Adj } S = \begin{bmatrix} A_{11} & A_{12} & A_{13} \\ A_{21} & A_{22} & A_{23} \\ A_{31} & A_{32} & A_{33} \end{bmatrix}'$$

$$= \begin{bmatrix} -1 & 1 & 1 \\ 1 & -1 & 1 \\ 1 & 1 & -1 \end{bmatrix}'$$

$$= \begin{bmatrix} -1 & 1 & 1 \\ 1 & -1 & 1 \\ 1 & 1 & -1 \end{bmatrix}$$

$$\therefore \quad S^{-1} = \frac{\text{Adj } S}{|S|}$$

$$= \frac{1}{2}\begin{bmatrix} -1 & 1 & 1 \\ 1 & -1 & 1 \\ 1 & 1 & -1 \end{bmatrix}$$

Again,

$$SA = \begin{bmatrix} 0 & 1 & 1 \\ 1 & 0 & 1 \\ 1 & 1 & 0 \end{bmatrix}\begin{bmatrix} b+c & c-a & b-a \\ c-b & c+a & a-b \\ b-c & a-c & a+b \end{bmatrix}$$

$$= \begin{bmatrix} \begin{matrix} 0+(c-b) \\ +(b-c) \end{matrix} & \begin{matrix} 0+(c+a) \\ +(a-c) \end{matrix} & 0+(a-b)+(a+b) \\ \begin{matrix} (b+c)+ \\ 0+(b-c) \end{matrix} & \begin{matrix} (c-a)+0 \\ +(a-c) \end{matrix} & (b-a)+0+(a+b) \\ \begin{matrix} (b+c)+ \\ (c-b)+0 \end{matrix} & \begin{matrix} (c-a)+ \\ (c+a)+0 \end{matrix} & (b-a)+(a-b)+0 \end{bmatrix}$$

$$= \begin{bmatrix} 0 & 2a & 2a \\ 2b & 0 & 2b \\ 2c & 2c & 0 \end{bmatrix}$$

$$\therefore \quad SAS^{-1} = \begin{bmatrix} 0 & 2a & 2a \\ 2b & 0 & 2b \\ 2c & 2c & 0 \end{bmatrix} \frac{1}{2} \begin{bmatrix} -1 & 1 & 1 \\ 1 & -1 & 1 \\ 1 & 1 & -1 \end{bmatrix}$$

$$= \begin{bmatrix} 0 & a & a \\ b & 0 & b \\ c & c & 0 \end{bmatrix} \begin{bmatrix} -1 & 1 & 1 \\ 1 & -1 & 1 \\ 1 & 1 & -1 \end{bmatrix}$$

$$= \begin{bmatrix} 0+a+a & 0-a+a & 0+a-a \\ -b+0+b & b+0+b & b+0-b \\ -c+c+0 & c-c+0 & c+c+0 \end{bmatrix}$$

$$= \begin{bmatrix} 2a & 0 & 0 \\ 0 & 2b & 0 \\ 0 & 0 & 2c \end{bmatrix}$$

$$= \text{diag}\ (2a,\ 2b,\ 2c)$$

Hence, SAS^{-1} is a diagonal matrix.

Example 12. Show that

$$\begin{bmatrix} \cos\theta & -\sin\theta \\ \sin\theta & \cos\theta \end{bmatrix} = \begin{bmatrix} 1 & -\tan\frac{\theta}{2} \\ \tan\frac{\theta}{2} & 1 \end{bmatrix} \begin{bmatrix} 1 & \tan\frac{\theta}{2} \\ -\tan\frac{\theta}{2} & 1 \end{bmatrix}^{-1}$$

Solution: We have

$$\begin{bmatrix} \cos\theta & -\sin\theta \\ \sin\theta & \cos\theta \end{bmatrix} \begin{bmatrix} 1 & \tan\frac{\theta}{2} \\ -\tan\frac{\theta}{2} & 1 \end{bmatrix}$$

$$= \begin{bmatrix} \cos\theta + \sin\theta \tan\dfrac{\theta}{2} & \cos\theta \tan\dfrac{\theta}{2} - \sin\theta \\ \sin\theta - \cos\theta \tan\dfrac{\theta}{2} & \sin\theta \tan\dfrac{\theta}{2} + \cos\theta \end{bmatrix}$$

$$= \begin{bmatrix} \dfrac{\cos\theta \cos\dfrac{\theta}{2} + \sin\theta \sin\dfrac{\theta}{2}}{\cos\dfrac{\theta}{2}} & \dfrac{\cos\theta \sin\dfrac{\theta}{2} - \sin\theta \cos\dfrac{\theta}{2}}{\cos\dfrac{\theta}{2}} \\ \dfrac{\sin\theta \cos\dfrac{\theta}{2} - \cos\theta \sin\dfrac{\theta}{2}}{\cos\dfrac{\theta}{2}} & \dfrac{\sin\theta \sin\dfrac{\theta}{2} + \cos\theta \cos\dfrac{\theta}{2}}{\cos\dfrac{\theta}{2}} \end{bmatrix}$$

$$= \begin{bmatrix} \dfrac{\cos\left(\theta - \dfrac{\theta}{2}\right)}{\cos\dfrac{\theta}{2}} & \dfrac{\sin\left(\dfrac{\theta}{2} - \theta\right)}{\cos\dfrac{\theta}{2}} \\ \dfrac{\sin\left(\theta - \dfrac{\theta}{2}\right)}{\cos\dfrac{\theta}{2}} & \dfrac{\cos\left(\theta - \dfrac{\theta}{2}\right)}{\cos\dfrac{\theta}{2}} \end{bmatrix}$$

$$= \begin{bmatrix} 1 & -\tan\dfrac{\theta}{2} \\ \tan\dfrac{\theta}{2} & 1 \end{bmatrix}$$

If we take $A = \begin{bmatrix} 1 & \tan\dfrac{\theta}{2} \\ -\tan\dfrac{\theta}{2} & 1 \end{bmatrix}$, then this result can be written as

$$\begin{bmatrix} \cos\theta & -\sin\theta \\ \sin\theta & \cos\theta \end{bmatrix} A = \begin{bmatrix} 1 & -\tan\frac{\theta}{2} \\ \tan\frac{\theta}{2} & 1 \end{bmatrix}$$

Post-multiplying both sides by A^{-1}, we have

$$\begin{bmatrix} \cos\theta & -\sin\theta \\ \sin\theta & \cos\theta \end{bmatrix} AA^{-1} = \begin{bmatrix} 1 & -\tan\frac{\theta}{2} \\ \tan\frac{\theta}{2} & 1 \end{bmatrix} A^{-1}$$

$$\Rightarrow \begin{bmatrix} \cos\theta & -\sin\theta \\ \sin\theta & \cos\theta \end{bmatrix} I = \begin{bmatrix} 1 & -\tan\frac{\theta}{2} \\ \tan\frac{\theta}{2} & 1 \end{bmatrix} \begin{bmatrix} 1 & \tan\frac{\theta}{2} \\ -\tan\frac{\theta}{2} & 1 \end{bmatrix}^{-1}$$

$$\Rightarrow \begin{bmatrix} \cos\theta & -\sin\theta \\ \sin\theta & \cos\theta \end{bmatrix} = \begin{bmatrix} 1 & -\tan\frac{\theta}{2} \\ \tan\frac{\theta}{2} & 1 \end{bmatrix} \begin{bmatrix} 1 & \tan\frac{\theta}{2} \\ -\tan\frac{\theta}{2} & 1 \end{bmatrix}^{-1}$$

EXERCISE 4.2

1. Find the adjoint and inverse of the matrix

   A, if $A = \begin{bmatrix} \cos\alpha & -\sin\alpha \\ \sin\alpha & \cos\alpha \end{bmatrix}$

2. Find the inverse of $\begin{bmatrix} \cos\alpha & \sin\alpha \\ \sin\alpha & \cos\alpha \end{bmatrix}$

3. Find the inverse of $\begin{bmatrix} a+ib & c+id \\ -c+id & a-ib \end{bmatrix}$, if $a^2 + b^2 + c^2 + d^2 = 1$

4. Find the adjoint of the matrix

$$A = \begin{bmatrix} 0 & 1 & 1 \\ 1 & 0 & 1 \\ 1 & 1 & 1 \end{bmatrix} \text{ and hence find } A^{-1}.$$

5. Find adj A and A^{-1} when $A = \begin{bmatrix} 1 & 3 & 3 \\ 1 & 4 & 3 \\ 1 & 3 & 4 \end{bmatrix}$.

6. If $A = \begin{bmatrix} 2 & 2 & 3 \\ 1 & -2 & 3 \\ 0 & 1 & -1 \end{bmatrix}$, find adj A and A^{-1}.

7. Find the adjoint of the matrix $A = \begin{bmatrix} 1 & 2 & 3 \\ 1 & 3 & 5 \\ 1 & 5 & 12 \end{bmatrix}$ and hence evaluate A^{-1}.

8. Show that $\begin{bmatrix} 1 & 2 & 3 \\ 2 & 5 & 7 \\ -2 & -4 & -5 \end{bmatrix}$ is the inverse of $\begin{bmatrix} 3 & -2 & -1 \\ -4 & 1 & -1 \\ 2 & 0 & 1 \end{bmatrix}$.

9. If α is not an odd multiple of $\frac{\pi}{2}$, and

$$A = \begin{bmatrix} 1 & 0 & 0 \\ 0 & \cos\alpha & -\sin\alpha \\ 0 & \sin\alpha & \cos\alpha \end{bmatrix},$$

show that $(I + A)$ is non-singular.

10. Find the inverse of the following matrices:

(a) $\begin{bmatrix} \cos h\alpha & \sin h\alpha \\ \sin h\alpha & \cos h\alpha \end{bmatrix}$

(b) $\begin{bmatrix} 3 & 5 & 7 \\ 2 & -3 & 1 \\ 1 & 1 & 2 \end{bmatrix}$

(c) $\begin{bmatrix} 1 & 2 & 3 \\ 2 & 4 & 5 \\ 3 & 5 & 6 \end{bmatrix}$

(d) $\begin{bmatrix} 1 & 0 & -1 \\ 3 & 4 & 5 \\ 0 & -6 & -7 \end{bmatrix}$

(e) $\begin{bmatrix} 1 & 2 & 1 \\ 3 & 2 & 3 \\ 1 & 1 & 2 \end{bmatrix}$

(f) $\begin{bmatrix} 2 & 3 & 1 \\ 1 & 2 & 3 \\ 3 & 1 & 2 \end{bmatrix}$

(g) $\begin{bmatrix} 1 & 0 & 0 \\ 1 & 1 & 0 \\ 1 & 0 & 1 \end{bmatrix}$

(h) $\begin{bmatrix} 0 & 1 & 2 \\ 1 & 2 & 3 \\ 3 & 1 & 1 \end{bmatrix}$

(i) $\begin{bmatrix} 1 & 3 & -2 \\ -3 & 0 & -5 \\ 2 & 5 & 0 \end{bmatrix}$

(j) $\begin{bmatrix} 1 & 0 & 2 \\ 2 & 1 & 0 \\ 3 & 2 & 1 \end{bmatrix}$

(k) $\begin{bmatrix} 1 & 0 & -1 \\ 3 & 4 & 5 \\ 0 & -6 & -7 \end{bmatrix}$

(l) $\begin{bmatrix} 9 & 7 & 6 \\ 7 & -1 & 8 \\ 3 & 4 & 2 \end{bmatrix}$

(m) $\begin{bmatrix} 2 & 2 & 2 \\ 2 & 5 & 5 \\ 2 & 5 & 11 \end{bmatrix}$

(n) $\begin{bmatrix} 1 & 2 & 3 \\ 1 & 3 & 5 \\ 1 & 5 & 12 \end{bmatrix}$

(o) $\begin{bmatrix} 3 & -2 & -1 \\ -4 & 1 & -1 \\ 2 & 0 & 1 \end{bmatrix}$

(p) $\begin{bmatrix} 3 & -2 & 1 \\ -4 & 1 & 1 \\ 2 & 0 & -1 \end{bmatrix}$

(q) $\begin{bmatrix} 1 & 2 & 3 \\ 2 & 4 & 5 \\ 3 & 5 & 6 \end{bmatrix}$

(r) $\begin{bmatrix} 1 & 2 & 3 \\ 1 & 3 & 4 \\ 1 & 4 & 3 \end{bmatrix}$

(s) $\begin{bmatrix} 1 & -2 & -1 \\ 2 & 3 & 1 \\ 0 & 5 & -2 \end{bmatrix}$

(t) $\begin{bmatrix} 1 & 1 & 1 \\ 2 & 2 & 3 \\ 1 & 4 & 9 \end{bmatrix}$

(u) $\begin{bmatrix} 1 & 2 & 1 \\ 3 & 2 & 3 \\ 1 & 1 & 2 \end{bmatrix}$

(v) $\begin{bmatrix} 2 & -4 & -2 \\ 4 & 6 & 2 \\ 0 & 10 & -4 \end{bmatrix}$

(w) $\begin{bmatrix} 2 & 1 & 2 \\ 2 & 2 & 1 \\ 1 & 2 & 2 \end{bmatrix}$

(x) $\begin{bmatrix} 1 & 2 & 4 \\ 5 & 7 & 8 \\ 9 & 10 & 12 \end{bmatrix}$

(y) $\begin{bmatrix} 1 & 0 & -1 \\ 3 & 4 & 5 \\ 0 & -6 & -7 \end{bmatrix}$

(z) $\begin{bmatrix} i & -1 & 2i \\ 2 & 0 & 2 \\ -1 & 0 & 1 \end{bmatrix}$

11. If $A = \begin{bmatrix} -1 & 2 & -2 \\ 4 & -3 & 4 \\ 4 & -4 & 5 \end{bmatrix}$, show that $A = A^{-1}$.

12. If $A = \begin{bmatrix} 1 & -1 & 1 \\ 2 & -1 & 0 \\ 1 & 0 & 1 \end{bmatrix}$, show that $A^2 = A^{-1}$.

13. A and B are two mutually reciprocal matrices. If $A = \begin{bmatrix} 1 & 0 & 0 \\ -1 & 1 & 0 \\ -1 & -1 & 1 \end{bmatrix}$, show that $(A+B)^2 = 4\begin{bmatrix} 1 & 0 & 0 \\ 0 & 1 & 0 \\ 1 & 0 & 1 \end{bmatrix}$.

14. If $A = \begin{bmatrix} 1 & -1 & 0 & 2 \\ 0 & 1 & 1 & -1 \\ 2 & 1 & 2 & 1 \\ 3 & -2 & 1 & 6 \end{bmatrix}$, find A^{-1}.

15. If $A = \begin{bmatrix} 0 & 2 & 1 & 3 \\ 1 & 1 & -1 & -2 \\ 1 & 2 & 0 & 1 \\ -1 & 1 & 2 & 6 \end{bmatrix}$, find A^{-1}.

16. If $A = \begin{bmatrix} 2 & 2 & 5 \\ 2 & 5 & 5 \\ 2 & 5 & 11 \end{bmatrix}$, show that $A^{-1} = \frac{1}{6}\begin{bmatrix} 5 & -2 & 0 \\ -2 & 3 & -1 \\ 0 & -1 & 1 \end{bmatrix}$ and verify that $AA^{-1} = A^{-1}A = I$.

17. If $A = \begin{bmatrix} 1 & 1 & 1 \\ 1 & 2 & 3 \\ 1 & 4 & 9 \end{bmatrix}$ and $B = \begin{bmatrix} 2 & 5 & 3 \\ 3 & 1 & 2 \\ 1 & 2 & 1 \end{bmatrix}$, then show that $(AB)^{-1} = B^{-1}A^{-1}$.

18. If A' denotes the transpose of a matrix A and
$A = \begin{bmatrix} 1 & -2 & 3 \\ 0 & -1 & 4 \\ -2 & 2 & 1 \end{bmatrix}$, find $(A')^{-1}$.

19. If A is a non-singular matrix of order n such that $AX = AY$, then show that $X = Y$.

20. Show that the inverse of a non-singular symmetric (hermitian) matrix is symmetric (hermitian).

21. Two matrices A and B are said to be similar if a non-singular matrix S exists such that $B = S^{-1}AS$. In this case show that $|A| = |B|$.

22. If A is a non-singular square matrix, show that
$A^{-1} = (A'A)^{-1}A' = A'\,(AA')^{-1}$

23. If A is a regular matrix, show that $(A^{-1})^* = (A^*)^{-1}$.

24. If A is a symmetric and B is a skew-symmetric matrix, both of order n such that $A + B$ is non-singular and $C = (A + B)^{-1}\,(A - B)$, then show that

(i) $C'\,(A + B)C = A + B$

(ii) $C'\,(A - B)C = A - B$

(iii) $C'AC = A$

25. The matrices A, B, $A + B$ are non-singular. Prove that
$[A(A + B)^{-1}A]^{-1} = A^{-1} + B^{-1}$.

26. If A and B are $n \times n$ matrices for which $AB = I$, then show that $AB = BA = A^{-1}A^{-1} = I$. Show that if $A = B$, then either it is a unit matrix or singular matrix.

27. Given two square matrices A and B such that $AB = A$ and $BA = B$. Show, by considering the product ABA, that $A^2 = A$. Further show that $B^2 = B$.

ANSWERS

1. $\text{Adj } A = \begin{bmatrix} \cos\alpha & \sin\alpha \\ -\sin\alpha & \cos\alpha \end{bmatrix}$

$A^{-1} = \begin{bmatrix} \cos\alpha & \sin\alpha \\ -\sin\alpha & \cos\alpha \end{bmatrix}$

2. $\sec 2\alpha \begin{bmatrix} \cos\alpha & -\sin\alpha \\ -\sin\alpha & \cos\alpha \end{bmatrix}$

3. $\begin{bmatrix} a-ib & -(c+id) \\ c-id & a+ib \end{bmatrix}$

4. $\text{adj } A = \begin{bmatrix} -1 & 1 & 1 \\ 1 & -1 & 1 \\ 1 & 1 & -1 \end{bmatrix}$

$A^{-1} = \frac{1}{2}\begin{bmatrix} -1 & 1 & 1 \\ 1 & -1 & 1 \\ 1 & 1 & -1 \end{bmatrix}$

5. $\text{adj } A = \begin{bmatrix} 7 & -3 & -3 \\ -1 & 1 & 0 \\ -1 & 0 & 1 \end{bmatrix}$

$A^{-1} = \begin{bmatrix} 7 & -3 & -3 \\ -1 & 1 & 0 \\ -1 & 0 & 1 \end{bmatrix}$

6. $\text{adj } A = \begin{bmatrix} -1 & 5 & 12 \\ 1 & -2 & -3 \\ 1 & -2 & -6 \end{bmatrix}$

$$A^{-1} = \frac{1}{3}\begin{bmatrix} -1 & 5 & 12 \\ 1 & -2 & -3 \\ 1 & -2 & -6 \end{bmatrix}$$

7. $$\text{adj } A = \begin{bmatrix} 11 & -9 & 1 \\ -7 & 9 & -2 \\ 2 & -3 & 1 \end{bmatrix}$$

$$A^{-1} = \frac{1}{3}\begin{bmatrix} 11 & -9 & 1 \\ -7 & 9 & -2 \\ 2 & -3 & 1 \end{bmatrix}$$

10. (a) $$\begin{bmatrix} \cos h\alpha & -\sin h\alpha \\ -\sin h\alpha & \cos h\alpha \end{bmatrix}$$

(b) $$\begin{bmatrix} 7 & 3 & -26 \\ 3 & 1 & -11 \\ -5 & -2 & 19 \end{bmatrix}$$

(c) $$\begin{bmatrix} 1 & -3 & 2 \\ -3 & 3 & -1 \\ 2 & -1 & 0 \end{bmatrix}$$

(d) $$\frac{1}{20}\begin{bmatrix} 2 & 6 & 4 \\ 21 & -7 & -8 \\ -18 & 6 & 4 \end{bmatrix}$$

(e) $$-\frac{1}{4}\begin{bmatrix} 1 & -3 & 4 \\ -3 & 1 & 0 \\ 1 & 1 & -4 \end{bmatrix}$$

(f) $$\frac{1}{18}\begin{bmatrix} 1 & -5 & 7 \\ 7 & 1 & -5 \\ -5 & 7 & 1 \end{bmatrix}$$

(g) $\begin{bmatrix} 1 & 0 & 0 \\ -1 & 1 & 0 \\ -1 & 0 & 1 \end{bmatrix}$

(h) $\begin{bmatrix} \frac{1}{2} & -\frac{1}{2} & \frac{1}{2} \\ -4 & 3 & -1 \\ \frac{5}{2} & -\frac{3}{2} & \frac{1}{2} \end{bmatrix}$

(i) $\frac{1}{25}\begin{bmatrix} 25 & -10 & -15 \\ -10 & 4 & 11 \\ -15 & 1 & 9 \end{bmatrix}$

(j) $\frac{1}{3}\begin{bmatrix} 1 & 4 & -2 \\ -2 & -5 & 4 \\ 1 & -2 & 1 \end{bmatrix}$

(k) $\frac{1}{20}\begin{bmatrix} 2 & 6 & 4 \\ 21 & -7 & -8 \\ -18 & 6 & 4 \end{bmatrix}$

(l) $-\frac{1}{50}\begin{bmatrix} 34 & 10 & 62 \\ 10 & 0 & -30 \\ 31 & -15 & -58 \end{bmatrix}$

(m) $\frac{1}{6}\begin{bmatrix} 5 & -2 & 0 \\ -2 & 3 & -1 \\ 0 & -1 & 1 \end{bmatrix}$

(n) $\frac{1}{3}\begin{bmatrix} 11 & -9 & 1 \\ -7 & 9 & -2 \\ 2 & -3 & 1 \end{bmatrix}$

(o) $\begin{bmatrix} 1 & 2 & 3 \\ 2 & 5 & 7 \\ -2 & -4 & -5 \end{bmatrix}$

(p) $\begin{bmatrix} 1 & 2 & 3 \\ 2 & 5 & 7 \\ -1 & -4 & -5 \end{bmatrix}$

(q) $\begin{bmatrix} 1 & -3 & 2 \\ -3 & 3 & -1 \\ 2 & -1 & 0 \end{bmatrix}$

(r) $-\frac{1}{2}\begin{bmatrix} -7 & 6 & -1 \\ 1 & 0 & -1 \\ 1 & -2 & 1 \end{bmatrix}$

(s) $\frac{1}{29}\begin{bmatrix} 11 & 9 & -1 \\ -4 & 2 & 3 \\ -10 & 5 & -7 \end{bmatrix}$

(t) $\begin{bmatrix} -2 & \frac{5}{2} & -\frac{1}{3} \\ 5 & -\frac{8}{3} & \frac{1}{3} \\ 2 & 1 & 0 \end{bmatrix}$

(u) $-\frac{1}{4}\begin{bmatrix} 1 & -3 & 4 \\ -3 & 1 & 0 \\ 1 & 1 & -4 \end{bmatrix}$

(v) $-\frac{1}{58}\begin{bmatrix} -11 & -9 & 1 \\ 4 & -2 & 1 \\ 10 & -5 & 7 \end{bmatrix}$

(w) $\frac{1}{5}\begin{bmatrix} 2 & 2 & -3 \\ -3 & 2 & 2 \\ 2 & -3 & 2 \end{bmatrix}$

(x) $\begin{bmatrix} -\frac{1}{6} & -\frac{2}{3} & \frac{1}{2} \\ -\frac{1}{2} & 1 & -\frac{1}{2} \\ \frac{13}{24} & -\frac{1}{3} & \frac{1}{3} \end{bmatrix}$

(y) $\frac{1}{20}\begin{bmatrix} 2 & 6 & 4 \\ 21 & -7 & -8 \\ -18 & 6 & 4 \end{bmatrix}$

(z) $\begin{bmatrix} 0 & \frac{1}{4} & -\frac{1}{2} \\ -1 & \frac{3}{4}i & \frac{1}{2}i \\ 0 & \frac{1}{4} & \frac{1}{2} \end{bmatrix}$

14. $\begin{bmatrix} 2 & -1 & 1 & -1 \\ -5 & -3 & 1 & 1 \\ 2 & 3 & -1 & 0 \\ -3 & -1 & 0 & 1 \end{bmatrix}$

15. $\begin{bmatrix} -1 & -3 & 3 & -1 \\ 1 & 1 & -1 & 0 \\ 2 & -5 & 2 & -3 \\ -1 & 1 & 0 & 1 \end{bmatrix}$

18. $\begin{bmatrix} -9 & -8 & -2 \\ 8 & 7 & 2 \\ -5 & -4 & -1 \end{bmatrix}$

4.5. Inversion of a Matrix by Solving Algebraic Equations

Consider the following system of n linear equations in n unknowns $x_1, x_2, x_3, \ldots\ldots, x_n$:

$$a_{11}x_1 + a_{12}x_2 + a_{13}x_3 + \ldots\ldots + a_{1n}\, x_n = b_1$$
$$a_{21}x_1 + a_{22}x_2 + a_{23}x_3 + \ldots\ldots + a_{2n}\, x_n = b_2$$
$$\ldots\ldots\ldots\ldots\ldots\ldots\ldots\ldots\ldots\ldots\ldots\ldots\ldots\ldots\ldots\ldots$$
$$a_{i1}x_1 + a_{i2}x_2 + a_{i3}x_3 + \ldots\ldots + a_{in}\, x_n = b_i$$
$$\ldots\ldots\ldots\ldots\ldots\ldots\ldots\ldots\ldots\ldots\ldots\ldots\ldots\ldots\ldots\ldots$$
$$a_{n1}x_1 + a_{n2}x_2 + a_{n3}x_3 + \ldots\ldots + a_{nn}\, x_n = b_n$$

By using the definition of matrix multiplication, these equations can be written as

$$\begin{bmatrix} a_{11} & a_{12} & a_{13} & \ldots\ldots & a_{1n} \\ a_{21} & a_{22} & a_{23} & \ldots\ldots & a_{2n} \\ \ldots\ldots & \ldots\ldots & \ldots\ldots & \ldots\ldots & \ldots\ldots \\ a_{i1} & a_{i2} & a_{i3} & \ldots\ldots & a_{in} \\ a_{n1} & a_{n2} & a_{n3} & \ldots\ldots & a_{nn} \end{bmatrix} \begin{bmatrix} x_1 \\ x_2 \\ x_3 \\ \vdots \\ x_n \end{bmatrix} = \begin{bmatrix} b_1 \\ b_2 \\ \vdots \\ b_i \\ \vdots \\ b_n \end{bmatrix}$$

OR

$$AX = B \qquad \ldots (4.21)$$

where,

$$A = \begin{bmatrix} a_{11} & a_{12} & a_{13} & \ldots\ldots & a_{1n} \\ a_{21} & a_{22} & a_{23} & \ldots\ldots & a_{2n} \\ \ldots\ldots & \ldots\ldots & \ldots\ldots & \ldots\ldots & \ldots\ldots \\ a_{i1} & a_{i2} & a_{i3} & \ldots\ldots & a_{in} \\ a_{n1} & a_{n2} & a_{n3} & \ldots\ldots & a_{nn} \end{bmatrix}$$

$$X = \begin{bmatrix} x_1 \\ x_2 \\ x_3 \\ \vdots \\ x_n \end{bmatrix} \text{ and } B = \begin{bmatrix} b_1 \\ b_2 \\ b_3 \\ \vdots \\ b_i \\ \vdots \\ b_n \end{bmatrix}$$

Let A be non-singular, then, $|A| \neq 0$.

$\therefore$ A^{-1} exists.

Hence, pre-multiplying both sides of the relation (Eq. (4.21) by A^{-1}, we obtain

$A^{-1}(AX) = A^{-1}B$

$\Rightarrow (A^{-1}A)X = A^{-1}B$ | By associative law of multiplication

$\Rightarrow IX = A^{-1}B$ | $\because A^{-1}A = I$

$\Rightarrow X = A^{-1}B$ | $\because IX = X$

This gives us the solution of the given system of equations as follows:

Express $x_1, x_2, x_3, \ldots, x_n$ in terms of $b_1, b_2, b_3, \ldots, b_n$ by elementary algebra. Then, the coefficient matrix of this latter system is the required inverse of A.

Uniqueness

Let X_1 and X_2 be two different solutions of $AX = B$. Then,

$AX_1 = B$

and,

$AX_2 = B$

$\therefore AX_1 = AX_2$

$\Rightarrow A^{-1}(AX_1) = A^{-1}(AX_2)$

$\Rightarrow (A^{-1}A)X_1 = (A^{-1}A)X_2$

$\Rightarrow IX_1 = IX_2$

$\Rightarrow X_1 = X_2$

Hence, the solution is unique.

ILLUSTRATIVE EXAMPLES

Example 1. Find the inverse of $A = \begin{bmatrix} 2 & 3 & 4 \\ 4 & 3 & 1 \\ 1 & 2 & 4 \end{bmatrix}$.

Solution: The matrix equation $AX = B$ is equivalent to the equations

$$2x_1 + 3x_2 + 4x_3 = b_1 \quad \text{... (4.22)}$$

$$4x_1 + 3x_2 + x_3 = b_2 \quad \text{... (4.23)}$$

$$x_1 + 2x_2 + 4x_3 = b_3 \quad \text{... (4.24)}$$

Substraction of Eqs. (4.22) and (4.24) gives

$$x_1 + x_2 = b_1 - b_3 \quad \text{... (4.25)}$$

$4 \times$ Eq. (4.23) – Eq. (4.24) gives

$$15x_1 + 10x_2 = 4b_2 - b_3 \quad \text{... (4.26)}$$

$10 \times$ Eq. (4.25) – Eq. (4.26) gives

$$-5x_1 = 10b_1 - 10b_3 - 4b_2 + b_3$$

$$\Rightarrow -5x_1 = 10b_1 - 4b_2 - 9b_3$$

$$\Rightarrow x_1 = -2b_1 + \frac{4}{5}b_2 + \frac{9}{5}b_3 \quad \text{... (4.27)}$$

Putting the value of x_1 in Eq. (4.25), we obtain

$$-2b_1 + \frac{4}{5}b_2 + \frac{9}{5}b_3 + x_2 = b_1 - b_3$$

$$\Rightarrow x_2 = 3b_1 - \frac{4}{5}b_2 - \frac{14}{5}b_3 \quad \text{... (4.28)}$$

Putting the values of x_1 and x_2 in Eq. (4.23), we obtain

$$4\left(-2b_1 + \frac{4}{5}b_2 + \frac{9}{5}b_3\right) + 3\left(3b_1 - \frac{4}{5}b_2 - \frac{14}{5}b_3\right) + x_3 = b_2$$

$$\Rightarrow -8b_1 + \frac{16}{5}b_2 + \frac{36}{5}b_3 + 9b_1 - \frac{12}{5}b_2 - \frac{42}{5}b_3 + x_3 = b_2$$

$$\Rightarrow b_1 + \frac{4}{5}b_2 - \frac{6}{5}b_3 + x_3 = b_2$$

$$\Rightarrow \quad x_3 = -b_1 + \frac{1}{5}b_2 + \frac{6}{5}b_3 \qquad \ldots (4.29)$$

From Eqs. (4.27), (4.28) and (4.29), we have

$$X \equiv \begin{bmatrix} x_1 \\ x_2 \\ x_3 \end{bmatrix} = \begin{bmatrix} -2b_1 + \frac{4}{5}b_2 + \frac{9}{5}b_3 \\ 3b_1 - \frac{4}{5}b_2 - \frac{14}{5}b_3 \\ -b_1 + \frac{1}{5}b_2 + \frac{6}{5}b_3 \end{bmatrix}$$

$$\Rightarrow \quad X \equiv \begin{bmatrix} x_1 \\ x_2 \\ x_3 \end{bmatrix} = \begin{bmatrix} -2 & \frac{4}{5} & \frac{9}{5} \\ 3 & -\frac{4}{5} & -\frac{14}{5} \\ -1 & \frac{1}{5} & \frac{6}{5} \end{bmatrix} \begin{bmatrix} b_1 \\ b_2 \\ b_3 \end{bmatrix}$$

$$\Rightarrow \quad X \equiv A^{-1}B$$

Hence,

$$A^{-1} = \begin{bmatrix} -2 & \frac{4}{5} & \frac{9}{5} \\ 3 & -\frac{4}{5} & -\frac{14}{5} \\ -1 & \frac{1}{5} & \frac{6}{5} \end{bmatrix}$$

$$\Rightarrow \quad A^{-1} = \frac{1}{5} \begin{bmatrix} -10 & 4 & 9 \\ 15 & -4 & -14 \\ -5 & 1 & 6 \end{bmatrix}$$

EXERCISE 4.3

Find the inverses of the following matrices by solving the corresponding matrix equations:

1. $\begin{bmatrix} 2 & -1 & 3 \\ 1 & 1 & 1 \\ 1 & -1 & 1 \end{bmatrix}$

2. $\begin{bmatrix} 1 & 0 & -1 \\ 3 & 4 & 5 \\ 0 & -6 & -7 \end{bmatrix}$

3. $\begin{bmatrix} 1 & 2 & 1 \\ 3 & 2 & 3 \\ 1 & 1 & 2 \end{bmatrix}$

4. $\begin{bmatrix} 1 & 2 & -2 \\ -1 & 3 & 0 \\ 0 & -2 & 1 \end{bmatrix}$

5. $\begin{bmatrix} 1 & -1 & 0 & 2 \\ 0 & 1 & 1 & -1 \\ 2 & 1 & 2 & 1 \\ 3 & -2 & 1 & 6 \end{bmatrix}$

6. $\begin{bmatrix} 0 & 2 & 1 & 3 \\ 1 & 1 & -1 & -2 \\ 1 & 2 & 0 & 1 \\ -1 & 1 & 2 & 6 \end{bmatrix}$

ANSWERS

1. $-\dfrac{1}{2}\begin{bmatrix} 2 & -2 & -4 \\ 0 & -1 & 1 \\ -2 & 1 & 3 \end{bmatrix}$

2. $\dfrac{1}{20}\begin{bmatrix} 2 & 6 & 4 \\ 21 & -7 & -8 \\ -18 & 6 & 4 \end{bmatrix}$

3. $\begin{bmatrix} -\dfrac{1}{4} & \dfrac{3}{4} & -1 \\ \dfrac{3}{4} & -\dfrac{1}{4} & 0 \\ -\dfrac{1}{4} & -\dfrac{1}{4} & 1 \end{bmatrix}$

4. $\begin{bmatrix} 3 & 2 & 6 \\ 1 & 1 & 2 \\ 2 & 2 & 5 \end{bmatrix}$

5. $\begin{bmatrix} 2 & -1 & 1 & -1 \\ -5 & -3 & 1 & 1 \\ 2 & 3 & -1 & 0 \\ -3 & -1 & 0 & 1 \end{bmatrix}$

6. $\begin{bmatrix} -1 & -3 & 3 & -1 \\ 1 & 1 & -1 & 0 \\ 2 & -5 & 2 & -3 \\ -1 & 1 & 0 & 1 \end{bmatrix}$

4.6. Elementary Operations (Transformations) and Elementary Matrices

The following three operations on a given matrix are known as elementary operations (transformations) or *E*-operations (transformations):

(i) Interchange of any two rows.

or

Interchange of any two columns.

(ii) Multiplication of any row by a non-zero scalar.

or

Multiplication of any column by a non-zero scalar.

(iii) Addition to the elements of one row, the corresponding elements of another row multiplied by any non-zero scalar.

or

Addition to the elements of one column, the corresponding elements of another column multiplied by any non-zero scalar.

Square matrices obtained from an identity matrix by any single elementary operation is known as elementary matrix (or an E-matrix).

4.7. Symbols to be Used for Elementary Transformations

We use the following notations to represent the elementary transformations:

(1) R_{ij} for the interchange of ith and j^{th} rows.

(2) $R_i(k)$ for the multiplication of the ith row by a non-zero scalar k.

(3) $R_{ij}(k)$ for the addition to the ith row, the products of the jth row by scalar $k(\neq 0)$.

Similarly, we use the symbols c_{ij}, $c_i(k)$ and $c_{ij}(k)$ for the corresponding column transformations.

4.8. Inverse of the Elementary Transformation

The elementary transformation which can undo a given elementary transformation is called the inverse of the given elementary transformation.

(1) In R_{ij}, we interchange the ith row and j^{th} row. So, if we again interchange these rows, we get back the original matrix. In other words, the inverse transformation of R_{ij} is R_{ij} itself.

(2) In $R_i(k)$, we multiply the ith row by k. So, if we multiply the same row again by $\frac{1}{k}$, we get back the

original matrix. Thus, the inverse transformation of $R_i(k)$ is $R_i\left(\frac{1}{k}\right)$.

(3) The inverse transformation of $R_{ij}(k)$ is $R_{ij}(-k)$.

Note: Exactly as in case of elementary row transformation, in case of elementary column transformations, we find that

(1) The inverse transformation of c_{ij} is c_{ij} itself.

(2) The inverse transformation of $c_i(k)$ is $c_i\left(\frac{1}{k}\right)$.

(3) The inverse transformation of $c_{ij}(k)$ is $c_{ij}(-k)$.

The above discussion and explanation suggests that if a matrix B can be obtained from another matrix A by the application of one or more of the above elementary transformations, then the matrix A can be got back from the matrix B by the application of the corresponding inverse elementary transformations.

4.9. Symbols for Elementary Matrices

(1) E_{ij} denotes the elementary matrix obtained from a unit matrix by interchanging its ith and j^{th} rows.

(2) $E_i(k)$ denotes the elementary matrix obtained by mutiplying the ith row of a unit matrix by k.

(3) $E_{ij}(k)$ denotes the elementary matrix obtained by adding to the elements of ith row of a unit matrix, k times the corresponding elements of the jth row.

As in case of elementary row operations on a unit matrix, we have the symbols for elementary column operations on a unit matrix as follows:

(1) E'_{ij} denotes the elementary matrix obtained from a unit matrix by interchanging its ith and j^{th} columns.

(2) $E'_i(k)$ denotes the elementary matrix obtained by multiplying the ith column of a unit matrix by k.

(3) $E'_{ij}(k)$ denotes the elementary matrix obtained by adding to the elements of ith column of a unit matrix, k times the corresponding elements of the jth column.

Illustration

We have

$$I_4 = \begin{bmatrix} 1 & 0 & 0 & 0 \\ 0 & 1 & 0 & 0 \\ 0 & 0 & 1 & 0 \\ 0 & 0 & 0 & 1 \end{bmatrix}$$

Then,

(1) By R_{12}, we get

$$R_{12}(I_4) = \begin{bmatrix} 0 & 1 & 0 & 0 \\ 1 & 0 & 0 & 0 \\ 0 & 0 & 1 & 0 \\ 0 & 0 & 0 & 1 \end{bmatrix} = E_{12}$$

(2) By $R_3(4)$, we get

$$R_3(4)(I_4) = \begin{bmatrix} 1 & 0 & 0 & 0 \\ 0 & 1 & 0 & 0 \\ 0 & 0 & 4 & 0 \\ 0 & 0 & 0 & 1 \end{bmatrix} = E_3(4)$$

(3) By $R_{12}(3)$, we get

$$R_{12}(3)(I_4) = \begin{bmatrix} 1 & 3 & 0 & 0 \\ 0 & 1 & 0 & 0 \\ 0 & 0 & 1 & 0 \\ 0 & 0 & 0 & 1 \end{bmatrix} = E_{12}(3)$$

Again, we have

$$I_3 = \begin{bmatrix} 1 & 0 & 0 \\ 0 & 1 & 0 \\ 0 & 0 & 1 \end{bmatrix}$$

Then,

(1) By C_{23}, we get

$$C_{23}(I_3) = \begin{bmatrix} 1 & 0 & 0 \\ 0 & 0 & 1 \\ 0 & 1 & 0 \end{bmatrix} = E'_{23}$$

(2) By $C_1(2)$, we get

$$C_1(2)(I_3) = \begin{bmatrix} 2 & 0 & 0 \\ 0 & 1 & 0 \\ 0 & 0 & 1 \end{bmatrix} = E'_1(2)$$

(3) By $C_{23}(2)$, we get

$$C_{23}(2)(I_3) = \begin{bmatrix} 1 & 0 & 0 \\ 0 & 1 & 0 \\ 0 & 2 & 1 \end{bmatrix} = E'_{23}(2)$$

4.10. Determinants of Elementary Matrices

$$|E_{ij}| = |E'_{ij}| = 1$$

$$|E_i(k)| = |E'_i(k)| = k$$

$$|E_{ij}(k)| = |E'_{ij}(k)| = 1$$

The above results show that the elementary matrices are non-singular.

4.11. Equivalent Matrices

Two matrices are said to be equivalent if one can be obtained from the other by applying a finite number of elementary transformations. If the matrices A and B are equivalent, then we write this fact symbolically as $A \sim B$.

4.12. Some Theorems on Elementary Operations

Theorem 1. Every elementary row (column) transformation of a matrix can be obtained by pre-multiplying (post-multiplying) by the corresponding elementary matrix of an appropriate order.

Proof. First of all, we shall prove a lemma.

Lemma. Every elementary row (column) transformation of the product of two matrices can be affected by subjecting the pre-factor (post-factor) to the same row (column) transformation.

Let $C = AB$ where $A = [a_{ij}]_{m \times n}$ and $B = [b_{jk}]_{n \times p}$.

We have,

$$A = \begin{bmatrix} R_1 \\ R_2 \\ \vdots \\ R_m \end{bmatrix}$$

where,

$$R_i = [a_{i1}, a_{i2}, \ldots\ldots, a_{in}]$$

and,

$$B = [C_1 \quad C_2 \quad \ldots\ldots \quad C_p]$$

where,

$$C_k = \begin{bmatrix} b_{1k} \\ b_{2k} \\ \vdots \\ b_{nk} \end{bmatrix}$$

$$\therefore \quad C = AB = \begin{bmatrix} R_1 \\ R_2 \\ \vdots \\ R_m \end{bmatrix} \begin{bmatrix} C_1 & C_2 & \ldots\ldots & C_p \end{bmatrix}$$

$$= \begin{bmatrix} R_1C_1 & R_1C_2 & \ldots\ldots & R_1C_p \\ R_2C_1 & R_2C_2 & \ldots\ldots & R_2C_p \\ \ldots\ldots & \ldots\ldots & \ldots\ldots & \ldots\ldots \\ R_mC_1 & R_mC_2 & \ldots\ldots & R_mC_p \end{bmatrix}$$

This shows that if the rows R_1, R_2, ..., R_m of A are subjected to any elementary row transformation, then the rows of AB are also subjected to the same transformation. Similarly, if the columns C_1, C_2, ..., C_p of B are subjected to any elementary column transformation, then the columns of AB are also subjected to the same transformation.

Hence, the lemma.

Proof of Main Theorem. We write $A = IA$, where I is the unit matrix.

Any elementary row transformation of A on L.H.S. can be obtained by applying the same row transformation on the rows of I, i.e. by pre-multiplying the matrix A in R.H.S. by an elementary matrix obtained from I by applying the same row transformation on I.

Hence, every row transformation on A can be affected by pre-multiplying A with the corresponding elementary matrix.

Similarly, by writing $A = AI$, we see that truth of the corresponding result for column transformations.

Illustration

Let us take

$$A = \begin{bmatrix} a_{11} & a_{12} & a_{13} & a_{14} \\ a_{21} & a_{22} & a_{23} & a_{24} \\ a_{31} & a_{32} & a_{33} & a_{34} \end{bmatrix},$$

$$I_3 = \begin{bmatrix} 1 & 0 & 0 \\ 0 & 1 & 0 \\ 0 & 0 & 1 \end{bmatrix}$$

and

$$I_4 = \begin{bmatrix} 1 & 0 & 0 & 0 \\ 0 & 1 & 0 & 0 \\ 0 & 0 & 1 & 0 \\ 0 & 0 & 0 & 1 \end{bmatrix}$$

(1) Let us apply R_{12} on I_3. Then, R_{12} on I_3 gives elementary matrix $E_{12} = \begin{bmatrix} 0 & 1 & 0 \\ 1 & 0 & 0 \\ 0 & 0 & 1 \end{bmatrix}$.

Now,

$$E_{12}A = \begin{bmatrix} 0 & 1 & 0 \\ 1 & 0 & 0 \\ 0 & 0 & 1 \end{bmatrix} \begin{bmatrix} a_{11} & a_{12} & a_{13} & a_{14} \\ a_{21} & a_{22} & a_{23} & a_{24} \\ a_{31} & a_{32} & a_{33} & a_{34} \end{bmatrix}$$

$$= \begin{bmatrix} a_{21} & a_{22} & a_{23} & a_{24} \\ a_{11} & a_{12} & a_{13} & a_{14} \\ a_{31} & a_{32} & a_{33} & a_{34} \end{bmatrix}$$

which is the same matrix as is obtained by applying R_{12} directly on A.

Again, let us apply C_{23} on I_4. We get an elementary matrix

$$E'_{23} = \begin{bmatrix} 1 & 0 & 0 & 0 \\ 0 & 0 & 1 & 0 \\ 0 & 1 & 0 & 0 \\ 0 & 0 & 0 & 1 \end{bmatrix}$$

Hence,

$$AE'_{23} = \begin{bmatrix} a_{11} & a_{12} & a_{13} & a_{14} \\ a_{21} & a_{22} & a_{23} & a_{24} \\ a_{31} & a_{32} & a_{33} & a_{34} \end{bmatrix} \begin{bmatrix} 1 & 0 & 0 & 0 \\ 0 & 0 & 1 & 0 \\ 0 & 1 & 0 & 0 \\ 0 & 0 & 0 & 1 \end{bmatrix}$$

$$= \begin{bmatrix} a_{11} & a_{12} & a_{13} & a_{14} \\ a_{21} & a_{22} & a_{23} & a_{24} \\ a_{31} & a_{32} & a_{33} & a_{34} \end{bmatrix}$$

which is the same as if C_{23} is applied directly on A.

(2) Let us apply $R_3(4)$ on I_3. Then $R_3(4)$ on I_3 gives elementary matrix $E_3(4) = \begin{bmatrix} 1 & 0 & 0 \\ 0 & 1 & 0 \\ 0 & 0 & 4 \end{bmatrix}$ and

$$E_3(4)A = \begin{bmatrix} 1 & 0 & 0 \\ 0 & 1 & 0 \\ 0 & 0 & 4 \end{bmatrix} \begin{bmatrix} a_{11} & a_{12} & a_{13} & a_{14} \\ a_{21} & a_{22} & a_{23} & a_{24} \\ a_{31} & a_{32} & a_{33} & a_{34} \end{bmatrix}$$

$$= \begin{bmatrix} a_{11} & a_{12} & a_{13} & a_{14} \\ a_{21} & a_{22} & a_{23} & a_{24} \\ 4a_{31} & 4a_{32} & 4a_{33} & 4a_{34} \end{bmatrix}$$

which is the same as obtained directly from A by applying $R_3(4)$.

Now, $E_2'(k)$ obtained from I_4 by applying $C_2(k)$ is given by

$$E_2'(k) = \begin{bmatrix} 1 & 0 & 0 & 0 \\ 0 & k & 0 & 0 \\ 0 & 0 & 1 & 0 \\ 0 & 0 & 0 & 1 \end{bmatrix}$$

Hence,

$$AE_2'(k) = \begin{bmatrix} a_{11} & a_{12} & a_{13} & a_{14} \\ a_{21} & a_{22} & a_{23} & a_{24} \\ a_{31} & a_{32} & a_{33} & a_{34} \end{bmatrix} \begin{bmatrix} 1 & 0 & 0 & 0 \\ 0 & k & 0 & 0 \\ 0 & 0 & 1 & 0 \\ 0 & 0 & 0 & 1 \end{bmatrix}$$

$$= \begin{bmatrix} a_{11} & ka_{12} & a_{13} & a_{14} \\ a_{21} & ka_{22} & a_{23} & a_{24} \\ a_{31} & ka_{32} & a_{33} & a_{34} \end{bmatrix}$$

which is the same as we get on applying $C_2(k)$ directly on A.

(3) Let us consider the transformation $R_{12}(1)$ and $C_{23}\left(-\frac{1}{2}\right)$.

We get

$$\begin{bmatrix} 1 & 1 & 0 \\ 0 & 1 & 0 \\ 0 & 0 & 1 \end{bmatrix} \begin{bmatrix} a_{11} & a_{12} & a_{13} & a_{14} \\ a_{21} & a_{22} & a_{23} & a_{24} \\ a_{31} & a_{32} & a_{33} & a_{34} \end{bmatrix}$$

$$= \begin{bmatrix} a_{11}+a_{21} & a_{12}+a_{22} & a_{13}+a_{23} & a_{14}+a_{24} \\ a_{21} & a_{22} & a_{23} & a_{24} \\ a_{31} & a_{32} & a_{33} & a_{34} \end{bmatrix}$$

and

$$\begin{bmatrix} a_{11} & a_{12} & a_{13} & a_{14} \\ a_{21} & a_{22} & a_{23} & a_{24} \\ a_{31} & a_{32} & a_{33} & a_{34} \end{bmatrix} \begin{bmatrix} 1 & 0 & 0 & 0 \\ 0 & 1 & 0 & 0 \\ 0 & -\frac{1}{2} & 1 & 0 \\ 0 & 0 & 0 & 1 \end{bmatrix}$$

$$= \begin{bmatrix} a_{11} & a_{12}-\frac{1}{2}a_{13} & a_{13} & a_{14} \\ a_{21} & a_{22}-\frac{1}{2}a_{23} & a_{23} & a_{24} \\ a_{31} & a_{32}-\frac{1}{2}a_{33} & a_{33} & a_{34} \end{bmatrix}$$

Hence, to effect any elementary operation on a given matrix A, we first perform the same operation on a unit matrix of appropriate order, then pre-multiply A by the elementary matrix if the operation is on rows, or post-multiply if it is on columns.

Theorem 2. The inverse of an elementary matrix is an elementary matrix.

Proof. Let I_n be a unit matrix of order n. Let E_{ij} be the resulting matrix obtained by applying the elementary operation R_{ij} on I_n. It is obvious that on applying the elementary transformation R_{ij} again on E_{ij}, we obtain the original matrix I_n. The latter transformation can be effected by pre-multiplying E_{ij} with E_{ij}. Thus,

$$E_{ij}\ E_{ij} = I_n$$

Thus, shows that E_{ij} is its non-inverse, i.e.

$$(E_{ij})^{-1} = E_{ij} \qquad \text{... (4.30)}$$

Again, let $E_i\ (k)$ denotes the matrix obtained on multiplying the ith row of I_n by k. $E_i(k)$ can be transformed into the unit matrix I_n on multiplying the ith row of $E_i(k)$ by $\frac{1}{k}$. The latter operation can be affected by pre-multiplying $E_i(k)$ with $E_i\left(\frac{1}{k}\right)$. Thus,

$$E_i\left(\frac{1}{k}\right) E_i\ (k) = I_n$$

This shows that

$$\{E_i\ (k)\}^{-1} = E_i\left(\frac{1}{k}\right) \qquad \text{... (4.31)}$$

Similarly, we can show that

$$\{E_{ij}\ (k)\}^{-1} = E_{ij}\ (-k) \qquad \text{... (4.32)}$$

Hence, the theorem.

4.13. Theorems on Equivalent Matrices

Theorem 1. If A and B be equivalent matrices, then there exist non-singular matrices R and C such that

$$B = RAC$$

Proof. Since A and B are equivalent matrices, therefore, B can be obtained from A by the application of a finite series of elementary row and column operation on A. But we know that any elementary row (column) operation A can be effected by pre (post) multiplication of A by elementary matrices of appropriate orders. Therefore,

$$(R_n\ .....\ R_2R_1)\ A\ (C_1\ C_2\ .....\ C_m) = B$$

Hence,

$$B = RAC$$

where,

$$R = R_n \;.....\; R_2R_1$$

and $C = C_1\, C_2 \;.....\; C_m$, being the products of elementary matrices of appropriate orders, are non-singular matrices.

Theorem 2. If A and B are equivalent matrices, then

$$A = R^{-1}BC^{-1}$$

Proof. Since A and B are equivalent matrices, therefore, by Theorem 1 above, we have

$$B = RAC \qquad ...\ (4.33)$$

where R and C are non-singular matrices. Consequently, their inverses respectively, R^{-1} and C^{-1} will exist.

Pre-multiplying both sides of Eq. (4.33) by R^{-1}, we get

$$\begin{aligned} R^{-1}B &= R^{-1}RAC \\ &= (R^{-1}R)AC && \mid \text{By associativity} \\ &= IAC \\ &= (IA)C \\ &= AC && \mid \because IA = A \end{aligned}$$

Now, post-multiplying both sides of the above relation by C^{-1}, we get

$$\begin{aligned} R^{-1}BC^{-1} &= ACI^{-1} \\ &= A(CC^{-1}) \\ &= AI \\ &= A \end{aligned}$$

Thus, we have

$$A = R^{-1}BC^{-1}$$

Hence, the theorem.

Theorem 3. Every non-singular square matrix can be expressed as the product of elementary matrices.

Proof. Let A be a non-singular square matrix of order. Let I_n be a unit matrix of order n. Since I_n can be obtained from A by applying a finite series of elementary row and column operation on A, therefore, A and I_n are equivalent matrices. Hence,

$$A = RI_nC$$

where, $R = R_p \dots R_2R_1$ and $C = C_1\ C_2 \dots C_m$ are the products of a number of elementary row matrices and elementary column matrices of appropriate orders, respectively.

Hence, the theorem.

Theorem 4. If A is a non-singular square matrix of order n, then there exist elementary matrices $E_1, E_2, \dots, E_k$ such that

$$E_k \dots E_2\ E_1\ A = I_n$$

where I_n is a unit matrix of order n, i.e.

$$EA = I_n, \text{ where } E = E_k \dots E_2E_1$$

Proof. Proof is obvious.

Theorem 5. If there exists a finite series of elementary matrices $E_1, E_2, \dots, E_k$ such that $(E_k \dots E_2E_1)A = I_n$ and A is non-singular square matrix of order n, then

$$A^{-1} = (E_k \dots E_2E_1)I_n$$

i.e. if a sequence of elementary operations on non-singular square matrix of order n transforms it to a unit matrix I_n, then the same sequence when applied on I transforms I to A^{-1}.

Proof. We have

$$(E_k \dots E_2E_1)A = I$$

$$\Rightarrow (E_k \dots E_2E_1)AA^{-1} = IA^{-1}$$

$$\Rightarrow (E_k \dots E_2E_1)I = A^{-1}$$

Hence, the theorem.

Note 1. This method is quite useful in finding the inverse of a non-singular square matrix A.

Note 2. Since I is obtained from A by elementary row operations, therefore, $A \sim I$. Hence, if the same set of elementary row operations is performed on I as on A, then A transforms to I and I to A^{-1}.

Note 3. We can similarly prove that

$$A(C_1C_2 \dots C_m) = I \Rightarrow A^{-1} = I(C_1C_2 \dots C_m)$$

ILLUSTRATIVE EXAMPLES

Example 1. Find the inverse of $A = \begin{bmatrix} 1 & 2 & -2 \\ -1 & 3 & 0 \\ 0 & -2 & 1 \end{bmatrix}$ using elementary transformations.

Solution: Let us write

$$\begin{bmatrix} 1 & 2 & -2 \\ -1 & 3 & 0 \\ 0 & -2 & 1 \end{bmatrix} = \begin{bmatrix} 1 & 0 & 0 \\ 0 & 1 & 0 \\ 0 & 0 & 1 \end{bmatrix} A$$

Applying R_{21}, we have

$$\begin{bmatrix} 1 & 2 & -2 \\ 0 & 5 & -2 \\ 0 & -2 & 1 \end{bmatrix} = \begin{bmatrix} 1 & 0 & 0 \\ 1 & 1 & 0 \\ 0 & 0 & 1 \end{bmatrix} A$$

Applying $R_{23}(2)$, we have

$$\begin{bmatrix} 1 & 0 & -1 \\ 0 & 1 & 0 \\ 0 & -2 & 1 \end{bmatrix} = \begin{bmatrix} 1 & 0 & 1 \\ 1 & 1 & 2 \\ 0 & 0 & 2 \end{bmatrix} A$$

Applying $R_{32}(2)$, we have

$$\begin{bmatrix} 1 & 0 & -1 \\ 0 & 1 & 0 \\ 0 & 0 & 1 \end{bmatrix} = \begin{bmatrix} 1 & 0 & 1 \\ 1 & 1 & 2 \\ 2 & 2 & 5 \end{bmatrix} A$$

Applying $R_{13}(1)$, we have

$$\begin{bmatrix} 1 & 0 & 0 \\ 0 & 1 & 0 \\ 0 & 0 & 1 \end{bmatrix} = \begin{bmatrix} 3 & 2 & 6 \\ 1 & 1 & 2 \\ 2 & 2 & 5 \end{bmatrix} A$$

Hence,

$$A^{-1} = \begin{bmatrix} 3 & 2 & 6 \\ 1 & 1 & 2 \\ 2 & 2 & 5 \end{bmatrix}$$

Example 2. With the help of elementary operations, find the inverse of $A = \begin{bmatrix} 1 & 2 & 1 \\ 3 & 2 & 3 \\ 1 & 1 & 2 \end{bmatrix}$.

Solution: Let us write

$$\begin{bmatrix} 1 & 2 & 1 \\ 3 & 2 & 3 \\ 1 & 1 & 2 \end{bmatrix} = \begin{bmatrix} 1 & 0 & 0 \\ 0 & 1 & 0 \\ 0 & 0 & 1 \end{bmatrix} A$$

Applying $R_{21}(-3)$ and $R_{31}(-1)$, we have

$$\begin{bmatrix} 1 & 2 & 1 \\ 0 & -4 & 0 \\ 0 & -1 & 1 \end{bmatrix} = \begin{bmatrix} 1 & 0 & 0 \\ -3 & 1 & 0 \\ -1 & 0 & 1 \end{bmatrix} A$$

Applying $R_2\left(-\frac{1}{4}\right)$, we have

$$\begin{bmatrix} 1 & 2 & 1 \\ 0 & 1 & 0 \\ 0 & -1 & 1 \end{bmatrix} = \begin{bmatrix} 1 & 0 & 0 \\ -\frac{3}{4} & -\frac{1}{4} & 0 \\ -1 & 0 & 1 \end{bmatrix} A$$

Applying $R_{32}(1)$ and $R_{12}(-2)$, we have

$$\begin{bmatrix} 1 & 0 & 1 \\ 0 & 1 & 0 \\ 0 & 0 & 1 \end{bmatrix} = \begin{bmatrix} -\frac{1}{2} & \frac{1}{2} & 0 \\ \frac{3}{4} & -\frac{1}{4} & 0 \\ -\frac{1}{4} & -\frac{1}{4} & 1 \end{bmatrix} A$$

Applying $R_{13}(-1)$, we have

$$\begin{bmatrix} 1 & 0 & 0 \\ 0 & 1 & 0 \\ 0 & 0 & 1 \end{bmatrix} = \begin{bmatrix} -\frac{1}{4} & \frac{3}{4} & -1 \\ \frac{3}{4} & -\frac{1}{4} & 0 \\ -\frac{1}{4} & -\frac{1}{4} & 1 \end{bmatrix} A$$

Hence,

$$A^{-1} = \begin{bmatrix} -\frac{1}{4} & \frac{3}{4} & -1 \\ \frac{3}{4} & -\frac{1}{4} & 0 \\ -\frac{1}{4} & -\frac{1}{4} & 0 \end{bmatrix}$$

Example 3. Using elementary transformtions, find the inverse of the matrix

$$A = \begin{bmatrix} 0 & 2 & 1 & 3 \\ 1 & 1 & -1 & -2 \\ 1 & 2 & 0 & 1 \\ -1 & 1 & 2 & 6 \end{bmatrix}$$

Solution: Let us write

$$\begin{bmatrix} 0 & 2 & 1 & 3 \\ 1 & 1 & -1 & -2 \\ 1 & 2 & 0 & 1 \\ -1 & 1 & 2 & 6 \end{bmatrix} = \begin{bmatrix} 1 & 0 & 0 & 0 \\ 0 & 1 & 0 & 0 \\ 0 & 0 & 1 & 0 \\ 0 & 0 & 0 & 1 \end{bmatrix} A$$

Applying R_{12}, we have

$$\begin{bmatrix} 1 & 1 & -1 & -2 \\ 0 & 2 & 1 & 3 \\ 1 & 2 & 0 & 1 \\ -1 & 1 & 2 & 6 \end{bmatrix} = \begin{bmatrix} 0 & 1 & 0 & 0 \\ 1 & 0 & 0 & 0 \\ 0 & 0 & 1 & 0 \\ 0 & 0 & 0 & 1 \end{bmatrix} A$$

Applying $R_{31}(-1)$ and $R_{41}(1)$, we have

$$\begin{bmatrix} 1 & 1 & -1 & -2 \\ 0 & 2 & 1 & 3 \\ 0 & 1 & 1 & 3 \\ 0 & 2 & 1 & 4 \end{bmatrix} = \begin{bmatrix} 0 & 1 & 0 & 0 \\ 1 & 0 & 0 & 0 \\ 0 & -1 & 1 & 0 \\ 0 & 1 & 0 & 1 \end{bmatrix} A$$

Applying $R_{42}(-1)$ and $R_{23}(-1)$, we have

$$\begin{bmatrix} 1 & 1 & -1 & -2 \\ 0 & 1 & 0 & 0 \\ 0 & 1 & 1 & 3 \\ 0 & 0 & 0 & 1 \end{bmatrix} = \begin{bmatrix} 0 & 1 & 0 & 0 \\ 1 & 1 & -1 & 0 \\ 0 & -1 & 1 & 0 \\ -1 & 1 & 0 & 1 \end{bmatrix} A$$

Applying $R_{12}(-1)$ and $R_{32}(-1)$, we have

$$\begin{bmatrix} 1 & 0 & -1 & -2 \\ 0 & 1 & 0 & 0 \\ 0 & 0 & 1 & 3 \\ 0 & 0 & 0 & 1 \end{bmatrix} = \begin{bmatrix} -1 & 0 & 1 & 0 \\ 1 & 1 & -1 & 0 \\ -1 & -2 & 2 & 0 \\ -1 & 1 & 0 & 1 \end{bmatrix} A$$

Applying $R_{14}(2)$ and $R_{34}(-3)$, we have

$$\begin{bmatrix} 1 & 0 & -1 & 0 \\ 0 & 1 & 0 & 0 \\ 0 & 0 & 1 & 0 \\ 0 & 0 & 0 & 1 \end{bmatrix} = \begin{bmatrix} -3 & 2 & 1 & 2 \\ 1 & 1 & -1 & 0 \\ 2 & -5 & 2 & -3 \\ -1 & 1 & 0 & 1 \end{bmatrix} A$$

Applying $R_{13}(1)$, we have

$$\begin{bmatrix} 1 & 0 & 0 & 0 \\ 0 & 1 & 0 & 0 \\ 0 & 0 & 1 & 0 \\ 0 & 0 & 0 & 1 \end{bmatrix} = \begin{bmatrix} -1 & -3 & 3 & -1 \\ 1 & 1 & -1 & 0 \\ 2 & -5 & 2 & -3 \\ -1 & 1 & 0 & 1 \end{bmatrix} A$$

Hence,

$$A^{-1} = \begin{bmatrix} -1 & -3 & 3 & -1 \\ 1 & 1 & -1 & 0 \\ 2 & -5 & 2 & -3 \\ -1 & 1 & 0 & 1 \end{bmatrix}$$

Example 4. Find the inverse of $A = \begin{bmatrix} 0 & 1 & 2 & 2 \\ 1 & 1 & 2 & 3 \\ 2 & 2 & 2 & 3 \\ 2 & 3 & 3 & 3 \end{bmatrix}$.

Solution: Let us write

$$\begin{bmatrix} 0 & 1 & 2 & 2 \\ 1 & 2 & 2 & 3 \\ 2 & 2 & 2 & 3 \\ 2 & 3 & 3 & 3 \end{bmatrix} = \begin{bmatrix} 1 & 0 & 0 & 0 \\ 0 & 1 & 0 & 0 \\ 0 & 0 & 1 & 0 \\ 0 & 0 & 0 & 1 \end{bmatrix} A$$

Applying R_{13}, we have

$$\begin{bmatrix} 1 & 1 & 2 & 3 \\ 0 & 1 & 2 & 2 \\ 2 & 2 & 2 & 3 \\ 2 & 3 & 3 & 3 \end{bmatrix} = \begin{bmatrix} 0 & 1 & 0 & 0 \\ 1 & 0 & 0 & 0 \\ 0 & 0 & 1 & 0 \\ 0 & 0 & 0 & 1 \end{bmatrix} A$$

Applying $R_{31}(-2)$ and $R_{41}(-2)$, we have

$$\begin{bmatrix} 1 & 1 & 2 & 3 \\ 0 & 1 & 2 & 2 \\ 0 & 0 & -2 & -3 \\ 0 & 1 & -1 & -3 \end{bmatrix} = \begin{bmatrix} 0 & 1 & 0 & 0 \\ 1 & 0 & 0 & 0 \\ 0 & -2 & 1 & 0 \\ 0 & -2 & 0 & 1 \end{bmatrix} A$$

Applying $R_{23}(1)$, we have

$$\begin{bmatrix} 1 & 1 & 2 & 3 \\ 0 & 1 & 0 & -1 \\ 0 & 0 & -2 & -3 \\ 0 & 1 & -1 & -3 \end{bmatrix} = \begin{bmatrix} 0 & 1 & 0 & 0 \\ 1 & -2 & 1 & 0 \\ 0 & -2 & 1 & 0 \\ 0 & -2 & 0 & 1 \end{bmatrix} A$$

Applying $R_{42}(-1)$, we have

$$\begin{bmatrix} 1 & 1 & 2 & 3 \\ 0 & 1 & 0 & -1 \\ 0 & 0 & -2 & -3 \\ 0 & 0 & -1 & -2 \end{bmatrix} = \begin{bmatrix} 0 & 1 & 0 & 0 \\ 1 & -2 & 1 & 0 \\ 0 & -2 & 1 & 0 \\ -1 & 0 & 1 & 1 \end{bmatrix} A$$

Applying $R_{13}(1)$, we have

$$\begin{bmatrix} 1 & 1 & 0 & 0 \\ 0 & 1 & 2 & -1 \\ 0 & 0 & -2 & -3 \\ 0 & 0 & -1 & -2 \end{bmatrix} = \begin{bmatrix} 0 & -1 & 1 & 0 \\ 1 & -2 & 1 & 0 \\ 0 & -2 & 1 & 0 \\ -1 & 0 & -1 & 1 \end{bmatrix} A$$

Applying $R_{43}(-1)$, we have

$$\begin{bmatrix} 1 & 1 & 0 & 0 \\ 0 & 1 & 0 & -1 \\ 3 & 0 & -2 & -3 \\ 0 & 0 & 1 & 1 \end{bmatrix} = \begin{bmatrix} 0 & -1 & 1 & 0 \\ 1 & -2 & 1 & 0 \\ 0 & -2 & 1 & 0 \\ -1 & 2 & -2 & 1 \end{bmatrix} A$$

Applying $R_{34}(2)$, we have

$$\begin{bmatrix} 1 & 1 & 0 & 0 \\ 0 & 1 & 0 & -1 \\ 0 & 0 & 0 & -1 \\ 0 & 0 & 1 & 1 \end{bmatrix} = \begin{bmatrix} 0 & -1 & 1 & 0 \\ 1 & -2 & 1 & 0 \\ -2 & 2 & -3 & 2 \\ -1 & 2 & -2 & 1 \end{bmatrix} A$$

Applying $R_{23}(-1)$ and $R_{43}(1)$, we have

$$\begin{bmatrix} 1 & 1 & 0 & 0 \\ 0 & 1 & 0 & 0 \\ 0 & 0 & 0 & -1 \\ 0 & 0 & 1 & 0 \end{bmatrix} = \begin{bmatrix} 0 & -1 & 1 & 2 \\ 3 & -4 & 4 & -2 \\ -2 & 2 & -3 & 2 \\ -3 & 4 & -5 & 3 \end{bmatrix} A$$

Applying $R_{12}(-1)$ and R_{34}, we have

$$\begin{bmatrix} 1 & 0 & 0 & 0 \\ 0 & 1 & 0 & 0 \\ 0 & 0 & 1 & 0 \\ 0 & 0 & 0 & -1 \end{bmatrix} = \begin{bmatrix} -3 & 3 & -3 & 2 \\ 3 & -4 & 4 & -2 \\ -3 & 4 & -5 & 3 \\ -2 & 2 & -3 & 2 \end{bmatrix} A$$

Applying $R_4(-1)$, we have

$$\begin{bmatrix} 1 & 0 & 0 & 0 \\ 0 & 1 & 0 & 0 \\ 1 & 0 & 1 & 0 \\ 0 & 0 & 0 & 1 \end{bmatrix} = \begin{bmatrix} -3 & 3 & -3 & 2 \\ 3 & -4 & 4 & -2 \\ -3 & 4 & -5 & 3 \\ 2 & -2 & 3 & -2 \end{bmatrix} A$$

Hence,

$$A^{-1} = \begin{bmatrix} -3 & 3 & -3 & 2 \\ 3 & -4 & 4 & -2 \\ -3 & 4 & -5 & 3 \\ 2 & -2 & 3 & -2 \end{bmatrix}$$

Example 5. Find the inverse of $A = \begin{bmatrix} 1 & -1 & 0 & 2 \\ 0 & 1 & 1 & -1 \\ 2 & 1 & 2 & 1 \\ 3 & -2 & 1 & 6 \end{bmatrix}$.

Solution: Let us write

$$\begin{bmatrix} 1 & -1 & 0 & 2 \\ 0 & 1 & 1 & -1 \\ 2 & 1 & 2 & 1 \\ 3 & -2 & 1 & 6 \end{bmatrix} = \begin{bmatrix} 1 & 0 & 0 & 0 \\ 0 & 1 & 0 & 0 \\ 0 & 0 & 1 & 0 \\ 0 & 0 & 0 & 1 \end{bmatrix} A$$

Applying $R_{31}(-1)$ and $R_{41}(-3)$, we have

$$\begin{bmatrix} 1 & -1 & 0 & 2 \\ 0 & 1 & 1 & -1 \\ 0 & 3 & 2 & -3 \\ 0 & 1 & 1 & 0 \end{bmatrix} = \begin{bmatrix} 1 & 0 & 0 & 0 \\ 0 & 1 & 0 & 0 \\ -2 & 0 & 1 & 0 \\ -3 & 0 & 0 & 1 \end{bmatrix} A$$

Applying $R_{32}(-3)$ and $R_{42}(-1)$, we have

$$\begin{bmatrix} 1 & -1 & 0 & 2 \\ 0 & 1 & 1 & -1 \\ 0 & 0 & -1 & 0 \\ 0 & 0 & 0 & 1 \end{bmatrix} = \begin{bmatrix} 1 & 0 & 0 & 0 \\ 0 & 1 & 0 & 0 \\ -2 & -3 & 1 & 0 \\ -3 & -1 & 3 & 1 \end{bmatrix} A$$

Applying $R_{14}(-2)$, $R_{24}(1)$ and $R_3(-1)$, we have

$$\begin{bmatrix} 1 & -1 & 0 & 0 \\ 0 & 1 & 1 & 0 \\ 0 & 0 & 1 & 0 \\ 0 & 0 & 0 & 1 \end{bmatrix} = \begin{bmatrix} 7 & 2 & 0 & -2 \\ -3 & 0 & 0 & 1 \\ 2 & 3 & -1 & 0 \\ -3 & -1 & 0 & 1 \end{bmatrix} A$$

Applying $R_{23}(-1)$, we have

$$\begin{bmatrix} 1 & -1 & 0 & 0 \\ 0 & 1 & 0 & 0 \\ 0 & 0 & 1 & 0 \\ 0 & 0 & 0 & 1 \end{bmatrix} = \begin{bmatrix} 7 & 2 & 0 & -2 \\ -5 & -3 & 1 & 1 \\ 2 & 3 & -1 & 0 \\ -3 & -1 & 0 & 1 \end{bmatrix} A$$

Applying $R_{12}(1)$, we have

$$\begin{bmatrix} 1 & 0 & 0 & 0 \\ 0 & 1 & 0 & 0 \\ 0 & 0 & 1 & 0 \\ 0 & 0 & 0 & 1 \end{bmatrix} = \begin{bmatrix} 2 & -1 & 1 & -1 \\ -5 & -3 & 1 & 1 \\ 2 & 3 & -1 & 0 \\ -3 & -1 & 0 & 1 \end{bmatrix} A$$

Hence,

$$A^{-1} = \begin{bmatrix} 2 & -1 & 1 & -1 \\ -5 & -3 & 1 & 1 \\ 2 & 3 & -1 & 0 \\ -3 & -1 & 0 & 1 \end{bmatrix}$$

Example 6. Find the inverse of the matrix

$$A = \begin{bmatrix} -1 & -3 & 3 & -1 \\ 1 & 1 & -1 & 0 \\ 2 & -5 & 2 & -3 \\ -1 & 1 & 0 & 1 \end{bmatrix}$$

by using E-transformations.

Solution: Let us write

$$\begin{bmatrix} -1 & -3 & 3 & -1 \\ 1 & 1 & -1 & 0 \\ 2 & -5 & 2 & -3 \\ -1 & 1 & 0 & 1 \end{bmatrix} = \begin{bmatrix} 1 & 0 & 0 & 0 \\ 0 & 1 & 0 & 0 \\ 0 & 0 & 1 & 0 \\ 0 & 0 & 0 & 1 \end{bmatrix} A$$

Applying $R_1(-1)$, we have

$$\begin{bmatrix} 1 & 3 & -3 & 1 \\ 1 & 1 & -1 & 0 \\ 2 & -5 & 2 & -3 \\ -1 & 1 & 0 & 1 \end{bmatrix} = \begin{bmatrix} -1 & 0 & 0 & 0 \\ 0 & 1 & 0 & 0 \\ 0 & 0 & 1 & 0 \\ 0 & 0 & 0 & 1 \end{bmatrix} A$$

Applying $R_{21}(-1)$, $R_{32}(-2)$ and $R_{41}(1)$, we have

$$\begin{bmatrix} 1 & 3 & -3 & 1 \\ 0 & -2 & 2 & -1 \\ 0 & -11 & 8 & -5 \\ 0 & 4 & -3 & 2 \end{bmatrix} = \begin{bmatrix} -1 & 0 & 0 & 0 \\ 1 & 1 & 0 & 0 \\ 2 & 0 & 1 & 0 \\ -1 & 0 & 0 & 1 \end{bmatrix} A$$

Applying $R_2\left(-\frac{1}{2}\right)$, we have

$$\begin{bmatrix} 1 & 3 & -3 & 1 \\ 0 & 1 & -1 & \frac{1}{2} \\ 0 & -11 & 8 & -5 \\ 0 & 4 & -3 & 2 \end{bmatrix} = \begin{bmatrix} -1 & 0 & 0 & 0 \\ -\frac{1}{2} & -\frac{1}{2} & 0 & 0 \\ 2 & 0 & 1 & 0 \\ -1 & 0 & 0 & 1 \end{bmatrix} A$$

Applying $R_{12}(-3)$, $R_{32}(11)$ and $R_{42}(-4)$, we have

$$\begin{bmatrix} 1 & 0 & 0 & -\frac{1}{2} \\ 0 & 1 & -1 & \frac{1}{2} \\ 0 & 0 & -3 & \frac{1}{2} \\ 0 & 0 & 1 & 0 \end{bmatrix} = \begin{bmatrix} \frac{1}{2} & \frac{3}{2} & 0 & 0 \\ -\frac{1}{2} & -\frac{1}{2} & 0 & 0 \\ -\frac{1}{2} & -\frac{11}{2} & 1 & 0 \\ 1 & 2 & 0 & 1 \end{bmatrix} A$$

Applying R_{34}, we have

$$\begin{bmatrix} 1 & 0 & 0 & -\frac{1}{2} \\ 0 & 1 & -1 & \frac{1}{2} \\ 0 & 0 & -3 & 0 \\ 0 & 0 & 1 & \frac{1}{2} \end{bmatrix} = \begin{bmatrix} \frac{1}{2} & \frac{3}{2} & 0 & 0 \\ -\frac{1}{2} & -\frac{1}{2} & 0 & 0 \\ 1 & 2 & 0 & 1 \\ -\frac{7}{2} & -\frac{11}{2} & 1 & 0 \end{bmatrix} A$$

Applying $R_{23}(1)$ and $R_{43}(3)$, we have

$$\begin{bmatrix} 1 & 0 & 0 & \frac{1}{2} \\ 0 & 1 & 0 & \frac{1}{2} \\ 0 & 0 & 1 & 0 \\ 0 & 0 & 0 & \frac{1}{2} \end{bmatrix} = \begin{bmatrix} \frac{1}{2} & \frac{3}{2} & 0 & 0 \\ \frac{1}{2} & \frac{3}{2} & 0 & 1 \\ 1 & 2 & 0 & 1 \\ -\frac{1}{2} & \frac{1}{2} & 1 & 3 \end{bmatrix} A$$

Applying $R_{24}(-1)$ and $R_{14}(1)$, we have

$$\begin{bmatrix} 1 & 0 & 0 & 0 \\ 0 & 1 & 0 & 0 \\ 0 & 0 & 1 & 0 \\ 0 & 0 & 1 & \frac{1}{2} \end{bmatrix} = \begin{bmatrix} 0 & 2 & 1 & 3 \\ 1 & 1 & -1 & -2 \\ 1 & 2 & 0 & 1 \\ -\frac{1}{2} & \frac{1}{2} & 1 & 3 \end{bmatrix} A$$

Applying $R_4(2)$, we have

$$\begin{bmatrix} 1 & 0 & 0 & 0 \\ 0 & 1 & 0 & 0 \\ 0 & 0 & 1 & 0 \\ 0 & 0 & 0 & 1 \end{bmatrix} = \begin{bmatrix} 0 & 2 & 1 & 3 \\ 1 & 1 & -1 & -2 \\ 1 & 2 & 0 & 1 \\ -1 & 1 & 2 & 6 \end{bmatrix} A$$

Hence,

$$A^{-1} = \begin{bmatrix} 0 & 2 & 1 & 3 \\ 1 & 1 & -1 & -2 \\ 1 & 2 & 0 & 1 \\ -1 & 1 & 2 & 6 \end{bmatrix}$$

Example 7. Find the inverse of the matrix product $\begin{bmatrix} 1 & 0 & K \\ 0 & 1 & 0 \\ 0 & 0 & 1 \end{bmatrix}$ $\begin{bmatrix} 1 & 0 & 0 \\ 0 & 1 & m \\ 0 & 0 & 1 \end{bmatrix}\begin{bmatrix} 1 & 0 & 0 \\ 0 & p & 0 \\ 0 & 0 & 1 \end{bmatrix}$ without first evaluating the product.

Solution: Let $A = \begin{bmatrix} 1 & 0 & K \\ 0 & 1 & 0 \\ 0 & 0 & 1 \end{bmatrix}\begin{bmatrix} 1 & 0 & 0 \\ 0 & 1 & m \\ 0 & 0 & 1 \end{bmatrix}\begin{bmatrix} 1 & 0 & 0 \\ 0 & p & 0 \\ 0 & 0 & 1 \end{bmatrix}$

Let us write

$$\begin{bmatrix} 1 & 0 & K \\ 0 & 1 & 0 \\ 0 & 0 & 1 \end{bmatrix}\begin{bmatrix} 1 & 0 & 0 \\ 0 & 1 & m \\ 0 & 0 & 1 \end{bmatrix}\begin{bmatrix} 1 & 0 & 0 \\ 0 & p & 0 \\ 0 & 0 & 1 \end{bmatrix} = \begin{bmatrix} 1 & 0 & 0 \\ 0 & 1 & 0 \\ 0 & 0 & 1 \end{bmatrix} A$$

Applying $R_{13}(-K)$, we have

$$\begin{bmatrix} 1 & 0 & 0 \\ 0 & 1 & 0 \\ 0 & 0 & 1 \end{bmatrix}\begin{bmatrix} 1 & 0 & 0 \\ 0 & 1 & m \\ 0 & 0 & 1 \end{bmatrix}\begin{bmatrix} 1 & 0 & 0 \\ 0 & p & 0 \\ 0 & 0 & 1 \end{bmatrix} = \begin{bmatrix} 1 & 0 & -K \\ 0 & 1 & 0 \\ 0 & 0 & 1 \end{bmatrix} A$$

$$\Rightarrow \begin{bmatrix} 1 & 0 & 0 \\ 0 & 1 & m \\ 0 & 0 & 1 \end{bmatrix}\begin{bmatrix} 1 & 0 & 0 \\ 0 & p & 0 \\ 0 & 0 & 1 \end{bmatrix} = \begin{bmatrix} 1 & 0 & -K \\ 0 & 1 & 0 \\ 0 & 0 & 1 \end{bmatrix} A \qquad |\because IX = X$$

Applying $R_{13}(-m)$, we have

$$\begin{bmatrix} 1 & 0 & 0 \\ 0 & 1 & 0 \\ 0 & 0 & 1 \end{bmatrix}\begin{bmatrix} 1 & 0 & 0 \\ 0 & p & 0 \\ 0 & 0 & 1 \end{bmatrix} = \begin{bmatrix} 1 & 0 & -K \\ 0 & 1 & -m \\ 0 & 0 & 1 \end{bmatrix} A$$

$$\Rightarrow \begin{bmatrix} 1 & 0 & 0 \\ 0 & p & 0 \\ 0 & 0 & 1 \end{bmatrix} = \begin{bmatrix} 1 & 0 & -K \\ 0 & 1 & -m \\ 0 & 0 & 1 \end{bmatrix} A \qquad | \because IX = X$$

Applying $R_2\left(\frac{1}{p}\right)$, we have

$$\begin{bmatrix} 1 & 0 & 0 \\ 0 & 1 & 0 \\ 0 & 0 & 1 \end{bmatrix} = \begin{bmatrix} 1 & 0 & -K \\ 0 & \frac{1}{p} & -\frac{m}{p} \\ 0 & 0 & 1 \end{bmatrix} A$$

Hence,

$$A^{-1} = \begin{bmatrix} 1 & 0 & -K \\ 0 & \frac{1}{p} & -\frac{m}{p} \\ 0 & 0 & 1 \end{bmatrix}$$

EXERCISE 4.4

Using elementary transformations, find the inverse of the following matrices, if possible:

1. $\begin{bmatrix} 1 & 2 & 3 \\ 1 & 3 & 4 \\ 1 & 4 & 3 \end{bmatrix}$

2. $\begin{bmatrix} 0 & 1 & 2 \\ 1 & 2 & 3 \\ 3 & 1 & 1 \end{bmatrix}$

3. $\begin{bmatrix} 2 & 0 & -1 \\ 5 & 1 & 0 \\ 0 & 1 & 3 \end{bmatrix}$

4. $\begin{bmatrix} 1 & -3 & 2 \\ 2 & 0 & 0 \\ 1 & 4 & 1 \end{bmatrix}$

5. $\begin{bmatrix} 1 & 0 & -1 \\ 3 & 4 & 5 \\ 0 & -6 & -7 \end{bmatrix}$

6. $\begin{bmatrix} 1 & 2 & 3 \\ 2 & 3 & 4 \\ 3 & 4 & 5 \end{bmatrix}$

7. $\begin{bmatrix} -1 & -2 & 3 \\ -2 & 1 & 1 \\ 4 & -5 & 2 \end{bmatrix}$

8. $\begin{bmatrix} 2 & -1 & 3 \\ 1 & 1 & 1 \\ 1 & -1 & 1 \end{bmatrix}$

9. $\begin{bmatrix} 3 & 3 & 4 \\ 2 & -3 & 4 \\ 0 & -1 & 1 \end{bmatrix}$

10. $\begin{bmatrix} 1 & 2 & 0 \\ 2 & -1 & 0 \\ 0 & 0 & 1 \end{bmatrix}$

11. $\begin{bmatrix} 1 & 2 & 3 & 1 \\ 1 & 3 & 3 & 2 \\ 2 & 4 & 3 & 3 \\ 1 & 1 & 1 & 1 \end{bmatrix}$

12. $\begin{bmatrix} 2 & 1 & -1 & 2 \\ 1 & 3 & 2 & -3 \\ -1 & 2 & 1 & -1 \\ 2 & -3 & -1 & 4 \end{bmatrix}$

13. Find the non-singular matrix P such that $PA = I$ where

$$A = \begin{bmatrix} 1 & -1 & 0 \\ 1 & -3 & 9 \\ 8 & 9 & 2 \end{bmatrix}.$$

14. Has the following matrix inverse?

$$A = \begin{bmatrix} 2 & 1 & 3 & 1 \\ 1 & 2 & -1 & 4 \\ 3 & 3 & 2 & 5 \\ 1 & -1 & 4 & -3 \end{bmatrix}$$

15. Find the inverse of the matrix

(i) $\begin{bmatrix} 3 & -2 & 0 & 1 \\ 0 & 2 & 2 & 1 \\ 1 & -2 & -3 & -2 \\ 0 & 1 & 2 & 1 \end{bmatrix}$

(ii) $\begin{bmatrix} 1 & 2 & 0 & 0 \\ 0 & 3 & 0 & 0 \\ 0 & 0 & 2 & 1 \\ 0 & 0 & 0 & 3 \end{bmatrix}$

ANSWERS

1. $\begin{bmatrix} \frac{7}{2} & -3 & -\frac{1}{2} \\ -\frac{1}{2} & 0 & \frac{1}{2} \\ -\frac{1}{2} & 0 & -\frac{1}{2} \end{bmatrix}$

2. $\begin{bmatrix} \frac{1}{2} & -\frac{1}{2} & -\frac{1}{2} \\ -4 & 3 & -1 \\ \frac{5}{2} & \frac{3}{2} & \frac{1}{2} \end{bmatrix}$

3. $\begin{bmatrix} 3 & -1 & 1 \\ -15 & 6 & -5 \\ 5 & -2 & 2 \end{bmatrix}$

4. $\begin{bmatrix} 0 & \frac{1}{2} & 0 \\ -\frac{1}{11} & -\frac{1}{22} & \frac{2}{11} \\ \frac{4}{11} & -\frac{7}{22} & \frac{3}{11} \end{bmatrix}$

5. $\frac{1}{20}\begin{bmatrix} 2 & 6 & 4 \\ 21 & -7 & -8 \\ -18 & 6 & 4 \end{bmatrix}$

6. Inverse is not possible since the matrix is singular.

7. $-\frac{1}{20}\begin{bmatrix} 7 & -11 & -5 \\ 8 & -14 & -5 \\ 6 & -13 & -5 \end{bmatrix}$

8. $-\frac{1}{2}\begin{bmatrix} -2 & 2 & 4 \\ 0 & 1 & -1 \\ 2 & -1 & -3 \end{bmatrix}$

9. $-\frac{1}{11}\begin{bmatrix} 1 & -7 & 24 \\ -2 & 3 & -4 \\ -2 & 3 & -15 \end{bmatrix}$

10. $-\frac{1}{5}\begin{bmatrix} -1 & -2 & 0 \\ -2 & 1 & 0 \\ 0 & 0 & -5 \end{bmatrix}$

11. $\begin{bmatrix} 1 & -2 & 1 & 0 \\ 1 & -2 & 2 & -3 \\ 0 & 1 & -1 & 1 \\ -2 & 3 & -2 & 3 \end{bmatrix}$

12. $\frac{1}{18}\begin{bmatrix} 2 & 5 & -7 & 1 \\ 5 & -1 & 5 & -2 \\ -7 & 5 & 11 & 10 \\ 1 & -2 & 10 & 5 \end{bmatrix}$

13. $\frac{1}{157}\begin{bmatrix} 87 & -2 & 9 \\ -70 & -2 & 9 \\ -33 & 17 & 2 \end{bmatrix}$

14. No

15. (i) $\begin{bmatrix} 1 & 1 & -2 & -4 \\ 0 & 1 & 0 & -1 \\ -1 & -1 & 3 & 2 \\ 2 & 1 & -6 & -10 \end{bmatrix}$

(ii) $\begin{bmatrix} 9 & -\frac{2}{3} & 0 & 0 \\ 9 & \frac{1}{3} & 0 & 0 \\ 0 & 0 & \frac{1}{2} & -\frac{1}{6} \\ 0 & 0 & 0 & \frac{1}{3} \end{bmatrix}$

4.14. Reduction of a Matrix to Triangular Form

Theorem. Every matrix can be reduced to triangular form by elementary row operations.

Proof. We shall prove this theorem by induction of m where m is the number of rows. For $m = 1$, the result is trivial as every matrix having only one row is a triangular matrix.

Let $A = [a_{ij}]_{m \times n}$. Let us assume that the theorem holds for all matrices having $(m - 1)$ rows.

Now there arise the following three cases:

Case I. If $a_{11} \neq 0$, then by applying the elementary row operation $R_1\left(\frac{1}{a_{11}}\right)$, A reduces to a matrix $B = [b_{ij}]_{m \times n}$ in which $b_{11} = 1$. Now by applying elementary row operations $R_{p1}(-b_{p1})$; $p = 2, 3, \ldots, n$, B reduces to $C = [c_{ij}]_{m \times n}$ in which $c_{p1} = 0$; $p > 1$. Thus, the matrix C is of the form

$$C = \begin{bmatrix} 1 & c_{12} & c_{13} & \ldots & c_{1n} \\ 0 & c_{22} & c_{23} & \ldots & c_{2n} \\ \vdots & \vdots & \vdots & \vdots & \vdots \\ 0 & c_{m2} & c_{m3} & \ldots & c_{mn} \end{bmatrix}$$

According to our hypothesis, the theorem holds for all matrices having $(m - 1)$ rows. Hence, the $(m - 1)$ rowed matrix

$$\begin{bmatrix} c_{21} & c_{23} & \cdots & c_{2n} \\ \vdots & & & \\ c_{m2} & c_{m3} & \cdots & c_{mn} \end{bmatrix}_{(m-1)\times n}$$

can be reduced to triangular form by applying elementary row operations. Hence, the corresponding elementary row operations when applied to c will reduce it to triangular form.

Case II. If $a_{11} = 0$ but $a_{p1} \neq 0$ for some p, then by elementary row transformation R_{1p}, the given matrix reduces to a matrix $D = [d_{ij}]_{m \times n}$ in which $d_{11} \neq 0$. D can now be reduced to triangular form as in Case I.

Case III. If $a_{p1} = 0$ for all p, then we have

$$A = \begin{bmatrix} 0 & a_{12} & \cdots & a_{1n} \\ 0 & a_{22} & \cdots & a_{2n} \\ \vdots & \vdots & & \\ 0 & a_{m2} & \cdots & a_{mn} \end{bmatrix}$$

By the assumption made in the beginning, the $(m - 1)$ rowed matrix $\begin{bmatrix} a_{22} & \cdots & a_{2n} \\ \vdots & \vdots & \vdots \\ a_{m2} & \cdots & a_{mn} \end{bmatrix}$ can be reduced to triangular form by applying row operations and the same elementary row operations when applied to A will reduce it to triangular form. Hence the theorem.

ILLUSTRATIVE EXAMPLE

Example. Reduce the matrix $A = \begin{bmatrix} 3 & 1 & 4 \\ 1 & 2 & -5 \\ 0 & 1 & 5 \end{bmatrix}$ to triangular form.

Solution: We have

$$A = \begin{bmatrix} 3 & 1 & 4 \\ 1 & 2 & -5 \\ 0 & 1 & 5 \end{bmatrix}$$

Applying R_{12}, we have

$$A \sim \begin{bmatrix} 1 & 2 & -5 \\ 3 & 1 & 4 \\ 0 & 1 & 5 \end{bmatrix}$$

Applying $R_{21}(-3)$, we have

$$A \sim \begin{bmatrix} 1 & 2 & -5 \\ 0 & -5 & 19 \\ 0 & 1 & 5 \end{bmatrix}$$

Applying R_{23}, we have

$$A \sim \begin{bmatrix} 1 & 2 & -5 \\ 0 & 1 & 5 \\ 0 & -5 & 19 \end{bmatrix}$$

Applying $R_{32}(5)$, we have

$$A \sim \begin{bmatrix} 1 & 2 & -5 \\ 0 & 1 & 5 \\ 0 & 0 & 44 \end{bmatrix}$$

EXERCISE 4.5

1. Reduce the matrix

(i) $A = \begin{bmatrix} 1 & 3 & 3 \\ 2 & 4 & 10 \\ 3 & 8 & 4 \end{bmatrix}$

(ii) $A = \begin{bmatrix} 1 & 2 & 3 \\ 2 & 5 & 7 \\ 3 & 1 & 2 \end{bmatrix}$

to triangular form.

2. Reduce the matrix

(i) $A = \begin{bmatrix} -1 & 2 & -2 \\ 1 & 2 & 1 \\ -1 & -1 & 0 \end{bmatrix}$

(ii) $A = \begin{bmatrix} 3 & 1 & 4 \\ 1 & 2 & -5 \\ 0 & 1 & 5 \end{bmatrix}$

to triangular form by using elementary row transformation.

ANSWERS

1. (i) $\begin{bmatrix} 1 & 0 & 0 \\ 0 & 1 & 0 \\ 0 & 0 & 1 \end{bmatrix}$ (ii) $\begin{bmatrix} 1 & 2 & 3 \\ 0 & 1 & 1 \\ 0 & 0 & -2 \end{bmatrix}$

2. (i) $\begin{bmatrix} -1 & 2 & -2 \\ 0 & 4 & -1 \\ 0 & 0 & 5 \end{bmatrix}$ (ii) $\begin{bmatrix} 0 & 1 & 4 \\ 0 & 5 & -19 \\ 0 & 0 & 22 \end{bmatrix}$

4.15. Partitioning of Matrices

Sometimes we sub-divide a matrix into rectangular blocks of elements by drawing lines parallel to the rows and columns of the matrix. These blocks are defined as sub-matrices of the given matrix. The dotted lines indicate the partitions of the given matrix. For example:

Let $A = [a_{ij}]_{m \times n}$. Then by drawing a horizontal line between r^{th} and $(r + 1)^{th}$ rows and a vertical line between s^{th}

and $(s + 1)^{th}$ columns, the matrix is partitioned as shown below:

$$A = \left[\begin{array}{cccc|ccc} a_{11} & a_{12} & \cdots\cdots & a_{1s} & a_{1s+1} & \cdots\cdots & a_{1n} \\ a_{21} & a_{22} & \cdots\cdots & a_{2s} & a_{2s+1} & \cdots\cdots & a_{2n} \\ \cdots & \cdots & \cdots & \cdots & \cdots & \cdots & \cdots \\ a_{r1} & a_{r2} & \cdots\cdots & a_{rs} & a_{rs+1} & \cdots\cdots & a_{rn} \\ \hline a_{r+1,1} & a_{r+1,2} & \cdots\cdots & a_{r+1,s} & a_{r+1,s+1} & \cdots\cdots & a_{r+1,n} \\ \cdots & \cdots & \cdots & \cdots & \cdots & \cdots & \cdots \\ a_{m1} & a_{m2} & & a_{ms} & a_{ms+1} & \cdots\cdots & a_{mn} \end{array}\right]$$

4.16. Identically Partitioned Matrices (Partitioning of Matrices for Addition)

Two matrices A and B of the same order are said to be identically partitioned, if the sub-matrices A_{ij} and B_{ij} are of the same order. Such matrices are said to be additively coherent (partitioned conformable for addition). If $A = \begin{bmatrix} A_{11} & A_{12} \\ A_{21} & A_{22} \end{bmatrix}$ and $B = \begin{bmatrix} B_{11} & B_{12} \\ B_{21} & B_{22} \end{bmatrix}$ are two identically partitioned matrices, then their sum is obtained by adding the corresponding sub-matrices. Thus,

$$A + B = \begin{bmatrix} A_{11} & A_{12} \\ A_{21} & A_{22} \end{bmatrix} + \begin{bmatrix} B_{11} & B_{12} \\ B_{21} & B_{22} \end{bmatrix}$$

$$= \begin{bmatrix} A_{11} + B_{11} & A_{12} + B_{12} \\ A_{21} + B_{21} & A_{22} + B_{22} \end{bmatrix}$$

Illustration

$$\text{Let } A = \left[\begin{array}{cc|c} 1 & 2 & 3 \\ 4 & 5 & 6 \\ \hline 7 & 8 & 9 \end{array}\right]$$

$$\text{and } B = \left[\begin{array}{cc|c} 10 & 11 & 12 \\ 13 & 14 & 15 \\ \hline 16 & 17 & 18 \end{array}\right]$$

$$\text{Then, } A + B = \begin{bmatrix} \begin{bmatrix} 1 & 2 \\ 4 & 5 \end{bmatrix} + \begin{bmatrix} 10 & 11 \\ 13 & 14 \end{bmatrix} & \begin{bmatrix} 3 \\ 6 \end{bmatrix} + \begin{bmatrix} 12 \\ 15 \end{bmatrix} \\ [7 \ 8] + [16 \ 17] & [9] + [18] \end{bmatrix}$$

$$= \begin{bmatrix} \begin{bmatrix} 1+10 & 2+11 \\ 4+13 & 5+14 \end{bmatrix} & \begin{bmatrix} 3+12 \\ 6+15 \end{bmatrix} \\ [7+16 \ \ 8+17] & [9+18] \end{bmatrix}$$

$$= \begin{bmatrix} \begin{bmatrix} 11 & 13 \\ 17 & 19 \end{bmatrix} & \begin{bmatrix} 15 \\ 21 \end{bmatrix} \\ [23 \ \ 25] & [27] \end{bmatrix}$$

$$= \begin{bmatrix} 11 & 13 & 15 \\ 17 & 19 & 21 \\ 23 & 25 & 27 \end{bmatrix}$$

4.17. Matrices Partitioned Conformably for Multiplication

Let A and B be $m \times n$ and $n \times p$ matrices respectively so that the product AB exists. We may partition the matrix A in any arbitrary manner and then the matrix B is partitioned in such a manner that the product of the sub-matrices of both A and B are defined. We then say that the matrices A and B are multiplicatively coherent, i.e. partitioned conformably for multiplication. This is done as follows:

Partition lines parallel to the column of A are in the same relative positions as the partition lines parallel to the rows of B. Such a partition is always possible because the number of columns in A is equal to the number of rows in B. The rows of A and columns of B may be partitioned in any arbitrary manner. For example:

$$\text{Let } A = \left[\begin{array}{cc|c} a_{11} & a_{12} & a_{13} \\ a_{21} & a_{22} & a_{23} \\ \hline a_{31} & a_{32} & a_{33} \end{array}\right]_{3\times 3} \quad \text{and } B = \left[\begin{array}{cc} b_{11} & b_{12} \\ b_{21} & b_{22} \\ \hline b_{31} & b_{32} \end{array}\right]_{3\times 2}$$

Here, in A, we have drawn a partition line after the second column. So we shall have to draw a partition line in B after the second row.

The horizontal partition in A and vertical partition in B is arbitrary. This breaks A into four sub-matrices A_{11}, A_{12}, A_{21}, A_{22} of orders 2×2, 2×1, 1×2, 1×1 respectively. Also, B is broken into two sub-matrices B_{11}, B_{21} of orders 2×2, 1×2 respectively. Here we have not drawn any vertical line to partition B though we could do so in any arbitrary manner. Thus,

$$A = \begin{bmatrix} A_{11} & A_{12} \\ A_{21} & A_{22} \end{bmatrix}_{2\times 2}, \quad B = \begin{bmatrix} B_{11} \\ B_{21} \end{bmatrix}_{2\times 1}$$

are 2×2, 2×1 matrices and as such they are conformable for multiplication. Hence,

$$AB = \begin{bmatrix} A_{11}B_{11} + A_{12}B_{21} \\ A_{12}B_{11} + A_{22}B_{21} \end{bmatrix}_{2\times 1}$$

$$= \begin{bmatrix} \begin{bmatrix} a_{11} & a_{12} \\ a_{22} & a_{22} \end{bmatrix} \begin{bmatrix} b_{11} & b_{12} \\ b_{21} & b_{22} \end{bmatrix} + \begin{bmatrix} a_{13} \\ a_{23} \end{bmatrix} \begin{bmatrix} b_{31} \\ b_{32} \end{bmatrix} \\ \begin{bmatrix} a_{31} & a_{32} \end{bmatrix} \begin{bmatrix} b_{11} & b_{12} \\ b_{21} & b_{22} \end{bmatrix} + \begin{bmatrix} a_{33} \end{bmatrix} \begin{bmatrix} b_{31} & b_{32} \end{bmatrix} \end{bmatrix}$$

$$= \begin{bmatrix} \begin{bmatrix} a_{11}b_{11} + a_{12}b_{21} & a_{11}b_{12} + a_{12}b_{22} \\ a_{21}b_{11} + a_{22}\, b_{21} & a_{21}b_{12} + a_{22}b_{2} \end{bmatrix} + \begin{bmatrix} a_{13}b_{31} & a_{13}b_{32} \\ a_{23}b_{31} & a_{23}b_{32} \end{bmatrix} \\ \begin{bmatrix} a_{31}b_{11} + a_{32}b_{21} & a_{31}b_{12} + a_{32}b_{22} \end{bmatrix} + \begin{bmatrix} a_{33}b_{31} & a_{33}b_{32} \end{bmatrix} \end{bmatrix}$$

$$= \begin{bmatrix} a_{11}b_{11} + a_{12}b_{21} + a_{13}b_{31} & a_{11}b_{12} + a_{12}b_{22} + a_{13}b_{32} \\ a_{21}b_{11} + a_{22}b_{21} + a_{23}b_{31} & a_{21}b_{12} + a_{22}b_{22} + a_{23}b_{32} \\ a_{31}b_{11} + a_{32}b_{21} + a_{33}b_{31} & a_{31}b_{12} + a_{32}b_{22} + a_{33}b_{32} \end{bmatrix}$$

Numerical Example

$$\text{Let } A = \left[\begin{array}{ccc|c} 1 & 2 & 3 & 5 \\ 4 & 5 & 9 & 0 \\ \hline 2 & 3 & 5 & 6 \\ 1 & -1 & 2 & -3 \\ \hline 4 & 5 & 0 & 7 \end{array}\right]_{5\times 4} \quad \text{and } B = \left[\begin{array}{cc|c} 1 & -1 & 2 \\ -3 & 4 & 0 \\ 3 & 6 & 7 \\ \hline 0 & 3 & 0 \end{array}\right]_{4\times 3}$$

Clearly AB is defined.

Now, A, B can be written as

$$A = \begin{bmatrix} A_{11} & A_{12} \\ A_{21} & A_{22} \\ A_{31} & A_{32} \end{bmatrix}_{3\times 2}, \quad B = \begin{bmatrix} B_{11} & B_{12} \\ B_{21} & B_{22} \end{bmatrix}_{2\times 2}$$

Hence,

$$AB = \begin{bmatrix} A_{11}B_{11} + A_{12}B_{21} & A_{11}B_{12} + A_{12}B_{22} \\ A_{21}B_{11} + A_{22}B_{21} & A_{21}B_{12} + A_{22}B_{22} \\ A_{31}B_{11} + A_{32}B_{21} & A_{31}B_{12} + A_{32}B_{22} \end{bmatrix}_{3\times 2}$$

We treat sub-matrices as if they were the elements

where,

$$A_{11}B_{11} = \begin{bmatrix} 1 & 2 & 3 \\ 4 & 5 & 9 \end{bmatrix} \begin{bmatrix} 1 & -1 \\ -3 & 4 \\ 5 & 6 \end{bmatrix} = \begin{bmatrix} 10 & 25 \\ 34 & 70 \end{bmatrix}$$

$$A_{12}B_{21} = \begin{bmatrix} 5 \\ 0 \end{bmatrix} \begin{bmatrix} 0 & 3 \end{bmatrix} = \begin{bmatrix} 0 & 15 \\ 0 & 0 \end{bmatrix}$$

$$A_{11}B_{12} = \begin{bmatrix} 1 & 2 & 3 \\ 4 & 5 & 9 \end{bmatrix} \begin{bmatrix} 2 \\ 0 \\ 7 \end{bmatrix} = \begin{bmatrix} 23 \\ 71 \end{bmatrix}$$

$$A_{12}B_{22} = \begin{bmatrix} 5 \\ 0 \end{bmatrix} [0] = \begin{bmatrix} 0 \\ 0 \end{bmatrix}$$

$$A_{12}B_{11} = \begin{bmatrix} 2 & 3 & 5 \\ 1 & -1 & 2 \end{bmatrix} \begin{bmatrix} 1 & -1 \\ -3 & -1 \\ 5 & 6 \end{bmatrix} = \begin{bmatrix} 18 & 40 \\ 14 & 7 \end{bmatrix}$$

$$A_{22}B_{21} = \begin{bmatrix} 6 \\ -3 \end{bmatrix} [0 \quad 3] = \begin{bmatrix} 0 & 18 \\ 0 & -9 \end{bmatrix}$$

$$A_{21}B_{12} = \begin{bmatrix} 2 & 3 & 5 \\ 1 & -1 & 2 \end{bmatrix} \begin{bmatrix} 2 \\ 0 \\ 7 \end{bmatrix} = \begin{bmatrix} 39 \\ 16 \end{bmatrix}$$

$$A_{22}B_{22} = \begin{bmatrix} 6 \\ -3 \end{bmatrix} [0] = \begin{bmatrix} 0 \\ 0 \end{bmatrix}$$

$$A_{31}B_{11} = [4 \quad 5 \quad 0] \begin{bmatrix} 1 & -1 \\ -3 & 4 \\ 5 & 6 \end{bmatrix} = [-11 \quad 16]$$

$$A_{32}B_{21} = [7][0 \quad 3] = [0 \quad 21]$$

$$A_{31}B_{12} = [4 \quad 5 \quad 0] \begin{bmatrix} 2 \\ 0 \\ 7 \end{bmatrix} = [8]$$

$$A_{32}B_{21} = [7][0] = [0]$$

$$A_{11}B_{11} + A_{12}B_{21} = \begin{bmatrix} 10 & 35 \\ 34 & 70 \end{bmatrix} + \begin{bmatrix} 0 & 15 \\ 0 & 0 \end{bmatrix} = \begin{bmatrix} 10 & 50 \\ 34 & 0 \end{bmatrix}$$

$$A_{12}B_{21} + A_{22}B_{21} = \begin{bmatrix} 18 & 40 \\ 14 & 7 \end{bmatrix} + \begin{bmatrix} 0 & 18 \\ 0 & -9 \end{bmatrix} = \begin{bmatrix} 18 & 58 \\ 14 & -2 \end{bmatrix}$$

$$A_{31}B_{11} + A_{32}B_{21} = [-11 \quad 16] + [0 \quad 21] = [-11 \quad 37]$$

$$A_{11}B_{12} + A_{12}B_{22} = \begin{bmatrix} 23 \\ 71 \end{bmatrix} + \begin{bmatrix} 0 \\ 0 \end{bmatrix} = \begin{bmatrix} 23 \\ 71 \end{bmatrix}$$

$$A_{21}B_{12} + A_{22}B_{22} = \begin{bmatrix} 39 \\ 16 \end{bmatrix} + \begin{bmatrix} 0 \\ 0 \end{bmatrix} = \begin{bmatrix} 39 \\ 16 \end{bmatrix}$$

$$A_{31}B_{12} + A_{32}B_{22} = [8] + [0] = [8]$$

Hence,

$$AB = \begin{bmatrix} 10 & 50 & 23 \\ 34 & 70 & 71 \\ 18 & 58 & 39 \\ 14 & -2 & 16 \\ -11 & 37 & 8 \end{bmatrix}_{3 \times 3}$$

It can be easily verified that the direct product of A and B also gives the same result.

ILLUSTRATIVE EXAMPLES

Example 1. If $A = \begin{bmatrix} A_{11} & A_{12} \\ A_{21} & A_{22} \end{bmatrix}$, where A_{12} and A_{21} are non-singular matrices, then find A^{-1}.

Solution: Let the orders of A_{12} and A_{21} be $m \times m$ and $n \times n$ respectively. Then the orders of A_{11}, A_{22} and A will be $m \times n$, $n \times m$ and $(m + n) \times (m + n)$, respectively. Now, the order of A^{-1} will be the same as that of A. Let us assume that A^{-1} is partitioned in such a way that the product AA^{-1} exists. Let

$A^{-1} = \begin{bmatrix} B_{11} & B_{12} \\ B_{21} & B_{22} \end{bmatrix}$, where B_{11}, B_{12}, B_{21}, B_{22} are of orders

$n \times m$, $n \times n$, $m \times m$, $m \times n$, respectively. Then, since $AA^{-1} = I_{m+n}$, on partitioning I_{m+n}, we have

$$\begin{bmatrix} A_{11} & A_{12} \\ A_{21} & A_{22} \end{bmatrix} \begin{bmatrix} B_{11} & B_{12} \\ B_{21} & B_{22} \end{bmatrix} = \begin{bmatrix} I_m & O \\ O & I_n \end{bmatrix}$$

This implies,

$$A_{11}B_{11} + A_{12}B_{21} = I_m \qquad \dots (4.34)$$

$$A_{11}B_{12} + A_{12}B_{22} = O \qquad \dots (4.35)$$

$$A_{21}B_{11} + A_{22}B_{21} = O \qquad \dots (4.36)$$

and $A_{21}B_{12} + A_{22}B_{22} = I_n \qquad \dots (4.37)$

From Eq. (4.36),

$$A_{21}B_{11} = O - A_{22}B_{21}$$

$$\Rightarrow \quad (A_{21}^{-1}A_{21})B_{11} = -A_{21}^{-1}(A_{22}B_{21})$$

$$\Rightarrow \quad B_{11} = -A_{21}^{-1}A_{22}B_{21} \qquad \dots (4.38)$$

Similarly, from Eq. (4.35)

$$B_{22} = -A_{12}^{-1}A_{11}B_{12} \qquad \dots (4.39)$$

From Eqs. (4.34) and (4.38), we have

$$[-A_{11}A_{21}^{-1}A_{22} + A_{12}]B_{21} = I_m$$

$$\Rightarrow \quad B_{21} = [A_{12} - A_{11}A_{21}^{-1}A_{22}]^{-1} = P \quad \text{(say)} \qquad \dots (4.40)$$

From Eqs. (4.37) and (4.39),

$$[A_{21} - A_{22}A_{12}^{-1}A_{11}]B_{12} = I_n$$

$$\Rightarrow \quad B_{12} = [A_{21} - A_{22}A_{12}^{-1}A_{11}]^{-1} = Q \quad \text{(say)} \qquad \dots (4.41)$$

From Eqs. (4.38) and (4.40), we have

$$B_{11} = -A_{21}^{-1}A_{22}P \qquad \dots (4.42)$$

From Eqs. (4.39) and (4.41), we have

$$B_{12} = -A_{12}^{-1}A_{11}Q \qquad \dots (4.43)$$

Hence,

$$A^{-1} = \begin{bmatrix} -A_{21}^{-1}A_{22}P & Q \\ P & -A_{12}^{-1}A_{11}Q \end{bmatrix}$$

Example 2. If P and Q are non-singular matrices and $A = \begin{bmatrix} P & O \\ O & Q \end{bmatrix}$, then show that $A^{-1} = \begin{bmatrix} P^{-1} & O \\ O & Q^{-1} \end{bmatrix}$.

Solution: Let $A^{-1} = \begin{bmatrix} M & N \\ R & S \end{bmatrix}$ ... (4.44)

where A^{-1} is partitioned in such a manner that A and A^{-1} are comformable for multiplication.

Since $A^{-1}A = I$

$$\therefore \quad \begin{bmatrix} M & N \\ R & S \end{bmatrix}\begin{bmatrix} P & O \\ O & Q \end{bmatrix} = \begin{bmatrix} I & O \\ O & I \end{bmatrix}$$

$$\Rightarrow \quad \begin{bmatrix} MP & NQ \\ RP & SQ \end{bmatrix} = \begin{bmatrix} I & O \\ O & I \end{bmatrix}$$

$\Rightarrow \quad MP = I$

$NQ = O$

$RP = O$

$SQ = I$

$\because \quad P$ is non-singular

$\therefore \quad MP = I$

$\Rightarrow \quad M = P^{-1}$

and $RP = O \Rightarrow R = O$

$\because \quad Q$ is non-singular

$\therefore \quad NQ = O$

$\Rightarrow \quad N = O$

and $SQ = I$

$\Rightarrow \quad S = Q^{-1}$

Hence, from Eq. (4.44),

$$A^{-1} = \begin{bmatrix} P^{-1} & O \\ O & Q^{-1} \end{bmatrix}$$

Example 3. If B and C are non-singular matrices, show that

$$\begin{bmatrix} A & B \\ C & O \end{bmatrix}^{-1} = \begin{bmatrix} O & C^{-1} \\ B^{-1} & B^{-1}AC^{-1} \end{bmatrix}$$

Solution:

$$\text{Let } L = \begin{bmatrix} A & B \\ C & O \end{bmatrix} \quad \text{... (4.45)}$$

$$\text{and } L^{-1} = \begin{bmatrix} M & N \\ R & S \end{bmatrix} \quad \text{... (4.46)}$$

where L^{-1} is partitioned in such a way that L and L^{-1} are conformable for multiplication.

Since $L^{-1}L = I$

$$\therefore \quad \begin{bmatrix} M & N \\ R & S \end{bmatrix}\begin{bmatrix} A & B \\ C & O \end{bmatrix} = \begin{bmatrix} I & O \\ O & I \end{bmatrix}$$

$$\Rightarrow \quad \begin{bmatrix} MA + NC & MB \\ RA + SC & RB \end{bmatrix} = \begin{bmatrix} I & O \\ O & I \end{bmatrix}$$

$\Rightarrow \quad MA + NC = I$ ... (4.47)

$MB = O$ ... (4.48)

$RA + SC = O$ ... (4.49)

$RB = I$ ... (4.50)

$\because \quad B$ is non-singular

$\therefore \quad$ Equation (4.48) gives $M = O$ ... (4.51)

and Eq. (4.50) gives $R = B^{-1}$ ... (4.52)

From Eqs. (4.47) and (4.51), we have

$NC = I$

$\Rightarrow N = C^{-1}$ $\quad$ | $\because$ C is non-singular

From Eqs. (4.49) and (4.52), we have

$SC = -RA$

$= -B^{-1}A$

$\Rightarrow S = -B^{-1}AC^{-1}$ $\quad$ | $\because$ C is non-singular

Hence, from Eq. (4.46),

$$L^{-1} = \begin{bmatrix} O & C^{-1} \\ B^{-1} & B^{-1}AC \end{bmatrix}$$

Example 4. If A, B, C are non-singular, then find

$$\begin{bmatrix} A & O & O \\ H & B & O \\ G & F & C \end{bmatrix}^{-1}$$

Solution: Let

$$P = \begin{bmatrix} A & O & O \\ H & B & O \\ G & F & C \end{bmatrix} \qquad \text{... (4.53)}$$

$$\text{and } P^{-1} = \begin{bmatrix} M & N & P \\ Q & R & S \\ T & U & V \end{bmatrix} \qquad \text{... (4.54)}$$

where P^{-1} is partitioned in such a way that P and P^{-1} are comformable for multiplication.

Since $P^{-1}P = I$

$$\therefore \quad \begin{bmatrix} M & N & P \\ Q & R & S \\ T & U & V \end{bmatrix}\begin{bmatrix} A & O & O \\ H & B & O \\ G & F & C \end{bmatrix} = \begin{bmatrix} I & O & O \\ O & I & O \\ O & O & I \end{bmatrix}$$

$$\Rightarrow \quad \begin{bmatrix} A & O & O \\ H & B & O \\ G & F & C \end{bmatrix}\begin{bmatrix} M & N & P \\ Q & R & S \\ T & U & V \end{bmatrix} = \begin{bmatrix} I & O & O \\ O & I & O \\ O & O & I \end{bmatrix} \qquad \left|\begin{array}{l} \because P^{-1}P = I \\ \Rightarrow PP^{-1} = I \end{array}\right.$$

$$\Rightarrow \quad \begin{bmatrix} AM & AN & AP \\ HM + BQ & HN + BR & HP + BS \\ GM + RQ + CT & GN + FR + CU & GP + FS + CV \end{bmatrix}$$

$$= \begin{bmatrix} I & O & O \\ O & I & O \\ O & O & I \end{bmatrix}$$

$\Rightarrow \quad AM = I$ ... (4.55)

$HM + BQ = O$ ... (4.56)

$GM + FQ + CT = O$ ... (4.57)

$AN = O$ ... (4.58)

$HN + BR = I$ ... (4.59)

$GN + FR + CU = O$ ... (4.60)

$AP = O$ ... (4.61)

$HP + BS = O$ ... (4.62)

$GP + FS + CV = I$ ... (4.63)

$\because$ A is non-singular

$\therefore$ From Eq. (4.55), $M = A^{-1}$ ... (4.64)

From Eq. (4.58), $N = O$ ... (4.65)

From Eq. (4.61), $P = O$ ... (4.66)

From Eqs. (4.56) and (4.64), we have

$HA^{-1} + BQ = O$

$\Rightarrow \quad Q = -B^{-1}HA^{-1}$ | $\because$ B is non-singular ... (4.67)

From Eqs. (4.59) and (4.65), we have

$O + BR = I$

$\Rightarrow \quad R = B^{-1}$ | $\because$ B is non-singular ... (4.68)

From Eqs. (4.66) and (4.62), we have

$O + BS = O$

$\Rightarrow \quad S = O$ ... (4.69)

From Eqs. (4.57), (4.64) and (4.67), we have

$GA^{-1} - FB^{-1}HA^{-1} + CT = O$

$\Rightarrow \quad CT = -GA^{-1} + FB^{-1}HA^{-1}$

$\Rightarrow \quad T = -C^{-1}GA^{-1} + C^{-1}FB^{-1}HA^{-1}$ | $\because$ C is non-singular ... (4.70)

From Eqs. (4.60), (4.65) and (4.68), we have

$$O + FB^{-1} + CU = O$$

$\Rightarrow$ $CU = -FB^{-1}$

$\Rightarrow$ $U = -C^{-1}FB^{-1}$ ... (4.71) | $\because$ C is non-singular

From Eqs. (4.63), (4.66) and (4.70), we have

$$O + U + CV = I$$

$\Rightarrow$ $V = C^{-1}$ ... (4.72) | $\because$ C is non-singular

Hence, from Eq. (4.54),

$$P^{-1} = \begin{bmatrix} A^{-1} & O & O \\ -B^{-1}AH^{-1} & B^{-1} & O \\ -C^{-1}GA^{-1} + C^{-1}FB^{-1}HA^{-1} & -C^{-1}FB^{-1} & -C^{-1} \end{bmatrix}$$

EXERCISE 4.6

1. If A and C are singular, prove that

$$\begin{bmatrix} A & O \\ B & C \end{bmatrix}^{-1} = \begin{bmatrix} A^{-1} & O \\ -C^{-1}BA^{-1} & C^{-1} \end{bmatrix}$$

2. If $\begin{bmatrix} A^{-1} & O \\ X & A^{-1} \end{bmatrix} = \begin{bmatrix} A & O \\ B & A \end{bmatrix}^{-1}$ and A is non-singular, prove that $X = -A^{-1}BA^{-1}$.

3. If $P = \begin{bmatrix} A & B \\ C & D \end{bmatrix}$, where A, B, C, D are square matrices of order n and L is any other square matrix of order n and

$$Q = \begin{bmatrix} A & B \\ LA + C & LB + D \end{bmatrix}, \text{ show that}$$

$$|Q| = |P|$$

Hence or otherwise show that if $AC = CA$, then

$$|P| = |AD - CB|.$$

5 RANK

5.1. Sub-Matrix

A matrix, which is obtained by deleting some rows or some columns or both of a matrix A, is called a sub-matrix of A. For example, if

$$A = \begin{bmatrix} 1 & 2 & 3 & 4 \\ 5 & 6 & 7 & 8 \\ 9 & 10 & 0 & 11 \end{bmatrix}, \text{ then}$$

$$\begin{bmatrix} 1 & 2 & 3 \\ 5 & 6 & 7 \\ 9 & 10 & 0 \end{bmatrix}, \begin{bmatrix} 2 & 3 \\ 6 & 7 \\ 10 & 0 \end{bmatrix}, \begin{bmatrix} 2 & 3 \\ 6 & 7 \end{bmatrix}, \begin{bmatrix} 7 & 8 \\ 0 & 11 \end{bmatrix}, \text{ etc. are all sub-}$$

matrices of the matrix A.

Particular Case. The matrix A is a sub-matrix of itself.

5.2. Minor of a Matrix

If any r rows and any r columns from an $m \times n$ matrix A are retained and the remaining $(m - r)$ rows and $(n - r)$ columns deleted, then the determinant of the remaining $r \times r$ sub-matrix of A is called a minor of A of order r. For example,

Let $A = \begin{bmatrix} a_{11} & a_{12} & a_{13} & a_{14} \\ a_{21} & a_{22} & a_{23} & a_{24} \\ a_{31} & a_{32} & a_{33} & a_{34} \\ a_{41} & a_{42} & a_{43} & a_{44} \\ a_{51} & a_{52} & a_{53} & a_{54} \end{bmatrix}_{5 \times 4}$, then

(i) The elements $a_{11}, a_{12}, a_{21}, a_{32}, a_{44}$, etc. are minors of A of order 1.

(ii) The determinants $\begin{vmatrix} a_{11} & a_{12} \\ a_{21} & a_{22} \end{vmatrix}, \begin{vmatrix} a_{11} & a_{13} \\ a_{21} & a_{23} \end{vmatrix}, \begin{vmatrix} a_{33} & a_{34} \\ a_{43} & a_{44} \end{vmatrix}$, $\begin{vmatrix} a_{13} & a_{14} \\ a_{53} & a_{54} \end{vmatrix}$, etc. are minors of A of order 2.

(iii) $\begin{vmatrix} a_{11} & a_{12} & a_{13} \\ a_{21} & a_{22} & a_{23} \\ a_{31} & a_{32} & a_{33} \end{vmatrix}, \begin{vmatrix} a_{11} & a_{12} & a_{13} \\ a_{41} & a_{42} & a_{43} \\ a_{51} & a_{52} & a_{53} \end{vmatrix}, \begin{vmatrix} a_{22} & a_{23} & a_{24} \\ a_{32} & a_{33} & a_{34} \\ a_{52} & a_{53} & a_{54} \end{vmatrix}$, etc. are minors of A of order 3.

(iv) $\begin{vmatrix} a_{11} & a_{12} & a_{13} & a_{14} \\ a_{21} & a_{22} & a_{23} & a_{24} \\ a_{31} & a_{32} & a_{33} & a_{34} \\ a_{41} & a_{42} & a_{43} & a_{44} \end{vmatrix}, \begin{vmatrix} a_{21} & a_{22} & a_{23} & a_{24} \\ a_{31} & a_{32} & a_{33} & a_{34} \\ a_{41} & a_{42} & a_{43} & a_{44} \\ a_{51} & a_{52} & a_{53} & a_{54} \end{vmatrix}$, etc. are minors of A of order 4.

Note. There cannot be any minor of order higher than 4 in the above example.

5.3. Rank of a Matrix

A natural number r is called the rank of the matrix A if

(i) There exists at least one non-zero minor of order r.

(ii) Every minor of order $(r + 1)$, if any, vanishes. The rank of the matrix A is denoted by $\rho(A)$ or rank (A).

Note 1. The rank of a zero (null) matrix of any order is taken to be zero. Hence,

$\rho(A) = 0$ when A is a zero matrix.

Note 2. $\rho(A) \geq$ when $A \neq O$.

Note 3. $\rho|A| \leq r$ when every minor of order $(r + 1)$ vanishes.

Note 4. $\rho(A) \geq r$ when there exists a non-zero minor of order r.

Note 5. $\rho(A) \leq m$ when A is a $m \times n$ matrix such that $m \leq n$.

Note 6. $\rho(A) \leq n$ when A is a $m \times n$ matrix such that $n \leq m$.

Note 7. $\rho(A') = \rho(A)$ where A' is the transpose of A.

Note 8. Rank of a matrix, whose every element is 1, is 1.

Note 9. If A is a square matrix of order n such that $|A| \neq 0$, then $\rho(A) = n$.

Note 10. If I_n is an identity matrix of order n, then $|I_n| = 1 \neq 0$ and therefore $\rho(I_n) = n$.

Note 11. If A is a diagonal matrix of order n with non-zero diagonal elements, then $|A| \neq 0$ and therefore $\rho(A) = n$.

Note 12. The property (ii) of the number r in the definition of rank of a matrix implies that every minor of order $(r + 2)$ vanishes since every minor of order $(r + 2)$ can be expressed as the sum of the multiples of minors of order $(r + 1)$. It is simple to visualise that every minor of order higher than r will vanish. Thus, the rank of a matrix is the largest order of a non-vanishing minor of a matrix.

5.4. Nullity of a Matrix

Let A be a square matrix of order n. Then $n - \rho(A)$ is called the nullity of the matrix A and is denoted by $N(A)$. We know that the rank of a non-singular square matrix of order n is n and therefore its nullity is equal to zero.

5.5. Some Theorems

Theorem 1. The rank of a matrix is equal to the rank of the transposed matrix.

OR

The rank of the transpose of a matrix is the same as the rank of the original matrix.

OR

$\rho(A) = \rho(A')$

Proof. We know that the transpose of a matrix is obtained by changing rows into columns and columns into rows. Also by a property of determinants, we know that the value of a determinant remains unchanged if its rows are changed into columns and columns into rows. So, by transposing a matrix, the values of its minors do not change. Hence, $\rho(A) = \rho(A')$.

Alternative Proof. Let $A = [a_{ij}]_{m \times n}$ be an $m \times n$ matrix. Let $\rho(A) = r$. Let A' be the transpose of A. Then, $A' = [a'_{ji}]_{n \times m}$. Therefore, there exists a non-singular square sub-matrix M_r of A. It shows that the matrix M'_r is also a non-singular sub-matrix of A', i.e.

$|M_r| = |M'_r| \neq 0$

Hence, $\rho(A') \geq r$ ... (5.1)

Now we consider a square sub-matrix A_{r+1} of A of order $(r + 1)$. Since $\rho(A) = r$, therefore, $|A_{r+1}| = 0$.

Then A'_{r+1} is a square sub-matrix of A' such that

$$|A'_{r+1}| = 0$$

It shows that $\rho(A') \leq r$ ... (5.2)

In view of Eqs. (5.1) and (5.2), we have

$$\rho(A') = r = \rho(A)$$

Theorem 2. $\rho(A^*) = \rho(A)$

Proof. We have proved in Theorem 1 that the rank of the transpose of a matrix is the same as the rank of the original matrix. So, to prove the theorem under consideration, what remains to prove for us is that the rank of the conjugate of a matrix is the same as the rank of the original matrix.

If A is real, then the result is trivial. If A is not real, then let us assume that the value of a minor of A with complex elements is $p + iq$. Then the value of the corresponding minor of the conjugate matrix of A is $p - iq$.

If $p + iq = 0$ then $p - iq = 0$

If $p + iq \neq 0$ then $p - iq \neq 0$

Hence,

$$\rho(\overline{A}) = \rho(A) \qquad \text{... (5.3)}$$

Also, $\rho(A') = \rho(A)$ ... (5.4)

In view of Eqs. (5.3) and (5.4), we have

$$\rho(A^*) = \rho(A)$$

Note. $\rho(A') = \rho(A^*) = \rho(A)$.

Theorem 3. If A is a non-zero column matrix and B is a non-zero row matrix, then show that $\rho(AB) = 1$.

Proof. Let $L = \begin{bmatrix} a_{11} \\ a_{21} \\ \vdots \\ a_{m1} \end{bmatrix}$ be a non-zero column matrix. Let $B = [b_{11} \ b_{12} \ \ldots\ldots \ b_{1n}]$ be a non-zero row matrix.

$\because$ A and B are both non-zero matrices.

$\therefore$ AB is also a non-zero matrix.

$\Rightarrow$ AB has at least one non-zero element.

$\Rightarrow$ AB will have at least one non-zero minor of order 1.

$\therefore$ $\rho(AB) \geq 1$ ... (5.5)

Now,

$$AB = \begin{bmatrix} a_{11}b_{11} & a_{11}b_{12} & \ldots\ldots & a_{11}b_{1n} \\ a_{21}b_{11} & a_{21}b_{12} & \ldots\ldots & a_{21}b_{1n} \\ \ldots\ldots & \ldots\ldots & \ldots\ldots & \ldots\ldots \\ a_{n1}b_{11} & a_{n1}b_{12} & \ldots\ldots & a_{n1}b_{1n} \end{bmatrix}$$

From the form of AB, it is clear that every minor of order 2 is zero.

$\therefore\ \rho(AB) < 2$ ... (5.6)

In view of Eqs. (5.5) and (5.6)

$$\rho(AB) = 1$$

Theorem 4. Show that the rank of any matrix $\geq$ rank of its every sub-matrix.

Proof. Let A be any $m \times n$ matrix. Let $\rho(A) = r$. Let A_0 be a sub-matrix of A. Let $\rho(A_0) = s$. Since every s-rowed minor of A_0 is a s-rowed minor of A, therefore, A_0 has at least one non-zero minor of order s. Consequently, A has at least one non-zero minor of order s such that $r = \rho(A) \geq s = \rho(A_0)$.

This implies that

$$r \geq s$$

or $\rho(A) \geq \rho(A_0)$

Hence, the theorem.

Theorem 5. If A is an n-square matrix of rank $(n - 1)$, show that adj $A \neq O$.

Proof. $\because$ A is an n-rowed square matrix of rank $(n - 1)$

$\therefore$ A has at least one non-zero minor of order $(n - 1)$.

But, every $(n - 1)$ rowed minor of matrix A = Co-factor of some element in $|A|$ in magnitude.

$\therefore$ At least one element in $|A|$ has its co-factor not equal to zero.

$\therefore$ At least one element of the matrix adj $A \neq 0$.

Hence, adj $A \neq O$.

Theorem 6. Prove that the rank of each of

$$\begin{bmatrix} A_1 & O \\ A_2 & O \end{bmatrix}, \begin{bmatrix} A_1 & B_1 \\ O & O \end{bmatrix}$$

is at most r; A_1 being an $r \times r$ matrix.

Proof. (i) Let $M = \begin{bmatrix} A_1 & O \\ A_2 & O \end{bmatrix}$

$\because$ A_1 is an $r \times r$ matrix

$\therefore$ The matrix A_2 will also have r non-zero columns.

$\Rightarrow$ Every $(r + 1)$-rowed square sub-matrix of M will have one column of zeroes.

$\Rightarrow$ Every $(r + 1)$-rowed minor of M vanishes.

Hence, $\rho(M) \le r$.

(ii) Let $N = \begin{bmatrix} A_1 & B_1 \\ O & O \end{bmatrix}$

$\because$ A_1 is $r \times r$ matrix.

$\therefore$ The matrix B_1 will also have r non-zero rows.

$\Rightarrow$ Every $(r + 1)$-rowed square sub-matrix of N will have one row of zeroes.

$\Rightarrow$ Every $(r + 1)$-rowed minor of N vanishes.

Hence, $\rho(N) \le r$

Theorem 7. Show that the rank of a skew-symmetric matrix cannot be one.

Solution: Let $A = \begin{bmatrix} 0 & a & b \\ -a & 0 & c \\ -b & -c & 0 \end{bmatrix}$ be a skew-symmetric matrix of order 3.

If $a = b = c = 0$, then $A = O$, which is not the case. Therefore, at least one of the members a, b, c is non-zero. Let $a \neq 0$ and $b = 0 = c$. Then, a second order minor $\begin{vmatrix} 0 & a \\ -a & 0 \end{vmatrix} = a^2 \neq 0$.

$\therefore$ $\rho(A) = 2$

$\Rightarrow$ $\rho(A) > 1$

This is true for every skew-symmetric matrix of every order.

Hence, the theorem.

ILLUSTRATIVE EXAMPLES

Example 1. Find the rank of the matrix A, where

$$A = \begin{bmatrix} 1 & 2 & 3 \\ 2 & 3 & 4 \\ 3 & 5 & 7 \end{bmatrix}$$

Solution: We have

$$A = \begin{bmatrix} 1 & 2 & 3 \\ 2 & 3 & 4 \\ 3 & 5 & 7 \end{bmatrix}$$

$$\therefore \quad |A| = \begin{vmatrix} 1 & 2 & 3 \\ 2 & 3 & 4 \\ 3 & 5 & 7 \end{vmatrix}$$

$$= \begin{vmatrix} 1 & 2 & 3 \\ 2 & 3 & 4 \\ 1 & 2 & 3 \end{vmatrix} \quad \Big| \text{ Operating } R_3 - R_1$$

$$= 0 \quad \Big| \because R_1 \text{ and } R_3 \text{ are identical}$$

$\therefore \quad \rho(A) \neq 3$

A minor of order 2 is $\begin{vmatrix} 1 & 2 \\ 2 & 3 \end{vmatrix}$ and $\begin{vmatrix} 1 & 2 \\ 2 & 3 \end{vmatrix} = 3 - 4 = -1 \neq 0$

$\therefore \quad \rho(A) = 2$

Example 2. Find the rank of the matrix A, where

$$A = \begin{bmatrix} 1 & 2 & 3 \\ 4 & 5 & 6 \\ 2 & 1 & 2 \end{bmatrix}$$

Solution:

$$|A| = \begin{vmatrix} 1 & 2 & 3 \\ 4 & 5 & 6 \\ 2 & 1 & 2 \end{vmatrix}$$

$= 1(10 - 6) + 2\ (12 - 8) + 3\ (4 - 10)$

$= 4 + 8 - 18$

$= 6 \neq 0$

$\therefore \quad \rho(A) = 3$

Example 3. Find the rank of the matrix A, where

$$A = \begin{bmatrix} 8 & 0 & 0 & 1 \\ 1 & 0 & 8 & 1 \\ 0 & 0 & 1 & 8 \\ 0 & 8 & 1 & 8 \end{bmatrix}$$

Solution:

$$|A| = \begin{vmatrix} 8 & 0 & 0 & 1 \\ 1 & 0 & 8 & 1 \\ 0 & 0 & 1 & 8 \\ 0 & 8 & 1 & 8 \end{vmatrix}$$

$$= 8 \begin{vmatrix} 0 & 8 & 1 \\ 0 & 1 & 8 \\ 8 & 1 & 8 \end{vmatrix} - 1 \begin{vmatrix} 1 & 0 & 8 \\ 0 & 0 & 1 \\ 0 & 8 & 1 \end{vmatrix}$$

$= 8[8(64 - 1)] - [1(0 - 8)]$

$= 4032 + 8$

$= 4040 \neq 0$

$\therefore \quad \rho(A) = 4$

Example 4. Find the rank of the matrix A, where

$$A = \begin{bmatrix} 6 & 1 & 3 & 8 \\ 4 & 2 & 6 & -1 \\ 10 & 3 & 9 & 7 \\ 16 & 4 & 12 & 15 \end{bmatrix}$$

Solution:

$$|A| = \begin{vmatrix} 6 & 1 & 3 & 8 \\ 4 & 2 & 6 & -1 \\ 10 & 3 & 9 & 7 \\ 16 & 4 & 12 & 15 \end{vmatrix}$$

$$= 3\begin{vmatrix} 6 & 1 & 1 & 8 \\ 4 & 2 & 2 & -1 \\ 10 & 3 & 3 & 7 \\ 16 & 4 & 4 & 15 \end{vmatrix} \qquad | \text{Taking 3 common from } c_3$$

$$= 3(0) \qquad | \because c_2 \text{ and } c_3 \text{ are identical}$$

$$= 0$$

$\therefore \quad \rho(A) \neq 4$

It is easy to see that all the minors of order 3 are zero-valued.

$\therefore \quad \rho(A) \neq 3$

There is a minor $\begin{vmatrix} 6 & 1 \\ 4 & 2 \end{vmatrix}$ of order 2 such that $\begin{vmatrix} 6 & 1 \\ 4 & 2 \end{vmatrix} = 12 - 4 = 8 \neq 0.$

Hence, $\rho(A) = 2$

Example 5. Find the rank of the matrix

$$A = \begin{bmatrix} 1 & -1 & 3 & 6 \\ 1 & 3 & -3 & -4 \\ 1 & 3 & 3 & 11 \end{bmatrix}$$

Solution: $\because$ The matrix A is or order 3×4

$\therefore \quad \rho(A) \leq 3$

A minor of order 3 is

$$\begin{vmatrix} 1 & -1 & 3 \\ 1 & 3 & -3 \\ 1 & 3 & 3 \end{vmatrix} = \begin{vmatrix} 1 & -1 & 3 \\ 0 & 4 & -6 \\ 0 & 4 & 0 \end{vmatrix} \qquad | \text{Operating } R_2 - R_1, R_3 - R_1$$

$$= 1\begin{vmatrix} 4 & -6 \\ 4 & 0 \end{vmatrix}$$

$$= 24 \neq 0$$

Hence, $\rho(A) = 3$

Example 6. Prove that the points (x_1, y_1), (x_2, y_2) and (x_3, y_3) are collinear if and only if the rank of the matrix $\begin{bmatrix} x_1 & y_1 & 1 \\ x_2 & y_2 & 1 \\ x_3 & y_3 & 1 \end{bmatrix}$ is less than 3.

Solution: *The condition is necessary.*

Let the points (x_1, y_1), (x_2, y_2) and (x_3, y_3) be collinear and lie on the line $ax + by + c = 0$.

Then,

$$ax_1 + by_1 + c = 0 \qquad \text{... (5.7)}$$

$$ax_2 + by_2 + c = 0 \qquad \text{... (5.8)}$$

$$ax_3 + by_3 + c = 0 \qquad \text{... (5.9)}$$

Eliminating a, b, c from Eqs. (5.7), (5.8) and (5.9), determinantically, we get,

$$\begin{vmatrix} x_1 & y_1 & 1 \\ x_2 & y_2 & 1 \\ x_3 & y_3 & 1 \end{vmatrix} = 0$$

Hence, the rank of the matrix

$\begin{bmatrix} x_1 & y_1 & 1 \\ x_2 & y_2 & 1 \\ x_3 & y_3 & 1 \end{bmatrix}$ is less than 3.

The condition is sufficient.

Since the rank of the matrix $\begin{bmatrix} x_1 & y_1 & 1 \\ x_2 & y_2 & 1 \\ x_3 & y_3 & 1 \end{bmatrix}$ is less than 3, therefore,

$$\begin{vmatrix} x_1 & y_1 & 1 \\ x_2 & y_2 & 1 \\ x_3 & y_3 & 1 \end{vmatrix} = 0$$

$$\Rightarrow \quad \frac{1}{2}\begin{vmatrix} x_1 & y_1 & 1 \\ x_2 & y_2 & 1 \\ x_3 & y_3 & 1 \end{vmatrix} = 0$$

$\Rightarrow$ Area of the triangle whose vertices are (x_1, y_1), (x_2, y_2) and (x_3, y_3) is 0.

Hence, the points (x_1, y_1), (x_2, y_2) and (x_3, y_3) are collinear.

EXERCISE 5.1

1. Find the rank of the following matrices:

(i) $\begin{bmatrix} 0 & 2 & 3 \\ 0 & 4 & 6 \\ 0 & 6 & 9 \end{bmatrix}$

(ii) $\begin{bmatrix} 1 & 0 & 0 \\ 0 & 1 & 0 \\ 0 & 0 & 1 \end{bmatrix}$

(iii) $\begin{bmatrix} 1 & 2 & 3 \\ 2 & 3 & 4 \\ 0 & 2 & 2 \end{bmatrix}$

(iv) $\begin{bmatrix} 2 & 1 & -1 \\ 0 & 3 & -2 \\ 2 & 4 & -3 \end{bmatrix}$

(v) $\begin{bmatrix} 0 & i & -i \\ -i & 0 & -i \\ i & -i & 0 \end{bmatrix}$ where $i^2 = -1$

(vi) $\begin{bmatrix} 1 & 2 & 4 \\ 2 & 5 & 6 \\ 4 & 8 & 12 \end{bmatrix}$

2. Determine the rank of the following matrices:

(i) $\begin{bmatrix} 1 & 2 & 3 & 1 \\ 2 & 4 & 6 & 2 \\ 1 & 2 & 3 & 2 \end{bmatrix}$

(ii) $\begin{bmatrix} 1 & 3 & 4 & 3 \\ 3 & 9 & 12 & 3 \\ 1 & 3 & 4 & 1 \end{bmatrix}$

(iii) $\begin{bmatrix} 1 & 2 & 3 & 4 \\ 2 & 4 & 6 & 8 \\ -1 & -2 & -3 & -4 \end{bmatrix}$

(iv) $\begin{bmatrix} 6 & 1 & 3 & 8 \\ 4 & 2 & 6 & -1 \\ 10 & 3 & 9 & 7 \\ 16 & 4 & 12 & 15 \end{bmatrix}$

(v) $\begin{bmatrix} 1 & 2 & 3 & 0 \\ 2 & 4 & 3 & 2 \\ 3 & 2 & 1 & 3 \\ 6 & 1 & 7 & 5 \end{bmatrix}$

(vi) $\begin{bmatrix} 2 & 3 & 4 & 5 \\ 1 & 2 & 3 & 4 \\ 1 & 1 & 1 & 1 \end{bmatrix}$

(vii) $\begin{bmatrix} 1 & a & b & 0 \\ 0 & c & a & 0 \\ 1 & a & b & 0 \\ 0 & c & a & 0 \end{bmatrix}$

3. If $A = \begin{bmatrix} 0 & 1 & 0 & 0 \\ 0 & 0 & 1 & 0 \\ 0 & 0 & 0 & 1 \\ 0 & 0 & 0 & 1 \end{bmatrix}$, find the ranks of A and A^2.

4. Prove that for an $m \times n$ matrix, whose every element is unity, the rank is 1.

[**Hint.** Every minor of order 2 is zero valued.]

ANSWERS

1. (i) 1
   (ii) 3
   (iii) 3
   (iv) 2
   (v) 2
   (vi) 3
2. (i) 2
   (ii) 2
   (iii) 1
   (iv) 2
   (v) 4
   (vi) 2
   (vii) 2
3. 3, 2

5.6. Invariance of Rank Through Elementary Transformations

To find out the rank of a matrix following the definition of rank, we require to compute the minors of the matrix. This computation can be simplified a lot by employing suitable elementary transformations on the basis of the following theorem.

5.7. Theorem

Elementary transformations do not alter the rank of a matrix.

OR

Equivalent matrices have the same rank.

OR

Rank of a matrix remains invariant under elementary transformations.

Proof. Firstly, we shall consider only elementary row transformations. The result will be established in three stages. Let A be any $m \times n$ matrix of rank r so that every minor of order $(r + 1)$ vanishes.

Case I. *Interchange of a pair of rows does not alter the rank of a matrix.*

Let B be the matrix which is obtained by the interchange of a pair of rows of A. Let $\rho(A) = r$ and $\rho(B) = r'$.

Consider any $(r + 1)$-rowed minor $|B_0|$ of B. The $(r + 1)$ rows of the sub-matrix B_0 of B are also the rows of some uniquely determined sub-matrix A_0 of A. The only difference between B_0 and A_0 may be that their identical rows occur in different relative positions. Since the interchange of two rows of a determinant changes possibly only the sign of the determinant, we have

$$|B_0| = |A_0| \text{ or } |B_0| = -|A_0| \quad \text{... (5.10)}$$

$\because \quad \rho(A) = r$

$\therefore \quad$ Every $(r + 1)$-rowed minor $|A_0|$ of A is zero.

It follows from Eq. (5.10) that every $(r + 1)$-rowed minor $|B_0|$ of B is also zero. Thus,

$$\rho(B) \le r = \rho(A)$$

$$\Rightarrow \rho(B) \le \rho(A)$$

$\Rightarrow\ r' \leq r$ ... (5.11)

i.e. the rank of a matrix cannot increase by an interchange of a pair of rows.

Again, since A can be obtained from B by an interchange of a pair of rows, therefore, we have

$r \leq r'$ ... (5.12)

In view of Eqs. (5.11) and (5.12), we have

$r = r'$

Case II. *Multiplication of the elements of a row by a non-zero number does not alter the rank.*

Let B be the matrix which is obtained by multiplying the elements of a row of A by a scalar $K \neq 0$.

Let $\rho(A) = r$ and $\rho(B) = r'$.

Consider any $(r + 1)$-rowed minor $|B_0|$ of B. Then, there exists a uniquely determined minor $|A_0|$ of A such that

$|B_0| = |A_0|$ or $|B_0| = K\ |A_0|$ ... (5.13)

according as B_0 does or does not contain the affected row.

$\because\ \rho(A) = r$

$\therefore$ Every minor $|A_0|$ of A of order $(r + 1)$ is zero.

$\Rightarrow\ |A_0| = 0$

We deduce from Eq. (5.13) that every minor $|B_0|$ of B of order $(r + 1)$ is also zero.

Thus,

$\rho(B) \leq r = \rho(A)$

$\Rightarrow\ \rho(B) \leq \rho(A)$

$\Rightarrow\ r' \leq r$ ... (5.14)

Again, since A can be obtained from B by a transformation of the same type, we have

$r \leq r'$ ... (5.15)

In view of Eqs. (5.14) and (5.15), we have

$r = r'$

Case III. *Addition to the elements of a row the product by a number of the corresponding elements of a row does not alter the rank.*

Let B be the matrix which is obtained by adding to the elements of the ith row, the products by K of the corresponding elements of its jth row.

Let $\rho(A) = r$. Let $\rho(B) = r'$.

Consider any $(r + 1)$-rowed minor $|B_0|$ of B and the corresponding minor $|A_0|$ of A. Then,

$|B_0| = |A_0|$ if no row of the sub-matrix A_0 is a part of the ith row of A, or if two rows of A_0 are parts of the ith and j^{th} rows of A.

And, $|B_0| = |A_0| + K\,|C_0|$ if a row of A_0 is a part of the ith row of A, but no row is a part of the jth row, where C_0 is an $(r + 1)$-rowed sub-matrix of A all of whose rows but one coincide with those of A_0.

$\because\ \rho(A) = r$

$\therefore$ Every $(r + 1)$-rowed minor of A is 0.

$\therefore$ Every $(r + 1)$-rowed minor of B is also 0, so that

$\rho(B) \le \rho(A)$

$\Rightarrow r' \le r$ ... (5.16)

Again, since A can be obtained from B by a transformation of the same type,

$\therefore\ r \le r'$ ... (5.17)

In view of Eqs. (5.16) and (5.17),

$r \le r'$

By making parallel arguments, we can establish that the elementary column operations do not alter the rank.

Hence, the theorem.

Note. Through judicious choice of elementary transformations, it may be possible to transform the given matrix to another with as many number of zero elements as possible, so that we can detect a non-zero minor with higher order minors all zero.

5.8. Normal Form

By a finite number of elementary transformations, every non-zero matrix A of order $m \times n$ and rank r (> 0) can be reduced to one of the following forms:

$$\left[\begin{array}{c|c} I_r & O \\ \hline O & O \end{array}\right], \left[\begin{array}{c} I_r \\ \hline O \end{array}\right], [I_r \mid O], [I_r]$$

where I_r denotes identity matrix of order r. Each one of these four forms is called *Normal Form* or *Canonical Form* or *Orthogonal Form*.

5.9. Procedure for Reduction to Normal Form

Let $A = [a_{ij}]$ be any matrix of order $m \times n$. Then, we can get the normal form of the matrix A by subjecting it to a finite number of elementary transformations in the following manner:

(1) We first interchange a pair of rows (or columns), if necessary, to obtain a non-zero element (preferably 1) in the first row and first column of the matrix A.

(2) Divide the first row by this non-zero element, if it is not 1.

(3) We subtract appropriate multiples of the elements of the first row from other rows so as to obtain zeroes in the remainder of the first column.

(4) We subtract appropriate multiples of the elements of the first column from other columns so as to obtain zeroes in the remainder of the first row.

(5) We repeat the above four steps starting with the element in the second row and the second column.

(6) Continue this process down the leading diagonal until the end of the diagonal is reached or until all the remaining elements in the matrix are zero.

Note 1. We know that the elementary transformations do not alter the rank or order of the matrix, therefore, the rank of the normal form will be the same as the rank of the given matrix A.

Note 2. In the process of evaluation of the rank of a matrix by means of elementary transformations (row or column), if certain rows or columns reduce to zero rows or zero columns, respectively, then we can delete these rows or columns without any effect on the rank of the matrix. This method is called *Sweep Out Method* or *Pivotal Method.*

5.10. Theorem

If A is any $m \times n$ matrix of rank r, then there exist non-singular matrices R and C such that

$$RAC = \left[\begin{array}{c|c} I_r & O \\ \hline O & O \end{array}\right]$$

Proof. If A is a matrix of rank r, then it can be transformed into the form $\left[\begin{array}{c|c} I_r & O \\ \hline O & O \end{array}\right]$ by means of elementary transformations. Since elementary row (or column) operations are equivalent to pre (or post) multiplication of the corresponding elementary matrices, therefore, we have the following result:

$$R_p \,.....\, R_2\, R_1\, A\, C_1\, C_2 \,.....\, C_q = \left[\begin{array}{c|c} I_r & O \\ \hline O & O \end{array}\right] \qquad ...\ (5.18)$$

where $R_1\ R_2\ .....\ R_p$; $C_1\ C_2\ .....\ C_q$ are elementary matrices corresponding to the row (or column) elementary transformations.

Since the elementary matrices are non-singular, therefore,

$$R_1\ R_2\ .....\ R_p = R \qquad ...\ (5.19)$$

$$\text{and}\quad C_1\ C_2\ .....\ C_q = C \qquad ...\ (5.20)$$

will be non-singular matrices. Hence, from Eqs. (5.18), (5.19) and (5.20),

$$RAC = \left[\begin{array}{c|c} I_r & O \\ \hline O & O \end{array}\right] \qquad ...\ (5.21)$$

The matrix $\left[\begin{array}{c|c} I_r & O \\ \hline O & O \end{array}\right]$ is of order $m \times n$. This matrix is called normal matrix and is denoted by N_r. Thus,

$$N_r = RAC \qquad ...\ (5.22)$$

Since R and C are non-singular, therefore, their inverses R^{-1} and C^{-1} exist. Hence, from Eq. (5.22), we have

$$A = R^{-1}N_rC^{-1} \quad \text{... (5.23)}$$

$$\Rightarrow A = EN_rF \quad \text{... (5.24)}$$

where $R^{-1} = E$ and $C^{-1} = F$

Equation (5.24) gives

$$N_r = E^{-1} AF^{-1} \quad \text{... (5.25)}$$

where E, F are the products of the elementary matrices of order m, n respectively.

Corollary 1. If A is a non-singular matrix, then we can put

$$A = E \quad \text{... (5.26)}$$

where E denotes a product of elementary matrices.

Proof. $\because$ E is a non-singular matrix of order n and its rank $r = n$.

$\therefore$ $N_r = I_n$

$\therefore$ From Eq. (5.24) above

$$A = EI_nF$$

which is of the form Eq. (5.26) as E and F are the products of elementary matrices.

Corollary 2. If two matrices A and B have the same order and the same rank, then there exists non-singular square matrices P and Q such that

$$A = PBQ, \; B = P^{-1}AQ^{-1} \quad \text{... (5.27)}$$

Proof. Let A and B both be of order $m \times n$ and rank r. Then, by Eq. (5.24), we can put

$$A = EN_rF \text{ and } B = E_1N_rF_1 \quad \text{... (5.28)}$$

where E, E_1 are products of elementary matrices of order m and F, F_1 are products of elementary matrices of order n. From, $B = E_1N_rF_1$, we have

$$N_r = E_1^{-1}B\, F_1^{-1}$$

Substituting this in $A = EN_rF$, we have,

$$A = EE_1^{-1}\, B\, F_1^{-1}\, F$$

which is of the form

$$A = PBQ$$

$$\Rightarrow B = P^{-1}AQ^{-1}$$

5.11. Rank of a Matrix Product

Theorem 1. The rank of the product of two matrices cannot exceed the rank of either matrix, i.e.

$$\rho(AB) \le \rho(A) \text{ and } \rho(AB) \le \rho(B)$$

Proof. Let r_1, r_2, r be the ranks of the matrices A, B, AB respectively. We have to show that

$$r \le r_1 \text{ and } r \le r_2$$

Lemma. If A be an $m \times n$ matrix of rank r, then there exists a non-zero matrix P such that

$$PA = \begin{bmatrix} G \\ O \end{bmatrix}$$

where G is an $r \times n$ matrix of rank r and O is a zero matrix of order $(m - r) \times n$.

Now, there exists a non-singular matrix P and a matrix G of rank r_1 and r_2 such that

$$PA = \begin{bmatrix} G \\ O \end{bmatrix}$$

The matrix P, being a product of elementary matrices, is non-singular.

We have

$$r = \rho(AB) = \rho(PAB)$$

Also,

$$PAB = \begin{bmatrix} G \\ O \end{bmatrix} B$$

has at the most r_1 non-zero rows which arise on multiplying the r_1 non-zero rows of G with columns of B so that

$$\rho(PAB) \le r_1$$

$$\Rightarrow r \le r_1$$

$$\Rightarrow \rho(AB) \le \rho(A)$$

Again,

$$\rho(AB) = \rho(AB)'$$

$$= \rho(B'A') \leq \rho(B') = \rho(B) \quad | \text{ as proved above}$$

$\therefore \quad \rho(AB) \leq \rho(B)$

$\Rightarrow r \leq r_2$

Theorem 2. The rank of a matrix does not alter by pre-multiplication or post-multiplication with any non-singular matrix.

Proof. Let A be a matrix of order $m \times n$. Let P be a singular matrix of order $n \times n$. Then, the product AP exists and is a $m \times n$ matrix. We have to prove that

Rank (AP) = Rank (A)

Let $B = AP$

Then,

$$BP^{-1} = APP^{-1} = AI = A$$

P^{-1} exists since P is non-singular.

Now, $B = AP$

$\Rightarrow$ Rank (B) = Rank $(AP) \leq$ Rank (A)

| By Theorem 1 above

$\Rightarrow$ Rank $(B) \leq$ Rank (A) ... (5.29)

Also,

$$A = BP^{-1}$$

$\Rightarrow$ Rank (A) = Rank $(BP^{-1}) \leq$ Rank B

| By Theorem 1 above

$\Rightarrow$ Rank $(A) \leq$ Rank (B) ... (5.30)

In view of Eqs. (5.29) and (5.30), we obtain

Rank (A) = Rank (B)

$\Rightarrow$ Rank (A) = Rank (AP)

Theorem 3. Prove that Rank (AA') = Rank (A)

Proof. Let $B = AA'$. Then,

Rank (B) = Rank (AA')

$\Rightarrow$ Rank $(B) \leq$ Rank (A) ... (5.31)

Again,

$$B = AA'$$
$$\Rightarrow A^{-1}B = A'$$
$$\therefore \text{Rank }(A) = \text{Rank }(A')$$
$$= \text{Rank }(A^{-1}B)$$
$$\leq \text{Rank }(B) \qquad \text{... (5.32)}$$

In view of Eqs. (5.31) and (5.32),

$$\text{Rank }(A) = \text{Rank }(B) = \text{Rank }(AA')$$

Theorem 4. Prove that Rank (AA^*) = Rank (A).

Proof. Let $C = AA^*$. Then,

$$\text{Rank }(C) = \text{Rank }(AA^*) \leq \text{Rank }(A)$$
$$\Rightarrow \text{Rank }(C) \leq \text{Rank }(A) \qquad \text{... (5.33)}$$

Again,

$$C = AA^*$$
$$\Rightarrow A^{-1}C = A^*$$
$$\therefore \text{Rank }(A^*) = \text{Rank }(A^{-1}C)$$
$$\leq \text{Rank }(C)$$
$$\Rightarrow \text{Rank }(A) \leq \text{Rank }(C) \qquad \text{... (5.34)}$$
$$| \because \text{Rank }(A^*) = \text{Rank }(A)$$

In view of Eqs. (5.33) and (5.34),

$$\text{Rank }(A) = \text{Rank }(C)$$
$$\Rightarrow \text{Rank }(A) = \text{Rank }(AA^*)$$

5.12. Theorem

Let A be a matrix of order $m \times p$ and of rank r. Let B be a matrix of order $p \times n$ such that $AB = O$. Then, prove that the rank of B cannot exceed $p - r$.

Proof. Since A is a matrix of rank r, therefore, there exist non-singular matrices P and Q such that PAQ is in the normal form. So,

$$PAQ = N = \left[\begin{array}{c|c} I_r & O \\ \hline O & O \end{array}\right]$$

$\Rightarrow A = P^{-1}NQ^{-1}$

$\Rightarrow AB = P^{-1}NQ^{-1}B$

$\Rightarrow O = P^{-1}NQ^{-1}B$ | $\because AB = O$ (given)

$\Rightarrow PO = PP^{-1}NQ^{-1}B$

$\Rightarrow O = NQ^{-1}B$

A is of order $m \times p$, Q is of order $p \times p$ and $Q^{-1}B$ is of order $p \times n$.

$NQ^{-1}B = O$ implies that the first r rows of $Q^{-1}B$ must be zeroes while the remaining $(p - r)$ rows may be arbitrary. Thus, the rank of $Q^{-1}B$ and hence the rank of B cannot exceed $p - r$.

Hence, the theorem.

5.13. Theorem

If A is of order n and rank $(n - 1)$, then prove that adj A is of rank 1.

Proof. $\because$ A is of rank $(n - 1)$.

$\therefore$ These exists at least one non-zero cofactor and $|A| = 0$.

Now,

A (adj A) $= |A|\, I = O$ | $\because |A| = O$

$\therefore$ Rank of adj $A = n - (n - 1)$ | By Th. 5.12.

$= 1$ | $\because \rho(A) = n - 1$

5.14. Theorem

If from a square matrix A of order n and rank r_A, a sub-matrix B consisting of s rows (columns) of A is selected, then prove that

$r_B \geq r_A + s - n$, where r_B is the rank of B.

Proof. $\because$ A is of rank r_A

$\therefore$ The normal form of A has $(n - r_A)$ rows which have all their elements zeroes.

Similarly, the normal form of B has $s - r_B$ rows whose elements are zeroes.

It is obvious that

$$n - r_A \geq s - r_B$$

$$\Rightarrow r_B \geq r_A + s - n$$

5.15. Theorem

Show that the equivalence of matrices is an equivalence relation.

Proof. Let A and B be any two matices of order $m \times n$ each. If there exist non-singular matrices P and Q such that $A = PBQ$, then we say that A is equivalent to B and denote it by $A \sim B$.

We see that

1. Reflexivity. For any matrix A of order $m \times n$, there exist two identity matrices I_m and I_n such that

$$A = I_m A I_n$$

$$\Rightarrow A = PAQ$$

where $P = I_m$, $Q = I_n$

So every matrix is equivalent to itself. Hence, the relation of equivalence is reflexive.

2. Symmetry. For any two $m \times n$ matrices A and B, $A \sim B$ $\Rightarrow A = PBQ$ for some non-singular matricces P and Q.

$$\Rightarrow P^{-1}AQ^{-1} = B$$

$$\Rightarrow B \sim A$$

Hence, the relation of equivalence is commutative.

3. Transitivity. For any three matrices of the same order $m \times n$,

$$A \sim B,\ B \sim C \Rightarrow A = PBQ \text{ and } B = P_1CQ_1$$

where P, Q, P_1 and Q_1 are non-singular.

$$\Rightarrow A = P(P_1CQ_1)Q$$

$$\Rightarrow A = (PP_1)\ C(Q_1Q)$$

$$\Rightarrow A \sim C \mid \because PP_1 \text{ and } Q_1Q \text{ are non-singular}$$

Hence, the relation of equivalence is transitive. Since the relation of equivalence is reflexive, symmetric and transitive, therefore, it is an equivalence relation.

Hence, the theorem.

ILLUSTRATIVE EXAMPLES

Example 1. Find the rank of the following matrix using elementary transformations:

$$A = \begin{bmatrix} 1 & 2 & 3 \\ 1 & 4 & 2 \\ 2 & 6 & 5 \end{bmatrix}$$

Solution: We have

$$A = \begin{bmatrix} 1 & 2 & 3 \\ 1 & 4 & 2 \\ 2 & 6 & 5 \end{bmatrix}$$

Operating $R_{21}(-1)$, $R_{31}(-2)$

$$A \sim \begin{bmatrix} 1 & 2 & 3 \\ 0 & 2 & -1 \\ 0 & 2 & -1 \end{bmatrix}$$

Operating $R_{32}(-1)$

$$A \sim \begin{bmatrix} 1 & 2 & 3 \\ 0 & 2 & -1 \\ 0 & 0 & 0 \end{bmatrix}$$

The single minor of order 3 is zero.

A minor of order 2 is

$$\begin{vmatrix} 1 & 2 \\ 0 & 2 \end{vmatrix} = 2 \neq 0$$

$\therefore \quad \rho(A) = 2$

Example 2. Find the rank of the matrix $A = \begin{bmatrix} 2 & 3 & 4 & -1 \\ 5 & 2 & 0 & -1 \\ -4 & 5 & 12 & -1 \end{bmatrix}$ employing elementary transformations.

Solution: We have

$$A = \begin{bmatrix} 2 & 3 & 4 & -1 \\ 5 & 2 & 0 & -1 \\ -4 & 5 & 12 & -1 \end{bmatrix}$$

Operating $R_{21}(-1)$, $R_{31}(-1)$

$$A \sim \begin{bmatrix} 2 & 3 & 4 & -1 \\ 3 & -1 & -4 & 0 \\ -6 & 2 & 8 & 0 \end{bmatrix}$$

Operating $R_{32}(2)$

$$A \sim \begin{bmatrix} 2 & 3 & 4 & -1 \\ 3 & -1 & -4 & 0 \\ 0 & 0 & 0 & 0 \end{bmatrix}$$

All the third order minors are zero but the second order minor $\begin{vmatrix} 4 & -1 \\ -4 & 0 \end{vmatrix} = -4 \neq 0$

$\therefore \quad \rho(A) = 2$

Example 3. Reduce the matrix $A = \begin{bmatrix} 8 & 1 & 3 & 6 \\ 0 & 3 & 2 & 2 \\ -8 & -1 & -3 & 4 \end{bmatrix}$ to normal form and find its rank.

Solution: We have

$$A = \begin{bmatrix} 8 & 1 & 3 & 6 \\ 0 & 3 & 2 & 2 \\ -8 & -1 & -3 & 4 \end{bmatrix}$$

Operating $R_{31}(1)$

$$A \sim \begin{bmatrix} 8 & 1 & 3 & 6 \\ 0 & 3 & 2 & 2 \\ 0 & 0 & 0 & 10 \end{bmatrix}$$

Operating $C_1\left(\frac{1}{8}\right), R_3\left(\frac{1}{10}\right)$

$$A \sim \begin{bmatrix} 1 & 1 & 3 & 6 \\ 0 & 3 & 2 & 2 \\ 0 & 0 & 0 & 1 \end{bmatrix}$$

Operating $C_{21}(-1),\ C_{31}(-3),\ C_{41}(-6)$

$$A \sim \begin{bmatrix} 1 & 0 & 0 & 0 \\ 0 & 3 & 2 & 2 \\ 0 & 0 & 0 & 1 \end{bmatrix}$$

Operating $R_{23}(-2)$

$$A \sim \begin{bmatrix} 1 & 0 & 0 & 0 \\ 0 & 3 & 2 & 0 \\ 0 & 0 & 0 & 1 \end{bmatrix}$$

Operating $C_2\left(\frac{1}{3}\right)$

$$A \sim \begin{bmatrix} 1 & 0 & 0 & 0 \\ 0 & 1 & 2 & 0 \\ 0 & 0 & 0 & 1 \end{bmatrix}$$

Operating $C_{32}(-2)$

$$A \sim \begin{bmatrix} 1 & 0 & 0 & 0 \\ 0 & 1 & 0 & 0 \\ 0 & 0 & 0 & 1 \end{bmatrix}$$

Operating C_{34}

$$A \sim \begin{bmatrix} 1 & 0 & 0 & 0 \\ 0 & 1 & 0 & 0 \\ 0 & 0 & 1 & 0 \end{bmatrix}$$

$\Rightarrow A \sim [I_3 \ O_{3\times 1}]$

which is the normal form.

Hence, $\rho(A) = 3$

Example 4. Reduce the matrix A to its normal form, where

$$A = \begin{bmatrix} 2 & 3 & -1 & -1 \\ 1 & -1 & -2 & -4 \\ 3 & 1 & 3 & -2 \\ 6 & 3 & 0 & -7 \end{bmatrix}$$ and hence find the rank of the matrix.

Solution: We have

$$A = \begin{bmatrix} 2 & 3 & -1 & -1 \\ 1 & -1 & -2 & -4 \\ 3 & 1 & 3 & -2 \\ 6 & 3 & 0 & -7 \end{bmatrix}$$

Operating R_{12}

$$A \sim \begin{bmatrix} 1 & -1 & -2 & -4 \\ 2 & 3 & -1 & -1 \\ 3 & 1 & 3 & -2 \\ 6 & 3 & 0 & -7 \end{bmatrix}$$

Operating $C_{21}(1)$, $C_{31}(2)$, $C_{41}(4)$

$$A \sim \begin{bmatrix} 1 & 0 & 0 & 0 \\ 2 & 5 & 3 & 7 \\ 3 & 4 & 9 & 10 \\ 6 & 9 & 12 & 17 \end{bmatrix}$$

Operating $R_{21}(-2)$, $R_{31}(-3)$, $R_{41}(-4)$

$$A \sim \begin{bmatrix} 1 & 0 & 0 & 0 \\ 0 & 5 & 3 & 7 \\ 0 & 4 & 9 & 10 \\ 0 & 9 & 12 & 17 \end{bmatrix}$$

Operating $R_{23}(-1)$, $R_{43}(-2)$

$$A \sim \begin{bmatrix} 1 & 0 & 0 & 0 \\ 0 & 1 & -6 & -3 \\ 0 & 4 & 9 & 10 \\ 0 & 1 & -6 & -3 \end{bmatrix}$$

Operating $C_{32}(6)$, $C_{42}(3)$

$$A \sim \begin{bmatrix} 1 & 0 & 0 & 0 \\ 0 & 1 & 0 & 0 \\ 0 & 4 & 33 & 22 \\ 0 & 1 & 0 & 0 \end{bmatrix}$$

Operating $R_{32}(-4)$, $R_{42}(-1)$

$$A \sim \begin{bmatrix} 1 & 0 & 0 & 0 \\ 0 & 1 & 0 & 0 \\ 0 & 0 & 33 & 22 \\ 0 & 0 & 0 & 0 \end{bmatrix}$$

Operating $C_3\left(\frac{1}{33}\right)$

$$A \sim \begin{bmatrix} 1 & 0 & 0 & 0 \\ 0 & 1 & 0 & 0 \\ 0 & 0 & 1 & 22 \\ 0 & 0 & 0 & 0 \end{bmatrix}$$

Operating $C_{43}(-22)$

$$A \sim \begin{bmatrix} 1 & 0 & 0 & 0 \\ 0 & 1 & 0 & 0 \\ 0 & 0 & 1 & 0 \\ 0 & 0 & 0 & 0 \end{bmatrix} = \begin{bmatrix} I_3 & O_{3\times1} \\ O_{1\times3} & O_{1\times1} \end{bmatrix}$$

which is the normal form.

$\therefore \quad \rho(A) = 3$

Example 5. Find the rank of the matrix $A = \begin{bmatrix} 1^2 & 2^2 & 3^2 & 4^2 \\ 2^2 & 3^2 & 4^2 & 5^2 \\ 3^2 & 4^2 & 5^2 & 6^2 \\ 4^2 & 5^2 & 6^2 & 7^2 \end{bmatrix}$

Solution: We have

$$A = \begin{bmatrix} 1^2 & 2^2 & 3^2 & 4^2 \\ 2^2 & 3^2 & 4^2 & 5^2 \\ 3^2 & 4^2 & 5^2 & 6^2 \\ 4^2 & 5^2 & 6^2 & 7^2 \end{bmatrix}$$

$$\Rightarrow A = \begin{bmatrix} 1 & 4 & 9 & 16 \\ 4 & 9 & 16 & 25 \\ 9 & 16 & 25 & 36 \\ 16 & 25 & 36 & 49 \end{bmatrix}$$

Operating $R_{21}(-4)$, $R_{31}(-9)$, $R_{41}(-16)$

$$A \sim \begin{bmatrix} 1 & 4 & 9 & 16 \\ 0 & -7 & -20 & -39 \\ 0 & -20 & -56 & -108 \\ 0 & -39 & -108 & -207 \end{bmatrix}$$

Operating $C_{21}(-4)$, $C_{31}(-9)$, $C_{41}(-16)$

$$A \sim \begin{bmatrix} 1 & 0 & 0 & 0 \\ 0 & -7 & -20 & -39 \\ 0 & -20 & -56 & -108 \\ 0 & -39 & -108 & -207 \end{bmatrix}$$

Operating $R_{32}(-3)$

$$A \sim \begin{bmatrix} 1 & 0 & 0 & 0 \\ 0 & -7 & -20 & -39 \\ 0 & 1 & 4 & 9 \\ 0 & -39 & -108 & -207 \end{bmatrix}$$

Operating R_{23}

$$A \sim \begin{bmatrix} 1 & 0 & 0 & 0 \\ 0 & 1 & 4 & 9 \\ 0 & -7 & -20 & -39 \\ 0 & -39 & -108 & -207 \end{bmatrix}$$

Operating $R_{32}(7)$, $R_{42}(39)$

$$A \sim \begin{bmatrix} 1 & 0 & 0 & 0 \\ 0 & 1 & 4 & 9 \\ 0 & 0 & 8 & 24 \\ 0 & 0 & 48 & 144 \end{bmatrix}$$

Operating $C_{32}(-4)$, $C_{42}(-9)$

$$A \sim \begin{bmatrix} 1 & 0 & 0 & 0 \\ 0 & 1 & 0 & 0 \\ 0 & 0 & 8 & 24 \\ 0 & 0 & 48 & 144 \end{bmatrix}$$

Operating $R_3\left(\frac{1}{8}\right)$

$$A \sim \begin{bmatrix} 1 & 0 & 0 & 0 \\ 0 & 1 & 0 & 0 \\ 0 & 0 & 1 & 3 \\ 0 & 0 & 48 & 144 \end{bmatrix}$$

Operating $R_{43}(-48)$

$$A \sim \begin{bmatrix} 1 & 0 & 0 & 0 \\ 0 & 1 & 0 & 0 \\ 0 & 0 & 1 & 3 \\ 0 & 0 & 0 & 0 \end{bmatrix}$$

Operating $C_{43}(-3)$

$$A \sim \begin{bmatrix} 1 & 0 & 0 & 0 \\ 0 & 1 & 0 & 0 \\ 0 & 0 & 1 & 0 \\ 0 & 0 & 0 & 0 \end{bmatrix} = \begin{bmatrix} I_3 & O_{3\times 1} \\ O_{1\times 3} & O_{1\times 1} \end{bmatrix}$$

which is the normal form.

$\therefore \quad \rho(A) = 3$

Example 6. Find the rank of the matrix $A = \begin{bmatrix} 1 & 1 & 1 \\ a & b & c \\ a^2 & b^2 & c^2 \end{bmatrix}$, where a, b, c are all real.

Solution: We have

$$A = \begin{bmatrix} 1 & 1 & 1 \\ a & b & c \\ a^2 & b^2 & c^2 \end{bmatrix}$$

$$\therefore \quad |A| = \begin{vmatrix} 1 & 1 & 1 \\ a & b & c \\ a^2 & b^2 & c^2 \end{vmatrix} = (a-b)(b-c)(c-a)(a+b+c)$$

Now the following cases arise:

Case I. *When* $a = b = c$

Then $|A| = \begin{vmatrix} 1 & 1 & 1 \\ a & b & c \\ a^2 & b^2 & c^2 \end{vmatrix} = 0 \qquad \Big|\ \because\ C_1$ and C_2 are identical

$\therefore \quad \rho(A) \neq 3$

Again, all the minors of order 2 are 0.

$\therefore \quad \rho(A) \neq 2$

Clearly A has non-zero minors of order 1.

$\therefore \quad \rho(A) = 1$

Case II. *When $a = b \neq c$*

Then $|A| = \begin{vmatrix} 1 & 1 & 1 \\ a & b & c \\ a^2 & b^2 & c^2 \end{vmatrix} = 0$ $\quad | \because C_1$ and C_2 are identical

$\therefore \quad \rho(A) \neq 3$

A non-zero minor of order 2 is

$$\begin{vmatrix} 1 & 1 \\ a & c \end{vmatrix} = c - a \neq 0 \qquad | \because a \neq c$$

$\therefore \quad \rho(A) = 2$

Similarly, $\rho(A) = 2$ when $b = c \neq a$ or $c = a \neq b$

Case III. *When a, b, c are all different but $a + b + c = 0$*

Then $|A| = 0$

$\therefore \quad \rho(A) \neq 3$

Also, a non-zero minor of order 2 is

$$\begin{vmatrix} 1 & 1 \\ a & b \end{vmatrix} = b - a \neq 0 \qquad | \because a \neq b$$

$\therefore \quad \rho(A) = 2$

Case IV. *When a, b, c are all different and $a + b + c \neq 0$*

Then $|A| \neq 0$, i.e. A has a non-zero minor of order 3.

Also, A has no minor of order higher than 3

$\therefore \quad \rho(A) = 3$

Example 7. Find the rank of $A = \begin{bmatrix} 0 & c & -b & a' \\ -c & 0 & a & b' \\ b & -a & 0 & c' \\ -a' & -b' & -c' & 0 \end{bmatrix}$ where

$a, b, c > 0$ and $\Sigma\, aa' = aa' + bb' + cc' = 0$

Solution: We have

$$A = \begin{bmatrix} 0 & c & -b & a' \\ -c & 0 & a & b' \\ b & -a & 0 & c' \\ -a' & -b' & -c' & 0 \end{bmatrix}$$

Operating $C_4(a)$

$$A \sim \begin{bmatrix} 0 & c & -b & aa' \\ -c & 0 & a & ab' \\ b & -a & 0 & ac' \\ -a' & -b' & -c' & 0 \end{bmatrix}$$

Operating $C_{43}(-b')$

$$A \sim \begin{bmatrix} 0 & c & -b & aa' + bb' \\ -c & 0 & a & 0 \\ b & -a & 0 & ac' \\ -a' & -b' & -c' & b'c' \end{bmatrix}$$

Operating $C_{42}(c')$

$$A \sim \begin{bmatrix} 0 & c & -b & aa' + bb' + cc' \\ -c & 0 & a & 0 \\ b & -a & 0 & 0 \\ -a' & -b' & -c' & 0 \end{bmatrix}$$

$$\Rightarrow A \sim \begin{bmatrix} 0 & c & -b & 0 \\ -c & 0 & a & 0 \\ b & -a & 0 & 0 \\ -a' & -b' & -c' & 0 \end{bmatrix} \quad \Big| \because \sum aa' = aa' + bb' + cc' = 0$$

Operating $C_3(c)$

$$A \sim \begin{bmatrix} 0 & c & -bc & 0 \\ -c & 0 & ac & 0 \\ b & -a & 0 & 0 \\ -a' & -b' & -cc' & 0 \end{bmatrix}$$

Operating $C_{32}(b)$

$$A \sim \begin{bmatrix} 0 & c & 0 & 0 \\ -c & 0 & ac & 0 \\ b & -a & -ab & 0 \\ -a' & -b' & -bb' - cc' & 0 \end{bmatrix}$$

Operating $C_{31}(a)$

$$A \sim \begin{bmatrix} 0 & c & 0 & 0 \\ -c & 0 & 0 & 0 \\ b & -a & 0 & 0 \\ -a' & -b' & -(aa' + bb' + cc') & 0 \end{bmatrix}$$

$$\Rightarrow A \sim \begin{bmatrix} 0 & c & 0 & 0 \\ -c & 0 & 0 & 0 \\ b & -a & 0 & 0 \\ -a' & -b' & 0 & 0 \end{bmatrix} \quad \Big| \because \sum aa' = aa' + bb' + cc' = 0$$

$$\Rightarrow A \sim \begin{bmatrix} 0 & c & 0 & 0 \\ -c & 0 & 0 & 0 \\ b & -a & 0 & 0 \\ -a' & -b' & 0 & 0 \end{bmatrix}$$

The only minor of order 4 is 0.

Every minor of order 3 is zero.

But a minor of order 2 is $\begin{vmatrix} 0 & c \\ -c & 0 \end{vmatrix} = c^2 \neq 0$

| $\because c > 0$, i.e. A has a non-zero minor of order 2

$\therefore \quad \rho(A) = 2$

Example 8. Find the rank of $\begin{bmatrix} 1 & 1 & 1 & 1 \\ 1 & 3 & -2 & a \\ 2 & 2a-2 & -a-2 & 3a-1 \\ 3 & a+2 & -3 & 2a+1 \end{bmatrix}$

Solution: Let

$$A = \begin{bmatrix} 1 & 1 & 1 & 1 \\ 1 & 3 & -2 & a \\ 2 & 2a-2 & -a-2 & 3a-1 \\ 3 & a+2 & -3 & 2a+1 \end{bmatrix}$$

Operating $C_{21}(-1)$, $C_{31}(-1)$, $C_{41}(-1)$

$$A \sim \begin{bmatrix} 1 & 0 & 0 & 0 \\ 1 & 2 & -3 & a-1 \\ 2 & 2a-4 & -a-4 & 3a-3 \\ 3 & a-1 & -6 & 2a-2 \end{bmatrix}$$

Operating $R_{21}(-1)$, $R_{31}(-2)$, $R_{41}(-3)$

$$A \sim \begin{bmatrix} 1 & 0 & 0 & 0 \\ 0 & 2 & -3 & a-1 \\ 0 & 2a-4 & -a-4 & 3a-3 \\ 0 & a-1 & -6 & 2a-2 \end{bmatrix}$$

Operating $R_{42}(-2)$

$$A \sim \begin{bmatrix} 1 & 0 & 0 & 0 \\ 0 & 2 & -3 & a-1 \\ 0 & 2a-4 & -a-4 & 3a-3 \\ 0 & a-5 & 0 & 0 \end{bmatrix}$$

Operating $C_2\left(\frac{1}{2}\right)$

$$A \sim \begin{bmatrix} 1 & 0 & 0 & 0 \\ 0 & 1 & -3 & a-1 \\ 0 & a-2 & -a-4 & 3a-3 \\ 0 & \frac{a-5}{2} & 0 & 0 \end{bmatrix}$$

Operating $C_{32}(3)$

$$A \sim \begin{bmatrix} 1 & 0 & 0 & 0 \\ 0 & 1 & 0 & a-1 \\ 0 & a-2 & 2a-10 & 3a-3 \\ 0 & \frac{a-5}{2} & \frac{3(a-5)}{2} & 0 \end{bmatrix}$$

Operating $R_4\left(\frac{a-5}{2}\right)$

$$A \sim \begin{bmatrix} 1 & 0 & 0 & 0 \\ 0 & 1 & 0 & a-1 \\ 0 & a-2 & 2a-10 & 3a-3 \\ 0 & 1 & 3 & 0 \end{bmatrix}$$

$$\therefore \quad |A| = \begin{vmatrix} 1 & 0 & a-1 \\ a-2 & 2a-10 & 3a-3 \\ 1 & 3 & 0 \end{vmatrix}$$

$$= 1\{0 - 3(3a - 3)\} + (a - 1)\{3(a - 2) - (2a - 10)\}$$
$$= -9a + 9 + (a - 1)(a + 4)$$
$$= -9a + 9 + a^2 + 3a - 4$$
$$= a^2 - 6a + 5$$
$$= (a - 1)(a - 5)$$

Now the following cases arise:

Case I. *When $a \neq 1, a \neq 5$*

Then $(a - 1)(a - 5) = 0$

$\therefore \quad \rho(A) = 4$

Case II. *When $a = 1, a \neq 5$*

Then $(a - 1)(a - 5) = 0$

$\therefore \quad \rho(A) \neq 4$

But a minor of order 3 is

$$\begin{vmatrix} 1 & 0 & 0 \\ 0 & 1 & 0 \\ 0 & a-2 & 2a-10 \end{vmatrix} = \begin{vmatrix} 1 & 0 & 0 \\ 0 & 1 & 0 \\ 0 & -1 & -8 \end{vmatrix}$$
$$= -8 \neq 0$$

$\therefore \quad \rho(A) = 3$

Case III. *When $a = 5, a \neq 1$*

Then $(a - 1)(a - 5) = 0$

Every minor of order 3 is 0. But a minor of order 2 is

$$\begin{vmatrix} 1 & 0 \\ 1 & 3 \end{vmatrix} = 3 \neq 0$$

$\therefore \quad \rho(A) = 2$

Example 9. For the matrix $A = \begin{bmatrix} 1 & 1 & 2 \\ 1 & 2 & 3 \\ 0 & -1 & -1 \end{bmatrix}$, find non-singular matrices P and Q such that PAQ is in the normal form.

Solution: We write

$$A = I_3 A I_3$$

$$\Rightarrow \begin{bmatrix} 1 & 1 & 2 \\ 1 & 2 & 3 \\ 0 & -1 & -1 \end{bmatrix} = \begin{bmatrix} 1 & 0 & 0 \\ 0 & 1 & 0 \\ 0 & 0 & 1 \end{bmatrix} A \begin{bmatrix} 1 & 0 & 0 \\ 0 & 1 & 0 \\ 0 & 0 & 1 \end{bmatrix}$$

Operating $C_{21}(-1)$, $C_{31}(-2)$

$$\begin{bmatrix} 1 & 0 & 0 \\ 1 & 1 & 1 \\ 0 & -1 & -1 \end{bmatrix} = \begin{bmatrix} 1 & 0 & 0 \\ 0 & 1 & 0 \\ 0 & 0 & 1 \end{bmatrix} A \begin{bmatrix} 1 & -1 & -2 \\ 0 & 1 & 0 \\ 0 & 0 & 1 \end{bmatrix}$$

Operating $R_{21}(-1)$

$$\begin{bmatrix} 1 & 0 & 0 \\ 0 & 1 & 1 \\ 0 & -1 & -1 \end{bmatrix} = \begin{bmatrix} 1 & 0 & 0 \\ -1 & 1 & 0 \\ 0 & 0 & 1 \end{bmatrix} A \begin{bmatrix} 1 & -1 & -2 \\ 0 & 1 & 0 \\ 0 & 0 & 1 \end{bmatrix}$$

Operating $C_{32}(-1)$

$$\begin{bmatrix} 1 & 0 & 0 \\ 0 & 1 & 0 \\ 0 & -1 & 0 \end{bmatrix} = \begin{bmatrix} 1 & 0 & 0 \\ -1 & 1 & 0 \\ 0 & 0 & 1 \end{bmatrix} A \begin{bmatrix} 1 & -1 & -1 \\ 0 & 1 & -1 \\ 0 & 0 & 1 \end{bmatrix}$$

Operating $R_{32}(1)$

$$\begin{bmatrix} 1 & 0 & 0 \\ 0 & 1 & 0 \\ 0 & 0 & 0 \end{bmatrix} = \begin{bmatrix} 1 & 0 & 0 \\ -1 & 1 & 0 \\ -1 & 1 & 0 \end{bmatrix} A \begin{bmatrix} 1 & -1 & -1 \\ 0 & 1 & -1 \\ 0 & 0 & 1 \end{bmatrix}$$

$$\Rightarrow \begin{bmatrix} I_2 & O_{2\times 1} \\ O_{1\times 2} & O_{1\times 1} \end{bmatrix} = PAQ$$

where

$$P = \begin{bmatrix} 1 & 0 & 0 \\ -1 & 1 & 0 \\ -1 & 1 & 1 \end{bmatrix}$$

$$\text{and } Q = \begin{bmatrix} 1 & -1 & -1 \\ 0 & 1 & -1 \\ 0 & 0 & 1 \end{bmatrix}$$

Example 10. If $A = \begin{bmatrix} 3 & -3 & 4 \\ 2 & -3 & 4 \\ 0 & -1 & 1 \end{bmatrix}$, determine two non-singular matrices P and Q such that $PAQ = I$. Hence, find A^{-1}.

Solution: Let us write

$$A = I_3 A I_3$$

$$\Rightarrow \begin{bmatrix} 3 & -3 & 4 \\ 2 & -3 & 4 \\ 0 & -1 & -1 \end{bmatrix} = \begin{bmatrix} 1 & 0 & 0 \\ 0 & 1 & 0 \\ 0 & 0 & 1 \end{bmatrix} A \begin{bmatrix} 1 & 0 & 0 \\ 0 & 1 & 0 \\ 0 & 0 & 1 \end{bmatrix}$$

Operating $R_{12}(-1)$

$$\begin{bmatrix} 1 & 0 & 0 \\ 2 & -3 & 4 \\ 0 & -1 & -1 \end{bmatrix} = \begin{bmatrix} 1 & -1 & 0 \\ 0 & 1 & 0 \\ 0 & 0 & 1 \end{bmatrix} A \begin{bmatrix} 1 & 0 & 0 \\ 0 & 1 & 0 \\ 0 & 0 & 1 \end{bmatrix}$$

Operating $R_{21}(-2)$

$$\begin{bmatrix} 1 & 0 & 0 \\ 0 & -3 & 4 \\ 0 & -1 & 1 \end{bmatrix} = \begin{bmatrix} 1 & -1 & 0 \\ -2 & 3 & 0 \\ 0 & 0 & 1 \end{bmatrix} A \begin{bmatrix} 1 & 0 & 0 \\ 0 & 1 & 0 \\ 0 & 0 & 1 \end{bmatrix}$$

Operating $R_{23}(-4)$

$$\begin{bmatrix} 1 & 0 & 0 \\ 0 & 1 & 0 \\ 0 & -1 & 1 \end{bmatrix} = \begin{bmatrix} 1 & -1 & 0 \\ -2 & 3 & -4 \\ 0 & 0 & 1 \end{bmatrix} A \begin{bmatrix} 1 & 0 & 0 \\ 0 & 1 & 0 \\ 0 & 0 & 1 \end{bmatrix}$$

Operating $C_{23}(1)$

$$\begin{bmatrix} 1 & 0 & 0 \\ 0 & 1 & 0 \\ 0 & 0 & 1 \end{bmatrix} = \begin{bmatrix} 1 & -1 & 0 \\ -2 & 3 & -4 \\ 0 & 0 & 1 \end{bmatrix} A \begin{bmatrix} 1 & 0 & 0 \\ 0 & 1 & 0 \\ 0 & 1 & 1 \end{bmatrix}$$

$\Rightarrow\ I = PAQ$

where

$$P = \begin{bmatrix} 1 & -1 & 0 \\ -2 & 3 & -4 \\ 0 & 0 & 1 \end{bmatrix}$$

$$\text{and } Q = \begin{bmatrix} 1 & 0 & 0 \\ 0 & 1 & 0 \\ 0 & 1 & 1 \end{bmatrix}$$

Now,

$$PAQ = I$$

Pre-multiplying by P^{-1},

$$P^{-1}PAQ = P^{-1}I$$

$\Rightarrow\ IAQ = P^{-1}I \quad | \because P^{-1}P = I$

$\Rightarrow\ AQ = P^{-1}$

Post-multiplying by P,

$$AQP = P^{-1}P$$

$\Rightarrow\ AQP = I$

Pre-multiplying by A^{-1},

$$A^{-1}AQP = A^{-1}I$$

$\Rightarrow\ IQP = A^{-1}I$

$\Rightarrow\ QP = A^{-1}$

$$\therefore\ A^{-1} = \begin{bmatrix} 1 & 0 & 0 \\ 0 & 1 & 0 \\ 0 & 1 & 1 \end{bmatrix}\begin{bmatrix} 1 & -1 & 0 \\ -2 & 3 & -4 \\ 0 & 0 & 1 \end{bmatrix} = \begin{bmatrix} 1 & -1 & 0 \\ -2 & 3 & -4 \\ -2 & 3 & -3 \end{bmatrix}$$

Example 11. Determine the non-singular matrices P and Q such that PAQ is in the normal form where $A = \begin{bmatrix} 3 & 2 & -1 & 5 \\ 5 & 1 & 4 & -2 \\ 1 & -4 & 11 & -19 \end{bmatrix}$. Hence, find the rank of A.

Solution:

$\therefore$ The order of A is 3×4

$\therefore$ We write

$A = I_3 A I_4$

$$\Rightarrow \begin{bmatrix} 3 & 2 & -1 & 5 \\ 5 & 1 & 4 & -2 \\ 1 & -4 & 11 & -19 \end{bmatrix} = \begin{bmatrix} 1 & 0 & 0 \\ 0 & 1 & 0 \\ 0 & 0 & 1 \end{bmatrix} A \begin{bmatrix} 1 & 0 & 0 & 0 \\ 0 & 1 & 0 & 0 \\ 0 & 0 & 1 & 0 \\ 0 & 0 & 0 & 1 \end{bmatrix}$$

Operating R_{13}

$$\begin{bmatrix} 1 & -4 & 11 & -19 \\ 5 & 1 & 4 & -2 \\ 1 & -4 & 11 & -19 \end{bmatrix} = \begin{bmatrix} 0 & 0 & 1 \\ 0 & 1 & 0 \\ 1 & 0 & 0 \end{bmatrix} A \begin{bmatrix} 1 & 0 & 0 & 0 \\ 0 & 1 & 0 & 0 \\ 0 & 0 & 1 & 0 \\ 0 & 0 & 0 & 1 \end{bmatrix}$$

Operating $C_{21}(4)$, $C_{31}(-11)$, $C_{41}(19)$

$$\begin{bmatrix} 1 & 0 & 0 & 0 \\ 5 & 21 & -51 & 93 \\ 3 & 14 & -34 & 62 \end{bmatrix} = \begin{bmatrix} 0 & 0 & 1 \\ 0 & 1 & 0 \\ 1 & 0 & 0 \end{bmatrix} A \begin{bmatrix} 1 & 4 & -11 & 19 \\ 0 & 1 & 0 & 0 \\ 0 & 0 & 0 & 0 \\ 0 & 0 & 1 & 1 \end{bmatrix}$$

Operating $R_{21}(-5)$, $R_{31}(-3)$

$$\begin{bmatrix} 1 & 0 & 0 & 0 \\ 0 & 21 & -51 & 93 \\ 0 & 14 & -34 & 62 \end{bmatrix} = \begin{bmatrix} 0 & 0 & 1 \\ 0 & 1 & -5 \\ 1 & 0 & -3 \end{bmatrix} A \begin{bmatrix} 1 & 4 & -11 & 19 \\ 0 & 1 & 0 & 0 \\ 0 & 0 & 0 & 0 \\ 0 & 0 & 1 & 1 \end{bmatrix}$$

Operating $C_2\left(\frac{1}{7}\right), C_3\left(-\frac{1}{17}\right), C_4\left(\frac{1}{31}\right)$

$$\begin{bmatrix} 1 & 0 & 0 & 0 \\ 0 & 3 & 3 & 3 \\ 0 & 2 & 2 & 2 \end{bmatrix} = \begin{bmatrix} 0 & 0 & 1 \\ 0 & 1 & -5 \\ 1 & 0 & -3 \end{bmatrix} A \begin{bmatrix} 1 & \frac{4}{7} & \frac{11}{17} & \frac{19}{31} \\ 0 & \frac{1}{7} & 0 & 0 \\ 0 & 0 & -\frac{1}{17} & 0 \\ 0 & 0 & 0 & \frac{1}{31} \end{bmatrix}$$

Operating $R_2\left(\frac{1}{3}\right), R_3\left(\frac{1}{2}\right)$

$$\begin{bmatrix} 1 & 0 & 0 & 0 \\ 0 & 1 & 1 & 1 \\ 0 & 1 & 1 & 1 \end{bmatrix} = \begin{bmatrix} 0 & 0 & 1 \\ 0 & \frac{1}{3} & \frac{-5}{3} \\ \frac{1}{2} & 0 & \frac{-3}{2} \end{bmatrix} A \begin{bmatrix} 1 & \frac{4}{7} & \frac{11}{17} & \frac{19}{31} \\ 0 & \frac{1}{7} & 0 & 0 \\ 0 & 0 & -\frac{1}{17} & 0 \\ 0 & 0 & 0 & \frac{1}{31} \end{bmatrix}$$

Operating $C_{32}(-1),\ C_{42}(-1)$

$$\begin{bmatrix} 1 & 0 & 0 & 0 \\ 0 & 1 & 0 & 0 \\ 0 & 1 & 0 & 0 \end{bmatrix} = \begin{bmatrix} 0 & 0 & 1 \\ 0 & \frac{1}{3} & \frac{-5}{3} \\ \frac{1}{2} & 0 & \frac{-3}{2} \end{bmatrix} A \begin{bmatrix} 1 & \frac{4}{7} & \frac{9}{119} & \frac{9}{217} \\ 0 & \frac{1}{7} & -\frac{1}{7} & -\frac{1}{7} \\ 0 & 0 & -\frac{1}{17} & 0 \\ 0 & 0 & 0 & \frac{1}{31} \end{bmatrix}$$

Operating $R_{32}(-1)$

$$\begin{bmatrix} 1 & 0 & 0 & 0 \\ 0 & 1 & 0 & 0 \\ 0 & 0 & 0 & 0 \end{bmatrix} = \begin{bmatrix} 0 & 0 & 1 \\ 0 & \frac{1}{3} & -\frac{5}{3} \\ \frac{1}{2} & -\frac{1}{3} & -\frac{1}{6} \end{bmatrix} A \begin{bmatrix} 1 & \frac{4}{7} & \frac{9}{119} & \frac{9}{217} \\ 0 & \frac{1}{7} & -\frac{1}{7} & -\frac{1}{7} \\ 0 & 0 & -\frac{1}{17} & 0 \\ 0 & 0 & 0 & \frac{1}{31} \end{bmatrix}$$

$$\Rightarrow \begin{bmatrix} I_{2\times 2} & O_{2\times 2} \\ O_{1\times 2} & O_{1\times 2} \end{bmatrix} = PAQ$$

where,

$$P = \begin{bmatrix} 0 & 0 & 1 \\ 0 & \frac{1}{3} & -\frac{5}{6} \\ \frac{1}{2} & -\frac{1}{3} & -\frac{1}{6} \end{bmatrix} \text{ and } Q = \begin{bmatrix} 1 & \frac{4}{7} & \frac{9}{119} & \frac{9}{217} \\ 0 & \frac{1}{7} & -\frac{1}{7} & -\frac{1}{7} \\ 0 & 0 & -\frac{1}{17} & 0 \\ 0 & 0 & 0 & \frac{1}{31} \end{bmatrix}$$

$\therefore \quad \rho(A) = 2$

Note: In such problems, other answers are also possible.

EXERCISE 5.2

1. Find the rank of the following matrices using elementary transformations:

(i) $\begin{bmatrix} 1 & 2 & 3 \\ 1 & 4 & 2 \\ 2 & 6 & 5 \end{bmatrix}$

(ii) $\begin{bmatrix} 1 & 1 & 1 \\ 2 & 2 & 2 \\ 3 & 3 & 3 \end{bmatrix}$

(iii) $\begin{bmatrix} -1 & -2 & -1 \\ 6 & 12 & 6 \\ 5 & 10 & 5 \end{bmatrix}$

(iv) $\begin{bmatrix} 1 & 2 & 3 \\ 2 & 4 & 7 \\ 3 & 6 & 10 \end{bmatrix}$

(v) $\begin{bmatrix} 3 & -1 & 2 \\ -6 & 2 & 4 \\ -3 & 1 & 2 \end{bmatrix}$

(vi) $\begin{bmatrix} 1 & 2 & 3 & 2 \\ 2 & 3 & 5 & 1 \\ 1 & 3 & 4 & 5 \end{bmatrix}$

(vii) $\begin{bmatrix} 1 & 2 & 0 & -1 \\ 3 & 4 & 1 & 2 \\ -2 & 3 & 2 & 5 \end{bmatrix}$

(viii) $\begin{bmatrix} 6 & 1 & 3 & 8 \\ 16 & 4 & 2 & 15 \\ 5 & 3 & 3 & 4 \\ 4 & 2 & 6 & -1 \end{bmatrix}$

(ix) $\begin{bmatrix} 1 & 1 & 2 & 3 \\ 1 & 3 & 0 & 3 \\ 1 & -2 & -3 & -3 \\ 1 & 1 & 2 & 3 \end{bmatrix}$

(x) $\begin{bmatrix} 3 & 4 & 5 & 6 & 7 \\ 4 & 5 & 6 & 7 & 8 \\ 5 & 6 & 7 & 8 & 9 \\ 10 & 11 & 12 & 13 & 14 \\ 15 & 16 & 17 & 18 & 19 \end{bmatrix}$

2. Reduce the following matrices to their normal forms and hence find their ranks:

(i) $\begin{bmatrix} 0 & 1 & -3 & -1 \\ 1 & 0 & 1 & 1 \\ 3 & 1 & 0 & 2 \\ 1 & 1 & -2 & 0 \end{bmatrix}$

(ii) $\begin{bmatrix} 1 & -1 & 3 & 6 \\ 1 & 3 & -3 & -4 \\ 5 & 3 & 3 & 11 \end{bmatrix}$

(iii) $\begin{bmatrix} 9 & -7 & 3 & 6 \\ 5 & -1 & 4 & 1 \\ 6 & 8 & 2 & 4 \end{bmatrix}$

(iv) $\begin{bmatrix} -2 & -1 & -3 & -1 \\ 1 & 2 & 3 & -1 \\ 1 & 0 & 1 & 1 \\ 0 & 1 & 1 & -1 \end{bmatrix}$

(v) $\begin{bmatrix} 1 & 2 & 0 & -1 \\ 3 & 4 & 1 & 2 \\ -2 & 3 & 2 & 5 \end{bmatrix}$

(vi) $\begin{bmatrix} 1 & 3 & 4 & 5 \\ 3 & 9 & 12 & 3 \\ 1 & 3 & 4 & 1 \end{bmatrix}$

(vii) $\begin{bmatrix} 1 & 2 & 1 & 2 \\ 1 & 3 & 2 & 2 \\ 2 & 4 & 3 & 4 \\ 3 & 7 & 4 & 6 \end{bmatrix}$

(viii) $\begin{bmatrix} 1 & 2 & 3 & 1 \\ 2 & 4 & 6 & 2 \\ 1 & 2 & 3 & 2 \end{bmatrix}$

(ix) $\begin{bmatrix} 3 & -2 & 0 & -1 & -7 \\ 0 & 2 & 2 & 1 & -5 \\ 1 & -2 & -3 & -2 & 1 \\ 0 & 1 & 2 & 1 & -6 \end{bmatrix}$

(x) $\begin{bmatrix} 1 & -1 & 2 & -3 \\ 4 & 1 & 0 & 2 \\ 0 & 3 & 0 & 4 \\ 0 & 1 & 0 & 2 \end{bmatrix}$

3. Find non-singular matrices P and Q so that PAQ is in the normal form where A is

(i) $\begin{bmatrix} 1 & 1 & 2 \\ 1 & 2 & 3 \\ 0 & -1 & -1 \end{bmatrix}$

(ii) $\begin{bmatrix} 1 & 2 & 3 \\ 3 & 2 & 1 \\ 1 & 3 & 2 \\ 2 & 1 & 3 \end{bmatrix}$

(iii) $\begin{bmatrix} 1 & 0 & -2 \\ 2 & 3 & -4 \\ 3 & 3 & -6 \end{bmatrix}$

(iv) $\begin{bmatrix} 1 & -1 & 2 & -1 \\ 4 & 2 & -1 & 2 \\ 2 & 2 & -2 & 0 \end{bmatrix}$

(v) $\begin{bmatrix} 3 & -1 & 2 & 1 \\ 1 & 4 & 6 & 1 \\ 7 & -11 & 6 & 1 \\ 7 & 2 & 12 & 3 \end{bmatrix}$

(vi) $\begin{bmatrix} 5 & 3 & 14 & 4 \\ 0 & 1 & 3 & 1 \\ 1 & -1 & 2 & 0 \end{bmatrix}$

4. If $A = \begin{bmatrix} 1 & 1 & -1 \\ 2 & -3 & 4 \\ 3 & -2 & 3 \end{bmatrix}$ and $B = \begin{bmatrix} -1 & -1 & -1 \\ 6 & 12 & 6 \\ 5 & 10 & 5 \end{bmatrix}$, then show that $\rho(AB) \neq \rho(BA)$, where ρ denotes its rank.

5. Find the ranks of A, B, $A + B$, AB and BA, where

$$A = \begin{bmatrix} 1 & 1 & -1 \\ 2 & -3 & 4 \\ 3 & -2 & 3 \end{bmatrix}, B = \begin{bmatrix} -1 & -2 & -1 \\ 6 & 12 & 6 \\ 5 & 10 & 5 \end{bmatrix}$$

6. Find the rank of the following matrices:

(i) $\begin{bmatrix} 6 & 1 & 3 & 8 \\ 4 & 2 & 6 & -1 \\ 10 & 3 & 9 & 7 \\ 16 & 4 & 12 & 15 \end{bmatrix}$

(ii) $\begin{bmatrix} 1 & 2 & 3 & 4 & 5 \\ 2 & 3 & 4 & 5 & 1 \\ 5 & 8 & 11 & 14 & 7 \end{bmatrix}$

(iii) $\begin{bmatrix} 0 & 0 & 0 & 0 & 0 \\ 0 & 1 & 2 & 3 & 4 \\ 0 & 2 & 3 & 4 & 1 \\ 0 & 3 & 4 & 1 & 2 \end{bmatrix}$

(iv) $\begin{bmatrix} 0 & 4 & -12 & 8 & 9 \\ 0 & 2 & -6 & 2 & 5 \\ 0 & 1 & -3 & 6 & 4 \\ 0 & -8 & 24 & 3 & 1 \end{bmatrix}$

(v) $\begin{bmatrix} 1 & 3 & 2 & 5 & 1 \\ 2 & 2 & -1 & 6 & 3 \\ 1 & 1 & 2 & 3 & -1 \\ 0 & 2 & 5 & 2 & -3 \end{bmatrix}$

7. Obtain a matrix N in the normal form equivalent to $A = \begin{bmatrix} 0 & 0 & 0 & 0 & 0 \\ 0 & 4 & 5 & 0 & 0 \\ 0 & 9 & 1 & -1 & 2 \\ 0 & 10 & 0 & 1 & 11 \end{bmatrix}$. Hence, find non-singular matrices P and Q such that $PAQ = N$.

ANSWERS

1. (i) 2 (ii) 1 (iii) 1
(iv) 2 (v) 2 (vi) 2
(vii) 3 (viii) 3 (ix) 3
(x) 2

2. (i) 2 (ii) 3 (iii) 2
(iv) 2 (v) 3 (vi) 2
(vii) 3 (viii) 2 (ix) 4
(x) 4

3. (i) $P = \begin{bmatrix} 1 & 0 & 0 \\ -1 & 1 & 0 \\ -1 & 1 & 1 \end{bmatrix}$

$Q = \begin{bmatrix} 1 & -1 & -1 \\ 0 & 1 & -1 \\ 0 & 0 & 1 \end{bmatrix}$

(ii) $P = \begin{bmatrix} 1 & 0 & 0 & 0 \\ \frac{3}{4} & -\frac{1}{4} & 0 & 0 \\ \frac{1}{12} & -\frac{1}{12} & -\frac{1}{3} & 0 \\ -\frac{3}{2} & -\frac{1}{2} & 1 & 1 \end{bmatrix}$

$Q = \begin{bmatrix} 1 & -2 & 1 \\ 0 & 1 & -2 \\ 0 & 0 & 1 \end{bmatrix}$

(iii) $P = \begin{bmatrix} 1 & 0 & 0 \\ 0 & 1 & 0 \\ -1 & -1 & 1 \end{bmatrix}$

$Q = \begin{bmatrix} 1 & 0 & 2 \\ -\frac{2}{3} & \frac{1}{3} & 0 \\ 0 & 0 & 1 \end{bmatrix}$

(iv) $P = \begin{bmatrix} 1 & 0 & 0 \\ -\frac{2}{3} & \frac{1}{6} & 0 \\ -\frac{1}{3} & \frac{1}{3} & -\frac{1}{2} \end{bmatrix}$

$$Q = \begin{bmatrix} 1 & 1 & 0 & -\frac{1}{2} \\ 0 & 1 & -1 & \frac{3}{2} \\ 0 & 0 & 0 & 1 \\ 0 & 0 & 1 & 0 \end{bmatrix}$$

(v) $P = \begin{bmatrix} 0 & 1 & 0 & 0 \\ 1 & -3 & 0 & 0 \\ 3 & 2 & 1 & 0 \end{bmatrix}$

$$Q = \begin{bmatrix} 1 & 3 & 2 & 5 \\ 0 & 1 & 0 & 2 \\ 0 & 0 & 1 & 0 \\ 0 & -7 & -8 & -13 \end{bmatrix}$$

(vi) $P = \begin{bmatrix} 1 & 0 & 4 \\ 0 & 1 & 0 \\ -7 & 0 & -27 \end{bmatrix}$

$$Q = \begin{bmatrix} 1 & -7 & -\frac{3}{4} & -1 \\ 0 & 1 & \frac{1}{4} & -3 \\ 0 & 0 & 0 & 1 \\ 0 & 0 & -\frac{1}{4} & 0 \end{bmatrix}$$

5. 2, 1, 2, 0, 1

6. (i) 2 (ii) 2 (iii) 3

(iv) 3 (v) 3

7. $P = \begin{bmatrix} 0 & 0 & 1 & 0 \\ 0 & -1 & 5 & -4 \\ 0 & 10 & -50 & 41 \\ 1 & 0 & 0 & 0 \end{bmatrix}$

$Q = \begin{bmatrix} 0 & 0 & 0 & 1 & 0 \\ 0 & 1 & 0 & 0 & 34 \\ 1 & -9 & 1 & 0 & -659 \\ 0 & 0 & 1 & 0 & -351 \\ 0 & 0 & 0 & 0 & 1 \end{bmatrix}$

6 LINEAR EQUATIONS

6.1. Linear Equation

An equation of first degree in n unknowns $x_1, x_2, x_3, \ldots\ldots, x_n$ is called a linear equation.

Thus,

$$a_{11}x_1 + a_{12}x_2 + a_{13}x_3 + \ldots\ldots + a_{1n}x_n = b_1 \quad \ldots (6.1)$$

is a linear equation in n unknowns $x_1, x_2, x_3, \ldots\ldots, x_n$ with coefficients $a_{11}, a_{12}, a_{13}, \ldots\ldots, a_{1n}$ and b_1 as constants.

If $b_1 = 0$, then Eq. (6.1) takes the form

$$a_{11}x_1 + a_{12}x_2 + a_{13}x_3 + \ldots\ldots + a_{1n}x_n = 0 \quad \ldots (6.2)$$

and is called a homogeneous linear equation in n unknowns $x_1, x_2, x_3, \ldots\ldots, x_n$.

Thus,

$2x + 3y + 4z = 20$ is an example of a non-homogeneous linear equation in 3 unknowns x, y and z whereas $x - y + z = 0$ is an example of a homogeneous linear equation in 3 unknowns x, y and z.

6.2. System of Linear Equations

Consider a system of m linear equations in n unknowns ($m > n$, $m = n$ or $m < n$) given below:

$$\left.\begin{array}{l} a_{11}x_1 + a_{12}x_2 + a_{13}x_3 + \ldots\ldots + a_{1n}x_n = b_1 \\ a_{21}x_1 + a_{22}x_2 + a_{23}x_3 + \ldots\ldots + a_{2n}x_n = b_2 \\ \ldots\ldots\ldots\ldots\ldots\ldots\ldots\ldots\ldots\ldots\ldots\ldots \\ \ldots\ldots\ldots\ldots\ldots\ldots\ldots\ldots\ldots\ldots\ldots\ldots \\ a_{m1}x_1 + a_{m2}x_2 + a_{m3}x_3 + \ldots\ldots + a_{mn}x_n = b_m \end{array}\right\} \quad \ldots(A)$$

In matrix notation, these equations can be put in the form

$$AX = B$$

where

$$A = \begin{bmatrix} a_{11} & a_{12} & a_{13} & \cdots & a_{1n} \\ a_{21} & a_{22} & a_{23} & \cdots & a_{2n} \\ \cdots & \cdots & \cdots & \cdots & \cdots \\ \cdots & \cdots & \cdots & \cdots & \cdots \\ a_{m1} & a_{m2} & a_{m3} & \cdots & a_{mn} \end{bmatrix}_{m\times n}$$

$$X = \begin{bmatrix} x_1 \\ x_2 \\ x_3 \\ \vdots \\ x_n \end{bmatrix}_{n\times 1} \quad \text{and} \quad B = \begin{bmatrix} b_1 \\ b_2 \\ \vdots \\ \vdots \\ b_m \end{bmatrix}_{m\times 1}$$

The matrix A is called the coefficient matrix. The matrix X is called the column matrix of n unknowns $x_1, x_2, x_3, \ldots,$ x_n. The matrix B is called the column matrix of m constants $b_1, b_2, \ldots, b_m$.

The matrix $C = [A : B]$ obtained by placing the constant column matrix B to the right of the matrix A is called augmented matrix. Thus, the matrix

$$C = [A : B] = \begin{bmatrix} a_{11} & a_{12} & a_{13} & \cdots & a_{1n} & : & b_1 \\ a_{21} & a_{22} & a_{23} & \cdots & a_{2n} & : & b_2 \\ \cdots & \cdots & \cdots & \cdots & \cdots & : & \cdots \\ \cdots & \cdots & \cdots & \cdots & \cdots & : & \cdots \\ a_{m1} & a_{m2} & a_{m3} & \cdots & a_{mn} & : & b_m \end{bmatrix}$$

is called the augmented matrix.

Any set of values of x_1, x_2, x_3, x_n which simultaneously satisfy the system of equation (A) is called the solution of the system (A). If the system has one or more solutions, it is called consistent. If it has no solution, it is called inconsistent. A consistent system has either one solution or infinitely many solutions.

Example

(i) The system of equations

$$x_1 + x_2 = 3$$
$$2x_1 + 3x_2 = 8$$

is consistent because it has a unique solution $x_1 = 1$, $x_2 = 2$.

(ii) The system of equations

$$2x_1 + 3x_2 = 5$$
$$6x_1 + 9x_2 = 15$$

is consistent because it has infinitely many solutions. Note that here the two equations are one and the same.

(iii) The system of equatins

$$x_1 - 4x_2 = 2$$
$$2x_1 - 8x_2 = 5$$

is inconsistent because it has no solution.

6.3. Non-singular or Regular System of Linear Equations

If we take $m = n$ in the system of equations (A), then we have

$$A = \begin{bmatrix} a_{11} & a_{12} & a_{13} & \cdots\cdots & a_{1n} \\ a_{21} & a_{22} & a_{23} & \cdots\cdots & a_{2n} \\ \cdots\cdots & \cdots\cdots & \cdots\cdots & \cdots\cdots & \cdots\cdots \\ \cdots\cdots & \cdots\cdots & \cdots\cdots & \cdots\cdots & \cdots\cdots \\ a_{n1} & a_{n2} & a_{n3} & \cdots\cdots & a_{nn} \end{bmatrix}$$

$$\therefore \quad |A| = \begin{vmatrix} a_{11} & a_{12} & a_{13} & \ldots\ldots & a_{1n} \\ a_{21} & a_{22} & a_{23} & \ldots\ldots & a_{2n} \\ \ldots\ldots & \ldots\ldots & \ldots\ldots & \ldots\ldots & \ldots\ldots \\ \ldots\ldots & \ldots\ldots & \ldots\ldots & \ldots\ldots & \ldots\ldots \\ a_{n1} & a_{n2} & a_{n3} & \ldots\ldots & a_{nn} \end{vmatrix}$$

$|A|$ is called the determinant of coefficients.

If $|A| \neq 0$, then the system of equations (when $m = n$) is called regular. This system has a unique solution given by

$\dfrac{x_1}{|A_1|} = \dfrac{x_2}{|A_2|} = \dfrac{x_3}{|A_3|} = \ldots\ldots = \dfrac{x_n}{|A_n|} = \dfrac{1}{|A|}$ where $|A_i|$ represents the determinant obtained by replacing the ith column of $|A|$ by the column of b's.

This is known as Cramer's Rule for solving a system of n linear equation in n unknowns.

Note. If $|A| = 0$, then Cramer's Rule fails.

When $|A| \neq 0$, then A^{-1} exists. Hence, pre-multiplying the matrix equation

$$AX = B$$

by A^{-1}, we obtain,

$$A^{-1}(AX) = A^{-1}B$$

$$\Rightarrow (A^{-1}A)X = A^{-1}B$$

$$\Rightarrow IX = A^{-1}B$$

$$\Rightarrow X = A^{-1}B$$

This gives the solution of the system of n equations in n unknowns when the system is non-singular (or regular).

6.4. Singular System of Linear Equations

If $|A| = 0$, the system of n equations in n unknowns is called singular. This case will be dealt with later on.

6.5. System of Linear Equations, in General

Consider the system of linear equations (A) as given in Section 6.2.

It is simple to see that the rank of the augmented matrix C cannot be less than the rank of the coefficient matrix A because every sub-matrix of A is also a sub-matrix of C.

Let $\rho(A) = r$. Then, by a suitable sequence of elementary row operations, the matrix A can be reduced to an equivalent matrix in which each of the first r elements of the leading diagonal is 1 and every element below this diagonal and/or below the rth row is zero. The matrix, so reduced, is said to be in *Echelon Form.*

If the same sequence of elementary operations is performed on the system of equations (A), then these will be transformed in the following form:

$$\left.\begin{aligned} y_1 + \alpha_{12}y_2 + \alpha_{13}y_3 + \ldots\ldots + \alpha_{1n}y_n &= \beta_1 \\ y_2 + \alpha_{23}y_3 + \ldots\ldots + \alpha_{2n}y_n &= \beta_2 \\ \ldots\ldots\ldots\ldots\ldots\ldots\ldots\ldots\ldots\ldots\ldots\ldots \\ y_r + \ldots\ldots + \alpha_{rn}y_n &= \beta_r \\ 0 &= \beta_{r+1} \\ \ldots\ldots &= \ldots\ldots \\ \ldots\ldots &= \ldots\ldots \\ 0 &= \beta_m \end{aligned}\right\} \quad \ldots \text{(B)}$$

in which $y_1, y_2, \ldots\ldots, y_n$ is some permutation of $x_1, x_2, \ldots\ldots, x_n$.

Also, the coefficient matrix and the augmented matrix of the system of equations (B) will be equivalent to A and C respectively.

Now the following cases arise:

Case I. When $r = 1$, then the system of equations (B) becomes,

$$\left.\begin{aligned} y_1 + \alpha_{12}y_2 + \alpha_{13}y_3 + \ldots\ldots + \alpha_{1n}y_n &= \beta_1 \\ 0 &= \beta_1 \\ 0 &= \beta_3 \\ &\vdots \\ &\vdots \\ 0 &= \beta_m \end{aligned}\right\} \quad \ldots \text{(C)}$$

In this case, $\rho(C) = 2$ or 1, since C has one column more than A.

When $\rho(C) = 2$, $\beta_2, \beta_3, \ldots\ldots, \beta_m$ cannot all be zero. Hence, the equations are inconsistent and there will be no solution.

When $\rho(C) = 2$, $\beta_2, \beta_3, \ldots\ldots, \beta_m$ will be all zero and the system of equations (B) will be equivalent to a single equation from which y_1 will be expressible in terms of $y_2, y_3, \ldots\ldots, y_n$ which can have arbitrary values.

Case II. When $r = 2$, then the system of equations (B) becomes

$$\left.\begin{array}{r} y_1 + \alpha_{12}y_2 + \alpha_{13}y_3 + \ldots\ldots + \alpha_{1n}y_n = \beta_1 \\ y_2 + \alpha_{23}y_3 + \ldots\ldots + \alpha_{2n}y_n = \beta_2 \\ 0 = \beta_3 \\ 0 = \beta_4 \\ \vdots \\ \vdots \\ 0 = \beta_m \end{array}\right\} \quad \ldots \text{(D)}$$

In this case, $\rho(C) = 3$ or 2.

When $\rho(C) = 3$, $\beta_3, \beta_4, \ldots\ldots, \beta_m$ cannot all be zero. Hence, the equations are inconsistent and there will be no solution.

But when $\rho(C) = 2$, $\beta_3, \beta_4, \ldots\ldots, \beta_m$ will be all zero and the equations will be equivalent to two independent equations from which y_1 and y_2 will be expressible in terms of $y_3, y_4, \ldots\ldots, y_n$ which can have arbitrary values.

Similarly, when $r = 3$, then $\rho(C)$ must also be 3 in order that the equations may be consistent and in that case y_1, y_2, y_3 will be expressible in terms of $y_4, y_5, \ldots\ldots, y_n$ which are arbitrary.

In general, the necessary and sufficient conditions that the equations (B) may be consistent is that $\rho(C) = \rho(A)$, i.e. if the coefficient matrix A and the augmented matrix C have the same rank and if each rank $= r$, the equations will be equivalent to r equations from which r unknowns can be expressed in terms of the remaining $(n - r)$ unknowns which are arbitrary.

We note that

(1) When $r < n$, the number of solutions is infinite.

(2) When $r = n$, there is only one solution (unique solution).

6.6. Homogeneous System of Linear Equations

If $b_1 = b_2 = \ldots\ldots = b_n = 0$, the system of equations (A) is said to be homogeneous. Then, this system of equations can be represented by the matrix equation

$$AX = O$$

For such a system, the rank of the coefficient matrix A and the rank of the augmented matrix B are equal. Hence, a system of homogeneous linear equation is always consistent. It is obvious that $X = 0$, i.e. $x_1 = x_2 = \ldots\ldots = x_n = 0$ is always a solution. But this solution is of no significance and is therefore called a *trivial (null) solution*. If A is a non-singular matrix of order n, then $\rho(A) = n$ and n equations of the system can be solved by Cramer's Rule to give the unique solution $x_1 = x_2 = \ldots\ldots x_n = 0$ and the system has only the trivial solutions. If $\rho(A) < n$, i.e. $|A| = 0$, then A can be reduced to a matrix which has r non-zero rows and $(n - r)$ zero rows. Consequently, the system is consistent and has infinitely many solutions. Hence, the necessary and sufficient condition for non-zero solutions (non-trivial solutions) is that $r < n$, i.e. the rank is less than the number of unknowns.

Also, when there are m $(< n)$ equations in n unknowns, then there are always non-trivial solutions because then the condition $r < n$ is automatically satisfied.

6.7. Aid to Memory

1.

A system of non-homogeneous linear equations $AX = B$

↓ Find $\rho(A)$ and $\rho(A:B)$

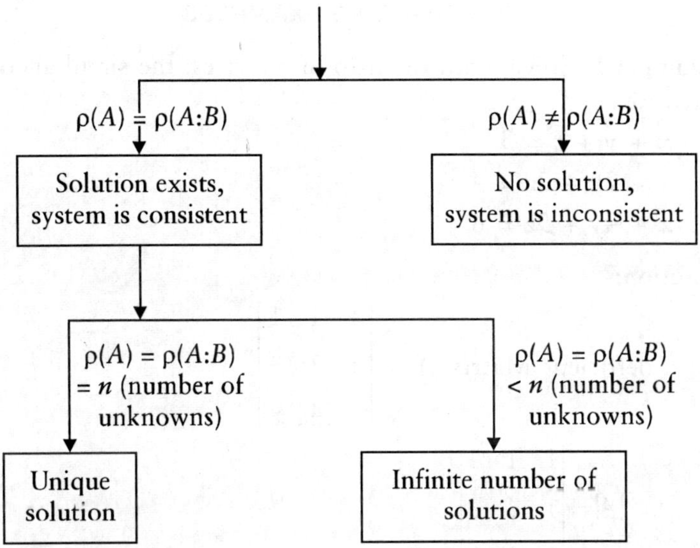
ρ(A) = ρ(A:B)
ρ(A) ≠ ρ(A:B)
Solution exists, system is consistent
No solution, system is inconsistent
ρ(A) = ρ(A:B) = n (number of unknowns)
ρ(A) = ρ(A:B) < n (number of unknowns)
Unique solution
Infinite number of solutions

2.

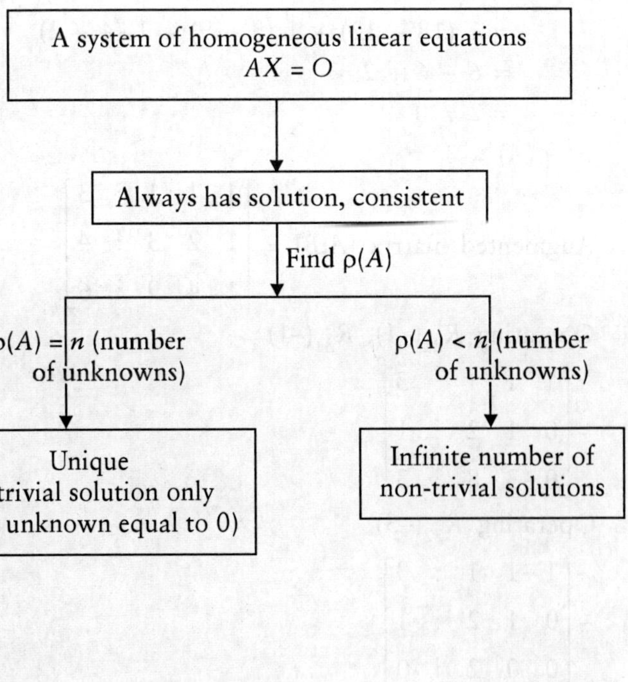
A system of homogeneous linear equations AX = O
Always has solution, consistent
Find ρ(A)
ρ(A) = n (number of unknowns)
ρ(A) < n (number of unknowns)
Unique or trivial solution only (each unknown equal to 0)
Infinite number of non-trivial solutions

ILLUSTRATIVE EXAMPLES

Example 1. Solve, with the help of matrices, the simultaneous equations:

$$x + y + z = 3$$
$$x + 2y + 3z = 4$$
$$x + 4y + 9z = 6$$

Solution:

$$\text{Coefficient Matrix } A = \begin{bmatrix} 1 & 1 & 1 \\ 1 & 2 & 3 \\ 1 & 4 & 9 \end{bmatrix}$$

$$\therefore \quad |A| = \begin{vmatrix} 1 & 1 & 1 \\ 1 & 2 & 3 \\ 1 & 4 & 9 \end{vmatrix}$$

$$= 1\,(18 - 12) + 1\,(3 - 9) + 1\,(4 - 2)$$
$$= 6 - 6 + 2$$
$$= 2 \neq 0$$

$$\therefore \quad \rho(A) = 3$$

$$\text{Augmented matrix } [A:B] = \begin{bmatrix} 1 & 1 & 1 & \vdots & 3 \\ 1 & 2 & 3 & \vdots & 4 \\ 1 & 4 & 9 & \vdots & 6 \end{bmatrix}$$

Operating $R_{21}(-1)$, $R_{31}(-1)$

$$\sim \begin{bmatrix} 1 & 1 & 1 & \vdots & 3 \\ 0 & 1 & 2 & \vdots & 1 \\ 0 & 3 & 8 & \vdots & 3 \end{bmatrix}$$

Operating $R_{32}(-3)$

$$\sim \begin{bmatrix} 1 & 1 & 1 & \vdots & 3 \\ 0 & 1 & 2 & \vdots & 1 \\ 0 & 0 & 2 & \vdots & 0 \end{bmatrix}$$

$\therefore \quad \rho[A:B] = 3$

$\because \quad \rho[A:B] = \rho[A] = 3$ (number of unknowns)

$\therefore$ The given system of equations is consistent and has a unique solution.

Equivalent system of equations is

$$\begin{bmatrix} 1 & 1 & 1 \\ 0 & 1 & 2 \\ 0 & 0 & 2 \end{bmatrix}\begin{bmatrix} x \\ y \\ z \end{bmatrix} = \begin{bmatrix} 3 \\ 1 \\ 0 \end{bmatrix}$$

$$\Rightarrow \quad x + y + z = 3$$

$$y + 2z = 1$$

$$2z = 0$$

$$\Rightarrow \quad x = 2,\ y = 1,\ z = 0$$

Example 2. Solve the system of equations by using matrix method:

$$2x_1 + x_2 + 2x_3 + x_4 = 6$$
$$6x_1 - 6x_2 + 6x_3 + 12x_4 = 36$$
$$4x_1 + 3x_2 + 3x_3 - 3x_4 = -1$$
$$2x_1 + 2x_2 - x_3 + x_4 = 10$$

Solution:

$$\text{Coefficient matrix } A = \begin{bmatrix} 2 & 1 & 2 & 1 \\ 6 & -6 & 6 & 12 \\ 4 & 3 & 3 & -3 \\ 2 & 2 & -1 & 1 \end{bmatrix}$$

$\because \quad |A| \neq 0$

$\therefore \quad \rho(A) = 4$

$$\text{Augmented matrix } [A:B] = \left[\begin{array}{cccc:c} 2 & 1 & 2 & 1 & 6 \\ 6 & -6 & 6 & 12 & 36 \\ 4 & 3 & 3 & -3 & -1 \\ 2 & 2 & 1 & 1 & 10 \end{array}\right]$$

Operating $R_{21}(-3)$, $R_{31}(-2)$, $R_{41}(-1)$

$$\sim \begin{bmatrix} 2 & 1 & 2 & 1 & \vdots & 6 \\ 0 & -9 & 0 & 9 & \vdots & 18 \\ 0 & 1 & -1 & -5 & \vdots & -13 \\ 0 & 1 & -3 & 0 & \vdots & 4 \end{bmatrix}$$

Operating $R_2\left(-\frac{1}{9}\right)$

$$\sim \begin{bmatrix} 2 & 1 & 2 & 1 & \vdots & 6 \\ 0 & 1 & 0 & -1 & \vdots & -2 \\ 0 & 1 & -1 & -5 & \vdots & -13 \\ 0 & 1 & -3 & 0 & \vdots & 4 \end{bmatrix}$$

Operating $R_{32}(-1)$, $R_{12}(-1)$

$$\sim \begin{bmatrix} 2 & 1 & 2 & 1 & \vdots & 6 \\ 0 & 1 & 0 & -1 & \vdots & -2 \\ 0 & 0 & -1 & -4 & \vdots & -11 \\ 0 & 0 & -3 & 1 & \vdots & 6 \end{bmatrix}$$

Operating $R_{43}(-3)$

$$\sim \begin{bmatrix} 2 & 1 & 2 & 1 & \vdots & 6 \\ 0 & 1 & 0 & -1 & \vdots & -2 \\ 0 & 0 & -1 & -4 & \vdots & -11 \\ 0 & 0 & 0 & 13 & \vdots & 39 \end{bmatrix}$$

which is Echelon Form.

$\therefore \quad \rho[A:B] = 4$

$\because \quad \rho[A:B] = \rho[A] = 4$ (number of variables)

$\therefore$ The system of equations is consistent and has a unique solution.

Equivalent system of equations is

$$\begin{bmatrix} 2 & 1 & 2 & 1 \\ 0 & 1 & 0 & -1 \\ 0 & 0 & -1 & -4 \\ 0 & 0 & 0 & 13 \end{bmatrix} \begin{bmatrix} x_1 \\ x_2 \\ x_3 \\ x_4 \end{bmatrix} = \begin{bmatrix} 6 \\ -2 \\ -11 \\ 39 \end{bmatrix}$$

$$\Rightarrow \quad 2x_1 + x_2 + 2x_3 + x_4 = 6$$

$$x_2 - x_4 = -2$$

$$-x_3 - 4x_4 = -11$$

$$13x_4 = 39$$

On solving, we get

$$x_1 = 2, x_2 = 1, x_3 = -1, x_4 = 3$$

Example 3. Using matrix method, show that the equations

$$3x + 3y + 2z = 1$$

$$x + 2y = 4$$

$$10y + 3z = -2$$

$$2x - 3y - z = 5$$

are consistent and hence obtain the solutions for x, y and z.

Solution:

$$\text{Coefficient matrix } A = \begin{bmatrix} 3 & 3 & 2 \\ 1 & 2 & 0 \\ 0 & 10 & 3 \\ 2 & -3 & -1 \end{bmatrix}$$

$$\because \quad \text{Minor} \begin{vmatrix} 1 & 2 & 0 \\ 0 & 10 & 3 \\ 2 & -3 & -1 \end{vmatrix} \neq 0$$

$$\therefore \quad \rho(A) = 3$$

$$\text{Augmented matrix } [A:B] = \begin{bmatrix} 3 & 3 & 2 & \vdots & 1 \\ 1 & 2 & 0 & \vdots & 4 \\ 0 & 10 & 3 & \vdots & -2 \\ 2 & -3 & -1 & \vdots & 5 \end{bmatrix}$$

Operating R_{12}

$$\sim \begin{bmatrix} 1 & 2 & 0 & \vdots & 4 \\ 3 & 3 & 2 & \vdots & 1 \\ 0 & 10 & 3 & \vdots & -2 \\ 2 & -3 & -1 & \vdots & 5 \end{bmatrix}$$

Operating $R_{21}(-3)$, $R_{41}(-2)$

$$\sim \begin{bmatrix} 1 & 2 & 0 & \vdots & 4 \\ 0 & -3 & 2 & \vdots & -11 \\ 0 & 10 & 3 & \vdots & -2 \\ 0 & -7 & -1 & \vdots & -3 \end{bmatrix}$$

Operating $R_{32}(3)$, $R_{12}(-2)$

$$\sim \begin{bmatrix} 1 & 2 & 0 & \vdots & 4 \\ 0 & -3 & 2 & \vdots & -11 \\ 0 & 1 & 9 & \vdots & -35 \\ 0 & -1 & -5 & \vdots & 19 \end{bmatrix}$$

Operating $R_{13}(-2)$, $R_{23}(3)$, $R_{43}(1)$

$$\sim \begin{bmatrix} 1 & 0 & -18 & \vdots & 74 \\ 0 & 0 & 29 & \vdots & -116 \\ 0 & 1 & 9 & \vdots & -35 \\ 0 & 0 & 4 & \vdots & -16 \end{bmatrix}$$

Operating R_{23}, $R_4\left(\frac{1}{4}\right)$

$$\sim \begin{bmatrix} 1 & 0 & -18 & \vdots & 74 \\ 0 & 1 & 9 & \vdots & -35 \\ 0 & 0 & 29 & \vdots & -116 \\ 0 & 0 & 1 & \vdots & -4 \end{bmatrix}$$

Operating $R_{43}\left(-\frac{1}{29}\right)$

$$\sim \begin{bmatrix} 1 & 0 & -18 & \vdots & 74 \\ 0 & 1 & 9 & \vdots & -35 \\ 0 & 0 & 29 & \vdots & -116 \\ 0 & 0 & 0 & \vdots & 0 \end{bmatrix}$$

which is Echelon Form.

$\therefore$ $\rho[A:B] = 3$

$\because$ $\rho[A:B] = \rho[A] = 3$ (no. of variables)

$\therefore$ The given system of equations is consistent and has a unique solution.

Equivalent system of equations is

$$\begin{bmatrix} 1 & 0 & -18 \\ 0 & 1 & 9 \\ 0 & 0 & 29 \\ 0 & 0 & 0 \end{bmatrix} \begin{bmatrix} x \\ y \\ z \end{bmatrix} = \begin{bmatrix} 74 \\ -35 \\ -116 \\ 0 \end{bmatrix}$$

$\Rightarrow$ $x - 18z = 74$

$y + 9z = -35$

$29z = -116$

$\Rightarrow$ $x = 2, y = 1, z = -4$

Example 4. Show that the following system of equations is inconsistent:

$$x_1 - 2x_2 + x_3 - x_4 + 1 = 0$$

$3x_1 - 2x_3 + 3x_4 + 4 = 0$

$5x_1 - 4x_2 + x_4 + 3 = 0$

Solution:

$$\text{Coefficient matrix } A = \begin{bmatrix} 1 & -2 & 1 & -1 \\ 3 & 0 & -2 & 3 \\ 5 & -4 & 0 & 1 \end{bmatrix}$$

$$\text{Augmented matrix } [A:B] = \begin{bmatrix} 1 & -2 & 1 & -1 & \vdots & -1 \\ 3 & 0 & -2 & 3 & \vdots & -4 \\ 5 & -4 & 0 & 1 & \vdots & -3 \end{bmatrix}$$

Operating $R_{21}(-3)$, $R_{31}(-5)$

$$\sim \begin{bmatrix} 1 & -2 & 1 & -1 & \vdots & -1 \\ 0 & 6 & -5 & 6 & \vdots & -1 \\ 0 & 6 & -5 & 6 & \vdots & 2 \end{bmatrix}$$

Operating $R_{32}(-1)$

$$\sim \begin{bmatrix} 1 & -2 & 1 & -1 & \vdots & -1 \\ 0 & 6 & -5 & 6 & \vdots & -1 \\ 0 & 0 & 0 & 0 & \vdots & 3 \end{bmatrix}$$

which is Echelon Form.

Clearly, $\rho(A) = 2$

$\rho(B) = 3$

$\therefore\ \rho(A) \neq \rho(B)$

Hence, the given system of equations is inconsistent.

Example 5. Investigate for consistency of the following equations and if possible, find the solutions:

$4x - 2y + 6z = 8$

$x + y - 3z = -1$

$15x - 3y + 9z = 21$

Solution:

$$\text{Coefficient matrix } A = \begin{bmatrix} 4 & -2 & 6 \\ 1 & 1 & -3 \\ 15 & -3 & 9 \end{bmatrix}$$

$$\text{Augmented matrix } [A:B] = \begin{bmatrix} 4 & -2 & 6 & \vdots & 8 \\ 1 & 1 & -3 & \vdots & -1 \\ 15 & -3 & 9 & \vdots & 21 \end{bmatrix}$$

Operating R_{12}

$$\sim \begin{bmatrix} 1 & 1 & -3 & \vdots & -1 \\ 4 & -2 & 6 & \vdots & 8 \\ 15 & -3 & 9 & \vdots & 21 \end{bmatrix}$$

Operating $R_{21}(-4)$, $R_{31}(-15)$

$$\sim \begin{bmatrix} 1 & 1 & -3 & \vdots & -1 \\ 0 & -6 & 18 & \vdots & 12 \\ 0 & -18 & 54 & \vdots & 36 \end{bmatrix}$$

Operating $R_{32}(-3)$

$$\sim \begin{bmatrix} 1 & 1 & -3 & \vdots & -1 \\ 0 & -6 & 18 & \vdots & 12 \\ 0 & 0 & 0 & \vdots & 0 \end{bmatrix}$$

which is Echelon Form.

Clearly, $\rho(A) = 2 = \rho[A:B] <$ (no. of variables)

Hence, the given system of equations is consistent and has an infinite number of solutions.

Equivalent system of equations is

$$\begin{bmatrix} 1 & 1 & -3 \\ 0 & -6 & 18 \\ 0 & 0 & 0 \end{bmatrix} \begin{bmatrix} x \\ y \\ z \end{bmatrix} = \begin{bmatrix} -1 \\ 12 \\ 0 \end{bmatrix}$$

$$\Rightarrow x + y - 3z = -1 \qquad \text{... (6.3)}$$

$$-6y + 18z = 12 \qquad \text{... (6.4)}$$

Clearly, r (=2) variables can be expressed in terms of $n - r$ (= 3 – 2 = 1) variable which is arbitrary.

Let $z = k$

Then, from Eq. (6.4),

$$-6y + 18k = 12$$

$$\Rightarrow 6y = 18k - 12$$

$$\Rightarrow y = 3k - 2$$

From Eq. (6.3),

$$x + 3k - 2 - 3k = -1$$

$$\Rightarrow x = 1$$

Hence, the required solutions are

$$x = 1$$

$$y = 3k - 2$$

$$z = k$$

where k is arbitrary.

Example 6. Solve the following system of equations:

$$x_1 - x_2 + x_3 = 0$$

$$x_1 + 2x_2 - x_3 = 0$$

$$2x_1 + x_2 + 3x_3 = 0$$

Solution:

$$\text{Coefficient matrix } A = \begin{bmatrix} 1 & -1 & 1 \\ 1 & 2 & -1 \\ 2 & 1 & 3 \end{bmatrix}$$

Operating $R_{21}(-1)$, $R_{31}(-2)$

$$\sim \begin{bmatrix} 1 & -1 & 1 \\ 0 & 3 & -2 \\ 0 & 3 & 1 \end{bmatrix}$$

Operating $R_{32}(-1)$

$$\sim \begin{bmatrix} 1 & -1 & 1 \\ 0 & 3 & -2 \\ 0 & 0 & 3 \end{bmatrix}$$

Operating $R_3\left(\frac{1}{3}\right)$

$$\sim \begin{bmatrix} 1 & -1 & 1 \\ 0 & 3 & -2 \\ 0 & 0 & 1 \end{bmatrix}$$

$\therefore \quad \rho(A) = 3 =$ No. of variables

Hence, the given system of equations has only trivial solutions given by

$x_1 = 0 = x_2 = x_3$

Example 7. Show that the homogeneous system of equations:

$$x + y \cos \gamma + z \cos \beta = 0$$
$$x \cos \gamma + y + z \cos \alpha = 0$$
$$x \cos \beta + y \cos \alpha + z = 0$$

has non-trivial solution if $\alpha + \beta + \gamma = 0$.

Solution: If the given system of homogeneous equations has non-trivial solutions, then the coefficient matrix must be singular.

$$\therefore \quad \begin{vmatrix} 1 & \cos\gamma & \cos\beta \\ \cos\gamma & 1 & \cos\alpha \\ \cos\beta & \cos\alpha & 1 \end{vmatrix} = 0$$

$$\Rightarrow \; 1-\cos^2\alpha + \cos\gamma(\cos\alpha\cos\beta - \cos\gamma)$$
$$+ \cos\beta(\cos\gamma\cos\alpha - \cos\beta) = 0$$

$$\Rightarrow \; \sin^2\alpha - \cos^2\beta - \cos^2\gamma + 2\cos\alpha\cos\beta\cos\gamma = 0$$

$$\Rightarrow \; -\left(\cos^2\beta - \sin^2\alpha\right) - \cos^2\gamma + 2\cos\alpha\cos\beta\cos\gamma = 0$$

$$\Rightarrow \; -\cos(\beta+\alpha)\cos(\beta-\alpha)-\cos^2\gamma + 2\cos\alpha\cos\beta\cos\gamma = 0$$

$$\Rightarrow \; -\cos(-\gamma)\cos(\beta-\alpha)-\cos^2\gamma+2\cos\alpha\cos\beta\cos\gamma = 0 \quad | \because \alpha+\beta+\gamma = 0$$

$$\Rightarrow \; -\cos\gamma\cos(\beta-\alpha)-\cos^2\gamma+2\cos\alpha\cos\beta\cos\gamma = 0$$

$$\Rightarrow \; -\cos\gamma\left[\cos(\beta-\alpha)+\cos\gamma\right]+2\cos\alpha\cos\beta\cos\gamma = 0$$

$$\Rightarrow \; -\cos\gamma\left[\cos(\beta-\alpha)-\cos\left(\pi-\overline{\alpha+\beta}\right)\right] + 2\cos\alpha\cos\beta\cos\gamma = 0 \quad | \because \alpha+\beta+\gamma = 0$$

$$\Rightarrow \; -\cos\gamma\left[\cos(\beta-\alpha)+\cos(\alpha+\beta)\right] + 2\cos\alpha\cos\beta\cos\gamma = 0$$

$$\Rightarrow \; -\cos\gamma\,(2\cos\alpha\cos\beta)+2\cos\alpha\cos\beta\cos\gamma = 0$$

$\Rightarrow \; 0 = 0$ which is true.

Hence, the result.

Example 8. Solve the following equations using matrix method:

$$x_1 + 3x_2 + 2x_3 = 0$$
$$2x_1 - x_2 + 3x_3 = 0$$
$$3x_1 - 5x_2 + 4x_3 = 0$$
$$x_1 + 17x_2 + 4x_3 = 0$$

Solution:

$$\text{Coefficient matrix } A = \begin{bmatrix} 1 & 3 & 2 \\ 2 & -1 & 3 \\ 3 & -5 & 4 \\ 1 & 17 & 4 \end{bmatrix}$$

Operating $R_{21}(-2)$, $R_{31}(-3)$, $R_{41}(-1)$

$$\sim \begin{bmatrix} 1 & 3 & 2 \\ 0 & -7 & -1 \\ 0 & -14 & -2 \\ 0 & 14 & 2 \end{bmatrix}$$

Operating $R_{32}(-2)$, $R_{42}(2)$

$$\sim \begin{bmatrix} 1 & 3 & 2 \\ 0 & -7 & -1 \\ 0 & 0 & 0 \\ 0 & 0 & 0 \end{bmatrix}$$

which is Echelon Form.

$\therefore\ \rho(A) = 2 <$ no. of unknowns

Hence, the given system has infinite number of non-trivial solutions given by

$$x_1 + 3x_2 + 2x_3 = 0 \qquad \text{... (6.5)}$$

$$-7x_2 - x_3 = 0 \qquad \text{... (6.6)}$$

Let $x_2 = k$. Then from Eq. (6.6),

$$-7k - x_3 = 0$$

$$\Rightarrow x_3 = -7k$$

$\therefore$ From Eq. (6.5),

$$x_1 + 3k - 14k = 0$$

$$\Rightarrow x_1 = 11k$$

Hence, the required solutions are

$$x_1 = 11k$$

$$x_2 = k$$

$$x_3 = -7k$$

where k is arbitrary. Different values of k give different solutions thus making the number of solutions infinite.

Example 9. Solve completely the following system of equations:

$$2w + 3x - y - z = 0$$

$$4w - 6x - 2y + 2z = 0$$

$$-6w + 12x + 3y - 4z = 0$$

Solution:

$$\text{Coefficient matrix } A = \begin{bmatrix} 2 & 3 & -1 & -1 \\ 4 & -6 & -2 & 2 \\ -6 & 12 & 3 & -4 \end{bmatrix}$$

Operating $R_{21}(-2)$, $R_{31}(3)$

$$\sim \begin{bmatrix} 2 & 3 & -1 & -1 \\ 0 & -12 & 0 & 4 \\ 0 & 21 & 0 & -7 \end{bmatrix}$$

Operating $R_2\left(-\frac{1}{4}\right)$, $R_3\left(\frac{1}{7}\right)$

$$\sim \begin{bmatrix} 2 & 3 & -1 & -1 \\ 0 & 3 & 0 & -1 \\ 0 & 3 & 0 & -1 \end{bmatrix}$$

Operating $R_{32}(-1)$

$$\sim \begin{bmatrix} 2 & 3 & -1 & -1 \\ 0 & 3 & 0 & -1 \\ 0 & 0 & 0 & 0 \end{bmatrix}$$

$\therefore\ \rho(A) = 2 < 4$ (number of variables)

Hence, the given system of equations is consistent and has an infinite number of solutions. Here, r (= 2) variables can be expressed in terms of $n - r$ (= 4 – 2 = 2) independent variables which are arbitrary.

The equivalent system of equations is

$$2w + 3x - y - z = 0 \qquad \text{... (6.7)}$$

$$3x - z = 0 \qquad \text{... (6.8)}$$

Take $z = k_1$, $y = k_2$

Then Eq. (6.8) gives

$$3x - k_1 = 0$$

$$\Rightarrow\ x = \frac{k_1}{3}$$

$\therefore$ Equation (6.7) gives

$$2w + k_1 - k_2 - k_1 = 0$$

$$\Rightarrow\ w = \frac{k_2}{2}$$

Hence, the complete solution is

$$x = \frac{k_1}{3}$$
$$y = k_2$$
$$z = k_1$$
$$w = \frac{k_2}{2}$$

Example 10. Investigate, for what values of λ and μ do the system of equations:

$$x + y + z = 6$$
$$x + 2y + 3z = 10$$
$$x + 2y + \lambda z = \mu$$

have

(i) no solution ?

(ii) unique solution ?

(iii) an infinity of solutions ?

Solution:

$$\text{Coefficient matrix } A = \begin{bmatrix} 1 & 1 & 1 \\ 1 & 2 & 3 \\ 1 & 2 & \lambda \end{bmatrix}$$

$$\text{Augmented matrix } [A:B] = \begin{bmatrix} 1 & 1 & 1 & : & 6 \\ 1 & 2 & 3 & : & 10 \\ 1 & 2 & \lambda & : & \mu \end{bmatrix}$$

Operating $R_{21}(-1)$, $R_{31}(-1)$

$$\sim \begin{bmatrix} 1 & 1 & 1 & : & 6 \\ 0 & 1 & 2 & : & 4 \\ 0 & 1 & \lambda - 1 & : & \mu - 6 \end{bmatrix}$$

Operating $R_{32}(-1)$

$$\sim \left[\begin{array}{ccc:c} 1 & 1 & 1 & 6 \\ 0 & 1 & 2 & 4 \\ 0 & 0 & \lambda - 3 & \mu - 10 \end{array}\right]$$

Now the following cases arise:

Case I. *When* $\lambda = 3$, $\mu \neq 10$

Then,

$$\rho(A) = 2$$
$$\rho[A:B] = 3$$
$$\therefore \quad \rho(A) \neq \rho[A:B]$$

$\therefore$ The system has no solution.

Case II. *When* $\lambda \neq 3$, μ *may have any value*

Then,

$$\rho(A) = \rho[A:B] = 3 = \text{No. of unknowns}$$

$\therefore$ The system has a unique solution.

Case III. *When* $\lambda = 3$, $\mu = 10$

Then,

$$\rho(A) = \rho[A:B] = 2 < \text{No. of variables}$$

$\therefore$ The system has an infinity of solutions.

Example 11. For what values of k, the equations

$$x + y + z = 1$$
$$2x + y + 4z = k$$
$$4x + y + 10z = k^2$$

have a solution and solve them completely in each case.

Solution:

$$\text{Coefficient matrix } A = \begin{bmatrix} 1 & 1 & 1 \\ 2 & 1 & 4 \\ 4 & 1 & 10 \end{bmatrix}$$

$$\text{Augmented matrix } [A:B] = \begin{bmatrix} 1 & 1 & 1 & : & 1 \\ 2 & 1 & 4 & : & k \\ 4 & 1 & 10 & : & k^2 \end{bmatrix}$$

Operating $R_{21}(-2)$, $R_{41}(-4)$

$$\sim \begin{bmatrix} 1 & 1 & 1 & : & 1 \\ 0 & -1 & 2 & : & k-2 \\ 0 & -3 & 6 & : & k^2-4 \end{bmatrix}$$

Operating $R_{32}(-3)$

$$\sim \begin{bmatrix} 1 & 1 & 1 & : & 1 \\ 0 & -1 & 2 & : & k-2 \\ 0 & 0 & 0 & : & k^2-3k+2 \end{bmatrix}$$

$\rho(A) = 2$

If the system is to have solution, then

$\rho[A:B] = 2$ for which $k^2 - 3k + 2 = 0$

which implies that $k = 1, 2$

Here, two variables can be expressed in terms of one independent variable which is arbitrary.

The equivalent system of equations is

$$\begin{bmatrix} 1 & 1 & 1 \\ 0 & -1 & 2 \\ 0 & 0 & 0 \end{bmatrix} \begin{bmatrix} x \\ y \\ z \end{bmatrix} = \begin{bmatrix} 1 \\ k-2 \\ k^2-3k+2 \end{bmatrix}$$

$\Rightarrow x + y + z = 1$ ... (6.9)

$-y + 2z = k - 2$ ... (6.10)

Case I. *When* $k = 1$

Then, we have from Eqs. (6.9) and (6.10),

$x + y + z = 1$ ... (6.11)

$-y + 2z = -1$ ... (6.12)

Let $y = \lambda$

Then, from Eq. (6.12),

$$-\lambda + 2z = -1$$

$$\Rightarrow 2z = \lambda - 1$$

$$\Rightarrow z = \frac{\lambda - 1}{2}$$

From Eq. (6.11),

$$x + \lambda + \frac{\lambda - 1}{2} = 1$$

$$\Rightarrow x + \frac{3\lambda - 1}{2} = 1$$

$$\Rightarrow x = 1 - \frac{3\lambda - 1}{2}$$

$$\Rightarrow x = \frac{3(1 - \lambda)}{2}$$

Hence, the complete solution is

$$x = \frac{3(1 - \lambda)}{2}$$

$$y = \lambda$$

$$z = \frac{\lambda - 1}{2}$$

where λ is arbitrary.

Case II. *When* $k = 2$

Then, we have from Eqs. (6.9) and (6.10),

$$x + y + z = 1 \quad \text{... (6.13)}$$

$$-y + 2z = 0 \quad \text{... (6.14)}$$

Put $z = \mu$

Then from Eq. (6.14)

$$-y + 2\mu = 0$$

$$\Rightarrow y = 2\mu$$

From Eq. (6.13),

$$x + 2\mu + \mu = 1$$

$$\Rightarrow x = 1 - 3\mu$$

Hence, the complete solution is

$$x = 1 - 3\mu$$
$$y = 2\mu$$
$$z = \mu$$

where μ is arbitrary.

Example 12. Show that the equations

$$-2x + y + z = a$$
$$x - 2y + z = b$$
$$x + y - 2z = c$$

have no solution unless $a + b + c = 0$. In which case they have infinitely many solutions? Find these solution when $a = 1$, $b = 1$, $c = 2$.

Solution:

$$\text{Coefficient matrix } A = \begin{bmatrix} -2 & 1 & 1 \\ 1 & -2 & 1 \\ 1 & 1 & -2 \end{bmatrix}$$

$$\text{Augmented matrix } [A:B] = \begin{bmatrix} -2 & 1 & 1 & \vdots & a \\ 1 & -2 & 1 & \vdots & b \\ 1 & 1 & -2 & \vdots & c \end{bmatrix}$$

Operating R_{13}

$$\sim \begin{bmatrix} 1 & 1 & -2 & \vdots & c \\ 1 & -2 & 1 & \vdots & b \\ -2 & 1 & 1 & \vdots & a \end{bmatrix}$$

Operating $R_{21}(-1)$, $R_{31}(2)$

$$\sim \begin{bmatrix} 1 & 1 & -2 & \vdots & c \\ 0 & -3 & 3 & \vdots & b-c \\ 0 & 3 & -3 & \vdots & a+2c \end{bmatrix}$$

Operating $R_{32}(1)$

$$\sim \left[\begin{array}{ccc:c} 1 & 1 & -2 & c \\ 0 & -3 & 3 & b-c \\ 0 & 0 & 0 & a+b+c \end{array}\right]$$

Case I. *When* $a + b + c \neq 0$

Then,

$$\rho(A) = 2, \rho[A:B] = 3$$

$$\therefore \rho(A) \neq \rho[A:B]$$

Hence, the given system of equations is inconsistent and consequently has no solution.

Case II. *When* $a + b + c = 0$

Then,

$$\rho(A) = \rho[A:B] = 2 < \text{Number of variables}$$

Hence, the given system of equations is consistent and has an infinite number of solutions.

Equivalent system of equations is

$$x + y - 2z = c = -2 \quad | \because c = -2 \quad \ldots (6.15)$$

$$-3y + 3z = b - c = 3 \quad | \because b = 1, c = -2 \quad \ldots (6.16)$$

Here, two variables can be expressed in terms of $3 - 2 = 1$ variable which is arbitrary.

Let $z = k$

Then Eq. (6.16) gives

$$-3y + 3k = 3 \Rightarrow y = k - 1$$

Also, Eq. (6.15) gives

$$x + k - 1 - 2k = -2$$

$$\Rightarrow x = k - 1$$

Hence, the solutions are

$x = k - 1, y = k - 1, z = k$ where k is arbitrary.

EXERCISE 6.1

1. Solve by matrix method:

(a) $x_1 - x_2 + x_3 = 2$

$3x_1 - x_2 + 2x_3 = -6$
$3x_1 + x_2 + x_3 = -18$

(b) $x + 2y + 3z = 14$
$3x + y + 2z = 11$
$2x + 3y + z = 11$

(c) $2x - y + 3z = 9$
$x + y + z = 6$
$x - y + z = 2$

(d) $x + y + z = 6$
$x + 2y + 3z = 14$
$x + 4y + 9z = 36$

(e) $x_1 + x_2 + x_3 = 0$
$2x_1 + 5x_2 + 6x_3 = 0$

(f) $x + y + z = 6$
$x - y + z = 2$
$2x + y - z = 1$

(g) $x + y + z = 3$
$x + 2y + 3z = 4$
$x + 4y + 9z = 6$

(h) $x + 2y + 3z = 4$
$2x + 3y + 8z = 7$
$x - y + 9z = 1$

(i) $4x + 2y + z + 34 = 0$
$6x + 3y + 4z + 74 = 0$
$2x + y + 4 = 0$

(j) $x_1 + x_2 + x_3 + x_4 = 1$
$2x_1 - x_2 + x_3 - 2x_4 = 2$
$3x_1 + 2x_2 - x_3 - x_4 = 3$

(k) $7x - 4y = 12$
$-4x + 12y - 6z = 0$
$-6y + 14z = 0$

(l) $x + y + z = 8$
$x - y + 2z = 6$
$3x + 5y - 7z = 14$

(m) $x + y + z = 6$
$x - y + 2z = 5$
$3x + y + z = 8$

(n) $x + 2y + 3z = 1$
$2x + 3y + 2z = 2$
$3x + 3y + 4z = 1$

(o) $x_1 + 2x_2 + x_3 = 0$
$3x_1 + x_2 - 2x_3 = 1$
$4x_1 - 3x_2 - x_3 = 3$
$2x_1 + 4x_2 + 2x_3 = 4$

(p) $2x + 4y - z = 9$
$3x - y + 5z = 5$
$8x + 2y + 9z = 19$

(q) $x + 3y + 2z = 0$
$x + 4y + 3z = 0$
$x + 5y + 4z = 0$

(r) $x + y + z = 0$
$4x + 5y + 2z = 0$
$2x + 3y = 0$

(s) $x + y + z = 0$
$2x - y - 3z = 0$
$3x - 5y + 4z = 0$
$x + 17y + 4z = 0$

(t) $2x + y + 5z + t = 5$
$x + y + 3z - 4t = -1$
$3x + 6y - 2z + t = 8$
$2x + 2y + 2z - 3t = 2$

(u) $2x - 2y + 5z + 3w = 0$
$4x - y + z + w = 0$
$3x - 2y + 3z + 4w = 0$
$x - 3y + 7z + 6w = 0$

(v) $3x + 4y - z - 6w = 0$
$2x + 3y + 2z - 3w = 0$
$2x + y - 14z - 9w = 0$
$x + 3y + 3z + 3w = 0$

(w) $x_1 + 2x_2 + x_3 = 4$
$x_1 - x_2 + x_3 = 5$
$2x_1 + 3x_2 - x_3 = 1$

(x) $2x - y + 3z = 8$
$-x + 2y + z = 4$
$3x + y - 4z = 0$

(y) $9x + 7y + 3z = 6$
$5x - y - 4z = 1$
$6x + 8y + 2z = 4$

(z) $x + 2y - z = 3$
$3x - y + 2z = 1$
$2x - 2y + 3z = 2$
$x - y + z = -1$

2. Test whether the following system of equations possesses a non-trivial solution:

$x_1 + x_2 + 2x_3 + 3x_4 = 0$
$3x_1 + 4x_2 + 7x_3 + 10x_4 = 0$
$5x_1 + 7x_2 + 11x_3 + 17x_4 = 0$
$6x_1 + 8x_2 + 13x_3 + 16x_4 = 0$

3. Find the values of k for which the system of equations

$(3k - 8)x + 3y + 3z = 0$
$3x + (3k - 8)y + 3z = 0$

$3x + 3y + (3k - 8)z = 0$

has a non-trivial solution.

4. If $A = \begin{bmatrix} -1 & 2 & 1 \\ 3 & -1 & 2 \\ 0 & 1 & \lambda \end{bmatrix}$, find the values of λ for which the matrix equation $AX = O$ has

(i) a unique solution

(ii) more than one solution.

5. Prove that the following system of equations is consistent and has infinite number of solutions:

$x_1 + 2x_2 + 3x_3 + 4x_4 = 5$

$6x_1 + 7x_2 + 8x_3 + 9x_4 = 10$

$11x_1 + 12x_2 + 13x_3 + 14x_4 = 15$

$16x_1 + 17x_2 + 18x_3 + 19x_4 = 20$

$21x_1 + 22x_2 + 23x_3 + 24x_4 = 25$

6. Determine the values of λ and μ such that the system of equations

$2x - 5y + 2z = 8$

$2x + 4y + 6z = 5$

$x + 2y + \lambda z = \mu$

has

(i) no solution

(ii) a unique solution

(iii) an infinite number of solutions.

7. Determine the values of a and b for which the system

$\begin{bmatrix} 3 & -2 & 1 \\ 5 & -8 & 9 \\ 2 & 1 & a \end{bmatrix} \begin{bmatrix} x \\ y \\ z \end{bmatrix} = \begin{bmatrix} b \\ 3 \\ -1 \end{bmatrix}$ has

(i) a unique solution

(ii) no solution

(iii) infinitely many solutions.

8. Find value of λ for which the following system of equations is consistent and has non-trivial solutions. Solve equations for all such values of λ:

$$(\lambda - 1)x + (3\lambda + 1)y + 2\lambda z = 0$$
$$(\lambda - 1)x + (4\lambda - 2)y + (\lambda + 3)z = 0$$
$$2x + (3\lambda + 1)y + 3(\lambda - 1)z = 0$$

9. Solve the following equations by matrix method:

$$\lambda x + 2y - 2z - 1 = 0$$
$$4x + 2\lambda y - z - 2 = 0$$
$$6x + 6y + \lambda z - 3 = 0$$

considering specially the case when $\lambda = 2$.

OR

Find the value of λ such that the following equations have unique solution:

$$\lambda x + 2y - 2z - 1 = 0$$
$$4x + 2\lambda y - z - 2 = 0$$
$$6x + 6y + \lambda z - 3 = 0$$

and use matrix method to solve these equations when $\lambda = 2$.

10. Solve

$$x - 2y + z - w = 0$$
$$x + y - 2z + 3w = 0$$
$$4x + y - 5z + 8w = 0$$
$$5x - 7y + 2z - w = 0$$

11. Prove that the matrix equation

$$\begin{bmatrix} 3 & 4 & 5 & 6 \\ 4 & 5 & 6 & 7 \\ 5 & 6 & 7 & 8 \\ 10 & 11 & 12 & 13 \\ 15 & 16 & 17 & 18 \end{bmatrix} \begin{bmatrix} x_1 \\ x_2 \\ x_3 \\ x_4 \end{bmatrix} = \begin{bmatrix} 7 \\ 8 \\ 9 \\ 14 \\ 19 \end{bmatrix}$$

is consistent and has infinitely many solutions.

12. Find the values of λ for which the equations

$(11 - \lambda)x - 4y - 7z = 0$

$7x - (\lambda + 2)y - 5z = 0$

$10x - 4y - (6 + \lambda)z = 0$

possesses a non-trivial solution.

For these value of λ, find the solutions also.

ANSWERS

1. (a) $x_1 = -\dfrac{x_3}{2} - 4$

$x_2 = \dfrac{x_3}{2} - 6$, x_3 being arbitrary

(b) $x = 1$

$y = 2$

$z = 3$

(c) $x = 1$

$y = 2$

$z = 3$

(d) $x = 1$

$y = 2$

$z = 3$

(e) $x_1 = \dfrac{k}{3}$

$x_2 = -\dfrac{4k}{3}$

$x_3 = k$, k being arbitrary

(f) $x = 1$

$y = 2$

$z = 3$

(g) $x = 2$

$y = 1$

$z = 0$

(h) $x = 2 - 7k$

$y = 1 + 2k$

$z = k$

(i) $x = \frac{k_2 - k_1}{2}$

$y = k_1$

$z = k_2$

$u = -k_2$; k_1 and k_2 being arbitrary

(j) $x_1 = -\frac{11 + 9k}{11}$

$x_2 = -\frac{12k}{11}$

$x_3 = -\frac{8k}{11}$

$x_4 = k$; k being arbitrary

(k) $x = \frac{396}{175}$

$y = \frac{24}{25}$

$z = \frac{72}{175}$

(l) $x = 5$

$y = \frac{5}{3}$

$z = \frac{4}{3}$

(m) $x = 1$

$y = 2$

$z = 3$

(n) $x = -\frac{3}{7}$

$y = \frac{8}{7}$

$z = -\frac{2}{7}$

(o) $x_1 = 1$

$x_2 = 0$

$x_3 = 1$

(p) $x = -\frac{19}{14}k + \frac{29}{14}$

$y = \frac{13}{14}k$

$z = k$; k being arbitrary

(q) $x = k$

$y = -k$

$z = k$

(r) $x = -3k$

$y = 2k$

$z = k$

(s) $x = 0 = y = z$

(t) $x = 2$

$y = \frac{1}{5}$

$z = 0$

$t = \frac{4}{5}$

(u) $x = -\frac{103}{9}w$

$y = 4w$

$z = \frac{7}{9}w$, w being arbitrary

(v) $x = 11k_1 + 6k_2$

$y = -8k_1 - 3k_2$

$z = k_1$

$w = k_2$, k_1 and k_2 being arbitrary

(w) $x_1 = \frac{20}{9}$

$$x_2 = -\frac{1}{3}$$

$$x_3 = \frac{22}{9}$$

(x) $x = 2$
$y = 2$
$z = 2$

(y) $x = 1$
$y = 0$
$z = -1$

(z) $x = -1$
$y = 4$
$z = 4$

2. No

3. $K = \frac{2}{3}, \frac{11}{3}, \frac{11}{3}$

4. (i) $\lambda \neq 1$
(ii) $\lambda = 1$

6. (i) $\lambda = 3, \mu \neq \frac{5}{2}$
(ii) $\lambda \neq 3$, μ may have any value
(iii) $\lambda = 3, \ \mu = \frac{5}{2}$

7. (i) a $\neq 3$, b may have any value
(ii) $a = -3, \ b \neq \frac{1}{3}$
(iii) $a = -3, b = \frac{1}{3}$

8. $\lambda = 0$; $x = k_1$, $y = k_1$, $z = k_1$; k_1 being arbitrary
$\lambda = 3$; $x = -5k_3 - 3k_2$
$y = k_3$
$z = k_2$; k_2, k_3 being arbitrary

9. $x = \frac{1}{2} + k_1 - k_2$

$y = k_2$

$z = k_1$; k_1 and k_2 being arbitrary

10. $x = \lambda - \frac{5}{3}\mu$

$y = \lambda - \frac{4}{3}\mu$

$z = \lambda$

$w = \mu$; λ and μ being arbitrary.

12. $\lambda = 0$; $x = k_1$, $y = k_1$, $z = k_1$; k_1 being arbitrary

$\lambda = 1$; $x = k_2$, $y = -k_2$, $z = 2k_2$; k_2 being arbitrary

$\lambda = 2$; $\lambda = 2k_3$, $y = k_3$, $z = 2k_3$; k_3 being arbitrary

7 LINEAR INDEPENDENCE AND DEPENDENCE OF VECTORS

7.1. Ordered Pair of Numbers

Let a, b be two different numbers. Then we can write them in two different ways:

(i) first a then b

(ii) first b then a

In case (i), we represent them as (a, b) while in case (ii), we represent them as (b, a). Here, (a, b) is called an ordered pair. The word ordered indicates the way in which the two numbers a and b are written. Similarly, (b, a) is an ordered pair. Note that (a, b) and (b, a) are entirely different unless $a = b$. In the ordered pair (a, b), a is called the first number and b is called the second number.

In analytical geometry, the ordered pair (x, y) of real numbers x and y is used to denote a point in two-dimensional cartesian plane. Similarly, the ordered triplet (x, y, z) of real numbers x, y and z is used to denote a point in three-dimensional space. In general, the ordered set $(x_1, x_2, x_3, ..., x_n)$ of n real numbers $x_1, x_2, x_3, ..., x_n$ (n-tuple) is used to denote a point in n-dimensional space.

7.2. Vector

An ordered set of n numbers (n-tuple of numbers) belonging to a field F is called an n-dimensional vector or n-vector or simply vector over the field F and is written as

$X = [x_1, x_2, x_3, ..., x_n]$

where the numbers $x_1, x_2, x_3, ..., x_n$ are called the components or elements or coordinates (first, second, third, ..., n^{th} respectively) of the vector X.

Illustrations

The ordered pair (x, y) is a vector of order 2. The triplet or triad (x, y, z) is a vector of order 3. The 4-tuple (1, 2, 3, 4) is a vector of order 4 and so on.

If each element of a vector is a real number, it is called a real vector or a vector over a real field. Similarly, if each element is an element of the field of complex numbers, then it is called a complex vector or a vector over a complex field.

Elements of a field are called scalars. Thus, the components of a vector are scalars.

7.3. Equality of Vectors

Two vectors X and Y are said to be equal if they have the same number of components and the corresponding components are equal. We express the equality of two vector X and Y symbolically as $X = Y$. Thus, if $X = [x_1, x_2, x_3, ..., x_n]$ and $Y = [y_1, y_2, y_3, ..., y_n]$ are two vectors, then $X = Y$ iff $x_1 = y_1$, $x_2 = y_2$, $x_3 = y_3$, ..., $x_n = y_n$.

Note: The vectors [1, 2, 3] and [2, 3, 1] are not equal although both have the same number of components because the corresponding components are not equal. Also, the vectors [1, 2] and [1, 2, 3] are obviously not equal because they do not have the same number of components although the corresponding first and second components are equal.

7.4. Row and Column Vectors

The vector $X = [x_1, x_2, x_3, ..., x_n]$ ... (7.1)

is called a row-vector or a row-matrix.

$$\text{Similarly, } X = \begin{bmatrix} x_1 \\ x_2 \\ x_3 \\ \vdots \\ x_n \end{bmatrix} \qquad \dots (7.2)$$

is called a column-vector or a column-matrix.

It is obvious that

$$[x_1, x_2, x_3, \dots, x_n]' = \begin{bmatrix} x_1 \\ x_2 \\ x_3 \\ \vdots \\ x_n \end{bmatrix}$$

and

$$\begin{bmatrix} x_1 \\ x_2 \\ x_3 \\ \vdots \\ x_n \end{bmatrix}' = [x_1, x_2, x_3, \dots, x_n]$$

i.e. the transpose of a row-matrix is a column matrix and vice-versa.

Note 1: Sometimes it is more convenient to write the components of a vector in a column.

Note 2: The notations (7.1) and (7.2) represent the same vector X.

Note 3: A matrix can be understood as a set of row vectors arranged in various columns. It can also be observed as a set of column vectors arranged in various rows. Thus, an $m \times n$ matrix defines m row vectors (each row vector being an n-vector) or n column vectors (each column vector being an m-vector).

7.5. Null Vector or Zero Vector

A vector all of whose components are zero is called a null vector. It is denoted by O. Thus,

$$O = [0, 0, 0, ..., 0]$$

is a null vector of order n.

7.6. The *n*-dimensional Vector Space

The set of all n-vectors over a firld F is called the n-vector space over F. It is dentoed by $V_n(F)$.

7.7. Operations on Vectors

1. Addition of Vectors

Let $X = [x_1, x_2, x_3, ..., x_n]$ and $Y = [y_1, y_2, y_3, ..., y_n]$ be two n-vectors over a field F. Then the sum of X and Y, denoted by $X + Y$, is obtained by adding the corresponding components. Thus,

$$X + Y = [x_1 + y_1, x_2 + y_2, x_3 + y_3, ..., x_n + y_n]$$

It is obvious that $X + Y$ is also an n-vector over the field F.

2. Scalar Multiplication

Let $K \in F$ be an arbitrary scalar. Let $X = [x_1, x_2, x_3, ..., x_n]$ be an n-vector over the field F. Then, the product of the scalar K and the vector X is called the scalar multiplication of X by K. It is denoted by KX and is defined as

$$KX = [Kx_1, Kx_2, Kx_3, ..., Kx_n]$$

Clearly KX is also an n-vector over the field F.

3. Negative of a Vector

The negative of a vector X, denoted by $-X$, is defined as

$$(-1)X = (-1)\ [x_1, x_2, x_3, ..., x_n]$$
$$= [-x_1, -x_2, -x_3, ..., -x_n]$$

Thus, the negative of a vector is obtained by reversing the signs of the elements of that vector.

Clearly $-X$ is also an n-vector over the field F.

4. Difference of Vectors

The difference of two vectors X and Y is defined as

$$X - Y = X + (-Y)$$

Thus, if $X = [x_1, x_2, x_3, ..., x_n]$ and

$Y = [y_1, y_2, y_3, ..., y_n]$, then

$$X - Y = X + (-Y)$$
$$= [x_1, x_2, x_3, ..., x_n] + [-y_1, -y_2, -y_3, ..., -y_n]$$
$$= [x_1 - y_1, x_2 - y_2, x_3 - y_3, ..., x_n - y_n]$$

Again, if $a, b \in F$ be any arbitrary scalars, then

$$ax + by = [ax_1 + by_1, ax_2 + by_2, ax_3 + by_3, ..., ax_n + by_n]$$

and,

$$ax - by = [ax_1 - by_1, ax_2 - by_2, ax_3 - by_3, ..., ax_n - by_n]$$

7.8. Fundamental Unit Vectors

n, n-vectors

$e_1 = [1, 0, 0, ..., 0]$

$e_2 = [0, 1, 0, ..., 0]$

$e_3 = [0, 0, 1, ..., 0]$

$\vdots$

$\vdots$

$e_n = [0, 0, 0, ..., 0]$

are called fundamental unit vectors or elementary vectors.

Note: By m, n-vectors, we mean that the number of n-dimensional vectos is m.

7.9. Vector Space Over a Field

Let F be a field. Let V be a non-empty set on which an operation of addition is defined. The elements of F and V may be called scalars and vectors respectively. We also suppose that there is also defined on V a scalar multiplication by elements of F, i.e. if $a \in F$ and $X \in V$, then aX is a uniquely determined element of V. The set V is then called a vector space over the field F if the following axioms are satisfied:

(V_1) addition is commutative, i.e.

$$X + Y = Y + X \ \forall \ X, Y \in V$$

(V_2) addition is asociative, i.e.

$$X + (Y + Z) = (X + Y) + Z \ \forall \ X, Y, Z \in V$$

(V_3) there exists a unique vector O in V, called the zero vector, such that

$$X + O = X \ \forall \ X \in V$$

(V_4) for each vector $X \in V$, there exists a unique vector $-X$ in V such that

$$X + (-X) = O$$

(V_5) $a(X + Y) = aX + aY \ \forall \ a \in F$ and $X, Y \in V$

(V_6) $(a + b)X = aX + bX \ \forall \ a, b \in F$ and $X \in V$

(V_7) $a(bX) = (ab)X \ \forall \ a, b \in F$ and $X \in V$

(V_8) for the unit scalar $1 \in F$, $1X = X \ \forall \ X$ in V.

Note 1: If V is a vector space over a field F, then we denote the vector space by $V(F)$ conventionally.

Note 2: If F is the field R of real numbers, then the vector space V is called a real vector space.

Note 3: If F is the field C of complex numbers, then the vector space V is called a complex vector space.

7.10. A Vector as a Linear Combination of a Set of Vectors

A vector X which can be expressed in the form

$$X = k_1X_1 + k_2X_2 + k_3X_3 + \ldots + k_mX_m$$

is called a linear combination over F of the set $[X_1, X_2, X_3, \ldots, X_m]$ of vectors $X_1, X_2, X_3, \ldots, X_m$, where $k_1, k_2, k_3, \ldots, k_m \in F$ are in arbitrary scalars, not all zero.

7.11. Linear Dependence and Independence of Vectors

The m n-vectors $X_1, X_2, X_3, \ldots, X_m$ defined over a field F and said to be linearly dependent over the field F, if there exist scalars $a_1, a_2, a_3, \ldots, a_m \in$ F, not all zero, such that

$$a_1X_1 + a_2X_2 + a_3X_3 + \ldots + a_mX_m = O$$

For example, the vectors $X_1 = [2, 6, -8]$ and $X_2 = [-3, -9, 12]$ are linearly dependent over the field F of real numbers since we have $3X_1 + 2X_2 = O$.

If the vectors $X_1, X_2, X_3, ..., X_m$ are not linearly dependent over F, then they are said to be linearly independent over F.

Consequently, the vectors $X_1, X_2, X_3, ..., X_m$ are linearly dependent if the relation of the form

$$k_1X_1 + k_2X_2 + k_3X_3 + ... + k_mX_m = O$$

$$\Rightarrow \quad k_1 = k_2 = k_3 = ... = k_m = O$$

where the scalars $k_1, k_2, k_3, ..., k_m \in F$.

7.12. Basis and Dimension of a Vector Space

A basis of a vector space is a linearly independent subset which generates the whole space. Thus, the set $\{X_1, X_2, X_3, ..., X_n\}$ of elements of a vector space V is a basis of V, if the following conditions are satisfied:

1. The set $\{X_1, X_2, X_3, ..., X_n\}$ is linearly independent.
2. V is generated by $\{X_1, X_2, X_3, ..., X_n\}$.

A vector space V is said to be n-dimensional or of finite dimension n (≥ 1), if V has a basis whose number of elements is n. It is denoted by the symbol dim V.

7.13. Some Basic Theorems on Linear Dependence and Independence of Vectors

Theorem 1. If the n-vectors $X_1, X_2, X_3, ..., X_m$ are linearly dependent over the field F, then at least one of them can be expressed as a linear combination of the remaining vectors.

Proof.

$\because$ The vectors $X_1, X_2, X_3, ..., X_m$ are linearly dependent over the field F.

$\therefore$ There exist scalars $k_1, k_2, k_3, ..., k_m \in F$, not all zero, such that

$k_1X_1 + k_2X_2 + k_3X_3 + ... + k_mX_m = O$

If $k_1 \neq O$, then

$$X_1 = \left(-\frac{k_2}{k_1}\right)X_2 + \left(-\frac{k_3}{k_1}\right)X_3 + \ldots + \left(-\frac{k_m}{k_1}\right)X_m$$

$\Rightarrow$ X_1 is expressible as a linear combination of the remaining vectors $X_2, X_3, ..., X_m$.

Theorem 2. If one of the $m + 1$, n-vectors $X_1, X_2, X_3, ..., X_m, X$ can be expressed as a linear combination of the remaining vectors, then the $m + 1$ vectors are linearly dependent.

Proof.

Let X be a linear combination of m vectors $X_1, X_2, X_3, ..., X_m$

$\therefore$ $X = k_1X_1 + k_2X_2 + k_3X_3 + ... + k_mX_m$

where $k_1, k_2, k_3, ..., k_m$ are arbitrary scalars, not all zero.

$\Rightarrow$ $k_1X_1 + k_2X_2 + k_3X_3 + ... + k_mX_m + (-1)X = O$

where $k_1, k_2, k_3, ..., k_m, -1$ are scalars, not all zero.

$\Rightarrow$ The $m + 1$ vectors $X_1, X_2, X_3, ..., X_m, X$ are linearly dependent.

Theorem 3. If the n-vectors $X_1, X_2, X_3, ..., X_m$ are linearly independent but the n-vectors $X_1, X_2, X_3, ..., X_m, X$ are linearly dependent, then X is a linear combination of $X_1, X_2, X_3, ..., X_m$.

Proof.

$\because$ $X_1, X_2, X_3, ..., X_m, X$ are linearly dependent.

$\therefore$ $k_1X_1 + k_2X_2 + k_3X_3 + ... + k_mX_m + kX = O$ ... (7.3)

where $k_1, k_2, k_3, ..., k_m, k$ are scalars, not all zero.

If $k = 0$, then we have

$$k_1X_1 + k_2X_2 + k_3X_3 + ... + k_mX_m = O$$

But $X_1, X_2, X_3, ..., X_m$ are linearly independent

$\therefore$ $k_1 = 0, k_2 = 0, k_3 = 0, ..., k_m = 0$

This contradicts the fact that $k_1, k_2, k_3, ..., k_m, k$ are not all zero.

Thus, $k = 0$ is impressible.

Hence, $k \neq 0$. Therefore Eq. (7.3) yields

$$X = -\frac{k_1}{k} X_1 - \frac{k_2}{k} X_2 - \frac{k_3}{k} X_3 - \ldots - \frac{k_m}{k} X_m$$

$\Rightarrow X$ is a linear combination of $X_1, X_2, X_3, \ldots, X_m$.

Theorem 4. If the set $\{X_1, X_2, X_3, \ldots, X_m\}$ of n-vectors is linearly independent over F, then any non-empty subset of this set is linearly independent.

OR

Any non-empty subset of a linearly independent set is linearly independent.

Proof.

Let $S_1 = \{X_1, X_2, X_3, \ldots, X_m\}$ be linearly independent.

Let the set S_2 consisting of r vectors be given by

$$S_2 = \{X_1, X_2, X_3, \ldots, X_r\} \text{ where } r < m$$

Clearly, S_2 is a subset of S_1. We are to prove that S_2 is linearly independent.

Now, let $k_1X_1 + k_2X_2 + k_3X_3 + \ldots k_rX_r = O \quad \ldots (7.4)$

This implies that

$$k_1X_1 + k_2X_2 + k_3X_3 + \ldots k_rX_r + OX_{r+1} + \ldots + OX_m = O \quad \ldots (7.5)$$

But S_1 is linearly independent, therefore Eq. (7.5) implies that

$$k_1 = 0, k_2 = 0, k_3 = 0, \ldots, k_r = 0$$

Hence, Eq. (7.5) is true only if all k's are zero.

Hence, set S_2 is also linearly independent.

Theorem 5. If $\{X_1, X_2, X_3, \ldots, X_m\} \subset \{X_1, X_2, X_3, \ldots, X_n\}$ where all X_i are n-vectors, $1 \leq m \leq n$ and if the set $\{X_1, X_2, X_3, \ldots, X_m\}$ is linearly dependent over F, then the set $\{X_1, X_2, X_3, \ldots, X_n\}$ is linearly dependent.

OR

Any super-set of a linearly dependent set of vectors is linearly dependent.

Proof.

$\because$ The set $\{X_1, X_2, X_3, ..., X_m\}$ is linearly dependent.

$\therefore$ There exist scalars $k_1, k_2, k_3, ..., k_m$, not all zero, such that

$$k_1X_1 + k_2X_2 + k_3X_3 + ... + k_mX_m = O$$

$$\Rightarrow k_1X_1 + k_2X_2 + k_3X_3 + ... + k_mX_m + OX_{m+1} + ... + OX_n = O$$

where all k's are not zero.

Hence, by definition, the set

$\{X_1, X_2, ..., X_n\}$ is linearly dependent.

Theorem 6. The set $\{X_1, X_2, X_3, ..., X_m\}$ of n-vectors is a linearly dependent set over F if at least one of the vectors of the set is the zero vector.

Proof.

Let $X_1 = O$

Then $k_1X_1 = O$, where $k_1 \neq 0$

Therefore,

$$k_1X_1 + OX_2 + OX_3 + ... + OX_m = O$$

where k_1, O, O, ..., O are scalars, not all zero.

Hence, the set $\{X_1, X_2, X_3, ..., X_m\}$ is a linearly dependent set over F.

Theorem 7. If the n-vectors $X_1, X_2, X_3, ..., X_m$ are linearly independent over F, then none of them can be the zero vector.

Proof.

Let $X_1 = O$ (say). Then,

$k_1X_1 + OX_2 + OX_3 + ... + OX_m = O$

where $k_1 \in F$ and $k_1 \neq 0$.

Hence, the vectors $X_1, X_2, X_3, ..., X_m$ are not linearly independent which is a contradiction as the vectors $X_1, X_2, X_3, ..., X_m$ are given to be linearly independent.

$\therefore \quad X_1 \neq 0$

But X_1 is arbitrary, therefore, none of the vectors X_1, X_2, X_3, ..., X_m is the zero vector.

Theorem 8. The set $\{X\}$, consisting of only one vector X, is linearly independent if and only if $X \neq O$.

Proof.

Let $X \neq O$.

Then, $kX = O \Rightarrow k = 0$.

Hence, the set $\{X\}$ is linearly independent.

Again, if the set $\{X\}$ is linearly independent, then by Theorem 7,

$X \neq O$

Hence, the theorem.

Theorem 9. The set consisting only of the zero vector, O, is linearly dependent.

Proof.

Let $X = \{0, 0, 0, ..., 0\}$ be an n-vector whose components are all zero. Then, $kX = O$ is true for some non-zero value of the scalar k. For example, $2X = O$ and $2 \neq 0$. Hence, the set $\{0\}$ is linearly dependent.

Theorem 10. The m n-vectors X_1, X_2, X_3, ..., X_m are linearly dependent if and only if the rank of the matrix $[X_1, X_2, X_3, ..., X_m]$ with given vectors and columns is less than m.

Proof.

Let

$$X_1 = \{a_{11}, a_{21}, a_{31}, ..., a_{n1}\}$$
$$X_2 = \{a_{12}, a_{22}, a_{32}, ..., a_{n2}\}$$
$$X_3 = \{a_{13}, a_{23}, a_{33}, ..., a_{n3}\}$$

....

....

$$X_m = \{a_{1m}, a_{2m}, a_{3m}, ..., a_{nm}\}$$

Let X_1, X_2, X_3, ..., X_m be linearly dependent.

Then, by definition, there exist arbitrary scalars $x_1, x_2, x_3, \ldots, x_m$, not all zero, such that

$$x_1X_1 + x_2X_2 + x_3X_3 + \ldots + x_mX_m = O \qquad \ldots (7.6)$$

The vector Eq. (or matrix Eq.) (7.6) is equivalent to n linear algebraic equations.

$$\left.\begin{array}{l} a_{11}x_1 + a_{12}x_2 + a_{13}x_3 + \ldots + a_{1m}x_m = 0 \\ a_{21}x_1 + a_{22}x_2 + a_{23}x_3 + \ldots + a_{2m}x_m = 0 \\ a_{31}x_1 + a_{32}x_2 + a_{33}x_3 + \ldots + a_{3m}x_m = 0 \\ \ldots\ldots\ldots\ldots\ldots\ldots\ldots\ldots\ldots\ldots\ldots\ldots \\ \ldots\ldots\ldots\ldots\ldots\ldots\ldots\ldots\ldots\ldots\ldots\ldots \\ a_{n1}x_1 + a_{n2}x_2 + a_{n3}x_3 + \ldots\ldots + a_{nm}x_m = 0 \end{array}\right\} \qquad \ldots (7.7)$$

$\because$ $x_1, x_2, x_3, \ldots, x_m$ are not all zero.

$\therefore$ The system of homogeneous linear Eq. (7.7) has at least one non-trivial solution for the x's, the condition for which is that the rank of the coefficient matrix $X = \{X_1, X_2, X_3, \ldots, X_m\}$ with the given vectors as columns must be less than m (the number of unknowns).

Conversely, if the rank of coefficient matrix of Eq. (7.7) is less than m, then the Eqs. (7.7) have a non-trivial solution, i.e. there exist $x_1, x_2, x_3, \ldots, x_m$, not all zero, which satisfy Eq. (7.7) and hence satisfy Eq. (7.6). Therefore, we conclude that $X_1, X_2, X_3, \ldots, X_m$ are linearly dependent.

Hence,

$$\text{rank of } [X_1, X_2, X_3, \ldots, X_m] < m \Leftrightarrow X_1, X_2, X_3, \ldots, X_m \text{ are linearly dependent.}$$

ILLUSTRATIVE EXAMPLES

Example 1. If $X = [0, -1, 2, 3] \in V_4(R)$ and

$$Y = [5, 1, 2, -3] \in V_4(R),$$

then find the value of $X + Y$ and $3X$.

Solution: We have

$$X + Y = [0, -1, 2, 3] + [5, 1, 2, -3]$$

$$= [0 + 5, -1 + 1, 2 + 2, 3 - 3]$$
$$= [5, 0, 4, 0]$$

Also,

$$3X = 3[0, -1, 2, 3]$$
$$= [0, -3, 6, 9]$$

Example 2. If $X_1 = [1, 0, 0]$, $X_2 = [0, 1, 0]$ and $X_3 = [0, 0, 1]$, find

(i) $X_1 + X_2 + X_3$

(ii) $2X_1 + 3X_2 - X_3$

Solution: (i) We have

$$X_1 + X_2 + X_3 = [1, 0, 0] + [0, 1, 0] + [0, 0, 1]$$
$$= [1 + 0 + 0, 0 + 1 + 0, 0 + 0 + 1]$$
$$= [1, 1, 1]$$

(ii) We have

$$2X_1 + 3X_2 - X_3 = 2[1, 0, 0] + 3[0, 1, 0] - [0, 0, 1]$$
$$= [2, 0, 0] + [0, 3, 0] - [0, 0, 1]$$
$$= [2, 3, -1]$$

Example 3. If $X_1 = [3, 1, -4]$, $X_2 = [2, 2, -3]$, $X_3 = [0, -4, 1]$ and $X_4 = [-4, -4, 6]$, then show that $2X_1 - X_2 - X_3 + X_4 = O$.

Solution: We have

$$2X_1 - X_2 - X_3 + X_4$$
$$= 2[3, 1, -4] - [2, 2, -3] - [0, -4, 1] + [-4, -4, 6]$$
$$= [6, 2, -8] - [2, 2, -3] - [0, -4, 1] + [-4, -4, 6]$$
$$= [6 - 2 - 4, 2 - 2 + 4 - 4, -8 + 3 - 1 + 6]$$
$$= [0, 0, 0] = O$$

Example 4. Show that the vectors $X_1 = [1, 2, -3]$ and $X_2 = [2, -2, 0]$ form a linearly independent set.

Solution: Let us assume that

$$k_1X_1 + k_2X_2 = O$$

$\Rightarrow k_1\,[1, 2, -3] + k_2\,[2, -2, 0] = [0, 0, 0]$

$\Rightarrow [k_1, 2k_1, -3k_1] + [2k_2, -2k_2, 0] = [0, 0, 0]$

$\Rightarrow [k_1 + 2k_2, 2k_1 - 2k_2, -3k_1] = [0, 0, 0]$

$\Rightarrow k_1 + 2k_2 = 0$

$2k_1 - 2k_2 = 0$

$-3k_1 = 0$

$\Rightarrow k_1 = 0, k_2 = 0$

Hence, the vectors X_1 and X_2 form a linearly independent set.

Example 5. Show that the vectors $X_1 = [1, 2, 4]$ and $X_2 = [3, 6, 12]$ are linearly dependent.

Solution: Let us assume that

$k_1X_1 + k_2X_2 = O$

$\Rightarrow k_1[1, 2, 4] + k_2[3, 6, 12] = [0, 0, 0]$

$\Rightarrow [k_1, 2k_1, 4k_1] + [3k_2, 6k_2, 12k_2] = [0, 0, 0]$

$\Rightarrow [k_1 + 3k_2, 2k_1 + 6k_2, 4k_1 + 12k_2] = [0, 0, 0]$

$\Rightarrow k_1 + 3k_2 = 0$

$2k_1 + 6k_2 = 0$

$4k_1 + 12k_2 = 0$

All these equations reduce to a single equation

$k_1 + 3k_2 = 0$

Let us take $k_1 = 3$, $k_2 = -1$. Then all these equations are satisfied and k_1, k_2 are not all zero.

Hence, the vectors X_1 and X_2 are linearly dependent.

Example 6. Find the condition that the vectors

$$X = \begin{bmatrix} a_1 \\ a_2 \end{bmatrix} \text{ and } Y = \begin{bmatrix} b_1 \\ b_2 \end{bmatrix} \text{ are linearly dependent.}$$

Solution: Let us assume that

$k_1X + k_2Y = O$

$$\Rightarrow k_1\begin{bmatrix} a_1 \\ a_2 \end{bmatrix} + k_2\begin{bmatrix} b_1 \\ b_2 \end{bmatrix} = \begin{bmatrix} 0 \\ 0 \end{bmatrix}$$

$$\Rightarrow \begin{bmatrix} k_1a_1 + k_2b_1 \\ k_1a_2 + k_2b_2 \end{bmatrix} = \begin{bmatrix} 0 \\ 0 \end{bmatrix}$$

$$\Rightarrow k_1a_1 + k_2b_1 = 0$$

$$k_1a_2 + k_2b_2 = 0$$

$$\Rightarrow \frac{k_1}{k_2} = -\frac{b_1}{a_1} = -\frac{b_2}{a_2}$$

Taking last two, we get

$$a_1b_2 - a_2b_1 = 0$$

which is the required condition.

Example 7. Prove that the vectors $X_1 = [1, 2, 3]$, $X_2 = [3, -2, 1]$ and $X_3 = [1, -6, -5]$ form a linearly dependent system.

Solution: Let us take

$$a_1X_1 + a_2X_2 + a_3X_3 = O \qquad \text{... (7.8)}$$

where a_1, a_2, a_3 are all scalars.

$$\Rightarrow a_1[1, 2, 3] + a_2[3, -2, 1] + a_3[1, -6, -5] = [0, 0, 0]$$

$$\Rightarrow a_1 + 3a_2 + a_3 = 0 \qquad \text{... (7.9)}$$

$$2a_1 - 2a_2 - 6a_3 = 0 \qquad \text{... (7.10)}$$

$$3a_1 + a_2 - 5a_3 = 0 \qquad \text{... (7.11)}$$

Equations (7.10) and (7.11), by cross-multiplication, we get

$$\frac{a_1}{10+6} = \frac{a_2}{-18+10} = \frac{a_3}{2+6}$$

$$\Rightarrow \frac{a_1}{2} = \frac{a_2}{-1} = \frac{a_3}{1} = \lambda \text{ (say)}$$

$$\Rightarrow a_1 = 2\lambda$$

$$a_2 = -\lambda$$

$$a_3 = \lambda$$

Substituting for a_1, a_2, a_3 in Eq. (7.9), we get

$$2\lambda - 3\lambda + \lambda = 0$$

$$\Rightarrow 0 = 0$$

Hence, Eq. (7.9) is satisfied for all values of λ implying that Eqs. (7.9), (7.10) and (7.11) are consistent.

If $\lambda = 1$, we have

$$a_1 = 2$$
$$a_2 = -1$$
$$a_3 = 1$$

which are not all zero.

Hence, the given vectors form a linearly dependent system.

The relation between the given vectors is given by

$$2X_1 - X_2 + X_3 = O$$
$$\Rightarrow X_2 = 2X_1 + X_3$$

Aliter.

$$\text{Coefficient matrix } A = \begin{bmatrix} 1 & 3 & 1 \\ 2 & -2 & -6 \\ 3 & 1 & -5 \end{bmatrix}$$

Operating $R_{21}(-2)$, $R_{31}(-3)$

$$A \sim \begin{bmatrix} 1 & 3 & 1 \\ 0 & -8 & -8 \\ 0 & -8 & -8 \end{bmatrix}$$

Operating $R_{32}(-1)$

$$A \sim \begin{bmatrix} 1 & 3 & 1 \\ 0 & -8 & -8 \\ 0 & 0 & 0 \end{bmatrix}$$

$\therefore$ $\rho(A) = 2 < 3$ (number of vectors)

Hence, the given vectors are linearly dependent.

Example 8. Show, using a matrix, that the set of vectors

$$X_1 = [1, 2, -3, 4]$$
$$X_2 = [3, -1, 2, 1]$$
$$X_3 = [1, -5, 8, -7]$$

is linearly dependent. Determine a maximum subset of linearly independent vectors and express the others as linear combination of these.

Solution:

$$\text{Coefficient of matrix } A = \begin{bmatrix} 1 & 2 & -3 & 4 \\ 3 & -1 & 2 & 1 \\ 1 & -5 & 8 & -7 \end{bmatrix} \qquad \dots (7.12)$$

Operating $R_{21}(-2)$

$$A \sim \begin{bmatrix} 1 & 2 & -3 & 4 \\ 1 & -5 & 8 & -7 \\ 1 & -5 & 8 & -7 \end{bmatrix} \qquad \dots (7.13)$$

Operating $R_{32}(-1)$

$$A \sim \begin{bmatrix} 1 & 2 & -3 & 4 \\ 1 & -5 & 8 & -7 \\ 0 & 0 & 0 & 0 \end{bmatrix}$$

This shows that determinant of every sub-matrix of order 3 is zero.

$$\text{Also} \begin{vmatrix} 1 & -2 \\ 1 & -5 \end{vmatrix} = -7 \neq 0$$

$\therefore \quad \rho(A) = 2 < 3$ (number of vectors)

Hence, the given vectors are linearly dependent.

Since $\rho(A) = 2$, there are two linearly independent vectors, say X_1 and X_2.

From Eqs. (7.12) and (7.13), it is clear that by performing the operation $R_{21}(-2)$, the second and third rows of the matrix A become identical, i.e. on multiplying the first row by -2 and adding to the second row, we obtain the third row. Since A is the matrix with the given vectors as rows, therefore, it follows that

$$X_3 = -2X_1 + X_2$$

Example 9. Show that the vectors $X_1 = [1, 2, 4]$, $X_2 = [2, -1, 3]$, $X_3 = [0, 1, 2]$ and $X_4 = [-3, 7, 2]$ are linearly dependent and find the relation between them.

Solution: Let us take

$$a_1X_1 + a_2X_2 + a_3X_3 + a_4X_4 = O \qquad \text{... (7.14)}$$

where a_1, a_2, a_3, a_4 are all scalars.

$$\Rightarrow a_1[1, 2, 4] + a_2[2, -1, 3] + a_3[0, 1, 2] + a_4[-3, 7, 2] = [0, 0, 0]$$

$$\Rightarrow a_1 + 2a_2 - 3a_4 = 0 \qquad \text{... (7.15)}$$

$$2a_1 - a_2 + a_3 + 7a_4 = 0 \qquad \text{... (7.16)}$$

$$4a_1 + 3a_2 + 2a_3 + 2a_4 = 0 \qquad \text{... (7.17)}$$

Multiplying Eq. (7.15) by 2 and subtracting from Eq. (7.17), we get

$$5a_2 - 12a_4 = 0 \qquad \text{... (7.18)}$$

Equations (7.15) and (7.18), using cross-multiplication, we get

$$\frac{a_1}{-9} = \frac{a_2}{12} = \frac{a_4}{5} = \lambda \quad \text{(say)}$$

$$\Rightarrow a_1 = -9\lambda$$

$$a_2 = 12\lambda$$

$$a_4 = 5\lambda$$

Substituting these values in Eq. (7.17), we get

$$-36\lambda + 36\lambda + 2a_3 + 10\lambda = 0$$

$$\Rightarrow a_3 = -5\lambda$$

Substituting for a_1, a_2, a_3, a_4 in Eq. (7.16), we get

$$2(-9\lambda) - 12\lambda - 5\lambda + 35\lambda = 0$$

$$\Rightarrow 0 = 0$$

Hence, Eq. (7.16) is satisfied for all values of λ implying that Eqs. (7.15), (7.16) and (7.17) are consistent.

If $\lambda = 1$, we have

$$a_1 = -9$$

$$a_2 = 12$$

$$a_3 = -5$$
$$a_4 = 5$$

which are not all zero.

Hence, the given vectors form a linearly dependent system.

The relation between vectors is given by

$$-9\lambda X_1 + 12\lambda X_2 - 5\lambda X_3 + 5\lambda X_4 = O$$
$$\Rightarrow 9X_1 - 12X_2 + 5X_3 - 5X_4 = O$$

Example 10. If $X_1 = [3, 1, -4]$, $X_2 = [2, 2, -3]$, $X_3 = [0, -4, 1]$, show that

(i) The vectors X_1 and X_2 are linearly independent over the field of rational numbers.

(ii) The vectors X_1, X_2 and X_3 are linearly dependent over the field of rational numbers.

Solution: (i) Let us assume that

$$k_1X_1 + k_1X_2 = O$$
$$\Rightarrow k_1[3, 1, -4] + k_2[2, 2, -3] = [0, 0, 0]$$
$$\Rightarrow [3k_1 + 2k_2, k_1 + 2k_2, -4k_1 - 3k_2] = [0, 0, 0]$$

$$\Rightarrow \left.\begin{array}{r} 3k_1 + 2k_2 = 0 \\ k_1 + 2k_2 = 0 \\ -4k_1 - 3k_2 = 0 \end{array}\right| \text{By definition of equality of two vectors}$$

On solving these linear equations, we obtain $k_1 = 0$ and $k_2 = 0$. Thus, $k_1X_1 + k_2X_2 = O$ implies that $k_1 = 0$, $k_2 = 0$.

Hence, by definition, the vectors X_1 and X_2 are linearly independent.

(ii) Let us assume that

$$k_1X_1 + k_2X_2 + k_3X_3 = O$$
$$\Rightarrow k_1[3, 1, -4] + k_2[2, 2, -3] + k_3[0, -4, 1] = [0, 0, 0]$$
$$\Rightarrow [3k_1 + 2k_2, k_1 + 2k_2 - 4k_3, -4k_1 - 3k_2 + k_3]$$
$$= [0, 0, 0]$$

$$\left.\begin{aligned} 3k_1 + 2k_2 &= 0 \\ \Rightarrow \quad k_1 + 2k_2 - 4k_3 &= 0 \\ -4k_1 - 3k_2 + k_3 &= 0 \end{aligned}\right| \text{By definition of equality of two vectors}$$

On solving these equations, we obtain

$$k_1 = -\frac{2}{3}k_2 = -2k_3 \neq 0$$

This shows that the scalars k_1, k_2, k_3, not all zero, exist such that $k_1X_1 + k_2X_2 + k_3X_3 = O$. Hence, by definition, the vectors X_1, X_2 and X_3 are linearly dependent.

Example 11. Show that the vectors $\alpha = [1 + i, 2i]$ and $\beta = [1, 1 + i]$ are linearly dependent over the complex field but are linearly independent over the real field.

Solution: Let us take

$$x\alpha + y\beta = O \qquad \text{... (7.19)}$$

where x, y are scalars.

$$\Rightarrow x[1 + i, 2i] + y[1, 1 + i] = [0, 0]$$

$$\Rightarrow x(1 + i) + y = 0 \qquad \text{... (7.20)}$$

$$x(2i) + y(1 + i) = 0 \qquad \text{... (7.21)}$$

From Eq. (7.20),

$$x(1 + i) = -y$$

$$\Rightarrow \frac{x}{-1} = \frac{y}{1+i} = \lambda \text{ (say)}$$

$$\Rightarrow x = -\lambda$$

$$y = (1 + i)\lambda$$

Substituting for x, y in Eq. (7.21) we get

$$-2i\lambda + (1 + i)^2\lambda = 0$$

$$\Rightarrow -2i\lambda + 2i\lambda = 0$$

$$\Rightarrow 0 = 0$$

which is true.

If $\lambda = 1$, $x = -1$, $y = 1 + i$

which are not all zero.

Hence, the vectors are linearly dependent over the complex field. However, if $\lambda = 0$, then $x = 0$, $y = 0$.

Here, the vectors are independent but over the real field.

EXERCISE 7

1. If $X_1 = [3, 1, -4]$, $X_2 = [2, 2, -3]$, $X_3 = [0, -4, 1]$, compute the vectors
   (i) $2X_1 - 5X_2$
   (ii) $2X_1 - 3X_2 - X_3$
2. If $X_1 = [1, 3, 4]$, $X_2 = [3, 1, 2]$, $X_3 = [1, 1, 2]$, find $X_1 - 2X_2 + 3X_3$.
3. If $X_1 = [1, 0, 0]$, $X_2 = [0, 1, 0]$, $X_3 = [0, 0, 1]$, compute the vectors:
   (i) $2X_1 + X_2 - X_3$
   (ii) $X_1 - 2X_2 + 3X_3$
4. If $X_1 = [1, 1, 2]$, $X_2 = [2, -1, -6]$, $X_3 = [13, 4, -4]$, prove that $7X_1 + 3X_2 = X_3$.
5. If $X_1 = [-4, 1, 3, 2]$, $X_2 = [2, 0, 0, 4]$, $X_3 = [4, 3, 2, 1]$ and $X_4 = [1, 1, 1, 1]$, then compute the following:
   (i) $X_1 + X_2 + X_3 + X_4$
   (ii) $2X_1 - 5X_2 - X_4$
   (iii) $2X_1 + X_2 - X_3 + 2X_4$
6. Show that the column vectors of $A = \begin{bmatrix} 1 & 0 & 0 \\ 6 & 2 & 1 \\ 4 & 3 & 2 \end{bmatrix}$ are linearly independent.
7. Show that the set of vectors [1, 2, 3], [3, 2, 1], [1, 1, 1] is linearly dependent.
8. Find whether the set of vectors [3, 2, 4], [1, 0, 2], [1, –1, –1] is linearly dependent or independent.

9. Show that the vectors [1, 2, 0], [0, 3, 1], [–1, 0, 1] are linearly independent.

10. Show that the vectors

$X_1 = [2, i, -i]$,

$X_2 = [2i, -1, 1]$

and $X_3 = [1, 2, 3]$

are linearly dependent.

11. Show that the vectors $X_1 = [3, 1, -4]$, $X_2 = [2, 2, -3]$ form a linearly independent set but $X_1 = [3, 1, -4]$, $X_2 = [2, 2, -3]$ and $X_3 = [0, -4, 1]$ are linearly dependent.

12. Show that [1, 2, 1, 2], [0, 1, 2, 0], [1, 4, 3, 2] are linearly independent.

13. Show that the vectors [1, 1, 0], [3, 1, 3], [5, 3, 3] are linearly dependent.

14. Show that the vectors [1, 0, –1], [2, 1, 3], [–1, 0, 0], [1, 0, 1] are linearly dependent.

15. Show that the set of vectors (1, 0, 0), (0, 1, 0), (0, 0, 1) is linearly independent.

16. Prove that the elementary vectors (unit vectors)

$E_1 = [1, 0, 0, ..., 0]$,

$E_2 = [0, 1, 0, ..., 0]$,

....

....

$E_n = [0, 0, 0, ..., 1]$

are linearly independent.

17. Prove that the four vectors $\alpha_1 = (1, 0, 0)$, $\alpha_2 = (0, 1, 0)$, $\alpha_3 = (0, 0, 1)$, $\alpha_4 = (1, 1, 1)$ in $V_3(R)$ form a linearly dependent set but any three of them are linearly independent.

18. Show, using a matrix, that the set of vectors $X_1 = [2, 3, 1, -1]$, $X_2 = [2, 3, 1, -2]$, $X_3 = [4, 6, 2, -3]$ is linearly

dependent. Determine a maximum subset of linearly independent vectors and express the others as a linear combination of these.

19. If the vectors (0, 1, *a*), (1, *a*, 1) and (*a*, 1, 0) are linearly dependent, then find the value of *a*.

20. Show that the vectors $X_1 = [2, 3, -1, -1]$, $X_2 = [1, -1, -2, -4]$, $X_3 = [3, 1, 3, -2]$, $X_4 = [6, 3, 0, -7]$ are linearly dependent. Also, express one of these as the linear combination of the others.

21. Prove that any *n*-dimensional vector *X* and the *n*-dimensional zero vector are linearly dependent.

ANSWERS

1. (i) [–4, –8, 7]
   (ii) [0, 0, 0]

2. [–2, –1, 6]

3. (i) [2, 1, –1]
   (ii) [1, –2, 3]

5. (i) [3, 5, 6, 8]
   (ii) [–17, –16, –11, 2]
   (iii) [–8, 1, 6, 9]

8. Linearly independent

18. $X_3 = X_1 + X_2$

19. 0, $\pm\sqrt{2}$

20. $X_4 = -X_1 - X_2 - X_3$

8 CHARACTERISTIC ROOTS AND VECTORS—CAYLEY-HAMILTON THEOREM

8.1. Matrix Polynomial

An expression of the form $F(\lambda) = A_0 + A_1\lambda + A_2\lambda^2 + ... + A_{m-1}\lambda^{m-1} + A_m\lambda^m$ is called a matrix polynomial of degree m if

(i) $A_0, A_1, A_2, ..., A_{m-1}, A_m$ all are square matrices of the same order n (say) and

(ii) $A_m \neq O$.

Such a matrix polynomial is called n-rowed and the symbol λ is called *intermediate*. A_m is called the leading coefficient.

Note: Every square matrix can be expressed as a polynomial of degree zero because if A is a square matrix, then we can write

$$A = \lambda^0 A$$

8.2. Equality of Two Matrix Polynomials

Two matrix polynomials are said to be equal if the coefficients of like powers of λ are the same. Thus, if $F(\lambda) = A_0 + A_1\lambda + A_2\lambda^2 + ... + A_{m-1}\lambda^{m-1} + A_m\lambda^m$ and $G(\lambda) = B_0 + B_1\lambda + B_2\lambda^2 + ... + B_{m-1}\lambda^{m-1} + B_m\lambda^m$, then we write $F(\lambda) = G(\lambda)$ if $A_r = B_r \ \forall \ r$ such that $0 \leq r \leq m$.

8.3. Theorem

Every square matrix whose elements are ordinary polynomials in λ can essentially be expressed as a matrix polynomial in λ of degree m where m is the highest power of λ occurring in any element of the matrix.

Proof. To prove this let us consider the matrix

$$A = \begin{bmatrix} 1 + 2\lambda + 3\lambda^2 & \lambda^2 & 4 + 6\lambda \\ 1 + \lambda^3 & 3 - 4\lambda^2 & 1 + 2\lambda - 4\lambda^3 \\ 2 + 3\lambda - 2\lambda^3 & 6 & -5 \end{bmatrix}$$

in which the highest power of λ occurring in any element is 3.

Rewriting each element as a cubic in λ supplying the missing coefficients with zeroes, we get

$$A = \begin{bmatrix} 1 + 2\lambda + 3\lambda^2 + 0\lambda^3 & 0 + 0\lambda + 1\lambda^2 + 0\lambda^3 & 4 + 6\lambda + 0\lambda^2 + 0\lambda^3 \\ 1 + 0\lambda + 0\lambda^2 + 1\lambda^3 & 3 + 0\lambda - 4\lambda^2 + 0\lambda^3 & 1 + 2\lambda + 0\lambda^2 - 4\lambda^3 \\ 2 + 3\lambda + 0\lambda^2 - 2\lambda^3 & 6 + 0\lambda + 0\lambda^2 + 0\lambda^3 & -5 + 0\lambda + 0\lambda^2 + 0\lambda^3 \end{bmatrix}$$

Obviously A can be written as a matrix polynomial as shown below:

$$A = \begin{bmatrix} 1 & 0 & 4 \\ 1 & 3 & 1 \\ 2 & 6 & -5 \end{bmatrix} + \lambda \begin{bmatrix} 2 & 0 & 6 \\ 0 & 0 & 2 \\ 3 & 0 & 0 \end{bmatrix} + \lambda^2 \begin{bmatrix} 3 & 1 & 0 \\ 0 & -4 & 0 \\ 0 & 0 & 0 \end{bmatrix}$$

$$+ \lambda^3 \begin{bmatrix} 0 & 0 & 0 \\ 1 & 0 & -4 \\ -2 & 0 & 0 \end{bmatrix}$$

Thus, when A is a square matrix whose elements are ordinary polynomials in λ such that the highest power of λ occurring in any element is 3, then A can expressed as a matrix polynomial in λ of degree 3.

The statement of the theorem is a straight forward generalisation of this.

8.4. Mapping or Function or Transformation

Let X and Y be two given sets. If by any given rule, there corresponds to each element x belonging to X a unique element y belonging to Y, then this correspondence is called a mapping or function or transformation of X to Y and is denoted by f. The set X is called the domain and the set Y is called the codomain of the function.

If the mapping f associates an element $x \in X$ with the element $y \in Y$, then y is called the f-image of x and we write

$$y = f(x)$$

The mapping of X to Y is denoted by

$$f : X \to Y$$

or

$$f(X) = Y$$

If the mapping $f : X \to Y$ is such that there is at least one element in Y which is not the f-image of any element in X, then f is called a mapping of X into Y. But if the mapping $f : X \to Y$ is such that each element in Y is the f-image of at lest one element in X, then f is called a mapping of X onto Y.

8.5. Linear Transformation

Let $X = [x_1, x_2, x_3, ..., x_n]'$ and $Y = [y_1, y_2, y_3, ..., y_n]'$ be two n-vectors with their components related by

$$\left.\begin{array}{l} y_1 = a_{11}x_1 + a_{12}x_2 + a_{13}x_3 + ... + a_{1n}x_n \\ y_2 = a_{21}x_1 + a_{22}x_2 + a_{23}x_3 + ... + a_{2n}x_n \\ . \quad . \quad . \quad . \quad . \quad . \\ . \quad . \quad . \quad . \quad . \quad . \\ y_n = a_{n1}x_1 + a_{n2}x_2 + a_{n3}x_3 + ... + a_{nn}x_n \end{array}\right\} \quad ... (8.1)$$

or, by $Y = AX$

where $A = [a_{ij}]_{m \times n}$, then Eq. (8.1) is called a linear transformation T which transforms any vector X into another vector Y.

If Eq. (8.1) transforms X_1 into Y_1 and X_2 into Y_2, then

(i) it will transform k_1X_1 into k_1Y_1 $\forall$ scalar k_1; and

(ii) it will transform $aX_1 + bX_2$ into $aY_1 + bY_2$ $\forall$ pair of scalars a and b.

This is why this transformation is called linear.

8.6. Characteristic Roots and Vectors

The linear transformation $Y = AX$ shows that a vector X transforms into another vector Y by the matrix A. Here, if A is an identity matrix, then the vector X will transform into X itself. This is true for any vector X. Thus, an identity matrix transforms any vector into itself. However, there exist matrices (other than the identity matrix) which transform some but not all vectors into themselves. It is clear from the following example.

$$\begin{bmatrix} 1 & 0 & 4 \\ 0 & 1 & 5 \\ 0 & 0 & 3 \end{bmatrix} \begin{bmatrix} x_1 \\ x_2 \\ 0 \end{bmatrix} = \begin{bmatrix} x_1 \\ x_2 \\ 0 \end{bmatrix}$$

From this example it follows that any vector with a zero third component will be transformed into itself by this matrix.

Now, if the diagonal elements 1 are replaced by 2, then the resulting matrix would transform 3×1 vectors multiplied by the scalar 2. Thus,

$$\begin{bmatrix} 2 & 0 & 4 \\ 0 & 2 & 5 \\ 0 & 0 & 3 \end{bmatrix} \begin{bmatrix} x_1 \\ x_2 \\ 0 \end{bmatrix} = \begin{bmatrix} 2x_1 \\ 2x_2 \\ 0 \end{bmatrix} = 2 \begin{bmatrix} x_1 \\ x_2 \\ 0 \end{bmatrix}$$

It is obvious that any scalar matrix would transform all vectors in this manner as shown below.

$$\begin{bmatrix} 2 & 0 & 0 \\ 0 & 2 & 0 \\ 0 & 0 & 2 \end{bmatrix} \begin{bmatrix} x_1 \\ x_2 \\ x_3 \end{bmatrix} = \begin{bmatrix} 2x_1 \\ 2x_2 \\ 2x_3 \end{bmatrix} = 2 \begin{bmatrix} x_1 \\ x_2 \\ x_3 \end{bmatrix}$$

For a general matrix, this takes us to a very important concept of characteristic roots and vectors.

8.7. Characteristic Value Problem

Let A be a square matrix of order n. We wish to determine the scalars λ and the non-zero vectors X which simultaneously satisfy the equation

$$AX = \lambda X \qquad \text{... (8.2)}$$

This is known as the characteristic value problem.

Let $A = [a_{ij}]_{m \times n}$; $i, j = 1, 2, ..., n$ and

$X = [x_1, x_2, ..., x_n]'$

$\because \quad X = I_n X$

$\therefore$ Equation (8.2) can be rewritten as

$$AX = \lambda I_n X$$

$$\Rightarrow \begin{bmatrix} a_{11} & a_{12} & \dots & a_{1n} \\ a_{21} & a_{22} & \dots & a_{2n} \\ \dots & \dots & \dots & \dots \\ a_{n1} & a_{n2} & \dots & a_{nn} \end{bmatrix} \begin{bmatrix} x_1 \\ x_2 \\ \dots \\ x_n \end{bmatrix} = \begin{bmatrix} \lambda & 0 & \dots & 0 \\ 0 & \lambda & \dots & 0 \\ \dots & \dots & \dots & \dots \\ 0 & 0 & \dots & \lambda \end{bmatrix} \begin{bmatrix} x_1 \\ x_2 \\ \dots \\ x_n \end{bmatrix}$$

$$\Rightarrow \begin{bmatrix} a_{11} - \lambda & a_{12} & \dots & a_{1n} \\ a_{21} & a_{22} - \lambda & \dots & a_{2n} \\ \dots & \dots & \dots & \dots \\ a_{n1} & a_{n2} & \dots & a_{nn} - \lambda \end{bmatrix} \begin{bmatrix} x_1 \\ x_2 \\ \dots \\ x_n \end{bmatrix} = \begin{bmatrix} 0 \\ 0 \\ \dots \\ 0 \end{bmatrix} \qquad \text{... (8.3)}$$

Alternatively

$$AX = \lambda I X$$

$$\Rightarrow \quad (A - \lambda I)X = 0 \qquad \text{... (8.4)}$$

This is a homogeneous system of linear equations whose coefficient matrix is $A - \lambda I$. Since we require a non-zero vector X, therefore, it is necessary that the determinant of this coefficient matrix is equal to zero. Thus,

$$|A - \lambda I| = \begin{vmatrix} a_{11} - \lambda & a_{12} & \dots & a_{1n} \\ a_{21} & a_{22} - \lambda & \dots & a_{2n} \\ \dots & \dots & \dots & \dots \\ a_{n1} & a_{n2} & \dots & a_{nn} - \lambda \end{vmatrix} = 0 \qquad \text{... (8.5)}$$

Some Definitions

1. Characteristic Matrix

The matrix $A - \lambda I$ is known as the characteristic matrix of A.

2. Characteristic Polynomial

The determinant of the matrix $A - \lambda I$, i.e. $|A - \lambda I|$ is known as the characteristic polynomial of A and is denoted by $\varphi(\lambda)$.

3. Characteristic Equation

The equation $\varphi(\lambda) = 0$, i.e. $|A - \lambda I| = 0$ is known as the characteristic equation (or secular equation) of A.

4. Characteristic Roots

The roots of the characteristic equation of A are called characteristic roots of A. These are also called as latent roots or invariant roots or proper roots or eigen values. The set of characteristic roots of A is called the spectrum of A.

5. Characteristic Vectors

Let $\lambda = \lambda_1$ be any characteristic root of A. Then, we have

$$(A - \lambda_1 I)X = O$$

The non-zero vector X which satisfies the above equation is called characteristic vector of A corresponding to the characteristic root $\lambda = \lambda_1$.

6. Characteristic Space

The collection of all X such that $AX = \lambda X$ is called the characteristic space associated with λ.

8.8. A Lemma

If A is a square matrix of order n, then the adjoint of the characteristic matrix $A - \lambda I$ can be expressed as a matrix polynomial in λ of degree $n - 1$.

Proof. Let us take

$$A = \begin{bmatrix} a_{11} & a_{12} & a_{13} \\ a_{21} & a_{22} & a_{23} \\ a_{31} & a_{32} & a_{33} \end{bmatrix}$$

and

$$|A| = \begin{vmatrix} a_{11} & a_{12} & a_{13} \\ a_{21} & a_{22} & a_{23} \\ a_{31} & a_{32} & a_{33} \end{vmatrix}$$

and,

$$A - \lambda I = \begin{bmatrix} a_{11} - \lambda & a_{12} & a_{13} \\ a_{21} & a_{22} - \lambda & a_{23} \\ a_{31} & a_{32} & a_{33} - \lambda \end{bmatrix}$$

$\therefore \quad adj\ (A - \lambda I)$

$$= \begin{bmatrix} \begin{matrix} \lambda^2 - \lambda(a_{22} + a_{33}) \\ + (a_{22}a_{33} - a_{23}a_{32}) \end{matrix} & \lambda a_{12} - (a_{12}a_{33} - a_{13}a_{32}) & \lambda a_{13} + (a_{32}a_{23} - a_{13}a_{22}) \\ \lambda a_{21} + (a_{23}a_{31} - a_{21}a_{33}) & \begin{matrix} \lambda^2 - \lambda(a_{11} + a_{33}) \\ - (a_{13}a_{31} - a_{11}a_{33}) \end{matrix} & \lambda a_{23} - (a_{21}a_{13} - a_{11}a_{23}) \\ \lambda a_{31} + (a_{32}a_{21} - a_{22}a_{31}) & \lambda a_{32} + (a_{21}a_{13} - a_{11}a_{32}) & \lambda^2 - \lambda(a_{11} + a_{22}) + (a_{11}a_{22} - a_{12}a_{21}) \end{bmatrix}$$

$$= \lambda^2 \begin{bmatrix} 1 & 0 & 0 \\ 0 & 1 & 0 \\ 0 & 0 & 1 \end{bmatrix} + \lambda \begin{bmatrix} a_{22} + a_{33} & a_{12} & a_{13} \\ a_{21} & -(a_{11} + a_{33}) & a_{23} \\ a_{31} & a_{32} & -(a_{11} + a_{12}) \end{bmatrix}$$

$$+ \begin{bmatrix} a_{22}a_{33} - a_{23}a_{32} & a_{12}a_{32} - a_{12}a_{33} & a_{12}a_{23} - a_{13}a_{22} \\ a_{23}a_{31} - a_{21}a_{33} & a_{11}a_{33} - a_{13}a_{31} & a_{21}a_{13} - a_{11}a_{23} \\ a_{21}a_{32} - a_{22}a_{31} & a_{21}a_{13} - a_{11}a_{32} & a_{11}a_{22} - a_{12}a_{21} \end{bmatrix}$$

which is obviously of the form $B_0\lambda^2 + B_1\lambda + B_2$ where B_0, B_1, B_2 are square matrices of order 3.

Thus, for a square matrix A of order 3, *adj* $(A - \lambda I)$ can be expressed as a matrix polynomial $B_0\lambda^2 + B_1\lambda + B_2$ of degree 2 in λ.

The statement of the lemma is a straight forward generalisation of this.

8.9. Cayley-Hamilton Theorem

Statement. Every square matrix satisfies its own characteristic equation.

OR

If $|A - \lambda I| = (-1)^n [\lambda^n + a_1\lambda^{n-1} + a_2\lambda^{n-2} + \ldots + a_n]$ be the characteristic polynomial of an $n \times n$ matrix $A = [a_{ij}]$, then the matrix equation

$$X^n + a_1X^{n-1} + \ldots + a_nI = O$$

is satisfied by $X = A$, i.e.

$$A^n + a_1A^{n-1} + \ldots + a_nI = O$$

Proof. Let $A = [a_{ij}]_{n \times n}$ be a square matrix of order n, I be an identity matrix of order n and λ be an intermediate. Let the characteristic polynomial of A be $\varphi(\lambda)$. Then,

$$\varphi(\lambda) = |A - \lambda I|$$

$$= \begin{vmatrix} a_{11} - \lambda & a_{12} & \ldots & a_{1n} \\ a_{21} & a_{22} - \lambda & \ldots & a_{2n} \\ \ldots & \ldots & \ldots & \ldots \\ a_{n1} & a_{n2} & \ldots & a_{nn} - \lambda \end{vmatrix}$$

Therefore, the characteristic equation is

$$|A - \lambda I| = 0$$

$$\Rightarrow \quad p_0\lambda^n + p_1\lambda^{n-1} + p_2\lambda^{n-2} + \ldots + p_n = 0$$

So, we have to prove that

$$p_0A^n + p_1A^{n-1} + p_2A^{n-2} + \ldots + p_nI = O$$

Since the elements of $(A - \lambda I)$ are polynomials atmost of the first degree in λ, therefore, the elements of *adj* $(A - \lambda I)$ are polynomials atmost of degree $(n - 1)$ in λ. Thus, *adj* $(A - \lambda I)$ can be expressed as a matrix polynomials in λ as

$$adj\ (A - \lambda I) = B_0\lambda^{n-1} + B_1\lambda^{n-2} + \dots + B_{n-1}$$

where $B_0, B_1, \dots, B_{n-1}$ are square matrices of the same order n, their elements being polynomials in the elements of A.

We know that

$$(A - \lambda I) \text{ adj } (A - \lambda I) = |A - \lambda I|\ I$$

$$\Rightarrow (A - \lambda \text{I}) (B_0\lambda^{n-1} + B_1\lambda^{n-2} + \dots + B_{n-1})$$
$$= (p_0\lambda^n + p_1\lambda^{n-1} + p_2\lambda^{n-2} + \dots + p_n)\ I$$

This is an identity in scalar λ. Therefore, equating the coefficients of like power of λ, we obtain

$$-B_0 = p_0 I$$
$$AB_0 - B_1 = p_1 I$$
$$AB_1 - B_2 = p_2 I$$
$$\vdots$$
$$\vdots$$
$$AB_{r-1} - B_r = p_r I$$
$$\vdots$$
$$\vdots$$
$$AB_{n-2} - B_{n-1} = p_{n-1} I$$
$$AB_{n-1} = p_n I$$

Pre-multiplying these equations by $A^n, A^{n-1}, A^{n-2}, \dots, A^{n-r}, \dots, A, I$ respectively and adding, we obtain

$$O = p_0A^n + p_1A^{n-1} + p_2A^{n-2} + \dots + p_{n-1}A + p_nI$$

which proves the theorem.

Corollary. *Computation of the inverse*

Let A be a non-singular square matrix of order n. Then, by Cayley-Hamilton theorem, we have

$$p_0A^n + p_1A^{n-1} + p_2A^{n-2} + \dots + p_{n-1}A + p_nI = O \quad \dots (8.6)$$

Multiplying Eq. (8.6) on both sides by A^{-1}, we obtain

$$p_0A^{n-1} + p_1A^{n-2} + p_2A^{n-3} + \dots + p_{n-1}I + p_nA^{-1} = O \quad \dots (8.7)$$

$$\Rightarrow A^{-1} = -\frac{1}{p_n}\left[p_0A^{n-1} + p_1A^{n-2} + p_2A^{n-3} + \dots + p_{n-1}\right]$$

Thus, A^{-1} can be evaluated.

Note: Successively multiplying Eq. (8.7) by A^{-1}, we may evaluate A^{-2}, A^{-3}, ... successively.

ILLUSTRATIVE EXAMPLES

Example 1. Verify Cayley-Hamilton Theorem for the matrix $A = \begin{bmatrix} 3 & 1 \\ -1 & 2 \end{bmatrix}$. Hence, express $2A^5 - 3A^4 + A^2 - 4I$ as a linear polynomial in A.

Solution: The characteristic equation of A is

$$|A - \lambda I| = 0$$

$$\Rightarrow \begin{vmatrix} 3-\lambda & 1 \\ -1 & 2-\lambda \end{vmatrix} = 0$$

$$\Rightarrow (3-\lambda)(2-\lambda) + 1 = 0$$

$$\Rightarrow \lambda^2 - 5\lambda + 7 = 0$$

To verify Cayley-Hamilton Theorem, we have to show that $A^2 - 5A + 7I = O$.

Now,

$$A^2 = \begin{bmatrix} 3 & 1 \\ -1 & 2 \end{bmatrix}\begin{bmatrix} 3 & 1 \\ -1 & 2 \end{bmatrix} = \begin{bmatrix} 8 & 5 \\ -5 & 3 \end{bmatrix}$$

$$\therefore\ A^2 - 5A + 7I = \begin{bmatrix} 8 & 5 \\ -5 & 3 \end{bmatrix} - 5\begin{bmatrix} 3 & 1 \\ -1 & 2 \end{bmatrix} + 7\begin{bmatrix} 1 & 0 \\ 0 & 1 \end{bmatrix}$$

$$= \begin{bmatrix} 0 & 0 \\ 0 & 0 \end{bmatrix} = O$$

This verifies Cayley-Hamilton Theorem.

We have,

$$A^2 - 5A + 7I = O \qquad \text{... (8.8)}$$

$$\Rightarrow A^2 = 5A - 7I \qquad \text{... (8.9)}$$

$$\Rightarrow A^4 = (5A - 7I)(5A - 7I)$$

$$\Rightarrow A^4 = 25A^2 + 49I - 70A$$

$$\Rightarrow A^4 = 25(5A - 7I) + 49I - 70A \quad | \text{ Using Eq. (8.9)}$$

$$\Rightarrow A^4 = 55A - 126I \qquad \text{... (8.10)}$$

Multiplying Eq. (8.10) on both sides by A, we get

$$A^5 = 55A^2 - 126A$$

$$\Rightarrow A^5 = 55(5A - 7I) - 126A \quad | \text{ Using Eq. (8.9)}$$

$$\Rightarrow A^5 = 149A - 385I \qquad \text{... (8.11)}$$

$$\therefore \quad 2A^5 - 3A^4 + A^2 - 4I$$

$$= 2(149A - 385I) - 3(55A - 126I) + (5A - 7I) - 4I$$

| Using Eqs. (8.9), (8.10) and (8.11)

$$= 138A - 403I$$

Example 2. If $a + b + c = 0$, find the characteristic roots of the matrix $A = \begin{bmatrix} a & c & b \\ c & b & a \\ b & a & c \end{bmatrix}$.

Solution: The characteristic equation of A is

$$|A - \lambda I| = 0$$

$$\Rightarrow \begin{vmatrix} a-\lambda & c & b \\ c & b-\lambda & a \\ b & a & c-\lambda \end{vmatrix} = 0$$

$$\Rightarrow \begin{vmatrix} a-\lambda+c+b & c & b \\ c+b-\lambda+a & b-\lambda & a \\ b+a+c-\lambda & a & c-\lambda \end{vmatrix} = 0$$

| Operating $C_1 + C_2 + C_3$

$$\Rightarrow \begin{vmatrix} -\lambda & c & b \\ -\lambda & b-\lambda & a \\ -\lambda & a & c-\lambda \end{vmatrix} = 0 \qquad | \because a+b+c=0$$

$$\Rightarrow \begin{vmatrix} -\lambda & c & b \\ 0 & b-\lambda-c & a-b \\ 0 & a-c & c-\lambda-b \end{vmatrix} = 0$$

| Operating $R_2 - R_1$, $R_3 - R_1$

$$\Rightarrow -\lambda\left[(b-\lambda-c)(c-\lambda-b)-(a-c)(a-b)\right]=0$$

$$\Rightarrow \lambda\left[\left(a^2+b^2+c^2-ab-bc-ca\right)-\lambda^2\right]=0$$

$$\Rightarrow \lambda\left[a^2+b^2+c^2+\frac{1}{2}\left(a^2+b^2+c^2\right)-\lambda^2\right]=0$$

$$\begin{aligned} &\because \quad a+b+c=0 \\ &\therefore \quad (a+b+c)^2=0 \\ &\Rightarrow \quad a^2+b^2+c^2+2ab+2bc+2ca=0 \\ &\Rightarrow \quad \frac{a^2+b^2+c^2}{2}=-(ab+bc+ca) \end{aligned}$$

$$\Rightarrow \lambda\left[\frac{3}{2}\left(a^2+b^2+c^2\right)-\lambda^2\right]=0$$

$$\Rightarrow \lambda = 0, \pm\sqrt{\frac{3}{2}\left(a^2+b^2+c^2\right)}$$

These are the required characteristic roots.

Example 3. Verify Cayley-Hamilton Theorem for the matrix

$$A = \begin{bmatrix} 2 & -1 & 1 \\ -1 & 2 & -1 \\ 1 & -1 & 2 \end{bmatrix}.$$ Hence, compute A^{-1}.

Solution: The characteristic equation of A is

$$|A - \lambda I| = 0$$

$$\Rightarrow \begin{vmatrix} 2-\lambda & -1 & 1 \\ -1 & 2-\lambda & -1 \\ 1 & -1 & 2-\lambda \end{vmatrix} = 0$$

$$\Rightarrow (2-\lambda)\left\{(2-\lambda)^2 - 1\right\} - \left\{-1 + (2-\lambda)\right\}$$
$$+ \left\{1 - (2-\lambda)\right\} = 0$$

$$\Rightarrow (2-\lambda)\left(\lambda^2 - 4\lambda + 3\right) - (1-\lambda) + (-1+\lambda) = 0$$

$$\Rightarrow 2\lambda^2 - 8\lambda + 6 - \lambda^3 + 4\lambda^2 - 3\lambda - 1 + \lambda - 1 + \lambda = 0$$

$$\Rightarrow -\lambda^3 + 6\lambda^2 - 9\lambda + 4 = 0$$

$$\Rightarrow \lambda^3 - 6\lambda^2 + 9\lambda - 4 = 0$$

To verify Cayley-Hamilton Theorem, we have to show that

$$A^3 - 6A^2 + 9A - 4I = O \qquad \text{... (8.12)}$$

Now,

$$A^2 = AA = \begin{bmatrix} 2 & -1 & 1 \\ -1 & 2 & -1 \\ 1 & -1 & 2 \end{bmatrix} \begin{bmatrix} 2 & -1 & 1 \\ -1 & 2 & -1 \\ 1 & -1 & 2 \end{bmatrix}$$

$$= \begin{bmatrix} 6 & -5 & 5 \\ -5 & 6 & -5 \\ 5 & -5 & 6 \end{bmatrix}$$

$$A^3 = A^2 A = \begin{bmatrix} 6 & -5 & 5 \\ -5 & 6 & -5 \\ 5 & -5 & 6 \end{bmatrix} \begin{bmatrix} 2 & -1 & 1 \\ -1 & 2 & -1 \\ 1 & -1 & 2 \end{bmatrix}$$

$$= \begin{bmatrix} 22 & -22 & 21 \\ -21 & 22 & -21 \\ 21 & -21 & 22 \end{bmatrix}$$

$$\therefore \quad A^3 - 6A^2 + 9A - 4I$$

$$= \begin{bmatrix} 22 & -21 & 21 \\ -21 & 22 & -21 \\ 21 & -21 & 22 \end{bmatrix} - 6\begin{bmatrix} 6 & -5 & 5 \\ -5 & 6 & -5 \\ 5 & -5 & 6 \end{bmatrix} + 9\begin{bmatrix} 2 & -1 & 1 \\ -1 & 2 & -1 \\ 1 & -1 & 2 \end{bmatrix} - 4\begin{bmatrix} 1 & 0 & 0 \\ 0 & 1 & 0 \\ 0 & 0 & 1 \end{bmatrix}$$

$$= \begin{bmatrix} 22 & -21 & 21 \\ -21 & 22 & -21 \\ 21 & -21 & 22 \end{bmatrix} + \begin{bmatrix} -36 & 30 & -30 \\ 30 & -36 & 30 \\ -30 & 30 & -36 \end{bmatrix} + \begin{bmatrix} 18 & -9 & 9 \\ -9 & 18 & -9 \\ 9 & -9 & 18 \end{bmatrix} + \begin{bmatrix} -4 & 0 & 0 \\ 0 & -4 & 0 \\ 0 & 0 & -4 \end{bmatrix}$$

$$= \begin{bmatrix} 22 - 36 + 18 - 4 & -21 + 30 - 9 + 0 & 21 - 30 + 9 + 0 \\ -21 + 30 - 9 + 0 & 22 - 36 + 18 - 4 & -21 + 30 \; 9 + 0 \\ 21 - 30 + 9 + 0 & -21 + 30 - 9 + 0 & 22 - 36 \; 18 - 4 \end{bmatrix}$$

$$= \begin{bmatrix} 0 & 0 & 0 \\ 0 & 0 & 0 \\ 0 & 0 & 0 \end{bmatrix} = O$$

This verifies Cayley-Hamilton Theorem for the matrix A.

Now, multiplying both sides of Eq. (8.12) by A^{-1}, we have

$$A^2 - 6A + 9I - 4A^{-1} = O$$

$$\Rightarrow \; 4A^{-1} = A^2 - 6A + 9I$$

$$\Rightarrow \; 4A^{-1} = \begin{bmatrix} 6 & -5 & 5 \\ -5 & 6 & -5 \\ 5 & -5 & 6 \end{bmatrix} - 6\begin{bmatrix} 2 & -1 & 1 \\ -1 & 2 & -1 \\ 1 & -1 & 2 \end{bmatrix} + 9\begin{bmatrix} 1 & 0 & 0 \\ 0 & 1 & 0 \\ 0 & 0 & 1 \end{bmatrix}$$

$$\Rightarrow \; 4A^{-1} = \begin{bmatrix} 6 & -5 & 5 \\ -5 & 6 & -5 \\ 5 & -5 & 6 \end{bmatrix} + \begin{bmatrix} -12 & 6 & -6 \\ 6 & -12 & 6 \\ -6 & 6 & -12 \end{bmatrix} + \begin{bmatrix} 9 & 0 & 0 \\ 0 & 9 & 0 \\ 0 & 0 & 9 \end{bmatrix}$$

$$\Rightarrow \; 4A^{-1} = \begin{bmatrix} 6-12+9 & -5+6+0 & 5-6+0 \\ -5+6+0 & 6-12+9 & -5+6+0 \\ 5-6+0 & -5+6+0 & 6+2+9 \end{bmatrix}$$

$$\Rightarrow \; 4A^{-1} = \begin{bmatrix} 3 & 1 & -1 \\ 1 & 3 & 1 \\ -1 & 1 & 3 \end{bmatrix}$$

$$\Rightarrow \; A^{-1} = \frac{1}{4}\begin{bmatrix} 3 & 1 & -1 \\ 1 & 3 & 1 \\ -1 & 1 & 3 \end{bmatrix}$$

Example 4. Show that the matrix $A = \begin{bmatrix} 0 & c & -b \\ -c & 0 & a \\ b & -a & 0 \end{bmatrix}$ satisfies Cayley-Hamilton Theorem.

Solution: The characteristic equation of A is

$$|A - \lambda I| = 0$$

$$\Rightarrow \begin{vmatrix} 0-\lambda & c & -b \\ -c & 0-\lambda & a \\ b & -a & 0-\lambda \end{vmatrix} = 0$$

$$\Rightarrow \begin{vmatrix} -\lambda & c & -b \\ -c & -\lambda & a \\ b & -a & -\lambda \end{vmatrix} = 0$$

$$\Rightarrow -\lambda\left(\lambda^2 - a^2\right) + c\left(ab - c\lambda\right) - b\left(ac + b\lambda\right) = 0$$

$$\Rightarrow -\lambda^3 - a^2\lambda + abc - c^2\lambda - abc - b^2\lambda = 0$$

$$\Rightarrow \lambda^3 + \left(a^2 + b^2 + c^2\right)\lambda = 0$$

To show that the matrix A satisfies Cayley-Hamilton Theorem, we need to prove that

$$A^3 + (a^2 + b^2 + c^2)A = O$$

Now,

$$A^2 = AA$$

$$= \begin{bmatrix} 0 & c & -b \\ -c & 0 & a \\ b & -a & 0 \end{bmatrix}\begin{bmatrix} 0 & c & -b \\ -c & 0 & a \\ b & -a & 0 \end{bmatrix}$$

$$= \begin{bmatrix} -c^2 - b^2 & ba & ca \\ ab & -c^2 - a^2 & cb \\ ac & bc & -b^2 - a^2 \end{bmatrix}$$

$$A^3 = A^2A$$

$$= \begin{bmatrix} -c^2 - b^2 & ba & ca \\ ab & -c^2 - a^2 & cb \\ ac & bc & -b^2 - a^2 \end{bmatrix}\begin{bmatrix} 0 & c & -b \\ -c & 0 & a \\ b & -a & 0 \end{bmatrix}$$

$$= \begin{bmatrix} 0 & -c^3 - b^2c - a^2c & c^2b + b^3 + a^2b \\ c^3 + a^2c + b^2c & 0 & -ab^2 - ac^2 - a^3 \\ -bc^2 - b^3 - a^2b & ac^2 + ab^2 + a^3 & 0 \end{bmatrix}$$

$$= \begin{bmatrix} 0 & \dfrac{-c}{(a^2+b^2+c^2)} & \dfrac{b}{(a^2+b^2+c^2)} \\ c(a^2+b^2+c^2) & 0 & \dfrac{-a}{(a^2+b^2+c^2)} \\ -b(a^2+b^2+c^2) & \dfrac{a}{(a^2+b^2+c^2)} & 0 \end{bmatrix}$$

$$= -(a^2+b^2+c^2)\begin{bmatrix} 0 & c & -b \\ -c & 0 & a \\ b & -a & 0 \end{bmatrix}$$

$$= -(a^2 + b^2 + c^2)A$$

$$\Rightarrow A^3 + (a^2 + b^2 + c^2)A = O$$

This verifies Cayley-Hamilton Theorem.

Example 5. Find the characteristic equation of the matrix $A = \begin{bmatrix} 2 & 1 & 1 \\ 0 & 1 & 0 \\ 1 & 1 & 2 \end{bmatrix}$ and, hence, compute A^{-1}. Also, find the matrix represented by $A^8 - 5A^7 + 7A^6 - 3A^5 + A^4 - 5A^3 + 8A^2 - 2A + I$.

Solution: The characteristic equation of A is

$$|A - \lambda I| = 0$$

$$\Rightarrow \begin{vmatrix} 2-\lambda & 1 & 1 \\ 0 & 1-\lambda & 0 \\ 1 & 1 & 2-\lambda \end{vmatrix} = 0$$

$$\Rightarrow \lambda^3 - 5\lambda^2 + 7\lambda - 3 = 0$$

Consequently, by Cayley-Hamilton Theorem, we have

$$A^3 - 5A^2 + 7A - 3I = O \qquad \text{... (8.13)}$$

Multiplying both sides of Eq. (8.13) by A^{-1}, we get

$$A^2 - 5A + 7I - 3A^{-1} = A^{-1}O$$

$$\Rightarrow \ A^2 - 5A + 7I - 3A^{-1} = O$$

$$\Rightarrow \ A^{-1} = \frac{1}{3}\left(A^2 - 5A + 7I\right) \qquad \text{... (8.14)}$$

Now,

$$A^2 = AA$$

$$= \begin{bmatrix} 2 & 1 & 1 \\ 0 & 1 & 0 \\ 1 & 1 & 2 \end{bmatrix}\begin{bmatrix} 2 & 1 & 1 \\ 0 & 1 & 0 \\ 1 & 1 & 2 \end{bmatrix}$$

$$= \begin{bmatrix} 5 & 4 & 4 \\ 0 & 1 & 0 \\ 4 & 4 & 5 \end{bmatrix}$$

From Eq. (8.14),

$$3A^{-1} = \begin{bmatrix} 5 & 4 & 4 \\ 0 & 1 & 0 \\ 4 & 4 & 5 \end{bmatrix} - 5\begin{bmatrix} 2 & 1 & 1 \\ 0 & 1 & 0 \\ 1 & 1 & 2 \end{bmatrix} + 7\begin{bmatrix} 1 & 0 & 0 \\ 0 & 1 & 0 \\ 0 & 0 & 1 \end{bmatrix}$$

$$= \begin{bmatrix} 2 & -1 & -1 \\ 0 & 3 & 0 \\ -1 & -1 & 2 \end{bmatrix}$$

$$\Rightarrow \ A^{-1} = \frac{1}{3}\begin{bmatrix} 2 & -1 & -1 \\ 0 & 3 & 0 \\ -1 & -1 & 2 \end{bmatrix}$$

Now,

$$A^8 - 5A^7 + 7A^6 - 3A^5 + A^4 - 5A^3 + 8A^2 - 2A + I$$

$$= A^5\left(A^3 - 5A^2 + 7A - 3I\right)$$

$$+ A\left(A^3 - 5A^2 + 7A - 3I\right) + \left(A^2 + A + I\right)$$

$$= A^2 + A + I \quad | \text{ Using Eq. (8.13)}$$

$$= \begin{bmatrix} 5 & 4 & 4 \\ 0 & 1 & 0 \\ 4 & 4 & 5 \end{bmatrix} + \begin{bmatrix} 2 & 1 & 1 \\ 0 & 1 & 0 \\ 1 & 1 & 2 \end{bmatrix} + \begin{bmatrix} 1 & 0 & 0 \\ 0 & 1 & 0 \\ 0 & 0 & 1 \end{bmatrix}$$

$$= \begin{bmatrix} 8 & 5 & 5 \\ 0 & 3 & 0 \\ 5 & 5 & 8 \end{bmatrix}$$

Example 6. Given $A = \begin{bmatrix} 1 & 2 & -1 \\ 0 & 1 & -1 \\ 3 & -1 & 1 \end{bmatrix}$, find adj A using Cayley-Hamilton Theorem.

Solution: The characteristic equation of A is

$$|A - \lambda I| = 0$$

$$\Rightarrow \begin{vmatrix} 1-\lambda & 2 & -1 \\ 0 & 1-\lambda & -1 \\ 3 & -1 & 1-\lambda \end{vmatrix} = 0$$

$$\Rightarrow \lambda^3 - 3\lambda^2 + 5\lambda + 3 = 0$$

$\therefore$ By Cayley-Hamilton Theorem,

$$A^3 - 3A^2 + 5A + 3I = O$$

Multiplying both sides by A^{-1}, we get

$$A^2 - 3A + 5I + 3A^{-1} = O$$

$$\Rightarrow A^{-1} = -\frac{1}{3}\left(A^2 - 3A + 5I\right)$$

Now,

$$A^2 = AA = \begin{bmatrix} 1 & 2 & -1 \\ 0 & 1 & -1 \\ 3 & -1 & 1 \end{bmatrix} \begin{bmatrix} 1 & 2 & -1 \\ 0 & 1 & -1 \\ 3 & -1 & 1 \end{bmatrix}$$

$$= \begin{bmatrix} -2 & 5 & -4 \\ -3 & 2 & -2 \\ 6 & 4 & -1 \end{bmatrix}$$

$$\therefore \quad A^{-1} = -\frac{1}{3}\left\{\begin{bmatrix} -2 & 5 & -4 \\ -3 & 2 & -2 \\ 6 & 4 & -1 \end{bmatrix} - 3\begin{bmatrix} 1 & 2 & -1 \\ 0 & 1 & -1 \\ 3 & -1 & 1 \end{bmatrix} + 5\begin{bmatrix} 1 & 0 & 0 \\ 0 & 1 & 0 \\ 0 & 0 & 1 \end{bmatrix}\right\}$$

$$= -\frac{1}{3}\begin{bmatrix} 0 & -1 & -1 \\ -3 & 4 & 1 \\ -3 & 7 & 1 \end{bmatrix}$$

Also, $|A| = \begin{vmatrix} 1 & 2 & -1 \\ 0 & 1 & -1 \\ 3 & -1 & 1 \end{vmatrix} = -3$

We know that

$$A^{-1} = \frac{\text{Adj } A}{|A|}$$

$$\therefore \quad \text{Adj } A = |A| \, A^{-1}$$

$$\Rightarrow \text{Adj } A = -3\left\{-\frac{1}{3}\begin{bmatrix} 0 & -1 & -1 \\ -3 & 4 & 1 \\ -3 & 7 & 1 \end{bmatrix}\right\}$$

$$\Rightarrow \text{Adj } A = \begin{bmatrix} 0 & -1 & -1 \\ -3 & 4 & 1 \\ -3 & 7 & 1 \end{bmatrix}$$

Example 7. Show that the matrix $A = \begin{bmatrix} 1 & 2 & 0 \\ 2 & -1 & 0 \\ 0 & 0 & -1 \end{bmatrix}$ satisfies its own characteristic equation and hence or otherwise obtain the value of A^{-2}.

Solution: The characteristic equation of the matrix A is

$$|A - \lambda I| = 0$$

$$\Rightarrow \begin{vmatrix} 1-\lambda & 2 & 0 \\ 2 & -1-\lambda & 0 \\ 0 & 0 & -1-\lambda \end{vmatrix} = 0$$

$$\Rightarrow \lambda^3 + \lambda^2 - 5\lambda - 5 = 0$$

To show that the matrix A satisfies its own characteristic equation, we have to establish that

$$A^3 + A^2 - 5A - 5I = O$$

Now,

$$A^2 = AA = \begin{bmatrix} 1 & 2 & 0 \\ 2 & -1 & 0 \\ 0 & 0 & -1 \end{bmatrix}\begin{bmatrix} 1 & 2 & 0 \\ 2 & -1 & 0 \\ 0 & 0 & -1 \end{bmatrix} = \begin{bmatrix} 5 & 0 & 0 \\ 0 & 5 & 0 \\ 0 & 0 & 1 \end{bmatrix}$$

$$A^3 = A^2A = \begin{bmatrix} 5 & 0 & 0 \\ 0 & 5 & 0 \\ 0 & 0 & 1 \end{bmatrix}\begin{bmatrix} 1 & 2 & 0 \\ 2 & -1 & 0 \\ 0 & 0 & -1 \end{bmatrix} = \begin{bmatrix} 5 & 10 & 0 \\ 10 & -5 & 0 \\ 0 & 0 & -1 \end{bmatrix}$$

$$\therefore \quad A^3 + A^2 - 5A - 5I$$

$$= \begin{bmatrix} 5 & 10 & 0 \\ 10 & -5 & 0 \\ 0 & 0 & -1 \end{bmatrix} + \begin{bmatrix} 5 & 0 & 0 \\ 0 & 5 & 0 \\ 0 & 0 & 1 \end{bmatrix} - 5\begin{bmatrix} 1 & 2 & 0 \\ 2 & -1 & 0 \\ 0 & 0 & -1 \end{bmatrix}$$

$$-5\begin{bmatrix} 1 & 0 & 0 \\ 0 & 1 & 0 \\ 0 & 0 & 0 \end{bmatrix} = O$$

Hence, the given matrix A satisfies its own characteristic equation.

Computation of A^{-2}

We have

$$A^3 + A^2 - 5A - 5I = O \qquad \text{... (8.15)}$$

Multiplying both sides of Eq. (8.15) by A^{-1}, we get

$$A^2 + A - 5I - 5A^{-1} = O$$

$$\Rightarrow \; A^{-1} = \frac{1}{5}\left(A^2 + A - 5I\right) \qquad \text{... (8.16)}$$

$$\Rightarrow \; A^{-1} = \frac{1}{5}\left\{\begin{bmatrix} 5 & 0 & 0 \\ 0 & 5 & 0 \\ 0 & 0 & 1 \end{bmatrix} + \begin{bmatrix} 1 & 2 & 0 \\ 2 & -1 & 0 \\ 0 & 0 & -1 \end{bmatrix} - 5\begin{bmatrix} 1 & 0 & 0 \\ 0 & 1 & 0 \\ 0 & 0 & 0 \end{bmatrix}\right\}$$

$$= \frac{1}{5}\begin{bmatrix} 1 & 2 & 0 \\ 2 & -1 & 0 \\ 0 & 0 & -1 \end{bmatrix} \qquad \text{... (8.17)}$$

Multiplying both sides of Eq. (8.16) by A^{-1}, we get

$$A^{-2} = \frac{1}{5}\left(A + I - 5A^{-1}\right)$$

$$= \frac{1}{5}\left\{\begin{bmatrix} 1 & 2 & 0 \\ 2 & -1 & 0 \\ 0 & 0 & -1 \end{bmatrix} + \begin{bmatrix} 1 & 0 & 0 \\ 0 & 1 & 0 \\ 0 & 0 & 1 \end{bmatrix} - 5\frac{1}{5}\begin{bmatrix} 1 & 2 & 0 \\ 2 & -1 & 0 \\ 0 & 0 & -1 \end{bmatrix}\right\}$$

$$= \frac{1}{5}\begin{bmatrix} 1 & 0 & 0 \\ 0 & 1 & 0 \\ 0 & 0 & -1 \end{bmatrix}$$

EXERCISE 8.1

1. Find the latent roots of $A = \begin{bmatrix} a & h & g \\ 0 & b & f \\ 0 & 0 & c \end{bmatrix}$.

2. Verify that the matrices $A = \begin{bmatrix} 0 & h & g \\ h & 0 & f \\ g & f & 0 \end{bmatrix}, B = \begin{bmatrix} 0 & f & h \\ f & 0 & g \\ h & g & 0 \end{bmatrix},$

$C = \begin{bmatrix} 0 & g & f \\ g & 0 & h \\ f & h & 0 \end{bmatrix}$ have the same characteristic equation

$\lambda^3 - (f^2 + g^2 + h^2)\lambda^2 - 2fgh = 0.$

3. Find the characteristic roots and inverse of the matrix

$A = \begin{bmatrix} 5 & 6 \\ 1 & 2 \end{bmatrix}.$

4. Find the eigen values of $A = \begin{bmatrix} 1 & 2 \\ 4 & 3 \end{bmatrix}.$

5. If $A = \begin{bmatrix} 1 & 2 \\ -1 & 3 \end{bmatrix}$, use Cayley-Hamilton Theorem to express $A^6 - 4A^5 + 8A^4 - 12A^3 + 14A^2$ as a linear polynomial in A.

6. Using Cayley-Hamilton Theorem, obtain A^{-1} where $A = \begin{bmatrix} 1 & 4 \\ 2 & 3 \end{bmatrix}$. Also express $A^5 - 4A^4 - 7A^3 + 11A^2 - A - 10I$ as a linear polynomial in A.

7. Verify Cayley-Hamilton Theorem for the matrix $A = \begin{bmatrix} 1 & 2 \\ 3 & 4 \end{bmatrix}$ and hence find A^{-1}.

8. Find A^{-1} by Cayley-Hamilton Theorem where $A = \begin{bmatrix} 1 & 1 \\ 1 & 0 \end{bmatrix}.$

9. Using the characteristic equation of the matrix $A = \begin{bmatrix} 1 & 0 & 1 \\ 0 & 1 & 0 \\ 0 & 0 & 1 \end{bmatrix}$, find A^{-1} and the latent roots.

10. Find the characteristic roots of the matrix $A = \begin{bmatrix} 2 & 2 & 1 \\ 1 & 3 & 1 \\ 1 & 2 & 2 \end{bmatrix}$ and show that it satisfies its own characteristic equation.

11. Using Cayley-Hamilton Theorem, find the inverse of $A = \begin{bmatrix} 1 & 2 & 3 \\ 1 & 3 & 5 \\ 1 & 5 & 12 \end{bmatrix}$.

12. Verify Cayley-Hamilton Theorem for the matrix $A = \begin{bmatrix} 8 & -6 & 2 \\ -6 & 7 & -4 \\ 2 & -4 & 3 \end{bmatrix}$. Find the latent roots and A^{-1} also.

13. For $A = \begin{bmatrix} 1 & 0 & 2 \\ 0 & 2 & 1 \\ 2 & 0 & 3 \end{bmatrix}$, verify the Cayley-Hamilton Theorem that A satisfies the equation $A^3 - 6A^2 + 7A + 2I = O$.

14. Find the characteristic equation of the matrix $A = \begin{bmatrix} 1 & 3 & 7 \\ 4 & 2 & 3 \\ 1 & 2 & 31 \end{bmatrix}$. Show that the equation is satisfied by A and hence obtain the value of A^{-1}.

15. If $A = \begin{bmatrix} 4 & -1 & -1 \\ -1 & 4 & -1 \\ -1 & -1 & 4 \end{bmatrix}$ and $B = I - \frac{1}{4}A$, then show that $\mu_i = 1 - \frac{1}{4}\lambda_i$, where λ_i and μ_i are the eigen values of A and B respectively.

ANSWERS

1. a, b, c

3. $\frac{7 \pm \sqrt{33}}{2}$, $A^{-1} = \frac{1}{4}\begin{bmatrix} 2 & -6 \\ -1 & 5 \end{bmatrix}$

4. $-1, 5$

5. $-4A + 5I$

6. $A^{-1} = \frac{1}{5}\begin{bmatrix} -3 & 4 \\ 2 & -1 \end{bmatrix}$, $A + 5I$

7. $\begin{bmatrix} 2 & -1 \\ -\frac{3}{2} & 1 \end{bmatrix}$

8. $\begin{bmatrix} 0 & 1 \\ 1 & -1 \end{bmatrix}$

9. $\begin{bmatrix} 1 & 0 & -1 \\ 0 & 1 & 0 \\ 0 & 0 & 1 \end{bmatrix}$; 1, 1, 1

10. 1, 1, 5

11. $\frac{1}{3}\begin{bmatrix} 11 & -9 & 1 \\ -7 & 9 & -2 \\ 2 & -3 & 1 \end{bmatrix}$

12. $0, 3, 15; \frac{1}{80}\begin{bmatrix} 11 & -10 & -34 \\ -2 & -20 & -52 \\ -10 & -20 & -20 \end{bmatrix}$

14. $\lambda^3 - 4\lambda^2 - 20\lambda - 35 = 0; A^{-1} = \frac{1}{35}\begin{bmatrix} -4 & 11 & -5 \\ -1 & -6 & 25 \\ 6 & 1 & -10 \end{bmatrix}$

8.10. Fundamental Theorems

Theorem 1. For a square matrix, every eigen vector corresponds to a unique eigen value.

Proof. Let there exist two distinct eigen values λ_1 and λ_2 corresponding to an eigen vector X of a square matrix A. Then, we have

$$AX = \lambda_1 X \quad \text{... (8.18)}$$

$$AX = \lambda_2 X \quad \text{... (8.19)} \qquad \Big| \because \lambda_1 \neq \lambda_2$$

In view of Eqs. (8.18) and (8.19), we have

$$\lambda_1 X = \lambda_2 X$$

$$\Rightarrow (\lambda_1 - \lambda_2)X = O$$

$$\Rightarrow X = O \qquad | \because \lambda_1 \neq \lambda_2$$

which is impossible since X is a non zero vector. Hence, every eigen vector corresponding to a unique eigen value.

Theorem 2. Show that for a square matrix, there are infinitely many eigen vectors corresponding to a single eigen value.

Proof. Let X be a characteristic vector of a square matrix A corresponding to a single eigen value λ. Then, we have

$$AX = \lambda X$$

Let k be an arbitrary non-zero scalar.

Then,

$$k(AX) = k(\lambda X)$$

$$\Rightarrow A(kX) = \lambda(kX)$$

Therefore, kX is also a characteristic vector of A corresponding to the same characteristic root λ.

Since k is an arbitrary non-zero scalar, therefore, there exist infinitely many eigen vectors corresponding to a single eigen value.

Theorem 3. The scalar λ is a characteristic root of the square matrix A if and only if there exists a non-zero vector X such that

$$AX = \lambda X$$

OR

The equation $AX = \lambda X$ has a non-trivial solution X if λ is a latent root of A.

OR

The scalar λ is a characteristic root of the square matrix A if and only if $A - \lambda I$ is singular.

Proof. Let λ be a latent root of a square matrix A. Then, by definition, λ must satisfy the characteristic equation of A, i.e.

$$|A - \lambda I| = 0$$

This implies that the matrix $A - \lambda I$ must be singular.

Hence, λ is a characteristic root of the square matrix A if $A - \lambda I$ is singular.

Therefore, the matrix equation $(A - \lambda I)X = O$ possesses a non-zero solution, i.e. there exists a non-zero vector X such that

$$(A - \lambda I)X = O$$

$$\Rightarrow AX - \lambda IX = O$$

$$\Rightarrow AX - \lambda(IX) = O$$

$$\Rightarrow AX - \lambda X = O$$

$$\Rightarrow AX = \lambda X$$

Conversely, If $|A - \lambda I| = 0$, then there exists a non-zero vector X such that

$$(A - \lambda I)X = O$$

$\Rightarrow\ AX = \lambda X$

$\Rightarrow\ \lambda$ is a characteristic root of the square matrix A.

Theorem 4. The product of all eigen values of the square matrix A is equal to determinant (A).

Proof. Let $A = [a_{ij}]_{n \times n}$ be the given square matrix. Let λ_1, λ_2, λ_3, ..., λ_n be its eigen values. Let $\varphi(\lambda)$ be the characteristic polynomial of A. Then,

$$\varphi(\lambda) = |A - \lambda I|$$

$$= \begin{vmatrix} a_{11} - \lambda & a_{12} & \cdots & a_{1n} \\ a_{21} & a_{22} - \lambda & \cdots & a_{2n} \\ \cdots & \cdots & \cdots & \cdots \\ a_{n1} & a_{n2} & \cdots & a_{nn} - \lambda \end{vmatrix}$$

$$= (-1)^n \{\lambda^n + p_1\lambda^{n-1} + p_2\lambda^{n-2} + \ldots + p_n\}$$

$$= (-1)^n \{(\lambda - \lambda_1)(\lambda - \lambda_2)(\lambda - \lambda_3) \ldots (\lambda - \lambda_n)\}$$

Putting $\lambda = 0$, we get

$$\varphi(0) = (-1)^n (-1)^n \lambda_1 \lambda_2 \lambda_3 \ldots \lambda_n$$

$$\Rightarrow |A| = \lambda_1 \lambda_2 \lambda_3 \ldots \lambda_n$$

Hence, the product of all eigen values of A is equal to the determinant (A).

Theorem 5. Prove that 0 is a characteristic root of the square matrix A iff the matrix A is singular.

Proof. The characteristic root λ of a matrix A is given by

$$|A - \lambda I| = 0 \qquad \ldots (8.20)$$

If $\lambda = 0$, then Eq. (8.20) gives

$$|A| = 0$$

$\Rightarrow$ A is singular

Conversely, if the matrix A is singular, then

$$|A| = 0$$

$$\therefore\ |A - \lambda I| = 0$$

$$\Rightarrow |A| - \lambda|I| = 0$$

$\Rightarrow\ 0 - \lambda 1 = 0$

$\Rightarrow\ -\lambda = 0$

$\Rightarrow\ \lambda = 0$

Hence, 0 is a characteristic root of the square matrix A.

Theorem 6. Show that the square matrices A and A' have the same eigen values.

Proof. Let A be a square matrix.

The characteristic equation of A is

$$|A - \lambda I| = 0 \qquad \text{... (8.21)}$$

Let A' be the transpose of A.

Then the characteristic equation of A' is

$$|A' - \lambda I| = 0 \qquad \text{... (8.22)}$$

Since the interchange of rows and columns does not alter the value of a determinant, therefore, we have

$$|A - \lambda I| = |A' - \lambda I| \qquad \left| \begin{aligned} |A - \lambda I| &= |(A - \lambda I)'| \\ &= |A' - \lambda I'| \\ &= |A' - \lambda I| \text{ as } I' = I \end{aligned} \right.$$

Hence, the eigen values of the square matrix A and its transpose A' are identical.

Theorem 7. The sum of the eigen values of the square matrix is equal to the sum of the elements of its principal diagonal.

Proof. Let $A = [a_{ij}]_{3 \times 3}$ be a square matrix of order 3. Then the characteristic equation of A is

$$|A - \lambda I| = 0$$

$$\Rightarrow \begin{vmatrix} a_{11} - \lambda & a_{12} & a_{13} \\ a_{21} & a_{22} - \lambda & a_{23} \\ a_{31} & a_{32} & a_{33} - \lambda \end{vmatrix} = 0$$

$$\Rightarrow -\lambda^3 + \lambda^2 \left(a_{11} + a_{22} + a_{33}\right) - \ldots = 0 \qquad \text{... (8.23)}$$

But we know that

$$|A - \lambda I| = (-1)^3 (\lambda - \lambda_1)(\lambda - \lambda_2)(\lambda - \lambda_3)$$

$$= -\lambda^3 + \lambda^2 (\lambda_1 + \lambda_2 + \lambda_3) - \ldots.. \qquad \ldots (8.24)$$

Comparing Eqs. (8.23) and (8.24), we get

$$\lambda_1 + \lambda_2 + \lambda_3 = a_{11} + a_{22} + a_{33}$$

Theorem 8. Prove that the characteristic roots of a hermitian matrix are all real.

Proof. Let A be a hermitian matrix. Then,

$$A^* = A \qquad \ldots (8.25)$$

Let λ be a characteristic root of the matrix A. Then, there exists a non-zero characteristic vector X such that

$$AX = \lambda X \qquad \ldots (8.26)$$

Pre-multiplying both sides of Eq. (8.26) by X^*, we obtain

$$X^*(AX) = X^*(\lambda X)$$

$$X^*AX = X^*\lambda X$$

$$(X^*AX)^* = (X^*\lambda X)^*$$

$$X^*A^*(X^*)^* = \bar{\lambda}X^*(X^*)^* \qquad | \text{ By Reversal Law for Tranjugate}$$

$$\Rightarrow X^*A^*X = \bar{\lambda}X^*X \qquad | \because (X^*)^* = X$$

$$\Rightarrow X^*AX = \bar{\lambda}X^*X \qquad | \text{ From Eq. (8.25)}$$

$$\Rightarrow X^*\lambda X = \bar{\lambda}X^*X \qquad | \text{ From Eq. (8.26)}$$

$$\Rightarrow \lambda X^*X = \bar{\lambda}X^*X$$

$$\Rightarrow (\lambda - \bar{\lambda})X^*X = O \qquad \ldots (8.27)$$

$\because$ X is a non-zero characteristic vector

$\therefore$ $X^*X \neq O$

$\therefore$ From Eq. (8.27), we have

$$\lambda - \bar{\lambda} = 0$$

$$\Rightarrow \lambda = \bar{\lambda}$$

$\Rightarrow$ λ is real.

Hence, the characteristic roots of a hermitian matrix are all real.

Theorem 9. Prove that the characteristic roots of a real symmetric matrix are all real.

Proof. Let A be real symmetric matrix.

$\because$ A is real

$\therefore$ $\overline{A} = A$

$\therefore$ $(\overline{A})' = A'$

$\Rightarrow$ $A^* = A$ $\quad\Big|$ $\because$ A is symmetric $\therefore A' = A$

$\Rightarrow$ A is hermitian

Hence, by Theorem 8 above, the characteristic roots of A are all real.

Theorem 10. The characteristic roots of a skew-hermitian matrix are either zero or purely imaginary.

Proof. Let A be a skew-hermitian matrix. Then,

$$A^* = A \qquad \text{... (8.28)}$$

Let λ be a characteristic root of the matrix A. Then, there exists a non-zero characteristic vector X such that

$$AX = \lambda X \qquad \text{... (8.29)}$$

Multiplying both sides of Eq. (8.29) by i, we get

$$i(AX) = i(\lambda X)$$

$$\Rightarrow (iA)X = (i\lambda)X \qquad \text{... (8.30)}$$

The relation (8.30) shows that $i\lambda$ is a characteristic root of iA.

Also,

$$(iA)^* = \overline{i}A^*$$

$$= -i(-A) \qquad \text{| From Eq. (8.28)}$$

$$= iA$$

This shows that iA is a hermitian matrix.

Hence, by Theorem 8, the characteristic roots of iA must be real.

Now, $i\lambda$ will be real if either $\lambda = 0$ or λ is purely imaginary.

This completes the proof.

Theorem 11. Prove that the characteristic roots of a real skew-symmetric matrix are either all zero or purely imaginary.

Proof. Let A be a real skew-symmetric matrix. Then,

$$A' = -A \qquad \text{... (8.31)}$$

and $A' = A$ ... (8.32)

Therefore,

$$\begin{aligned} A^* &= (\overline{A})' \\ &= A' && \text{| From Eq. (8.31)} \\ &= -A && \text{| From Eq. (8.32)} \end{aligned}$$

$\Rightarrow$ A is skew-hermitian

Hence, by Theorem 10 above, the characteristic roots of A are either all zero or purely imaginary.

Theorem 12. Prove that the characteristic roots of an orthogonal matrix are of unit modulus.

Proof. Let A be an orthogonal matrix. Then,

$$A'A = AA' = I \qquad \text{... (8.33)}$$

Let λ be a characteristic root of the matrix A. Then there exists a corresponding non-zero characteristic vector X such that

$$AX = \lambda X \qquad \text{... (8.34)}$$

Taking transpose of both sides of Eq. (8.34), we get

$$(AX)' = (\lambda X)' \qquad \text{... (8.35)}$$

Multiplying Eqs. (8.34) and (8.35), we get

$$(AX)'(AX) = (\lambda X)'(\lambda X)$$

$$\Rightarrow (X'A')(AX) = (\lambda X')(\lambda X)$$

$$\Rightarrow X'(A'A)X = \lambda^2 X'X$$

$$\Rightarrow X'IX = \lambda^2 X'X \qquad \text{| From Eq. (8.33)}$$

$$\Rightarrow X'X = \lambda^2 X'X$$

$$\Rightarrow (1 - \lambda^2)\, X'X = O \qquad \text{... (8.36)}$$

Since X is a non-zero characteristic vector

$\therefore$ $X \neq O$

Consequently, $X'X \neq O$

$\therefore$ From Eq. (8.36), we get

$$1 - \lambda^2 = 0$$

$$\Rightarrow \lambda = \pm 1$$

$$\Rightarrow |A| = 1$$

Hence, the theorem.

Theorem 13. Prove that the characteristic roots of an orthogonal real matrix are of unit modulus.

Proof. Let A be an orthogonal real matrix. Then,

$$A'A = AA' = I \quad \text{... (8.37)}$$

and

$$\bar{A} = A \quad \text{... (8.38)}$$

Taking conjugate of both sides of Eq. (8.37), we obtain

$$\overline{(A'A)} = \bar{I}$$

$$\Rightarrow \bar{A}\,\overline{(A')} = I$$

$$\Rightarrow \bar{A}\,A^* = I$$

$$\Rightarrow AA^* = I \qquad | \text{ From Eq. (8.38)}$$

Similarly,

$$A^*A = I$$

$$\therefore AA^* = A^*A = I$$

$\Rightarrow$ The matrix A is unitary

Hence, by Theorem 13 above, the characteristic root of A are of unit modulus.

Therom 14. Prove that the characteritic roots of a unitary matrix are of unit modulus.

Proof. Let A be a unitary matrix. Then,

$$A^*A = AA^* = I \quad \text{... (8.39)}$$

Let λ be a characteristic root of A and X be its corresponding characteristic vector. Then,

$$AX = \lambda X \quad \text{... (8.40)}$$

Taking transposed conjugate of Eq. (8.40), we get

$$(AX)^* = (\lambda X)^*$$

$$\Rightarrow \quad X^* A^* = \bar{\lambda} X^* \qquad \ldots (8.41)$$

Multiplying Eqs. (8.40) and (8.41), we get

$$(X^* A^*)(AX) = (\bar{\lambda} X^*)(\lambda X)$$

$$\Rightarrow \quad X^*(A^* A) X = \lambda\bar{\lambda}(X^* X)$$

$$\Rightarrow \quad X^* I X = \lambda\bar{\lambda}(X^* X) \qquad | \text{ From Eq. (8.39)}$$

$$\Rightarrow \quad X^* X = \lambda\bar{\lambda}(X^* X)$$

$$\Rightarrow \quad (1 - \lambda\bar{\lambda}) X^* X = O \qquad \ldots (8.42)$$

Since X is a non-zero characteristic vector.

$\therefore \quad X \neq O$

Consequently, $X^* X \neq O$

$\therefore$ From Eq. (8.42), we obtain

$$1 - \lambda\bar{\lambda} = 0$$

$$\Rightarrow \quad \lambda\bar{\lambda} = 1$$

$$\Rightarrow \quad |\lambda|^2 = 1$$

$$\Rightarrow \quad |\lambda| = 1$$

Hence, the theorem.

Theorem 15. Prove that the characteristic roots of an idempotent matrix are either zero or unity.

Proof. Let A be an idempotent matrix. Then,

$$A^2 = A \qquad \ldots (8.43)$$

Let λ be a characteristic root of A and X be its corresponding characteristic non-zero vector. Then,

$$AX = \lambda X \qquad \ldots (8.44)$$

Pre-multiplying both sides of Eq. (8.44) by A, we get

$$A(AX) = A(\lambda X)$$

$$\Rightarrow \quad (AA)X = \lambda(AX)$$

$$\Rightarrow \quad A^2 X = \lambda(\lambda X) \qquad | \text{ From Eq. (8.44)}$$

$$\Rightarrow \quad AX = \lambda^2 X \qquad | \text{ From Eq. (8.43)}$$

$$\Rightarrow \quad \lambda X = \lambda^2 X \qquad | \text{ From Eq. (8.44)}$$

$$\Rightarrow \quad (\lambda^2 - \lambda)X = O \qquad \ldots (8.45)$$

Since X is a non-zero characteristic vector.

$\therefore \quad X \neq O$

$\therefore$ From Eq. (8.44), we obtain

$$\lambda^2 - \lambda = 0$$

$$\lambda(\lambda - 1) = 0$$

$$\lambda = 0, 1$$

ILLUSTRATIVE EXAMPLES

Example 1. If A and B are square matrices of the same order and if P is invertible, then prove that A and $P^{-1}AP$ have the same eigen values.

Solution: Let $B = P^{-1}AP$

Then,

$$\begin{aligned} B - \lambda I &= P^{-1}AP - \lambda I \\ &= P^{-1}AP - \lambda I\,(P^{-1}P) \\ &= P^{-1}AP - P^{-1}\lambda\, IP \\ &= P^{-1}(A - \lambda I)P \end{aligned}$$

$$\begin{aligned} \Rightarrow \quad |B - \lambda I| &= |P^{-1}(A - \lambda I)P| \\ &= |P^{-1}|\;|A - \lambda I|\;|P| \\ &= |A - \lambda I|\;|P^{-1}|\;|P| \\ &= |A - \lambda I|\;|P^{-1}P| \\ &= |A - \lambda I|\;|I| \\ &= |A - \lambda I| \end{aligned}$$

Thus, the two matrices A and B ($= P^{-1}AP$) have the same characteristic determinants and hence the same characteristic equations and consequently the same characteristic roots.

Example 2. Show that if $\lambda_1, \lambda_2, \ldots\ldots, \lambda_n$ are the latent roots of the matrix A, then A^3 has the latent roots $\lambda_1^3, \lambda_2^3, \ldots\ldots, \lambda_n^3$.

Solution: Let λ be a latent root of the matrix A. Then there exists a non-zero corresponding vector X such that

$$AX = \lambda X \qquad \ldots (8.46)$$

$\Rightarrow\ A^2(AX) = A^2(\lambda X)$

$\Rightarrow\ (A^2A)X = \lambda(A^2X)$

$\Rightarrow\ A^3X = \lambda(A^2X)$

$\Rightarrow\ A^3X = A\{A(AX)\}$

$\Rightarrow\ A^3X = A\{A(\lambda X)\}$ | From Eq. (8.46)

$\Rightarrow\ A^3X = A\{\lambda(AX)\}$

$\Rightarrow\ A^3X = A\{\lambda(\lambda X)\}$ | From Eq. (8.46)

$\Rightarrow\ A^3X = A(\lambda^2X)$

$\Rightarrow\ A^3X = \lambda^2(AX)$

$\Rightarrow\ A^3X = \lambda^2(\lambda X)$ | From Eq. (8.46)

$\Rightarrow\ A^3X = \lambda^3X$

$\Rightarrow\ \lambda^3$ is a latent root of A^3.

Hence, if $\lambda_1, \lambda_2, \ldots\ldots, \lambda_n$ are the latent roots of A, then, $\lambda_1^3, \lambda_2^3, \ldots\ldots, \lambda_n^3$ are the latent roots of A^3.

Example 3. If $\lambda_1, \lambda_2, \ldots\ldots, \lambda_n$ are the eigen values of the matrix A, then find the eigen values of the matrix $(A - \lambda I)^2$.

Solution: We have

$$(A - \lambda I)^2 = A^2 - 2\lambda AI + \lambda^2 I^2$$
$$= A^2 - 2\lambda A + \lambda^2 I$$

Eigen values of A^2 are $\lambda_1^2, \lambda_2^2, \ldots\ldots, \lambda_n^2$

Eigen values of $2\lambda A$ are $2\lambda\lambda_1, 2\lambda\lambda_2, \ldots\ldots, 2\lambda\lambda_n$

Eigen values of $\lambda^2 I$ are λ^2

$\therefore$ Eigen values of $(A - \lambda I)^2$ are

$\lambda_1^2 - 2\lambda\lambda_1 + \lambda^2, \lambda_2^2 - 2\lambda\lambda_2 + \lambda^2, \ldots\ldots, \lambda_n^2 - 2\lambda\lambda_n + \lambda^2$

i.e. $(\lambda_1 - \lambda)^2, (\lambda_2 - \lambda)^2, \ldots\ldots, (\lambda_n - \lambda)^2$

Example 4. If λ be an eigen value of a non-singular matrix A, show that

(i) λ^{-1} is an eigen value of A^{-1}.

(ii) $\dfrac{|A|}{\lambda}$ is an eigen value of adj A.

Solution:

(i) λ is an eigen value of A

$\Rightarrow$ There exists a non-zero corresponding characteristic vector X such that

$AX = \lambda X$

$\Rightarrow A^{-1}(AX) = A^{-1}(\lambda X)$

$\Rightarrow (A^{-1}A)X = \lambda(A^{-1}X)$

$\Rightarrow IX = \lambda(A^{-1}X)$

$\Rightarrow X = \lambda(A^{-1}X)$

$\Rightarrow \dfrac{1}{\lambda}X = A^{-1}X$

$\Rightarrow \lambda^{-1}X = A^{-1}X$

$\Rightarrow \lambda^{-1}$ is an eigen value of A^{-1}.

(ii) λ is an eigen value of X

$\Rightarrow$ There exists a non-zero corresponding characteristic vector X such that

$AX = \lambda X$

$\Rightarrow (\text{adj } A)\ (AX) = (\text{adj } A)\ (\lambda X)$

$\Rightarrow \{(\text{adj } A)A\}X = \lambda\{(\text{adj } A)X\}$

$\Rightarrow |A|IX = \lambda\{(\text{adj } A)X\}$

$\Rightarrow |A|X = \lambda\{(\text{adj } A)X\}$

$\Rightarrow \dfrac{|A|}{\lambda}X = (\text{adj } A)X$

$\Rightarrow (\text{adj } A)X = \dfrac{|A|}{\lambda}X$

$\Rightarrow \dfrac{|A|}{\lambda}$ is an eigen value of adj A.

Example 5. Show that the characteristic roots of an upper or lower triangular matrix are just the diagonal elements of the matrix.

Solution: Let us consider a triangular matrix

$$A = \begin{bmatrix} a_{11} & a_{12} & \cdots & a_{1n} \\ 0 & a_{22} & \cdots & a_{2n} \\ \cdots & \cdots & \cdots & \cdots \\ \cdots & \cdots & \cdots & \cdots \\ 0 & 0 & \cdots & a_{nn} \end{bmatrix}_{n \times n} \text{ of order } n$$

Then,

$$A - \lambda I = \begin{bmatrix} a_{11} & a_{12} & \cdots & a_{1n} \\ 0 & a_{22} & \cdots & a_{2n} \\ \cdots & \cdots & \cdots & \cdots \\ \cdots & \cdots & \cdots & \cdots \\ 0 & 0 & \cdots & a_{nn} \end{bmatrix} - \lambda \begin{bmatrix} 1 & 0 & \cdots & 0 \\ 0 & 1 & \cdots & 0 \\ \cdots & \cdots & \cdots & \cdots \\ \cdots & \cdots & \cdots & \cdots \\ 0 & 0 & \cdots & 1 \end{bmatrix}$$

$$= \begin{bmatrix} a_{11} - \lambda & a_{12} & \cdots & a_{1n} \\ 0 & a_{22} - \lambda & \cdots & a_{2n} \\ \cdots & \cdots & \cdots & \cdots \\ \cdots & \cdots & \cdots & \cdots \\ 0 & 0 & \cdots & a_{nn} - \lambda \end{bmatrix}$$

$\therefore \quad |A - \lambda I| = 0$ gives

$$\begin{vmatrix} a_{11} - \lambda & a_{12} & \cdots & a_{1n} \\ 0 & a_{22} - \lambda & \cdots & a_{2n} \\ \cdots & \cdots & \cdots & \cdots \\ \cdots & \cdots & \cdots & \cdots \\ 0 & 0 & \cdots & a_{nn} - \lambda \end{vmatrix} = 0$$

$$\Rightarrow \quad (a_{11} - \lambda)\,(a_{22} - \lambda)\,\cdots\,(a_{nn} - \lambda) = 0$$

$$\lambda = a_{11}, a_{22}, \ldots, a_{nn}$$

Hence, the characteristic roots of A are just the diagonal elements of A.

Example 6. Let A and B be square matrices of order n. Show that AB and BA have the same characteristic roots.

Solution: We know that

(i) The product of non-singular matrices is non-singular.

and

(ii) If 0 is a characteristic root of a matrix A, then A is singular.

There arise two cases.

Case I. If 0 is a characteristic root of AB, then AB is singular.

$\Rightarrow$ A is singular or B is singular.

$\Rightarrow$ BA is singular.

$\Rightarrow$ 0 is a characteristic root of BA.

Case II. If λ is a non-zero characteristic root of AB, then there exists a non-zero corresponding characteristic vector X such that

$$ABX = \lambda X \quad \text{... (8.47)}$$

Let $BX = Y$

Then

$$AY = ABX$$
$$= \lambda X$$
$$\neq O \quad | \because \lambda \neq 0 \text{ and } X \neq O$$
$$\Rightarrow Y \neq O \quad | \because A \neq O$$

Also,

$$BAY = BA\ (BX)$$
$$= B(ABX)$$
$$= B(\lambda X) \quad | \text{ From Eq. (8.47)}$$
$$= \lambda(BX)$$
$$= \lambda Y$$

Hence, λ is a characteristic root of BA.

Since λ is arbitrary, therefore, any non-zero characteristic root of AB is also a characteristic root of BA. Thus, AB and BA have the same characteristic roots.

Aliter.

We have

$$AB = IAB$$
$$= B^{-1}B\ (AB)$$
$$= B^{-1}(BA)B \qquad \text{... (8.48)}$$

But by Example 1, BA and $B^{-1}(BA)B$ have the same characteristic roots, therefore BA and AB by Eq. (8.48) have the same characteristic roots.

Example 7. Any two characteristic vectors corresponding to two distinct characteristic roots of a hermitian matrix are orthogonal and linearly independent.

Solution: Let A be a hermitian matrix. Then,

$$A^* = A \qquad \text{... (8.49)}$$

Let λ and μ be two distinct characteristic roots of the hermitian matrix A. Then, λ and μ are real numbers since the characteristic roots of a hermitian matrix are all real. Therefore,

$$\bar{\lambda} = \lambda \qquad \text{... (8.50)}$$

and

$$\bar{\mu} = \mu \qquad \text{... (8.51)}$$

Let X and Y be the non-zero characteristic vectors corresponding to the latent roots λ and μ respectively. Then,

$$AX = \lambda X \qquad \text{... (8.52)}$$

and

$$AY = \mu Y \qquad \text{... (8.53)}$$

First Part. *To prove that X and Y are linearly independent*

Let us assume that

$$aX + bY = O \qquad \text{... (8.54)}$$

where a, b are scalars.

$\Rightarrow A(aX + bY) = AO$

$\Rightarrow aAX + bAY = O$

$\Rightarrow a\lambda X + b\mu Y = O$ | From Eqs. (8.52) and (8.53)

$\Rightarrow \lambda(-bY) + b\mu Y = O$ | From Eq. (8.54)

$\Rightarrow b(\mu - \lambda)Y = O$

$\Rightarrow bY = O$ | $\because \mu - \lambda \neq 0$; μ, λ being distinct

$\Rightarrow b = 0$ | $\because Y \neq O$

$\therefore$ Equation (8.54) $\Rightarrow aX = O$

$\Rightarrow a = 0$ | $\because X \neq O$

Hence, by definition, X and Y are linearly independent.

Second Part. *To prove that X and Y are orthogonal*

We have

$$AX = \lambda X$$

$$\Rightarrow Y^*AX = Y^*\lambda X$$

$$\Rightarrow Y^*AX = \lambda Y^*X \quad \text{... (8.55)}$$

and

$$AY = \mu Y$$

$$\Rightarrow X^*AY = \mu X^*Y \quad \text{... (8.56)}$$

Equation (8.55)

$$\Rightarrow (Y^*AX)^* = (\lambda Y^*X)^*$$

$$\Rightarrow X^*A^*Y = \bar{\lambda} X^*Y$$

$$\Rightarrow X^*AY = \lambda X^*Y$$

| From Eqs. (8.49) and (8.50) ... (8.57)

In view of Eqs. (8.56) and (8.59), we get

$$\lambda X^*Y = \mu X^*Y$$

$$\Rightarrow (\lambda - \mu)\, X^*Y = O$$

$\Rightarrow X^*Y = O$ | $\because \lambda - \mu \neq 0$

Hence, the result.

Example 8. Find the eigen values and eigen vectors of the matrix $A = \begin{bmatrix} 1 & -2 \\ -5 & 4 \end{bmatrix}$.

Solution: The characteristic equation of the given matrix is

$$|A - \lambda I| = 0$$

$$\Rightarrow \begin{vmatrix} 1-\lambda & -2 \\ -5 & 4-\lambda \end{vmatrix} = 0$$

$$\Rightarrow \lambda^2 - 5\lambda - 6 = 0$$

$$\Rightarrow \lambda = 6, -1$$

Hence, the eigen values of A are 6, –1.

Corresponding to $\lambda = 6$, the eigen vector X_1 is given by

$$(A - 6I)\, X_1 = O$$

$$\Rightarrow \begin{bmatrix} 1-6 & -2 \\ -5 & 4-6 \end{bmatrix} \begin{bmatrix} x_1 \\ x_2 \end{bmatrix} = \begin{bmatrix} 0 \\ 0 \end{bmatrix}$$

$$\Rightarrow \begin{bmatrix} -5 & -2 \\ -5 & -2 \end{bmatrix} \begin{bmatrix} x_1 \\ x_2 \end{bmatrix} = \begin{bmatrix} 0 \\ 0 \end{bmatrix}$$

$$\Rightarrow -5x_1 - 2x_2 = 0$$

$$\Rightarrow \frac{x_1}{2} = \frac{x_2}{-5} = k_1 \text{ (say) where } k_1 \neq 0$$

$$\Rightarrow x_1 = 2k_1$$

$$x_2 = -5k_1$$

$$\therefore \quad X_1 = \begin{bmatrix} x_1 \\ x_2 \end{bmatrix} = \begin{bmatrix} 2k_1 \\ -5k_1 \end{bmatrix} = k_1 \begin{bmatrix} 2 \\ -5 \end{bmatrix}$$

Corresponding to $\lambda = -1$, the eigen vector X_2 is given by

$$(A + I)X_2 = O$$

$$\Rightarrow \begin{bmatrix} 1+1 & -2 \\ -5 & 4+1 \end{bmatrix} \begin{bmatrix} x_1 \\ x_2 \end{bmatrix} = \begin{bmatrix} 0 \\ 0 \end{bmatrix}$$

$$\Rightarrow \begin{bmatrix} 2 & -2 \\ -5 & 5 \end{bmatrix} \begin{bmatrix} x_1 \\ x_2 \end{bmatrix} = \begin{bmatrix} 0 \\ 0 \end{bmatrix}$$

$$\Rightarrow x_1 - x_2 = 0$$

$$\Rightarrow \frac{x_1}{1} = \frac{x_2}{1} = k_2 \text{ (say)}$$

$$\therefore \quad X_2 = \begin{bmatrix} x_1 \\ x_2 \end{bmatrix} = \begin{bmatrix} k_2 \\ k_2 \end{bmatrix} = k_2 \begin{bmatrix} 1 \\ 1 \end{bmatrix}$$

Example 9. Find the eigen values and eigen vectors of the matrix $A = \begin{bmatrix} 8 & -6 & 2 \\ -6 & 7 & -4 \\ 2 & -4 & 3 \end{bmatrix}$.

Solution: The characteristic equation of the given matrix A is

$$|A - \lambda I| = 0$$

$$\Rightarrow \begin{vmatrix} 8-\lambda & -6 & 2 \\ -6 & 7-\lambda & -4 \\ 2 & -4 & 3-\lambda \end{vmatrix} = 0$$

$$\Rightarrow \lambda^3 - 18\lambda^2 + 45\lambda = 0$$

$$\Rightarrow (\lambda)(\lambda - 3)(\lambda - 15) = 0$$

$$\Rightarrow \lambda = 0, 3, 15$$

Hence, the eigen values are $\lambda_1 = 0, \lambda_2 = 3, \lambda_3 = 15.$

The eigen vector X_1 corresponding to $\lambda_1 = 0$ is given by

$$(A - \lambda_1 I)X_1 = O$$

$$\Rightarrow \begin{bmatrix} 8 & -6 & 2 \\ -6 & 7 & -4 \\ 2 & -4 & 3 \end{bmatrix} \begin{bmatrix} x_1 \\ x_2 \\ x_3 \end{bmatrix} = \begin{bmatrix} 0 \\ 0 \\ 0 \end{bmatrix}$$

$$\Rightarrow 8x_1 - 6x_2 + 2x_3 = 0 \qquad \text{... (8.58)}$$

$$-6x_1 + 7x_2 - 4x_3 = 0 \qquad \text{... (8.59)}$$

$$2x_1 - 4x_2 + 3x_3 = 0 \qquad \text{... (8.60)}$$

Equations (8.58) and (8.59), by cross-multiplication, we get

$$\frac{x_1}{24 - 14} = \frac{x_2}{-12 + 32} = \frac{x_3}{56 - 36}$$

$$\Rightarrow \frac{x_1}{1} = \frac{x_2}{2} = \frac{x_3}{2} = k_1 \text{ (say) where } k_1 \neq 0$$

$$\Rightarrow \quad x_1 = k_1$$
$$x_2 = 2k_1$$
$$x_3 = 2k_1$$

These values of x_1, x_2, x_3 satisfy Eq. (8.60).

$$\therefore \quad X_1 = \begin{bmatrix} x_1 \\ x_2 \\ x_3 \end{bmatrix} = \begin{bmatrix} k_1 \\ 2k_1 \\ 2k_1 \end{bmatrix} = k_1 \begin{bmatrix} 1 \\ 2 \\ 2 \end{bmatrix}$$

The eigen vector X_2 corresponding to $\lambda_2 = 3$ is given by

$$(A - \lambda_2 I) X_2 = O$$

$$\Rightarrow \begin{bmatrix} 5 & -6 & 2 \\ -6 & 4 & -4 \\ 2 & -4 & 0 \end{bmatrix} \begin{bmatrix} x_1 \\ x_2 \\ x_3 \end{bmatrix} = \begin{bmatrix} 0 \\ 0 \\ 0 \end{bmatrix}$$

$$\Rightarrow \quad 5x_1 - 6x_2 + 2x_3 = 0 \quad \text{... (8.61)}$$
$$-6x_1 + 4x_2 - 4x_3 = 0 \quad \text{... (8.62)}$$
$$2x_1 - 4x_2 = 0 \quad \text{... (8.63)}$$

Equations (8.61) and (8.62), by cross-multiplication, we get

$$\frac{x_1}{24 - 8} = \frac{x_2}{-12 + 20} = \frac{x_3}{20 - 36}$$

$$\Rightarrow \frac{x_1}{2} = \frac{x_2}{1} = \frac{x_3}{-2} = k_2 \text{ (say) where } k_2 \neq 0$$

$$\Rightarrow \quad x_1 = 2k_2$$
$$x_2 = k_2$$
$$x_3 = -2k_2$$

These values satisfy Eq. (8.63).

$$\therefore \quad X_2 = \begin{bmatrix} x_1 \\ x_2 \\ x_3 \end{bmatrix} = \begin{bmatrix} 2k_2 \\ k_2 \\ -2k_2 \end{bmatrix} = k_2 \begin{bmatrix} 2 \\ 1 \\ -2 \end{bmatrix}$$

The eigen vector X_3 corresponding to $\lambda_3 = 15$ is given by

$$(A - \lambda_3 I) X_3 = O$$

$$\Rightarrow \begin{bmatrix} -7 & -6 & 2 \\ -6 & -8 & -4 \\ 2 & -4 & -12 \end{bmatrix} \begin{bmatrix} x_1 \\ x_2 \\ x_3 \end{bmatrix} = \begin{bmatrix} 0 \\ 0 \\ 0 \end{bmatrix}$$

$$\Rightarrow -7x_1 - 6x_2 + 2x_3 = 0 \qquad \text{... (8.64)}$$

$$-6x_1 - 8x_2 - 4x_3 = 0 \qquad \text{... (8.65)}$$

$$2x_1 - 4x_2 - 12x_3 = 0 \qquad \text{... (8.66)}$$

Equations (8.64) and (8.65), by cross-multiplication, we get

$$\frac{x_1}{24 + 16} = \frac{x_2}{-12 - 28} = \frac{x_3}{56 - 36}$$

$$\Rightarrow \frac{x_1}{2} = \frac{x_2}{-2} = \frac{x_3}{1} = k_3 \text{ (say) where } k_3 \neq 0$$

$$\Rightarrow x_1 = 2k_3$$

$$x_2 = -2k_3$$

$$x_3 = k_3$$

These values satisfy Eq. (8.66)

$$\therefore \quad X_3 = \begin{bmatrix} x_1 \\ x_2 \\ x_3 \end{bmatrix} = \begin{bmatrix} 2k_3 \\ -2k_3 \\ k_3 \end{bmatrix} = k_3 \begin{bmatrix} 2 \\ -2 \\ 1 \end{bmatrix}$$

Example 10. Determine the characteristic roots and the corresponding characteristic vectors of the matrix

$$A = \begin{bmatrix} -2 & 2 & -3 \\ 2 & 1 & -6 \\ -1 & -2 & 0 \end{bmatrix}.$$

Solution: The characteristic equation of the given matrix A is

$$|A - \lambda I| = 0$$

$$\Rightarrow \begin{vmatrix} -2-\lambda & 2 & -3 \\ 2 & 1-\lambda & -6 \\ -1 & -2 & 0-\lambda \end{vmatrix} = 0$$

$$\Rightarrow \lambda^3 + \lambda^2 - 21\lambda - 45 = 0$$

$$\Rightarrow (\lambda + 3)(\lambda + 3)(\lambda - 5) = 0$$

$$\Rightarrow \lambda = -3, -3, 5$$

Hence, the characteristic roots are

$$\lambda_1 = -3 = \lambda_2, \lambda_3 = 5$$

The eigen vector $X_1 = X_2$ corresponding to $\lambda_1 = -3 = \lambda_2$ is given by

$$(A - \lambda_1 I)X_1 = O; X_1 = X_2$$

$$\Rightarrow \begin{bmatrix} 1 & 2 & -3 \\ 2 & 4 & -6 \\ -1 & -2 & 3 \end{bmatrix} \begin{bmatrix} x_1 \\ x_2 \\ x_3 \end{bmatrix} = \begin{bmatrix} 0 \\ 0 \\ 0 \end{bmatrix}$$

$$\Rightarrow x_1 + 2x_2 - 3x_3 = 0$$

$$2x_1 + 4x_2 - 6x_3 = 0$$

$$-x_1 - 2x_2 + 3x_3 = 0$$

These equations are equivalent to a single equation.

$$x_1 + 2x_2 - 3x_3 = 0$$

Clearly, out of the three unknowns x_1, x_2, x_3, one can be expressed in terms of arbitrary values of the other two.

So, let $x_3 = k_1$

$$x_2 = k_2$$

where k_1, k_2 are arbitrary scalars.

Then, $x_1 = 3k_1 - 2k_2$

$$\therefore \quad X_1 = X_2 = \begin{bmatrix} x_1 \\ x_2 \\ x_3 \end{bmatrix} = \begin{bmatrix} 3k_1 - 2k_2 \\ k_2 \\ k_1 \end{bmatrix}$$

$$= k_1 \begin{bmatrix} 3 \\ 0 \\ 1 \end{bmatrix} + k_2 \begin{bmatrix} -2 \\ 1 \\ 0 \end{bmatrix}$$

The eigen vector X_3 corresponding to $\lambda_3 = 5$ is given by

$$(A - \lambda_3 I)X_3 = O$$

$$\Rightarrow \begin{bmatrix} -7 & 2 & -3 \\ 2 & -4 & -6 \\ -1 & -2 & -5 \end{bmatrix} \begin{bmatrix} x_1 \\ x_2 \\ x_3 \end{bmatrix} = \begin{bmatrix} 0 \\ 0 \\ 0 \end{bmatrix}$$

$$\Rightarrow -7x_1 + 2x_2 - 3x_3 = 0 \qquad \text{... (8.67)}$$

$$2x_1 - 4x_2 - 6x_3 = 0 \qquad \text{... (8.68)}$$

$$-x_1 - 2x_2 - 5x_3 = 0 \qquad \text{... (8.69)}$$

Equations (8.67) and (8.68), by cross-multiplication, we get

$$\frac{x_1}{10-6} = \frac{x_2}{3+5} = \frac{x_3}{-2-2}$$

$$\Rightarrow \frac{x_1}{1} = \frac{x_2}{2} = \frac{x_3}{-1} = k_3 \text{ (say) where } k_3 \neq 0$$

$$\Rightarrow x_1 = k_3$$

$$x_2 = 2k_3$$

$$x_3 = -k_3$$

These values satisfy the Eq. (8.69).

$$\therefore \quad X_3 = \begin{bmatrix} x_1 \\ x_2 \\ x_3 \end{bmatrix} = \begin{bmatrix} k_3 \\ 2k_3 \\ -k_3 \end{bmatrix} = k_3 \begin{bmatrix} 1 \\ 2 \\ -1 \end{bmatrix}$$

Example 11. Find out the latent roots and the corresponding latent vectors of the matrix $A = \begin{bmatrix} 3 & 1 & 4 \\ 0 & 2 & 6 \\ 0 & 0 & 5 \end{bmatrix}$.

Solution: The characteristic equation of the given matrix A is

$$|A - \lambda I| = 0$$

$$\Rightarrow \begin{vmatrix} 3-\lambda & 1 & 4 \\ 0 & 2-\lambda & 6 \\ 0 & 0 & 5-\lambda \end{vmatrix} = 0$$

$\Rightarrow (3 - \lambda)(2 - \lambda)(5 - \lambda) = 0$

$\Rightarrow \lambda = 3, 2, 5$

Hence, the latent roots are $\lambda_1 = 3$, $\lambda_2 = 2$, $\lambda_3 = 5$.

The latent vector X_1 corresponding to $\lambda_1 = 3$ is given by

$$(A - \lambda_1 I)X_1 = O \text{ where } X_1 = [x_1\ x_2\ x_3]' = \begin{bmatrix} x_1 \\ x_2 \\ x_3 \end{bmatrix}$$

$$\Rightarrow \begin{bmatrix} 0 & 1 & 4 \\ 0 & -1 & 6 \\ 0 & 0 & 2 \end{bmatrix} \begin{bmatrix} x_1 \\ x_2 \\ x_3 \end{bmatrix} = \begin{bmatrix} 0 \\ 0 \\ 0 \end{bmatrix}$$

$$\Rightarrow x_2 + 4x_3 = 0$$
$$-x_2 + 6x_3 = 0$$
$$2x_3 = 0$$
$$\Rightarrow x_3 = 0$$
$$x_2 = 0$$

Let $x_1 = k_1$ where k_1 is an arbitrary scalar.

$$\therefore \quad X_1 = \begin{bmatrix} x_1 \\ x_2 \\ x_3 \end{bmatrix} = \begin{bmatrix} k_1 \\ 0 \\ 0 \end{bmatrix} = k_1 \begin{bmatrix} 1 \\ 0 \\ 0 \end{bmatrix}$$

The latent vector X_2 corresponding to $\lambda_2 = 2$ is given by

$$(A - \lambda_2 I)X_2 = O$$
$$\Rightarrow (A - 2I)X_2 = O$$

$$\Rightarrow \begin{bmatrix} 1 & 1 & 4 \\ 0 & 0 & 6 \\ 0 & 0 & 3 \end{bmatrix} \begin{bmatrix} x_1 \\ x_2 \\ x_3 \end{bmatrix} = \begin{bmatrix} 0 \\ 0 \\ 0 \end{bmatrix}$$

$$\Rightarrow x_1 + x_2 + 4x_3 = 0$$
$$6x_3 = 0$$
$$3x_3 = 0$$
$$\Rightarrow x_3 = 0$$
$$x_1 + x_2 = 0$$

$$\Rightarrow \frac{x_1}{1} = \frac{x_2}{-1} = \frac{x_3}{0} = k_2 \text{ (say) where } k_2 \neq 0$$

$$\Rightarrow x_1 = k_2$$
$$x_2 = -k_2$$
$$x_3 = 0$$

$$\therefore \quad X_2 = \begin{bmatrix} x_1 \\ x_2 \\ x_3 \end{bmatrix} = \begin{bmatrix} k_2 \\ -k_2 \\ 0 \end{bmatrix} = k_2 \begin{bmatrix} 1 \\ -1 \\ 0 \end{bmatrix}$$

The latent vector corresponding to $\lambda_3 = 5$ is given by

$$(A - \lambda_3 I)X_3 = O$$

$$\Rightarrow (A - 5I)X_3 = O$$

$$\Rightarrow \begin{bmatrix} -2 & 1 & 4 \\ 0 & -3 & 6 \\ 0 & 0 & 0 \end{bmatrix} \begin{bmatrix} x_1 \\ x_2 \\ x_3 \end{bmatrix} = \begin{bmatrix} 0 \\ 0 \\ 0 \end{bmatrix}$$

$$\Rightarrow -2x_1 + x_2 + 4x_3 = 0$$
$$-3x_2 + 6x_3 = 0$$

These equations, by cross-multiplication, we get

$$\frac{x_1}{6 + 12} = \frac{x_2}{12} = \frac{x_3}{6}$$

$$\Rightarrow \frac{x_1}{3} = \frac{x_2}{2} = \frac{x_3}{1} = k_3 \text{ (say) where } k_3 \neq 0$$

$$\Rightarrow x_1 = 3k_3$$
$$x_2 = 2k_3$$
$$x_3 = k_3$$

$$\therefore \quad X_3 = \begin{bmatrix} x_1 \\ x_2 \\ x_3 \end{bmatrix} = \begin{bmatrix} 3k_3 \\ 2k_3 \\ k_3 \end{bmatrix} = k_3 \begin{bmatrix} 3 \\ 2 \\ 1 \end{bmatrix}$$

Example 12. Find the latent roots and latent vectors of the matrix $A = \begin{bmatrix} a & h & g \\ 0 & b & 0 \\ 0 & 0 & c \end{bmatrix}$.

Solution: $\because$ A is a triangular matrix

$\therefore$ Characteristic roots of A are the diagonal elements, i.e. $\lambda_1 = a$, $\lambda_2 = b$, $\lambda_3 = c$.

The latent vector X_1 corresponding to $\lambda_1 = a$ is given by

$$(A - \lambda_1 I)X_1 = O$$

$$\Rightarrow (A - aI)X_1 = O$$

$$\Rightarrow \begin{bmatrix} a-a & h & g \\ 0 & b-a & 0 \\ 0 & 0 & c-a \end{bmatrix} \begin{bmatrix} x_1 \\ x_2 \\ x_3 \end{bmatrix} = \begin{bmatrix} 0 \\ 0 \\ 0 \end{bmatrix}$$

$$\Rightarrow hx_2 + gx_3 = 0$$

$$(b - a)x_2 = 0$$

$$(c - a)x_3 = 0$$

$$\Rightarrow x_2 = 0 \qquad \because a \neq b \neq c$$

$$x_3 = 0$$

Let $x_1 = k_1$ where k_1 is an arbitrary scalar

$$\therefore \quad X_1 = \begin{bmatrix} x_1 \\ x_2 \\ x_3 \end{bmatrix} = \begin{bmatrix} k_1 \\ 0 \\ 0 \end{bmatrix} = k_1 \begin{bmatrix} 1 \\ 0 \\ 0 \end{bmatrix}$$

The latent vector X_2 corresponding to $\lambda_2 = b$ is given by

$$(A - \lambda_2 I)X_2 = O$$

$$\Rightarrow (A - bI)X_2 = O$$

$$\Rightarrow \begin{bmatrix} a-b & h & g \\ 0 & b-b & 0 \\ 0 & 0 & c-b \end{bmatrix} \begin{bmatrix} x_1 \\ x_2 \\ x_3 \end{bmatrix} = \begin{bmatrix} 0 \\ 0 \\ 0 \end{bmatrix}$$

$$\Rightarrow (a - b)x_1 + hx_2 + gx_3 = 0$$

$$(c - b)x_3 = 0$$

$$\Rightarrow x_3 = 0 \qquad \because b \neq c$$

$$(a - b)x_1 + hx_2 = 0$$

$$\Rightarrow \frac{x_1}{h} = \frac{x_2}{b - a} = k_2 \text{ (say) where } k_2 \neq 0$$

$\Rightarrow x_1 = k_2 h$

$x_2 = k_2(b - a)$

$k_3 = 0$

$$\therefore \quad X_2 = \begin{bmatrix} x_1 \\ x_2 \\ x_3 \end{bmatrix} = \begin{bmatrix} k_2 h \\ k_2(b-a) \\ 0 \end{bmatrix} = k_2 \begin{bmatrix} h \\ b-a \\ 0 \end{bmatrix}$$

The latent vector X_3 corresponding to $\lambda_3 = c$ is given by

$(A - \lambda_3 I)X_3 = O$

$\Rightarrow (A - cI)X_3 = O$

$$\Rightarrow \begin{bmatrix} a-c & h & g \\ 0 & b-c & 0 \\ 0 & 0 & c-c \end{bmatrix} \begin{bmatrix} x_1 \\ x_2 \\ x_3 \end{bmatrix} = \begin{bmatrix} 0 \\ 0 \\ 0 \end{bmatrix}$$

$\Rightarrow (a - c)x_1 + hx_2 + gx_3 = 0$

$(b - c)x_2 = 0$

$\Rightarrow x_2 = 0 \qquad | \because b \neq c$

$(a - c)x_1 + gx_3 = 0$

$$\Rightarrow \frac{x_1}{g} = \frac{x_3}{c-a} = k_3 \text{ (say) where } k_3 \neq 0$$

$\Rightarrow x_1 = k_3 g$

$x_3 = k_3(c - a)$

$x_2 = 0$

$$\therefore \quad X_3 = \begin{bmatrix} x_1 \\ x_2 \\ x_3 \end{bmatrix} = \begin{bmatrix} k_3 g \\ 0 \\ k_3(c-a) \end{bmatrix} = k_3 \begin{bmatrix} g \\ 0 \\ c-a \end{bmatrix}$$

Example 13. If $B = \begin{bmatrix} 2 & \sqrt{2} \\ \sqrt{2} & 1 \end{bmatrix}$, then find the characteristic equation of B and verify that the matrix B satisfies this equation. Also find the characteristic roots and the corresponding characteristic vectors of B.

Solution: The characteristic equation of B is

$$|B - \lambda I| = 0$$

$$\Rightarrow \begin{vmatrix} 2-\lambda & \sqrt{2} \\ \sqrt{2} & 1-\lambda \end{vmatrix} = 0$$

$$\Rightarrow \lambda^2 - 3\lambda = 0$$

$$\Rightarrow \lambda(\lambda - 3) = 0$$

$$\Rightarrow \lambda = 0, 3$$

Hence, the characteristic roots of B are

$$\lambda_1 = 0, \lambda_2 = 3$$

To verify that the matrix B satisfies this equation, we must establish that

$$B^2 - 3B = O$$

Now,

$$B^2 = BB = \begin{bmatrix} 2 & \sqrt{2} \\ \sqrt{2} & 1 \end{bmatrix}\begin{bmatrix} 2 & \sqrt{2} \\ \sqrt{2} & 1 \end{bmatrix}$$

$$= \begin{bmatrix} 6 & 3\sqrt{2} \\ 3\sqrt{2} & 3 \end{bmatrix}$$

$$= 3\begin{bmatrix} 2 & \sqrt{2} \\ \sqrt{2} & 1 \end{bmatrix} = 3B$$

$$\Rightarrow B^2 - 3B = O$$

Hence, the given matrix B satisfies its own characteristic equation.

The characteristic vector X_1 corresponding to $\lambda_1 = 0$ is given by

$$(B - \lambda_1 I)X_1 = O$$

$$\Rightarrow \begin{bmatrix} 2 & \sqrt{2} \\ \sqrt{2} & 1 \end{bmatrix}\begin{bmatrix} x_1 \\ x_2 \end{bmatrix} = \begin{bmatrix} 0 \\ 0 \end{bmatrix}$$

$$\Rightarrow 2x_1 + \sqrt{2}x_2 = 0$$

$$\sqrt{2}x_1 + x_2 = 0$$

These two equations reduce to a single equation

$$\sqrt{2}x_1 + x_2 = 0$$

$$\Rightarrow \frac{x_1}{1} = \frac{x_2}{-\sqrt{2}} = k_1 \text{ (say) where } k_1 \neq 0$$

$$\Rightarrow x_1 = k_1$$

$$x_2 = -\sqrt{2}k_1$$

$$\therefore \quad X_1 = \begin{bmatrix} x_1 \\ x_2 \end{bmatrix} = \begin{bmatrix} k_1 \\ -\sqrt{2}k_1 \end{bmatrix} = k_1 \begin{bmatrix} 1 \\ -\sqrt{2} \end{bmatrix}$$

The characteritic vector X_2 corresponding to $\lambda_2 = 3$ is given by

$$(B - \lambda_2 I)X_2 = O$$

$$\Rightarrow (B - 3I)X_2 = O$$

$$\Rightarrow \begin{bmatrix} 2-3 & \sqrt{2} \\ \sqrt{2} & 1-3 \end{bmatrix} \begin{bmatrix} x_1 \\ x_2 \end{bmatrix} = \begin{bmatrix} 0 \\ 0 \end{bmatrix}$$

$$\Rightarrow \begin{bmatrix} -1 & \sqrt{2} \\ \sqrt{2} & -2 \end{bmatrix} \begin{bmatrix} x_1 \\ x_2 \end{bmatrix} = \begin{bmatrix} 0 \\ 0 \end{bmatrix}$$

$$\Rightarrow -x_1 + \sqrt{2}x_2 = 0$$

$$\sqrt{2}x_1 - 2x_2 = 0$$

These two equations are equivalent to a single equation

$$-x_1 + \sqrt{2}x_2 = 0$$

$$\Rightarrow \frac{x_1}{\sqrt{2}} = \frac{x_2}{1} = k_2 \text{ (say) where } k_2 \neq 0$$

$$\Rightarrow x_1 = \sqrt{2}k_2$$

$$x_2 = k_2$$

$$\therefore \quad X_2 = \begin{bmatrix} x_1 \\ x_2 \end{bmatrix} = \begin{bmatrix} \sqrt{2}k_2 \\ k_2 \end{bmatrix} = k_2 \begin{bmatrix} \sqrt{2} \\ 1 \end{bmatrix}$$

EXERCISE 8.2

1. Prove that the characteristic roots of a diagonal matrix are precisely the diagonal elements of the matrix.

2. Find the characteristic roots and the corresponding characteristic vectors of the matrix $A = \begin{bmatrix} -2 & -1 \\ 5 & 4 \end{bmatrix}$.

3. Find eigen values of $A = \begin{bmatrix} 1 & 2 \\ 2 & 1 \end{bmatrix}$. Also find eigen vectors.

4. Find the eigen values of $3A^3 + 5A^2 - 6A + 2I$ where $A = \begin{bmatrix} 1 & 2 & -3 \\ 0 & 3 & 2 \\ 0 & 0 & -2 \end{bmatrix}$.

5. Show that if λ is a characteristic root of the matrix A, then $\lambda \pm k$ is a characteristic root of the matrix $A \pm kI$.

6. Show that if $\lambda_1, \lambda_2, \ldots\ldots, \lambda_n$ are the eigen values of the matrix A, then A^m has the eigen values $\lambda_1^m, \lambda_2^m, \ldots\ldots, \lambda_n^m$ (m being a positive integer).

7. Determine the characteristic roots and the associated characteristic vectors for the matrix $A = \begin{bmatrix} 2 & 2 & 1 \\ 1 & 3 & 1 \\ 1 & 2 & 2 \end{bmatrix}$.

8. Determine the latent roots and the corresponding characteristic vectors for the matrix $A = \begin{bmatrix} 2 & -1 & 1 \\ -1 & 2 & -1 \\ 1 & -1 & 2 \end{bmatrix}$.

9. Find the eigen values and eigen vectors of $A = \begin{bmatrix} 1 & -1 & -1 \\ 1 & -1 & 0 \\ 1 & 0 & -1 \end{bmatrix}$.

10. Determine the characteristic roots and the corresponding characteristic vectors of the matrix $A = \begin{bmatrix} 6 & -2 & 2 \\ -2 & 3 & -1 \\ 2 & -1 & 3 \end{bmatrix}$.

11. Find the latent roots and the corresponding latent vectors of the matrix $A = \begin{bmatrix} 1 & 2 & 3 \\ 0 & 2 & 3 \\ 0 & 0 & 2 \end{bmatrix}$.

12. Find the latent roots and the corresponding latent vectors for the matrix $A = \begin{bmatrix} 2 & 1 & 0 \\ 0 & 2 & 1 \\ 0 & 0 & 2 \end{bmatrix}$.

13. Obtain the eigen values of A^3 where $A = \begin{bmatrix} 3 & 2 \\ 1 & 2 \end{bmatrix}$.

14. Two eigen values of the matrix $A = \begin{bmatrix} 2 & 2 & 1 \\ 1 & 3 & 1 \\ 1 & 2 & 2 \end{bmatrix}$ are equal to 1 each. Find the eigen values of A^{-1}.

15. Find the eigen vectors of

(i) $A = \begin{bmatrix} 3 & 1 & 4 \\ 0 & 2 & 0 \\ 0 & 0 & 5 \end{bmatrix}$

(ii) $A = \begin{bmatrix} 2 & 5 & 1 \\ 0 & 3 & 0 \\ 0 & 0 & 4 \end{bmatrix}$

(iii) $A = \begin{bmatrix} -2 & 2 & -3 \\ 2 & 1 & -6 \\ -1 & -2 & 0 \end{bmatrix}$

(iv) $A = \begin{bmatrix} 1 & 2 & 0 \\ 2 & -1 & 0 \\ 0 & 0 & 1 \end{bmatrix}$

(v) $A = \begin{bmatrix} 3 & 10 & 5 \\ -2 & -3 & -4 \\ 3 & 5 & 7 \end{bmatrix}$

(vi) $A = \begin{bmatrix} 2 & 1 & -1 \\ 0 & 3 & -2 \\ 2 & 4 & -3 \end{bmatrix}$

16. If $\mu = \begin{bmatrix} 0 & 1 & 1 \\ 1 & 0 & 1 \\ 1 & 1 & 0 \end{bmatrix}$ and $P = \frac{1}{2}\begin{bmatrix} b+c & c-a & b-a \\ c-b & c+a & a-b \\ b-c & a-c & a+b \end{bmatrix}$, show that the transform of P by M, i.e. MPM^{-1} is a diagonal matrix and hence find the eigen values of P.

17. If A is a skew-symmetric matrix of order n, then show that $|A - \lambda I| = (-1)^n |A + \lambda I|$. Deduce that if μ is a latent root of A, then $-\mu$ is another.

18. If k is a scalar, prove that the characteristic roots of kA are k times the characteristic roots of A.

[**Hint.** $|kA - k\lambda I| = k^n |A - \lambda I|$]

19. Prove that

(i) The characteristic roots of A^*A are all non-negative.

(ii) The characteristic roots of A^* are the conjugates of those of A.

20. If A and B are n-square matrices and A is non-singular, then $A^{-1}B$ and BA^{-1} have the same characteristic roots. Prove.

ANSWERS

2. $-1, 3; \begin{bmatrix} 1 \\ -1 \end{bmatrix}, \begin{bmatrix} 1 \\ -5 \end{bmatrix}$

3. $-1, 3; -1 \begin{bmatrix} -k_1 \\ k_1 \end{bmatrix}, 3 \begin{bmatrix} k_2 \\ k_2 \end{bmatrix}$

4. 4, 110, 10

7. $5, 1, 1; X_1 = k_1 \begin{bmatrix} 1 \\ 1 \\ 1 \end{bmatrix}, X_2 = X_3 = k_2 \begin{bmatrix} 2 \\ -1 \\ 0 \end{bmatrix} + k_3 \begin{bmatrix} 1 \\ 0 \\ -1 \end{bmatrix}$

8. $1, 1, 4; X_1 = X_2 = k_1 \begin{bmatrix} 1 \\ 0 \\ -1 \end{bmatrix} + k_2 \begin{bmatrix} 0 \\ 1 \\ 1 \end{bmatrix}, X_3 = \begin{bmatrix} 1 \\ -1 \\ 1 \end{bmatrix}$

9. $-1, i, -i; X_1 = \begin{bmatrix} 0 \\ 1 \\ -1 \end{bmatrix}, X_2 = \begin{bmatrix} 1+i \\ 1 \\ 1 \end{bmatrix}, X_3 = \begin{bmatrix} 1-i \\ 1 \\ 1 \end{bmatrix}$

10. $2, 2, 8; X_1 = X_2 = k_1 \begin{bmatrix} 1 \\ 2 \\ 0 \end{bmatrix} + k_2 \begin{bmatrix} 1 \\ 0 \\ -2 \end{bmatrix}; X_3 = k_3 \begin{bmatrix} 2 \\ -1 \\ 1 \end{bmatrix}$

11. $1, 2, 2; X_1 = k_1 \begin{bmatrix} 1 \\ 0 \\ 0 \end{bmatrix}, X_2 = X_3 = k_2 \begin{bmatrix} 2 \\ 1 \\ 0 \end{bmatrix}$

12. 2, 2, 2; $X_1 = X_2 = X_3 = k \begin{bmatrix} 1 \\ 0 \\ 0 \end{bmatrix}$

13. 1, 64

14. 1, 1, $\frac{1}{5}$

15. (i) 2, 3, 5; $k_1 \begin{bmatrix} 1 \\ -1 \\ 0 \end{bmatrix}, k_2 \begin{bmatrix} 1 \\ 0 \\ 0 \end{bmatrix}, k_3 \begin{bmatrix} 3 \\ 2 \\ 1 \end{bmatrix}$

(ii) 2, 3, 4; $k_1 \begin{bmatrix} 1 \\ 0 \\ 0 \end{bmatrix}, k_2 \begin{bmatrix} 5 \\ 1 \\ 0 \end{bmatrix}, k_3 \begin{bmatrix} 1 \\ 0 \\ 2 \end{bmatrix}$

(iii) 5, – 3, – 4; $k_1 \begin{bmatrix} -1 \\ -2 \\ 1 \end{bmatrix}, k_2 \begin{bmatrix} -2 \\ 1 \\ 0 \end{bmatrix}, k_3 \begin{bmatrix} 3 \\ 0 \\ 1 \end{bmatrix}$

(iv) 1, $\sqrt{5}$, $-\sqrt{5}$; $\begin{bmatrix} 0 \\ 0 \\ 0 \end{bmatrix}, k_2 \begin{bmatrix} 2 \\ 1-\sqrt{5} \\ 0 \end{bmatrix}, k_3 \begin{bmatrix} 2 \\ 1+\sqrt{5} \\ 0 \end{bmatrix}$

(v) 2, 2, 3; $X_1 = X_2 = k_1 \begin{bmatrix} 5 \\ 2 \\ -5 \end{bmatrix}, X_3 = k_2 \begin{bmatrix} 1 \\ 1 \\ -2 \end{bmatrix}$

(vi) 0, 1, 1; $X_1 = k_1 \begin{bmatrix} 1 \\ 2 \\ 3 \end{bmatrix}, X_2 = X_3 = k_2 \begin{bmatrix} 0 \\ 1 \\ 1 \end{bmatrix}$

16. a, b, c

9 QUADRATIC FORMS

9.1. Introduction

The concept of homogeneous forms is very important in Mathematics. These involve linear combinations of variables where the coefficients belong to a field. The homogeneous forms are of several types. Each homogeneous form is characterised by the degree of the variables involved. Among the homogeneous forms encounteted most frequently are:

(i) linear forms

(ii) bilinear forms

(iii) quadratic forms

9.2. Linear Form

A linear form in n variables $x_1, x_2, x_3, ..., x_n$ is a homogeneous polynomial of the type

$$\sum_{i=1}^{n} a_i x_i = a_1x_1 + a_2x_2 + a_3x_3 + ... + a_nx_n \qquad ... (9.1)$$

where the coefficients $a_1, a_2, a_3, ..., a_n$ belong to a field F.

Illustrations

(i) $x_1 + 2x_2$ is a linear form in two variables x_1 and x_2.

(ii) $x_1 - 2x_2 + 3x_3$ is a liner form in three variables x_1, x_2 and x_3.

(iii) Let $x_1, x_2, ..., x_n$ be n-variables. Let their arithmatic mean be m_x. Then, we have,

$$m_x = \frac{x_1 + x_2 + ... + x_n}{n}$$

$$= \frac{1}{n} \sum_{i=1}^{n} x_i$$

$$= \frac{1}{n} x_1 + \frac{1}{n} x_2 + \ldots + \frac{1}{n} x_n$$

Here, m_x is a linear form in $x_1, x_2, \ldots, x_n$ with all the coefficients equal to $\frac{1}{n}$.

9.3. Linear Form as a Matrix Product

Let $A = [a_1, a_2, a_3, \ldots, a_n]_{1 \times n}$

and

$$X = \begin{bmatrix} x_1 \\ x_2 \\ x_3 \\ \vdots \\ x_n \end{bmatrix}_{n \times 1}$$

Then,

$$AX = [a_1, a_2, a_3, \ldots, a_n]_{1 \times n} \begin{bmatrix} x_1 \\ x_2 \\ x_3 \\ \vdots \\ x_n \end{bmatrix}_{n \times 1}$$

$$= a_1x_1 + a_2x_2 + a_3x_3 + \ldots + a_nx_n$$

which is nothing but the linear form given by Eq. (9.1). Thus, the linear form of Eq. (9.1) can be expressed as a matrix product AX.

Here, the vector X is called the variables of the linear form. The matrix X is called the matrix of the linear form.

We write Eq. (9.1) as

$$f(X) = a_1x_1 + a_2x_2 + a_3x_3 + \ldots + a_nx_n$$

9.4. Bilinear Form

In this form two sets of variables are involved. Each term in the form has one and only one variable to the first power from each set. In the term 'bilinear', 'bi' indicates that two sets of variables are involved and 'linear' indicates that the degree of each variable in each term is one. Thus, a bilinear form in two sets of variables $x_1, x_2, x_3, ..., x_m$ and $y_1, y_2, y_3, ..., y_n$ is a polynomial of the type

$$\sum_{i=1}^{m} \sum_{j=1}^{n} a_{ij} x_i y_j \qquad \text{... (9.2)}$$

Clearly, it is linear and homogeneous in each of the two sets of variables.

Illustrations

$f(X, Y) = x_1y_1 - 2x_1y_2 + 4x_2y_1$ is a bilinear form over the real field in the two sets of variables x_1, x_2 and y_1, y_2.

9.5. Bilinear Form as a Matrix Product

Let us take

$$X = \begin{bmatrix} x_1 \\ x_2 \\ \vdots \\ x_m \end{bmatrix}_{m \times 1}, \quad Y = \begin{bmatrix} y_1 \\ y_2 \\ \vdots \\ y_n \end{bmatrix}_{n \times 1}$$

and

$$A = \begin{bmatrix} a_{11} & a_{12} & \cdots & a_{1n} \\ a_{21} & a_{22} & \cdots & a_{2n} \\ \cdots & \cdots & \cdots & \cdots \\ a_{m1} & a_{m2} & \cdots & a_{mn} \end{bmatrix}_{m \times n}$$

Then,

$$\begin{aligned} X'AY &= X'(AY) \\ &= \sum_{i=1}^{m} \left(\sum_{j=1}^{n} a_{ij} y_j \right) x_i \end{aligned}$$

$$= \sum_{i=1}^{m} \sum_{j=1}^{n} a_{ij} x_i y_j$$

which is nothing but the bilinear form given by Eq. (9.2).

Thus, the bilinear form in Eq. (9.2) can be expressed as a matrix product $X'AY$.

Here, the matrix A of the coefficients is called the matrix of the bilinear form. The rank of A is called the rank of the form.

Example. Consider the bilinear form

$$x_1y_1 + x_1y_2 + x_1y_3 + x_2y_1 + x_2y_2 + x_3y_2$$

$$= [x_1 \; x_2 \; x_3] \begin{bmatrix} 1 & 1 & 1 \\ 1 & 0 & 1 \\ 0 & 1 & 1 \end{bmatrix} \begin{bmatrix} y_1 \\ y_2 \\ y_3 \end{bmatrix}$$

$$= X'AY$$

$\because \quad \rho(A) = 2$

$\therefore \quad$ Rank of the bilinear form $X'AY$ is 2.

9.6. Quadratic Form

A homogeneous polynomial of second degree in any number of variables is called a quadratic form. For example,

(i) $ax^2 + 2hxy + by^2$

(ii) $ax^2 + by^2 + cz^2 + 2hxy + 2fyz + 2gzx$

and

(iii) $ax^2 + by^2 + cz^2 + dw^2 + 2hxy + 2gyz + 2fzx + 2lxw + 2myw + 2nzw$

are quadratic forms in two, three and four variables, respectively.

In n variables $x_1, x_2, ..., x_n$, the general quadratic form over a field F is a homogeneous polynomial of the type

$$\sum_{i=1}^{n} \sum_{j=1}^{n} a_{ij} x_i x_j \qquad ... (9.3)$$

whose coefficients a_{ij} are the element of F. The expression (9.3) is denoted by q.

Characteristics of q

(i) The suffix i varies from 1 to n.

(ii) The suffix j varies from 1 to n.

(iii) The coefficients of the square terms $x_1^2, x_2^2, ..., x_n^2$ which occur when $i = j$ are $a_{11}, a_{22}, ..., a_{nn}$, respectively.

(iv) The coefficient of each cross-product term or mixed product term $x_i x_j$, $i \neq j$ is $a_{ij} + a_{ji}$. (Note that $x_i x_j = x_j x_i$.)

9.7. Quadratic Form as a Matrix Product

Let

$$X = \begin{bmatrix} x_1 \\ x_2 \\ \vdots \\ x_n \end{bmatrix}_{n \times 1} \quad \text{and } A = \begin{bmatrix} a_{11} & a_{12} & \cdots & a_{1n} \\ a_{21} & a_{22} & \cdots & a_{2n} \\ \cdots & \cdots & \cdots & \cdots \\ a_{n1} & a_{n2} & \cdots & a_{nn} \end{bmatrix}_{n \times n}$$

Then,

$$\begin{aligned} X'AX &= X'(AX) \\ &= \sum_{i=1}^{n} \left(\sum_{j=1}^{n} a_{ij} x_j \right) x_i \\ &= \sum_{i=1}^{n} \sum_{j=1}^{n} a_{ij} x_i x_j \end{aligned}$$

Thus, the quadratic form of Eq. (9.3) can be expressed as a matrix product $X'AX$. Here, the matrix A of the coefficients is called the matrix of the quadratic form. A is a symmetric matrix as $a_{ij} = a_{ji}$. Thus, for a quadratic form $A' = A$. The determinant $|A|$ is called the discriminant or modulus of the quadratic form. The rank of the matrix A is called the rank of the quadratic form. If $|A| \neq 0$, the quadratic form is said to be non-singular.

Note 1. In a quadratic form in n variables, there are n square terms and $\frac{1}{2} n(n-1)$ cross-product terms. Thus, the total number of terms in a quadratic form in n variables is

$$n + \frac{1}{2} n (n - 1) = \frac{1}{2} n (n + 1)$$

Note 2. A quadratic form q may be expressed as a matrix product $X'AX$ in infinitely many ways by breaking each cross-product term in two parts arbitrarily.

Note 3. The rows and columns of the symmetric matrix of a quadratic form q are the coefficients of $x_1, x_2, ..., x_n$ in $\frac{1}{2}\frac{\partial q}{\partial x_1}, \frac{1}{2}\frac{\partial q}{\partial x_2}, ..., \frac{1}{2}\frac{\partial q}{\partial x_n}$, respectively.

Note 4. The quadratic form may be regarded as a special case of bilinear form in which $X = Y = X$ so that

$$f(X, X) = X'AX$$

where A is a square matrix.

Note 5. We can write the examples of qudratic forms given in Section 9.6 in matrix form as follows:

(i) $ax^2 + 2hxy + by^2 = [x\ y]\begin{bmatrix} a & h \\ h & b \end{bmatrix}\begin{bmatrix} x \\ y \end{bmatrix}$

(ii) $ax^2 + by^2 + cz^2 + 2hxy + 2fyz + 2gzx$

$$= [x\ y\ z]\begin{bmatrix} a & h & f \\ h & b & g \\ f & g & c \end{bmatrix}\begin{bmatrix} x \\ y \\ z \end{bmatrix}$$

(iii) $ax^2 + by^2 + cz^2 + dw^2 + 2hxy + 2gyz + 2fzx + 2lxw + 2myw + 2nzw$

$$= [x\ y\ z\ w]\begin{bmatrix} a & h & f & l \\ h & b & g & m \\ f & g & c & n \\ l & m & n & d \end{bmatrix}\begin{bmatrix} x \\ y \\ z \\ w \end{bmatrix}$$

Note 6. In the quadratic form of Eq. (9.3), if we replace a_{ij} and a_{ji} both, $i \neq j$, by their mean $\frac{1}{2}(a_{ji} + a_{ji})$, then we find that there is no loss of generality because

$$a_{ij}x_ix_j + a_{ji}x_jx_i \equiv \frac{1}{2}\left(a_{ij} + a_{ji}\right)x_ix_j + \frac{1}{2}\left(a_{ij} + a_{ji}\right)x_jx_i$$

Note that for $i = j$,

$$a_{ij} = \frac{1}{2}\left(a_{ij} + a_{ji}\right)$$

and $a_{ji} = \frac{1}{2}\left(a_{ij} + a_{ji}\right)$

Note 7. We always separate the cross-product terms of a quadratic form so that $a_{ij} = a_{ji}$.

The quadratic form $q = \sum\sum a_{ji}x_ix_j$ with $a_{ij} = a_{ji}$ can be written in full as

$$\begin{aligned} q &= a_{11}x_1^2 + a_{12}x_1x_2 + \ldots + a_{1n}x_1x_n \\ &\quad + a_{21}x_2x_1 + a_{22}x_2^2 + \ldots + a_{2n}x_2x_n \\ &\quad + \ldots\ldots\ldots\ldots\ldots\ldots\ldots\ldots\ldots\ldots \\ &\quad + a_{n1}x_nx_1 + a_{n2}x_nx_2 + \ldots + a_{nn}x_n^2 \\ &= a_{11}x_1^2 + a_{22}x_2^2 + \ldots + 2\,a_{12}x_1x_1x_2 + \ldots \end{aligned}$$

$\Big|\ \because a_{ij} = a_{ji}$ (assumed)

$$= \sum_{i=1}^{n} a_{ii}x_i^2 + 2\sum a_{ij}x_ix_j,$$

where in the second summation i varies from 1 to $n - 1$ while j varies from 1 to n $(i < j)$.

In particular, the quadratic form in two variables x_1, x_2 is given by

$$\begin{aligned} q &= a_{11}x_1^2 + a_{12}x_1x_2 + a_{21}x_2x_1 + a_{22}x_2^2 \\ &= a_{11}x_1^2 + 2a_{12}x_1x_2 + a_{22}x_2^2 \end{aligned}$$

Here, the matrix of coefficients is $\begin{bmatrix} a_{11} & a_{12} \\ a_{21} & a_{22} \end{bmatrix}$ where $a_{12} = a_{21}$.

9.8. Linear Transformations

A set of n linear equations of the form

$$\left.\begin{aligned} x_1 &= b_{11}\,y_1 + b_{12}\,y_2 + \ldots + b_{1n}y_n \\ x_2 &= b_{21}\,y_1 + b_{22}\,y_2 + \ldots + b_{2n}y_n \\ &\ldots\ldots\ldots\ldots\ldots\ldots\ldots\ldots\ldots\ldots \\ x_n &= b_{n1}\,y_1 + b_{n2}\,y_2 + \ldots + b_{nn}\,y_n \end{aligned}\right\} \quad \ldots (9.4)$$

is called a linear transformation from the x-variables to the y-variables.

Let

$$X = [x_1, x_2, \ldots, x_n]' = \begin{bmatrix} x_1 \\ x_2 \\ \vdots \\ x_n \end{bmatrix},$$

$$Y = [y_1, y_2, \ldots, y_n]' = \begin{bmatrix} y_1 \\ y_2 \\ \vdots \\ y_n \end{bmatrix}$$

and $B = [b_{ij}]_{n \times n}$

Then, in matrix notation, the set of Eqs. (9.4) can be written in compact form as

$$X = BY \quad \ldots (9.5)$$

The n-square matrix B of coefficients is called the matrix of the transformation. $|B|$ is called the discriminant or modulus of the transformation. The transformation is said to be non-singular or singular according as B is non-singular or singular.

If B is non-singular, then pre-multiplying Eq. (9.5) by B^{-1}, we obtain

$$B^{-1}X = B^{-1}(BY)$$

$$\Rightarrow \quad B^{-1}X = Y$$

$$\Rightarrow \quad Y = B^{-1}X$$

This is called the inverse transformation. This is also a linear transformation.

Also, if B is non-singular, then the following results are obvious: (Refer chapter 6).

(i) to any set of values of $y_1, y_2, ..., y_n$ corresponds a unique set of values $x_1, x_2, ..., x_n$ and conversely.

(ii) to the set of values $y_1 = 0, y_2 = 0, ..., y_n = 0,$ corresponds the set of values $x_1 = 0, x_2 = 0, ...,$ $x_n = 0$ and conversely.

(iii) if either set of values is non-zero (not all zeros), then the other set of values is also non-zero.

9.9. Orthogonal Transformation

If the matrix of the linear transformation is orthogonal, then the transformation is said to be orthogonal. The inverse transformation is also orthogonal.

If the transformation is orthogonal and $|B| = 1$, then the transformation is called a rotation.

9.10. Linear Transformation of a Given Quadratic Form

Theorem 1. The linear transformation $X = BY$ transforms the original quadratic form in x-variables into a quadratic form in y-variables.

OR

The linear transformation $X = BY$ transforms the quadratic form $X'AX$ with symmetric matrix A into the quadratic form $Y'PY$ with symmetric matrix $P = B'AB$.

Proof. Let $q = \sum_{j=1}^{n} \sum_{i=1}^{n} a_{ij}x_ix_j$ be a quadratic form. Let B be its symmetric matrix. Then, we have

$$q = X'AX \quad ... (9.6)$$

Let us apply the linear transformation $X = BY$ to the quadratic form (9.6) where

$$B = [b_{ij}]_{n \times n}$$

and $Y = [y_1, y_2, ..., y_n]' = \begin{bmatrix} y_1 \\ y_2 \\ \vdots \\ y_n \end{bmatrix}$

Then, we have

$$q = X'AX$$
$$= (BY)' A(BY)$$
$$= Y'B' A BY \qquad | \text{ By Reversal Law}$$
$$= Y'(B'AB)Y \qquad | \text{ By Associative Law}$$
$$= Y'PY$$

where

$$P = B'AB$$

Since

$$P' = (B'AB)'$$
$$= B'A'(B')' \qquad | \text{ By Reversal Law}$$
$$= B'A'B$$
$$= B'AB \qquad | \because A \text{ is symmetric}$$
$$= P$$

Therefore, P is symmetric.

Theorem 2. When a quadratic form is changed to new variables by a non-singular linear transformation, its discriminant is multiplied by the square of the modulus of the transformtion.

Proof. We have

$$P = P' = B'AB \quad | \text{ Refer Theorem 1 above}$$
$$\therefore \quad |P| = |B'AB|$$
$$= |B'|\,|A|\,|B|$$
$$= |B|\,|A|\,|B| \qquad | \because |B'| = |B|$$
$$= |B^2|\,|A|$$

Theorem 3. The definiteness of a quadratic form is invariant under non-singular linear transformation.

Proof. Let $q = \sum_{i=1}^{n} \sum_{j=1}^{n} a_{ij}x_i x_j$ be a quadratic form. Let A be the matrix of the form. Then A is a symmetric matrix such that

$$q = X'AX$$

Let $X = BY$ be a non-singular linear transformation. Then, B is a non-singular matrix of order n so that

$$X = 0 \Rightarrow Y = 0$$

If $X'AX = f$ for some X, then for $Y = B^{-1}X$, we have

$$\begin{aligned} Y'PY &= (B^{-1}X)' P (B^{-1}X) \\ &= X'(B^{-1})' P B^{-1}X \\ &= X'(B')^{-1} PB^{-1}X \\ &= X'(B')^{-1} B'ABB^{-1}X && | \because P = B'AB \\ &= X'AX \\ &= f \end{aligned}$$

Conversely, if $Y'PY = f$, then there exists an X such that

$$X'AX = f$$

Thus, the values assumed by $X'AX$ for a non-zero matrix X are the same as those of $Y'PY$ for a non-zero matrix Y.

Hence, the quadratic form $q = X'AX$ is invariant under non-singular linear transformation.

Theorem 4. The rank of a quadratic form is invariant under non-singular linear transformation.

Proof. Let $q = X'AX$ be a given quadratic form where A is a symmetric matrix. On applying a non-singular linear transformation $X = BY$ from the x-variables to the y-variables to q, $X'AX$ is transformed to $Y'PY$ where $P = B'AB$

$$\begin{aligned} \therefore \quad \text{rank}\,(P) &= \text{rank}\,(B'AB) \\ &= \text{rank}\,(B'A) && | \because B \text{ is non-singular} \\ &= \text{rank}\,(A) && | \because B' \text{ is also non-singular} \end{aligned}$$

9.11. Successive Linear Transformation on a Quadratic Form

Let the quadratic form $A(x, x)$ [in x-variables] be transformed to another quadratic form $B(y, y)$ [in y-variables] by the linear transformation $X = PY$ where P is the matrix of transformation. Again, by using the linear transformation $Y = RZ$, let the quadratic form $B(y, y)$ be transformed to a quadratic form $C(z, z)$ [in z-variables]. Then, $A(x, x)$ can be transformed into $C(z, z)$ directly by the linear transformation $X = (PR)Y$.

Since $A(x, x) = X'AX$ transforms to $B(y, y) = Y'BY$ by the transformation $X = PY$, we have

$$B = P'AP \qquad \text{... (9.7)}$$

Again, since $B(y, y)$ transforms to $C(z, z) = Z'CZ$ by the transformation $Y = RZ$, we have

$$C = R'BR \qquad \text{... (9.8)}$$

Thus,

$$\begin{aligned} C &= R'\,(P'AP)R && \mid \text{From Eq. (9.7)} \\ &= R'P'\,APR \\ &= (PR)'\,A(PR) && \mid \text{By Reversal Law} \quad \text{... (9.9)} \end{aligned}$$

This shows that $A(x, x)$ can be transformed into $C(z, z)$ directly by the linear transformation $X = (PR)Z$. Hence, the effect of applying linear transformation in succession is the same as the effect of applying a single linear transformation whose matrix is the product of the matrices of the linear transformations applied in succession in the order in which they are applied.

The resulting transformation $X = (PR)Z$ is called the product transformation of $X = PY$ and $Y = RZ$. It is obvious that if these transformations are non-singular, then the product transformation will also be non-singular.

9.12. Diagonal Reduction of a Symmetric Matrix

Every symmetric matrix of rank r can be reduced to a diagonal matrix having exactly r non-zero elements in the diagonal.

Let the given quadratic form be $q = X'AX$ where A is the n-square symmetric matrix of rank r of the quadratic form. First, we shall obtain an n-square non-singular matrix B such that

$$B'AB = \text{diag}\,(d_1, d_2, d_3, ..., d_r, 0, 0, ..., 0).$$

Let us write

$$A = I'AI \qquad ...\ (9.10)$$

Take a non-zero diagonal element as pivot and apply the sweep out method to reduce the elements lying in the same row and the same column to zeroes except the diagonal elements by elementary transformations. Since A is a symmetric matrix, therefore, $A' = A$ and hence to reduce two similarly situated elements of A to zeroes by the pivot, we require two similar elementary transformations one for the row and the other for the column. Such similar transformations can be carried out by pre- and post-multiplying the right-hand side of Eq. (9.10) by elementary matrices which will be transposes of each other. This procedure will be repeated whenever a non-zero diagonal element is obtained.

At any stage when all the diagonal elements of the matrix so obtained from A become zero, we bring a non-zero element in the diagonal place by suitable similar elementary row and column transformations keeping the resulting matrix symmetric. This can be carried out by pre- and post-multiplying the R.H.S. of the equation so obtained from Eq. (9.10) by symmetric elementary matrices.

This procedure is continued till A is reduced to its diagonal form. Note that if the rank of the matrix A is r, we shall get

$$\text{diag}\,(d_1, d_2, d_3, ..., d_r, 0, 0, ..., 0) = B'AB$$

where B will be a non-singular matrix, it being the product of elementary matrices.

9.13. Reduction of Quadratic Form into Sum of Squares Form (or Canonical Form or Principal Axes Form or Standard Form)

Let $q = X'AX$ be a given quadratic form where $A = [a_{ij}]_{n \times n}$ is a symmetric matrix of rank r. By the method of diagonal reduction, it is evident that there exists a non-singular matrix B such that

$$B'AB = \text{diag } (d_1, d_2, d_3, ..., d_r, 0, 0, ..., 0) \quad ... (9.11)$$

Now consider the non-singular linear transformation $X = BY$ from the x-variables to the y-variables. Then, from Eq. (9.11), we have

$$\begin{aligned} q &= X'AX \\ &= Y'(B'AB)Y \\ &= Y' \text{ diag } (d_1, d_2, ..., d_r, 0, 0, ..., 0) Y \\ &= d_1y_1^2 + d_2y_2^2 + ... + d_ry_r^2 \\ &= \sum_{i=1}^{r} d_iy_i \end{aligned}$$

ILLUSTRATIVE EXAMPLES

Example 1. Write down the symmetric matrix of the quadratic form

$$q = x_1^2 + 2x_2^2 - 7x_3^2 - 4x_1x_2 + 8x_1x_3 + 5x_2x_3.$$

Solution: We know that the quadratic form in three variables x_1, x_2, x_3 is

$$\begin{aligned} q = a_{11}x_1^2 + a_{22}x_2^2 + a_{33}x_3^2 + 2a_{12}x_1x_2 \\ + 2a_{13}x_1x_3 + 2a_{23}x_2x_3 \end{aligned} \quad ... (9.12)$$

The given quadratic form is

$$q = x_1^2 + 2x_2^2 - 7x_3^2 - 4x_1x_2 + 8x_1x_3 + 5x_2x_3 \quad ... (9.13)$$

Comparing Eqs. (9.12) and (9.13), we obtain

$$\begin{aligned} a_{11} &= \text{Coefficient of } x_1^2 = 1 \\ a_{22} &= \text{Coefficient of } x_2^2 = 2 \\ a_{33} &= \text{Coefficient of } x_3^2 = -7 \\ a_{12} &= \frac{1}{2} \text{ coefficient of } x_1x_2 = \frac{1}{2}(-4) = -2 \\ a_{13} &= \frac{1}{2} \text{ coefficient of } x_1x_3 = \frac{1}{2}(8) = 4 \end{aligned}$$

$$a_{23} = \frac{1}{2} \text{ coefficient of } x_2x_3 = \frac{1}{2}(5) = \frac{5}{2}$$

Hence, the required symmetric matrix of the quadratic form is

$$A = \begin{bmatrix} a_{11} & a_{12} & a_{13} \\ a_{21} & a_{22} & a_{23} \\ a_{31} & a_{32} & a_{33} \end{bmatrix} = \begin{bmatrix} 1 & -2 & 4 \\ -2 & 2 & \frac{5}{2} \\ 4 & \frac{5}{2} & -7 \end{bmatrix}$$

and

$$q = X'AX \text{ where } X' = [x_1, x_2, x_3]$$

Example 2. Write down the quadratic form corresponding to the matrix $A = \begin{bmatrix} 1 & 2 & 5 \\ 2 & 0 & 3 \\ 5 & 3 & 4 \end{bmatrix}$.

Solution: Required quadratic form

$$= X'AX$$

$$= [x_1, x_2, x_3] \begin{bmatrix} 1 & 2 & 5 \\ 2 & 0 & 3 \\ 5 & 3 & 4 \end{bmatrix} \begin{bmatrix} x_1 \\ x_2 \\ x_3 \end{bmatrix}$$

$$= x_1^2 + 4x_3^2 + 4x_1x_2 + 10x_1x_3 + 6x_2x_3$$

Aliter.

We know that the quadratic form corresponding to the matrix

$$A = \begin{bmatrix} a_{11} & a_{12} & a_{13} \\ a_{21} & a_{22} & a_{23} \\ a_{31} & a_{32} & a_{33} \end{bmatrix}$$

in three variables x_1, x_2, x_3 is

$$a_{11}x_1^2 + a_{22}x_2^2 + a_{33}x_3^2 + 2a_{12}x_1x_2 + 2a_{13}x_1x_3 + 2a_{23}x_2x_3$$

Here,

$$a_{11} = 1$$
$$a_{12} = 2$$
$$a_{13} = 5$$
$$a_{22} = 0$$
$$a_{23} = 3$$
$$a_{33} = 4$$

Example 3. Reduce the quadratic form

$$q = 6x_1^2 + 3x_2^2 + 3x_3^2 - 4x_1x_2 - 2x_2x_3 + 4x_3x_1$$

to the sum of the squares.

Solution: The matrix of the given quadratic form q is

$$A = \begin{bmatrix} 6 & -2 & 2 \\ -2 & 3 & -1 \\ 2 & -1 & 3 \end{bmatrix}$$

Let us write

$$A = I'AI$$

$$\Rightarrow \begin{bmatrix} 6 & -2 & 2 \\ -2 & 3 & -1 \\ 2 & -1 & 3 \end{bmatrix} = \begin{bmatrix} 1 & 0 & 0 \\ 0 & 1 & 0 \\ 0 & 0 & 1 \end{bmatrix} A \begin{bmatrix} 1 & 0 & 0 \\ 0 & 1 & 0 \\ 0 & 0 & 1 \end{bmatrix}$$

Operating $R_{21}\left(\frac{1}{3}\right)$, $R_{31}\left(-\frac{1}{3}\right)$

$$\begin{bmatrix} 6 & -2 & 2 \\ 0 & \frac{7}{3} & -\frac{1}{3} \\ 0 & -\frac{1}{3} & \frac{7}{3} \end{bmatrix} = \begin{bmatrix} 1 & 0 & 0 \\ \frac{1}{3} & 1 & 0 \\ -\frac{1}{3} & 0 & 1 \end{bmatrix} A \begin{bmatrix} 1 & 0 & 0 \\ 0 & 1 & 0 \\ 0 & 0 & 1 \end{bmatrix}$$

Operating $C_{21}\left(\frac{1}{3}\right), C_{31}\left(-\frac{1}{3}\right)$

$$\begin{bmatrix} 6 & 0 & 0 \\ 0 & \frac{7}{3} & -\frac{1}{3} \\ 0 & -\frac{1}{3} & \frac{7}{3} \end{bmatrix} = \begin{bmatrix} 1 & 0 & 0 \\ \frac{1}{3} & 1 & 0 \\ -\frac{1}{3} & 0 & 1 \end{bmatrix} A \begin{bmatrix} 1 & \frac{1}{3} & -\frac{1}{3} \\ 0 & 1 & 0 \\ 0 & 0 & 1 \end{bmatrix}$$

Operating $R_{32}\left(\frac{1}{7}\right)$

$$\begin{bmatrix} 6 & 0 & 0 \\ 0 & \frac{7}{3} & -\frac{1}{3} \\ 0 & 0 & \frac{16}{7} \end{bmatrix} = \begin{bmatrix} 1 & 0 & 0 \\ \frac{1}{3} & 1 & 0 \\ -\frac{2}{7} & \frac{1}{7} & 1 \end{bmatrix} A \begin{bmatrix} 1 & \frac{1}{3} & -\frac{1}{3} \\ 0 & 1 & 0 \\ 0 & 0 & 1 \end{bmatrix}$$

Operating $C_{32}\left(\frac{1}{7}\right)$

$$\begin{bmatrix} 6 & 0 & 0 \\ 0 & \frac{7}{3} & 0 \\ 0 & 0 & \frac{16}{7} \end{bmatrix} = \begin{bmatrix} 1 & 0 & 0 \\ \frac{1}{3} & 1 & 0 \\ -\frac{2}{7} & \frac{1}{7} & 1 \end{bmatrix} A \begin{bmatrix} 1 & \frac{1}{3} & -\frac{2}{7} \\ 0 & 1 & \frac{1}{7} \\ 0 & 0 & 1 \end{bmatrix}$$

or, $\text{diag}\left(6, \frac{7}{3}, \frac{16}{7}\right) = B'AB$

Hence, by the linear transformation $X = BY$, i.e.

$$\begin{bmatrix} x_1 \\ x_2 \\ x_3 \end{bmatrix} = \begin{bmatrix} 1 & \frac{1}{3} & -\frac{2}{7} \\ 0 & 1 & \frac{1}{7} \\ 0 & 0 & 1 \end{bmatrix} \begin{bmatrix} y_1 \\ y_2 \\ y_3 \end{bmatrix}$$

or $x_1 = y_1 + \frac{1}{3}y_2 - \frac{2}{7}y_3$

$x_2 = y_2 + \frac{1}{7}y_3$

$x_3 = y_3,$

we have

$$\begin{aligned} q &= X'AX \\ &= Y'(B'AB)Y \\ &= Y' \operatorname{diag}\left(6, \frac{7}{3}, \frac{16}{7}\right) Y \\ &= [y_1\ y_2\ y_3] \begin{bmatrix} 0 & \frac{1}{3} & -\frac{2}{7} \\ 0 & 1 & \frac{1}{7} \\ 0 & 0 & 1 \end{bmatrix} \begin{bmatrix} y_1 \\ y_2 \\ y_3 \end{bmatrix} \\ &= 6y_1^2 + \frac{7}{3}y_2^2 + \frac{16}{7}y_3^2 \end{aligned}$$

Example 4. Reduce to sum of squares the quadratic form $q = x_1^2 + 2x_2^2 - 7x_3^2 - 4x_1x_2 + 8x_1x_3$.

Solution: The matrix of the given quadratic form q is

$$A = \begin{bmatrix} 1 & -2 & 4 \\ -2 & 2 & 0 \\ 4 & 0 & -7 \end{bmatrix}$$

Let us write

$$A = I'AI$$

$$\Rightarrow \begin{bmatrix} 1 & -2 & 4 \\ -2 & 2 & 0 \\ 4 & 0 & -7 \end{bmatrix} = \begin{bmatrix} 1 & 0 & 0 \\ 0 & 1 & 0 \\ 0 & 0 & 1 \end{bmatrix} A \begin{bmatrix} 1 & 0 & 0 \\ 0 & 1 & 0 \\ 0 & 0 & 1 \end{bmatrix}$$

Operating $R_{21}(2)$, $R_{31}(-4)$

$$\begin{bmatrix} 1 & -2 & 4 \\ 0 & -2 & 8 \\ 0 & 8 & -23 \end{bmatrix} = \begin{bmatrix} 1 & 0 & 0 \\ 2 & 1 & 0 \\ -4 & 0 & 1 \end{bmatrix} A \begin{bmatrix} 1 & 0 & 0 \\ 0 & 1 & 0 \\ 0 & 0 & 1 \end{bmatrix}$$

Operating $C_{21}(2)$, $C_{31}(-4)$

$$\begin{bmatrix} 1 & 0 & 0 \\ 0 & -2 & 8 \\ 0 & 8 & -23 \end{bmatrix} = \begin{bmatrix} 1 & 0 & 0 \\ 2 & 1 & 0 \\ -4 & 0 & 1 \end{bmatrix} A \begin{bmatrix} 1 & 2 & -4 \\ 0 & 1 & 0 \\ 0 & 0 & 1 \end{bmatrix}$$

Operating $R_{32}(4)$

$$\begin{bmatrix} 1 & 0 & 0 \\ 0 & -2 & 8 \\ 0 & 0 & 9 \end{bmatrix} = \begin{bmatrix} 1 & 0 & 0 \\ 2 & 1 & 0 \\ 4 & 4 & 1 \end{bmatrix} A \begin{bmatrix} 1 & 2 & -4 \\ 0 & 1 & 0 \\ 0 & 0 & 1 \end{bmatrix}$$

Operating $C_{32}(4)$

$$\begin{bmatrix} 1 & 0 & 0 \\ 0 & -2 & 0 \\ 0 & 0 & 9 \end{bmatrix} = \begin{bmatrix} 1 & 0 & 0 \\ 2 & 1 & 0 \\ 4 & 4 & 1 \end{bmatrix} A \begin{bmatrix} 1 & 2 & 4 \\ 0 & 1 & 4 \\ 0 & 0 & 1 \end{bmatrix}$$

or, $\text{diag}\ (1, -2, 9) = B'AB$

Hence, by the linear transformation

$$X = BY$$

i.e. $$\begin{bmatrix} x_1 \\ x_2 \\ x_3 \end{bmatrix} = \begin{bmatrix} 1 & 2 & 4 \\ 0 & 1 & 4 \\ 0 & 0 & 1 \end{bmatrix} \begin{bmatrix} y_1 \\ y_2 \\ y_3 \end{bmatrix}$$

or, $x_1 = y_1 + 2y_2 + 4y_3$

$x_2 = y_2 + 4y_3$

$x_3 = y_3,$

we have

$$\begin{aligned} q &= X'AX \\ &= Y'(B'AB)Y \\ &= Y'\ \text{diag}\ (1, -2, 9)\, Y \end{aligned}$$

$$= [y_1, y_2, y_3]\begin{bmatrix} 1 & 0 & 0 \\ 0 & -2 & 0 \\ 0 & 0 & 9 \end{bmatrix}\begin{bmatrix} y_1 \\ y_2 \\ y_3 \end{bmatrix}$$

$$= y_1^2 - 2y_2^2 + 9y_3^2$$

Example 5. Reduce $3x^2 + 3z^2 + 4xy + 8xz + 8yz$ into canonical form.

Solution: The given quadratic form can be written as $X'AX$ where $X' = [x, y, z]$ and the symmetric matrix

$$A = \begin{bmatrix} 3 & 2 & 4 \\ 2 & 0 & 4 \\ 4 & 4 & 3 \end{bmatrix}$$

Now we shall reduce A into diagonal matrix.

Let us write

$$A = I'AI$$

$$\Rightarrow \begin{bmatrix} 3 & 2 & 4 \\ 2 & 0 & 4 \\ 4 & 4 & 3 \end{bmatrix} = \begin{bmatrix} 1 & 0 & 0 \\ 0 & 1 & 0 \\ 0 & 0 & 1 \end{bmatrix} A \begin{bmatrix} 1 & 0 & 0 \\ 0 & 1 & 0 \\ 0 & 0 & 1 \end{bmatrix}$$

Operating $R_{21}\left(-\frac{2}{3}\right), R_{31}\left(-\frac{4}{3}\right)$

$$\begin{bmatrix} 3 & 2 & 4 \\ 0 & -\frac{4}{3} & \frac{4}{3} \\ 0 & \frac{4}{3} & -\frac{7}{3} \end{bmatrix} = \begin{bmatrix} 1 & 0 & 0 \\ -\frac{2}{3} & 1 & 0 \\ -\frac{4}{3} & 0 & 1 \end{bmatrix} A \begin{bmatrix} 1 & 0 & 0 \\ 0 & 1 & 0 \\ 0 & 0 & 1 \end{bmatrix}$$

Operating $C_{21}\left(-\frac{2}{3}\right), C_{31}\left(-\frac{4}{3}\right)$

$$\begin{bmatrix} 3 & 0 & 0 \\ 0 & -\frac{4}{3} & \frac{4}{3} \\ 0 & \frac{4}{3} & -\frac{7}{3} \end{bmatrix} = \begin{bmatrix} 1 & 0 & 0 \\ -\frac{2}{3} & 1 & 0 \\ -\frac{4}{3} & 0 & 1 \end{bmatrix} A \begin{bmatrix} 1 & -\frac{2}{3} & -\frac{4}{3} \\ 0 & 1 & 0 \\ 0 & 0 & 1 \end{bmatrix}$$

Operating $R_{32}(1)$

$$\begin{bmatrix} 3 & 0 & 0 \\ 0 & -\frac{4}{3} & \frac{4}{3} \\ 0 & 0 & -1 \end{bmatrix} = \begin{bmatrix} 1 & 0 & 0 \\ -\frac{2}{3} & 1 & 0 \\ -2 & 1 & 1 \end{bmatrix} A \begin{bmatrix} 1 & -\frac{2}{3} & -\frac{4}{3} \\ 0 & 1 & 0 \\ 0 & 0 & 1 \end{bmatrix}$$

Operating $C_{32}(1)$

$$\begin{bmatrix} 3 & 0 & 0 \\ 0 & -\frac{4}{3} & 0 \\ 0 & 0 & -1 \end{bmatrix} = \begin{bmatrix} 1 & 0 & 0 \\ -\frac{2}{3} & 1 & 0 \\ -2 & 1 & 1 \end{bmatrix} A \begin{bmatrix} 1 & -\frac{2}{3} & -2 \\ 0 & 1 & 1 \\ 0 & 0 & 1 \end{bmatrix}$$

or, $\operatorname{diag}\left(3, -\frac{4}{3}, -1\right) = B'AB$

Hence, by the linear transformation

$$X = BY$$

i.e. $$\begin{bmatrix} x \\ y \\ z \end{bmatrix} = \begin{bmatrix} 1 & -\frac{2}{3} & -2 \\ 0 & 1 & 1 \\ 0 & 0 & 1 \end{bmatrix} \begin{bmatrix} u \\ v \\ w \end{bmatrix}$$

or $x = u - \frac{2}{3}v - 2w$

$y = v$

$z = w,$

we have

$$\begin{aligned} q &= X'AX \\ &= Y'(B'AB)Y \\ &= Y' \operatorname{diag}\left(3, -\frac{4}{3}, -1\right) Y \\ &= [u, v, w] \begin{bmatrix} 3 & 0 & 0 \\ 0 & -\frac{4}{3} & 0 \\ 0 & 0 & -1 \end{bmatrix} \begin{bmatrix} u \\ v \\ w \end{bmatrix} \\ &= 3u^2 - \frac{4}{3}v^2 - w^2 \end{aligned}$$

Example 6. Reduce the quadratic form $x^2 - 4y^2 + 6z^2 + 2xy - 4xz + 2w^2 - 6zw$ into sum of squares.

Solution: The matrix form of the given quadratic form is $X'AX$, where $X' = [x, y, z, w]$ and

$$A = \begin{bmatrix} 1 & 1 & -2 & 0 \\ 1 & -4 & 0 & 0 \\ -2 & 0 & 6 & -3 \\ 0 & 0 & -3 & 2 \end{bmatrix}$$

Now we shall reduce A into diagonal matrix.

Let us write

$$A = I'AI$$

$$\Rightarrow \begin{bmatrix} 1 & 1 & -2 & 0 \\ 1 & -4 & 0 & 0 \\ -2 & 0 & 6 & -3 \\ 0 & 0 & -3 & 2 \end{bmatrix} = \begin{bmatrix} 1 & 0 & 0 & 0 \\ 0 & 1 & 0 & 0 \\ 0 & 0 & 1 & 0 \\ 0 & 0 & 0 & 1 \end{bmatrix} A \begin{bmatrix} 1 & 0 & 0 & 0 \\ 0 & 1 & 0 & 0 \\ 0 & 0 & 1 & 0 \\ 0 & 0 & 0 & 1 \end{bmatrix}$$

Operating $R_{21}(-1)$, $R_{31}(2)$

$$\begin{bmatrix} 1 & 1 & -2 & 0 \\ 0 & -5 & 2 & 0 \\ 0 & 2 & 2 & -3 \\ 0 & 0 & -3 & 2 \end{bmatrix} = \begin{bmatrix} 1 & 0 & 0 & 0 \\ -1 & 1 & 0 & 0 \\ 2 & 0 & 1 & 0 \\ 0 & 0 & 0 & 1 \end{bmatrix} A \begin{bmatrix} 1 & 0 & 0 & 0 \\ 0 & 1 & 0 & 0 \\ 0 & 0 & 1 & 0 \\ 0 & 0 & 0 & 1 \end{bmatrix}$$

Operating $C_{21}(-1)$, $C_{31}(2)$

$$\begin{bmatrix} 1 & 0 & 0 & 0 \\ 0 & -5 & 2 & 0 \\ 0 & 2 & 2 & -3 \\ 0 & 0 & -3 & 2 \end{bmatrix} = \begin{bmatrix} 1 & 0 & 0 & 0 \\ -1 & 1 & 0 & 0 \\ 2 & 0 & 1 & 0 \\ 0 & 0 & 0 & 1 \end{bmatrix} A \begin{bmatrix} 1 & -1 & 2 & 0 \\ 0 & 1 & 0 & 0 \\ 0 & 0 & 1 & 0 \\ 0 & 0 & 0 & 1 \end{bmatrix}$$

Operating $R_{32}\left(\frac{2}{5}\right)$

$$\begin{bmatrix} 1 & 0 & 0 & 0 \\ 0 & -5 & 2 & 0 \\ 0 & 0 & \frac{14}{5} & -3 \\ 0 & 0 & -3 & 2 \end{bmatrix} = \begin{bmatrix} 1 & 0 & 0 & 0 \\ -1 & 1 & 0 & 0 \\ \frac{8}{5} & \frac{2}{5} & 1 & 0 \\ 0 & 0 & 0 & 1 \end{bmatrix} A \begin{bmatrix} 1 & -1 & 2 & 0 \\ 0 & 1 & 0 & 0 \\ 0 & 0 & 1 & 0 \\ 0 & 0 & 0 & 1 \end{bmatrix}$$

Operating $C_{32}\left(\frac{2}{5}\right)$

$$\begin{bmatrix} 1 & 0 & 0 & 0 \\ 0 & -5 & 0 & 0 \\ 0 & 0 & \frac{14}{5} & -3 \\ 0 & 0 & -3 & 2 \end{bmatrix} = \begin{bmatrix} 1 & 0 & 0 & 0 \\ -1 & 1 & 0 & 0 \\ \frac{8}{5} & \frac{2}{5} & 1 & 0 \\ 0 & 0 & 0 & 1 \end{bmatrix} A \begin{bmatrix} 1 & -1 & \frac{8}{5} & 0 \\ 0 & 1 & \frac{2}{5} & 0 \\ 0 & 0 & 1 & 0 \\ 0 & 0 & 0 & 1 \end{bmatrix}$$

Operating $R_{43}\left(\frac{15}{14}\right)$

$$\begin{bmatrix} 1 & 0 & 0 & 0 \\ 0 & -5 & 0 & 0 \\ 0 & 0 & \frac{14}{5} & -3 \\ 0 & 0 & 0 & -\frac{17}{14} \end{bmatrix} = \begin{bmatrix} 1 & 0 & 0 & 0 \\ -1 & 1 & 0 & 0 \\ \frac{8}{5} & \frac{2}{5} & 1 & 0 \\ \frac{12}{7} & \frac{3}{7} & \frac{15}{14} & 1 \end{bmatrix} A \begin{bmatrix} 1 & -1 & \frac{8}{5} & 0 \\ 0 & 1 & \frac{2}{5} & 0 \\ 0 & 0 & 1 & 0 \\ 0 & 0 & 0 & 1 \end{bmatrix}$$

Operating $C_{43}\left(\frac{15}{14}\right)$

$$\begin{bmatrix} 1 & 0 & 0 & 0 \\ 0 & -5 & 0 & 0 \\ 0 & 0 & \frac{14}{5} & -3 \\ 0 & 0 & 0 & -\frac{17}{14} \end{bmatrix} = \begin{bmatrix} 1 & 0 & 0 & 0 \\ -1 & 1 & 0 & 0 \\ \frac{8}{5} & \frac{2}{5} & 1 & 0 \\ \frac{12}{7} & \frac{3}{7} & \frac{15}{14} & 1 \end{bmatrix} A \begin{bmatrix} 1 & -1 & \frac{8}{5} & \frac{12}{7} \\ 0 & 1 & \frac{2}{5} & \frac{3}{7} \\ 0 & 0 & 1 & \frac{15}{14} \\ 0 & 0 & 0 & 1 \end{bmatrix}$$

or, $\text{diag}\left(1, -5, \frac{14}{5}, -\frac{17}{14}\right) = B'AB$

Hence, by the linear transformation

$X = BY$

i.e. $$\begin{bmatrix} x \\ y \\ z \\ w \end{bmatrix} = \begin{bmatrix} 1 & -1 & \frac{8}{5} & \frac{12}{7} \\ 0 & 1 & \frac{2}{5} & \frac{3}{7} \\ 0 & 0 & 1 & \frac{15}{14} \\ 0 & 0 & 0 & 1 \end{bmatrix} \begin{bmatrix} y_1 \\ y_2 \\ y_3 \\ y_4 \end{bmatrix}$$

or $x = y_1 - y_2 + \frac{8}{5} y_3 + \frac{12}{7} y_4$

$$y = y_2 + \frac{2}{5} y_3 + \frac{3}{7} y_4$$

$$z = y_3 + \frac{15}{4} y_4$$

$$w = y_4,$$

we have

$$q = X'AX$$

$$= Y'.(B'AB)Y$$

$$= Y' \text{ diag}\left(1, -5, \frac{14}{5}, -\frac{17}{14}\right)Y$$

$$= [y_1, y_2, y_3, y_4]\begin{bmatrix} 1 & 0 & 0 & 0 \\ 0 & -5 & 0 & 0 \\ 0 & 0 & \frac{14}{5} & 0 \\ 0 & 0 & 0 & -\frac{17}{14} \end{bmatrix}\begin{bmatrix} y_1 \\ y_2 \\ y_3 \\ y_4 \end{bmatrix}$$

$$= y_1^2 - 5y_2^2 + \frac{14}{5} y_3^2 - \frac{17}{14} y_4^2,$$

which is the sum of the squares.

EXERCISE 9.1

1. Write down the matrix of the quadratic form

   $$2x^2 + 3y^2 + 6xy$$

2. Write down the matrix of the quadratic form

   $$2x^2 + 5y^2 - 6z^2 - 2xy - yz + 8zx$$

3. Write down the matrix of the quadratic form

   $$x_1^2 + 2x_2^2 - 7x_3^2 + x_4^2 - 4x_1x_2 + 8x_1x_3 - 6x_3x_4$$

4. Write down the quadratic form corresponding to the matrix $\begin{bmatrix} 2 & 4 & 5 \\ 4 & 3 & 1 \\ 5 & 1 & 1 \end{bmatrix}$.

5. Write down the quadratic form corresponding to the matrix $\begin{bmatrix} 1 & 1 & -2 & 0 \\ 1 & -4 & 0 & 0 \\ -2 & 0 & 6 & -3 \\ 0 & 0 & -3 & 2 \end{bmatrix}$.

6. Reduce to sum of squares the quadratic form
$x_1x_2 + x_2x_3 + x_3x_1$

7. Reduce to canonical form the quadratic form
$x_1^2 + 6x_2^2 + 18x_3^2 + 4x_1x_2 + 8x_1x_3 - 4x_2x_3$

8. Diagnolise the quadratic form $x_1^2 + 4x_2^2 + 4x_3^2 + 4x_1x_2 + 4x_1x_3 + 16x_2x_3$ by linear transfomation and write the linear transformation.

9. Reduce to sum of squares the quadratic form $q = x^2 + y^2 + 4z^2 + 9t^2 - 2xy - 4yz + 6yt - 6tx - 12tz$.

10. Reduce to sum of multiples of squares the quadratic form
$yz - 2zx + xy$

11. Reduce to principal axes form the quadratic form
$12x_1^2 + 4x_2^2 + 5x_3^2 - 4x_2x_3 + 6x_1x_3 - 6x_1x_2$

ANSWERS

1. $\begin{bmatrix} 2 & 3 \\ 3 & 3 \end{bmatrix}$

2. $\begin{bmatrix} 2 & -1 & 4 \\ -1 & 5 & -\frac{1}{2} \\ 4 & -\frac{1}{2} & -6 \end{bmatrix}$

3. $\begin{bmatrix} 1 & -2 & 4 & 0 \\ -2 & 2 & 0 & 0 \\ 4 & 0 & -7 & -3 \\ 0 & 0 & -3 & 1 \end{bmatrix}$

4. $2x^2 + 3y^2 + z^2 + 8xy + 2yz + 10xz$

5. $x_1^2 - 4x_2^2 + 6x_3^2 + 2x_4^2 + 2x_1x_2 - 4x_1x_3 - 6x_3x_4$

6. $y_1^2 - \frac{1}{4}y_2^2 - y_3^2$

7. $y_1^2 + 2y_2^2 - 48y_3^2$

8. $y_1^2 + 8y_2^2 - 2y_3^2$; $X = \begin{bmatrix} 1 & -4 & 0 \\ 0 & 1 & -\frac{1}{2} \\ 0 & 1 & \frac{1}{2} \end{bmatrix} Y$

9. $u^2 + 4v^2 - w^2$

10. $2u^2 - \frac{1}{8}v^2 + 2w^2$

11. $12y_1^2 + \frac{13}{4}y_2^2 + \frac{49}{13}y_3^2$

9.14. Index and Signature of the Form

Let a real quadratic form $q = X'AX$ of rank r be reduced by a real non-singular transformation to the form

$$q = c_1y_1^2 + c_2y_2^2 + \dots + c_ry_r^2 \qquad \dots (9.14)$$

If one or more of c_i are negative, then, there exists a non-singular transformation $X = PZ$ where P is obtained from R by a sequence of row and column operations which carries q into

$$q = h_1z_1^2 + \dots + h_kz_k^2 - h_{k+1}z_{k+1}^2 - \dots - h_rz_r^2 \qquad \dots (9.15)$$

where each $h_i > 0$.

When q is reduced to the form of Eq. (9.15), the number k of positive terms is called the *index* of the form and the difference between the number of positive and negative terms, $p - (r - p)$, is called the *signature* of the form.

9.15. Canonical Form

The non-singular transformation

$$w_i = z_i\sqrt{h_i};\ i = 1, 2, \dots, r \qquad \dots (9.16)$$

reduces the form of Eq. (9.15) into the canonical form given by

$$q = w_1^2 + w_2^2 + \dots + w_k^2 - w_{k+1}^2 - \dots - w_r^2 \quad \dots (9.17)$$

Since the product of non-singular transformations is a non-singular transformation, it follows that "Every real quadratic form can be reduced to the canonical form of Eq. (9.17) by a real non-singular linear transformation where k is the index and r is the rank of the given quadratic form."

Note. In canonical form of Eq. (9.17), all the positive terms in the new variables are followed by all the negative terms in the new variables.

9.16. Sylvester's Law of Inertia of Quadratic Form

Theorem. If a real quadratic form is reduced by two real non-singular transformations to canonical forms, they have the same rank and the same index.

Proof. Let a real quadratic form $q = X'AX$ be reduced into two distinct canonical forms given by

$$y_1^2 + y_2^2 + \dots + y_p^2 - y_{p+1}^2 - \dots - y_r^2 \quad \dots (9.18)$$

$$y_1^2 + y_2^2 + \dots + y_q^2 - y_{q+1}^2 - \dots - y_r^2 \quad \dots (9.19)$$

by two non-singular transformations $X = FY$ and $X = GY$ respectively. Then, the transformations

$$Y = \begin{bmatrix} y_1 \\ y_2 \\ \vdots \\ y_n \end{bmatrix} = F^{-1}X = \left.\begin{matrix} b_{11}x_1 + b_{12}x_2 + \dots + b_{1n}x_n \\ b_{21}x_1 + b_{22}x_2 + \dots + b_{2n}x_n \\ \dots\dots\dots\dots\dots\dots\dots\dots \\ b_{n1}x_1 + b_{n2}x_2 + \dots + b_{nn}x_n \end{matrix}\right\} \quad \dots (9.20)$$

and

$$Y = \begin{bmatrix} y_1 \\ y_2 \\ \vdots \\ y_n \end{bmatrix} = G^{-1}X = \left.\begin{matrix} c_{11}x_1 + c_{12}x_2 + \dots + c_{1n}x_n \\ c_{21}x_1 + c_{22}x_2 + \dots + c_{2n}x_n \\ \dots\dots\dots\dots\dots\dots\dots\dots \\ c_{n1}x_1 + c_{n2}x_2 + \dots + c_{nn}x_n \end{matrix}\right\} \quad \dots (9.21)$$

respectively carry Eqs. (9.18) and (9.19) back into q.

Substituting the values of $y_1, y_2, ..., y_n$ from Eqs. (9.20) and (9.21) into Eqs. (9.18) and (9.19) respectively, we obtain

$$\begin{aligned}&\left(b_{11}x_1 + b_{12}x_2 + ... + b_{1n}x_n\right)^2 + ... + \left(b_{p1}x_1 + b_{p2}x_2\right.\\&\left.+ ... + b_{pn}x_n\right)^2 - \left(b_{p+1,1}x_1 + b_{p+1,2}x_2 + ...\right.\\&\left.+ b_{p+1,n}x_n\right)^2 - ... \left(b_{r_1}x_1 + b_{r_2}x_2 + ... + b_{r_n}x_n\right)^2\\&= \left(c_{11}x_1 + c_{12}x_2 + ... + c_{1n}x_{n1}\right)^2 + ...\\&\quad + \left(c_{k_1}x_1 + c_{k_2}x_2 + ... + c_{k_n}x_n\right)^2 - \left(c_{k+1,1}x_1\right.\\&\qquad \left.+ c_{k+1,2}x_2 + ... + c_{k+1,n}x_n\right)^2 - ... - \left(c_{r_1}x_1 + c_{r_2}x_2\right.\\&\qquad\quad \left.+ ... + c_{r_n}x_n\right)^2 \qquad ... (9.22)\end{aligned}$$

Now consider the following $r - q + p < n$ equations

$$\left.\begin{aligned}b_{11}x_1 + b_{12}x_2 + ... + b_{1n}x_n &= 0\\ b_{21}x_1 + b_{22}x_2 + ... + b_{2n}x_n &= 0\\ \dots\dots\dots\dots\dots\dots\dots\dots\dots\\ b_{p_1}x_1 + b_{p_2}x_2 + ... + b_{p_n}x_n &= 0\end{aligned}\right\}$$

$$\left.\begin{aligned}c_{k+1,1}\,x_1 + c_{k+1,2}\,x_2 + ... + c_{k+1,n}\,x_n &= 0\\ c_{k+2,1}\,x_1 + c_{k+2,2}\,x_2 + ... + c_{k+2,n}\,x_n &= 0\\ \dots\dots\dots\dots\dots\dots\dots\dots\dots\dots\dots\dots\\ c_{n_1}\,x_1 + c_{n_2}\,x_2 + ... + c_{nn}\,x_n &= 0\end{aligned}\right\}$$

They have a non-trivial solution, say, $(k_1, k_2, ..., k_n)$. When this solution is substituted in Eq. (9.22), we have

$$\begin{aligned}&-\left(b_{p+1,1}k_1 + b_{p+1,2}\,k_2 + ... + b_{p+1,n}\,k_n\right)^2 - ... -\\&\left(b_{r_1}k_1 + b_{r_2}k_2 + ... + b_{r_n}k_n\right)^2\\&\qquad = \left(c_{11}k_1 + c_{12}k_2 + ... + c_{1n}k_n\right)^2 + ... +\\&\qquad\qquad \left(c_{q_1}k_1 + c_{q_2}k_2 + ... + c_{q_n}k_n\right)^2\end{aligned}$$

Clearly, this requires that each of the squared terms is zero. But then neither F nor G is non-singular; contrary to the hypothesis. Thus, $q \leq p$. A repetition of the above argument under the assumption that $q > p$ will also lead to a contradiction. Hence, $q = p$.

9.17. Definite, Semi-definite and Indefinite Real Quadratic Forms

Let $X'AX$ be a real quadratic form in n variables $x_1, x_2, \ldots, x_n$ with rank r and index p. The form is said to be

1. Positive Definite Form. If $r = p = n$, i.e. if the rank and index of the quadratic form are equal. So by suitable transformation $X = QY$, the $X'AX$ reduces to $y_1^2 + y_2^2 + \ldots + y_n^2$. Thus, positive definite form is always real non-singular quadratic form.

2. Negative Definite Form. If $r = n$, $p = 0$, i.e. the index is zero. So by suitable transformation, the form is reduced to

$$-y_1^2 - y_2^2 - \ldots - y_n^2$$

Thus, if the quadratic form is negative definite, it must be non-singular.

3. Positive Semi-definite Form. If $r = p < n$, i.e. the real quadratic form $X'AX$ is singular (i.e. $|A| = 0$). The index is equal to the rank means that by suitable transformation $X = PY$, $X'AX$ reduces to

$$Y'(P'AP)Y = y_1^2 + y_2^2 + \ldots + y_r^2$$

4. Negative Semi-definite Form. If $r < n$, $p = 0$, i.e. the index is zero and by non-singular transformation $X = PY$, the form is reduced to $-y_1^2 - y_2^2 - \ldots - y_r^2$.

5. Indefinite Form. If the canonical form contains both positive and negative terms, clearly, the quadratic form is indefinite if it is positive for some sets of x's and negative for others.

9.18. Theorem

If $q = X'AX$ is positive definite, then

$|A| > 0$

Proof. When q is positive definite, then there exists a non-singular transformation $X = BY$ such that

$$X'AX = Y'(B'AB)Y$$
$$= Y'(I_n)Y$$

Hence,

$$B'AB = I_n$$
$$\Rightarrow |B'AB| = |I_n|$$
$$\Rightarrow |B'| \, |A| \, |B| = 1$$
$$\Rightarrow |B| \, |A| \, |B| = 1 \qquad | \because |B'| = |B|$$
$$\Rightarrow |A| \, |B|^2 = 1$$
$$\Rightarrow |A| = |B|^{-2} > 0$$

9.19. Principal Minor

A minor of matrix A is called principal if it is obtained by deleting certain rows and the same numbered columns of A. Thus, the diagonal elements of a principal minor of A are diagonal elements of A.

9.20. Leading Principal Minors

Let $A = [a_{ij}]_{n \times n}$ be a square matrix of order n. Then, the leading principal minors are defined as

$$p_0 = 1$$
$$p_1 = a_{11}$$
$$p_2 = \begin{vmatrix} a_{11} & a_{12} \\ a_{21} & a_{22} \end{vmatrix}$$
$$p_3 = \begin{vmatrix} a_{11} & a_{12} & a_{13} \\ a_{21} & a_{22} & a_{23} \\ a_{31} & a_{32} & a_{33} \end{vmatrix}$$
$$\vdots$$
$$p_n = |A|$$

9.21. Theorem

If $q = X'AX$ is positive definite, then every principal minor determinant of A is positive.

Proof. Such a minor is the determinant of the matrix of the quadratic form obtained by making one or more of the variables $x_1, x_2, ..., x_n$ equal to zero. The resulting quadratic form is positive definite in the remaining variables. By Theorem 9.17, the determinant of the resulting form must be positive.

Corollary. If $q = X'AX$ is positive definite, then each $a_{ii} > 0$; $i = 1, 2, ..., n$.

9.22. Theorem

If $q = X'AX$ is positive semi-definite, every principal minor determinant of $A \geq 0$.

Proof. If $q = X'AX$ is positive semi-definite, then there exists a non-singular transformation $X = BY$ such that

$$\begin{aligned} q &= X'AX \\ &= Y'(B'AB)Y \\ &= Y' \text{ diag } (d_1, d_2, ..., d_r, 0, 0, ..., 0)Y \end{aligned}$$

where r is the rank of A and each d_i is positive.

Consequently,

$$|B'AB| = |\text{diag } (d_1, d_2, ..., d_r, 0, 0, ..., 0)|$$

$$\Rightarrow |A| = |\text{diag } (d_1, d_2, ..., d_r, 0, 0, ..., 0)| \; |B|^{-2}$$

It is clear therefore that $|A| = 0$ if $r < n$ and $|A| > 0$ if $r = n$. This shows that for positive semi-definite form, $|A| = 0$ and for positive definite form, $|A| > 0$.

Now, any principal minor of A is the determinant of the matrix of the quadratic form obtained by making one or more of the variables $x_1, x_2, ..., x_n$ zero. Such a quadratic form is either positive semi-definite or positive definite in the remaining variables. Hence, the principal minor must be either zero or positive.

9.23. Theorem

The necessary and sufficient condition for a red quadratic form $q = X'AX$ to be positive definite is that every leading principal minor determinant of A is positive, i.e.

$$a_{11} > 0, \begin{vmatrix} a_{11} & a_{12} \\ a_{21} & a_{22} \end{vmatrix} > 0, \begin{vmatrix} a_{11} & a_{12} & a_{13} \\ a_{21} & a_{22} & a_{23} \\ a_{31} & a_{32} & a_{33} \end{vmatrix} > 0, ...$$

9.24. Lagrange's Reduction

Let $q = f(x_1, x_2, ..., x_n) = \sum_{i=1}^{n}\sum_{j=1}^{n} a_{ij}x_ix_j$ be a quadratic form in n variables $x_1, x_2, ..., x_n$ where the coefficients a_{ij} may be real or complex, then q can be transformed to the form

$$c_1y_1^2 + c_2y_2^2 + ... + c_ny_n^2$$

by a non-singular linear transformation.

Proof. Case I. *When q contains at least one square term $a_{ii}x_i^2$ with $a_{ii} \neq 0$*

Then, the only term, containing x_i in q are

$$2a_{i1}x_ix_1, 2a_{i2}x_ix_2, ..., a_{ij}x_i^2$$

and

$$2a_{in}x_ix_n$$

Hence, the difference

$$f(x_1, x_2, ..., x_n) - \frac{1}{a_{ii}}(a_{i1}\,x_1 + a_{i2}\,x_2 + ... + a_{in}x_n)^2$$

is independent of x_i. Clearly, this is a quadratic form in $n(n-1)$ variables $x_1, x_2, ..., x_{i-1}, x_{i+1}, ..., x_n$. Let us denote it by $f_1(x_1, x_2, ..., x_{i-1}, x_{i+1}, ..., x_n)$.

We apply the following non-singular transformations to f_1:

$$\begin{aligned}
x_1' &= a_{i1}\,x_1 + a_{i2}\,x_2 + ... + a_{in}\,x_n\\
x_2' &= x_2\\
&\vdots\\
x_{i-1}' &= x_{i-1}\\
x_i' &= x_i\\
x_{i+1}' &= x_{i+1}\\
&\vdots\\
x_n' &= x_n
\end{aligned}$$

Then f_1 reduces to the form

$$f(x_1, x_2, ..., x_n) = \frac{1}{a_{ii}} x_1' + f_1(x_2', ..., x_n')$$

where $f_1(x_2', x_3', ..., x_n')$ is identically zero or is a quadratic form in $(n - 1)$ variables and is independent of x_1'.

If it is zero, we have obtained the required form. If not, we apply the same procedure to $f_1(x_2', x_3', ..., x_n')$ repeatedly unless the coefficients of all the square terms are zero. Thus, by a number of successive non-singular linear transformtions, q can be reduced to the form

$$c_1 y_1^2 + c_2 y_2^2 + ... + c_n y_n^2$$

provided that in each successive reduced form, at least one of the square terms is non-zero.

Case II. When q contains no square terms, i.e. $a_{ii} = 0$; $i = 1, 2, ..., n$, and also let $a_{12} \neq 0$.

Then,

$$\begin{aligned} f(x_1, x_2, ..., x_n) &= 2a_{12} x_1 x_2 + 2x_1 (a_{13} x_1 + a_{14} x_4 \\ &+ ... + a_{1n} x_n) + 2x_2 (a_{23} x_3 + a_{24} x_4 + ... + a_{2n} x_n) \\ &+ \sum_{i \neq j = 3}^{n} a_{ij} x_i x_j = \frac{2}{a_{12}} (a_{12} x_2 + a_{13} x_3 + ... + a_{1n} x_n) \\ &\qquad (a_{21} x_n + a_{23} x_3 + ... + a_{2n} x_n) \\ &\qquad + f_1(x_3, x_4, ..., x_n) \quad ... (9.23) \end{aligned}$$

where $f_1(x_3, x_4, ..., x_n)$ is a quadratic form in $(n - 2)$ variables and is independent of x_1 and x_2.

Let us now consider the following linear transformation

$$x_1' = a_{12} x_2 + a_{13} x_3 + ... + a_{1n} x_n$$

$$x_2' = a_{21} x_1 + a_{23} x_3 + ... + a_{2n} x_n$$

....

$$x_i' = x_i;\ i = 3, 4, ..., n$$

which is non-singular, its modulus being

$$-a_{12}^2 \neq 0$$

By applying this transformation, the Eq. (9.23) reduces to

$$f = \frac{2}{a_{12}} x_1' x_2' + f_1(x_3', x_4', ..., x_n') \quad ... (9.24)$$

Again, consider the linear transformation

$$x_1'' = x_1' + x_2'$$
$$x_2'' = x_1' - x_2'$$
$$\vdots$$
$$x_i'' = x_i'; \; i = 3, 4, ..., n$$

This transformation is clearly non-singular, its modulus being –2. On applying this transformation, the Eq. (9.24) reduces to

$$f = -\frac{1}{a_{12}} x_1''^2 - \frac{1}{2a_{12}} x_2''^2 + f_1(x_3'', x_4'', ..., x_n'') \quad ... (9.25)$$

Equation (9.25) shows that f can be expressed as the sum of two squares plus a quadratic form in $(n - 1)$ variables, which can be disposed by Case I or Case II whichever is applicable.

Thus, we finally have

$$q = c_1 y_1^2 + c_2 y_2^2 + ... + c_n y_n^2$$

Note. The form $c_1 y_1^2 + c_2 y_2^2 + ... + c_n y_n^2$ of q is called its canonical form. The number of non-zero c_i's in the canonical form of q is equal to its rank.

Putting $\sqrt{c_i}\, y_i = y_i'; \; i = 1, 2, ..., n,$ we get

$$q = y_1'^2 + y_2'^2 + ... + y_n'^2$$

which is called the normal form of the quadratic form.

9.25. Kronecker's Reduction

If $q = X'AX$ is a real quadratic form in n-variables with rank $r < n$ having a non-singular leading principal sub-matrix P of order r, then there exists a non-singular linear transformation which transforms q to $q' = Y'CY$ where

$C = \begin{bmatrix} P & O \\ O & O \end{bmatrix}$ and q' is a non-singular quadratic form in r variables.

Proof. Let $A = [a_1, a_2, ..., a_n] = \begin{bmatrix} P & Q \\ Q' & R \end{bmatrix}$

Since P is a non-singular matrix of order r, therefore, a_1, a_2, ..., a_r are linearly independent and $a_{r+1}, a_{r+2}, ..., a_n$ can be expressed in the form

$$a_{r+i} = a_{r+i,1}\, a_1 + a_{r+i,2}\, a_2 + ... + a_{r+i,n} a_n;\ i = 1, 2, ...$$

$$\therefore \quad [a_1, a_2, ..., a_n] = \begin{bmatrix} -a_{r+1,1} & -a_{r+1,1} & \cdots & a_{n1} \\ \cdots & \cdots & \cdots & \cdots \\ -a_{r+1,r} & -a_{r+1,r} & \cdots & -a_{nr} \\ 1 & 0 & \cdots & 0 \\ 0 & 1 & \cdots & 0 \\ \cdots & \cdots & \cdots & \cdots \\ 0 & 0 & \cdots & 1 \end{bmatrix}$$

$$= [0, 0, ..., 0]$$

$$\Rightarrow \begin{bmatrix} P & Q \\ Q' & R \end{bmatrix} \begin{bmatrix} -G \\ I_{n-r} \end{bmatrix} = \begin{bmatrix} O \\ O \end{bmatrix} \text{ where } G = \begin{bmatrix} a_{r+1,1} & \cdots & a_{n1} \\ a_{r+1,r} & \cdots & a_{nr} \end{bmatrix}$$

$$\therefore \left.\begin{matrix} -PG + Q = O \\ Q'G + R = O \end{matrix}\right\} \qquad \text{... (9.26)}$$

Now applying the non-singular linear transformation $X = BY$ where

$$X = \begin{bmatrix} I_r & -G' \\ O & I_{n-r} \end{bmatrix} \text{ to } X'AX, \text{ we obtain } Y'CY \text{ where}$$

$$C = B'AB$$

$$= \begin{bmatrix} I_r & O \\ -G' & I_{n-r} \end{bmatrix} \begin{bmatrix} P & Q \\ Q' & R \end{bmatrix} \begin{bmatrix} I_r & -G \\ O & I_{n-r} \end{bmatrix}$$

$$= \begin{bmatrix} I_r & O \\ -G' & I_{n-r} \end{bmatrix} \begin{bmatrix} P & O \\ Q' & O \end{bmatrix} \qquad | \text{ Using Eq. (9.26)}$$

$$= \begin{bmatrix} P & O \\ -G'P + Q' & O \end{bmatrix}$$

$$= \begin{bmatrix} P & O \\ O & O \end{bmatrix} \qquad \left| \begin{array}{l} \because Q' - G'P \\ = (-PG + Q)' \\ = O \end{array} \right.$$

Hence, the theorem.

ILLUSTRATIVE EXAMPLES

Example 1. Test for the positive definiteness of the quadratic form

$$q = 2x^2 + y^2 + 2z^2 + 2xy - 2zx$$

Solution: The matrix of the quadratic form is

$$A = \begin{bmatrix} 2 & 1 & -1 \\ 1 & 1 & 0 \\ -1 & 0 & 2 \end{bmatrix}$$

$$p_1 = 2 > 0$$

$$p_2 = \begin{vmatrix} 2 & 1 \\ 1 & 1 \end{vmatrix} = 1 > 0$$

$$p_3 = |A| = \begin{vmatrix} 2 & 1 & -1 \\ 1 & 1 & 0 \\ -1 & 0 & 2 \end{vmatrix} = 1 > 0$$

Hence, the given quadratic form is positive definite.

Example 2. Examine whether the quadratic form $q = 4x^2 + 9y^2 + 2z^2 + 8yz + 6zx + 6xy$ is positive definite.

Solution: The matrix of the quadratic form is

$$A = \begin{bmatrix} 4 & 3 & 3 \\ 3 & 9 & 4 \\ 3 & 4 & 2 \end{bmatrix}$$

$$\therefore \quad p_1 = 4 > 0$$

$$p_2 = \begin{vmatrix} 4 & 3 \\ 3 & 9 \end{vmatrix} = 27 > 0$$

$$p_3 = |A| = \begin{vmatrix} 4 & 3 & 3 \\ 3 & 9 & 4 \\ 3 & 4 & 2 \end{vmatrix} = -19 < 0$$

Hence, the given quadratic form is not positive definite.

Example 3. Reduce to canonical (normal) form and find the rank, index and signature of the quadratic form $q = x^2 - 2y^2 + 3z^2 - 4yz + 6zx$.

Solution: The symmetric matrix of the quadratic form is

$$A = \begin{bmatrix} 1 & 0 & 3 \\ 0 & -2 & -2 \\ 3 & -2 & 3 \end{bmatrix}$$

A can be written as $I'AI$. Thus,

$$\begin{bmatrix} 1 & 0 & 3 \\ 0 & -2 & -2 \\ 3 & -2 & 3 \end{bmatrix} = \begin{bmatrix} 1 & 0 & 0 \\ 0 & 1 & 0 \\ 0 & 0 & 1 \end{bmatrix} A \begin{bmatrix} 1 & 0 & 0 \\ 0 & 1 & 0 \\ 0 & 0 & 1 \end{bmatrix}$$

Operating $R_{31}(-3)$, $C_{31}(-3)$

$$\begin{bmatrix} 1 & 0 & 0 \\ 0 & -2 & -2 \\ 0 & -2 & 3 \end{bmatrix} = \begin{bmatrix} 1 & 0 & 0 \\ 0 & 1 & 0 \\ -3 & 0 & 1 \end{bmatrix} A \begin{bmatrix} 1 & 0 & -3 \\ 0 & 1 & 0 \\ 0 & 0 & 1 \end{bmatrix}$$

Operating $R_2(-1)$, $C_{32}(-1)$

$$\begin{bmatrix} 1 & 0 & 0 \\ 0 & -2 & 0 \\ 0 & 0 & -4 \end{bmatrix} = \begin{bmatrix} 1 & 0 & 0 \\ 0 & 1 & 0 \\ -3 & -1 & 1 \end{bmatrix} A \begin{bmatrix} 1 & 0 & -3 \\ 0 & 1 & -1 \\ 0 & 0 & 1 \end{bmatrix}$$

or, diag $(1, -2, -4) = B'AB$ (say) where

$$B = \begin{bmatrix} 1 & 0 & -3 \\ 0 & 1 & -1 \\ 0 & 0 & 1 \end{bmatrix}$$

Hence, the non-singular transformation

$$X = BY$$

$$\text{i.e.} \begin{bmatrix} x \\ y \\ z \end{bmatrix} = \begin{bmatrix} 1 & 0 & -3 \\ 0 & 1 & -1 \\ 0 & 0 & 1 \end{bmatrix} \begin{bmatrix} \bar{x} \\ \bar{y} \\ \bar{z} \end{bmatrix} \quad \ldots (9.27)$$

reduces the given quadratic form q into

$$q = \bar{x}^2 - 2\bar{y}^2 - 4\bar{z}^2 \quad \ldots (9.28)$$

Also, by the non-singular transformation

$$\bar{x} = u$$

$$\bar{y} = \frac{1}{\sqrt{2}} v$$

$$\bar{z} = \frac{1}{2} w,$$

q is reduced to the canonical form

$$q = u^2 - v^2 - w^2 \quad \ldots (9.29)$$

Combining the above non-singular transformations, we have

$$\left.\begin{aligned} x &= \bar{x} - 3\bar{z} = u - \frac{3}{2} w \\ y &= \bar{y} - \bar{z} = \frac{1}{\sqrt{2}} v - \frac{1}{2} w \\ z &= \bar{z} = \frac{1}{2} w \end{aligned}\right\} \quad \ldots (9.30)$$

Thus, the transformation.

$$\begin{bmatrix} x \\ y \\ z \end{bmatrix} = \begin{bmatrix} 1 & 0 & -\frac{3}{2} \\ 1 & \frac{1}{\sqrt{2}} & -\frac{1}{2} \\ 0 & 0 & \frac{1}{2} \end{bmatrix} \begin{bmatrix} u \\ v \\ w \end{bmatrix}$$

reduces q in the canonical form

$$q = u^2 - v^2 - w^2$$

in one step.

From the canonical form, it is clear that the rank of the form $r = 3$, index $= p$ = number of positive terms = 1 and signature = number of positive terms – number of negative terms $= p - (r - p) = 1 - 2 = -1$.

Note. Evidently, the given quadratic form is indefinite, since we can find out values of u, v, w which make the form positive, negative or zero, i.e.

when $u = 1, v = 0, w = 0, q > 0$

when $u = 0, v = 0, w = 1, q < 0$

when $u = 1, v = 1, w = 0, q = 0$

The corresponding set of values of x, y, z can be obtained by substituting these values in Eq. (9.30).

Example 4. Show that the form

$$5x_1^2 + 26x_2^2 + 10x_3^2 + 4x_2x_3 + 14x_3x_1 + 6x_1x_2$$

is positive semi-definite.

Solution: The matrix of the quadratic form is

$$A = \begin{bmatrix} 5 & 3 & 7 \\ 3 & 26 & 2 \\ 7 & 2 & 10 \end{bmatrix}$$

A can be written as $I'AI$. Thus,

$$\begin{bmatrix} 5 & 3 & 7 \\ 3 & 26 & 2 \\ 7 & 2 & 10 \end{bmatrix} = \begin{bmatrix} 1 & 0 & 0 \\ 0 & 1 & 0 \\ 0 & 0 & 1 \end{bmatrix} A \begin{bmatrix} 1 & 0 & 0 \\ 0 & 1 & 0 \\ 0 & 0 & 1 \end{bmatrix}$$

Operating $R_{21}\left(-\frac{3}{5}\right)$, $R_{31}\left(-\frac{7}{5}\right)$, $C_{21}\left(-\frac{3}{5}\right)$, $C_{31}\left(-\frac{7}{5}\right)$

$$\begin{bmatrix} 5 & 0 & 0 \\ 0 & \frac{121}{5} & -\frac{11}{5} \\ 0 & -\frac{11}{5} & \frac{1}{5} \end{bmatrix} = \begin{bmatrix} 1 & 0 & 0 \\ -\frac{3}{5} & 1 & 0 \\ -\frac{7}{5} & 0 & 1 \end{bmatrix} A \begin{bmatrix} 1 & -\frac{3}{5} & -\frac{7}{5} \\ 0 & 1 & 0 \\ 0 & 0 & 1 \end{bmatrix}$$

Operating $R_{32}\left(\frac{1}{11}\right)$, $C_{32}\left(\frac{1}{11}\right)$

$$\begin{bmatrix} 5 & 0 & 0 \\ 0 & \frac{121}{5} & 0 \\ 0 & 0 & 0 \end{bmatrix} = \begin{bmatrix} 1 & 0 & 0 \\ -\frac{3}{5} & 1 & 0 \\ -\frac{16}{11} & \frac{1}{11} & 1 \end{bmatrix} A \begin{bmatrix} 1 & -\frac{3}{5} & -\frac{16}{11} \\ 0 & 1 & \frac{1}{11} \\ 0 & 0 & 1 \end{bmatrix}$$

or, $\text{diag}\left(5, \frac{121}{5}, 0\right) = B'AB$ (say) ... (9.31)

where

$$B = \begin{bmatrix} 1 & -\frac{3}{5} & -\frac{16}{11} \\ 0 & 1 & \frac{1}{11} \\ 0 & 0 & 1 \end{bmatrix}$$

Hence, the non-singular linear transformation

$$X = BY$$

$$\text{i.e.} \begin{bmatrix} x_1 \\ x_2 \\ x_3 \end{bmatrix} = \begin{bmatrix} 1 & -\frac{3}{5} & -\frac{16}{11} \\ 0 & 1 & \frac{1}{11} \\ 0 & 0 & 1 \end{bmatrix} \begin{bmatrix} y_1 \\ y_2 \\ y_3 \end{bmatrix}$$

$$\left.\begin{aligned} \text{or } x_1 &= y_1 - \frac{3}{5} y_2 - \frac{16}{11} y_3 \\ x_2 &= y_2 + \frac{1}{11} y_3 \\ x_3 &= y_3 \end{aligned}\right\} \quad \dots (9.32)$$

reduces q into

$$\begin{aligned} X'AX &= Y'(B'AB)Y \\ &= Y' \operatorname{diag}\left(5, \frac{121}{5}, 0\right) Y \\ &= [y_1, y_2, y_3] \begin{bmatrix} 5 & 0 & 0 \\ 0 & \frac{121}{5} & 0 \\ 0 & 0 & 0 \end{bmatrix} \begin{bmatrix} y_1 \\ y_2 \\ y_3 \end{bmatrix} \\ &= 5y_1^2 + \frac{121}{5} y_2^2 \end{aligned} \quad \dots (9.33)$$

From Eq. (9.33), it is clear that the rank of the form $r = 2$, index $= p =$ number of positive terms $= 2$. Also, $n = 3$. Hence, $r = p < n$. Thus, the given quadratic form is semi-definite.

Example 5. Using Lagrange's reduction, reduce the quadratic form

$$q = x^2 - 4y^2 + 6z^2 + 2xy - 4xz + 2w^2 - 6zw$$

into sum of squares.

Solution: Let

$$\begin{aligned} f(x, y, z, w) &= x^2 - 4y^2 + 6z^2 + 2xy - 4xz + 2w^2 - 6zw \\ &= (x + y - 2z)^2 + f_1(y, z, w) \end{aligned}$$

where,

$$f_1(y, z, w) = -5y^2 + 4yz + 2z^2 + 2w^2 - 6zw$$
$$= -\frac{1}{5}(5y - 2z)^2 + f_2(y, z, w)$$

where,

$$f_2(y, z, w) = \frac{14}{5}z^2 - 6zw + 2w^2$$
$$= \frac{5}{14}\left(\frac{14}{5}z - 3w\right)^2 - \frac{w^2}{2}$$

Thus,

$$f(x, y, z, w) = (x + y - 2z)^2 - \frac{1}{5}(5y - 2z^2)$$
$$+ \frac{5}{14}\left(\frac{14}{5}z - 3w\right)^2 - \frac{w^2}{2} \qquad \text{... (9.34)}$$

Now, we consider the following non-singular transformations

$$\left.\begin{aligned} x' &= x + y - 2z \\ y' &= 5y - 2z \\ z' &= \frac{14}{5}z - 2w \\ w' &= w \end{aligned}\right\}$$

Applying this transformation to Eq. (9.34), we get

$$f'(x', y', z', w') = x'^2 - \frac{1}{5}y'^2 + \frac{5}{14}z'^2 - \frac{w'^2}{2}$$

Example 6. Using Kronecker's reduction, reduce

$$q = X'\begin{bmatrix} 2 & 1 & 7 \\ 1 & 1 & 2 \\ 7 & 2 & 29 \end{bmatrix} X \text{ to}$$

$q' = Y'CY$ form.

Solution: Let $q = X'AX$

Then,

$$A = \begin{bmatrix} 2 & 1 & 7 \\ 1 & 1 & 2 \\ 7 & 2 & 29 \end{bmatrix}$$

Clearly, rank of $A = 3$ and, therefore, the leading principal sub-matrix say, P, is non-singular. Hence, the third column can be linearly expressed in terms of first and second columns. Thus,

$$\begin{bmatrix} 7 \\ 2 \\ 29 \end{bmatrix} = K_1 \begin{bmatrix} 2 \\ 1 \\ 7 \end{bmatrix} + K_2 \begin{bmatrix} 1 \\ 1 \\ 2 \end{bmatrix}$$

$$\Rightarrow \quad 2K_1 + K_2 = 7$$

$$K_1 + K_2 = 2$$

$$7K_1 + 2K_2 = 29$$

$$\Rightarrow \quad K_1 = 5, K_2 = -3$$

$$\therefore \quad C_3 = 5C_1 - 3C_2$$

$$\Rightarrow \quad -5C_1 + 3C_2 + C_3 = 0$$

$$\Rightarrow \quad [C_1\ C_2\ C_3] \begin{bmatrix} -5 \\ 3 \\ 1 \end{bmatrix} = 0$$

So, the non-singular linear transformation is

$$X = BY$$

where

$$B = \begin{bmatrix} 1 & 0 & -5 \\ 0 & 1 & 3 \\ 0 & 0 & 1 \end{bmatrix}$$

Hence, the given quadratic form is carried into $Y'CY$ where

$$C = \begin{bmatrix} 2 & 1 & 0 \\ 1 & 1 & 0 \\ 0 & 0 & 0 \end{bmatrix}.$$

i.e. q is reduced to $2Y_1^2 + 2Y_1Y_2 + Y_2^2$.

EXERCISE 9.2

1. Prove that the quadratic form $6x_1^2 + 3x_2^2 + 3x_3^2 - 4x_1x_2 - 2x_2x_3 + 4x_3x_1$ is positive definite. Find a transformation to reduce this form to $c_1y_1^2 + c_2y_2^2 + c_3y_3^3$.
2. Prove that the quadratic forms

$$2x^2 - 4xy + 3xz + 6y^2 - 6yz + 8z^2$$

and

$$2x_1^2 + x_2^2 - 3x_3^2 - 8x_2x_3 + 4x_3x_1 + 2x_1x_2$$

are positive definite.
3. Show that the quadratic form

$$q = -21x_1^2 + 30x_1x_2 - 12x_1x_3 - 11x_2^2 + 8x_2x_3 - 2x_3^2$$

is negative semi-definite. Find the rank and index also.
4. Prove that the quadratic forms

$$6x^2 + 35y^2 + 11z^2 + 34yz$$

and

$$6x^2 + 49y^2 + 51z^2 - 82yz + 20zx - 4xy$$

are positive definite.
5. Find whether each of the following forms is
(i) positive semi-definite
(ii) positive definite
(iii) neither

(a) $x^2 + y^2 + z^2 + yz - zx - xy$

(b) $-3x^2 - 4y^2 + 2z^2 - 2yz + zx + 7xy$

(c) $9x^2 + y^2 + 4z^2 + 6xy - 12xz - 4yz$

6. Determine the rank and signature of the quadratic form $x_1x_2 - 4x_1x_4 - 2x_2x_3 + 12x_3x_4$. Use Lagrange's Reduction.

7. (a) Reduce to canonical form the quadratic form
$$q = x_1^2 + 2x_2^2 - 7x_3^2 - 4x_1x_2 + 8x_1x_3$$
Also find its rank, index and signature.

(b) Define similar matrices and similarity transformation.

8. Find the rank and index of the following quadratic forms:

(a) $6x_1^2 + 3x_2^2 + 14x_3^2 + 4x_2x_3 + 18x_3x_1 + 4x_1x_2$

(b) $2x_1^2 + 12x_1x_2 + x_2^2 - 4x_1x_3 - 8x_2x_3 - 3x_3^2$

9. Reduce to canonical form the quadratic form
$$x^2 + y^2 + 4z^2 - 9t^2 - 2xy - 4yz + 6yt - 6tx - 12tz$$
Find also its rank, index and signature.

10. Reduce the quadratic form $q = 2x_1^2 - 2x_2^2 - 48x_3^2 - 22x_2x_3 + 4x_3x_1 + 3x_1x_2$ by Kronecker's Reduction.

11. Show that the quadratic form $11x^2 + 14xy + 8yz + 14xz$ is indefinite.

12. Under what circumstances will a real matrix of the type
$$A = \begin{bmatrix} x & a & a & \dots & a \\ a & x & a & \dots & a \\ \dots & \dots & \dots & \dots & \dots \\ a & a & a & \dots & x \end{bmatrix}_{n \times n} \quad \text{be}$$

(i) positive definite?

(ii) positive semi-definite?

ANSWERS

1. $X = BY$, where

$$B = \begin{bmatrix} 1 & \frac{1}{3} & -\frac{2}{7} \\ 0 & 1 & \frac{1}{7} \\ 0 & 0 & 1 \end{bmatrix}$$

Reduced form $6y_1^2 + \frac{7}{3}y_2^2 + \frac{16}{7}y_3^2$

3. rank = 2, index = 0

5. (a) Positive-definite
   (b) Neither
   (c) Positive semi-definite

6. 4, 0

7. (a) $u^2 - 2v^2 + 9w^2$; 3, 2, 1
   (b) The n-square matrix B is said to be similar to n-square matix A if there exists a non-singular matrix M such that $B = M'AM$ ... (9.35).
   Equation (9.35) is called a similarity transformation.

8. (a) 3, 3
   (b) 3, 1

9. 4, 2, 0

10. $2u^2 + 3uv - 2w^2$

12. (i) $x > 0$, $x > a$, $x > -(n - 1)\ a$; a may be positive or negative.
    (ii) $x = a > 0$; $x = -(n - 1)\ a$, $a < 0$